Communication Yearbook 28

Communication
Yearbook
28

PAMELA J. KALBFLEISCH

EDITOR

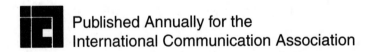

Published Annually for the
International Communication Association

LEA
LAWRENCE ERLBAUM ASSOCIATES, PUBLISHERS
2004   Mahwah, New Jersey   London

Copyright © 2004 by The International Communication Association

Lawrence Erlbaum Associates, Inc., Publishers
10 Industrial Avenue
Mahwah, NJ 07430

Library of Congress:
ISSN: 0147-4642
ISBN: 0-8058-5121-6 (hardcover)

Cover design by Kathryn Houghtaling-Lacey

Books published by Lawrence Erlbaum Associates are printed on acid-free paper, and their bindings are chosen for strength and durability.

Printed in the United States of America
10 9 8 7 6 5 4 3 2 1

Managing Editor: Barbara Stooksberry, ICA Headquarters
Copy & Production Editor: Matthew Katz, ICA Headquarters

CONTENTS

THE INTERNATIONAL COMMUNICATION ASSOCIATION

The International Communication Association (ICA) was formed in 1950, bringing together academics and other professionals whose interests focus on human communication. The Association maintains an active membership of more than 3,000 individuals, of whom some two thirds are teaching and conducting research in colleges, universities, and schools around the world. Other members are in government, law, medicine, and other professions. The wide professional and geographic distribution of the membership provides the basic strength of the ICA. The Association is a meeting ground for sharing research and useful dialogue about communication interests.

Through its divisions and interest groups, publications, annual conferences, and relations with other associations around the world, the ICA promotes the systemic study of communication theories, processes, and skills. In addition to *Communication Yearbook,* the Association publishes the *Journal of Communication, Human Communication Research, Communication Theory, Journal of Computer-Mediated Communication, A Guide to Publishing in Scholarly Communication Journals*, and the *ICA Newsletter.*

For additional information about the ICA and its activities, visit online at www.icahdq.org or contact Michael L. Haley, Executive Director, International Communication Association, 1730 Rhode Island NW, Suite 300, Washington, DC 20036 USA; phone (202) 530-9855; fax (202) 530-9851; email: ica@icahdq.org.

Editors of the *Communication Yearbook* series:

Volumes 1 and 2, Brent D. Ruben
Volumes 3 and 4, Dan Nimmo
Volumes 5 and 6, Michael Burgoon
Volumes 7 and 8, Robert N. Bostrom
Volumes 9 and 10, Margaret L. McLaughlin
Volumes 11, 12, 13, and 14, James A. Anderson
Volumes 15, 16, and 17, Stanley A. Deetz
Volumes 18, 19, and 20, Brant R. Burleson
Volumes 21, 22, and 23, Michael E. Roloff
Volumes 24, 25, and 26, William B. Gudykunst
Volumes 27, 28, and 29, Pamela J. Kalbfleisch

CONSULTING EDITORS

The following scholars have kindly shared their time and talents in consulting with the editor and in refereeing manuscripts for this volume of *Communication Yearbook.*

Terrance L. Albrecht, *University of South Florida*
James Anderson, *University of Utah*
Robert Anderson, *Saint Louis University*
Taik Sup Auh, *Korea University*
Stephen P. Banks, *University of Idaho*
R. Warwick Blood, *University of Canberra*
Mary E. Burman, *University of Wyoming*
Patrice M. Buzzanell, *Purdue University*
Martha Burkle, *Monterrey Insitute of Technologies*
Carolyn M. Byerly , *University of Maryland*
Kevin Carragee, *Suffolk University*
François Cooren, *University at Albany, SUNY*
Janet Cotterill, *Cardiff University*
Kent Drummond , *University of Wyoming*
William Eadie, *San Diego State University*
Eric Eisenberg, *University of South Florida*
Donald Ellis, *University of Hartford*
John Nguyet Erni, *City University of Hong Kong*
Larry Frey, *University of Colorado, Boulder*
Kristine Fitch, *University of Iowa*
Darek Galasinski, *University of Wolverhampton*
Jennifer Garst, *University of Maryland*
Danna M. Gibson, *Columbia State University*
James E. Grunig, *University of Maryland*
Roderick P. Hart, *University of Texas at Austin*
Tadasu Todd Imahori, *Seinan Gakuin University*
Tomas L. Jacobson, *University at Buffalo, SUNY*
Fred Jandt, *California State University, San Bernardino*
Adam Jaworski, *Cardiff University*
Min-Sun Kim, *University of Hawaii, Manoa*
Yungwook Kim, *Ewha Womans University*
Erika L. Kirby, *Creighton University*
Randy Kluver, *Nanyang Technological University*
Thomas Knieper, *University of Munich*
Ascan Koerner, *University of Minnesota*
Anita Lee, *University of Hong Kong*

Jae-Won Lee, *University of Cleveland*
Wendy Leeds-Hurwitz, *University of Wisconsin, Parkside*
Dong Hoon Ma, *Chonbuk National University*
Edward A. Mabry, *University of Wisconsin, Milwaukee*
Jenny Mandelbaum, *Rutgers University*
Valerie Manusov, *University of Washington*
Lynda McCrosky, *California State University, Long Beach*
Ed McLuskie, *Boise State University*
Caryn Medved, *Ohio University*
Frank Millar, *University of Wyoming*
Yoko Nadamitsu, *Josai International University*
James Neuliep, *St. Norbert College*
Richard M. Perloff, *Cleveland State University*
Joseph J. Pilotta, *Ohio State University*
Donnalyn Pompper, *Florida State University*
Maili Pörhölä, *University of Jyvaskyla*
Cindy Price, *University of Wyoming*
William K. Rawlins, *Purdue University*
John Reinard, *California State University, Fullerton*
Ralph Renger, *University of Arizona*
Randell Rogan, *Wake Forest University*
Eric Rothenbuhler, *The New School*
Abran J. Salazar, *University of Rhode Island*
Bill Sharkey, *University of Hawaii, Manoa*
Chris Segrin, *University of Arizona*
Gregory J. Shepard, *Ohio University*
Kenneth Smith, *University of Wyoming*
Pradeep Sopory, *University of Memphis*
Glen H. Stamp, *Ball State University*
Matt Stanndard, *University of Wyoming*
Karen Tracy, *University of Colorado, Boulder*
Arthur VanLear, *University of Connecticut*
Dejan Vercic, *University of Ljubljana*
Lynne M. Webb, *University of Arkansas*
Laurie J. Wilson, *Brigham Young University*
Brenda J. Wrigley, *Michigan State University*

COMMUNICATION AND COMMUNITY: AN INTRODUCTION

Communities are composed of connected individuals. The communication that exists within these communities, about these communities, and between these communities is at the heart of this volume of *Communication Yearbook*. The chapters in this volume draw from the broad range encompassed by the communication discipline to review literature that has something to say about community and what the communication discipline has to contribute to understanding this human connection.

This volume opens with Carl and Duck presenting an influence model addressing the most basic level of community, the personal relationship. This is followed by Stafford's review of the literature on romantic and parent-child relationships at a distance. This review considers the alienating nature of community for those trying to keep connection with distant loved ones.

From loved ones living apart to alternative organizational communities, Edley, Hylmö, and Newsom address community in terms of those working at home and telecommuting, running home-based businesses, and participating in online communities. Collectivist organizing and telework take on intriguing implications as one considers the community connection and lack of connection for those working at distance from others.

Tracy and Dimock take us to the social milieu of the meeting in their literature review addressing this communicative venue for community building and fragmentation. Social capital and tolerance is then examined by St. John and Shepherd in their review and critique of tolerance as an approach to civic interaction. These authors end up recommending transcendence as a more pragmatic schema for facilitating communication within community.

Heath and Frey review the literature on collaboration, examining this communicative performance in community groups. Hallahan then addresses community as a foundation for the study of public relations theory and practice.

The visual images of community and what they suggest about these communities to those looking in from the outside are considered by Mullen in his essay on this burgeoning area of communication research. Katz, Rice, Acord, Dasgupta, and David follow this essay with a literature review considering the role new technology plays in maintaining community. These authors address technological advances in personal mediated devices and ho users communicate via the Internet, mobile phones, and the like to build mobile based communities and social capital.

This volume then closes with two literature reviews addressing community contexts. Kassing, Billings, Brown, Halone, Harrison, Krizek, Mean, and Turman consider the community of sport and the communication research addressing the sports community and our perceptions of the sports community as a whole. Milburn then addresses a community of scholars and the study of speech community and the attendant communication of its scholars.

The call for manuscripts for this volume was a popular one in the communication discipline, drawing submissions from authors representing all 18 divisions and interest groups of the International Communication Association. There are many other worthy essays on communication and community beyond those presented in this volume that I hope find suitable publication outlets. The rejection rate for the blind, peer reviewed manuscripts in this volume was 85%. The chapters included in this volume represent the very best of the literature reviews submitted in response to the published call for reviews of communication research addressing the theme of community.

In addition, this volume contains invited literature reviews from four sets of internationally known scholars actively engaged in communication research that addresses community. Walter J. Carl and Steve Duck, Karen Tracy and Aaron Dimock, Jeffrey St. John and Gregory J. Shepherd, and the collaborative team of James E. Katz, Ronald E. Rice, Sophia Acord, Kiku Dasgupta, and Kalpana David were all kind enough to share their research experience with the readers of the *Communication Yearbook* series with their commissioned literature reviews of communication and community as addressed by their domain of the communication discipline.

It is my hope that by examining what we have to say as a discipline about selected areas of public interest such as community, the field of communication can have a greater impact in the lives of others and that we can realize the full potential of communication as a field of scholarly endeavor.

ACKNOWLEDGMENTS

Two universities supported the editing of this volume of *Communication Yearbook*. The year *Communication Yearbook 28* was edited, I moved from my longtime home as a professor at the University of Wyoming to a new post as professor and director of the School of Communication at the University of North Dakota. My editorial assistant, Anita Herold, moved with me and subsequently changed graduate programs to continue her work as editorial assistant for the *Communication Yearbook*.

The deans of the Colleges of Arts and Sciences at both universities provided generous support for the two editorial offices of the *Communication Yearbook*. The contributors kept track of my move and sent their manuscripts to the correct locations. The production editors at the International Communication Association offices and at Lawrence Erlbaum Associate Publishers were also most helpful in this move. All involved worked to make sure we could make all our deadlines and honor our commitments to blind peer review, speedy processing of manuscripts, and a high quality publication I would like to thank them all for their unselfish support of my editorial responsibilities.

I would also like to thank my editorial assistants Valina K. Eckley, who worked on the early submissions to this volume, and Anita Herold, who worked on the later submissions to this volume and helped me see it to completion. Both are excellent new scholars that you are sure to hear more from in the coming years. Jan Gierman provided excellent technical support for this volume with his software program designed to manage the blind review process. Finally, my mother Marian Kalbfleisch continues her personal support for my professional endeavors and is delighted to know I am happily writing and editing manuscripts in my new home on the Dakota prairie.

Pamela J. Kalbfleisch
Grand Forks, ND

CHAPTER CONTENTS

1 How to Do Things With Relationships . . . and How Relationships Do Things With Us

WALTER J. CARL
Northeastern University

STEVE DUCK
University of Iowa

A community is made up of actively connected personal relationships. These relationships significantly shape how people come to understand their world, gain a sense of the validity and verifiability of their ideas, and become accountable for changes in their attitudes and behaviors. Acknowledgment of the relational underpinnings of such communication processes forces us to revise common understandings of relationships as places where individuals have their personal needs fulfilled and instead conceive of relationships as a form of action, which emphasizes the integral connections between the study of rhetoric and relationships. We explore the ways in which everyday communication draws substantially on these relational underpinnings that have been historically underdeveloped in theories of interpersonal influence and propose a new model of influence, the social consequences of interpersonal influence (SCIPI) model that recognizes the powerful role of one's relational network in individual decision making and realizing attitudinal and behavioral changes. This model suggests a productive way to reconsider studies of interpersonal influence, communication, and community, as well as a number of different threads in the communication discipline as a whole, including the impact of media messages, and health communication campaigns, as well as group decision making.

The term *community* has many common uses that do not denote one specific concept in a truly scientific and accurate manner. For example, the term is used loosely to refer to members of any large universal group (hence, the gay community, the student community, the Black community) where there is no

AUTHORS' NOTE: The authors thank Julia Wood, Pamela Kalbfleisch, and Lise VanderVoort for their insightful comments on earlier drafts of this manuscript.

Correspondence: Walter J. Carl, 101 Lake Hall, Department of Communication Studies, Northeastern University, Boston, MA 02115; email w.carl@neu.edu indication of interaction among all members, merely an identification of a common membership characteristic. On the other hand, people sometimes use the word community to imply common rights, common interest, or common habitat with an implication that patterns of interaction may exist as a result (this retirement community, the neighborhood community, the local community). The word community is also used to mean fellowship, common fate, or mutual interest in the good of each person (a supportive community). Then the word can also be used to denote the associates of a specific person as a network of real and actively connected relationships, whether or not there is any intimacy among them: "When he died the word spread rapidly through his community." Finally, the term is sometimes employed as an indication of intimacy or close-knit membership ("We are a close community"). There are other meanings also for the term as used in communication studies, where the etymological connection between "community" and "communication" is often noted as meaningful.

In the present chapter we are specifically concerned only with the usage that connotes a community of real and actively connected relationships, whether the targets are intimate partners, relatives, or acquaintances. We do not restrict ourselves to intimate ones as long as they exert some kind of referent power over the target individual. Using that meaning, we will here explore the ways in which everyday communication draws substantially on relational underpinnings that have been ignored for too long in theories of interpersonal influence.

Miller and Steinberg (1975) noted that "[t]he basic function of all communication is to control the environment so as to realize certain physical, economic, or social rewards from it" (p. 12). Amending this quote, this chapter argues that the basic function of all communication is to seek a sense of control of the environment and of the rightness of one's views of it, judgments of "rightness" being the issue that brings communication into contact with community. Other functions of communication are subordinate to this goal and depend upon it but connect very significantly with matters of interpersonal influence. We argue that these goals are achieved through relationships with other people in the community and through their influence on us and our influence on them. We argue also that relational contexts affect people in ways not normally a part of the conscious or intentional matrix of interpersonal communication. For these reasons we emphasize the interpersonal workings of community through the everyday glue provided by relational communication or through communication with the community as it is represented by interpersonal relationships. For people at large, community influence is, we contend, represented by the interactions that they have with other people who are in their relational networks and we stress these proximal community influences over those provided at a distance by media.

Accordingly, because we see community as a network of real and actively connected relationships, we review some underlying themes of the interpersonal communication research to draw out features specifically from the relationships literature and to connect these to, inter alia, the ways in which interpersonal influence works in everyday encounters. A primary intent is to urge consideration of the community from the point of view of everyday network activity that is involved in relationships and from which the partners derive a sense of their location and the validity of their ideas. We review a number of different strands of communication research and expose their underlying relational dynamics, arguing that relationships are the engine of much that is of concern to communication studies in understanding communities, such as interpersonal influence, media influences, impact of health messages, group decision making, and the proliferation of innovations or the impact of gossip and opinion. The chapter argues that the relational interactions that constitute daily life experience are the unexamined basis of many processes that have hitherto been explained by use of specific theories of communication and community about the above topics.

We will argue that the community of relationships is *epistemic*: That is to say, the conduct of relationships not only instantiates a person's way of knowing the world but also represents a foundation for new forms of knowledge. As a part of this process, we propose that people not only do, but expect to, present accounts and rationales for their positions and behaviors to other people in their community network, an observation that is both at one level rather pedestrian and at another quite profound in its implications for the conduct of research in interpersonal communication and communication theory more generally. It is pedestrian because it focuses us on the mundane as the locus of interpersonal communication and also as the source of a sense of community membership and responsibility. At the same time, it is profound because it suggests that the everyday business of life is doing something fundamental for people (e.g., helping them to manage and comprehend substantial questions of meaning and understanding). In particular, the fact that relationships are epistemic creates the foundation for other forms of knowledge, whether derived apparently from media or other community sources because the acceptance and processing of information from such sources are ultimately referred to, and assessed via, a relational epistemic base that the community of relationships provides. In other words, the claim that a person knows something is ultimately an appeal to a relational base where the person can reliably assume that others will endorse the claim to knowledge.

We will further argue that relationships and communities are *rhetorical* and not only pervade everyday episodic action in life but are intimately connected with the broad representation of one's knowledge to others and, as such, serve a persuasive (rhetorical) function in the discourses of everyday life. In making this point, some scholars have observed that life's pedestrianism disguises the important function of the presentational nature of talk, where each utterance by a given person is an implicit rhetorical vision of the world (Duck & Pond, 1989) that embodies the speaker's approach to life. Such talk is inherently rhetorical in that it implicitly offers a persuasive account of a view and hence is an effort to attempt to persuade others to support said view of the world or of self. In this light, practices of talk are not unimportant nor are they confined to the significant exposition of, for instance, self-disclosure or explicit persuasive attempts. Instead, everyday talk is a matter of continuously seeking confirmation of a self in relation to others. Despite the appearance of pedestrianism, all remarks and choices of topic serve to take a position, to espouse beliefs, and to promulgate attitudes and opinions, and are inherently rhetorical or sermonic—which is to say, are inherently intended to persuade or align an audience with a particular outlook (Hauser, 1986). For example, one author has an acquaintance who over a period of years has raised issues and made comments that bespeak an underlying rhetorical vision of self-as-victim-of-life. Things are always coming out as bad breaks; unlucky turns of events surprise every well-laid plan; colds and diseases that are going around always head straight for her first; every pain is more deeply felt than anyone else's; undeserved misfortune is never far away. "Poor you. What a hero to put up with it all!" seems to be the desired ego-supportive response. Such a rhetorical vision may be presented to the community of others either consciously or unconsciously, yet it exposes not only an individual's specific thinking but also general attitudes and ones that, in the conduct of that particular relationship, frame discourse, make it relevant or irrelevant, and provide a context in which one's discourse and engagement with the other person are conducted. Such presentations of a general world view are subject to moral (good or bad), probabilistic (likely or unlikely to be right), and logical (accurate or inaccurate) evaluation, endorsement, or critique—just as are the specific statements made by a person at any time (Shotter, 1992). In essence, this position leads us to argue that the role of relationships in interpersonal influence has been underestimated and that relationships and interpersonal influence are wrongly separated conceptually (Chang & Duck, in prep; Duck, 1998, 2002b): Relationships are intricately involved in interpersonal influence; everyday instances of interpersonal influence are ultimately about relationships and the accounts that are given in them during the commerce of daily life. Although researchers in interpersonal influence (since Miller, 1987) have long emphasized "interpersonal factors" in interpersonal influence, exploration of these has largely been confined to such matters as power, credibility, and attraction in affecting decisions. We are arguing something else: In addition to interpersonally relevant forces such as these, the community of interpersonal relationships is a basis for interpersonal influence per se, in many different ways that we will explore here.

A number of consequences follow from these premises. One involves us in the discussion of differences and similarities between relationship conduct and the conduct of influence attempts, whether conscious or not. We then outline a number of places in the communication literature where the conceptualization of relationships as both epistemic and rhetorical can influence our understanding of the activities of interpersonal communication in the relational community more broadly. We end the chapter with some suggestions for larger issues that connect community and communication practice and theory, such as health campaigns, commercial advertising, political advertising, and models of interpersonal influence. The model that we will propose, the social consequences of interpersonal influence model (SCIPI), suggests a redirection of attention from messages, campaigns, and ideas that persuade and toward the social antecedents, processes, and consequences of attitude change, attitude consistency, or attitudinal expression in the social context of everyday life living in an active relational community.

In sum, this approach reconceptualizes the conduct of relational life as an epistemic and rhetorical enterprise in which the interpersonal influence of other people toward one's view of the world is a perpetual but hidden and not always conscious activity running alongside the social and relational consequences of the moral, rational, probabilistic, and logical accounting about our views and behaviors that is carried out by the community of others in our relational world. Likewise, relationships, whether conceived as relatively independent dyads or as open systems placed in the context of a larger social network, can be understood in the same way. That is, rather than being understood as a container for individuals to seek out and fulfill personal emotional needs, relationships are better conceptualized as active loci of performance, where people not only do relating but also express identity and advance and negotiate an understanding of the world. Relationships are a perpetual site for presentational rhetoric (VanderVoort & Duck, 2000) and as such there is much interpersonal influence going on all the time about both explicit and implicit topics.

At this point we need to explicate different elements of our above claims about interpersonal influence: (a) Interpersonal influence occurs in relationships in some obvious ways (e.g., during conflict) that concern us less here than other overlooked modes; (b) interpersonal influence exists in relationships when one partner reaffirms (hence, countering the opposite supposition) the existence of the relationship in a particular form; (c) interpersonal influence occurs through the demonstration to other people of the existence of a relationship (for example, the exhibition of a relationship through tie-signs [Goffman, 1959a] "persuades" others that boundaries exist around the partners); (d) interpersonal influence occurs in relationships when one person is affected by the other's presence to act in a particular way, rather than some other way that would occur in the presence of a different partner or the same partner were she or he to act differently; and (e) interpersonal influence is also evident through relationships when a person processes information to develop a perspective, opinion, or position with another person through discourse. This claim considerably broadens the notion of what counts as interpersonal influence for communication studies, essentially proposing that interpersonal influence is a community activity that is a perpetual attendant at every everyday conversation in some form.

EVERYDAY RELATIONSHIPS, RELATIONSHIP PRACTICES, AND COMMUNITY

The conceptual contributions of rhetoric, social accountability, and personal relationships should already be evident in this preliminary outline of our approach to the intersection of communication and community. We define rhetoric as the unfinished, ongoing process of presenting particular versions of ourselves, situations, the world, and so on, to others for their inspection, revision, acceptance, and rejection (Duck, 1994). Social accountability refers to the ways in which members of social networks hold one another responsible for their own and others' actions through provision of accounts to one another (Antaki, 1994; Buttny, 1993). An important assumption of our approach is that accountability is a pervasive feature of interaction in a community and not just something called out when a specific extraordinary event happens. Generally speaking, behaviors that are considered normal, routine, and representative of the individual will normally pass without a requirement that accounts be provided to the community, whereas actions that are considered nonroutine, exceptional, and out of the ordinary require a suitable account to be made.

However, even the normal can be called to account whenever required or made focal, as by a predicament, face threat, humorous observation, or dramaturgical slippage (Cupach & Metts, 1994). Duck (2002a) has described this feature of social life in terms of the fact that everyday discourse contains marked hypertext that can be read either as an accepted part of the ordinary content of conversation or else as an item that can be clicked to several further levels of meaning otherwise hidden, including a need for accounts. Such hypertext can, of course, be clicked or called to account when any participant chooses to do so. One hypertextual element of all everyday conversation, we assume, is the awareness of others' judgments and assessments that shape a person's responses and behaviors. Another hypertextual referent suggested by Wood (personal communication) is provided by the rhetorical construct of the enthymeme. In relationships, we often make statements of identity, perspective, intent, and so forth with a suppressed hypertextual premise (or even the suppressed first and second premises, with only the conclusion explicated) that our community of familiars understands about us. The suppressed premise in enthymematic discourse can be called out for inspection and justification, when required. For example, if a cat lover remarks to a partner, "We should adopt a kitten," then among the many suppressed premises are that cats deserve good homes and that speaker and partner are people who take care of animals. The speaker's wily partner could call the premises to an accounting by saying, "But adopting another cat would be hurtful to our present cats, who have a good home now and wouldn't with a new cat added to it." This argues that taking care of a new kitten would amount to a dereliction of care of the two already resident cats.

We take personal relationships to be coherent systems of norms and premises that serve as a basis for understanding, showing support, disagreement, and controversy among the relationship parties (Fitch, 2003). The identified conceptual underpinnings (rhetoric, accountability) are important to our project because accounts for behavior are always placed in a context of alternative versions that could be provided to the community of others who either have a right to expect them or else, in the course of everyday life, run into and need to address them. Further, personal relationships provide the basis, worked out over time and through interaction, upon which certain accounts will be treated as intelligible and appropriate within that community. For instance, during the dissolution of relationships, a large concern of participants is the provision to outsiders of an acceptable, face-saving account of the break-up (La Gaipa, 1982) or of the postdissolution format of a romance now reconstructed as a truly friendly relationship (Masuda, 2000), and accounts are formed so as to appeal to the relevant audience. It is a feature of relationships, then, that when we are "in" them, we are constantly presenting accounts and attempting to gain acceptance or approval from the community for our accounts not only of our own behavior but also of "the world" and that these activities impinge upon our social face.

Everyday Practices of Influence in Relationships

Given these claims, the rest of this section will call attention to the fact that everyday practices of relationships not only are drawn from dyadic conversations but also occur within a communal network of informational exchange and in the context of the daily performance of community through specific relationships. Daily conversation and coordinated relational practices convey to participants the underlying sense of a community's understanding of, and interaction with, the world and do so constantly in ways that provide a continuous basis for other experience. The role of everyday conversations is proposed to be a nontrivial influence on the ways in which people not only think about issues but receive the opinions of others in their relational community and discuss the matters that are relevant to their worldviews. In this sense, for example, the nature of social support is not simply a decontextualized specific act of support but, as Leatham and Duck (1990) argued, fundamentally buried in the history of everyday interactions that render the asking for any acute support possible (or not). Hence we also offer an approach to social support that intensifies attention to the background of everyday life experiences upon which any acute demands for social support are drawn.

In contrast to the above position, the relationships literature explains the attractiveness of, and needs for, relationships in terms of the relationships' provisions, on the assumption that relationships are places or things through which an individual satisfies various psychological needs and motivations. Weiss (1974), for example, proposed seven provisions of relationships based on a belief that there are fundamental human needs that in some sense explain why people connect with one another and seek out the company of others:

1. Belonging and a sense of reliable alliance. People need to feel that they have others to whom they can turn and to whom their existence matters. We would reinterpret this as meaning that people need a set of others who endorse their rhetorical visions of the world.

2. Emotional integration and stability. People need a sounding board against which to evaluate their emotional reactions to the situations that they encounter in life. Self-evidently, this provision is a reflection of the argument that we are making here, that people need others against whom to assess the validity of their reactions and worldview.

3. Opportunities for communication about self. This provision is clearly consistent with our broader claims, namely that people need a chance to have their rhetorical visions certified by other people.

4. Provision of assistance and physical support. Even in providing physical support (as, for example, in helping us to move a piano) friends offer us ratification of our worth as people. Obviously our associates would not help us unless they regarded us as worthy of support.

5. Reassurance of worth and value. Clearly this provision ratifies several of the others in that the various activities of friendship previously described reaffirm the value in which we are held by our acquaintances. Any of the above activities is an essentially implicit statement of the worth and value in which we are held by those people who respond to the foregoing needs.

6. Opportunity to help others. Weiss regarded this as a separate provision but it is hard to see how some of the other provisions are not instances of this. For example, provision of assistance and physical support can be a way of satisfying our need to help others and thereby maintain our and others' views of us as helpful persons.

7. Personality support. Seen in terms of traditional views of personality, this provision simply means that actions of friendship and closeness represent the supporting of a person's personality needs and values. Seen from the point of view of those approaches to personality that treat it as epistemic (i.e., as a way of knowing the world, see Kelly, 1969; Duck, 1994), this provision amounts to the idea that a person's rhetorical visions are validated in social interactions by those people to whom they are offered and that this validation is regarded as satisfying by those who offer their visions.

By and large, these seven provisions are reinterpretable in our new analysis as in service of personal epistemic needs that can be understood as satisfying global aspects of human nature in which the individual simply participates. Daily life experience is constantly facing people with their needs for self-validation and everyday discourse offers the chance of satisfying those needs. We suggest that the underlying and primary functions of sociality, at least as far as communication studies is concerned, are those that provide a sense of knowledge of the world, particularly those that provide emotional integration and stability within relevant cultural contexts. Others of Weiss's provisions, such as help and support or behavioral indications of a shared or supported view of the world, serve these major needs while communication is both a valuable instrument through which the other provisions are provided, obtained, or elicited and also a means through which one's beliefs and positions are presented to the outside world. While making communication central to social life, we also recognize that its deployment can serve several psychological and practical needs.

Now that researchers in communication studies, especially interpersonal communication, are recognizing the importance of relational communication, even to the extent of asking if it is in any significant ways different from or less than interpersonal communication as a whole (Wilson, 2000), our proposal shifts thinking about the nature of relationships away from the popular confessional-talk-show view, in which the seeking of affection and the need for integration and ability to express one's inner experience to others are the primal benefits of relationships. Relationships can, instead, be reconceptualized as so fundamental to human experience as to be the basis of understanding, or of making sense of the world, including oneself within it. Mead's (1934; Miller, 1980) early suggestions that the self and mind both spring from sociality, and not the reverse, entail the underlying claim that the self arises from social embeddedness and the use of collective, significant symbols. In this view, the self, or one's sense of individuality, is in a sense inherently social. This view implicitly places a community of relationships at the center of the individual's ongoing existential experience of the world and of the self, not just at the center of daily conduct.

Everyday Communication and the Practice of Relationships: The Importance of the Mundane

What, then, are the features of such daily life communication that characterize relationships? Studies of everyday life communication have confirmed, at once depressingly and excitingly, the news that most daily lives, although not necessarily filled with the quiet desperation identified by Thoreau (1986), are nonetheless not, at least on the surface, the cockpits of importance and plutonial significance that some focused research might have led us to believe. Conversations are typically not only unexciting and meandering but also largely about pedestrian matters. Despite tendencies of research to focus on the decontextualized importance of decision making, conflict, social support, persuasive attempts, and attitude change, it is, we argue, more important for us to understand the mundane than it is to continue to decontextualize special occasions from their everyday context. Several scholars have already substantiated this point. For example, Dainton (2000) noted the central importance of routine in the maintenance and praxis of relationships, and Dindia (2000) has argued that although self-disclosure is important, it is also rare (Dindia, Fitzpatrick, & Kenny, 1989), at least as studied in the prototypical research in the 1980s when we were all apparently having peak, meaningful experiences all the time. Indeed the experiences that we have may be meaningful but without the accompaniment of the sounds of dramatic music and swelling signs of significance. Life is routine; life is normally pedestrian; life is not larded with obvious signs of importance most of the time.

For this reason, the true significance of the mundane has been overlooked as researchers have sought out the exciting and important while failing to acknowledge the rarity of these events. The mundane and the routine events constitute our typical experience and they are important for that reason—notwithstanding that rare and occasional events can, of course, be truly significant life events or may provide the markers of life's turning points, but they do not give life its character (Kelly, 1969). In the language of figure-ground, the mundane serves as the ground upon which the figure stands out; without the ground, the figure could not be perceived or articulated. The decontextualized momentous occurrences may be remarkable for those few moments in every life that are memorable and metamorphosing, but like the rising of Moby Dick from an ocean of ordinariness, they emphasize the whale without noticing the significance of the ocean. Even big moments, such as the news of a serious or chronic illness, should be understood in terms of how these moments affect, and equally importantly, draw on, the existing mundane patterns of interaction. For instance, researchers have overlooked the degree to which a diagnosis of serious or chronic illness reorganizes the patterns of interaction within a family at the same time as it places the patient at the center of family business, and also presents the family with operational dilemmas that have significance and impact on the ways in which support is defined, offered, and operationalized (Lyons, Mickelson, Sullivan, & Coyne, 1998).

All of these ideas have the common themes of emphasizing that the proper study of humankind is humankind's tendency to the pedestrian. Research that immoderately or exclusively seeks out the exciting but atypical aspects of life for experimental reproduction has missed the point. In order to understand the true nature of human life, we believe that human life in all its extent and banality needs to be not only studied but also theorized as it stands, not glorified into what it is not before such theorizing.

Commentators who make similar claims then go on to note the significant impact of everyday life experiences, despite their evident insignificance, in the conduct of life (Acitelli, Duck, & West, 2000). Others go further and suggest that the pedestrian quality of life is in fact the fundamental process that characterizes relationships and that it should not be overlooked nor denigrated because of its seeming ordinariness to great interpersonal and relational communicative moments (Baxter & Montgomery, 1996). It is, in short, the everyday communication within a relationship, which is seemingly unimportant, that gives the relationship its form and its life and so provides the recognizable continuity to the experience of individuals as they continue to believe day to day that they are "in" a relationship.

Relationships as Performative

Once an emphasis is placed on the unremarkable, the center of attention in research becomes more about the performance of everyday life than about the acute execution of specifically dramatic aspects of life (Senchea, 1998). This refocusing onto the practical aspects of life has many implications, but we select as crucial the focus on the omnipresent needs for self-validation and reinforcement. However, a secondary emphasis of our analysis falls also on the everyday practices of life that serve persuasive functions.

All the routine, pedestrian, and rhythmic aspects of the practices of everyday talk are importantly differentiable in communication theory, and everyday talk can be reevaluated as concerned with the interpersonal influence or alignment of other people toward the positions relevant to the speaker: Interpersonal influence does not have to be construed as a special activity at all times. Nor should one assume that these alignments are not conducted collaboratively. As Goffman (1959a) pointed out, interaction is grounded on alignments and teamwork, such that interpersonal influence can be collaboratively conducted. Our analysis, of course, implies that collaboration is an implicitly persuasive enterprise that involves one person aligning with another attitudinally and behaviorally. Recent studies of identity management in discourse indicate strongly the ways in which interpersonal negotiation is involved in the construction of identity (Mokros, 2003). Although there are times when interpersonal influence is the sole and explicit purpose of discourse (for example, compliance gaining or seeking, conflict management, all of which of course can be studied particularly and decontextually), it is a mistake to observe only the intentionally persuasive communication that occurs in relationships. All communication occurs within a context of other discourse from the network, the implied *generalized other* of Mead (1934), and hence communication is conducted within an epistemic framework in which the person strives to understand the world not only for him- or herself but also in the context of the discourse of networks and cultures to which the person is exposed and pays attention.

In the context of our earlier observations, the form of discourse in a relationship is also a relevant persuasive element of the everyday discourse that we regard as primary (cf. Gronbeck, 1997, on the form of local news broadcasts). Whether scholars examine the (dis)affiliative effects of accommodative speech forms (Giles, Taylor, & Bourhis, 1973), the relational boundary functions of personal idioms (Hopper, Knapp & Scott, 1981), or routine forms of relational maintenance brought about in mundane conversation (Dainton, 2000), it is clear that the form of language carries relational messages and so meets our criteria for presenting the relationship to outsiders in rhetorical, sermonic, and epistemic ways. Such an idea can be stitched into the broader tapestry offered above. The very form of talk in relationships can offer support (e.g., comfort, Burleson, 1990; advice, Goldsmith & Fitch, 1997) or can exemplify emotional integration (as, for example, in the management of risks in seeking social support, Goldsmith & Parks, 1990)

These forms and performances of everyday talk rely on practical epistemics, that is to say, their basis is in practical knowledge of the world that is shared (or presumed to be shared) by communicators. The enactment of relationships is predicated on shared understanding that, although previously expressed only as a cause of relationships (e.g., Byrne, 1997, on attitude similarity or Berscheid & Walster, 1974, on physical attractiveness), is actually a substrate of all relationships activity, and hence of all processes that are founded on interpersonal relationships, which, we will argue, extend to media influences, public address, and health communication. Communication between people can truly occur only when they share some sense of the meaning of underlying terms and referents and ways of making sense of the world and its happenings. Of course, misunderstanding or miscommunication occurs, but, not to let the tail wag the cat, these instances are innumerably small compared to those cases where the partners evidently understand each other sufficiently well that the commerce of interpersonal discourse can occur quite adequately and effectively. Indeed, the tendency to focus on misunderstandings is somewhat similar to emphasizing self-disclosure; that is, researchers tend to focus on the atypical over the typical.

All the way from Mead's (1934) claim that the self derives from social interaction to more recent claims that the personal is the social (Milardo & Wellman, 1992), it is self-evident that interpersonal communication is founded on sociality, on a process that requires shared meaning and awareness of one's accountability to others. All meaningful symbolic engagements within a given culture require that the participants understand together the referents of their discourse and the rules that govern its procedure. Discourse between any two individuals, however personally it may be shaped by use of idioms or personal tie signs of intimacy (Hopper, Knapp, & Scott, 1981), nevertheless refers to a broader discourse outside the dyad and pays its respects to the schemes of knowledge and reference that circulate in the wider culture and more specifically in the networks to which the partners belong (Fitch, 2003). This view requires that one assume that daily social commerce presumes a set of underlying assumptions about the nature of the world and how it should be known. To the extent that partners attempt even implicitly to persuade one another about the best way to know the world, the epistemology that they portray is an essential part of daily life.

Relationships as Rhetorical Action

In the perspective that we have sketched, relationships are action: They are performed, done, and get accomplished in and through communication. Communication is not merely transmitting information, but is relational action that simultaneously reflects and constitutes the relationship and all of its entailed history and understandings of conduct, parallel in force to the "symbolic action" identified by Burke (1966). In other words, when people are in relationships, they are not only part of a relational entity that has a recognizable social form, but they are also part of a shared knowledge system that distinguishes itself from other relational groupings by its taken-for-granted, but actually quite laboriously worked out, assumptions of what is known and how it is known.

By treating communication as relational action we redescribe relationships as symbolic forms that are ever in process and change, subject to systematic variation and variable forces that influence outcomes of interpersonal discourse. People talk of the relationship as static, but we (analysts and relationship partners) can also talk of relating (Duck, West, & Acitelli, 1997). Talk is extremely flexible and malleable. For example, one account of why the relationship ended can be used to assign blame and responsibility, whereas another account might be used to mitigate responsibility by constructing a version in which there was never a relationship to begin with (Potter & Wetherell, 1987). Though there are always rival versions of what counts as a relationship, relationship ending, or relationship problem—and others may deny the existence of a relationship or problem, as when we dismiss a teenager's profession of love as "just puppy love" or a friend's major concern as "not a serious problem"—relationship activity necessarily involves a constructed and shared sense of self and connectivity to others. In the course of this everyday communication, people attend to and are aware of the relationship implications of their actions to some degree, significantly in some cases and nonsignificantly in others. Thus, for example, a person making choices between possible courses of action may make a final decision on the basis of expectations that the chosen course will benefit a relationship partner, further a relationship, or cause fewest relationship problems.

When we begin to understand communication as action, we catch a glimpse of its rhetorical force and its ultimate dependence on some acceptance of rhetorics of connectivity. Talk serves to mark the version of events or relationship or person or identity that is subscribed to at the time by the speakers. Importantly, communication also presupposes such understanding or versions of events and is possible only when participants—whether in interpersonal contexts, mediated contexts, public address, or information transmission—share or show signs acknowledging, if not actually endorsing, such understandings or versions (Cissna & Sieburg, 1981). Thus, talk is used to state what kind of relationship this is, as opposed to other versions of what the relationship could be, but is also formed and enacted on the basis of acceptance of versions of other features of the environment. This implies that if we want to understand what a relationship is, we must understand that relationships have their life primarily through communication and that the talk depicts or marks its relevant form at a given moment (Duck, 1995). We deliberately do not use the term "constructs" here because we do not believe that relationships are constructed in talk in the usual sense. Rather they are marked, and versions of events are called out, not only by the talk just of the partners, but also of others (or third parties; see below on gossip).

The interlacing of personal relationships and rhetoric also has another twist. When we view relationships in this way, we see how people perform actions for each other based on the relationship they share or have negotiated with each other historically (Duck, 2002a). We feel obliged to do things for our friends that we would not do for strangers, and vice versa. We can understand this persuasive element of relationships through reference to the history of interaction. For example, the direct use of relational terms in forming requests (Sahlstein, 1999), and accounting for, or justifying, a request through invoking the history of the relationship are examples of the ways in which two kinds of history influence given interactions (History B, relational history, and History C, interaction sequencing, in Duck's 2002a terms). Likewise, network marketing business practices exploit the time-extended nature of the relationship by blurring the social and economic functions (many sets of steak knives have been sold like this; Biggart, 1989; Carl, 2001; Cialdini, 1993; Taylor, 1978). In this way, the relationship speaks for itself. The relationship has not only rhetorical force but also epistemic and ontological implications.

Another way to understand relationships in a rhetorical manner is to recognize that the use of relational terms as categories, such as close friend versus friend versus acquaintance, carry certain expectations and entitlements (Potter, 1996; Tracy

& Anderson, 1999) and that these are marked (not constructed but marked) or called out by discourse. Of course categories can also construct a relationship, or argue for a particular construction or transformation in the understanding of a relationship, as when X first says to Y "You are my best friend" or "I love you" or "Let's just be friends." When a relationship is being defined or redefined, partners' efforts to reach agreement about the epistemic nature of their relationships may involve extensive discourse, and influence attempts, to articulate and ratify a shared view of who we are.

Yet another connection between rhetoric and relationships is that talk is an index of relationship development. People tend to self-disclose more frequently earlier in relationships rather than later, but they also transact relational business through self-disclosure sequences (Dindia, 2000; Petronio, 2002). People tend to engage in certain types of talk to gain support for their version of what happened in the relationship, particularly in the social and grave-dressing processes of relationship dissolution (Duck, 1998). Instead of seeing self-disclosure as a transmission of information that is intimate, we see it as a marking of a relational form and an implicitly influential offering of an intimate form, if the hearer is willing to collaborate in and accept that version of the relationship between speaker and hearer.

Relationships as Conversational Resources

In our view, interpersonal influence is not most fruitfully understood in terms of attitude change, at the level of cognitions, but rather in terms of both drawing on, first, and then, second, freely providing conversational resources for people to account to their relational networks and partners for targeted changes in social actions. Thus the process of changing people's attitudes and beliefs about smoking, for example, is less about interpersonal influence as normally understood (which we term light coercion) and more about creating messages and resources that provide (un)suitable accounts or make such accounts available as resources in conversation. Using these accounts, one can then explain to others in one's social network why one no longer wants to or needs to smoke. Although this is an important reconceptualization of the interpersonal influence process, it is enabled by our focus on the community of relationships as the center of social being. Because changes of behavior need to be accounted for to the social network, our approach recognizes that attitude change is partly cognitive and partly behaviors that have to be performed in the presence of those who might otherwise have expected the individual to offer an account or else to do something else. In this sense, attitude change is always partly relational. One example is the grave-dressing processes of relationship dissolution (Duck, 1998), in which the breakup of a relationship entails a need to offer an explanation to those in the breakup parties' social networks.

Our approach above recommends reinterpretation of interpersonal influence by any one of three means: traditional direct attitude change; self-persuasions as a result of reflecting on the (group) discussion; or relational rhetoric (Duck, 1998; Sahlstein, 1999). This latter concept, especially the notion of rhetorical relational terms (RRTs), used by Sahlstein (1999), emphasizes the ways in which relationships themselves can be persuasive. Not only are explicit references to relationships persuasive ("You're my friend, please do me this favor" or "Buddy, can you spare a dime?"), but also the implicit contextual existence of the relationship can produce the same effects. Clearly, people willingly do favors for their friends unasked and are prepared to respond to requests from friends that would be unacceptable if asked by a stranger. The obligations of friendship do not need to be directly invoked for this to occur (Roloff, Janiszewski, McGrath, Burns, & Manrai, 1988; Surra, 1988). Various exclusion rituals—for example, shunning by the Amish, the scarlet letter for Hester Prynne, excommunication by the Catholic church—emphasize that an individual's or relationship parties' attitudes, behaviors, or statements meet the disapproval of acquaintances, and such exclusions are purposeful and direct uses of relational rhetorics. As such, they are persuasive and influential devices because we prefer not to experience, even if we do not actually fear, ostracism. One smoker friend of ours once commented gratefully to one of us, "Thanks for not making me feel like a jerk because I smoke." Such social concerns about image may be daily more persuasive than distant invocations from governments to which the person does not feel attached personally. Health warnings on consumables are therefore likely to be relatively ineffective when judged against means based on interpersonal involvement at a closer level, such as peer group membership in adolescence (Miller, Alberts, Hecht, & Trost, 2000).

When people make changes to their behavior, other members of their network make comments and ask questions about why they made those changes (as predictable from Mead's, 1934, discussion of the generalized other) and people can be expected to have to answer. Interpersonal influence and campaign research can take this idea and pay closer attention to the role of personal relationships in encouraging others to participate in, or not participate in, certain kinds of behavior. This includes not only supporting in the traditional sense by agreeing, or comforting, or helping patients to adhere to regimens, or offering emotional support, but by accepting an account of change, something that normally occurs in the everyday pedestrian conversational activity that we have stressed. The first point to note here then is that the everyday context provides frequent and unexpected occasions for people to present accounts to others for behavior change or attitudinal readjustment. A second implication of this point for interpersonal influence and also for research on competence is that people who have greater conversational resources and skills to provide suitable accounts for their friends, family members, and coworkers—and who are actively encouraged to do so—will be in a better position to remain committed to particular behavior changes and to receive support for those changes.

There is an even more fundamental point to be made about interpersonal influence, relationship networks, and accountability, however. This point concerns actions that fall into or out of the realm of persuadables. Fitch (2003) argued that within any speech community, particular actions can be placed along a continuum for which interpersonal influence is possible (relational persuadables), not possible (that is, coercion would be required), or not necessary (because the action is already consistent with relationship-specific premises and norms). A goal of persuasive campaigns would be to move desirable actions currently in the realm of the persuadable into the realm of taken-for-granted premises where the action is considered routine and ordinary so that no further persuasive attempts are necessary. Alternatively, if the undesirable behavior is currently deemed acceptable and taken for granted, the goal is to create messages and campaigns that call into question the relationship-specific premises that permit the action to go unchallenged.

In summary, this first section has provided a set of claims that frame the central argument of our chapter. We began by noting that, in contrast to a psychological, needs-based view of relationships, our communication-centered view highlights how the everyday communicative performance of relationships serves the important function of endorsing one's rhetorical visions of the self and world. Thus, the conduct of relationships, we claimed, is the basis for understanding our world, but the importance of this is often lost on the everyday, pedestrian nature or relational activity, most notably, talk. We also argued against common understandings of relationships as containers in which individuals have their personal needs fulfilled, and instead argued that relationships are a form of action, which emphasizes the strong connections between the study of rhetoric and relationships. Finally, we proposed that relationships are resources for the process of interpersonal influence. Once we acknowledge that people are embedded in a network of relations and that their actions are subject to the process of social accountability, the targets of influence cease to be the individual, but rather the focus is on the community network of relations in which the individual is embedded and the accounts that those in that relational network treat as meaningful and influential.

EVERYDAY PERSUASIVE PRACTICES

The purpose of this section is to provide further evidence to support our claim that the conduct of specific dyadic relationships is embedded within a larger relational network and is a site of everyday persuasive practices. As discussed above, there is a growing recognition that everyday life interactions with others are important and consequential to our lives (Duck, Rutt, Hurst, & Strejc, 1991). Further, in these everyday, informal conversations individuals collaborate to present rhetorical versions of themselves, others, and their general, perhaps moral, outlook on life (Duck & Pond, 1989; Hauser, 1986). Mundane and seemingly trivial daily conversations with friends, acquaintances, and colleagues serve to reinforce those relationships and do so in ways not dependent on deep self-disclosures or strong statements of positive affect. These interactions serve to reinscribe the relationship simply by their occurrence, and they are missed when they do not occur. More than this, individuals conduct themselves in an interpersonal environment where their behaviors are subject to the evaluation and critique of other people with whom they choose to associate and also with people with whom they interact by force of circumstance rather than free choice (e.g., Hepburn & Crepin, 1984). Such circumstances may result from relatively involuntary contact with disliked colleagues at work, in the neighborhood, or in the extended family as well as from casual contact with unknown others who choose to voice their opinions about the person's behavior.

The study of gossip (Bergmann, 1993) provides an excellent way to illustrate how behavior is conducted within this context of a network of relationships and is subject to evaluation, and hence influence, by those network members. Gossip is a pervasive practice in everyday life and represents a special genre of communication that needs to be distinguished both at the level of content (for example, information of a personal, private nature) and, importantly, at the level of the relational configuration of those sharing the content. For example, if a husband has an extramarital affair, the communication by friends and neighbors about this could be considered gossip, but communication between the wife and her divorce lawyer would not be viewed as gossip. Thus, the relationship of the parties communicating is central to the definition of whether something is gossip.

In his study of gossip-communication, Bergmann (1993) noted that there are always at least three parties implicated in the structure of gossip, forming a gossip triad: gossip producer (A), gossip recipient (B), and gossip subject (C). In other words, gossip takes place when A discloses private information about an absent friend or acquaintance (C), to another friend or acquaintance (B). All parties to gossip form a network of acquaintanceship such that any one of the parties could identify any other based on prior knowledge or a previous encounter. An exception to this acquaintanceship rule occurs when the talk is about a celebrity or well-known person, rather than an acquaintance. Further, an exception to the absence rule takes place when an intimate of the absent other (C) shows up. In this situation, the gossip about C usually stops because, when C's intimate arrives, C is made vicariously present in the interaction. Due to the high face-threat of the interaction, people tend not to gossip in front of the gossip-subject or their intimate stand-in. Interestingly, those people without family members or close friends are favorite targets of gossip in a community because there is no one who could present themselves in order to inhibit gossip about them (Campbell, 1964; Wolf, 1972). Noting these two exceptions, gossip communication occurs "only through friends and acquaintances and only with friends and acquaintances" (Bergman, 1993, p. 70). According to Bergmann, gossip is a privilege extended only to those who "mutually recognize themselves as members of this relational network" (p. 70). A stranger or neophyte member of a network, who happens to be in the presence of people gossiping, soon realizes that he or she does not (yet) belong. Thus, gossip is always gossip-for-a-relational-network.

The fact that gossip communication always takes place in the context of a relational network actually creates the conditions for the (re)emergence of gossip and implies a cultural understanding of rights and obligations regarding features of personal relationships (Fitch, 1998, 2003). Through interaction with friends and acquaintances, we acquire private, intimate information that, if shared, could have negative or disastrous consequences for those friends and acquaintances. Because a characteristic feature of friendship is trust, there is a cultural presumption that the private information would be kept in confidence. Disclosing a friend's private information would betray that trust which, in turn, would put the friendship in jeopardy (Dindia, 2000). However, when the members of a relational network are all friends or acquaintances, to varying degrees, there are multiple competing expectations about relational rights and obligations. Specifically, in the same way friends are not to disclose certain secrets or personal information with others, there is a rule that friends should not withhold information from another friend (Baxter, Dun, & Sahlstein, 2001). Withholding information from a friend would also violate trust and a friend's sense of loyalty. Thus, in concealing what information A knows about friend C, A also conceals that s/he knows some information from another friend B (Bergmann, 1993). A's telling B personal information about C is a form of indiscretion toward C. At the same time, to be selective about telling B the information because B is A's friend and not just any random person, A is also being discreet. This contradictory and paradoxical structure of loyalty for friends and acquaintances in the context of a relational network, that is, how a friend can be both discreet and indiscreet simultaneously, accounts for the equivocal nature of gossip—how gossip is condemned as immoral, but is entertaining and universally practiced—as well as the continued (re)creation of gossip as a genre of communication (Bergmann, 1993).

These relational network structures and the cultural systems of meaning regarding personal relationships have implications for how gossip is influential. In addition to our common sense understandings of gossip, empirical studies confirm that the manner in which gossip is shared is not neutral (Bergmann, 1993; Goldsmith, 1990; Goodman & Ben-Ze'ev, 1994). Rather, gossip producers and recipients collaboratively construct a version of what-happened-and-who-did-what-to-whom in order to assign (ir)responsibility, to assess (im)morality, and to determine (in)appropriateness of activities done by others in their relational networks (Bergmann, 1993; Fitch, 2003). Naturalistic studies of gossip sequences reveal that they consist largely of turns that comment on and evaluate the talked-aboutactivity, and then generalize the information to socially categorize the talked-about other as a particular type of person or belonging to a specific group of people, such as brats, jerks, sluts, studs, assholes, pricks, saints, and heroes (Bergmann, 1993; Senchea, 1998; Winters & Duck, 2001). Thus a persuasive impact of gossip in a relational network lies in its moral persuasion; a force that encourages conformity and both judges and discourages inappropriate activity (Duck & VanderVoort, 2002).

In examining actual gossip in interaction, however, there is a curious finding about the extent of the condemnation. Bergmann (1993) found that gossip sequences also always express some element of sympathy and understanding for the talked-about-other. He found that the condemnation of the gossip subject is later softened or revised in the gossip sequence. The reason for this, Bergmann claims, is due to the very relational structure that contributed to the gossip in the first place. That is, although gossipers consistently made moral judgments of the talked-about other, this is tempered by the fact that the gossip-subject is one of their acquaintances. Thus, the gossip producer (A) today could be the target of gossip tomorrow (C). Further, A's talk about C could get back to C later and then A would have to account for such behavior, or it might decrease the likelihood that C would become the next partner with whom A can share gossip. Additionally, gossip producers manage a delicate balance between dishing out gossip, and attempting not to be seen as the type of person who gossips because of the social disdain for the practice. Thus, "it is the gossip triad's particular personal constellation that makes the 'sins' of an acquaintance socially relevant to it, but, at the same time, it also prevents this acquaintance from being morally condemned in gossip mercilessly" (Bergmann, 1993, p. 133).

To sum up, gossip as an everyday practice of communication in a relational network is influential in two ways: First, participants in gossip collaborate to construct particular versions of events in order to cast an absent other as indicative of a type of person with associated (often disparaging) characteristics. These versions of events are highly selective and actively construct a lapse in the moral order such that indignation is an appropriate response. That is, gossip communication does not simply represent in talk a violation of the social or moral order, to which people then respond. Rather gossip is a rhetorical, presentational enterprise in which gossipers actively "situate, interpret, and thus transform [the violation of a norm] into something relevant to them, against the background of their own social position and interests" (Bergman, 1993, p. 134). Secondly, gossip producers and recipients apply communal meaning systems of rights, obligations, and morality to assess and evaluate behavior. People's knowledge of how one's conduct may be (re)presented in gossip communication can powerfully shape their actions. Thus, a person may act in such a way so that her or his reputation is not soiled or so that she or he will not be grouped into an undesirable category of persons (see, for example, Senchea's, 1998, analysis of teenage girls' moral accounting of one another by use of derogatory nicknames). Conversely, a person may act in such a way so that their reputation is enhanced among their network members and so that their exploits would group them into a socially desirable category of people. Thus, because of such concerns, gossip serves to create a moral climate in which the social group enforces or sanctions behaviors and attitudes. In their own way such TV programs as *Jerry Springer* and the British red-top tabloid newspapers act as such good gossips: The parading of the abnormal or dispreferred forms of behaviors in such outlets serves not only to fuel media survival, but also act as an arena where broad social norms and rebukes can be screamed at reprobates by audiences and sanctimonious editors alike, thus effectively reinforcing normativity (Liss, 2000).

In addition to gossip, another example of how relational networks are persuasive is interpersonal violence (West, 1995; Wood, 2001). West's (1995) study of relational violence and interpersonal ideology found that members of the relational network, including family members and clergy, sought to influence a partner to stay in a violent relationship. One of his informants, Jenni, described an interaction between her and her priest:

And I said, "I can't. What am I supposed to do if he's cheating on me and hits me?" He [the priest] said, "You should forgive him." And I said, "What if he continues to do it?" Then he said, "You should pray that he'll stop" [sarcastic laughter]. I said, "I'm sorry, I'm sorry, I've waited for a long time for him to stop and he hasn't and I'm not going back." Then he told me that I was very selfish and all I cared about was myself and what I was doing. You know, so it was really hard. The priest was mad, my parents were mad, my brother [who was best friends with her husband] didn't talk to me for a long time, I mean he would say, "Hi, how's it going?" Once in a while he would make rude comments. I mean here I was brought up believing, I mean my parents always said you come from a large family, you work together, there's no one like your family, only your family does things for you, you know, really ingrained, the family, the family, the family, and all of a sudden to have part of my family not just pissed but totally sided with my ex was tough. (pp. 129–130)

Additionally, Wood's (2001) work on narratives and relational violence showed that women's views of what behavior was deemed (un)acceptable for an intimate relationship was shaped by what their friends said to them as well as what they anticipated their friends and family members would say about their violent partner and their relationship.

Although gossip and interpersonal violence are especially compelling examples of the role of the network in the performance of dyadic relationships and also about the persuasive force of everyday communication in those relationships, there are many other examples of everyday communication that make the same point. For example, deception in relationships has been analyzed as intended to persuade (West, 1996), and so have compliments (Knapp, Hopper, & Bell, 1984), and, to a lesser extent, bullshit (Frankfurt, 1986). More general forms of communication such as narratives and accounts have also been analyzed in ways that happen to point out their persuasive undertones, but these have not typically been made a major focus of the analysis (Fitch, 2003).

The central purpose of this section is to claim that relationships are conducted in broader networks beyond the dyad and these relationships are a primary site for practices of interpersonal influence, such as gossip and managing identities. In the next section, we will extend this claim by reviewing literature that treats the fundamental nature of interpersonal influence as relationally based.

INTERPERSONAL INFLUENCE AS RELATIONALLY BASED

Our approach holds that the fundamental basis of interpersonal influence is located in relationships and identity management. As indicated in the preceding section, this claim refers to the general tenor of large classes of communication such as gossip and also to specific instances of behavior such as compliance-seeking episodes. To support our broad claim, we will review work that shows how people understand the world in ways specific to particular relationships; contrast early views of interpersonal influence that do not situate the process in the social context of relational networks with those that do; and then reconceptualize traditional understandings of ethos in light of our relationship-as-epistemic approach.

As discussed above, rather than being understood as a container for individuals to seek out and fulfill personal needs, relationships are better conceptualized as actively shaping our understanding of the world and as a site for presentational rhetoric (Duck & Pond, 1989; VanderVoort & Duck, 2000). To illustrate this claim, consider work on the notion of face, or the versions of self that we present to others, and the emergence of relationship-specific ways of understanding and acting in the world. Researchers have identified three different aspects or kinds of face that people display in social interaction: *solidarity* (being liked, appreciated, or included), *autonomy* (not being imposed upon), and *competence* (being seen as knowledgeable or skilled; Brown & Levinson, 1987; Lim & Bowers, 1991).

Cupach and Metts (1994) argued that people draw on different interpretive frameworks when interacting with strangers and nonintimates than when interacting with intimate partners, such as a romantic partner, spouse, family member, or close friend. They claim that as we develop more intimate relationships with people, we simultaneously develop associated sets of assumptions, inferences, and expectations that are specific to relational partners. With nonintimates, we present a *social face* through which we are likely to enact broader, conventional understandings of what constitutes polite forms of social interaction. With people who are acquaintances, we present a *relational face* that may relax or modify conventional understandings and expectations of what counts as appropriate and inappropriate interaction. With intimate partners and people we know well, we enact a *relationship-specific face*, or set of patterns, understandings, and codes that are relatively unique to the particular relationship shared by the partners (Baxter, 1987; Duck, 1994; Fitch, 2003; Wood, 1982). As partners become closer, their communication patterns are marked by less concern for making impositions on the other, greater openness and directness, as well as less tact (Cupach & Metts, 1994).

Cupach and Metts (1994) made another important point as well, concerning how close personal relationships affect how partners make sense of each other's actions. They claim that the "level of intimacy in a relationship influences what a person considers to be face-threatening as well as the degree of face threat attached to a particular behavior" (p. 99). To illustrate this claim, consider their research finding that as relationships develop over time, they tend to become more resilient in that they can withstand greater threats to the other's autonomy face. They contend that asking a favor from an acquaintance constitutes a greater threat to their autonomy face, and therefore requires greater displays of politeness, whereas asking the same favor of an intimate counts as only a minor face threat or none at all. Indeed, the very nature of face changes in intimacy as a result of the relational culture partners collaboratively construct. If partners construct a relational culture with understood rules/norms, such as, "We need and depend on each other," "We like to help each other out," then autonomy is not an aspect of face within that particular relationship. Conversely, in the relatively rare cases in which the requested action is viewed by the intimate partner as a very large imposition, that partner might also feel that the relationship has either been taken advantage of or that it has not been taken into consideration. Thus, the degree of closeness that we share with a relational partner shapes what we see as an imposition and what we see as an appropriate response to that imposition.

The claim that humans enact relationship-specific ways of understanding the world has important implications for how we conceptualize interpersonal influence. Early views of persuasion, dating back to Ancient Greece, focused on senders as the source of a message and their ability to craft messages in ways compelling to an audience. Later views, however, significantly changed this source-oriented view of persuasion and instead emphasized the symbolic and cooperative process that takes place between the sender and receiver. For example, according to Burke (1945/1969), persuasion works through the related processes of identification and consubstantiality. To the extent that the receiver perceives substantial similarity with the speaker's values, the receiver comes to identify with the views of the sender and considers the sender's views also her or his own. Pragmatically, the identification process is successful to the extent that both the speaker and audience create a personal, positive relationship with one another. This is often done through the use of symbols that highlight how the speaker is like the audience member and shares their values. Thus, rather than understanding the influence process in terms of one person attempting to convince another to adopt a particular view, Burke offered a collaborative view that stresses the importance of managing the identifications of both the speaker and audience.

Our argument builds on Burke's notions of identification and consubstantiality by recognizing the importance of the network relationships to the process of persuasion. If one inspects the relational context for such things, then the impact of messages, from whatever source, comes to be seen as potentially influential only to the extent that their adoption or espousal will not conflict with the person's established ways of operating in the social network. That is, messages will be accepted only if they do not require that any attitude change by the person violates the underlying beliefs and expectations of the group and so threatens the person's membership and inclusion in that group. For example, a person may be uninfluenced by an otherwise persuasive message about smoking simply because that person lives in a relational context where smoking is a normal, and even desirable, symbol of group membership and acceptance of the practices and preferences of others. Thus, the identification process is successful to the extent that a speaker creates a personal, positive relationship with the audience members and recognizes that they have relational contexts in which they will respond to and evaluate the message.

Influence in interpersonal settings, often referred to as compliance gaining, has historically focused on strategies that senders use to get others (or, targets) to do something for them (Edgar & Fitzpatrick, 1988; Gass & Seiter, 1999; Miller, Boster, Roloff, & Seibold, 1977; Seibold, Cantrill, & Meyers, 1994). More recent work in compliance gaining has built on this foundation to show also the fundamental basis of relational and identity concerns (Sanders & Fitch, 2001; Wilson, Aleman, & Leatham, 1998). For example, Wilson et al. (1998) offered a contextualized view for how multiple face threats are managed because of the specific goals of speakers and targets in a compliance-gaining interaction. These researchers contend that each person enacts tacit knowledge that defines and creates the context of the compliance-gaining episode. In the process of giving advice, for example, the targets may infer that they are the type of people who need advice and that senders are in the position to provide that advice. Alternatively, by asking a favor, senders run the risk of implying that they cannot deal with the situation themselves, and thereby may appear lazy or incompetent. Thus, this work shows how talk must be understood simultaneously at two levels: the content level (e.g., the words used to request a favor, solicit advice, or enforce an unfulfilled obligation) as well as the relational level (or what the communication says about the relationship and identities of the people speaking; Watzlawick, Beavin, & Jackson, 1967).

A study by Sanders and Fitch (2001) illustrates how compliance gaining is rich with relational and identity concerns. They argued that compliance gaining, or what they call compliance seeking, episodes are collaboratively built up, turn by turn, in an interactive manner. They base their theory of compliance seeking upon what they refer to as the influential meanings postulate. Drawing on the work of both Mead (1934) and Goffman (1959b, 1967), they state this postulate and their rationale for it in this way:

> Person P's likelihood of saying or doing X depends on what P projects the social meaning of his/her doing or saying X would be for relevant others (i.e., what they could infer about P's identity, character, or relationship with others). This is because the way others treat P depends on their belief about P's identity, character, and relationship with others. (p. 265)

To illustrate this postulate, consider the following scenario adapted from Sanders and Fitch (2001, p. 267). Suppose that the target person (T) had previously said getting a cat for a household pet was not something T wanted to do, and that the compliance seeker (CS) has requested that the couple get a cat. Also suppose that the sequential position of the request in the interaction implied that the CS's need to get a cat was more important than T's desire not to get one. Thus, if the target were to comply at that moment in the interaction, the inference could be drawn that T's needs were less important than CS's. To the extent that T evaluated this as an undesirable inference, T might resist the request for just that reason. Now suppose that CS made the point that T had earlier promised to get the cat as a pet in an effort to induce T to comply. In doing so, CS has put T in a position that, were T to comply at that point in the interaction, T could not do so out of T's own good will. Rather, T's compliance would be out of fulfillment of an earlier obligation. If T wanted the compliance to imply good will, then T might be less likely to comply at that point in the interaction.

Thus, to understand adequately the process of interpersonal influence, it is essential to take into account the social meanings implied by particular actions at specific points in an interactional sequence as well as the significance of these social meanings to relevant others in one's social network. Further, the influential meanings postulate highlights that there are certain premises common to cultures, networks, relationships, and so forth that simultaneously enable and constrain what could be considered appropriate and sensible kinds of actions to be solicited and how to go about seeking those actions—for example, what kinds of inducements to offer. The actions one solicits and the inducements offered implicate how the compliance seeker understands the identity, the nature of the relationship, and each party's rights and obligations. Thus, if the solicitations or inducements "are not congruent with cultural premises about the target person's rights and obligations in the relationship or identity he or she claims, compliance would implicate that the person's claim to that relationship or identity is spurious" (Sanders & Fitch, 2001, p. 268). To the extent that such relational implications are not adequately taken into consideration, efforts at seeking and gaining compliance will be impaired.

Our claim that interpersonal influence is fundamentally based in relationships and identity management leads us to reconceptualize a foundational concept of interpersonal influence: *ethos*. Aristotle identified ethos as one of the artistic proofs or appeals that a speaker is able to manipulate or change to bolster a rhetor's attempt to persuade an audience. According to Aristotle, the ethos a speaker brings to a persuasive presentation was known as the speaker's reputation (Larson, 1989). Aristotle also discussed how ethos could be developed in the delivery of the presentation itself through the use of clever arguments, gestures, and eloquent language choices. Since Aristotle's initial work, researchers have conceptualized ethos in terms of the credibility of a message source, which can be further broken down into such characteristics as expertness, trustworthiness, and dynamism.

In contrast to these views of ethos as the abstract credibility of a speaker, we want to argue that ethos is ultimately better understood as the relational force of sources of information. Effects of ethos derive from the relationship of the speaker to the audience. This revised view has two important implications. First, it highlights the significance of network relationships to our understanding of the world, especially in relation to abstract entities or personalities. For example, although the U.S. surgeon general may be presented in a public health campaign as a credible expert on the topic of smoking and disease, it is the relational force of the norms and premises that circulate in the talk of the social network that will have a greater impact on how the message is understood and addressed. For instance, if a friendship group holds the surgeon general in contempt for some reason, then the impact of any statements made by the surgeon general is likely to be minimal in that group irrespective of their scientific value. Second, it is through our talk with others in our web of relationships that our rhetorical visions of the world are (dis)confirmed and (de)legitimated. In powerful ways, our peers and colleagues can validate or invalidate our experiences and shape our understanding of the world.

In sum, then, the previous sections have noted the persuasiveness of relational forces in interpersonal influence, seen both as a general background in everyday life communication and as specific instances of attempts at influence. We have argued that interpersonal influence exists in the very essence of relationships and that its force and effects are interlaced with relationship forces in ways more often unified than disparate. Accordingly, we are now ready to argue a more general case.

A GENERAL MODEL OF THE SOCIAL CONSEQUENCES OF INTERPERSONAL INFLUENCE

We can now extend the principles argued above to broader matters of interpersonal influence, especially in relation to health communication and media theories. An important theory in relation to health communication messages has been Babrow's (1992, 1995, 2001) problematic integration theory (PIT). A novel approach to the classic tensions between evaluation and probability (cf. Petty & Cacioppo, 1981), PIT notes that individuals are often faced with problems of integrating (i.e., reconciling) information when the evaluation (positive or negative) of an event or piece of information may conflict with the probabilistic assessment of its likelihood of occurrence. Babrow noted that in the course of everyday life, people are exposed to "chaining," that is, multiple considerations of particular issues on the basis of the relevance of information and the source of the opinions whether contrary or supportive (of the change from one to the other). The problem here may be the integration of advice from different sources who are weighted differently according to what is known, relationally and personally, about the source as well as the topic. Searcy (2003) extended this idea to note that chaining may lead a person or a group of people to adopt particular self-referential metaphors that metaintegrate the relevant information and address the issue of process. For instance, by repeated exposure of one's own ideas to those of other people in the network, a person may come to see integration as based on teamwork or on the notion of the family (a family decides things together by mutual arrangement). Searcy's claim alerts us to the fact that the integration of information is not simply an individual's task, but one that nods toward one's social membership and its accompanying obligations, such that information is treated as a collective good and one that must be integrated in ways that are acceptable within the social network's frameworks of understanding also.

In a separate venture that we can now reinterpret as relevant here, intermedia theory (Gumpert & Cathcart, 1986) supposes that media messages have their influence at least in part from the extent to which they stimulate discussion in a network of acquaintances. Instead of media messages having a direct hypodermic effect, or acting directly on the cognitive mechanics of the individual, intermedia theory supposes that people in everyday life discuss things that they have seen on television, email, Web, or newspapers or have heard on the radio or by word of mouth. A person is more likely to be influenced by messages that stimulate discussion between the individual and his or her groups of significant others or associates such that interpersonal influence or adoption of the message's rhetorical vision becomes more likely. McMahan (2001) discovered that media tracings (i.e., references to situations, people, and phrases found on TV, radio, or film) were a substantial part of everyday conversations. To the extent that media tracings can be directed or encouraged in the conversation of groups of associates, the influence of particular messages should be enhanced. Thus, consistent with our earlier claims, a model of interpersonal influence that attends to the daily conversations of friends and acquaintances and their influence upon one another will be more likely to predict the ultimate influence of messages, whether mass mediated or delivered interpersonally. A recent and cogent example is provided by 9/11. Many watched coverage and talked to others almost continuously while trying to attach meaning to the assault on the United States. Talk with others became a primary means by which we arrived at understandings of media images and messages.

Duck (2002b) proposed that intermedia theory is usefully supplemented by the recognition of the fact that individuals converse with their friends and social acquaintances about incoming information, from whatever source. Thus information is evaluated by the individual not only in ways that are accounted for by Babrow's proposals but are (perhaps first, or perhaps second) assessed against the likelihood of reception by the social network. On this view, a person not only integrates information according to its informational characteristics but takes account of its likely social effects within the network. A person assessing information therefore takes account of the ways in which its ultimate integration may affect that person's social life. Its import is likely to be at least discussed with friends and the results of dealing with the information in one way or another will also be assessed for the likely social consequences.

In this sense the relationship between people can exert a perpetually influential effect on their acceptance of, or resistance to, persuasion attempts. For instance, a person may be exposed to messages about the benefits of stopping smoking and yet belong to a group that performs its friendship in places where smoking is part of the performance. The impact of messages as pieces of pure information may well be moderated by the perceived impact upon the friendship of accepting the information, and hence the social influence of the relationships may overpower the cognitive effects of the information. The person may prefer to continue the friendship rather than quit smoking on the basis of information about health risks and may in fact prefer to devalue the information (Duck, 2002b). Thus the impact of the health message is moderated by the silent but powerful influence exerted by the person's desire to remain friends with a social network. Indeed, Pechmann, Zhao, Goldberg, & Reibling (2003) showed that adolescents particularly are more likely to be influenced by antismoking ads that stress adolescents' perceptions that smoking poses severe risks of social disapproval. Those ads that presented information about health risks had no influence on the adolescents at all. Additionally, Miller's (1998) work has found that adolescents perceive that refusing offers of alcohol, tobacco, and other drugs has significant relational implications and that generating effective refusal strategies involves competency in understanding the relational and identity consequences of acceptance or refusal.

Reconstructing Interpersonal Influence in Multiple Contexts

Our proposals have a number of consequences for a variety of lines of inquiry in communication studies, including the study of interpersonal influence, communication, and community, as well as a number of different threads in the communication discipline as a whole. First, for the study of interpersonal influence, we urge more studies that closely investigate the accounts provided to others in the social network about attitude and behavior change. Our SCIPI (social consequences of interpersonal influence) model recognizes that to effect attitude or behavior change in a target individual, that change must be accounted for in the target person's community of relationships in order to be realized. Further, because attitude and behavior change always implicates the relationships and identities of the target persons, it is important to understand what accounts are treated as acceptable or unacceptable in specific relational configurations.

Our claims in this chapter also suggest a particular rendering of the concept of community as real and active relationships in one's social network. Other commentators on community (e.g., Bellah, Madsen, Sullivan, Swidler, & Tipton, 1985) have argued that close, intimate relationships and individual experiences have become a substitute for membership in a larger community or public life. We, however, are making a different point: Community needs to be understood not as a label to designate membership in a social group or geographical unit, or to imply common rights or interests, but, in this discipline, as the network of real and actively connected relationships, be they intimate, acquaintance, or familial. It is this matrix of relationships that serves as the grounding for our knowledge of the world and our place and value in it. Communication researchers are urged to consider this conceptualization of community and to consider the active, relational dynamics that constitute such communities.

Further, our emphasis on the importance of relationships to the process of interpersonal influence has a number of implications for the communication discipline as a whole; these will be discussed in the remainder of this section. For one thing, the recognition of the importance of the social relational substratum of individual decision making requires us to theorize the social relational effects of messages, whether directed at healthy behavior or at acceptance of messages about products or other aspects of attitude change. We submit that theories of the impact of messages about health, for example, will be influential and effective only to the extent that they recognize a person's embedding in a social and relational network that may view the messages in particular lights, whether these are the same ones intended by the source or not. We also suggest that models of media effects are deficient to the extent that they fail to acknowledge the interpersonal context in which individuals make decisions about such mediated messages and discuss the content of media programs. Although mediated messages may indeed occasionally connect directly with an individual's psyche (as suggested by hypodermic models), we suggest that important messages are more frequently run past the network by receivers and their implications and possible meanings discussed therein before an individual makes a binding decision about their treatment, let alone adoption. We further suggest that when an individual processes such information alone, he or she at least weighs into the equation the likely effects of any adoption or rejection of the message upon his or her standing within important social relationships.

Our suggestions also offer a different perspective on group decision making. If one saw an important substrate of relationship issues operating in any context of interpersonal influence, then one would turn to some underlying relational dynamics as an addendum to any theories of group decision making that had previously focused only on the assimilation of information by individuals, groups, or collectives. Thus decisions that are incompetent or nonfunctional from the point of view of usage of information (Hirokawa, 1988) may be rendered more sensible by reference to the relational concerns of those involved (Duck, 1998). The fact that individuals in a group do not consider all relevant information can be ascribed to the relevance of the preservation of interpersonal relationships with other group members, for example. An individual may defer to a powerful group member because it is more important to that person to stay on good terms with the powerful person than it is to use information effectively as judged outside of relational context.

In the case of jury decision making, this analysis would suggest that the relational activities carried out in juries might ultimately be as persuasive as the arguments offered by particular people. It has always been observed that juries spend a disproportionate amount of time talking about things other than the case at hand (James, 1959), but previous analyses have not suspected that this time is spent forming relationships or moral judgments of the companion jurors (Duck, 1998). If instead of reproaching juries for wasting time, researchers accepted that this is probably time spent building relationships, then the analysis of jury decisions could be more firmly based on the everyday relationship practices that we have analyzed here. This would have the implication that jury selection should focus not only on the personal characteristics and attitudes of individual jurors but also on their ethos and likelihood of appealing to other jury members as authoritative or trustworthy sources.

Yet another area of research that would be affected by our analysis above concerns the spread of innovations, which can also be understood better by reference to the relational linkages in a network. Those who are opinion leaders (Katz & Lazarsfeld, 1955) for a particular individual may or may not be the marked leaders in the relevant community and are as likely to be the people whom each individual severally trusts and looks to for self-sustaining discourse about everyday life. Hence rather than identifying opinion leaders by their role occupancy in general terms, we would propose identifying them by means of their relational connections to a target individual. The individual is more likely to be influenced by the opinion leaders with whom he or she interacts most often about a range of things or by individuals to whom the person accords great credibility on particular matters or topics and by those whose opinions and knowledge are trusted as informed and reliable on the topic in question (Duck, 2002b).

If we extend our earlier discussion of Bergmann's (1993) analysis of the ways in which gossip works, then social conformity can result not from the rational evaluation of pieces of information but on the basis of expectations of social consequences for treating information a particular way, as noted earlier. This observation has several important consequences for other areas of research in communication studies in addition to those already discussed above, and we select the following nonexhaustive examples. First, health communication and messages related to health would be enhanced to the extent that they attend to the relational dynamics noted in this chapter, both in terms of the contrast of official sources versus the opinions about such sources held in the networks of relationships in which the person operates and in terms of the relational consequences of adopting or rejecting a particular message. Second, media and the intermedia approach to messages can be modified in the terms that we have proposed earlier to take account of the ways in which relational embeddedness generates and also affects people's likelihood of discussing mediated messages with one another, and effective campaigns will, we propose, be those that target the network and stimulate discussion there. Third, consideration of the role of social sanctions such as gossip (foreshadowed above) as a means of social control and also as an influence on the spread or inhibition of information and behavior change about key topics.

Further, the field of marketing has seen an explosion of concepts related to relationships, including network marketing (Frenzen & Davis, 1990), relationship marketing (Barnes, 2001), advertising (Scott, 2003), as well as word of mouth in the development of products and their impact (Murray, 1991), loyalty to brands and organizations (Fournier, 1998), and viral marketing (Helm, 2000). Scott (2003) has noted that a large emphasis of modern advertising is on the relationship between the customer and the organization or on brand loyalty, a relationship of customer to product. She notes that "recent research has touted the power of warm advertising to boost sales of familiar brands given increased media weight and that a useful framing is provided by intimacy in psychology, creative strategy (appeal) and involvement in advertising, and relationship development in services marketing. Many businesses now see the task of relationship marketing advertising as one that transforms impersonal mass communication into representations of personal discourse." Despite the obvious emphasis of communication concepts in this approach, communication scholars have been left largely aside in the developments here. Our analysis gives us a foothold in this expanding area because it places and interprets the role of relationships somewhat differently from its placement by the marketers. The emphasis on the social context of living takes circumstances of everyday life into account and makes them a sleeping, but significant, part of work on interpersonal influence and interpersonal communication by marketers and others.

AND SO . . .

Our claims have been that relationship life is epistemic, that it provides persons with a sense of the validity and verifiability of their ideas as indicated by both Festinger (1954) and a variety of communication theorists. We have attempted to show that the leaching of the epistemic into everyday life experience provides persons with a large range of references upon which to sound, and ground, their attitudes and beliefs, including those in transition. That set of referees exerts an influence on the individual that affects choices made at the individual level. In acknowledging this influence, we are forced to revise common understandings of relationships as containers in which individuals have their personal needs fulfilled. Instead, we have conceived of relationships as a form of action—which emphasizes the integral connections between the study of rhetoric and relationships— and we have reformulated individual decision making as relationally grounded. Our bottom-line position, then, is that the relational bases of individual decision making are not only overlooked but also extremely powerful ways to extend communication theory and the practical world beyond.

REFERENCES

Acitelli, L. K., Duck, S. W., & West, D. L. (2000). Embracing the social in personal relationships and research. In W. Ickes & S. W. Duck (Eds.), *Social psychology and personal relationships* (pp. 215–227). Chichester, UK: Wiley.

Antaki, C. (1994). *Explaining and arguing: The social organization of accounts*. London: Sage.

Babrow, A. S. (1992). Communication and problematic integration: Understanding diverging probability and value, ambiguity, ambivalence, and impossibility. *Communication Theory, 2,* 95–130.

Babrow, A. S. (1995). Communication and problematic integration: Milan Kundera's "Lost Letters" in *The Book of Laughter and Forgetting. Communication Monographs, 62,* 283–300.

Babrow, A. S. (2001). Uncertainty, value, communication, and problematic integration. *Journal of Communication, 51,* 553–573.

Barnes, J. G. (2001). *Secrets of customer relationship management: It's all about how you make them feel.* New York: McGraw-Hill.

Baxter, L. A. (1987). Symbols of relationship identity in relationship cultures. *Journal of Social and Personal Relationships, 4,* 261–280.

Baxter, L. A., Dun, T., & Sahlstein, E. (2001). Rules for relating communicated among social network members. *Journal of Social and Personal Relationships, 18(2),* 173–199.

Baxter, L. A., & Montgomery, B. M. (1996). *Relating: Dialogues and dialectics.* New York: Guilford Press.

Bellah, R. N., Madsen, R., Sullivan, W. M., Swidler, A., & Tipton, S. M. (1985). *Habits of the heart: Individualism and commitment in American life.* New York: Harper & Row.

Bergmann, J. R. (1993). *Discreet indiscretions: The social organization of gossip.* New York: Aldine de Gruyter.

Berscheid, E., & Walster [Hatfield], E. (1974). Physical attractiveness. In L. Berkowitz (Ed.), *Advances in Experimental Social Psychology* (pp. 158–216). New York: Academic Press.

Biggart, N. W. (1989). *Charismatic capitalism: Direct selling organizations in America*. Chicago: University of Chicago Press.

Brown, P., & Levinson, S. C. (1987). *Universals in language usage: Politeness phenomena*. Cambridge, UK: Cambridge University Press.

Burke, K. (1945/1969). *A grammar of motives*. Berkeley: University of California Press.

Burke, K. (1966). *Language as symbolic action*. Berkeley: University of California Press.

Burleson, B. R. (1990). Comforting as social support: Relational consequences of supportive behaviors. In S. W. Duck & W. R. C. Silver (Eds.), *Personal relationships and social support* (pp. 66–82) London: Sage.

Buttny, R. (1993). *Social accountability in communication*. London: Sage.

Byrne, D. (1997). An overview (and underview) of research and theory within the attraction paradigm. *Journal of Social and Personal Relationships, 14*, 417–431.

Campbell, J. K. (1964). *Honor, family, and patronage: A study of institutions and moral values in a Greek mountain community*. Oxford, UK: Oxford University Press.

Carl, W. J. (2001). *The (interactional) business of doing business: A rhetorical discursive action analysis of an e-commerce business opportunity* (Doctoral dissertation, University of Iowa, Iowa City, IA), [Online]. Retrieved April 20, 2001 from http://etd.lib.uiowa.edu/etd.html

Chang, Y., & Duck, S. W. *Beyond what's said purposefully: Interpersonal influence revisited*. Manuscript in preparation. University of Iowa.

Cialdini, R. B. (1993). *Influence: Science and practice*. New York: Harper Collins.

Cissna, K., & Sieburg, E. (1981). Patterns of interactional confirmation and disconfirmation. In C. Wilder-Mott & J. Weakland (Eds.), *Rigor and imagination: Essays from the legacy of Gregory Bateson* (pp. 65–91). New York: Praeger.

Cupach, W. R., & Metts, S. (1994). *Facework*. Thousand Oaks, CA: Sage.

Dainton, M. (2000). Maintenance behaviors, expectations for maintenance, and satisfaction: Linking comparison levels to relational maintenance strategies. *Journal of Social and Personal Relationships, 17*, 827–842.

Dindia, K. (2000). Self-disclosure, identity, and relationship development: A dialectical perspective. In K. Dindia & S. W. Duck (Eds.), *Communication and personal relationships* (pp. 147–162). Chichester, UK: Wiley.

Dindia, K., Fitzpatrick, M. A., & Kenny, D. A. (1989, May). *Self-disclosure in spouse and stranger dyads: A social relations analysis*. Paper presented at the annual conference of the International Communication Association, San Francisco, CA.

Duck, S. W. (1994). *Meaningful relationships: Talking, sense, and relating*. Thousand Oaks, CA: Sage.

Duck, S. W. (1995). Talking relationships into being. *Journal of Social and Personal Relationships, 12*, 535–540.

Duck, S. W. (1998). *Human relationships* (3rd ed.). London: Sage

Duck, S. W. (2002a). Hypertext in the key of G: Three types of "history" as influences on conversational structure and flow. *Communication Theory, 12*(1), 41–62.

Duck, S. W. (2002b, November). *Meaning[ful], relationships and health*. Paper presented at the annual conference of the National Communication Association, New Orleans, LA.

Duck, S. W., & Pond, K. (1989). Friends, Romans, countrymen; lend me your retrospective data: Rhetoric and reality in personal relationships. In C. Hendrick (Ed.), *Close relationships* (pp. 17–38). Newbury Park, CA: Sage.

Duck, S. W., Rutt, D. J., Hurst, M., & Strejc, H. (1991). Some evident truths about conversations in everyday relationships: All communication is not created equal. *Human Communication Research, 18*, 228–267.

Duck, S. W., & VanderVoort, L. A. (2002). Scarlet letters and whited sepulchers: The social marking of relationships as "inappropriate." In R. Goodwin & D. Cramer, *Inappropriate relationships: The unconventional, the disapproved, and the forbidden* (pp. 3–24). Mahwah, NJ, Erlbaum.

Duck, S., West, L., & Acitelli, L. (1997). Sewing the field: The tapestry of relationships in life and research. In S. W. Duck (Ed.), *Handbook of personal relationships* (2nd ed., pp. 1–27). Chichester, UK: Wiley.

Edgar, T., & Fitzpatrick, M. A. (1988). Compliance-gaining in relational interaction: When your life depends on it. *Southern Speech Communication Journal, 53*, 385–405.

Festinger, L. (1954). A theory of social comparison processes. *Human Relations, 7*, 117–40.

Fitch, K. L. (1998). *Speaking relationally: Culture, communication, and interpersonal connection.* New York: Guilford.

Fitch, K. L. (2003). Cultural persuadables. *Communication Theory, 1*, 100–123.

Fournier, S. (1998). Consumers and their brands: Developing relationship theory in consumer research. *Journal of Consumer Research, 24*, 343–373.

Frankfurt, H. (1986, February). Reflections on bullshit. *Harper's Magazine*, 14–17.

Frenzen, J. R., & Davis, H. L. (1990). Purchasing behavior in embedded markets. *Journal of Consumer Research, 17*, 1–12.

Gass, R. H., & Seiter, J. S. (1999). *Persuasion, social influence, and compliance-gaining.* Boston: Allyn & Bacon.

Giles, H., Taylor, D. M., & Bourhis, R. Y. (1973). Towards a theory of interpersonal accommodation through language use. *Language in Society, 2*, 177–192.

Goffman, E. (1959a). *Behaviour in public places.* Harmondsworth, UK: Penguin.

Goffman, E. (1959b). *The presentation of self in everyday life.* New York: Overlook.

Goffman, E. (1967). *Interaction ritual: Essays on face-to-face behavior.* New York: Pantheon.

Goldsmith, D. (1990). Gossip from the native's point of view: A comparative analysis. *Research on Language and Social Interaction, 23*, 163–194.

Goldsmith, D. J., & Fitch, K. (1997). The normative context of advice as social support. *Human Communication Research, 23*, 454–476.

Goldsmith, D., & Parks, M. (1990). Communicative strategies for managing the risks of seeking social support. In S. W. Duck & W. R. C. Silver (Eds.), *Personal relationships and social support* (pp. 104–121). Newbury Park, CA: Sage.

Goodman, R. F., & Ben-Ze'ev, A. (Eds.). (1994). *Good gossip.* Lawrence: University Press of Kansas.

Gronbeck, B. E. (1997). Tradition and technology in local news: The social psychology of form. *Sociological Quarterly, 38*, 361–374.

Gumpert, G., & Cathcart, R. (Eds.). (1986). *Inter/Media: Interpersonal communication in a media world* (3rd ed.). New York: Oxford University Press.

Hauser, G. (1986). *Introduction to rhetorical theory.* New York: Harper & Row.

Helm, S. (2000). Viral marketing: Establishing customer relationships by "word-of-mouse." *Electronic Markets, 10(3)*, 158–161.

Hepburn, J. R., & Crepin, A. E. (1984). Relationship strategies in a coercive institution: A study of dependence among prison guards. *Journal of Social and Personal Relationships, 1*, 139–158.

Hirokawa, R. Y. (1988). Group communication and decision-making performance: A continued test of the functional perspective. *Human Communication Research, 14*, 487–515.

Hopper, R., Knapp, M. L., & Scott, L. (1981). Couples' personal idioms: exploring intimate talk. *Journal of Communication, 31*(1), 23–33.

James, R. M. (1959). Status and competence of jurors. *American Journal of Sociology, 64*, 563–570.

Katz, E., & Lazarsfeld, P. F. (1955). *Personal influence: The part played by people in the flow of mass communication.* Glencoe, IL: Free Press.

Kelly, G. A. (1969). Ontological acceleration. In B. Maher (Ed.), *Clinical psychology and personality: The collected papers of George Kelly* (pp. 7–45). New York: Wiley.

Knapp, M. L., Hopper, R., & Bell, R. A. (1984). Compliments: A descriptive taxonomy. *Journal of Communication, 34*(4), 12–31.

La Gaipa, J. J. (1982). Rules and rituals in disengaging from relationships. In S. W. Duck (Ed.), *Personal relationships 4: Dissolving personal relationships* (pp. 189–209). London: Academic Press.

Larson, C. U. (1989). *Persuasion: Reception and responsibility.* Belmont, CA: Wadsworth.

Leatham, G. B., & Duck, S. W. (1990). Conversations with friends and the dynamics of social support. In S. W. Duck & W. R. C. Silver (Eds.), *Personal relationships and social support* (pp. 1–29). London: Sage.

Lim, T. S., & Bowers, J. W. (1991). Facework, solidarity, approbation, and tact. Human *Communication Research, 17*, 415–450.

Liss, B. (2000). *Popular TV talk-shows as moral resources.* Unpublished doctoral dissertation, University of Colorado, Boulder.

Lyons, R. F., Mickelson, K. D., Sullivan, M. J. L., & Coyne, J. C. (1998). Coping as a communal process. *Journal of Social and Personal Relationships, 15*, 579–605.

Masuda, M. (2000). *Post dissolution relationships as rhetorical situations.* Unpublished doctoral dissertation, University of Iowa, Iowa City.

McMahan, D. T. (2001). *Where's the beef?* Unpublished doctoral dissertation, University of Iowa, Iowa City, IA.

Mead, G. H. (1934). *Mind, self and society.* Chicago: University of Chicago Press.

Milardo, R. M., & Wellman, B. (1992). The personal is social. *Journal of Social and Personal Relationships, 9*, 339–42.

Miller, D. L. (Ed.). (1980). *The individual and the social self: Unpublished work of G. H. Mead.* Chicago: University of Chicago Press.

Miller, G. R. (1987). Persuasion. In C. R. Berger & S. Chaffee (Eds.), *Handbook of communication science* (pp. 446–483). Newbury Park, CA, Sage.

Miller, G. R., Boster, F., Roloff, M., & Seibold, D. (1977). Compliance-gaining message strategies: A typology and some findings concerning effects of situational differences. *Communication Monographs, 44*, 37–51.

Miller, G. R., & Steinberg, M. (1975). *Between people: A new analysis of interpersonal communication.* Chicago: Science Research Associates.

Miller, M. A. (1998). The social process of drug resistance in a relational context. *Communication Studies, 49*, 358–375.

Miller, M., Alberts, J. Hecht, M., & Trost, M. (2000). *Adolescent relationships and drug resistance.* Mahwah, NJ: Erlbaum.

Mokros, H. B. (Ed.). (2003). *Identity matters: Communication based explorations and explanations.* Cresskill, NJ: Hampton Press.

Murray, K. (1991). Consumer information acquisition activities. *Journal of Marketing, 55*, 10–21.

Pechmann, C., Zhao, G., Goldberg, M. E., & Reibling, E. T. (2003). What to convey in antismoking advertisements for adolescents: The use of protection motivation theory to identify effective message themes. *Journal of Marketing, 67*, 1–18.

Petronio, S. (2002). *Boundaries of privacy.* Albany: State University of New York Press.

Petty, R. E., & Cacioppo, J. T. (1981). *Attitudes and persuasion: Classic and contemporary approaches.* Dubuque, IA: W.C. Brown.

Potter, J. (1996). *Representing reality: Discourse, rhetoric and social construction.* London: Sage.

Potter, J., & Wetherell, M. (1987). *Discourse and social psychology.* London: Sage.

Roloff, M. E., Janiszewski, C. A., McGrath, A. M., Burns, C. S., & Manrai, L. A. (1988). Acquiring resources from intimates: When obligation substitutes for persuasion. *Human Communication Research, 14*, 364–396.

Sahlstein, E. (1999, November). *The relationship in talk: Explicit and implicit influences on persuasion.* Paper presented at the annual conference of the National Communication Association, Chicago, IL.

Sanders, R. E., & Fitch, K. L. (2001). The actual practice of compliance seeking. *Communication Theory, 11*(3), 263–289.

Scott, A. (2003). *Relationship marketing.* Unpublished doctoral dissertation, University of Florida, Gainesville.

Searcy, M. (2003, April). *The social problematic integration theory (SPIT) model.* Paper presented at the annual conference of the Central States Communication Association, Omaha, NE.

Seibold, D. R., Cantrill, J. G., & Meyers, R. A. (1994). Communication and interpersonal influence. In M. L. Knapp & G. R. Miller (Eds.), *Handbook of interpersonal communication* (2nd ed., pp. 542–588). Thousand Oaks, CA: Sage.

Senchea, J. A. (1998). *Gendered constructions of sexuality in adolescent girls' talk.* Unpublished doctoral dissertation, University of Iowa, Iowa City.

Shotter, J. (1992). What is a "personal" relationship? A rhetorical-responsive account of "unfinished business." In J. H. Harvey, T. L. Orbuch, & A. L. Weber (Eds.), *Attributions, accounts, and close relationships* (pp. 19–39). New York: Springer-Verlag.

Surra, C. A. (1988). The influence of the interactive network on developing relationships. In R. Milardo (Ed.), *Families and social networks* (pp. 48–82). Newbury Park, CA: Sage.

Taylor, R. (1978). Marilyn's friends and Rita's customers: A study of party selling as play and as work. *Sociological Review, 26*, 573–611.

Thoreau, H. D. (1986). *Walden.* Cutchogue, NY: Buccaneer Books.

Tracy, K., & Anderson, D. L. (1999). Relational positioning strategies in police calls: A dilemma. *Discourse Studies, 1*, 201–225.

VanderVoort, L. A., & Duck, S. W. (2000). Talking about "relationships": Variations on a theme. In K. Dindia & S. W. Duck (Eds.), *Communication and personal relationships* (pp. 1–12). Chichester, UK: Wiley.

Watzlawick, P., Beavin, J., & Jackson, D. (1967). *Pragmatics of human communication.* New York: W. W. Norton.

Weiss, R. S. (1974). The provisions of social relationships. In Z. Rubin (Ed.), *Doing unto others* (pp. 17–26). New Jersey: Prentice Hall.

West, J. T. (1995). Understanding how the dynamics of ideology influence violence between intimates. *Confronting Relationship Challenges* (Vol. 5, pp. 129–149). Newbury Park, CA: Sage.

West, L. (1996, November). *Deception as a social practice.* Paper presented at the annual conference of the Speech Communication Association, San Antonio, TX.

Wilson, S. R. (2000). *Is there a difference between relational communication and interpersonal communication?* Paper presented at the annual conference of the Central States Communication Association, Detroit, MI.

Wilson, S. R., Aleman, C. G., & Leatham, G. B. (1998). Identity implications of influence goals: A revised analysis of face-threatening acts and application to seeking compliance gaining with same sex friends. *Human Communication Research, 25*(1), 64–92.

Winters, A. M., & Duck, S. W. (2001). You ****!!! Swearing as an aversive and a relational activity. In R. Kowalski (Ed.), *Behaving badly: Aversive behaviors in interpersonal relationships* (pp. 59–77). Washington, DC: APA Books.

Wolf, M. (1972). *Women and the family in rural Taiwan.* Stanford, CA: Stanford University Press.

Wood, J. T. (1982). Communication and relational culture: Bases for the study of human relationships. *Communication Quarterly, 30*, 75–83.

Wood, J. T. (2001). The normalization of violence in heterosexual romantic relationships: Women's narratives of love and violence. *Journal of Social and Personal Relationships, 18*, 239–261.

CHAPTER CONTENTS

2 Romantic and Parent-Child Relationships at a Distance

LAURA STAFFORD
The Ohio State University

Cultural expectations in U.S. society dictate that communication should be frequent and face-to-face in order to sustain close relationships, romantic partners should live in geographic proximity, and married individuals and parents and young children should share a residence. Such conceptions about communication in and residential structures of close relationships immediately call into question how geographically separated individuals can maintain close relational ties. Numerous types of long-distance relationships are reviewed, including dating relationships, dual-career couples, and spouses separated due to military deployments or incarceration. Parents and young children may also encounter separations because of divorce, military deployment, or imprisonment. The variety of long-distance relationships (LDRs) and families calls us to reconsider traditional views of the role of communication in close relationships and family structures. Research must go beyond frequency, amount, or mode of interaction. Vague, positive communication may help sustain LDRs as it fosters idealized images. The usual criterion of relational stability as success is simplistic, as success may be defined in numerous ways. Relational dissolution or lessened contact may be considered a success in certain circumstances. The proximal community plays a significant, albeit not always helpful role for individuals in long-distance relationships.

I n U.S. society, face-to-face interaction is the preferred primary mode of communication in intimate relationships (O'Sullivan, 2000). Communication should also be frequent and in-depth for close relationships to thrive (Parks, 1995). In addition, casual talk or small talk on a daily basis is a presumed relational necessity (Duck & Pittman, 1994). Concomitantly, infrequent contact, increases in distance, and increases in time between interactions have been seen as classic hallmarks of relational demise (Miller & Parks, 1982). Such conceptions about communication in personal relationships immediately calls into question how geographically separated individuals can maintain close relational ties.

Correspondence: Laura Stafford, The Ohio State University, 3016 Derby Hall, 154 N. Oval Mall, Columbus, OH; email: Stafford.3@osu.edu

This review compiles what is known about communication in selected long-distance relationships and considers the role community plays in these relationships, as proximal networks may play a more influential role in long-distance relationships (LDRs) than in geographically close relationships. The LDRs considered herein are romantic partners, both dating and married, and parent-child relationships. The family as a whole is considered when sufficient research allows. Social science research has predominantly focused on the successes of long-distance relationships (LDRs), on ramifications of separation on romantic partners or on children, and on how individuals cope with separation. Interests in sustaining LDRs and in coping with effects of separations upon individuals involved in LDRs leads directly to consideration of community.

An additional goal of this review is to delineate various types of success in LDRs, as the usual criteria of stability and satisfaction are simplistic at best, and irrelevant or potentially harmful at worst. The ultimate goal then is to consider the role of communication in the success of LDRs, note deficits in current literature, and offer conclusions and suggestions for future study.

After delineating the scope of this review, I outline various types of LDRs, then consider selected U.S. cultural expectations that are particularly relevant to LDRs. Multiple levels of success are then differentiated and the little that is known about communication and success is explicated. Because roles are often problematic in LDRs, I include a brief discussion. I will also take a look at the manner in which community and proximal relationships support or hinder individuals in LDRs. Finally, I suggest future directions of research and offer conclusions.

SCOPE AND DEFINITIONS

This review considers long-distance dating relationships and selected family relationships in U.S. culture. Within the family, I consider marital partners and parents and their relatively young children (whether the parents are married or not), as well as the family as a whole when sufficient research allows. Given the scarcity of research on long-distance families as a whole, focus is predominantly upon two types of LDRs: romantic and young child-parent.

The exact definition of a long-distance romantic relationship varies from report to report. Some research has considered long-distance marriages as those in which the couple spends at least three nights per week in separate residences (Gerstel & Gross, 1984). Definitions for long-distance dating relationships do not hinge upon residences, but rather on other physical parameters such as mileage (Carpenter & Knox, 1986). Others have defined long-distance romantic relationships as those which participants consider long distance (Dellmann-Jenkins, Bernard-Paolucci, & Rushing, 1994). Such a definition likely captures relational reality better than researcher-imposed constructions.

Definitions for long-distance parent-child relationships have not been attempted in the literature. Children are generally only considered secondarily in long-distance romantic relationships in terms of how their mere existence or age affects long-distance couples and only a few studies have examined the long-distance family as a whole.

In addition to children of long-distance partners, parents and children may be separated when the parents are no longer romantically involved, as in the case of divorced or never-married partners. Children may live many miles from one parent or within a few blocks, but due to court restrictions or other factors have limited access to that parent. Long-distance parent-child relationships may also occur when a parent is imprisoned, whether or not the child's parents have a continued romantic involvement. In all of these cases, a child has restricted communication opportunities with at least one parent.

As is readily apparent, relationships at a distance or long-distance relationships defy precise definitions. Long-distance relationships may best be considered as an injunctive construct. "All injunctively defined concepts lack a sharp borderline but merge by graduation into neighboring concepts" (Lorenz, 1966, p. 276). Long-distance relationships are a fuzzy set; no formal definition will be attempted here. Rather as a guiding principle, relationships are considered long distance when communication opportunities are restricted in the view of the individuals involved, because of geographic parameters, and the individuals within the relationship have expectations of a continued close connection.

All studies of romantic LDRs reference heterosexual relationships; I located no research on long-distance homosexual relationships. Moreover, research on dating relationships and dual-career relationships is based almost exclusively on White, middle-class samples. I found only one study examining African American dual career-dual residence (DCDR) couples (Jackson, Brown, & Patterson-Stewart, 2000). Studies concerning separation due to military deployment and incarceration include a broader racial spectrum.

It is not my intent to privilege one group or type of relationship or family form over another. Rather, space limitations and a deficit of research in some areas dictate a relatively narrow scope. The relationships considered herein offer potential for insight into current conceptions of relational communication as, in general, these are in conflict with societal expectations about communication in relationships and views of relational structures.

Invoking perceptions of restricted communication with the expectation of continued close ties yields numerous long-distance relational forms beyond those considered here. Research is beginning to emerge on grandparent-grandchild ties (Harwood, 2000), adult children's relationships with their elderly parents (Mickus & Luz, 2002; Williams & Nussbaum, 2001), and young adult children's or college-aged children's relationships with their middle-aged parents (Graber & Dubas, 1996). Other parent-child long-distance arrangements, such as interaction between parents and children in foster care (Leathers, 2002), have received limited attention.

LDRs may also occur among adult friends (Dugan & Kivett, 1998; Johnson, 2001) and adult siblings (Cicirelli, 1991). Additionally, LDRs may be initiated and developed through computer-mediated communication (Dainton & Aylor, 2002; Parks & Floyd, 1996; Parks & Roberts, 1998).

TYPE AND FREQUENCY ESTIMATES OF LDRS

More research has been conducted on long-distance romantic relationships than other forms of long-distance relationships. The field of communication has spent the most energy investigating premarital or dating relationships (Aylor, 2003). To date, the extant literature within the field of communication has focused almost exclusively on dyads in which at least one member is a college student. College LDRs are accessible and ubiquitous; reports estimate that anywhere from 25% to 50% of college students are involved in a long-distance romantic relationships at any given point (Dellmann-Jenkins et al., 1994), and 75% of college students have at some time been involved in at least one long-distance romantic relationship (Guldner & Swensen, 1995).

In addition to college dating LDRs, married individuals are often geographically separated. Estimates put the number of married persons living apart for reasons other than consideration of divorce at 2.4 million in 1998, a rise of 18% since 1994 (Fields & Casper, 2001). The two most common reasons for marital noncohabitation are military service[1] and incarceration[2] (Rindfuss & Stephen, 1990). However, the exact number of long-distance marriages or families in the United States is difficult to obtain because many forms are not recognized as a category by the U.S. Census Bureau. For example, families who have one residence from which one member travels extensively are not captured in census numbers, nor are dual-residence, dual-career married couples.

Gross (1980) classified long-distance marriages, and implicitly families with children, into two major types. The first is single-residence, single-career families in which, most often, the wife-mother remains at the primary residence and the occupational demands of the husband-father require his extended absence. Two general variations of this single-residence, single-career, long-distance family exist: civilian and military. Some civilian occupations, such as professional sports, politics, merchant marines, and some business professions, require various periods of separation (Gerstel & Gross, 1984). These separations might be regular, frequent, and short, such as when business professionals are gone for several days a week (Boss, McCubbin, & Lester, 1979; Roehling & Bultman, 2002), or they might involve individuals who are absent for months at a time, such as offshore oil workers (Lowenstein, 1986; Morrice & Taylor, 1978; Vormbrock, 1993). Civilian separations may also occur because of imprisonment of one partner (Lowenstein, 1986).

Given the relative deficit of literature, especially recent literature, on civilian forms of single-residence long-distance couples, research on military families is predominantly considered here, although I offer insights from civilian forms when applicable and available. The ramifications of deployment on military families have a long research tradition (Waller, 1940). Separations are simply part of military life. The number of married personnel in the armed forces has increased in the past few decades. For example, 16% of Vietnam soldiers were married with children, compared to 60% of Gulf War soldiers (Cooper & Ward-Zuckerman, 2001).

The second global type of long-distance marriage or family is the dual-career, dual-residence one (DCDR).[3] These arrangements refer to married individuals, with or without children, who voluntarily maintain two distinct residences, intend to stay married, and are both committed to careers. They choose to live separately because of difficulties finding suitable career opportunities for both partners in the same geographic location (Anderson & Spruill, 1993; Gross, 1980; Taylor & Lounsbury, 1988). Estimates place the number of DCDR couples around 700,000 (Maines, 1993) to 1 million (Stroh, 1999).

Beginning with Rapoport and Rapoport's (1969) conceptualization of the dual-career couple, extensive research has focused upon this type of marriage (Gilbert, 1993). The specific focus on the subset of dual-career, dual-residence couples has been somewhat meager. Research peaked during the late 1970s to mid 1980s (Douvan & Pleck, 1978; Farris, 1978; Gerstel, 1978, 1979; Gerstel & Gross, 1982, 1983,1984,1987; Kirschner & Walum, 1978; Winfield, 1985) but has lessened in recent years. Interest, however, may be re-emerging (Magnuson & Norem, 1999; Rhodes, 2002).

The lack of research on dual-career, dual-residence marriages is somewhat surprising given the increasing number of dual-career academicians. Approximately 40% of academic women are married to academic partners, which results in many DCDR marriages (Astin & Milem, 1997). The situation is so prevalent that physicists and other scientists have punfully labeled the dual-career problem the "dual-body" problem (McNeil & Sher, 1999).

Two other types of long-distance romantic relationship have escaped much study and thus receive only passing consideration here. The first is the long-distance cohabiting couple. Although this may seem oxymoronic, such couples are those who have cohabitated and then moved to separate geographic vicinities, not due to discord or intent to dissolve the union, but often for career or educational reasons. A cohabiting couple may resume coresidence with marriage or without marriage (Binstock & Thornton, 2003). The extent to which studies of long-distance dating relationships or marriages include prior cohabiters is not known because information about prior cohabitation is generally not reported.

Another type of couple not formally recognized is "living apart together" couples or LATs. LATs may or may not be married, may be heterosexual or homosexual, and might or might not have children, are self-defined as a couple, and both partners have their own primary residence (Levin & Trost, 1999). Dual-career dual-residence marriages would not be considered a LAT couple if one residence was primary and another secondary. Moreover, LATs exist for many reasons beyond career concerns, military duty, or incarceration. For example, a couple formed later in life may desire to maintain separate homes in order to live in proximity to children or grandchildren. Apparently The Netherlands is the only place that has a term for this type of couple, though certainly such couples exist in the U.S. (See Levin & Trost for a review of types of and reasons for LATs).

Just as it is difficult to determine the precise number of marital couples living apart, it is equally difficult to know the number of young children who spend a significant amount of time away from at least one parent. In 2000, 28% of children under 18 lived with one parent—23% lived with the mother, 5% with the father—4% lived with neither parent (Fields & Casper, 2001). These numbers include children whose parent is absent due to divorce, nonmarital childbirth, or death. However, the number of children who live away from at least one parent for extended periods of time because of parental military deployment, incarceration, or occupational demands is not represented in reports of children's living arrangements (Fields & Casper).

The fastest growing reason children are separated from a parent is incarceration (Brenner, 2001). The number of fathers in prison grew by 61% in the 1990s and the number of imprisoned mothers grew by 85% (Mumola, 2000). Approximately one third of fathers and just over one half of mothers in state prisons report that at least one minor child lived with them at the time of their arrest (Mumola). About 2% of U.S. children have one or both parents incarcerated (Reed & Reed, 1997).

When considering children separated from a parent because of military duties, the presumption has been that the deployed parent was the father. However, the Gulf War became dubbed the "mommy war" because during this conflict, 40,793 women were deployed and approximately one third of these had one or more dependent children (Pierce, Vinokur, & Buck, 1998; U.S. Presidential Commission, 1993). Both the number of dual-military couples and the number of married women in military service are increasing. As of 2001, 5.7% of active duty personnel were in dual-military marriages. The percentage of women on active duty and in the reserves continued to increase from 1980 to 2001. The number of women in the reserves rose from 6.3% to 17.5%, and the number of enlisted women from 8.3% to 17.5% (Military Family Resource Center, 2002).

CULTURAL EXPECTATIONS

Long-distance relationships are of particular interest to students of communication and family as they exist in contradiction to two societal expectations: (a) Face-to-face communication is necessary for close relational ties, and (b) family members share a residence.

Close Relationships and Face-to-Face Communication

A long-standing assumption is that close relationships are characterized by frequent face-to-face contact and, reciprocally, frequent face-to-face contact is necessary for the continuance of close relationships (Parks, 1995). However, clearly relationships do not cease to exist simply because relational partners are not in each other's immediate physical presence. Relationships have often been thought to be mental constructions (Berger & Kellner, 1964; Berger & Luckmann, 1966) that exist beyond copresence (Sigman, 1991; Wilmot, 1995). However, it is through daily talk that such mental creations of relationships are thought to occur and stabilize (Duck & Pittman, 1994). As Sahlstein (in press) reminds us, copresence is conspicuously absent in LDRs. In addition to the simple continuance of relationships, face-to face interaction has generally been tied to relational satisfaction. Studies have indicated that satisfied couples engage in more conversation across a greater variety of topics than dissatisfied couples and spend more time in the evening talking about their day (Richmond, 1995; Vangelisti & Banski, 1993). Individuals perceive daily talk with relational partners as an indication of the healthy continuation of their relationship (Duck, Rutt, Hurst, & Strejc, 1991)

Talk is not the only valued aspect of daily interaction. Simply spending time together is a commonly reported means of maintaining relationships (Dainton & Stafford, 1993; Dindia & Baxter, 1987). In summarizing research, Vangelisti (2002) concluded the "amount of time couples spend engaged in various activities together on a day-to-day basis" (p. 658) has served as a global indicator of relational satisfaction; "people who are happy with their relationships not only spend more time together, they engage in activities that make their time together particularly rewarding" (p. 660). In their review of the literature on marriage, Reissman, Aron, and Bergen (1993) reached a similar conclusion: The time couples spend engaging in leisure activities, such as talking or sharing tasks, is related to their relational satisfaction.

Such expectations are not limited to romantic relationships. Parental time spent interacting with children is considered an indicator of child well-being by U.S. government offices (Fields, Smith, Bass, & Lugaila, 2001). Family academicians concur that routinized, frequent, positive interactions between parents and children lay the foundation for numerous aspects of child's development (Satir, 1988). Though clearly all interaction between parents and children is not positive, again frequency or amount of contact is the most studied aspect of communication in relationships between nonresidential parents and children. By and large, the U.S. societal view is that even among divorced or never married parents, children's overall adjustment is facilitated when frequent contact with both parents is maintained (Hetherington & Stanley-Hagan, 1997).

Families are also defined through interaction, though they are seldom studied as a whole. Burgess (1926) observed that any given family may be best thought of as a set of "interacting personalities" (p. 3). This view still holds: "A family's construction of social reality is represented in the family member's interactions. The social construction of reality is indicated by the lexical speech, the nonlexical speech, and the nonverbal behavior of family members as it is organized into recurring patterns" (Fitzpatrick & Caughlin, 2002, p. 745). Maintenance of family relationships is assumed to be achieved via face-to-face interaction (Vogl-Bauer, 2003).

This is not to say that frequency (or quantity) of face-to-face contact is the only communication construct of relevance in close relationships, nor is it necessarily the most important. Nor is frequency of interaction consistently defined or operationalized. It is, however, the single most often examined variable in research on various forms of LDRs. Perhaps this is because the ambiguous construct of "frequent" face-to-face interaction is at the core of current cultural conceptualization of close relationships, even in an era of increasing technological interactions (O'Sullivan, 2000). Scholars have viewed strong ties as those that are usually in near proximity and offer easily available frequent access (Granovetter, 1973) in order to provide companionship, social support, advice, and emotional assistance (Wellman, 1999).

Individuals have implicit theories of relationships (Fletcher & Thomas, 1996). Though not all cocultural groups within a society share such conceptions to the same extent, and certainly neither do any two relational partners, general societal assumptions influence, at least partially, individuals' expectations of their relationships as well as expectations of members external to those relationships (Reis & Knee, 1996). In other words, most people have significant social and cultural knowledge about what certain types of relationships should be like. This knowledge influences individual expectations or implicit theories and subsequent behavior as well as interpretations of behaviors (Fitzpatrick & Koerner, 2002).

Current societal expectations for romantic partners, whether married or not, are based on companionship, love, and intimacy. Most college students consider friendship and passionate love as important aspects of their relationships (Hendrick & Hendrick, 1992; Sprecher & Regan, 1998). Societal expectations include providing care, both in terms of instrumental and emotional support, and affection in both marriage and dating relationships (Cutrona, 1996).

Long-distance relationships are in danger of failing to meet society's typical relational expectations. Le and Agnew (2001) concluded, "It may be more difficult for partners to fulfill each other's relationship-related needs when separated by great geographic distance" and "suggest that one's relational partner needs to be physically accessible for need fulfillment" (p. 436). Disadvantages are assumed to be experienced by individuals DRDC marriages in emotional and social realms. Such individuals face a lack of companionship and emotional support (Groves & Horm-Wingerd, 1991). Partners of military personnel and incarcerated individuals experience similar losses; however, the severity or magnitude is likely greater.

Expectations for companionship extend to parent-child relationships and the family as a whole. The family has shifted from an institution based on law and custom to one based on companionship and love (Burgess, Locke, & Thomes, 1971). Fitzpatrick and Caughlin (2002) endorsed Wamboldt and Reiss's (1989) conceptualization of a family, which, like marital dyads, emphasizes intimacy, interdependence or commitment, group identity, a sense of history, and interactions that affect other family members. This view of the family places an incredible emphasis upon communication as the means through which such facets are achieved

(Fitzpatrick & Caughlin, 2002). In short, romantic dyads, whether dating or married, and families, with or without children or with or without married parents, are conceived in U.S. culture as contingent upon interaction, companionship, and intimacy, all of which presume some degree of face-to-face contact. The absence of this supposed necessary condition is exactly what makes long distance relationships of particular interest to students of communication and close relationships: Long-distance relationships contravene culturally held beliefs about the role of interpersonal communication in relationships.

Shared Residences and Geographic Proximity

Long-distance relationships are not only at odds with many cultural expectations for close ties; they also violate cultural views of the structure of close relationships, especially family relationships. One presumption is that DCDR couples desire to live together at some point (Winfield, 1985), although one study found a small percentage of couples who desired the commuting arrangement to be permanent (Farris, 1978). Research on LATs in the Netherlands revealed that many couples desire to continue separate residences indefinitely, if not permanently (Levin & Trost, 1999). The extent to which multiple forms of romantic LDRs and families desire eventual shared residence or prefer to live apart is in need of investigation. Moreover, for many variations of LDR families, such as nonresidential parents and children, shared residence is not an eventual goal.

In point of fact, a proportion of romantic partners and families have not shared residences for extended periods since antiquity. Even Homer's Penelope awaited the return of Odysseus when duty called him away to save Troy and rescue Helen (Homer, trans. 1948). Certainly in select cultures and historical periods husband and wife have not always lived together, nor have parent and child; the Israeli Kibbutz serves as one example (Spiro, 1954). Nonetheless "almost all standard sociological definitions of 'marriage' or a 'married couple' include co-residence as a component" (Rindfuss & Stephen, 1990). Rindfuss and Stephen argued that, given the number of married individuals who live apart for numerous reasons, aside from consideration of divorce, cohabitation should not be assumed to be a defining characteristic of marriage, but rather a variable within marriage.

Families with children, especially young children, are also expected to share the same residence. The classic definition of a family as a "social group characterized by common residence, economic cooperation, and reproduction" (Murdock, 1949, p.1) has stood as a standard for many years. This definition was reinforced by functional approach to families (Parsons, 1965). As Gerstel and Gross (1984) point out, Parsons assumes that a single shared residence is necessary for "the performance of family functions" (p. 199). Gerstel and Gross trace this U.S. sociological assumption to Cooley's (1909) definition of primary groups. Cooley explained a primary group as one "characterized by intimate, face to face association and cooperation" (p. 24). Until quite recently family textbooks have defined the family in terms of a single-residence, although, of late, the term *binuclear* has been invoked to recognize children of divorced parents. "In spite of the obvious problems, most family research still uses 'the household' as the working definition of the family" (Fitzpatrick & Caughlin, 2002, p. 727), as does the U.S. government. The U.S. Census Bureau offers the following definition: "Family. A family is a group of two people or more (one of whom is the householder) related by birth, marriage, or adoption and *residing together*" (italics added, U.S. Census Bureau, 2002).

Family scholars have recognized that families may span households, primarily because of divorce or nonmarital childbirth. However, if parents are married, it is assumed that a single residence is shared by all. Apparently, marital or family noncohabitation is a concept most Americans find difficult to grasp. Unless separated due to the traditional occupational demands of the husband, such as military duty, individuals in such relationships often encounter resistance or at least curiosity, if not suspicion from their extended families or social networks.

If children do not live with both parents, the mother is the culturally preferred primary caregiver. Thus, most research on nonresidential parents examines father absence. (The exception has been the recent upsurge in research on the military mother). The concept of mother absence has generally been considered outlandish given the "tender years doctrine," which privileges child and mother as the natural unit that is inherently best for the children.[4] The tender years doctrine, although historically recent, has often preempted the separation of mothers and children whether through court decisions or family ones. Nonetheless a significant number of mothers are separated from their children because of employment (military or dual-career), divorce, or incarceration.

In current U.S. society we accept or expect friends, adult children, and adult siblings to live in different residences or different geographic locations. We do not expect romantic partners or *nuclear* families to live apart. By definition, a nuclear family is one that shares a residence (Fitzpatrick & Caughlin, 2002). Even in the case of divorced families, an expectation exists that children will remain emotionally close to both parents, and contact with both parents is considered optimal for the child.

Given the expectations for the type of communication and for the type of structural living arrangements necessary to sustain close relationships, LDRs provide a natural experimental condition under which to examine assumptions about the role of communication in close relationships. Such relationships also provide an opportunity to examine the community, as community may be of greater significance to LDRs than geographically close ones. Long-distance relationships may well be sustained and individuals in these relationships better adjusted, as much if not more, through their proximal community ties than through communication with their relational counterparts. Conversely, many individuals in various types of LDRs feel stigmatized by their community and potential proximal support networks, resulting in isolation. In either situation, community plays a prominent role in these relationships.

SUCCESS

What people want to know most about long-distance relationships is "Do they work?" (Guldner, 2001). In order to answer that question, one must define "work." Guldner considers long-distance romantic relationships as working if the couple remains intact. Undoubtedly, the same criterion for success is not necessarily held by all involved in, or impacted by, the LDR. From an ecological systemic perspective (Bronfenbrenner, 1979) individuals, families, and the society in which they are located are all interrelated. Thus, to consider success only as romantic relationship stability misses much of the picture of some LDRs, and is not even relevant for other LDRs.

In general, individuals in the U.S. adhere to an individualistic view of selves in romantic relationships; relationships exist to meet individual needs (Gergen, 1991). Research grounded in social exchange is certainly based in the premise that individuals within relationships desire to maximize their own profits (Wilmot, 1995).

Success may also be considered in terms of ramifications for children in LDR families. Though individual children often report feelings of loss or sadness with parental separation, nonresidential parent-child relationships might be considered successful if children are well-adjusted. Long-term socialization of the child is generally considered as the benchmark of successful parenting (Fitzpatrick & Caughlin, 2002).

For corporations or the military, successful LDRs are those that result in job retention and job performance. Even society at large has a yardstick for success. For example, family relationships with an incarcerated family member might be considered successful if such connections lower recidivism rates or curb potential criminal activity among children.

Adult Individuals' Success

Much concern has been expressed over the dysfunction, or depression which may accompany romantic separations. Thus one emphasis in work on LDRs has been upon individual coping with separation. Two issues emerge: First, among some relational forms, distress has been assumed rather than verified. Second, the stressors present among differing types of long-distance relationships are not of equal type or magnitude.

For the most part, distress among individuals in LDR dating relationships has not been documented. The presumption of stress in long-distance dating relationships might be traced to Wendel (1975). She was interested in the feelings of high school sweethearts when one or both went away to college. She concluded that students felt a sense of "separateness and distance" (p. 45).

The legacy of dysfunction and depression among LDR dating couples became entrenched with the findings of Westefeld and Liddell (1982). As college counselors, they reported being confronted by students in angst over their long-distance romances. They began conducting workshops as a forum for students to exchange advice about the difficulties they encountered. Westefeld and Liddell summarized the students' recommendations for coping strategies. Advice included simply recognizing and accepting that the situation is stressful; developing support networks in their present community; developing "creative ways of communication while at a distance" (p. 550); setting rules for the separation in advance, while being aware these might need to be flexible; using their limited time together wisely; and being honest and open with each other. They also advised focusing on the positive aspects of the separation and attempting to be optimistic about the relationship. Though often repeated (Aylor, 2003; Rohfling, 1995), these suggestions remain to be studied as actually beneficial.

Holt and Stone's (1988) findings challenge the assumption that students involved in LDRs have problems to any greater extent than geographically close relationships. Holt and Stone found the less satisfied students were with the LDR, the more likely they were to seek counseling. Because Westefeld and Liddell (1982) drew their conclusions about the need for coping based only upon individuals who sought counseling, their conclusions drawn about LDRs may be overstated. Although Guldner (1996) did find that students involved in LDRs reported "feeling blue" more often than students in proximal relationships, he did report major depression to be no more frequent among LDRs than among those in geographically proximal relationships.

Sahlstein's (in press) findings challenge the view that most college LDRs are filled with stressed, depressed individuals. She found that college students enumerated both advantages and disadvantages of their relationships, with an advantage being the ability to focus upon their academics. Other studies have supported her findings that individuals in LDRs are better rested and perform better academically than those in geographically close relationships (Guldner, 1992, 1996; Guldner & Swensen, 1995).

DCDR couples are assumed to experience greater stress and dissatisfaction than single-residence, dual-career couples (Bunker, Zubek, Vanderslice, & Rice, 1992). Again, this has not been substantiated. On the contrary, the DCDR couples may be the most likely LDR form to reap benefits; they are voluntarily separated precisely for the benefits they hope to incur.[5] In current U.S. culture, marriages are concurrently supposed to provide individual self-fulfillment and growth as well as intense emotional intimacy (Cate & Lloyd, 1992). DCDR marriages, in theory, allow for both.

Overwhelmingly, DCDR couples report the major benefit of the arrangement is the career opportunities and career development. The dual-residences allow them the independence, time, and flexibility to focus on careers, thus meeting desires for personal fulfillment (Groves & Horm-Wingerd, 1991). Separate job locations allow the ability to focus on their careers and segment family life. Work is prioritized when apart, and family is prioritized when together (Gerstel & Gross, 1984). Bunker et al. (1992) found DCDR couples to be more satisfied with their work than dual-career, single-residence couples. In the one study of an African American sample of DCDR couples, a stated benefit of their arrangement was combating racial stereotypes and racial oppression as the geographic separation allowed them to pursue higher level, higher paying jobs than only seeking jobs in the same location would have allowed (Jackson et al., 2000).

The intent is not to imply that DCDR couples are void of any difficulties. Some stress is inevitable in any relationship. The severity of stress may be contingent upon the factors surrounding the separation, and one major factor is the presence and age of children.

For couples with children, a DCDR arrangement is generally more difficult than for those without (Rotter, Barnett, & Fawcett, 1998). If the couple has children, those in the later stages of the family cycle (i.e., with older children) fare better than those with younger children (Anderson, 1992). When children are involved, the marital relationship becomes less egalitarian and more like a dual-career, single-residence couple, as the children live in one home that serves as the primary residence (Rotter et al.). The partner living away from the children is able to focus more on career, and the noncommuter (usually the mother) resides with the children and becomes in many ways like a single parent. She is faced with practical childcare arrangements and is less able to focus on her career. Thus, the primary benefit of entering the arrangement is predominately lost. In such cases resentment often results (Rhodes, 2002).

There are costs for the commuting parent as well. Traveling parents report missing the day-to-day aspects of their children's development and suffer feelings of guilt. Viewing the separation as short term and best for the family in the long run alleviates some of these feelings (Rhodes, 2002; Rotter et al., 1998). Gerstel (1978) found the "best fit" of career cycle and family life cycle to be after children have left home. However, most dual-career, dual-residence couples are in their 30s and approximately 50% have children (Anderson & Spruill, 1993; Forsyth & Gramling, 1987).

Factors other than mere presence or absence of children, or age of children, may come into play. The literature provides a general profile of successful DCDR marriages. Available data indicate that successful DCDR couples hold less traditional and more egalitarian sex roles, are well educated, and engage in planning and joint decision making about the separation (Anderson & Spruill, 1993; Forsyth & Gramling, 1987). Those with greater financial resources or flexible job schedules experience fewer difficulties (Anderson, 1992). In addition, the more difficult and trying the commute, the greater dissatisfaction with the lifestyle (Groves & Horm-Wingerd, 1991). Roehling and Bultman (2002) found marital satisfaction among individuals in dual-career commuting couples differed depending upon both the spouse's gender role attitudes and which spouse traveled.

Counterintuitively, Bunker et al. (1992) found individuals in single-residence dual-career couples actually faced more role overload and stress than dual-career, dual resident couples. However, in this study, the DCDR couples had significantly fewer children than the single-residence couples, and when children were present they were significantly older, which may account for the greater overload and stress among the single-residence couples.

Unlike assumptions concerning college students and DCDR couples, the symptoms of distress are well documented among the families of deployed military personnel and single-residence civilian families with extended separations. In both of these families, the at-home parent, usually the mother, often encounters severe depression, loneliness, role changes, overload, financial concerns, and increased parenting demands with diminished parenting abilities. She may experience a wide range of emotions, including worry about the spouse as well as detachment and resentment (see Vormbrock, 1993, for a review). The term "submariners' wives syndrome" has been coined by psychiatrists to refer to such symptoms of dysphoria, which accompany long-term separations (Isay, 1968). Husband or father distress during women's deployment has received minimal attention. Additional stresses for military families include frustration with bureaucracy and fears about safety (Drummet, Coleman, & Cable, 2003; Hunter, 1982). Family members of incarcerated individuals report similar strains, with the added burdens of stigmatization and lack of support (Hairston, 1991). Success for these individuals is not achieving fulfillment through career goals, but simply making it through the day. Clearly these forms are not equivalent to college student or DCDR couples. They vary in the degree to which the separation is voluntary, societal perceptions and community support, and resources available.

In sum, individual success for adults in LDRs ranges from the absence of pathologies to self-actualization through meeting career goals. Individual level measures of success for children of long-distance families are in some ways similar and in other ways different.

Children's Success

From a child's perspective, separation is virtually always involuntary. Regardless of the reason for separation, most children undoubtedly suffer immediate sadness and dissatisfaction over lost connections with a parent. As noted, generally society considers adequate socialization and asymptomatic behaviors as success. Children may be more concerned with their relationship with the absent parent or their immediate happiness. Unfortunately, research from children's perspectives is sorely lacking.

The effect of the separation on the child seems to be quite dependent upon the child's age, development, and reason for separation. Older children may fare better as they are more likely to understand the reasons for the parental absence. As a general rule, the more influence and control children have over factors surrounding their circumstances during the separation, the better adjusted they tend to be (Ursano & Norwood, 1996). In addition, it seems likely that children's adjustment, and family disruption overall, is in part contingent upon reasons for separation. Parental absence due to socially acceptable reasons in general, does not have the same ramifications as those that are socially stigmatized (Lowenstein, 1986).

Only one study was located that directly examined children's perspectives of DCDR parents. Jackson et al. (2000) interviewed children of four DCDR families.

The children reported feeling that the traveling parent did not care about them and reported feelings of neglect, anger, and disappointment. On the other hand, children also said they felt unique and important among their peers as they viewed their parents as holding important jobs. These children's experiences stand in stark contrast to children of incarcerated parents who are often embarrassed or ashamed.

Historically, more research has been conducted on paternal military duty than maternal. Military children are presumed to be affected both directly from their deployed father's absence as well as indirectly by their mother's stress and depression, which interferes with her parenting abilities (Black, 1993; Schumm, Bell, Knott, & Rice, 1996). Children whose fathers are deployed in times of combat experience more difficulties than those whose fathers are on routine deployments; maternal dysfunction is greater as well, thus indirectly affecting the children (Kelley, Herzog-Simmer, & Harris, 1994).

Given the rise in maternal deployments, research attention has turned to child outcomes of maternal absence (Applewhite & Mays, 1996; Kelley et al., 1994). Male civilian spouses are less likely than female civilian spouses to live in a military community or to take advantage of military support systems for parents. They are also less likely to take over childcare responsibilities. Thus, these children may be at greater risk than children whose fathers are deployed. Yet, to date, significant differences between children of deployed fathers and of deployed mothers have not been found (Applewhite & Mays). Children at greatest risk are those of single parents, and those of dual-military parents. Such children must change residences to live with extended family members, and perhaps change schools and communities, adding to the disruption in their lives (Defense Manpower Data Center, 1999; Martin & McClure, 2000).

Children of divorce also have been reported to have numerous adjustment difficulties (see Amato & Keith, 1991); however, it is unknown the extent to which children's problems are a result of parental absence per se or related factors. Lamb (1997) reviewed previous research on divorced residential parents and concluded that divorce often results in the lack of another adult with whom to share instrumental tasks and parental decision making, resulting in overload. This stress has spillover effects for the children, as in the case of deployed spouses. Others have surmised that problems generally associated with the divorce are due to parental conflict either before or continuing after the divorce (Amato & Rezac, 1994).

Little consensus exists as to the extent of the impact of parental incarceration on children. Research is scarce, and that which has been conducted is based upon small samples, anecdotal evidence, indirect methods of assessment, and a lack of longitudinal work (Seymour, 1998). Some conclude that the impact on romantic partners and children of parental imprisonment is well documented (Snyder, Carlo, & Coats, 2001). Others argue that many prisoners had no relationship with their children prior to incarceration, thus the impact is not as pervasive as some have claimed (Paylor & Smith, 1994).

Though the scope of the problem may not be as widespread as some have claimed, this does not negate the reality for those who are affected. Limited evidence appears to suggest that at least some children of incarcerated parents, most notably those living with the parent prior to incarceration, face many obstacles and have numerous emotional and behavioral problems (Seymour, 1998). For children with close ties to the incarcerated parent prior to imprisonment the separation is traumatic. Parental incarceration contributes to "traumatic separation and negative child outcomes such as poor academic performance, emotional suffering, alcohol and drug abuse" (Arditti, Lambert-Shute, & Joest, 2003), as well as denial, depression, sleeplessness, and anger (Brooks, 1993; Snyder et al., 2001). Children of incarcerated individuals often feel embarrassed or stigmatized (Gabel, 1992). In efforts to protect, some children are not told the reason for the parent's absence (Gabel).

Single mothers, whether divorced, never married, or functionally single with an incarcerated partner, have the lowest household income per capita and most are below poverty level (Arditti et al., 2003; Lamb, 1997). Poverty is not a factor among children separated from parents in dual-career families, and although income may be low among deployed military families, abject poverty is not usually an issue. All parent-child separations clearly are not equal.

Romantic Dyadic Success

At the romantic dyadic level, research has often focused on success as stability and satisfaction of marital (Fitzpatrick & Caughlin, 2002; Vangelisti, 2002) and dating partners (Cate, Levin, & Richmond, 2002). The search for factors contributing to stability and satisfaction appears to have begun in the 1930s (Broderick, 1988; Perlman, 2001). In the past few decades, literally hundreds of studies have examined stability and satisfaction as the primary construct of interest in romantic relationships (Canary & Stafford, 1994).

Defining dating LDRs as successful if they remain intact (Guldner, 2001) is the commonly invoked measure of success. Most studies of dating relationships have reported equal or greater levels of relational qualities such as satisfaction, commitment, or trust in long-distance dating relationships compared to geographically close ones (Guldner & Swensen, 1995; Lydon, Pierce, & O'Regan, 1997; Schwebel, Dunn, Moss, & Renner, 1992; Stafford & Reske, 1990; Stephen, 1986; c.f., VanHorn et al., 1997). Stephen (1986) found that long-distance college romantic relationships were more stable across time than geographically close ones. Stafford and Reske's (1990) findings supported Stephen's. VanHorn et al. did not replicate these findings. However, the time frame of the study was 3 months compared to 2 years for Stephen's study and 9 months for the Stafford and Reske study, which may account for the differences in relational dissolution rate.

Knox, Zusman, Daniels, and Brantley (2002) reported separation to be damaging for dating relationships. By 5 months, approximately 20% ended their relationships and another 20% reported their relationships were worse. Of note, however, is that nearly 20% also indicated the separation made their relationship better and nearly one third gave mixed responses. Sahlstein (in press) interviewed 20 long-distance college dating couples and found both positive and negative aspects of LDRs.

Considering marital partners, Rindfuss and Stephen (1990) found that noncohabitating spouses have a divorce rate twice that of cohabiting spouses within 3 years of separation. Yet they drew their conclusions largely on military personnel and incarcerated individuals, both of whom have higher divorce rates than the population at large. Although Bunker et al. (1992) found DCDR couples to be less satisfied with their partners, Govaerts and Dixon (1988) reported similar marital satisfaction levels for DCDR couples and single-residence couples. DCDR marriages and LDR college couples may be somewhat similar in that they are voluntarily separated in order to achieve individual goals and have the most potential access to means of interaction. Nonetheless, a deficit of longitudinal research on college LDRs and DCDR marriages exists.

More research is available on military deployments. Although divorces seldom occur during deployment, divorce rates are higher among military personnel who have returned from deployments than among those who have not been deployed. Divorces spiked upon the demobilization following WWII (DaVanzo & Rahman, 1993). Angrist and Johnson (2000) found male deployments were not related to divorce following the Gulf War, but female deployments were. There is some evidence that combat experience hurts marital relationships to a greater extent than those deployed in noncombat units (Gimbel & Booth, 1994).

Institutional and Societal Success

Within corporate America, DCDR relationships are successful for the company if job retention is achieved and job performance is high. Approximately 8% of job relocations result in DCDR families (Stroh, 1999). Taylor and Lounsbury (1988) found participants in an executive development program rated applicants for transfer more negatively if a DCDR marriage would result. They felt the employee would be likely to leave the company, become divorced, or be unable to offer the company peak performance skills.

Retention and performance are also key issues in the military. Given the U.S. volunteer armed forces, it would seem that great attention would be accorded to factors affecting reenlistment. "There is no question that the service member's family satisfaction with the military is a major factor in the service member's decision to choose a military career" (Command Briefing Resources, 2000). Deployments are a major contributor to dissatisfaction with military life (Etheridge, 1989). Spousal attitudes following deployment are also a major predictor of retention in the reserves (Kirby & Naftel, 2000). Family and spousal satisfaction is also related to soldier job performance (Bell & Schumm, 2000; Bell, Schumm, Knott, & Ender, 1999; Ursano & Norwood, 1996). Despite these findings, the military has failed to adequately consider or research the importance of family relationships and instead has overrated job-related factors in terms of retention (Kelley, Hock, Smith, Jarvis, Bonney, & Gaffney, 2001).

Societal interest in successful marital and family relationships may be best illustrated by consideration of incarcerated individuals (Segrin & Flora, 2001). Review of the little previous work to date revealed that a supportive, satisfying marriage is highly associated with "successful rehabilitation and unlikely recidivism," whereas mere marital status is not (p. 153). Brenner (2001) reported that eight states currently have programs promoting father-child involvement and parenting skills. The hope is that increasing the fathers' commitment to parenting will lower recidivism rates, thus benefiting the parent, the child, and society.

Children of prisoners are six times more likely to become criminals than children in the general population (Reed & Reed, 1997). Given that violent criminals are predominately males who grew up without fathers (Brenner, 2001), speculation has been offered that since paternal imprisonment separates children from fathers, incarceration may be feeding a cycle of criminal behavior into the next generation as opposed to curbing it (Davidson, 1990).

Arditti et al. (2003) argued that current penal policies create more harm than good and alternative policies and approaches need to be adapted. They conclude that the evidence suggests, given the negative family and societal ramifications of the current penal system, imprisonment should be considered a last resort. Rather than imprisonment, emphasis should be upon harm reduction and intervention (Lenton, 2003). Restorative justice models ensure that incarceration does no more harm than the crime and concentration is shifted to intervention (Arditti et al., 2003). Of course, others have argued that there is little support for such dire unintended impacts on family (Segal, 2001). In either case, the well-being of the incarcerated individual, children, family members, and society are all taken into account (Hairston, 2001b). Such approaches illustrate systemic consideration of the various levels and meanings of success.

Summary

Despite the usual focus on stability and satisfaction as markers of successful relationships, success has a variety of meanings to the numerous parties involved in, or affected by, the LDR. Success for individuals might mean the ability to focus upon personal goals such as career fulfillment or may mean merely the ability to function adequately. Society considers adequate socialization as success for children, whereas the children may be more concerned about their relationships with parents and their own immediate happiness. For romantic dyads, whether married or not, success has generally been defined as stability or satisfaction. For businesses and the military, long-distance arrangements for employees often serve the employer's interests and are considered successful if they achieve retention and job performance. In the case of incarceration, success is achieved at all levels when satisfactory marital or parent-child bonds aid in the reintegrating the incarcerated individual into family life. With that should come a reduction in recidivism rates and preemption of child criminal behavior, which benefits the adult, the child, the family, and society.

COMMUNICATION AND SUCCESS

Little research has examined long-distance family systems as a whole. Rather, it has primarily focused on either the effects of parental stress or conflict on the child or on roles and boundaries. Communication among long-distance family members that might facilitate a healthy family environment is a needed area of research. Given the absence of such research, communication and success is considered in terms of two dyads: the romantic pair and the parent-child dyad.

Communication and Success: Young Children and Parents

Two cultural assumptions are especially relevant to LDRs between parents and children. First, it is assumed that if parents care about their children, they will stay in contact. This presumption ignores the difficulties of maintaining parent-child bonds when parent and child live apart (Leite & McKenry, 2002). The nonresidential parent's own perception of the nature of his or her role can hamper interaction, as can an uncooperative residential parent who controls access to the child or relocates, thus complicating custody and visitation (Dudley, 1991; Wolchik, Fenaughty, & Braver, 1996). Similar factors influence never-married noncustodial parents. Incarcerated parents face even more logistical, legal, and emotional barriers.

The second assumption is that frequent contact between children and a nonresidential parent is good, and many investigations track only that. Frequency of contact alone, however, is not a strong predictor of child outcomes or of the strength of the parent-child relationship (Arendell, 1997).

By far more research has been conducted on parental-child contact when separated due to divorce than contact during separation for any other reason. In the case of nonresidential parents due to divorce, there is little debate that ideally and in theory it is in a child's best interest for both parents to stay involved in the child's life. A consistent finding is that the chief complaint about divorce from children is the loss of contact with their fathers (Kelly, 1993). Children overwhelmingly experience a sense of loss when, because of divorce, contact with a nonresidential parent diminishes or is cut off (Wolchik et al. 1996).

Seltzer (1991) reported that 37% of children of divorced parents had no contact of any kind with their fathers in a given year, and about 25% have contact of some kind at least once a week. Geographic proximity has been strongly related to parental contact (Cooksey & Craig, 1998), and fathers seldom use other means to compensate for distance. If fathers live too far away for regular visits, they also tend not to communicate by telephone or mail; those who do visit regularly tend to communicate through other modes as well (King & Heard, 1999). Pragmatically, paternal-child contact is highly correlated with payment of child support among both divorced and never married fathers (Seltzer, Schaeffer, & Charng, 1989). Thus, one potential benefit of contact is a lessened probability of poverty.

However, the extent to which contact actually incurs benefits for children is highly questionable. Studies have produced mixed findings. Adverse effects for parental conflict between married parents on child adjustment and behavior are well documented (Grych & Fincham, 1990). There is no reason to suspect that conflict between divorced parents would be any less damaging to the child than conflict between married parents. Indeed, child adjustment seems to be better predicted by parental conflict than by family structure (Kot & Shoemaker, 1999). Amato and Rezac (1994) reviewed 33 studies that directly examined the hypothesis that frequency of contact with the nonresidential parent was positively correlated with the child's well-being. In all but one study the father was the nonresident parent. Although 18 of the studies supported the hypothesis, 9 studies reported no association, and 6 studies found that the greater the contact from the nonresident parents, the greater the problems for the child. The researchers recognized that some methodological or sample differences might explain some of these effects, yet they proposed that most of the effect was due to the relationship between the parents. In situations of parental hostility, the child may actually fare better with decreased parental contact because increased contact with children generally involves increased contact and coordination among the divorced spouses. The potential benefits of nonresidential parental contact are thus often negated by the increased hostilities. Hostile interactions and legal battles between current or ex-spouses appear to be directly linked to poor psychological and emotional adjustment and behavior problems in their children (Buchanan & Heiges, 2001; Furstenberg & Nord, 1985). Sometimes in cases of divorce, the child and nonresident parent actually become closer and engage in more frequent contact because the parents are no longing living together promoting daily friction (Hetherington, Cox, & Cox, 1982).

Unquestioningly, children desire unrestricted and flexible access to both parents (Neugebauer, 1989), and increasing paternal involvement in children's lives is precisely the reason joint legal custody is beginning to happen more frequently (Braver & O'Connell, 1998). The number of parents with joint physical custody is still low (approximately 7%), but joint legal custody still does little to involve the nonresidential parent on a daily basis.

Evidence indicates that when such arrangements are exercised cooperatively, mother, father, and child benefit (Kelly, 2000). Arendell (1997) summarized research on joint custody and reported: "Probably the best conclusion that can be drawn from existing research is that joint custody appears to be preferable when both parents elect this option but that joint custody should not be imposed on unwilling parents in mediation or in a court hearing" (p. 26). When parents cooperate—keeping conflict at a minimum or at least hidden from the children—and children truly share their time in the homes of both parents, the parents and the children benefit (Buchanan, 2000; Buchanan, Maccoby, & Dornbusch, 1996; Kelly, 2000). This suggests parent-child relationships may best be facilitated by improving the coparental relationship, and simply mandating joint custody, hence joint decision making, does not accomplish this goal. When the parents remain hostile, this arrangement can actually be negative for the child (Emery, 1994).

Unequivocally, fathers who remain involved in children's lives with a collegial relationship with the children's mothers contribute to the adjustment and happiness of the children (DeFrain & Olson, 1999). Researchers who have studied the role fathers play in adolescent development suggest that a supportive relationship with the father, regardless of whether or not he lives with his children, is beneficial for the child (Lamb, 1986; Lund, 1987; Shulman & Seiffge-Krenke, 1997; Zimmerman, Salem, & Notaro, 2000).

Even though a father who does not live at home may not take part in monitoring his adolescent's daily activities, he may, nonetheless, help link his child to the larger community. Nonresident fathers may also provide support and guidance, communicate values and attitudes (e.g., education, career, and future), and spend time with their children. (Zimmerman et al., 2000, p. 241)

Recent studies have emphasized the child's perception of the father or the symbolic contact between father and child. When noncustodial parents take care to communicate the importance of their relationships with their children, this may help children adjust almost as much as continuing, frequent contact. Buchanan et al. (1996) found that when noncustodial parents (mothers or fathers) remember special days such as holidays and birthdays, children are better adjusted, even in the absence of frequent contact (Buchanan, 2000). Children's perception of bonds with their nonresidential parent is a better predictor of their well-being than actual frequency of contact (Amato & Rezac, 1994).

The question of child contact with incarcerated parents, especially visits in prison, is an even more hotly debated topic. The vast majority of imprisoned parents, fathers and mothers, have some sort of contact (e.g., letters) at least monthly with their children, yet approximately 55% of both mothers and fathers have never received an in-person visit from their children (Mumola, 2000). Visitation increases the likelihood of family reunification or, if the parents are no longer romantically involved, which is the vast majority (Mumola, 2000), continued parent-child contact after release (Hairston, 2001a). Communication by phone, cards, and letters and by visits help incarcerated parents remain emotionally attached to children (Hairston, 2001a). Visitation and other means of contact are frequently supported only in theory; actual institutional practices often impede rather than promote family ties (Hairston, 2001b).

However, many imprisoned parents do not want their children to see them incarcerated because they fear the experience will be emotionally painful or damaging for the child. Sometimes the custodial parent or extended family networks also believe visitation would be detrimental for the child, as do many professionals within corrections and social services (Hairston, 2001b). In fact, many institutional policies serve to make family or child visits uncomfortable, difficult, or even degrading and humiliating. Nonetheless, the limited evidence available suggests that visitation facilitates child adjustment and parent-child bonds. Given a deficit of large-scale longitudinal research, however, and the wide range of circumstances, one cannot reach a blanket conclusion that increased contact facilitates child adjustment; each situation must be considered on a case-by-case basis.

Summary

Whether parents and children live apart from each other, regardless of reason, it is clear that children desire contact with their fathers and their mothers. Arguments have been made both for increased and decreased parent-child involvement when parents are incarcerated, or when parents are not married and child benefit appear contingent on a complex host of understudied factors. Extant research relies more upon frequency of the contact, rather than nature of the contact.

The extent to which contact facilitates child adjustment appears contingent both on the relationship between the parents and the parenting behaviors of the nonresidential parent. When the quality of the communication has been examined, the maintenance of symbolic affectionate ties seems to be more important than actual interaction, as long as needs are met by other community members.

Given the number of military personnel, DCDR couples with children, and the number of incarcerated parents, the lack of research on parent-child contact during separation is surprising. How these parents and children maintain relationships is unexplored aside from the speculation that symbolic communication and family rituals may help facilitate a feeling of togetherness in parent-child separation (Rotter et al., 1998).

The permanently nonresidential parent faces different obstacles in maintaining contact with children than the temporarily separated parent, including complex barriers created by geographical constraints. It is undeniable that positive, cooperative, consistent coparenting increases parental involvement with children and is in children's and parents' best interests. Unfortunately, conflict between the parents often makes this difficult. For divorced parents, never-married parents, and imprisoned parents, contact often is contingent on circumstances beyond their control. Despite the dearth of research on various types of separations, I would speculate that even simply symbolic communication, such as sending a birthday card, recognizes a relationship and is beneficial, regardless of reason for separation.

Communication and Success: Romantic Long-distance Relationships

As I noted previously, frequency of contact is by far the most often studied communication construct in long-distance romantic relationships, and face-to-face contact has been presumed as necessary for satisfactory relationships. After I consider face-to-face communication, I then turn attention to the link between various modes of communication and idealization.

Holt and Stone (1988) reported that college partners who physically saw each other less than once a month and lived under 250 miles apart were less satisfied than dating partners who saw each other more frequently. One month also seems to be the maximum time most DCDR couples can cope with separation (Magnuson & Norem, 1999). Individuals report feeling out of touch, begin to develop separate relational realities, and feel more like they are single as opposed to in a stable relationship (Magnuson & Norem).

Similarly, Dainton and Aylor (2002) asked how often college LDR individuals saw each other and found that those who answered "never" were less satisfied and less committed than individuals with "periodic face to face contact" (p. 127). They found face-to-face contact to be positively associated with "relational success" as defined by increased satisfaction, trust, commitment, and lowered jealousy. However, their findings were not longitudinal. Carpenter and Knox (1986) found, through retrospective accounts of college students, that frequency of face-to-face interaction was associated with stability for men, but not for women. Dainton and Aylor (2002) found that even when college students used the Internet, some "periodic face to face contact" was needed for satisfaction and commitment.

Not all concur with this finding. Guldner and Swenson (1995) concluded, "Some individuals can apparently maintain perfectly satisfying relationships with very little face-to-face contact, at least for periods of 3 to 4 months" (p. 319). They noted this situation is rare: "Clearly, relationships require some level of (face-to-face) contact and extremely infrequent contact probably does ultimately result in relationship instability" (p. 319).

This infrequent face-to-face contact is normative in selected civilian single-career commuting occupations (e.g., off-shore oil workers), military deployments, and incarceration. The long-distance couple that has garnered the most research attention is the military couple. Considering the emphasis on face-to-face contact, the military has attempted to allow physical copresence during deployment, but spousal visitations to the base for a few days during peacetime has been of questionable benefit. Some partners actually see each other little during their visits because of the soldier's assignments. Thus, morale for both is lowered (Carlson & Carlson, 2002).

Conclusions are mixed about mid-deployment or R&R leaves. Spouses are overwhelmingly in support of the program, and one third take advantage of it; however, families dislike the lack of control over when the visits are scheduled, the lack of advance notice about the visit, and the fact they are not compensatory. As to the visits themselves, they last about 10 days. This can be quite unsettling after months of separation and are especially difficult for young children to understand. Such rapid and brief contact can inflict more trauma on all involved than the initial separation. Overall, studies have found that following such leaves, depression and stress levels tend to increase and desire to stay in the military decreases (Bell, Bartone, Bartone, Schumm, & Gade, 1997).

Idealization is a theme that implicitly emerges in many studies of long-distance relationships, especially college ones. All LDRs, by default, have restricted face-to-face communication. Various relationships have varying access to mediated communication. Knox et al. (2002) reported that only 10% of college LDRs saw each other weekly, but that approximately 10% talked via telephone several times a day, 22% talked at least once a day, and just over 50% talked on the phone and e-mailed their partners several times a week. Similarly, many DCDR couples report talking on the phone daily (Gerstel & Gross, 1984). Both college dating relationships and DCDR individuals likely have greater access to both phone and computer-mediated communication (CMC) than incarcerated individuals and deployed military personnel.

Despite defining long-distance dating relationships as successful if they are intact, Guldner (1996) also pointed out that dating relationships have a high rate of dissolution in general. Much interest in premarital relationships has been their predictive ability for marital stability (Cate et al., 2002). An often repeated finding is that the length of dating prior to marriage is associated with marital success stability (Cate et al., 2002; Larson & Holman, 1994). It undoubtedly is not the passage of time per se that is important, but rather the interaction that takes place during this time. LDRs have restricted interaction. Perhaps a better question to explore is if long-distance dating relationships allow individuals to become acquainted well enough to make an informed decision about marriage.

Restricted communication facilitates idealized images and high expectations. Idealized images contribute to relational stability, which is not necessarily a marker of success. Idealization plays both positive and negative roles in LDRs. This line of reasoning is explicated.

Some longitudinal research has found decreased communication among dating couples to be associated with relational stability. Stephen (1986) found that long-distance dating couples were more stable after 2 years than geographically close ones in spite of restraints on their communication. He proposed that such individuals might come to "see talk as less critical" (p. 207). Stafford and Reske (1990) found the greater the proportion of interaction spent face-to-face compared to other modes, the less satisfied with the relationship, the less satisfied with the communication, and the more likely the demise of the relationship by 9 months. They also found face-to-face interaction to be negatively associated with measures of idealization. They also expressed concern over the notion that it was in the student's best interest to sustain the long-distance relationship. They found restricted communication to be associated with idealized images. They proposed that perhaps these positive illusions accounted for the longevity of geographically separated dating relationships. In other words, perhaps the lack of communication preempted couples from getting to know each other.

LDRs have less face-to-face interaction, more mediated communication, and may avoid conflict, putting their best foot forward in their limited time together (Dainton & Aylor, 2002; Stafford & Reske, 1990). Sahlstein (in press) similarly reported long-distance partners avoid negative interactions when face-to-face so as not to have their time together ruined, and they feel a tremendous pressure to have quality time when together. When apart they may focus on plans for when together and invoke relational memories of being together to sustain them while apart (Sahlstein). Daydreaming has been found to aid in maintaining these relationships (Holt & Stone, 1988).

Schwebel et al. (1992) found that relational satisfaction among college students prior to separation in the fall was strongly related to the survival of the relationship throughout the school term. Dainton and Aylor (2002) returned to concerns of idealization, proposing that perhaps even long-distance couples with frequent, short, face-to-face visits may be acting on their "best behavior," allowing idealization to continue instead of actually becoming better acquainted with their partners. Perhaps the satisfaction from the fall is perpetuated through a lack of interaction.

In short, restricted communication appears to promote positive illusions, and positive illusions have been found to promote premarital stability (Murray & Holmes, 1996). However, "[p]eople need to spend sufficient time before marriage developing essential processes that will enhance their marriage" (Cate et al., 2002, p. 262). The avoidance of conflict in premarital stages of relationships is a risk subsequently (Gottman & Krokoff, 1989). Everyday casual interaction can provide a safe context within which more specific discussions can occur and partners can learn about one another (Duck, 1990). Everyday casual interaction is sorely lacking in LDRs.

Thus, emphasis on commitment, satisfaction, relational stability, and the like as indicators of relational success in premarital relationships is puzzling. There is little debate that interaction is necessary to acquire knowledge about one's partner, and "depth of acquaintance" has remained a consistent predictor of later marital quality and stability (Larson & Holman, 1994). Nevertheless, in the face of restricted communication, long-distance college dating couples have been found to know their partners less well, but to be more confident than geographically proximal pairs that they know them well (Stafford & Reske, 1990). One must also question the extent to which commitment is "good" in long-distance dating relationships. Most students who experienced long-distance relationship break-ups reported they would "never again" attempt a long-distance romance (Knox et al., 2002).

Longitudinal research on the rates of marriage and subsequent divorce of college dating relationships are nonexistent. Although undergraduate students generally desire to know how to make their relationships work, sustaining these relationships may not be in their best long-term interests, or the best question for the academician. Perhaps continued focus on coping strategies for individuals who do report feelings of stress and isolation, as well as understanding ramifications for the long-term future of the relationship may be more worthwhile directions of research than simply ascertaining how such relationships are preserved. As Hill, Rubin, & Peplau (1976) remarked, "The best divorce is one you get before you get married" (p. 168).

College dating relationships are not the only LDRs in which individuals idealize their partner or their relationships. Such idealization serves both to sustain a relationship as well as to promote potentially damaging, overly high expectations. Gross (1980) reported DCDR couples have high expectations about the quality of their time together when they reunite. And both DCDR marriages and single-career, single-resident marriages with frequent, predictable, and short separations often experience a honeymoon-like reunion, putting their best fronts on, similar to dating couples (Gerstel & Gross, 1984; Vormbrock, 1993).

Unrealistic images of the partner and the time they will have together increase as time apart increases; this can lead to disillusionment and disappointment when they see each other (Gerstel & Gross, 1984). The reunion is greatly anticipated and then, after an initial honeymoon period, a time of conflict and renegotiation of roles ensues (Gross, 1980). Studies of military personnel report similar findings (Wood, Scarville, & Gravino, 1995), as do those of long-distance dating couples (Sahlstein, in press).

Dainton and Aylor (2002) found telephone time among dating partners was positively associated with "relational success" as defined by increased satisfaction, trust, and commitment, and decreased jealousy. However, the college students in that sample also had some face-to-face contact. Telephone use may operate differently in extended separations. Although Gerstel and Gross (1984) found DCDR couples talked on the telephone daily, the couples did not find the conversations to be particularly satisfying as the focus was upon practical concerns and did not result in feelings of emotional closeness.

Pincus, House, Christenson, and Adler (2001) offer mixed results of phone use among deployed soldiers in Bosnia. For some spouses at home, phone calls had a "stabilizing experience." Conversely, other spouses and soldiers reported having predominantly "bad phone calls" that only made things worse (Pincus & Nam, 1999). Other problems included increased frustration by the spouse because the phone contact could only be initiated by military personnel. Spouses reported feeling confined to the house because they might miss a call, given that they had little or no notice when or if a call would be placed. If the spouse was not home when a call was attempted, soldiers reported feelings of abandonment and isolation.

Moreover, increased phone time allows for increased opportunities for conflict (Pincus et al., 2001). The "disadvantage of easy phone access is the immediacy and proximity to unsettling events at home or in theater" (p. 3), despite the potential for positive outcomes from conversations. Phone calls seem to be beneficial if the conversations are simply to "stay in touch" or to recognize special days such as birthdays and anniversaries (Pincus et al.).

Unlike phone calls, letters have been consistently associated with relational satisfaction. This may be because letters lend themselves to the creation or perpetuation of idealized images. Among dating couples, Stafford and Reske (1990) found letters to be more highly associated with feelings of satisfaction, love, satisfaction with communication, and idealization in the relationship than face-to-face or telephone contact. LDR dating couples who exchange letters are more likely to stay together (Guldner, 1992, as cited in Guldner, 1996).

Letters have been found to be positively associated with relational features among military and prison populations for whom phone access is limited. For individuals with an incarcerated partner, maintaining any type of contact is often the most difficult obstacle: Phone calls are expensive, and visits may be logistically impossible due to the geographic distance or the expense of traveling. Cards and letters are the primary means of demonstrating caring and connection. Holding on to positive perceptions of relational histories, which may be perpetuated through a lack of other modes of interactions, buffers incarcerated individuals against a sense of loneliness (Segrin & Flora, 2001). Although not tested, Segrin and Flora have proposed that hope of reuniting sustains couples during this time of limited communication. One report found that 90% of "significant women" (i.e., wives and lovers) expected to reunite with their partners upon release (Hairston, 1995).

Naval spouses and deployed naval personnel reported higher marital satisfaction with letters rather than with phone calls (Stafford & Yost, 1990). Letters contained vague, loving, reassuring statements. Letters could be edited by the writer, contained more positive emotional tones, and avoided the delivery of negative or upsetting news.

Dainton and Aylor (2002) did not find the same positive associations with letters, but did for email use between dating couples. This may be a function of expectations and availability. Access to email was greater on college campuses at the time of the Dainton and Aylor study than when the Stafford and Reske (1990) study was conducted. In fact, Stafford and Reske did not even ask about email usage.

Asynchronous email may have similar properties to letters and thus may also foster idealization. Dainton and Aylor (2002) found correlations among the written channels of Internet and letters supporting Westmyer, DiCioccio, and Rubin's (1998) contention that these two channels are functional equivalents. Pincus et al. (2001) proposed email may be a better method of communication among deployed families than telephone contact, as timing is not an issue. Moreover, with email, one can edit and reread to "filter out intense emotions that may be unnecessarily disturbing" (Pincus et al., p. 4) prior to sending the email. The ability to reread and edit allows more room for impression management than face-to-face contact (Rabby & Walther, 2003).

Rabby and Walther (2003) noted that the computer-mediated communication (CMC) may facilitate maintenance of relationships that originated offline. Romantic partners may use email to stay in touch, and simply sending a CMC message lets the other know the relationship exists and the other is being thought about (Rabby & Walther, 2003). However, based upon Gunn & Gunn's (2000) study, Rabby and Walther raised the possibility that couples who have gone for extended periods of time without face-to-face contact may tend to idealize their relationships. With email, individuals tend complete missing information in desirable ways. (Rabby, 1997) found email messages among romantic partners to be virtually never negative. Rabby and Walther proposed that email messages lend an emphasis on the positive and contribute to idealized images and expectations. "When one communicates largely through email he or she loses the sense of that partner's . . . undesirable habits" (p. 154).

The greatest desire during deployments for both military personnel and spouses is for increased access to communication through telephone and email, and military personal are beginning to expect the availability of such contact (Cooper & Ward-Zuckerman, 2001; Ross, 2001) Jacobs and Hicks (1987) found military personnel reported the inability to engage in regular communication a contributing factor to feeling less intimacy with their partners.

Rohall, Segal, and Segal (1999) found that soldiers who experienced "satisfaction with resources to communicate home" were more positively adjusted than "those who experienced dissatisfaction with communication resources." In other words, "Soldiers who feel that they are able to communicate more readily with the families find it [the separation] less difficult" (p. 59), regardless of whether or not they actually take advantage of the communication opportunities.

Ross (2001) found the benefits of increased access to email to be questionable. Approximately one half of both sailors and spouses reported that email did not meet their expectations. Ross's overall conclusion was that email increased the quality of life for many families. On the other hand, expectations for email availability were related to morale problems when systems were down or unavailable.

Summary and Conclusions

It remains to be seen if increasing frequency of interaction is beneficial for long-distance romantic relationships. The possibility is raised that DCDR marriages can reach a point of too much contact, thus interfering with the one advantage of separation, segmentation in order to focus on careers.

Dating couples, like military couples, desire increased contact, as do imprisoned personnel. Although some research has reported that dating individuals are more satisfied with increased contact, some have found restricted communication to be related to relational longevity among dating couples. Only longitudinal studies will reveal if increased communication facilitates dating couples' movement through the premarital trajectory. The limited research allows one to tentatively conclude that letters and email may be more strongly associated with relational satisfaction in military couples than short face-to-face visits or even telephone calls. During military separations, too much contact may actually be harmful for all involved because increased contact may lead to the exchange of negative information and emotionally upsetting interactions, creating more stress, depression, and distraction. Overall, some form of positive or nurturing contact or even mere one-way information from home, such as a positive letter, "care packages," or news relayed through others simply to say that their family is doing well, is associated with positive morale of military individuals (Ursano & Norwood, 1996). Letters to partners in prison help individuals hold onto positive relational images. In sum, restricted communication does seem to be related to positive images and expectations, and such images also may serve to preserve the relationship.

However, idealized images may also contribute to unrealistic expectations, and unrealistic expectations tend to be associated with relational dissatisfaction (Vangelisti, 2002). As a consequence, LDRs may be especially at risk upon reunification. Le and Agnew (2001) found, among dating individuals, geographically close partners were better able to meet needs for companionship, sexual activity, security, and emotional involvement. Nevertheless, the failure to meet these needs was not associated with negative emotions among LDR couples. Le and Agnew propose that "a temporary reduction or virtual absence of need fulfillment may be perceived as tolerable to protect relationship stability" (p. 438). In other words, perhaps some partners in LDRs may not have the same expectations of need fulfillment that proximal partners do, at least not immediately. Rather, Le and Agnew conjecture that needs may be expected to be met at some point in the future; positive emotions in the short run may come from "talking on the phone, writing, and receiving letters, making plans, and thinking about the partner" (p. 436). Supporting the contention that individuals in LDRs may not have the same need expectations, autonomously oriented individuals appear to fair better in long-distance marital relationships (Magnuson & Norem, 1999). It is unclear if these individuals are already autonomous or if they develop autonomy in response to the separation. It must be noted that in these situations (dating and DCDR) separation is voluntary.

Regarding communication per se, the nature, frequency, and mode of communication may vary with the type of separation encountered. Nevertheless, it appears that restricted communication fosters pleasant, reassuring, and perhaps even vague messages to stay in touch, which in turn promotes positive mental reconstructions of relationships. Couples recreate each other and their relationship and areas of conflict are avoided (Schulman, 1974). Idealization has generally been thought to occur in early stages of relationships and then to dissipate with increased interactions. Restricted communication does not allow for such disillusionment in dating couples, and apparently restricted communication may reinstantiate idealized images among married partners with infrequent face-to-face contact. Letters and asynchronous email may be especially prone to the facilitation of idealization. This is precisely the type of communication the military desires in order to keep soldiers satisfied and not preoccupied with problems at home.

Such communication, however, may contribute to problems upon reunion. Then again, these hazy, romanticized messages seem to sustain the relationships during separation. It has been argued that benevolent misconceptions (Ickes & Simpson, 1997) protect even geographically close relationships. A certain amount of misunderstanding or optimistic adoration may well be necessary for the preservation of relationships in general (Sillars, 1998).

REGULATION OF ROLES AND POWER STRUCTURES

Reunions have often been found to be characterized by turbulence. However, reintegration into the relational and family dynamics involves redefining roles, power structures, and boundary regulations, resulting in tumultuous reunions. Difficult adjustments to reunions have repeatedly been found as part of an entire cycle of separation and reunion.

Hill (1945, 1949, 1958) was the first to identify and discuss patterns or stages during the deployment cycle, now considered a normal part of military life. Hill (1958) described the deployment cycle as a roller coaster-like ride. Hill was also the first to examine coping behaviors of the spouse at home during deployment, which at that time was almost exclusively the wife. He identified three patterns. Some women held onto traditional sex roles and attempted to adapt without making substantive adjustments. These women felt helpless, and the family was in turmoil as the women felt incapable of operating without their husbands' input, which was generally impossible to gain. At the other extreme, husbands were excluded psychologically and his roles and duties were divided among children and the wife. This family appeared to function quite well in the deployed soldier's absence. Yet, they encountered the most traumatic readjustment upon his return.

Hill surmised a third pattern was most successful. These families included the father symbolically and psychologically, and continued affectionate contact through regular letters. The mother made decisions and exercised power and authority in his absence. Here the families did experience more difficulty with the father's absence than did families that shut the father out entirely. Alternatively, they also experienced fewer difficulties adjusting to the father's reintegration into the family.

Role adjustments continue to be a problem in today's military families. Roles, routines, authority, and power structures must all be renegotiated upon a spouse's departure, return, and departure again. The returning solider unrealistically expects everything to be the same as before deployment. Surprisingly, he finds many of his duties to be reassigned to extended family, the spouse, or children, and often actually feels bored and restless after a brief period at home (Wood et al., 1995). The spouse who remains at home may desire admiration or appreciation for successfully accomplishing family tasks. Instead she discovers her military partner wants to resume these tasks, and she becomes resentful and feels unappreciated (Wood et al.).

Forsyth and Gramling (1987) offered a summary of coping patterns based upon both military and long-term civilian separations several decades after Hill. Their findings are remarkably similar to his. They noted that the occupations that required prolonged separation tended to be working-class families who generally adhere to traditional sex-role power and authority structures. Like Hill, their overall conclusion was that prolonged separations disrupt this power structure and thus family dynamics revolve around adaptation to changing roles. Forsyth and Gramling (1987) reported five types of family adaptation among single-residence, commuting couples.

The first is the "replacement husband father." During times of absence, a male or males from the extended family act as the base of power and authority. Another type of adaptation process occurs when "contingent authority" is granted to the wife. She takes on the traditional authority granted the male, to some extent, in limited areas and only during his absence; she remains traditional in most ways. The children in such families tend to develop quite a bit of power, given the wife's discomfort in the role as disciplinarian. A third type of adaptation is "alternating authority." Here power and authority are passed back and forth between husband and wife. She does act as the decision maker, disciplinarian, and the family authority in his absence, but these roles are handed over to the father on his return. Forsyth and Gramling noted this to be most common when separations are short and predictable. The fourth pattern is one characterized by conflict. In this case, the wife takes on the same roles as in the alternating authority model, yet she does not relinquish the roles upon the father's return. Conflict ensues as the husband expects to resume his traditional roles. The last family type portrayed is that of the father as "periodic guest." In this case, the mother takes on all the roles of the traditional mother and father (aside from primary wage earner). The father's reunion is anticipated and is enjoyed at first. However, his presence becomes difficult and problematic as he disrupts the family system that has emerged; family members have settled into roles, routines, social networks, and activities that don't include him. The mother-children boundaries may have merged as the mother has come to rely upon and consult the children about household concerns. In essence, the father is a guest in his own home and after a while, anxiously awaits his next departure.

Families separated by incarceration also must deal with role changes. Many men provided the sole financial support prior to their imprisonment. The inability to provide for the family contributes to feeling unneeded and less connected (Fishman, 1990). The remaining family members encounter role renegotiations similar to those of military families during deployments. Children of incarcerated parents have difficulty delineating roles; they often attempt to take over role responsibilities of the incarcerated member (Brooks, 1993).

Children and parents separated by divorce must also address many role issues. The quality of contact is related to the "role" of the father as reciprocally defined by self, society, the mother, and the parental relationship. This is potentially of great consequence. As some research suggests, it appears that the maternal satisfaction with the paternal contact is more predictive of the child's well-being than the actual paternal contact. Unfortunately, there is little actual research to draw conclusions from the father's point of view about his reasons for involvement, or lack thereof; scant research has included the father directly. Gordon (2000) reviewed five major family and child development journals from 1993 to 1997 and found 304 articles concerned with caregiver or family influences on child or adolescence development. Only six of these articles included data collected from the fathers.

In the absence of a marital union with the mother, a father who sees his role as parent and husband may have difficulty maintaining a cohesive father-child bond (Kissman, 1997). Restrictions on the amount of time father and children have together, as well as legal limitations in cases of sole maternal custody, also play into this role ambiguity. Fathers report feeling like a visitor in their children's lives instead of a parent (Arendell, 1997). Thus, their role often disintegrates into the overly permissive, entertaining, and fun visiting relative rather than teacher or authority figure (Hetherington & Stanley-Hagen, 1997). The father may experience great role confusion and feel he has no place in the child's life except as an occasional guest (Hetherington & Stanley-Hagen).

Another obstacle to parental involvement related to roles is remarriage of either parent (Cooksey & Craig, 1998). With remarriage, and especially with the presence of new biological children or stepchildren, the role as father and husband is once more psychologically completed, thus reducing the father's need for contact with his other children (Kissman, 1997). It also reduces the amount of time, money, and availability of the father (Cooksey & Craig 1998). Kissman (1997) proposes that the extent to which expectations of fatherhood become important as opposed to being both father and husband, the more fathers will be able to maintain contact with their children.

Kissman (1997) reported nonresidential mothers suffer role and identity issues as well. Noncustodial mothers suffer almost unbearable guilt for relinquishing or not succeeding in attaining custody, and such guilt has a debilitating effect. The guilt and self-blame may affect their ability to become involved with their children.

Summary

Inappropriate role boundaries and ambiguous role definitions apparently plague most LDR families. When only one parental figure is present, whether due to divorce, incarceration, or occupational or military duty, the at-home parent and the children readjust boundaries. Children and primary parents may become autonomous units. In the case of divorce, parents may have difficulty defining their own roles as the roles of parent and spouse are perceived as intertwined, resulting in difficulty enacting one role in the absence of the other role. Families facing frequent cycles of departure and return may feel in a constant state of upheaval because power dynamics are in a perpetual state of major renegotiation. Although spouses in short-term frequent separations have less depression and less pronounced distress, recurrent short separations seem to make it especially difficult for the at home spouses to deal with stress and responsibility as power structures and roles are in a constant state of adaptation to arrivals and departures. Disagreement over child-rearing practices may be frequent (Vormbrock, 1993). Though all families renegotiate roles and power structures with developmental and family life-cycle changes, families with long-distance members provide a unique forum for studying family roles, power, and boundary negotiations. Considering Olson's (2000) circumplex model, it would seem such a family would be characterized by perpetually high levels of adaptability with widely fluctuating levels of cohesion. Families maintaining relationships from a distance provide an interesting arena for the study of family system dynamics.

THE ROLE OF COMMUNITY

Although community support is usually beneficial, support is contingent upon the nature of and reason for separations. The extent to which community support is needed and offered also varies among LDR types. In addition, it has been proposed that community and extended family may actually provide too much support in the case of frequent temporary separations, inadvertently contributing to the demise of the relationships among the separated parties.

Westefeld and Liddell (1982) reported that they believed that the primary benefit of the student forums was the connections among the students who attended them. The importance of developing proximal community ties for the provision of companionship, support, and the like among LDR dating partners remains consistently advised (Aylor, 2003; Carpenter & Knox, 1986; Holt & Stone, 1988; Schwebel et al., 1992; Wilmot & Carbaugh, 1986).

The advice that involvement with local networks may lesson stress and alleviate isolation may be sound, but it has not been empirically verified. Moreover, one must wonder if increased involvement in proximal relationships might also be related to relational dissolution, depending on whether such networks support the relationship or meet needs too well. Sahlstein (in press) reported that long-distance dating partners find their immediate social networks play both a positive and a negative role in their situations.

Given that LDRs violate norms of proximity, individuals are not always validated by their proximal networks. Though not tested in regard to LDRs, approval of friendship networks has repeatedly been found to play a role in the stability of dating relationships in general (Cate et al., 2002; Felmlee, 2001; Sprecher & Felmlee, 2000). Because of the ubiquitous nature of LDRs among college students, individuals in dating LDRs are surrounded by others in similar circumstances with whom to commiserate. "Perhaps the unique college environment inoculates these relationships against the impact of deficits in time spent together" (Guldner & Swensen, 1995, p. 319).

DCDR marriages may encounter less societal support than dating couples, given that norms for marital cohabitation are stronger than norms for dating couple proximity. "Social disapproval . . . is seen by most sociologists and psychologists as the most difficult problem the DCDR couple has to face" (Winfield, 1985, p. 168). Similarly, Bunker et al. (1992) reported that popular images of the commuting family are "generally pessimistic" (p. 339). As a result, they speculate that DCDR families may limit contact with community to avoid such explicit or implicit criticism. The limited contact in turn reduces potential support networks for childcare and other practical problems. Indeed, Gerstel and Gross (1984) found that personal networks, the workplace, and society in general do not support DCDR marriages. Friends and family members often question the wisdom of such a nonconventional lifestyle (Gerstel & Gross) and perceive the decision to reside apart as a lack of interest in or commitment to the marriage or as an early warning sign of an impending divorce (Groves & Horm-Wingerd, 1991). However, Groves and Horm-Wingerd also found that although society at large is not accepting of the marital commuting lifestyle, on a case-by-case basis family and friends provide comfort.

Although not examined in conjunction with long-distance marriages, evidence indicates that network overlap is related to marital satisfaction (Milardo & Helms-Erikson, 2000). By default, these individuals in long-distance marriages have less network overlap. DCDR couples are also less likely to know individuals in similar situations than are college dating couples or military personnel. The picture of societal support for DCDR marriages is a bleak one, although arguably, they are in less need of community support than many other types of LDRs because of their relatively high incomes and ease of contact compared to families with an incarcerated member, military families, or many divorced or never-married parents and their children.

In the case of nonresidential parents due to divorce or of never-married parents, community support systems tend to focus on the residential parent through the provision of monetary, instrumental, and emotional support. When the residential parent can adequately function through the help of others, a positive spillover effect occurs for children. When children in divorced families have community support in emotional and financial areas, and the involvement of other caregivers, such as grandparents, the direct effects of the lack of paternal involvement may be mitigated (Cowen, Pedro-Carroll, & Alpert-Gillis, 1990; Drapeau & Bouchard, 1993; Kot & Shoemaker, 1999).

Unlike most other forms of LDRs, military personnel have institutionalized support systems, and most often, societal approval for the separation. The military attempts to create and involve the family in support services. Much of this support is emotional. Some is instrumental, such as providing group day care or car maintenance (Reed & Segal, 2000).

The dissemination of information by the military is another form of assistance. Communication from the military unit to the spouse appears to alleviate marital distress. Such communication may involve direct communication, such as newsletters from the unit, or it may involve the facilitation of communication among the families, such as by setting up support groups. Calling trees or circles among spouses to disseminate information and make spouses aware of military support systems and opportunities have also been organized by military command. Dissemination of information can be especially helpful for younger, recently married spouses facing their first deployment, as well as civilian husbands and reservists' spouses as they tend to be the least integrated into military life and thus know the least about support opportunities while being the most at risk (Black, 1993; Knox & Price, 1995).

Although community support appears beneficial (Rosen & Moghadam, 1988), today's military is faced with the problem of maintaining a sense of military community. Approximately 50% of military families live in civilian communities as opposed to military communities (Martin & McClure, 2000). Of those families who were living on base prior to a spouse's overseas deployment, many move away from the base during the deployment (Schumm, Bell, & Knott, 2000). These families have decreased connection and cohesion with other military families. Therefore, an increasing challenge for the military is to develop means to disseminate information to these families and encourage involvement in military support systems (Ursano & Norwood, 1996).

Because of the dispersion of the military community, even though more services are offered today than ever before, the spouse is more in need of comfort and assistance from the civilian community. Living off base is not necessarily detrimental. Many spouses chose to move closer to relatives for instrumental support as well as emotional support. This can actually benefit both the family and the military (Bell & Schumm, 1999). Often military spouses attribute successful separations to their local social support networks of friends, family, and church communities, rather than military networks (Wood et al., 1995). Disadvantages for the spouse and the military can also result as families off base have decreased access to information and military support groups. These families also no longer have access to lower priced medical treatment and other services (Schumm et al., 2000). Spouses and families who fare separations best rely on a combination of formal and informal military networks, formal civilian support programs, backing from their own employers, and informal assistance of friends and family (Martin & McClure, 2000).

A unique form of community support often available to military families is overall societal support; missions that are popularly endorsed or at least understood by the individual's community foster a helpful climate for the family. Of course, this is not true of all deployments. Deployments that are not seen as "legitimate," or those that are not popular (e.g., Vietnam) or not well understood by the community (e.g., Somalia) create more difficulties for the spouse at home than those that are endorsed and embraced by society at large (e.g., World War II; Ursano & Norwood, 1996).

Although societal support of specific deployments may ebb and flow, families separated due to incarceration, despite their readily apparent needs, receive virtually no community support, institutional or otherwise. For the most part, they receive quite the opposite. Families with an incarcerated member often become isolated because they lack institutional, community, or family support resources (Western & McLanahan, 2000). Families of incarcerated persons encounter social stigma, lack of sympathy, lack of social support, involuntary single parenting, and poverty (Arditti et al., 2003). Family members of incarcerated individuals have difficulty in acquiring both information about policies and practices of the correctional system and information about their particular family member (Hairston, 2001b). Uncertainty about rules and policies and about their incarcerated member's status are predominant concerns of family members (Fishman, 1990), yet families have fewer resources to turn to than military families. Some do not seek public assistance because they lack information about the assistance; others are suspicious of formal organizations (Beckerman, 1994).

Some states offer programs designed to provide support for families of incarcerated members. These programs range from instrumental help, such as the providing food and clothing, to facilitating contact among the incarcerated prisoners and family members, and to aiding the formation of support groups among family members of incarcerated individuals. Psychological intervention for children of incarcerated parents is another form of support. Other programs facilitate visitation by providing information on visitation policies, intervening in problems with visitation, facilitating more family-friendly visits, or paying for children's visits. Some states facilitate family support groups connecting families of incarcerated prisoners with each other. Such programs are rare and often underfunded.

According to Arditti et al. (2003), the most likely successful arena of intervention is "enhancing naturally occurring networks of support for these families" (p. 202). The provision of social support alleviates some emotional distress, helps to reduce isolation, increases parenting abilities, and often prevents poverty. Despite the potential individual and societal benefits, such support is seldom available.

Although most scholars contend that community support and involvement are beneficial for virtually all types of LDR couples and families, Vormbrock (1993) cautioned against too much proximal support. She concluded, from her review of numerous types of long-distance marriages, that for individuals in routine long separations, the family members at home can actually become overly reliant upon proximal social support. This excess dependency on family and community blurs boundaries and roles and makes reunion more difficult. Family members at home may have fewer immediate difficulties and may be distracted from their loneliness through such involvements. However, Vormbrock found some individuals to become less attached and less emotionally involved with the absent member over time. This detachment feeds a cycle of finding reasons to stay apart and decreasing reliance and attachment to the absent member. This is reminiscent of the patterns identified by Forsyth and Gramling (1987) wherein returning members feel like a guests in their own homes and looked forward to departing again. Thus, the proximal network can dysfunctionally enable separation as opposed to functionally supporting individuals involved in the separation.

Summary

Across couple types and relationships, the role of the proximal community has the potential incredible influence. Clearly, at least some individuals in LDR dating relationships experience difficulties and the proximal community has been proposed to alleviate some feelings of loneliness, although this is yet to be verified. For DCDR couples, the role of community support is relatively unexplored. However, it appears that although society in general is not particularly accepting of such arrangements, individuals within proximal networks are. Perhaps because of the relative acceptance of the reasons for separation, community provision of emotional and tangible instrumental support is more available for families separated because of military duties than other types of LDRs. Some of this aid comes simply from friends, family, and other community members being sympathetic to the couple's separation. Community support is more likely to be offered if the deployment is perceived to be for a just and understandable cause.

Though not necessarily direct support, network overlap also warrants consideration as overlap has been associated with positive relational properties (Milardo & Helms-Erikson, 2000). Separated couples of all kinds, by default, would have less network overlap than proximal couples and thus may be more at risk.

Families have become less involved in communities over time in the United States. Family historians do not agree on the degree to which family and community were more connected earlier in U.S. history, nor on the extent to which family and community are now isolated from each other, or the exact time frame in which this gradual shift occurred. Nonetheless, family historians in general agree that the immediate or nuclear family has become more privatized, and primacy of the "nuclear" family has resulted in "weakening influence of extended kin, friends, and neighbors on family ties, and to an isolation of the family from interaction with the community" (Haveran, 1987, p. 54). As a result, today's family relationships often embody a plethora of expectations and needs to be provided by other family members. Perhaps successful long-distance families mirror an era in which the immediate family was more intertwined with extended family and community.

CONCLUSIONS AND FUTURE DIRECTIONS

It would be unethical and impossible to create experimental groups of couples or families who reside apart in order to examine communication processes or community support. Therefore, we must be content with examining the numerous existing relationships. These relationships lend themselves as natural laboratories for exploration of communication practices from multiple theoretical perspectives.

Although differing theoretical orientations certainly ask and answer different questions, to date a deficit of theoretically guided research into virtually every aspect of long-distance relationships exists. Exceptions include Vormbrock's (1993) examination of attachment theory, Stephen's (1986) consideration of symbolic interdependence, Dainton and Aylor's (2001) examination of uncertainty reduction theory, and Sahlstein's (in press) application of relational dialectics. Even when theory is considered, communication scholars are too often confined to college dating relationships and limited conceptions of success.

The study of LDRs of all varieties is timely because the sheer number of LDRs is on the rise. Although divorce rates appear to have stabilized, the number of children born to never married or noncohabiting parents is increasing. As a result, the number of children living away from at least one parent is also rising. Incarceration is growing at record rates in the United States. In addition, the increasing number of dual-career marriages, both in civilian and military domains, increases the likelihood of families living apart. The rate of cohabitation is also climbing, hence the number of long-distance unmarried committed relationships, past the college years, will likely grow as well. Both college dating relationships and DCDR marriages are the most voluntary forms of separation. These two forms of LDRs offer the most potential for fulfillment of individual goals. Other LDRs studied in the U.S. are relatively involuntary. Yet the study of Dutch LATs has revealed numerous reasons for voluntary separations aside from fulfillment of individual goals (Levin & Trost, 1999). Continued research will likely discover additional reasons for voluntary LDRs in U.S. society as well. For example, committed gay and lesbian couples, whether defined as married or not, may also have LDRs. In short, numerous societal factors are converging that will most likely result in a higher proportion of the population involved in some type of personal relationship enacted at a distance.

Not only do the circumstances of personal relationships among individuals living apart provide students of communication the opportunity to test and develop theory, communication scholars may also offer applied research to help in the formulation of policies and intervention in multiple domains. Roloff (2002) observed that interpersonal communication scholars have contributed relatively little directly to socially significant problems and urged us to "overcome our own inertia" (p. 440).

As has been a theme throughout, actual communication is seldom studied in long-distance relationships. When communication is the focus of study, it is often merely the frequency of contact, particularly face-to-face contact, that is considered. Of course, it is and always has been absurd to equate frequency of communication with intimacy of relationships, yet as Parks (1995) has made clear, ours is a culture plagued by the ideology of intimacy, and frequent, in-depth, face-to-face communication is seen as a must for "true" meaningful relationships. Parks acknowledged that, although such beliefs are beginning to dissipate from the thinking of communication researchers, they remain firmly implanted in most introductory communication texts and popular culture. In spite of this, reported findings indicate that neither frequency, nor depth, nor face-to-face communication are defining hallmarks of success (regardless of type of success) in long-distance relationships.

More sophisticated conceptions of communication and investigations of actual interaction between separated parties, as well as communication in the home concerning the separated parties, are sorely needed, as is additional research from the perspectives of all parties involved. Researchers must recognize that there are numerous types of LDRs and that there are important distinctions among them, even in similar relationship types—such as DCDR marriages and single-residence, dual-earner marriages with one commuting partner. Not all military marriages are the same; differences exist among active duty personal and reservists, between those deployed in combat versus noncombat units, and those that are dual-career, single-career, or single-parent families. Such simplistic markers as miles apart or frequency of interaction do not adequately capture the distinctions nor do they allow exploration of the plethora of potential patterns of interaction and community support possible. A systems perspective to understanding the role of communication and community among various types of families attempting to maintain close ties at a distance is warranted. Dialectical perspectives (Baxter & Montgomery, 1996) that consider the pushes and pulls upon these relationships offer a potentially insightful research heuristic.

Definitive conclusions are limited, yet some tentative ones are offered. As stated at the onset, a purpose of this synthesis was to delineate the role of communication in long-distance relationships. First, actual interaction or facets of communication are seldom studied. Sheer frequency of contact, both face-to-face and mediated, is the most predominant focus in all areas. To the extent that content has been assessed, it appears that vague, positive communication may help sustain many LDRs as such communication fosters optimistic images of the partner and the relationship. Idealization has some dangers. Dating couples may not be truly gaining knowledge about their partner in order to make informed decisions about marriage. Another risk of idealization is that when reunited, the risk of expectations exceeding enactment is incurred. However, it might be argued that some idealization or positive illusions are necessary for sustaining most relationships. Seeing our romantic partners through rose colored glasses has many benefits (Hendrick & Hendrick, 1988). Third, idealization may come into play among separated parents and children as well. The remembrance of birthdays, enactment of inclusive rituals and the like, seems to facilitate affectionate ties even in the absence of much interaction.

Fourth, the usual criterion of relational stability as success is simplistic at best. It fails to capture various systemic levels of success and ignores the possibility that relational dissolution or lessened contact may be considered successful in certain circumstances. Fifth, just as the conception of success as stability is overly simplistic, so are most conceptions of long-distance relationships. We have barely begun to tap the multitude of differences among differing long-distance forms, and some long-distance relationships have remained completely unstudied.

Finally, whatever the type of relationship and whatever criterion of success invoked, the proximal community plays a significant, albeit not always helpful role. Community support may be helpful in most circumstances. However, the community can also be cold and unsympathetic creating additional distress for some children, parents, or partners. Proximal community ties may also be too helpful causing rifts among the separated individuals. In sum, the vast number and variety of long-distance relationships and family forms should call us to reconsider the traditionally conceived views of family structure, the role of communication in close relationships, and the presumption that community necessarily plays a positive role in the lives of those involved such relationships.

NOTES

1. A subset of military personnel separated from their families is POWs and MIAs. Obviously these marital partners and children experience stresses and strains quite different from other long-distance families, including a greater uncertainty of eventual return and legal complications unmatched by those with an absent, yet accounted for spouse or parent. Given a focus here is upon communication, and communication with such individuals is almost always impossible, research surrounding MIAs and POWs is not reviewed here. This is meant in no way to lesson the importance of research on coping and community support for families in this situation. In fact, it is likely that a supportive community is especially relevant in these families. (McCubbin, Dahl, Lester, Benson, & Robertson, 1976).

2. Interaction with family members of incarcerated individuals on death row is not considered here. These family members face prolonged and distorted grief, with no societal accepted modes of mourning. They encounter extreme senses of guilt, isolation, and feelings of powerlessness and psychological problems (Smykla, 1987).

3. Gerstel and Gross (1984) use the term "commuter" marriage to refer to these couple types. Yet the term commuter marriage is used inconsistently in the literature, resulting in confusion between

DCDR couples and single-residence couples in which one member commutes on a regular basis. Thus, this review examines dual-career, dual-residence marriages dubbed with the acronym DCDR.

4. In early U.S. history, in the case of divorce, common law and common practice recognized the father as custodian. In a landmark case, *Pennsylvania v. Addicks* (1813), Chief Justice William Tilghman awarded custody to the mother: "[I]t appears to us that considering their (the two daughters') tender age, they stand in need of that kind of assistance, which can be afforded by none so well as a mother" (Frost-Knappman & Cullen-Dupont, 1997). This case was significant in many ways: First, the court took into account the children's best interests; second, common law precedence was changed from the presumption of the father as custodian to mother; and third, the concept that the mother and father cooperate in the father's visitation of the children was included. Tilghman declared that the mother should not interfere with the father's right to see his children, she should accommodate his visits or allow the children to visit him, and he should not attempt to remove the children to another geographic location. The "tender years" doctrine took root here and by the turn of the 20th century the presumption of the "natural" custodian had shifted from the father to the mother.

5. Voluntary is subjective. These relationships are referred to here as voluntary as no higher authority, such as the government or one's parents, dictates their separations. Gerstel and Gross (1984) point out that the individuals within dual-career, dual-residence marriages may not feel that their separations are voluntary; they may perceive no other options as viable.

REFERENCES

Amato, P. R., & Keith, B. (1991). Parental divorce and well-being of children: A meta-analysis. *Psychological Bulletin, 110*, 26–46.

Amato, P. R., & Rezac, S. J. (1994). Contact with nonresident parents, interparental conflict, and children's behavior. *Journal of Family Issues, 15*, 191–207.

Anderson, E. A. (1992). Decision-making style: Impact on satisfaction of the commuter couples' lifestyle. *Journal of Family and Economic Issues, 13*, 5–21.

Anderson, E. A., & Spruill, J. W. (1993). The dual-career commuter family: A lifestyle on the move. *Marriage and Family Review, 19*, 131–147.

Angrist, J. D., & Johnson, J. H. (2000). Effects of work-related absences on families: Evidence from the Gulf War. *Industrial and Labor Relations Review, 54*, 41–58.

Applewhite, L. W., Jr., & Mays, R. A. (1996). Parent–child separation: A comparison of maternally and paternally separated children in military families. *Child Adolescent Social Work Journal, 13*, 23–39.

Arditti, J. A., Lambert-Shute, J., & Joest, K. (2003). Saturday morning at the jail: Implications of incarceration for families and children. *Family Relations, 52*, 195–204.

Arendell, T. (1997). The new father. In T. Arendell (Ed.), *Contemporary parenting: Challenges and issues* (pp. 154–195). Thousand Oaks, CA: Sage.

Astin, H. S., & Milem, J. F. (1997). The status of academic couples in U.S. institutions. In M. A. Ferber & J. W. Loeb (Eds.), *Academic couples: Problems and promise* (pp. 128–155). Champaign: University of Illinois Press.

Aylor, D. (2003). Maintaining long-distance relationships. In D. J. Canary & M. Dainton (Eds.), *Maintaining relationships through communication: Relational, contextual, and cultural variations* (pp. 127–140). Mahwah, NJ: Erlbaum.

Baxter, L. A., & Montgomery, B. M. (1996). *Relating: Dialogues and dialects*. New York: Guilford Press.

Beckerman, A. (1994). Mothers in prison: Meeting the prerequisite conditions for permanency planning. *Social Work, 39*, 9–14.

Bell, D. B., Bartone, J., Bartone, P. T., Schumm, W. R., & Gade, P. A. (1997). *USAREUR family support during Operation Joint Endeavor: A summary report*. Alexandria, VA: U.S. Army Research Institute for the Behavioral and Social Science.

Bell, D. B., & Schumm, W. R. (1999). Family adaptation to deployments. In I. P. McClure (Ed.), *Pathways to the future: A review of military family research* (pp. 109–131). Scranton, PA: Military Family Institute.

Bell, D. B., & Schumm, W. R. (2000). Providing family support during military deployments. In J. A. Martin, L. N. Rosen, & L. R. Sparacino (Eds.), *The military family: A practice guide for human service providers* (pp. 139–152). Westport, CT: Praeger.

Bell, D. B., Schumm, W. R., Knott, B., & Ender, M. G. (1999). The desert fax: A research note on calling home from Somalia. *Armed Forces and Society, 25*, 509–521.

Berger, P. L., & Kellner, H. (1964). Marriage and the construction of reality. *Diogenes, 64*, 1–4.

Berger, P. L., & Luckmann, T. (1966). *The social construction of reality: A treatise in the sociology of knowledge.* Garden City, NY: Doubleday.

Binstock, G., & Thornton, A. (2003). Separations, reconciliations, and living apart in cohabitating and marital unions. *Journal of Marriage and Family, 65*, 432–473.

Black, W. (1993). Military-induced family separation: A stress reduction intervention. *Social Work, 38*, 273–280.

Boss, P., McCubbin, H. I., & Lester, G. (1979). The corporate executive wife's coping patterns in response to routine husband-father absence: Implications for family stress theory. *Family Process, 18*, 79–86.

Braver, S. L., & O'Connell, D. (1998). *Divorced dads: Shattering the myths.* New York: Jeremy P. Tarcher.

Brenner, E. (2001). *Fathers in prison: A review of the data.* Philadelphia: National Center on Fathers and Families.

Broderick, C. B. (1988). To arrive where we started: The field of family studies in the 1930s. *Journal of Marriage and the Family, 50*, 569–584.

Bronfenbrenner, U. (1979). *The ecology of human development: Experiments by nature and by design.* Cambridge, MA: Harvard University Press.

Brooks, M. K. (1993). *How can I help? Working with children of incarcerated parents.* New York: Osborne Association.

Buchanan, C. M. (2000). Adolescent's adjustment to divorce. In R. D. Taylor & M. C. Wang (Eds.), *Resilience across contexts: Family, work, culture, and community* (pp. 179–216). Mahwah, NJ: Erlbaum.

Buchanan, C. M., & Heiges, K. L. (2001). When conflict continues after the marriage ends: Effects of post-divorce conflict on children. In J. H. Grych & F. D. Fincham (Eds.), *Interparental conflict and child development* (pp. 337–362). Cambridge, UK: Cambridge University Press.

Buchanan, C. M., Maccoby, E. E., & Dornbusch, S. M. (1996). *Adolescents after divorce.* Cambridge, MA: Harvard University Press.

Bunker, B. B., Zubek, J. M., Vanderslice, V. A., & Rice, R. W. (1992). Quality of life in dual-career families: Commuting versus single-residence couples. *Journal of Marriage and Family, 54*, 339–407.

Burgess, E. W. (1926). The family as a unit of interacting personalities. *The Family, 7*, 3–9.

Burgess, E. W., Locke, H. J., & Thomes, M. M. (1971). *The family: From traditional to companionship* (4th ed.). New York: Van Nostrand Reinhold.

Canary, D. J., & Stafford, L. (1994). Maintaining relationships through strategic and routine interaction. In D. J. Canary & L. Stafford (Eds.), *Communication and relational maintenance* (pp. 3–22). San Diego, CA: Academic Press.

Carlson, E., & Carlson, R. (2002). *Navy marriages and deployments* (Rev. ed.). New York: University of America Press.

Carpenter, D., & Knox, D. (1986). Relationship maintenance of college students separated during courtship. *College Student Journal, 20*, 86–88.

Cate, R. M., & Lloyd, S. A. (1992). *Courtship.* Newbury Park, CA: Sage.

Cate, R. M., Levin, L. A., & Richmond, L. S. (2002). Premarital relationship stability: A review of recent research. *Journal of Social and Personal Relationships, 19*, 261–284.

Cicirelli, V. G. (1991). Sibling relationships in adulthood. In S. K. Pfeifer & M. B. Sussman (Eds.), *Families: Intergenerational and generational connections* (pp. 291–309). New York: Hayworth Press.

Command Briefing Resources. (2000). *Deployment and families: Research and implications.* Arlington, VA: Military Family Resource Center.

Cooksey, E. C., & Craig, P. H. (1998). Parenting from a distance: The effects of paternal characteristics on contact between nonresidential fathers and children. *Demography, 35,* 187–200.

Cooley, C. (1909). *Social organization.* New York: Scribner.

Cooper, C., & Ward-Zuckerman, B. (2001). *Military personnel: Actions needed to achieve greater results from Air Force family needs assessments.* Washington, DC: U.S. General Accounting Office.

Cowen, E. L., Pedro-Carroll, J. L., & Alpert-Gillis, L. J. (1990). Relationships between support and adjustment among children of divorce. *Journal of Child Psychology and Psychiatry and Allied Disciplines, 31,* 727–735.

Cutrona, C. E. (1996). *Social support in couples: Marriages as a resources in times of need.* Thousand Oaks, CA: Sage.

Dainton, M., & Aylor, B. (2001). A relational uncertainty analysis of jealousy, trust, and maintenance in long-distance versus geographically close relationships. *Communication Quarterly, 49,* 172–188.

Dainton, M., & Aylor, B. (2002). Patterns of communication channel use in the maintenance of long-distance relationships. *Communication Research Reports, 19,* 118–129.

Dainton, M., & Stafford, L. (1993). Routine maintenance behaviors: A comparison of relationship type, partner similarity, and sex differences. *Journal of Social and Personal Relationships, 10,* 255–272.

DaVanzo, J., & Rahman, M. O. (1993). American families: Trends and correlates. *Population Index, 59,* 350–386.

Davidson, N. (1990). Life without father: America's greatest social catastrophe. *Policy Review, 51,* 40–44.

Defense Manpower Data Center. (1999). *Effective strategies to assist spouses of junior enlisted members with employment.* Alexandria, VA: Survey and Program Evaluation Division.

DeFrain, J., & Olson, D. H. (1999). Contemporary family patterns and relationships. In M. B. Sussman, S. Steinmetz, & G. Peterson (Eds.), *Handbook of marriage and the family* (2nd ed., pp. 309–326). New York: Plenum.

Dellmann-Jenkins, M., Bernard-Paolucci, T. S., & Rushing, B. (1994). Does distance make the heart grow fonder? A comparison of college students in long-distance and geographically-close dating relationships. *College Student Journal, 28,* 212–219.

Dindia, K., & Baxter, L. A. (1987). Strategies for repairing and maintaining marital relationships. *Journal of Social and Personal Relationships, 4,* 143–158.

Douvan, E., & Pleck, J. (1978). Separation as support. In R. Rapoport & R. Rapoport (Eds.), *Working couples* (pp. 138–146). New York: Harper & Row.

Drapeau, S., & Bouchard, C. (1993). Support networks and adjustment among 6 to 11 year-olds from maritally-disrupted and intact families. *Journal of Divorce and Remarriage, 19,* 75–97.

Drummet, A. R., Coleman, M., & Cable, S. (2003). Military families under stress: Implications for family life education. *Family Relations, 52,* 279–287.

Duck, S. W. (1990). Where do all the kisses go? Rapport, positivity and relational level of analysis of interpersonal enmeshment. *Psychological Inquiry, 1,* 47–53.

Duck, S. W., & Pittman, G. (1994). Social and personal relationships. In M. L. Knapp & G. R. Miller (Eds.), *Handbook of interpersonal communication* (2nd ed., pp. 676–695). Thousand Oaks, CA: Sage.

Duck, S. W., Rutt, D. J., Hurst, M. H., & Strejc, H. (1991). Some evident truths about everyday conversation: All communications are not created equal. *Human. Communication Research, 18,* 228–267.

Dudley, J. R. (1991). Increasing our understanding of divorced fathers who have infrequent contact with their children. *Family Relations, 40,* 279–285.

Dugan, E., & Kivett, V. R. (1998). Implementing the Adams and Blieszner conceptual model: Predicting interactive friendship processes of older adults. *Journal of Social and Personal Relationships, 15,* 607–622.

Emery, R. E. (1994). *Renegotiation family relationships: Divorce, child custody, and mediation.* New York: Guilford Press.

Etheridge, R. M. (1989). *Family factors affecting retention: A review of the literature.* Alexandria, VA: U.S. Army Research Institute for the Behavior and Social Science.

Farris, A. (1978). Commuting. In R. Rapoport & R. Rapoport (Eds.), *Working couples* (pp. 100–107). London: Routledge & Kegan Paul.

Felmlee, D. H. (2001). No couple is an island: A social network perspective on dyadic stability. *Social Forces, 79,* 1259–1287.

Fields, J., & Casper, L. M. (2001). *America's families and living arrangements: March 2000.* Washington, DC: U.S. Census Bureau.

Fields, J., Smith, K., Bass, L. E., & Lugaila, T. (2001). *A child's day: Home, school, and play (selected indicators of child well-being).* Washington, DC: U.S. Census Bureau.

Fishman, L. T. (1990). *Women at the wall: A study of prisoners' wives doing time on the outside.* Albany: State University of New York Press.

Fitzpatrick, M. A., & Caughlin, J. P. (2002). Interpersonal communication in family relationships. In M. L. Knapp & J. A. Daly (Eds.), *The handbook of interpersonal communication* (3rd ed., pp. 726–777). Thousand Oaks, CA: Sage.

Fitzpatrick, M. A., & Koerner, A. F. (2002). Toward a theory of family communication. *Communication Theory, 12,* 70–91.

Fletcher, G. J. O., & Thomas, G. (1996). Close relationship laid theories: Their structure and function. In G. J. O. Fletcher & J. Fitness (Eds.), *Knowledge structures in close relationships: A social psychological approach* (pp. 3–24). Mahwah, NJ: Erlbaum.

Forsyth, C. J., & Gramling, R. (1987). Feast or famine: Alternative management techniques among periodic-father absence single career families. *International Journal of Sociology of the Family, 17,* 183–196.

Frost-Knappman, E., & Cullen-Dupont, K. (Eds.). (1997). *Women's rights on trial: 101 historic trials from Anne Hutchinson to the Virginia Military Institute cadets.* Detroit, MI: Gale.

Furstenberg, F. F., Jr., & Nord, C. W. (1985). Parenting apart: Patterns of child-rearing after marital disruption. *Journal of Marriage and the Family, 47,* 893–904.

Gabel, S. (1992). Children of incarcerated and criminal parents: Adjustment, behavior, and prognosis. *Bulletin of the American Academy of Psychiatry Law, 20,* 33–45.

Gergen, K. J. (1991). *The saturated self: Dilemmas of identity in contemporary life.* New York: Basic Books.

Gerstel, N. (1978). The feasibility of commuter marriage. In P. J. Stein, J. Richman, & N. Hannon (Eds.), *The family, functions and conflicts and symbols* (pp. 357–367). Reading, MA: Addison-Wesley.

Gerstel, N. (1979). Marital Alternatives and the regulation of sex: Commuter couples as a test case. *Alternative Lifestyles, 2,* 145–176.

Gerstel, N., & Gross, H. (1982). Commuter marriages: A review. *Marriage and Family Review, 5,* 71–93.

Gerstel, N., & Gross, H. (1983). Commuter marriage: Couples who live apart. In E. D. Macklin & R. H. Rubin (Eds.), *Contemporary families and alternative lifestyles* (pp. 180–193). Beverly Hills, CA: Sage.

Gerstel, N., & Gross, H. (1984). *Commuter marriage: A study of work and family.* New York: Guilford Press.

Gerstel, N., & Gross, H. (1987). Commuter marriage: A microcosm of career and family conflict. In N. Gerstel & H. Gross (Eds.), *Families and work.* Philadelphia: Temple University Press.

Gilbert, L. A. (1993). *Two careers, one family: The promise of gender equality.* Newbury Park, CA: Sage.

Gimbel, C., & Booth, A. (1994). Why does military combat experience adversely affect marital relations? *Journal of Marriage and Family, 56,* 691–703.

Gordon, E. W. (2000). The myths and realities of African-American fatherhood. In R. D. Taylor & M. C. Wang (Eds.), *Resilience across contexts: Family, work, culture, and community* (pp. 217–232). Mahwah, NJ: Erlbaum.

Gottman, J. M., & Krokoff, L. J. (1989). Marital interaction and satisfaction: A longitudinal view. *Journal of Consulting and Clinical Psychology, 41,* 47–52.

Govaerts, K., & Dixon, D. N. (1988). Until careers do us part: Vocational and marital satisfaction in the dual-career commuter marriage. *International Journal for Advanced Counseling,* 11, 265–281.

Graber, J. A., & Dubas, J. S. (1996). *Leaving home: Understanding the transition to adulthood.* San Francisco: Jossey-Bass.

Granovetter, M. S. (1973). The strength of weak ties. *American Journal of Sociology, 78,* 1360–1380.

Gross, H. (1980). Dual-career couples who live apart: Two types. *Journal of Marriage and the Family, 42,* 567–576.

Groves, M. M., & Horm-Wingerd, D. M. (1991). Commuter marriages: Personal, family, and career issues. *Sociology and Social Research, 75,* 212–217.

Grych, J. H., & Fincham, F. D. (1990). Marital conflict and children's adjustment: A cognitive contextual framework. *Psychological Bulletin, 108,* 267–290.

Guldner, G. T. (1992). *Propinquity and dating relationships: Toward a theory of long-distance romantic relationships including an exploratory study of college students' relationships-at-a-distance.* Unpublished manuscript, West Lafayette, IN.

Guldner, G. T. (1996). Long-distance romantic relationships: Prevalence and separation-related symptoms in college students. *Journal of College Student Development, 37,* 289–295.

Guldner, G. T. (2001). Long-distance relationships and emergency medicine residency. *Annals of Emergency Medicine, 37,* 103–106.

Guldner, G. T., & Swensen, C. H. (1995). Time spent together and relationship quality: Long-distance relationships as a test case. *Journal of Social and Personal Relationships, 12,* 313–320.

Gunn, D., & Gunn, C. (2000, September). *The quality of electronically maintained relationships.* Paper presented at the Association of Internet Researchers, Lawrence, KS.

Hairston, C. (1991). Family ties during imprisonment: Important to whom and for what? *Journal of Sociology and Social Welfare, 18,* 87–104.

Hairston, C. (2001a). Fathers in prison: Responsible fatherhood and responsible public policies. *Marriage and Family Review, 32,* 111–136.

Hairston, C. F. (1995). Fathers in prison. In D. Johnson & K. Gables (Eds.), *Children of incarcerated parents* (pp. 31–40). Lexington, MA: Lexington Books.

Harwood, J. (2000). Communication media use in the grandparent-grandchild relationship. *Journal of Communication, 50,* 56–78.

Haveran, T. K. (1987). Historical analysis of the family. In M. B. Sussman & S. Steinmetz (Eds.), *Handbook of marriage and the family* (pp. 37–57). New York: Plenum Press.

Hendrick, C., & Hendrick, S. S. (1988). Lovers wear rose colored glasses. *Journal of Social and Personal Relationships, 5,* 161–184.

Hendrick, S., & Hendrick, C. (1992). *Romantic love.* Newbury Park, CA: Sage.

Hetherington, E. M., & Stanley-Hagen, M. (1997). The effects of divorce on fathers and their children. In M. E. Lamb (Ed.), *The role of fathers in child development* (pp. 191–244). New York: Wiley.

Hetherington, E. M., Cox, M., & Cox, R. (1982). Effects of divorce on parents and children. In M. E. Lamb (Ed.), *Nontraditional families* (pp. 233–288). Hillsdale, NJ: Erlbaum.

Hill, C. T., Rubin, Z., & Peplau, L. (1976). Breakups before marriage: The end of 103 affairs. *Journal of Social Issues, 32,* 147–168.

Hill, R. (1945). The returning father and his family. *Marriage and Family Living, 7,* 31–34.

Hill, R. (1949). *Families under stress: Adjustment to the crises of war separation and reunion.* New York: Harper.

Hill, R. (1958). Social stresses on the family: Generic features of families under stress. *Social Casework, 39,* 139–150.

Holt, P. A., & Stone, G. L. (1988). Needs, coping strategies, and coping outcomes associated with long-distance relationships. *Journal of College Student Development, 29,* 136–141.

Homer. (1948). *Odyssey,* (S. O. Andrew, Trans.). London: Dent.

Hunter, E. J. (1982). *Families under the flag: A review of military family literature.* New York: Praeger.

Ickes, W., & Simpson, J. A. (1997). Managing empathic accuracy in close relationships. In W. Ickes (Ed.), *Empathetic accuracy* (pp. 218–250). New York: Guilford Press.

Isay, R. (1968). The submariners' wives syndrome. *Psychiatric Quarterly, 42,* 647–652.

Jackson, A. P., Brown, R. P., & Patterson-Stewart, K. E. (2000). African Americans in dual-career commuter marriages: An investigation of their experiences. *Family Journal, 8,* 22–36.

Jacobs, E. W., & Hicks, M. W. (1987). Periodic family separation: The importance of beliefs in determining outcomes. *Military Family, 7*(2), 3–5.

Johnson, A. J. (2001). Examining the maintenance of friendships: Are there differences between geographically close and long-distance friends? *Communication Quarterly, 49,* 424–435.

Kelley, M. L., Herzog-Simmer, P. A., & Harris, M. A. (1994). Effects of military-induced separation on the parenting stress and family functioning of deploying mothers. *Military Psychology, 6*(2), 125–138.

Kelley, M. L., Hock, E., Smith, K. M., Jarvis, B. S., Bonney, J. F., & Gaffney, M. A. (2001). Internalizing and externalizing behavior of children with enlisted navy mothers experiencing military-induced separation. *Journal of the American Academy of Child and Adolescent Psychiatry, 40,* 464–471.

Kelly, J. B. (1993). Current research on children's post-divorce adjustment. *Family and Conciliation Courts Review, 31,* 29–49.

Kelly, J. B. (2000). Children's adjustment in conflicted marriage and divorce: A decade review of research. *Journal of the American Academy of Child and Adolescent Psychiatry, 39,* 963–973.

King, V., & Heard, H. E. (1999). Nonresident father visitation, parental conflict, and mother's satisfaction: What's best for child well-being? *Journal of Marriage and the Family, 61,* 385–396.

Kirby, S. N., & Naftel, S. (2000). The impact of deployment on the retention of military reservists. *Armed Forces and Society, 26,* 259–284.

Kirschner, B. F., & Walum, L. M. (1978). Two-location families. *Alternative Lifestyles, 1,* 513–525.

Kissman, K. (1997). Noncustodial fatherhood: Research trends and issues. *Journal of Divorce and Remarriage, 28,* 77–88.

Knox, D., Zusman, M. E., Daniels, V., & Brantley, A. (2002). Absence makes the heart grow fonder? Long distance dating relationships among college students. *College Student Journal, 36,* 364–367.

Knox, J., & Price, D. H. (1995). The changing American military family: Opportunities for social work. *Social Service Review, 69,* 479–497.

Kot, L., & Shoemaker, H. M. (1999). Children of divorce: An investigation of the developmental effects from infancy through adulthood. *Journal of Divorce and Remarriage, 31,* 161–178.

Lamb, M. E. (Ed.). (1986). *The father's role: Applied perspectives.* New York: Wiley.

Lamb, M. E. (1997). Fathers and child development: An introductory overview and guide. In M. E. Lamb (Ed.), *The role of the father in child development* (3rd ed., pp. 1–18). New York: Wiley.

Larson, J. H., & Holman, T. B. (1994). Premarital predictors of marital quality and stability. *Family Relations, 43,* 228–237.

Le, B., & Agnew, C. R. (2001). Need fulfillment and emotional experience in interdependent romantic relationships. *Journal of Social and Personal Relationships, 18,* 423–440.

Leathers, S. J. (2002). Parental visiting and family reunification: Could inclusive practice make a difference? *Child Welfare, 81,* 595–616.

Leite, R. W., & McKenry, P. C. (2002). Aspects of father status and post divorce father involvement with children. *Journal of Family Issues, 23,* 601–623.

Lenton, S. (2003). Policy from a harm reduction perspective. *Current Opinion in Psychiatry, 16,* 271–278.

Levin, I., & Trost, J. (1999). Living together apart. *Community, Work, and Family, 2,* 279–292.

Lorenz, K. Z. (1966). Evolution of ritualization in the biological and cultural spheres. In J. Huxley (Ed.), *A discussion on ritualization of behaviour in animals and man: Philosophical transactions of the Royal Society of London Series B* (pp. 273–284).

Lowenstein, A. (1986). Temporary single parenthood: The case of prisoner's families. *Family Relations, 35,* 79–85.

Lund, M. (1987). The non-custodial father: Common challenges in parenting after divorce. In C. Lewis & M. O'Brien (Ed.), *Reassessing fatherhood: New observations on fathers and the modern family* (pp. 212–224). Thousand Oaks, CA: Sage.

Lydon, J., Pierce, T., & O'Regan, S. (1997). Coping with moral commitment to long-distance dating relationships. *Journal of Personality and Social Psychology, 73,* 104–113.

Magnuson, S., & Norem, K. (1999). Challenges of higher-education couples in commuter marriages: Insights for couples and counselors who work with them. *Family Journal, 7,* 125–134.

Maines, J. (1993). Long-distance romances. *American Demographics, 15,* 47.

Martin, J., & McClure, P. (2000). Today's active duty military family: The evolving challenges of military family life. In J. A. Martin, L. N. Rosen & L. R. Sparacino (Eds.), *The military family, a practice guide for human service providers.*(pp. 3–24). Westport, CO: Praeger.

McCubbin, H. I., Dahl, B. B., Lester, G. R., Benson, D., & Robertson, M. L. (1976). Coping repertoires of families adapting to prolonged war-induced separations. *Journal of Marriage and the Family, 38,* 461–471.

McNeil, L., & Sher, M. (1999). The dual-career-couple problem. *Physics Today, 52,* 32–37.

Mickus, M. A., & Luz, C. C. (2002). Televisits: Sustaining long distance family relationships among institutional elders through technology. *Aging and Mental Health, 6,* 387–396.

Milardo, R. M., & Helms-Erikson, H. (2000). Close relationships: A source book. In C. Hendrick & S. Hendrick (Eds.), *Network overlap and third-party influence in close relationships* (pp. 33–45). Thousand Oaks, CA: Sage.

Military Family Resource Center. (2002). *Profile of the military community: 2001 demographics.* Retrieved September, 2002, from http://www.mfrc-dodqol.org

Miller, G. R., & Parks, M. R. (1982). Personal relationships: Dissolving personal relationships. In S. W. Duck (Ed.), *Communication in dissolving relationships* (Vol. 4, pp. 127–154). London: Academic Press.

Morrice, J. K. W., & Taylor, J. C. (1978). The intermittent husband syndrome. *New Society, 43,* 12–13.

Mumola, C. J. (2000). *Bureau of Justice statistics special report: Incarcerated parents and their children.* Washington, DC: U.S. Department of Justice, Office of Justice Programs.

Murdock, G. P. (1949). *Social structure.* New York: Macmillan.

Murray, S. L., & Holmes, J. G. (1996). The construction of relationship realities. In G. J. O. Fletcher & J. Fitness (Eds.), *Knowledge structures in close relationships: A social psychological approach* (pp. 91–120). Mahwah, NJ: Erlbaum.

Neugebauer, R. (1989). Divorce, custody, and visitation: The child's point of view. *Journal of Divorce, 12,* 153–168.

Olson, D. H. (2000). Circumplex model of marital and family systems. *Journal of Family Therapy, 22,* 144–167.

O'Sullivan, P. (2000). What you don't know won't hurt me: Impression management functions of communication channels in relationships. *Human Communication Research, 26,* 403–431.

Parks, M. R. (1995). Ideology in interpersonal communication: Beyond the couches, talk shows, and bunkers. In B. Burleson (Ed.), *Communication yearbook 18* (pp. 480–497). Thousand Oaks, CA: Sage.

Parks, M. R., & Floyd, K. (1996). Making friends in cyberspace. *Journal of Communication, 46,* 80–97.

Parks, M. R., & Roberts, L. D. (1998). 'Making MOOsic': The development of personal relationships on-line and comparison to their off-line counterparts. *Journal of Social and Personal Relationships, 15,* 517–537.

Parsons, T. (1965). The normal American family. In F. Farber, P. Mustacchi & R. Wilson (Eds.), *Man and civilization* (pp. 31–50). New York: McGraw Hill.

Paylor, I., & Smith, D. (1994). Who are prisoners' families. *Journal of Social Welfare and Family Law, 2,* 131–144.

Perlman, D. (2001). Maintaining and enhancing relationships: Concluding commentary. In J. Harvey & A. Wenzel (Eds.), *Close romantic relationships: Maintaining and enhancement* (pp. 357–378). Mahawh, NJ: Erlbaum.

Pierce, P. F., Vinokur, A. D., & Buck, C. L. (1998). Effects of war-induced maternal separation on children's adjustment during the gulf war and two years later. *Journal of Applied Social Psychology, 28,* 1286–1311.

Pincus, S. H., & Nam, T. A. (1999). Psychological aspects of deployment: The Bosnian experience. *Journal of the United States Army Medical Department, 1–3,* 38–44.

Pincus, S. H., House, R., Christenson, J., & Adler, L. E. (2001). The emotional cycle of deployment: A military family perspective. *U.S. Army Medical Department Journal, 4–6,* 15–23.

Rabby, M. K. (1997, November). *Maintaining relationships via electronic mail.* Paper presented at the annual conference of the National Communication Association, Chicago.

Rabby, M. K., & Walther, J. B. (2003). Computer-mediated effects on relationship formation and maintenance. In D. J. Canary & M. Dainton (Eds.), *Maintaining relationships through communication: Relational, contextual, and cultural variations* (pp. 141–162). Mahwah, NJ: Erlbaum.

Rapoport, R., & Rapoport, R. N. (1969). The dual-career family. *Human Relations, 22,* 3–33.

Reed, B. J., & Segal, D. R. (2000). The impact of multiple deployments of solders' peacekeeping attitudes, morale, and retention. *Armed Forces and Society, 27,* 57–78.

Reed, D. F., & Reed, E. L. (1997). Children of incarcerated parents. *Social Justice, 24,* 152–169.

Reis, H. T., & Knee, C. R. (1996). What we know, what we don't know, and what we need to know about relationship knowledge structures. In G. J. O. Fletcher & J. Fitness (Eds.), *Knowledge structures in close relationships: A sociological approach* (pp. 169–191). Mahwah, NJ: Erlbaum.

Reissman, C., Aron, A., & Bergen, M. R. (1993). Shared activities and marital satisfaction: Causal direction and self-expansion versus boredom. *Journal of Social and Personal Relationships, 10,* 243–254.

Rhodes, A. R. (2002). Long-distance relationships in dual-career commuter couples: A review of counseling issues. *Family Journal, 8,* 398–404.

Richmond, V. P. (1995). Amount of communication in marital dyads as a function of dyadic and individual marital satisfaction. *Communication Reports, 13,* 152–159.

Rindfuss, R. R., & Stephen, E. H. (1990). Marital noncohabitation: Separation does not make the heart grow fonder. *Journal of Marriage and the Family, 52,* 259–270.

Roehling, P. V., & Bultman, M. (2002). Does absence make the heart grow fonder? Work-related travel and marital satisfaction. *Sex Roles, 46,* 279–293.

Rohall, D. E., Segal, M. W., & Segal, D. R. (1999). Examining the importance of organizational supports on family adjustment to army life in a period of increasing separation. *Journal of Political and Military Sociology, 27,* 49–65.

Rohfling, M. (1995). "Doesn't anybody stay in one place anymore?" An exploration of under-studied phenomenon of long-distance relationships. In J. Wood & S. W. Duck (Eds.), *Under-studied relationships: Off the beaten track* (pp. 173–196). Thousand Oaks, CA: Sage.

Roloff, M. E. (2002). The state of the art of interpersonal communication research, Are we addressing socially significant issues? In M. Allen, R. W. Preiss, B. M. Gayle, & N. Burrell (Eds.), *Interpersonal communication research: Advances through meta-analysis* (pp. 423–445). Mahwah, NJ: Erlbaum.

Rosen, L. N., & Moghadam, L. Z. (1988). Social support, family separation, and well-being among military wives. *Behavioral Medicine, 14,* 64–70.

Ross, B. J. (2001). The emotional impact of e-mail on deployment. *Proceedings of the Naval Institute, 127,* 85–86.

Rotter, J. C., Barnett, D. E., & Fawcett, M. L. (1998). On the road again: Dual-career commuter relationships. *Family Journal, 6,* 46–49.

Satir, V. (1988). *The new peoplemaking.* Mountain View, CA: Science & Behavior Books.

Sahlstein, E. (in press). *Journal of Social and Personal Relationships.*

Schulman, M. L. (1974). Idealization in engaged couples. *Journal of Marriage and Family, 36,* 139–147.

Schumm, W. R., Bell, D. B., & Knott, B. (2000). Factors associated with spouses moving away from their military installation during an overseas deployment. *Psychological Reports, 86,* 1275–1282.

Schumm, W. R., Bell, D. B., Knott, B., & Rice, R. E. (1996). The perceived effect of stressors on marital satisfaction among civilian wives of enlisted soldiers deployed to Somalia for Operation Restore Hope. *Military Medicine, 161,* 601–606.

Schwebel, A. I., Dunn, R. L., Moss, B. F., & Renner, M. A. (1992). Factors associated with relational stability in geographically separated couples. *Journal of College Student Development, 33,* 222–230.

Segal, J. A. (2001). Family ties and federal sentencing: A critique of the literature. *Federal Sentencing Reporter, 13,* 258–267.

Segrin, C., & Flora, J. (2001). Perceptions of relational histories, marital quality, and loneliness when communication is limited: An examination of married prison inmates. *Journal of Family Communication, 1,* 151–174.

Seltzer, J. A. (1991). Relationships between fathers and children who live apart: The father's role after separation. *Journal of Marriage and Family, 53,* 79–101.

Seltzer, J. A., Schaeffer, N. C., & Charng, H. (1989), Family ties after divorce: The relationship between visiting and paying child support. *Journal of Marriage and the Family, 51.* 1013–1032.

Seymour, C. (1998). Children with parents in prison: Child welfare policy, program, and practice issues. *Child Welfare, 77,* 469–493.

Shulman, S., & Seiffge-Krenke, I. (1997). *Fathers and adolescents: Developmental and clinical perspectives.* New York: Routledge.

Sigman, S. J. (1991). Handling the discontinuous aspects of continuing social relationships: Towards research of the persistence of social forms. *Communication Theory, 1,* 106–127.

Sillars, A. L. (1998). (Mis)understanding. In B. H. Spitzberg & W. R. Cupach (Eds.), *The dark side of close relationships* (pp. 73–102). Mahwah, NJ: Erlbaum.

Smykla, J.O. (1987). The human impact of capital punishment: Interviews with families of persons on death row. *Journal of Criminal Justice, 15,* 331–346.

Snyder, Z. K., Carlo, T. A., & Coats, M. M. (2001). Parenting from prison: An examination of children's visitation program at a women's correctional facility. *Marriage and Family Review, 32,* 33–61.

Spiro, M. E. (1954). Is the family universal? *American Anthropologist, 56,* 839–846.

Sprecher, S., & Felmlee, D. (2000). Romantic partners' perceptions of social network attributes with the passage of time and relationship transitions. *Personal Relationships, 7,* 325–340.

Sprecher, S., & Regan, P. C. (1998). Passionate and companionate love in courting and young married couples. *Sociological Inquiry, 68,* 163–185.

Stafford, L., & Reske, J. R. (1990). Idealization and communication in long-distance premarital relationships. *Family Relations, 39,* 274–279.

Stafford, L., & Yost, S. (1990, November). The role of communication in naval couple's marital satisfaction. Paper presented at the annual conference of the National Communication Association, Chicago.

Stephen, T. (1986). Communication and interdependence in geographically separated relationships. *Human Communication Research, 13,* 191–210.

Stroh, L. K. (1999). A review of relocation: The impact on work and family. *Human Resource Management Review, 9,* 279–308.

Taylor, A. S., & Lounsbury, J. W. (1988). Dual-career couples and geographic transfer: Executives' reactions to commuter marriage and attitude toward the move. *Human Relations, 47,* 407–424.

U.S. Census Bureau. (2002). Current population survey (CPS): Definitions and explanations. Retrieved August 2, 2003, from http://www.census.gov/population/www/cps/cpsdef.html

U.S. Presidential Commission. (1993). *Women in combat: report to the president.* Washington, DC: Brassey's.

Ursano, R. J., & Norwood, A. E. (1996). *Emotional aftermath of the Persian Gulf War: Veterans, families, communities and nations.* Washington, DC: American Psychiatric Press.

Vangelisti, A. (2002). Interpersonal processes in romantic relationships. In M. Knapp & J. Daly (Eds.), *Handbook of interpersonal communication* (pp. 643–679). Thousand Oaks, CA: Sage.

Vangelisti, A. L., & Banski, M. (1993). Couples' debriefing conversations: The impact of gender, occupation, and demographic characteristics. *Family Relations, 42,* 149–157.

VanHorn, K. R., Arnone, A., Nesbitt, K., Desilets, L., Sears, T., Griffin, M., et al. (1997). Physical distance and interpersonal characteristics in college students' romantic relationships. *Personal Relationships, 4,* 25–34.

Vogl-Bauer, S. (2003). Maintaining family relationships. In D. J. Canary & M. Dainton (Eds.), *Maintaining relationships through communication: Relational, contextual, and cultural variations* (pp. 31–50). Mahwah, NJ: Erlbaum.

Vormbrock, J. K. (1993). Attachment theory as applied to wartime and job-related marital separation. *Psychological Bulletin, 114,* 122–144.

Waller, W. (1940). *War and the family.* New York: Dryden Press.

Wamboldt, F. S., & Reiss, D. (1989). Defining a family heritage and a new relationship identity: Two central tasks in the making of a marriage. *Family Process, 28,* 317–335.

Wellman, B. (1999). The network community: An introduction. In B. Wellman (Ed.), *Networks in the global community* (pp. 1–47). Boulder, CO: Westview.

Wendel, W. C. (1975). High school sweethearts: A study in separation and commitment. *Journal of Clinical Child Psychology, 4,* 45–46.

Westefeld, J. S., & Liddell, D. (1982). Coping with long-distance relationships. *Journal of College Student Development, 23,* 550–551.

Western, B., & McLanahan, S. (2000). Fathers behind bars: The impact of incarceration on family formation. *Contemporary Perspectives in Family Research, 2,* 307–322.

Westmyer, S., DiCioccio, R., & Rubin, R. (1998). Appropriateness and effectiveness of communication channels in competent interpersonal communication. *Journal of Communication, 48,* 27–48.

Williams, A., & Nussbaum, J. N. (2001). *Intergenerational communication across the life span.* Mahwah, NJ: Erlbaum.

Wilmot, W. W. (1995). *Relational communication.* New York: McGraw-Hill.

Wilmot, W. W., & Carbaugh, D. (1986). Long-distance lovers: Predicting the dissolution of relationships. *Journal of Northwest Communication Association, 14,* 43–59.

Winfield, F. E. (1985). *Commuter marriage: Living together, apart.* New York: Columbia University Press.

Wolchik, S. A., Fenaughty, A. M., & Braver, S. L. (1996). Residential and nonresidential parents' perspectives on visitation problems. *Family Relations, 45,* 230–237.

Wood, S., Scarville, J., & Gravino, K. S. (1995). Waiting wives: Separation and reunion among Army wives. *Armed Forces and Society, 21,* 217–236.

Zimmerman, M. A., Salem, D., & Notaro, P. (2000). Make room for daddy II: The positive effects of fathers' role in adolescent development. In R. Taylor & M. Wang (Eds.), *Resilience across contexts: Family, work, culture, and community* (pp. 233–252). Mahwah, NJ: Erlbaum.

CHAPTER CONTENTS

3 Alternative Organizing Communities: Collectivist Organizing, Telework, Home-Based Internet Businesses, and Online Communities

PAIGE P. EDLEY
ANNIKA HYLMÖ
Loyola Marymount University

VICTORIA ANN NEWSOM
Bowling Green State University

Alternative work communities encompass various organizing forms, including democratic organizing practices, participative decision making, feminist organizing principles, and technological alternatives, such as telecommuting and Internet businesses. These nontraditional organizing practices discursively construct identity and community in the day-to-day negotiation of the tensions of technological empowerment and organizational control. This review of literature pulls together varied, multidisciplinary sources from organizational communication, critical management studies, feminist theory, and gender studies, as well as business, organization studies, and sociology to aid in the development of future research in gender and organizational communication studies or, as Martin and Collinson (2002) referred to this growing area of study, gendered organizational studies.

E mployment and participation in nontraditional organizing communities is rapidly growing and largely can be attributed to organizational downsizing, as well as to women's resistance to the glass ceiling (Powell, 1999; Silver, 1994). Participation in alternative organizing communities especially relates to women's resistance to their lack of authority in traditional organizations and their desire to become their own boss and to choose an alternative to the workaholic lifestyle that is often rewarded in traditional organizations. This gendered phenomenon not only can cause women to start their own businesses, but also can lead to their working out of their homes, telecommuting, starting Internet businesses, and participating in online communities. These individuals are choosing to

Correspondence: Paige Edley, Loyola Marymount University, Department of Communication Studies, One LMU Drive, Foley Hall/MS 3231, Los Angeles, CA 90045-2695; email: pedley@lmu.edu

Communication Yearbook 28, pp. 87–125

reevaluate their organizational, societal, environmental, and familial relationships and reassess what is valued and what is healthy in one's life. They are choosing to live a healthier, balanced life while attending to the whole person, not just the needs of the organization. (see Buzzanell, 2000; Deetz, 1992; Edley, 2001, 2003). We argue that by choosing alternative career paths, and alternative work communities over, as well as within the context of, traditional organizational structures and corporate control practices, individuals are seeking (and achieving) a more rewarding life outside the traditional organization.

Clearly, the issue of gender and alternative organizations affects working people around the world. For the purpose of the present essay, however, we are focusing on the U.S. context while recognizing the constraints that imposes. We will return to the problems raised by our limited focus in the conclusion of our work.

International Data Corporation (IDC) reported in 2001 that 12.6 million American households contained at least one parent (with dependent children) working at home (cited in Edwards, Edwards, & Roberts, 2002, p. 5). Edwards, Edwards, and Roberts (2002) estimated that 10 million entrepreneurial parents (both men and women) work from home in Internet-based businesses. Cyber Dialogue, Inc. found that of the 84.9 million adults working on-line, 57% were fathers and 43% were mothers. Despite Edwards et al.'s own study that found 80% of those parents working from home were work-at-home moms (WAHMs), the authors still argue that working at home is a gender blind option. We disagree. We argue that, although both men and women may be working at home and simultaneously caring for young children, women's rationale for leaving their paid jobs outside the home is a form of resistance to the glass ceiling and a way to combine childcare and eldercare with paid work in a more humane and less stressful way.

In this essay we develop a review of the literature of alternative organizing practices from a critical feminist perspective that distinguishes traditional, patriarchal, and bureaucratic organizing structures and practices as not being conducive to living full productive lives as whole persons, as friends, sisters, mothers, loving partners, and daughters. Our method of selecting the literature is informed by feminist and critical perspectives of organizational communication. The selection process is bound by our own limits as White, middle-class, academic, heterosexual women situated in the U.S. We seek to offer alternative forms of organizing and resistance to traditional (read masculine) views of work and career. Organizational studies and the work-life balance literature are often presented with a blind eye to power and gender. In this extensive review of literature we seek to address these imperative issues, along with promoting alternative organizing communities that value nonwork contexts and relationships, and with work contexts and relationships. In the next section we develop our definition of community.

COMMUNITY

Many technology-based home workers and teleworkers discursively construct a sense of *community* among other entrepreneurial parents, other telecommuting professionals, and in the case of teleworkers, also their onsite coworkers. These online and face-to-face communities create a sense of connection among and between each other to form a system of professional and personal support. Before we go any further we need to distinguish how we define community.

We built our definition of alternative organizing communities on the basic building blocks of Rheingold's (1993) definition of virtual communities as "social aggregations that emerge from the Net when enough people carry on those public discussions long enough, with sufficient human feelings, to form webs of personal relationships in cyberspace" (p. 5). However, our definition of the alternative organizing community is not exclusively bounded within cyberspace nor is it conceived of as simply a social aggregate. Our concept of community is constituted in interpersonal relationships and a sense of *belonging* rather than simply as a social aggregate. Shotter (1993) defined this sense of belonging as

> a sense of "being at home" in a reality that one's actions help both to reproduce and to develop. To live within a community which one senses as being one's own—as both "mine" and "yours," as "ours," rather than "theirs" . . . Part of a sense of "belonging," of a sense of "being at home" in one's own community, is that one has an automatic right of initial access to the community simply by virtue of having contributed [to it] . . . not having a sense of being an intrusive alien, [rather] of having worth as who one is. (p. 163)

This sense of belonging and contribution also brings to mind Csikszentmihalyi's (1990) argument that community provides people with "a chance to enjoy as many aspects of their lives as possible, while allowing them to develop their potential in the pursuit of ever greater challenges" (p. 191). Adelman and Frey (1997) described community as "a web spun of space, identity, emotional connection, interdependence, common symbols, and mutual influence" (p. 5), whereas Van Maanen and Barley's (1984) concept of "occupational community" emphasized shared values and blurred boundaries between work and nonwork contexts:

> a group of people engaged in the same sort of work; whose identity is drawn from the work; who share with one another a set of values, norms, and perspectives that apply to but extend beyond work related matters; and whose social relationships meld work and leisure. (p. 287)

These communicative webs of connection include coworkers, family, friends, and outreach and volunteer group relationships. In addition Mumby (2000) described a study by Maguire and Mohtar (1994) in which they reconceptualized organizational community as:

> a constellation of discursive moments...[as] the relation between the public and private realms becom[ing] problematized. The members of this community blur the boundaries between the economic, political, and domestic realms, discursively positioning themselves as challenging and resisting liberal conceptions of what 'counts' as appropriate issues for public debate. (p. 22)

Furthermore, within these protean alternative work communities, members nego-tiate movement across, among, and between the fluid and permeable boundaries of work and nonwork contexts as they navigate the dialectics of community, in which individuals negotiate the contradictions and tensions of everyday life (Adelman & Frey, 1997). Similarly, Goodall (1999) credited a conversation with Eisenberg with teaching him that organizational community is something that looks from the outside "very much like a conflict of opposing interests that pit the indi-vidual against the social unit" (p. 485). This metaphor of conflict is not necessarily a negative concept but rather is a dialogic process of constant negotiation and jug-gling work and life issues. Anderson's (1991) "imagined community" suggests more of the social support network that we envision an alternative organizing com-munity to be, what Matei, Ball-Rokeach, Wilson, Gibbs, and Hoyt (2001) described as the communication infrastructure that people use to construct "belonging rela-tionships." (p. 2)

Many technology-based, protean communities are assembled through alterna-tive, nonbureaucratic organizing practices allowing process-oriented decision-making and nonhierarchical power structures (Buzzanell, 1995; Iannello, 1992). Members of these communities live and work in the borderlands (Anzaldua, 1987; Clark, 2000). They constantly negotiate the movement within, between, and among the fluid boundaries of work and nonwork/life discourses. These include the dis-courses of family, friends, neighbors, and outreach and volunteer group relation-ships that are just as valued and valid as work discourses.

The protean metaphor works with this concept not in that it lacks structure, but that the structures are blurred, blended, and boundless. Moreover, many feminists and women's groups who find traditional bureaucratic structures to be a male-defined and male-dominated form of organizing have embraced nonhierarchical forms of organizing (Buzzanell, 1994, 1995; Ferguson, 1984; Padavic & Reskin, 2002; Powell & Graves, 2003). These gendered spaces are constituted as alterna-tive communities that provide a rich context for organizational communication, critical, and feminist scholars to explore how relational, gendered, social, and tech-nological implications emerge within nontraditional forms of organizing. Ground-ing future organizational communication research in both traditional and nontradi-tional organizing practices is imperative to understanding the constant flux in con-temporary organizing.

The term *alternative* includes democratic, collectivist, feminist, political, and technologically based organizing processes. Some of these organizational com-munities employ a limited number of employees and, rather than a strict division of labor, everyone does a little bit of everything. Decisions are made consensually in a democratic process in which all members have input. Furthermore, alternative organizing communities also include nontraditional organizing practices such as telecommuting or working collaboratively in online work communities. Telecommuting consists of working from a computer and modem at home a few days a week or working at home after hours and on weekends. Deming (1994) reported that 23.7 million home workers are categorized as corporate after-hours home workers, although 14.2 million are self-employed home workers, and only 9.1 million are telecommuters. Apgar (1998) suggested that 30 to 40 million people in the U.S. currently work at home as self-employed home workers and telecommuters. The American Management Association forecasts 118% annual growth in the number of telecommuters over the next few years ("The Telecommuting Paradox," 1998). We argue that these corporate after-hours home workers consist of caregivers who are putting in another shift of work at home after caring for children and elderly parents.

By introducing the teleworking component of alternative organizing communities, we emphasize the tensions of work-life balance. Technology allows them to extend the workplace into the home in order to spend time with family. It also allows them to be more productive and to work harder and longer hours for their employers. Technology both empowers and controls employees. It also both reinforces and permeates the boundaries of traditionally gendered spaces by blurring the normative standards of workspaces.

GENDERED SPACES: THE PUBLIC-PRIVATE SPHERE(S)

Historically, the public and private spheres have been separated into diametrically opposed realms of public discourse and private, family-related discourses. However, today men and women both are blending their public and private roles in such a way that the two cannot be separated. Yet societal attitudes and biases still favor the forced divisions of public and private. As Martin (1990) argued, this construction of the public and private as two mutually exclusive spheres is a false dichotomy. Furthermore, the private sphere, in particular, is a feminine gendered space. Spain (1994) discussed gendered space as a geographical area with established boundaries between women's and men's knowledge. Cultural constructions and stereotypes determine how a space is defined and gendered: "Domestic architecture mediates social relations, specifically those between women and men. Houses are the spatial context within which the social order is reproduced" (p. 140). Kitchens, for example, are gendered female in many societies because there is a strong traditional link between the activities performed in the space and women's daily lives.

The double standard concerning privatization of corporate values creates a devaluing of family discourses. The devaluing of all things feminine is prevalent in a patriarchal society and this includes the gendered discourses of home and family. The traditional feminization of home and family is then juxtaposed with the masculinization of the traditional, male-dominated bureaucratic workplace. This leaves working parents wondering how they might balance work and family responsibilities when family discourse is generally frowned upon within organizational systems of domination. Moreover, Martin (1990) discussed the problem of reifying the gendered public–private dichotomy in the workplace and constructing pregnancy, childbirth, childcare, and female sexuality as taboo in organizational contexts. The public–private and masculine–feminine dichotomies serve as "a linch-pin of gender discrimination" (p. 350). Martin argues that parents' daycare needs become the needs of the corporation—just as a parent needs to take care of a sick child, the need to take the child to the doctor or dentist, and the need for parent-teacher conferences all have an effect on the public organization.

As the private sphere needs affect the needs of the public organization, the private and public spheres become intertwined. Thus the presentation of the spheres as separate is a false dichotomy. Instead, the gendering of spaces becomes a method of patriarchal oppression and an attempt to keep women in their place, so they cannot be a threat to patriarchal society (Martin, 1990, 1994). However, women are resisting these discriminating practices. One way of resisting this false dichotomy, as Deetz (1992) argued, is when both men and women reject the discourse of managerialism by choosing "balanced lives, and they pay for it primarily in the financial code favored by management, but they are happier people" (p. 337). Thus, employees often reject the workaholic experience in favor of a more comfortable work-life balance.

Another way women and men are resisting is in choosing to work part-time and choosing to work in more flexible, more "family-friendly" workplaces. Often this means constructing alternative organizing opportunities, such as telework, creating more flexible work schedules, being accessible to work by cell phone, or making a breakthrough in entrepreneurialism. A form of resistance could be in the construction of and participation in alternative work communities, such as home-based businesses and online communities.

FEMINIST VIEWS OF POWER AND ORGANIZATIONAL COMMUNICATION

As a result of the blurring of boundaries between public–private and masculine–feminine spaces, a focus on the gendered nature of organizational spaces and processes needs to be emphasized. Many traditional organizational communication studies fail to recognize gender as a political construction; however, a few studies have addressed gender issues in organizations, but have not addressed the blurring of boundaries between home and work or the need for alternative, nontraditional organizing communities. Feminist organizational communication and management scholars argue that organizations and work are gendered, thus it is imperative for organizational communication scholars to emphasize a gender analysis of organizing (Acker, 1990, 1995; Allen, 1998, 2000; Ashcraft, 1998; Buzzanell, 1995, 2000; Calás & Smircich, 1992; Clair, 1998; Ferree & Martin, 1995; Martin, 1994; Martin & Collinson, 2002; Mumby, 1996; Mumby & Stohl, 1998; Padavic & Reskin, 2002; Sotirin, 2000; Trethewey, 1999; Wanca-Thibault & Thompkins, 1998). These scholars uncover the hidden political structures of gender within organizational contexts, and it becomes evident that institutions employ strict boundaries and stratification regarding the enactment of power and gender-specific roles. Not unlike the division of labor between masculine and feminine gendered space, men do historically situated men's work, and women do traditional women's work within organizations.

Furthermore, power differentials weigh in the men's favor, while women play secondary and often subjugated and discriminated roles. Similarly, organizational communication theory is gendered with its roots firmly planted within the dominant, White male perspective. Thus, an alternative work community viewpoint that encompasses gender analysis is an important addition to the organizational communication literature. This approach helps to identify problems and to expose and to understand the gendered nature of alternative work communities.

Organizational communication and management scholars suggest that women's organizational practices and management styles differ from those of men (Buzzanell, 1994; Eisenberg & Goodall, 2001; Powell & Graves, 2003). Some studies argue that women share power and information with coworkers and enhance the socioemotional climate (see Buzzanell, 1994; Ferguson, 1984; Helgesen, 1990; Kanter, 1977; Padavic & Reskin, 1998; Powell & Graves, 2003). Also, instead of hierarchical views of power as dominance over people, many scholars view women in power as the center of concentric webs or networks of power (Ferguson, 1984; Helgeson, 1990). According to Kanter (1977), this is a form of empowerment—the power to accomplish things and to guide people rather than the power to dominate them. Further, feminist scholars suggest that empowerment carries out women's values by nurturing coworkers, a web-like leadership, rather than linear hierarchies, and a service orientation to clients.

ALTERNATIVE, NONHIERARCHICAL FORMS OF ORGANIZING

Buzzanell (1995) and Mumby (1996) both have articulated a need for research on nonhierarchical, or alternative, organizational communities, especially from a feminist perspective. Although neither scholar articulated a specific definition of an alternative organization, nor defined it in terms of what it was not, Buzzanell developed a list of alternatives to bureaucratic structures based on studies by Bantz (1989), Garfield (1992), Helgeson (1990), Morgan (1986, 1993), and Weick (1989), all cited in Buzzanell. Her list includes self-designing, ad hocratic, improvisational, and web forms. These nonhierarchical organizing forms "redesign corporations around core issues of permeable boundaries and inclusionary values. . . . In each nontraditional form, successful work completion is dependent on interconnectedness as well as on utilization of the most appropriate members for specific problem solving" (Buzzanell, p. 335). These organizational forms facilitate "personal growth, diminished status differences, awareness of others' talents, and redefinitions of self in relation to others as work needs shift" (p. 335) and also are important parts of community building in terms of mutual respect and connection.

Many alternative organizing communities exhibit a need to adapt throughout their life cycles. Three nontraditional forms in Buzzanell's typology, self-designing, ad hocratic, and improvisational, also emphasize a temporal quality of semipermanence or temporary status. Self-designing organizations are semipermanent. These are the "'dream teams' that redesign work processes with union and management collaboration; flexible church teams that appear disorganized but are based on strong, coherent, and shared values; and organizations such as Semco S/A, PC Connection, and The Body Shop" (1995, p. 335). Ad hocracies consist of project teams from the aerospace and electronic industries, as well as research and development groups that dissolve after project completion and then regroup with new members as new projects are assigned. Improvisation organizations are self-guided teams that constantly adjust to "changing individual and team interactions" (1995, p. 335). Each of these organizational forms serves a particular purpose within a specific temporal framework. The last entry in Buzzanell's list, the web form, is grounded in feminist philosophies of leadership that "encourage integrative communication practices, fairness in collaborating with organizational members, and responsibility to work, family, and community" (p. 335). Each of these four forms is based on egalitarian values, collaborative ethics, and the ability to be flexible and willing to adapt—all components of the enactment of alternative organizing communities.

Another characteristic for many alternative organizations is political origin. Many alternative organizations originated as a voice for some political cause. Many developed out of the antiwar, antiestablishment movement of the mid-1960s (Iannello, 1992; Lont, 1988; Rothschild-Whitt, 1979). These alternative organizational communities "resolved to exist without the bureaucratic authority and profit motive found in standard organizations" (Lont, 1988, p. 233). Yet, even with politically motivated origins, many alternative organizations found that perhaps survival was a key concept. Many politically motivated organizations "had to modify their original goals, become more profit-oriented, or cease to exist" (p. 233). Thus, the "everyday" political motivation of providing for one's own future or that of one's children and elderly parents can be an important factor in creating a new work community. Other political motivations include explicit opposition to hierarchy and commitment to activism, community outreach, and volunteerism.

Power Relations and the Collectivist Model

Participants in feminist organizations argue that feminism operates within organizations as an ideology rooted in the acknowledgement of gender inequity and other forms of inequity and oppression. For example, a participant claims that an organization is feminist because the organization empowers people and allows everybody to be heard so that responsibility is shared (Staggenborg, 1995). Feminist organizing generally promotes collective organizing and alternative methods of maintaining control. Collectives focus on maintaining equality of status for all members (Rothschild-Whitt, 1979). All members are recognized as important and valuable to the whole, and there is a strong focus on teamwork and cooperation. According to Staggenborg (1995), collective organizations stress collective decision making and the empowerment of all individuals within the organization.

Kerri (1976) provided an overview of collectivist associations. These organizations are likely to function in modern societies because they provide a common interest outlet. Industrial and technological societies create specific rigid structures in which people are forced to participate. Collectivism provides outlets for individual creativity and shared ideals. Further, Kerri argued that common interest organizations are not rigidly structured and both encourage voluntary membership and help these organizations to survive general societal tensions.

Staggenborg (1995) argued that the distinction between bureaucratic and collectivist feminist organizations is problematic because success seems to occur when both styles are used. Collectives are often short-lived since they focus on group work and often fail to maintain other goals. Bureaucratic organizations tend to be more stable. Collectivist organizations focus on ideals of egalitarianism and collective decision making (Acker, 1990; 1995; Martin, 1990; Rothschild-Whitt, 1979). Because of the stability and longevity of bureaucracies in relation to many collectives, we argue that it is possible, and even imperative, for alternative organizing communities to develop within as well as outside of traditional bureaucratic structures. Collective organizations also have a homogenous nature, which is important because members all need to agree on the goals of the organization. Collective organizations also are primarily democratic in nature, with elected officers (Acker, 1990; Bart, 1987; Britton, 2000; Rothschild-Whitt, 1979).

Bart (1987) explained that satisfaction of members is a major ideal. All members must find satisfaction within the organization because that is their major compensation. Bart's own study focused on an illegal abortion clinic in which the illegality itself provided a sense of satisfaction for members. She suggested that "[b]ecause the group was illegal, it was cohesive and efficient" (p. 346), and the women were grateful that this organization avoided the legal and political hassles with licensing agencies and provided an alternative to standard bureaucratic organizations. The illegality of the organization provided members with support and a collective sense of purpose that they could not acquire through other means. This aspect of collective organizing may be one of the most significant. The organization must offer something that can only be found in the organization itself. This sense of support, and collective sense of purpose, created a sense of community in this organization.

Consistent with Bart's argument that extreme challenges such as protecting the organization from illegal activity enhance collectivity, Ferree and Martin (1995) argued that the feminist movement is a multiplistic collection of mobilizations related to equality of the sexes, races, classes, and age groups. They argued: "Many feminist organizations founded in the decade 1965 to 1975 are celebrating their twentieth or twenty-fifth anniversaries. Their survival provides evidence that they became institutionalized in at least some respects" (p. 6). Again, the sense of support and purpose create a sense of community for organizational members. Also, the collective system "enables women who individually lack the capital and/or training to begin a business, to do so as a group, sharing the leadership, the work, and the financial burden" (Eastland, 1991, p. 25). The collective system of egalitarianism thus also aids in the construction of community.

Rothschild-Whitt's collectivist-bureaucratic model stipulates that alternative institutions have at least eight characteristics that distinguish them from bureaucratic organizations. These characteristics represent an ideal type, just as bureaucracy is an ideal type. The collectivist ideal type is based on Weber's concept of value rationality an approach to social action that differs from the organizational rationality model of decision making that excludes relational values, intuition, and gut feelings (Mumby & Putnam, 1992; Rothschild-Whitt, 1979; Rothschild & Whitt, 1986). Several of Rothschild-Whitt's (1979) characteristics of collectivist organizing apply to our concept of gendered alternative organizing communities in their enactment of authority within the group as a whole rather than in an individual. The group has no hierarchy and, thus, decisions are made through a "'consensus process' in which all members participate in the collective formulation of problems and negotiation of decisions" (p. 512). Collectivist communities also minimize rules and govern themselves by a sense of "substantive ethic" in that decisions are made on an ad hoc basis. In addition, unobtrusive social control tends to follow the pattern of peer pressure, rather than direct supervision or the enforcement of standardized rules. Moreover, relationships among members are personal, emotional, holistic, and valued. Recruitment and advancement are not based on credentials or skills but rather is accomplished through friendship networks and a sharing of social and political values.

In summary, collectivist organizing is enacted through egalitarian work practices and consensual decision making. With the focus on a democratic organizing process, collectivist communities are often politically motivated through feminist and critical ideologies.

Gender Politics and Alternative Work Communities

Martin (1994) defined gender as a cultural overlay "that is associated with and modifies or supplements these physiological sex differences. . . . Because gender involves a process of social construction, it is often used as an adjective ('gendered') or a verb ('gendering'), rather than as a noun" (p. 405). Although physical differences do exist, they are "'meaningless' until social practices associate power inequalities with particular physiological characteristics" (p. 408). In this respect, we realize that gendered meanings and inequalities become embedded within our social structure and thus render the construction of gender to be a political construction. Gender relations are power relations and, within the politics of everyday life, we construct knowledge through gendered, embodied experience. Our experiences are how we come to know the world around us, and within this gendered social system we also construct gendered organizations.

Acker (1990) defined the gendered organization as recognition that "advantage and disadvantage, exploitation and control, action and emotion, meaning and identity, are patterned through and in terms of distinction between male and female, masculine and feminine" (p. 146). From the performance perspective, often people "do" whatever gender is expected of them. We enact the categories of men and women in the politics of everyday life. Within the organization, "gender is a central feature of institutional life" (Mumby, 1996, p. 259). Furthermore, with the devaluation of women's experiences, women and other subordinate members of society often take on the voice of dominant society and thus articulate the dominant society's meanings and reality as their own. The reality constituted in the discourse of dominant members of a culture is privileged over that of nondominant members of the culture. These nondominant members are often referred to as marginalized, while the dominant groups are constructed as powerful. The dominant group is considered to be mainstream society, the norm as defined by male-dominated ways of thinking. While dominant members make up the mainstream society, nondominant members are relegated to life in the margins, an area designated as not the norm.

Fraser (1990/91) related the concept of women's voice to resistance in her development of the concept of the subaltern counterpublic, a form of women's resistance within the public sphere of discourse, which she built on from the theorizing of Spivak (1995) and Habermas (1987). The subaltern organizations are "parallel discursive arenas where members of subordinated social groups invent and circulate counter discourses, which in turn permit them to formulate oppositional interpretations of their identities, interests, and needs" (Fraser, 1990/91, p. 67). In these subaltern groups, a form of alternative organizing, "counterpublics emerge in response to exclusions within dominant publics, [and] they help expand discursive space" (Fraser, 1990/91, p. 67). Participating in these counter publics means "being able to speak 'in one's own voice,' thereby simultaneously constructing and expressing one's cultural identity through idiom and style" (Fraser, 1990/91, p. 69). Therefore, according to Fraser, participating in an alternative organization is a form of resistance.

Ultimately, what makes an organization feminist is the ideology enacted by its participants. Staggenborg explains that a participant in her study of a women's organization claims that an organization is feminist because the organization empowers people and allows everybody to be heard, so that responsibility is shared. This central goal is the motivating factor that keeps people returning to work for the organization.

TECHNOLOGICAL ALTERNATIVES IN ORGANIZING

Organizational communication scholarship enters into technology studies discourse on multiple levels, but mostly on interpersonal and organizational levels. Interpersonal issues range from coworker interactions to boss-direct report relationships and concomitant promotional ability assessments. The concept of cyberidentity also enters into this discourse when organizational studies focus on community building and identity construction within organizations. For instance, communication is viewed as problematic when telecommuters have difficulty maintaining contact with in-house workers (Cleaver, 2000) or maintaining a solid work-family balance (Edley, 2001; Edley & Newsom, 2003). The time one spends in the workplace, in the technological workspaces, and in home spaces all need to be balanced.

Furthermore, technology promotes the development of spaces for voluntary and nonhierarchical organizing. Feminist organizations have been developed in Web spaces and have no offline physical presence (Newsom, 2003). Moreover, Web spaces invite alternative organizing processes because they can be perceived as spaces outside of the hierarchical or patriarchal norms. These spaces can be created with feminine or feminist empowerment in mind; they can be created as gendered spaces with intentionally inherent alternative values. This allows alternative organizations to thrive in Internet spaces.

Further, Internet spaces allow normative space-time practices and values to be recreated. Time allocated to work and home cannot be as easily distinguished if the physical spaces used are not distinguished. Space and time become interrelated, and time becomes a more significant factor in determining activity. Workplace time can be discussed in terms of concurrency (accomplishing single or multiple tasks; Ballard & Seibold, 2000; see also Hall, 1981, 1989), linearity (segmenting time into smaller units, as established by clocks and calendars; Hassard, 1996), and cyclicality (referring to the ongoing, dynamic nature of time related to natural cycles of earth and the moon; Hassard, 1996). Each characteristic of time has implications for organizational functioning as work communities create their approaches to time through discursive interactions. Time is inherently situated in discourses of power and can be used for purposes of subordination and domination (Glucksmann, 1998; Perlow, 1998; Sahay, 1997). Control of time is not limited to predetermined amounts of time but is often embedded in discourses about expected overtime, early morning meetings, commitment to work teams, and promotability. All of these determine how much time is available to the employee outside of the office (Perlow, 1998). The control of time is central to why managers are reluctant to allow telecommuting (Egan, Miles, Birstler, & Klayton-Mi, 1998; Maruca, 1998).

Space also is socially constructed: "Space is neither absolute, relative or relational in itself, but it can become one or all simultaneously, depending on the circumstances" (Sahay, 1997, p. 240). Different cultures construct the use of space differently to indicate power by size, location, or structured use of office space (Hall, 1989). Examples of different uses and meanings of space can be seen in the extent to which organizations allow for personal decorations in their offices and decision making with regard to type, amount, and location of office space. Being invited to lunch is a discursive practice that invites participation in a specific personal sphere, just as a closed door serves as a tool to exclude communicative interaction (Munro, 1999). Space can control employees through designation of membership. Both Kunda (1992) and Garsten (1999) have shown how temporary employees are not considered full-fledged members of the organization by virtue of their temporary status. The temporary status is upheld regardless of the number of years that the temporary employee has been with the organization. As such, the temporary status serves as a discursive marker to exclude full access to organizational space and hence to full identification as a member. In other words, space can be used to isolate by including as well as excluding, depending on how organization members socially construct inclusion and isolation (Vega & Brennan, 2000).

In short, time and space are socially and discursively constructed. Giddens noted that "contextuality of time-space, and especially the connection between time-space, location, and milieux of action, are not just uninteresting boundaries of social life, but are inherently involved in its constitution and reproduction" (cited in Sahay, 1997, p. 242). Communicative action is situated simultaneously and continuously within time and space and becomes a series of presences and absences that work together to create meaning that is patterned in time and space within a given organizational context. These patterns are created through social interactions and serve as boundaries for action and for the creation of new patterns of meaning and identities.

Cyborgs and Web Organizing: Gendered Spaces and Identities Online

Ideally the Internet is a space that eliminates gendered, racist, ageist, and all other oppressions. However, the Web has taken on a distinctly gendered nature, and, moreover, individual Web sites have taken on gendered presentations. The technology of the Web carries a number of patriarchal and masculine connotations. Individual sites often reflect an active gendered nature, illustrated in the images, sounds, language, and color schemes used on the sites. This gendering of the Web is often intentional, as in the case of a number of feminist sites. Organizations that maintain these sites use their Internet space as gendered sites for negotiating feminist ideologies with the gendered nature of reality.

Feminist Internet spaces are primarily female oriented and gendered feminine to build a feminist identity in cyberspace to function as ideal feminist space. Feminist voices seek spaces where they can be heard outside the patriarchal structures of the physical world. The construction of gendered spaces is a process of interaction between the physical space and the gendered identity of those participating in the space. Umiker-Sebeok (1996) identified how power operates in and through gendered spaces as the ability to control movement through space and time. This control allows access to resources that are necessary for survival in spaces. Thus, power may be seen as gendered in spaces where access to resources is gendered.

Information is the primary resource of the Internet or cyberspace. Information builds and operates cyberspace through its construction and distribution. However, offline realities define the value of online information. Although historically women have been active in the construction of the Web (Myburgh, 1998), they have not been viewed as the producers of meaning in Web spaces. The Internet, initially viewed as part of the public sphere, serves as a tool of patriarchy. However, with feminist standpoint theories viewing gender as performative, feminists have determined it is possible to build identities online, masked in patriarchal characteristics so as to access power and generate feminist ideals.

Cyberspace is discussed among feminists as a logical place for women to gather and discuss gender issues. Virtual identities—the identities people take on while in cyberspace—are theoretically not tied to "real self" factors such as gender, age, profession, disability, sexuality, or race. Scholars disagree that physical characteristics of the Internet user are completely erased online. These characteristics may be masked or hidden by the perception of a new cyberidentity. McGerty (2000) argued that researchers have come to acknowledge that Internet users actually negotiate between their physical and perceived identities. Online contexts are partially determined by offline characteristics; those aspects of identities that are important offline are also important online. Kendall (1999) explained, "Nobody lives only in cyberspace" (p. 58). Reality in cyberspace is defined by information, but information is valued and gendered offline.

The perception of gender-free space online is then threatened by the reality of gendered constructs of the world in which cyberspace operates. Men in Western society are the Internet's primary users. As a form of information technology, cyberspace operates as a means to perpetuate the structural norms of Western society. The Internet is a powerful tool and is therefore viewed as a primarily masculine space that serves the needs of the patriarchal structure in which it operates. *Cyberfeminisms* are a contemporary feminist attempt to disrupt the technological power structures and alter technology that is often hostile to feminist viewpoints.

Plant (1995) introduced the concept of cyberfeminism as a set of practices intended to generate nonoppressive alternatives to the power structure of the Internet. Cyberfeminisms are viewed as women-centered spaces within the Internet, where women's issues can prevail and not fall under patriarchal control. Plant (1996) views cyberspace as a gendered space that destroys the identity of the patriarchal figure through the Web's fluidity. Patriarchy requires fixed structures in order to function and sets rules and norms to maintain male domination. For Plant the Internet is too easily changeable for patriarchy to maintain dominance.

Other scholars disagree on the fluidity of the Internet. Matheson (1992) contended that cyberspace generates highly stereotypical gender roles tied to the identity chosen by the user. Persons who enter cyberspace with male cybernames act stereotypically male, and female names indicate hyperfeminine characteristics. Cyberfeminists seek to alter this power structure by including more gender issues and practices in cyberspace. Crow (1998) discussed the increase in female-centered discussion groups and workshops on the Web, specifically arguing that politicizing the Web is a means of dismantling the power structures invested in cyberspace. Using the Web as an activist tool is a way for feminists to deconstruct patriarchal power.

Crow argued that language of the Web and the facility for women to access the Web are two prevalent factors that need to be altered for feminist cyberspaces to function. Myburgh (1998) explained, "Cyberculture is reliant only on the structures of linguistics and semiotics in order to have meaning" (p. 2). Therefore, altering the meaning of cyberspace requires altering the images and language used to be more feminist and feminine in order to disrupt the power structures and to welcome women online. Women need to feel comfortable online so that women-centered messages can reach them through the Internet. For the ability of the space to be truly female gendered, getting women to participate in the cyber-gendered spaces is key.

Cyberspace as a gendered space is further complicated by cultural understandings of how gendered spaces function. In offline reality, female spaces are generally found in the private sphere and male spaces in the public. On the World Wide Web, this balance is upset. The Web is a public space but female-oriented spaces exist within that sphere. Activities associated with the Web are not activities that, offline, function solely in one sphere or the other. The binary division between the spheres cannot function online because cyberspace is a fusion of traditionally female or private technologies and information sciences (the telephone, the VCR) and traditionally male or public ones. Myburgh (1998) further explained:

> The net is patriarchal to the extent that the machines have been dominated by pale males for some time, although many women have been involved in inventing, designing and using them. There is not equality in cyberspace to the extent that the majority of users are still male and harassment is not unknown. On the other hand, women can use this tool as they wish and they clearly do. (p. 3)

Myburgh cautioned, however, that McLuhan's (1965) myth of the Global Village is not real, and the Internet is primarily an elite space. Although the Internet is a powerful political tool, it is still constructed through patriarchy. Women need to use this tool with that in mind. She explained, "Women are now in a position where they can own the means of production" (p. 3). If women can produce meaning online, using patriarchal means, they can potentially generate a new understanding that may be able to apply offline as well.

In order to maintain a comfort level online, women must be familiar with the ideals being presented to them in the online spaces. This identity becomes part of the cyberidentities, or cyborg identities, of those participating in the site, and the sites' generated feminist ideals flow between the identities of people online and their physical identities. Hence, women develop empowered constructions of "natural-technical objects of knowledge in which the difference between machine and organism is thoroughly blurred; mind, body, and tool are on very intimate terms" (Haraway, 1990, p. 207). Cyborgs are potent political identities that are "synthesized from fusions of outsider identities" (p. 216) and survive by "seizing the tools to mark the world that marked them as other" (p. 217). A virtual or cybersociety is constructed by cyborgs interacting online and engaging in alternative work communities and identity construction.

Online Organizing: Fragmented Identities, Fragmented Communities

Online organizational practices, telecommuting, and home-based work are arrangements suited to changing organizational and workforce demands. These organizational styles are distinct for two reasons: Work and communication are accomplished and transported technologically, while time-space relations are being reconsidered and recreated within specific organizational cultures. Whereas management and communication accounts and investigations of technology have centered on instrumental directives associated with telecommuting practices (and associated with conduit and linkage metaphors), they have failed to account for the differential experiences of organizational participants with cyborg identities, especially when those identities become the organization's identity. The problems of organizational communication assist in ferreting out the complexities of technological advances embedded within organizational cultural assumptions.

Complex, ambiguous, and fluid meaning systems are the keys to the technological organizational community. As new categories of relationships among organizational community members and other stakeholders develop (e.g., independent contractors and telecommuters), these categories continue to blur distinctions between insiders and outsiders. As a hospital social worker remarked about the lack of a clear center in her work environment:

> It just seems to me like social workers are always a little bit on the fringe; they're part of the institution but they're not. You know they have to be part of the institution in order to really get what they need for their clients, but basically they're usually at odds with the institution. You have to remain affiliated with the institution in order to work the system. So it's like we are in the institution, but not of it. (Meyerson, 1991, p. 140)

Being in, but not of, the employing organization characterizes the lived experience of many outsiders within who express very different realities than dominant organization members (see Allen, 2000; Collins, 1991; Orbe, 1998). As organizations become more diverse, global, technology-infused, and distributed in terms of work arrangements, face-to-face interactions may become increasingly fewer, momentary, and shallow.

Fragmentation scholars note that organizational community members vary in the types of ambiguities they see and how they react to them over time. Organization members may question decision-making criteria and the extent to which these criteria are incommensurable (e.g., Eisenberg, Murphy, & Andrews, 1998). Organization members may express ambiguity, confusion, and contradiction as they are in the process of making sense and developing causal maps retrospectively of organizational happenings (see Weick, 1995).

Martin (1992) identified fragmentation as a framework depicting culture in terms of confusion, paradox, obscurity, tension, and conflicts. In short, fragmentation explores the role of ambiguity, inconsistency, and multiplicity of culture, identities, causal attributions, and subgroup memberships in organizational contexts. Hylmö (2001) found that telecommuters could describe different outsider-within experiences. Their identities could become even more fragmented than the telecommuter versus in-house employees that one would assume from a differentiation approach.

Indeed, gender, race, organizational status, and other factors might influence the degrees and types of ambiguity they see surrounding work arrangements.

Home-based entrepreneurs encompass a growing number of employed parents. Most of these entrepreneurs start their own businesses to spend more time with their families. For some women the catalyst is a newborn baby whom they do not want to leave. For others, commuting long distances wastes valuable time that could be spent caring for children and elderly parents. Still others just want to be their own bosses. What many of these women crave is a way to blend simultaneously work and family responsibilities. They seek to break down the boundaries that separate work and home, public and private, and professional and family.

Entrepreneurial cyborgs use the master's tool, the computer, to make their marks on the business world and change women's experiences: "The cyborg is our ontology; it gives us our politics. The cyborg is a condensed image of both imagination and material reality, the two joined centers structuring any possibility of historical transformation" (Haraway, 1991, pp. 149150). She exists in a postgender world that is no longer structured by artificial, polarized boundaries of public and private. In this world, the cyborg is empowered—she has agency.

Technology both empowers and constrains employed parents and entrepreneurial mothers. Rakow and Navarro (1993) argued that new technologies have created remote mothering in which mothers manage their home responsibilities while at work. Their participants like being "available to [their] children by having a cellular telephone" (p. 153) in a space between public and private. Similarly, Edley (2001) reported the use of the cell phone as an electronic baby sitter and one mother's paying the price when her child called in the middle of her presentation to the board of directors. Edley (2003) explored entrepreneurial Web sites as computer-mediated communication that marks not only a viable terrain for work and client interactions, but the online communicative process also enacts a sense of community building and identity construction for these entrepreneurial mothers.

Furthermore, Markham (1998) argued "in text-based spaces, self is constructed through dialogue and...on-line or off-line, all of us make sense of our experiences and tell the stories of our lives in self-centered and self-understood ways" (p. 210). She added:

> Technologies extend our physical capacities....As an augmentation of the self that is situated outside the body, online communication technology offers a powerful means of control over the text, over the performance of self through the text, and control over Others' capacities as well. (pp. 213–214)

Markham's online ethnography found that participants believed they could control their online self-presentations more than their offline face-to-face interactions: "Control is wielded by the user of the tool, the one writing the text, the one writing the script for the performance—a distinctly non-interactive, non-transactional view of communication" (p. 214). She contended that this control is illusory: "Online, we begin to exist as a persona when others respond to us; being, in this sense, is relational and dialogic" (p. 214). She concluded that the illusion of control is all that is necessary. Even with careful online self-monitoring and constant editing individuals are still not in control of their self-production. Construction of the self is a dialogic process offline and online.

Women home-based business owners report that they often function as "virtual corporations" and are just as likely to use communication technology as men home-based business owners (National Foundation of Women Business Owners, 2000). According to a study conducted by the NFWBO (2000), "[h]ome-based businesses owned by women are providing employment and fostering economic development in their communities, and they owe a lot of their businesses' growth to technology." The study determined that home-based businesses are not limited to start-ups and began as home-based businesses. Furthermore, owners preferred working from home and claimed they would remain home-based indefinitely.

Ironically, the appeal of technology to make our lives easier also serves to complicate our lives and make us work harder and longer hours—at home. Technology provides both temporal and spatial extensions of work into the home and during leisure and family time—during weekends, evenings, and predawn hours in order to balance work and family responsibilities. Society treats these socially constructed terms of *work, family, public,* and *private* as if they are natural and real. By so doing, we ignore the negotiated tensions and contradictions that employed parents and adult children of elderly parents engage in as we attempt to balance the multiple roles, emotions, and social constraints produced and reproduced in the gendered discourses of work/family.

Drawing on Habermas's (1987) work, Deetz (1992) defined corporate colonization of the lifeworld in which organizational values and practices "extend into nonwork life through time structuring, educational content, economic distributions, product development, and creation of needs. Modern corporations affect society by both their products and their income distribution but also by the practices internal to them" (pp. 113–114). Not only is corporate colonization influencing the decisions that employees make regarding their private lives, organizations also are seducing working women and men into believing that they can have it all. Organizations have seduced working parents with technology and have gained their consent to be controlled through the illusion of removing spatial and temporal constraints.

Alternative Work: Telecommuting

The idea of employees doing paid work at home is nothing new. During the 15th to 18th centuries, entrepreneurs often relied on home workers to produce cloth from raw materials delivered by an entrepreneur to a worker's cottage (Snizek, 1995). The entrepreneur would then pick up the finished goods for delivery to market and the worker would be paid for the labor. Similar labor practices have been used by the apparel industry more recently, such as by home knitters in Vermont (Loker, 2000).

Cottage workers of past and present are not the only groups that can be compared to telecommuters. During the 20th century, corporations became more international; multinational corporations rely on expatriates who worked outside their home countries but still connected to organizational headquarters (see Keough, 1998). Like expatriates, telecommuters work at sites away from headquarters. While telecommuters and expatriates are expected to act as boundary spanners between headquarters and clients or local organizational members, their geographic distance from the core organizing communities leads to concerns that these employees could lose touch with the central organizational culture and thus be less loyal (Banai & Reisel, 1993; Dutton, 1994; Gregersen & Black, 1992; Kugelmass, 1995). Also, they may build stronger attachments to their professional communities than with the employing organizations, which may lead to increased turnover rates (Olson & Primps, 1984; Russo, 1998).

In recent years dramatic changes have occurred in the organizational environment, particularly with regard to alternative work arrangements such as telecommuting, home-based businesses, and Web-based businesses. As organizations are becoming more reliant on distribution of knowledge and the use of technology, telecommuting (or teleworking) becomes a logical next step (Kompast & Wagner, 1998). Telecommuting occurs when a worker completes the majority of work-related tasks away from the company headquarters or other centralized office and relies on technology to transfer the work, in contrast to traditional forms of work completed while the employee is physically located in a company office (Nilles, 1988; Qvartrop, 1998). Telecommuting has become widespread among organizations of various types and sizes, ranging from large corporations such as IBM and AT&T (Biddle, 1999) to chambers of commerce (Apgar, 1998) and the U.S. Army (Apgar, 1998).

There are several different categories of telecommuters based on amount of time spent working away from the office, including those who work at home part-time, who bring work home after hours, and those who work at home full-time. Telecommuters may be fully integrated members of the organizational community, or they may be piece- or contract workers, or self-employed entrepreneurs (Kraut & Grambsch, 1987). Most jobs qualified for telecommuting are white-collar executive or professional positions (Bredin, 1996) at medium or higher salary levels (Weijers, Meijer, & Spoelman, 1992), or low-tech clerical jobs such as claims processing (Dutton, 1994). Telecommuters may work out of their home offices, at telecommuting centers implemented by the employing organization or local chamber of commerce, or in mobile offices where work takes place on the road. The majority of people who telecommute spend a few days each week in the office with coworkers (Bredin, 1996). It also is not unusual for full-time telecommuting to last only for the duration of a particular project (Dutton, 1994).

Technology is increasing in quality to the point that it is possible for more people to telecommute than in previous years; however, there are those who suggest that until broadband technology is widely available in the home, we are unlikely to see a more extensive transition to teleworking (Biddle, 1999). Nevertheless, telework centers already are appearing across the U.S. and worldwide (Aichholzer, 1998). These centers make it easy for employees to rent a desk close to home and complete work-related tasks with all the amenities available in a regular office. Regional and national governments are promoting telecommuting for political reasons. Benefits include helping communities maintain a clean environment, increasing flexibility for parents and others with domestic needs, and reducing long commutes. Furthermore, economic reports support the viability of telecommuting ("Employers Save $10,000 Per Teleworker," 1999).

Though telecommuting has been an accepted phenomenon since the oil crisis of the early 1970s (Nilles, 1977), most of what is known about telecommuting is largely anecdotal. The popular business press has published stories about the success of telecommuting or provided how-to lists, but very few theoretically grounded studies have been conducted (Ellison, 1999). Of the few studies that have been theoretically grounded, most have used quantitative data to focus on social presence and information richness (see Duxbury, Higgins, & Neufield, 1998; Scott & Timmerman, 1999; Wiesenfeld, Raghuram, & Garud, 1998). A few theoretically grounded, qualitative studies have focused on relationships between home and work for telecommuters (Haddon & Silverstone, 1995; Hylmö, 2001; Hylmö & Buzzanell, 2002; Mirchandani, 1998a). These studies found telecommuters often have difficulty maintaining boundaries between work and home life and strive to reify traditional boundaries so they will not give the impression of being too committed to work. This body of literature is especially gendered in nature.

Gendered Examinations of Telecommuting

The literature examining telecommuting and gender tends to fall into two broad categories. One way that this relationship has been examined can be found in the argument that telecommuters are in a position to challenge the dichotomy between work and home and to actualize a feminist vision of eradicating arbitrarily placed boundaries between the two realms (Mirchandani, 1999). The other way that gender tends to be examined in the context of telecommuting is in relation to organizational culture (Mirchandani, 1998a).

The first way that the current body of literature has examined the relationship between home and work is as a relationship that operates along a dichotomous continuum. At one end, the two realms of home and work are fully integrated with no distinct boundaries. At the other end, the two worlds are completely distinct and segmented from one another (Nippert-Eng, 1996). The dichotomous body of literature may examine the link between household and job-related work activities, such as the relationship between working at home and caring for children and other family members. For example, studies have shown that even when they are telecommuting at home, women still tend to work more hours doing household tasks than men do, even when the men espouse an equal division of chores (Perin, 1998). Other studies have examined the importance of telecommuting for some women to experience a stronger sense of connectedness with their families by being more involved in their children's lives (Mirchandani, 1998b) or by incorporating their children into their workday as a way to reduce stress (Hochschild, 1997).

The second way that the literature has examined gender and telecommuting points out telecommuters are still located within a specific organizational culture even as they are working at home. From this view, telecommuting men and women are regarded as seeking out alternative workweek schedules that better accommodate their private lives while remaining members of a cultural environment that permits this change in work-related behavior (Friedman, Christensen, & DeGroot, 1998). Mirchandani (1998a) drew on the work of Mills and Murgatroyd (1991) to identify two ways that gendered organizational cultures are manifest in the telecommuting experience: the necessity to be fully immersed in the work process and the assumption that concerns of the family take second place to work concerns. Both views are patriarchal in nature.

A patriarchal view of work emphasizes engrossment in work (Mirchandani, 1999) as represented by the emphasis on dedication to work and presenting telecommuting as beneficial to organizational productivity (Bredin, 1996). However, telecommuters often work longer hours because of the availability of work (Kurland & Bailey, 1999) or because working behind a closed door at home may lead to fewer cultural cues to stop working, such as coworkers saying good-bye (Hill, Miller, Weiner, & Colihan, 1998). A lack of boundaries may be particularly problematic for many women who often emphasize the need to separate work and home, but then find that work invades home as they see themselves as being on call for the benefit of colleagues (Mirchandani, 1998b).

More recently, work by Hylmö (2003) and Hylmö and Buzzanell (2002) has challenged the distinctions drawn by previous literature that focused primarily on either the distinctions drawn between home and work or the experiences of telecommuters in terms of their ability to be productive members of an organization. Hylmö and Buzzanell have argued that telecommuting organizations should be understood as holistic entities typically comprised of both in-house and telecommuting employees embedded in a given organizational culture. Their research revealed that the challenges faced by alternative organizations include traditionally gendered expectations of clear divisions between home and work reinforced by perceptions that employees choosing to be on a promotion-oriented track would retain a clear distinction between home and work. The expectation, largely, was that the distinction be made geographically (in-house versus telecommuting). To many of the employees studied, telecommuting was something that people who were stagnant in their careers would embrace. However, the study also revealed that some women felt that they would be able both to telecommute and have an advancing career, as long as they maintained the appearance of strict boundaries. These women would attempt to do so by keeping strict hours while working at home, not engaging in any activities that could appear nonwork related during those hours, and by keeping a clear demarcation between home and work by closing office doors even at home. Such perceptions were contradictory to the dominant culture and could present additional challenges to alternative forms of work when members, typically women, believe in existing promotion myths that may have little to do with reality (Buzzanell & Goldzwig, 1991).

Technological Impact on Communication for Telecommuters

Telecommuters rely on technology to complete and transfer their work as well as to communicate with various stakeholders in their work processes. However, the amount and type of technology on which employees rely varies (Bredin, 1996). Most telecommuters use their own equipment. Among telecommuting employees of the City of Long Beach, California, 73% used their own computers rather than equipment purchased by the city (Dutton, 1994). In the past few years, companies appear more willing to absorb some of the cost of the technology, at least for those telecommuters who are part of formal programs (Paik, 2000).

Technology is not only used to complete task-related functions, but also to communicate with coworkers. A study by Pacific Bell found telecommuters primarily used technology to communicate with their coworkers (Meade, 1993). Communication was most commonplace via e-mail (90%), followed by the telephone (87%). Meeting face-to-face was slightly less frequent (83%), and voice mail (57%) even less so. This pattern of media use suggests that telecommuters rely more on mediated communication that is less rich in information than on face-to-face interaction common to everyday encounters in a traditional office (see Daft & Lengel, 1984).

Regardless of the way one telecommutes, being physically apart from the employing organization may create a complex set of tensions and opportunities for both employee and organization. Hylmö and Buzzanell (2002) emphasize the discursive constructions of the complexities of everyday life, individual identity, organizational practices, and cultural belonging among all organizational members. For example, the use of technology may be serving patriarchal interests that emphasize the importance of work over nonwork life by reinforcing existing emphases on productivity that can be measured quantitatively through billing by the hour (Bailyn, 1993). Employees may feel pressured to maintain such billability, even when using technology that is less advanced or efficient than that which is available in a central office, and work longer hours in order to appear extra productive in exchange for the privilege of working elsewhere (Hylmö, 2001, 2003).

Telecommuters are apt to feel lonely and disconnected from their coworkers (Kugelmass, 1995; Schepp, 1990), which may cause telecommuting employees to feel less identification with their coworkers. This may especially be the case for those employees who are telecommuting full-time, since part-time telecommuters seem to be better able to develop continuing attachments to their workgroups and the organization (Scott et al., 1999).

Because discussions about technological equipment, costs, and communication support have occupied a prominent place in writings on telecommuting and other alternative work arrangements, the accompanying work on communication has been relatively unsophisticated. In general, communication is depicted in terms of conduit and linkage metaphors—that is, in terms of how to best provide information or alleviate perceptions of isolation and lack of person-organization attachments, rather than the construction of multiple realities through discursive processes (see Putnam, Phillips, & Chapman, 1996). Given the varied forms of telecommuting that are enacted differently by diverse workforce members, it is not surprising that findings from studies searching for telecommuting communication prescriptions would seem simplistic.

Hierarchical communication also changes with telecommuting. Managing telecommuters means new forms of interactions and surveillance are developed, because the traditional forms of control with managers supervising on-site employees no longer apply (Froggatt, 2000). Because face-to-face monitoring is impossible, tendencies to micromanage telecommuters are strong (Siskos, 2001). In addition, managers express concern about disruptions that telecommuting brings to other organizational activities (e.g., rescheduling and restructuring; see Powell & Mainiero, 1999) to the extent that they resist implementation of telecommuting programs (Barr, 2000) and urge their organizations to withdraw telecommuting options (Darrow, 2001).

Although much has been written about the importance of communication to the success of telecommuting programs (Cascio, 2000; Staples, 2001), most materials focus on instrumental communication, particularly how different kinds of exchanges are useful in managing and controlling telecommuters as well as developing work arrangements that suit employees' central life interests (Friedman, Christensen, & DeGroot, 1998; Maruca, 1998). Communication is important in both the formal and the informal sense, so that telecommuters and in-house employees know what is expected and how to produce informal, personalized boss-subordinate exchanges. Formal communication can alleviate telecommuters' fears that they may be excluded from promotions (Lee, 2001; see also Roberts, 2001c, for telecommuters' higher expectations of promotion based on productivity) and corporate concerns about legal obligations for workers' safety in home offices (Murphy, 2001). Communication on interpersonal and organizational levels is compounded by the fact that telecommuting often operates in virtual settings in which formal, instrumental communication is dysfunctional (Davenport & Pearlson, 1998) and in time-space dislocations that add unprecedented complexity to communication.

THE POLITICS AND PARADOXES OF ALTERNATIVE ORGANIZING

The goal of political engagement in feminist organizing is to maximize autonomy for the movement, while challenging institutional practices. Power for feminists has come to be defined as the ability to act, rather than as a competitive state. The state becomes viewed as a site of political struggle, and then engagement occurs. Radical feminist ideals were often incorporated into feminist collective organizations, as radical feminism pushed for political change. Reinelt (1995) explained:

> In addition to the ideological, economic, and political forces that have made it difficult to imple-
> ment radical feminist political practices fully, there are problematic aspects to radical feminist
> practice itself. Consensus decision-making, a hallmark of radical feminist practice, may em-
> power group members and challenge hierarchical structure of decision-making, but as early as
> 1972 feminists also identified negative aspects. Resolving conflict is difficult…participation is
> very time-consuming . . . and homogeneity is fostered. Many shelter organizations have thus
> moved away from pure consensus-based decision-making (p. 89).

Reinelt explained that the boundaries between the women's movement and the hierarchical institutions that feminism opposes have become blurred. This blur-ring may indicate a type of paradox, or a situation based in interaction, where the pursuit of one goal enters into the pursuit of a competing goal and thereby uninten-tionally undermines it (Stohl & Cheney, 2001). To deal with paradox and still be functional, political organizing exhibits combinations of both hierarchical and con-sensual organizing practices.

Stohl and Cheney (2001) have identified four types of organizational paradoxes relating to participation: structure, agency, identity, and power. *Paradoxes of struc-ture* are directly concerned with the design of participation in the organization, a rubric that encompasses four aspects of structural paradoxes together: design, ad-aptation, punctuation, and formalization. The *paradox of design* notes that some grassroots participation programs may, in fact, be imposed from the top of the organization when management develops new programs that are intended to pro-vide employees with more opportunities to participate. For example, management may initiate alternative work arrangements such as telecommuting programs that allow for worker participation in an effort to enhance quality of work life (Cleaver, 2000; Langhoff, 1996). The *paradox of adaptation* exists when organizations at-tempt to change to address external expectations but lose the heart of the organiza-tion. In other words, organizations experience tension between the need to adjust to the external environment and the need to focus on what the organization was set up to do. For example, it may be difficult for organizations to adapt to external pressures such as allowing employees more personal flexibility or getting people off the roads in an effort to reduce congestion, while retaining a core sense of what the organization itself is about (Shear, 2000; Wolf, 2001).

Another way that organizations may experience paradoxes emerges from the way that groups punctuate, or perceive, temporal patterns and sequences of inter-action (Watzlawick, Beavin, & Jackson, cited in Stohl & Cheney, 2001). Group members participate in procedures intended to increase efficiency, but these pro-cedures may instead reduce efficiency so that the group members become less likely to participate in them. By resisting participation in punctuating events (e.g., meetings or training sessions), group members increasingly become powerless as they become less organized than they would have if they had continued with the initial procedures. Thus the *paradox of punctuation* refers to the possibility of the participatory process being cut short in organizations so that the vitality of the organization is lost over time. One way that alternative organizations may experience the paradox of punctuation might be found in the forms of communication media that the members use. By relying on quick email messages or telephone calls from cell phones on the run rather than longer face-to-face interaction, the members may lose vitality as a group because face-to-face may be more appropriate to the generation of new ideas (Kayany, Wotring, & Forrest, 1996; Khatri, 2000).

Finally, organizations experience the *paradox of formalization* when opportunities for spontaneous interaction become too routine (Stohl & Cheney, 2001). Instead of chance encounters, members rely on formalized, ritualized meetings. An example of the formalization paradox might be when a part-time telecommuter who at one time had the option to work at home at the spur-of-the-moment now has to go through an application process to get prior approval from a manager (e.g., Cascio, 2000; Powell & Mainiero, 1999; Wolfe, 2001). By going through a manager with a formal application, the process may become so formalized that the potential benefits of telecommuting as increased flexibility and productivity are lost.

Paradoxes of agency concern an individual's perception of efficiency within the organization. There are four paradoxes of agency that Stohl and Cheney (2001) identify: responsibility, cooperation, sociality, and autonomy. The *paradox of responsibility* finds that even as groups are dependent on individuals to function, they function by voluntary subordination on the individual's part. Hence, as management identifies the best way to telecommute, the individual has to accept it, even if the individual feels that she or he has a better way to implement a flexible work schedule (Rose, 1996; Sheley, 1996). Similarly, online communities are struggling to find appropriate female discursive spaces that are devoid of existing masculine norms (Plant, 1996). Next, the *paradox of cooperation* means that the very procedures set in place to foster cooperation may in fact hinder it. The procedures that allow alternative organizing practices such as telecommuting programs to exist can actually increase job satisfaction (Weijers et al., 1992). However, by distancing the telecommuting employee from the rest of the work community, the employee may be hindered from fully participating in some work-related activities (Vega & Brennan, 2000). Similarly, the cyborg mother finds that the option to work via technology simultaneously enables her to remain in contact with her family and constrains her by increasing her availability to coworkers and clients (Edley, 2001).

The *paradox of sociality*, Stohl and Cheney (2001) suggested, tends to arise most frequently in organizations in which the employees are highly committed to participation, but participation leads to social burnout. For example, telecommuters may find that even as they relish telecommuting as a way to spend more time with their families, they may actually spend less time with their families because work is always available (Hill, Hawkins, & Miller, 1996; Silver, Cohen, & Crutchfield,

1994). Last, the *paradox of autonomy* means that in order to gain something in terms of power, a certain amount of independence is sacrificed. Some telecommuters may feel that it is difficult to retain visibility, and to be considered for promotions, when working outside of the main office where power and decision making are located (Roberts, 2001a). Likewise, many working women are struggling with societal expectations to be not only working but mothers as well. On top of that, they are expected to be on a rising career path that eventually may turn out to be more of a myth than a reality (Buzzanell, 1995; Buzzanell & Goldzwig, 1991).

The *identity set of paradoxes* refers to tensions that are experienced by individuals attempting to balance a sense of self with a sense of being part of a group (Stohl & Cheney, 2001). Three identity paradoxes exist: commitment, representation, and compatibility. The *paradox of commitment* suggests that organizational members are expected to commit to sharing diverse ideas and open discussions, and at the same time commit to a singular idea. In the latter case, disagreements may be reframed as resistance or lack of loyalty. For some members of organizations, commitment may mean working in a colocated space (see Perlow, 1998). However, telecommuters may find that their lack of colocation with other organizational members brands them as being disloyal and uncommitted to the organization's ideals (Franco, 1997; Hylmö & Buzzanell, 2002; Roberts, 2001b). Working mothers are expected to put work ahead of family and eradicate all signs to the contrary (Bailyn, 1993; Edley, 2001). If they do not, they are expected to pay the price.

Next, the *paradox of representation* suggests that rather than having a voice, some groups may find themselves with no voice or an imagined voice (Stohl & Cheney, 2001). For example, the Internet may give the impression that individuals have more of a voice than is really the case. Alternative organizations for women are finding themselves embedded in a patriarchal environment that is consistently reified as normative. Although the appearance may be that everyone has a voice, in reality that voice may be submerged or ignored on a larger scale. Even women business owners may be challenged in this regard as they strive to be recognized in the world by working from their homes away from many spheres of ongoing face-to-face interaction. In many organizations, telecommuting may appear as the result of employee initiatives and as a way of giving voice to the needs of the employees. Ironically, once the telecommuters begin to work outside the central office, they may find they are losing that voice as their remaining coworkers and managers no longer remember to take the voice of the telecommuters into consideration when making decisions (Ellison, 1999; Parr, 1999).

That leads to the last of the three paradoxes of identity, the *compatibility paradox*, which notes that organizational strategy and cultural values overlap and become compatible. The problem is that cultural values take much longer to change than do organizational strategies. As a result, when organizational strategies change, these strategies are implemented in a cultural environment that may represent cultural values that are incommensurable with the new values of the changed strategy (Stohl & Cheney, 2001). When telecommuters work outside of the office as part of a changing organizational strategy, the organizational values may remain the same as before telecommuting was allowed, or evolve slowly to coincide with the new organizational structure. These values may include an emphasis on colocation of members and a sense of separation between organizational and home life (Hill et al., 1998; Kompast & Wagner, 1998). In accordance with the compatibility paradox, when telecommuting programs are implemented, organizational members are expected to act in agreement with the newly implemented program, even though it may be in conflict with deeper values embedded in the organization's culture. Clearly, the compatibility paradox may be the most challenging paradox to alternative organizations as women are asserting themselves and their right to lead balanced lives, with or without an employing organization or children at home. Women are taking the lead in expecting organizations to rise to the opportunity to present their employees with the means to have both a work life and a nonwork life. It may be that it is just a matter of organizations struggling to catch up to meet an inevitable challenge.

Paradoxes of power focus on the location and exercise of power in the organization. These include, but are not limited to, issues of voice, allocation and availability of resources, and relationship dynamics. Stohl and Cheney (2001) identified three paradoxes of power: control, leadership, and homogeneity. The *paradox of control* suggests that even as shared control among employees and managers is at the core of participation, team-based control may end up being even tighter than managerially driven control as members control each other (Barker, 1993; Papa, Auwal, & Singhal, 1997). From a telecommuting perspective, the paradox of control may have interesting implications. For example, it is possible that even as management endorses telecommuting and provides it as an option, it is the organizational members who determine who may actually participate in the telecommuting program. Similarly, as Bailyn (1993) and others have shown (e.g., Odih, 1999; Rapoport, Bailyn, Fletcher, & Pruitt, 2002), it is often a matter of how an individual's coworkers react that will impact on another's ability to balance work and nonwork life. Men are often expected to come in to work during the weekend on projects that need to be finished, whereas women are expected to take maternity leave and therefore not be considered in line for a promotion. Closely related to the paradox of control is the *paradox of leadership*, in which some organizations expect a charismatic leader to trigger the creation of democracy rather than the employees who are going to be participating in it (Stohl & Cheney, 2001). As some organizations are still contemplating whether or not to implement telecommuting in an effort to democratize the employees' ability to choose where and when to work, the implementation of such a program often has to be developed by one or more particularly inspired leaders. The implementation of the democratic telecommuting program then often comes from the top (Cascio, 2000; Davenport & Pearlson, 1998).

The final paradox of power is the *paradox of homogeneity*. This paradox posits that even as organizations strive toward unity, that unity may be limiting in that too much unity may lead to groupthink or a lack of consciousness and alternative viewpoints (Janis, 1982). This paradox presents an interesting challenge for telecommuting organizations (Haddon & Silverstone, 1995; Janss, 2001). As telecommuting is implemented, it will most likely be presented to the members in terms of organizational unity, as something that they should all appreciate and rally behind as being beneficial to the organization and its members.

The discourses and practices of telecommuting often are paradoxical (Hylmö, 2001; Hylmö & Buzzanell, 2002). Khaifa and Davidson (2000) pointed out that, although a large number of organizations present themselves as supportive of telecommuting, very few organizations actually allow telecommuting to permeate organizational life. The reasons why so many organizations are reluctant to embrace telecommuting may be due to the ambiguities and uncertainties that accompany this work arrangement. With too much unity on the benefits to the organization, some of the potential problems and challenges may be over-shadowed until it becomes too late to develop alternative solutions. As Stohl and Cheney (2001) put it:

> the webs we weave will come to constrain us, often in unforeseen ways. Paradox delimits options for participants in a system, particularly if there is little awareness of what is happening or if members are unable to comment on it. (p. 352)

The paradox of homogeneity also presents an important challenge to feminist theorizing about alternative organizations. Too often the assumption about gender and women in organizations is one that tends to homogenize female experiences into one. Much of our literature on work-life balance focuses on women with families, with an underlying assumption that by families we mean the nuclear family with children, wife, and husband. However, as Israel (2002) has pointed out, most women are likely to be single women at one point or other in our lives and often working at the same time. We know that some women never have children, but still work and are productive members of society. In addition, many women come to realize the role reversal of taking care of their elderly parents as the older generation comes to depend on their help with everyday life functions. Also, women's realities in different countries around the world vary greatly, for better or for worse. We know that we are all subject to the paradox of homogeneity, and that we must take on the challenge to diversify our ways of thinking and examining alternative organizational forms (Allen, 1998, 2000).

CONCLUSION

Our extensive review of literature has positioned telework, home-based businesses, and online work communities as gendered work spaces within which many working women seek to produce empowered identities and communities of commitment and belonging. Such communities could serve as alternatives to, as well as function within, traditional organizing structures. The community practices may also create alternatives to existing conditions of workaholism and corporate control. Alternative communities construct a holistic blend of multiple discourses of work, outreach, and volunteerism, interwoven with family, friends, and other interpersonal relationships. These connections serve as an interrelated and interdependent system of physical, emotional, and cooperative collaboration.

To engage in nonhierarchical organizing practices involves commitment—commitment to change, to engage in healthy balances among all the many responsibilities and activities that connect individuals in relationships of belonging and support. Sometimes it is a commitment to particular critical and/or feminist ideologies a commitment to succeed, and a commitment to take time to relax, relate, and reconnect.

Theoretical Implications and Need for Future Research

The present essay has served to bring together the state of the art of three bodies of literature (the cyborg, telecommuters, and online communities) from a feminist perspective. While collectivist organizing can serve an important purpose in developing new forms of community, other alternative contexts may be fraught with unforeseen challenges. We have pointed out the tensions experienced by the cyborg mother struggling to juggle technology for work and family purposes as she attempts to multitask her life. We explored online communities as a possible forum for women to develop connections and new spaces for themselves, and the challenges that such communities face in a normatively masculine environment. Finally, we found that telecommuters use the same technology as the cyborg and the online communities, in an effort to balance paid and nonpaid labor. Such efforts often include a mythological view of advancement opportunities that might never materialize because of decreased face-to-face interactions.

Our essay has drawn on Shotter's (1993), Csikszentmihalyi's (1990), and others' definitions of community to argue that all individuals have a right to be involved and to enjoy their participation as worthy human beings. Acknowledging the importance of full participation in this way further means that individuals are recognized as unique participants who contribute to the success of organizations. Furthermore, it means recognizing that individuals will be able to contribute the most when their relationships with others in a multitude of contexts are appreciated and validated. Such recognition serves to uphold the uniqueness factor of individuals as imperative to dynamic organizational environments while preserving an emphasis on moral respect and interdependency on others for maximum achievement. Reaffirming the existence of blurred boundaries provides the potential for simultaneously balancing work-life contributions and creates a relationship nexus of community, social support, and professional networking, guidance, and cooperation.

Future studies need to continue to develop theory that explores and embraces a sense of holistic thinking and valuing of individuals comprising a web of relationships within which individuals and organizations are situated. We argue that feminist theory needs to continue to develop a challenge to traditional organizational theory by maintaining a focus on the multiplicity engendered by those webs. Such a focus is still limited within the bodies of literature that we have available to us to date.

Our review of the literature has pointed out the need to continue to examine relationship webs as a form of community by deepening existing research. For example, the paradox of homogeneity (Stohl & Cheney, 2001) reveals a narrow focus on a specific type of family among much of the current research in all areas of organizational and community life. Most studies focus on the experiences of White, middle-class, professional women with children living at home in the U.S. We lack studies focusing on people of color, working or upper class, men and women with or without children, with or without spouses, and nonnuclear/traditional families, as well as international contexts. Additionally, we are lacking studies focusing on gay, lesbian, bisexual, and transgendered couples. There is, furthermore, a scarcity of studies that focus on changes over the lifespan, including ageism and eldercare.

From an international perspective, we need to recognize that the current body of communication literature focuses on a limited part of the global population. There is an underlying assumption that people everywhere share the same experiences; however, different cultural values and national policies lead us to believe otherwise. For example, Swedish women often work part-time as it is. and both men and women in Sweden have extended parental leaves available to them, even though women tend to take the majority of the family leave (Stier & Lewin-Epstein, 2001). That reality affects organizational life in that women may find it harder to advance in a context where they are expected to be absent for extended periods of time devoted to childcare (Acker, 1998; Ivarsson, 2001; Sundström, 1999). The question remains how such different national policies and cultures affect the cyborg mother, online communities, and telecommuting from a communication perspective.

One way that the limitations in the current body of literature may be addressed is by drawing more extensively on feminist standpoint theory while attempting to be more inclusive in terms of the multiple positions examined. Organizational communication research in general is devoid of work that highlights and represents marginalized groups. We argue that such a lack is to the detriment of the field as a whole. Work by Allen (1998, 2000), Orbe and Warren (Orbe 1998; Orbe & Warren, 2000) and Hendrix (2002) pointed us to important ways that standpoint theory serves to highlight and validate different experiences. Clair (1998) explored the different realities of Native Americans; Parker (2001) examined the discursive experiences of African American women in leadership positions. Research by Aoki (2000) examined the complex nexus created by family, work, and religions for Mexican Americans. Such work needs to be extended and embraced much further by exploring issues such as the impact of technology on currently underrepresented communities and organizational members.

Practical Implications

Women in general tend to value supportive environments, not only in our work, but also in supporting each other as people. Significantly, women value the individual input that each organizational member makes to the whole. Implicit is that without each individual's contribution, the organization would be weaker and less able fully to attain its goals. Valuing individual efforts means that the strength of the organization is found in its webs of connection among unique members that enables the whole to reach new heights. Furthermore, it means recognizing individual members' lived experiences in and out of the organization and what those experiences represent. Women tend to respect the diversity of our lived experiences and our needs as individuals to accommodate the expectations that our lives hold.

For this area of research to impact women's everyday lives, it is imperative that corporations and governments adopt policies to make the work–life balance easier to achieve. Such policies must be inclusive of all lived experiences. Not only must corporations be held accountable for their frequent lack of holistic lifestyle policies, but government legislation also must uphold policies that benefit all stakeholders. Corporations need to understand the need for rest and a healthy lifestyle for employees to be productive, whole persons. Promoting and rewarding workaholic climates should not be tolerated. It is our hope and desire that this article can manifest some real changes in people's lives.

REFERENCES

Acker, J. (1990). Hierarchies, bodies, and jobs: A gendered theory of organizations. *Gender & Society, 4,* 139–158.

Acker, J. (1995). Feminist goals and organizing processes. In M. M. Ferree & P. Y. Martin (Eds.), *Feminist organizations: Harvest of the new women's movement* (pp. 137–144). Philadelphia: Temple University Press.

Acker, J. (1998). The future of "gender and organizations": Connections and boundaries. *Gender, Work & Organization, 5,* 195–206.

Adelman, M. B., & Frey, L. R. (1997). Foreward: Communication and community building. In L. A. Jason (Ed.), *Community building: Values for a sustainable future* (pp. ix–xii). New York: Praeger.

Aichholzer, G. (1998). A social innovation in its infancy: Experiences with telework centres. In P. J. Jackson & J. M. Van der Wielen (Eds.), *Teleworking: International perspectives* (pp. 292–302). London: Routledge.

Allen, B. J. (1998). Black womanhood and feminist standpoint. *Management Communication Quarterly, 11,* 575–586.

Allen, B. J. (2000). "Learning the ropes": A black feminist standpoint analysis. In P. M. Buzzanell (Ed.), *Rethinking organizational and managerial communication from feminist perspectives* (pp. 177–208). Thousand Oaks, CA: Sage.

Anderson, B. (1991). *Imagined communities.* New York: Verso.

Anzaldua, G. (1987). *Borderlands/La frontera.* San Francisco: Spinsters/Aunt Lute.

Aoki, E. (2000). Mexican American ethnicity in Biola, CA: An ethnographic account of hard work, family, and religion. *Howard Journal of Communication, 11,* 207–227.

Apgar, M. (1998, May–June). The alternative workplace: Changing where and how people work. *Harvard Business Review, 76,* 121–136.

Ashcraft, K. L. (1998). "I wouldn't say I'm a feminist, but . . .": Organizational micropractice and gender identity. *Management Communication Quarterly, 11*, 587–597.

Bailyn, L. (1993). *Breaking the mold: Women, men, and time in the new corporate world.* New York: Free Press.

Ballard, D. I., & Seibold, D. R. (2000). Time orientation and temporal variation across work groups: Implications for group and organizational communication. *Western Journal of Communication, 64*, 218–242.

Banai, M., & Reisel, W. D. (1993). Expatriate managers' loyalty to the MNC: Myth or reality? An exploratory study. *Journal of International Business Studies, 22*, 233–248.

Barker, J. R. (1993). Tightening the iron cage: Concertive control in self-managing teams. *Administrative Science Quarterly, 21*, 223–240.

Barr, S. (2000, August 2). Resistance from middle managers impedes growth of telecommuting, report says. *Washington Post*, p. B2.

Bart, P. B. (1987). Seizing the means of reproduction: An illegal feminist abortion collective-how and why it worked. *Qualitative Sociology, 10*, 339–357.

Biddle, F. M. (1999, October 26). Work week. *Wall Street Journal*, p. A1.

Bredin, A. (1996). *The virtual office survival handbook*. New York: Wiley.

Britton, D. (2000). The epistemology of the gendered organization. *Gender and Society, 14*, 418–434.

Buzzanell, P. M. (1994). Gaining a voice: Feminist organizational communication theorizing. *Management Communication Quarterly, 7*, 339–383.

Buzzanell, P. M. (1995). Reframing the glass ceiling as a socially constructed process: Implications for understanding and change. *Communication Monographs, 62*, 327–354.

Buzzanell, P. M. (2000). The promise and practice of the new career and social contract: Illusions exposed and suggestions for reform. In P. M. Buzzanell (Ed.), *Rethinking organizational & managerial communication from feminist perspectives*, (pp. 209–235). Thousand Oaks, CA: Sage.

Buzzanell, P. M., & Goldzwig, S. (1991). Linear and non-linear career models: Metaphors, paradigms, and ideologies. *Management Communication Quarterly, 4*, 466–505.

Calás, M. B., & Smircich, L. (1992). Using the "F" word: Feminist theories and the social consequences of organizational research. In A. J. Mills & P. Tancred (Eds.), *Gendering organizational analysis* (pp. 222–234). Newbury Park, CA: Sage.

Cascio, W. F. (2000). Managing a virtual workplace. *Academy of Management Executive, 14*(3), 81–90.

Clair, R. P. (1998). *Organizing silence: A world of possibilities*. Albany: State University of New York Press.

Clark, S. (2000). Work/family border theory: A new theory of work/family balance. *Human Relations, 53*, 747–770.

Cleaver, J. (2000). Out of sight: When teams of employees telecommute, it's great for the bottom line but tough on communication. *Crain's New York Business, 16*, 31.

Collins, P. H. (1991). *Black feminist thought: Knowledge, consciousness, and the politics of empowerment*. New York: Routledge.

Crow, B. (1998) Politicizing the internet: Getting women on-line. *Women and Environments International, 42*–43. Retrieved from http://80-Web6.epnet.com.proxy.ohiolink.edu:9099.

Csikszentmihalyi, M. (1990). *Flow: The psychology of optimal experience*. New York: Harper & Row.

Daft, R. L., & Lengel, R. H. (1984). Information richness: A new approach to managerial behavior and organization design. *Research in Organizational Behavior, 6*, 191–233.

Darrow, B. (2001, March 16). Telecommuters are heading back to the office. *TechWeb*. Retrieved June 7, 2001, from http://content.techWeb.com/wire/story/TWB20010316S0009

Davenport, T. H., & Pearlson, K. (1998). Two cheers for the virtual office. *Sloan Management Review, 39*(4), 51–64.

Deetz, S. A. (1992). *Democracy in an age of corporate colonization: Developments in communication and the politics of everyday life*. Albany: State University of New York Press.

Deming, W. G. (1994, February). Work at home: Data from the CPS. *Monthly Labor Review, 14*–20.

Dutton, G. (1994). Can California change its corporate culture? *Management Review, 83*(6) 49–54.

Duxbury, L., Higgins, C., & Neufield, D. (1998). Telework and the balance between work and family: Is telework part of the problem or part of the solution? In M. Igbara & M. Tan (Eds.), *The virtual workplace* (pp. 218–255). Hershey, PA: Idea Group.

Eastland, L. (1991). *Communication, organization, and change within a feminist context: A participant observation of a feminist collective.* Lewiston, NY: Edwin Mellen Press.

Edley, P. P. (2001). Technology, working mothers, and corporate colonization of the lifeworld: A gendered paradox of work and family balance. *Women and Language, 24,* 28–35.

Edley, P. P. (2003). Entrepreneurial mothers' balance of work and family: Discursive constructions of time, mothering, and identity. In P. Buzzanell, H. Sterk, & L. Turner's (Eds.) *Gendered approaches to applied communication* (pp. 255–274). Thousand Oaks, CA: Sage.

Edley, P. P., & Newsom, V. A. (2003). Work-family balance: A third wave feminist agenda. Unpublished manuscript.

Edwards, P., Edwards, S., & Roberts, L. (2002). The entrepreneurial parent: How to earn your living from home and still enjoy your family, your work, and your life. New York: Tarcher/Putnam.

Egan, R. M., Miles, W., Birstler, J. R., & Klayton-Mi, M. (1998, July-August). Can the rift between Allison and Penny be mended? Four experts offer their advice on the complexities of managing off-site employees. *Harvard Business Review, 76,* 28–32.

Eisenberg, E. M., & Goodall, H. L., Jr. (2001). *Organizational communication: Balancing creativity and constraint* (3rd. ed.). New York: Bedford/St. Martin's Press.

Eisenberg, E. M., Murphy, A., & Andrews, L. (1998). Openness and decision making in the search for a university provost. *Communication Monographs, 65,* 1–23.

Ellison, N. B. (1999). Social impacts: New perspectives on telework. *Social Science Computer Review, 17,* 338–356.

Employers save $10,000 per teleworker in reduced absenteeism and retention costs. (1999, October 27). International Telework Association & Council. Retrieved August 15, 2000, from http://www.telecommute.org/TeleworkAmerica/twa_research_results.htm

Ferguson, K. E. (1984). *The feminist case against bureaucracy.* Philadelphia: Temple University Press.

Ferree, M. M., & Martin, P. Y. (1995). Doing the work of the movement: Feminist organizations. In M. M. Ferree & P. Y. Martin (Eds.), *Feminist organizations: Harvest of the new women's movement.* Philadelphia: Temple University Press.

Franco, R. l. (1997, June 16). No, really, I am working. *Forbes, 159,* 39.

Fraser, N. (1990/91). Rethinking the public sphere: A contribution to the critique of actually existing democracy. *Social Text, 25–26,* 56–80.

Friedman, S. D., Christensen, P., & DeGroot, J. (1998, November-December). Work and life: The end of the zero-sum game. *Harvard Business Review, 76,* 119–129.

Froggatt, C. (2000). Telework: Distance makes a difference. *Home Office Computing, 18*(8), 20.

Garsten, C. (1999). Betwixt and between: Temporary employees as liminal subjects in flexible organizations. *Organization Studies, 20,* 601–617.

Glucksmann, M. A. (1998). "What a difference a day makes": A theoretical and historical exploration of temporality and gender. *Sociology, 32,* 239–258.

Goodall, H. L., Jr. (1999). Casing the academy for community. *Communication Theory, 9,* 463–494.

Gregersen, H. B., & Black, J. S. (1992). Antecedents to commitment to a parent company and a foreign operation. *Academy of Management Journal, 35,* 65–90.

Habermas, J. (1987). *The theory of communicative action, Vol. 2: Lifeworld and system* (Thomas McCarthy, Trans.). Boston: Beacon Press.

Haddon, L., & Silverstone, R. (1995). Telework and the changing relation of home and work. In N. Heap, R. Thomas, G. Einon, R. Mason, & H. Mackay (Eds.), *Information technology and society: A reader* (pp. 400–412). London: Open University.

Hall, E. T. (1981). *Beyond culture.* New York: Anchor Books.

Hall, E. T. (1989). *The silent language.* New York: Anchor Books.

Haraway, D. (1990). Manifesto for cyborgs: Science, technology, and socialist feminism in the 1980s. In N. Fraser & L. J. Nicholson (Eds.), *Feminism/postmodernism* (pp. 190–233). New York: Routledge.

Haraway, D. (1991). *Simians, cyborgs, and women: The reinvention of nature*. New York: Routledge.
Hassard, J. (1996). Images of time in work and organization. In S. R. Clegg, C. Hardy, & W. R. Nord (Eds.), *Handbook of Organization Studies* (pp. 581–598). Thousand Oaks, CA: Sage.
Helgesen, S. (1990). *The female advantage: Women's ways of leadership*. New York: Doubleday.
Hendrix, K. E. (2002). "Did being Black introduce bias into your study?": Attempting to mute the race-related research of Black scholars. *Howard Journal of Communication, 13*, 153–171.
Hill, E. J., Hawkins, A. J., & Miller, B. C. (1996). Work and family in the virtual office: Perceived influences of mobile telework. *Family Relations, 45*, 293–301.
Hill, E. J., Miller, B. C., Weiner, S. P., & Colihan, J. (1998). Influences of the virtual office on aspects of work and work/life balance. *Personnel Psychology, 51*, 667–683.
Hochschild, A. R. (1997). *The time bind: When work becomes home and home becomes work*. New York: Henry Holt.
Hylmö, A. (2001). *Telecommuting as viewed through cultural lenses: Discourses of utopia, identity, and mystery*. Unpublished doctoral dissertation, Purdue University, West Lafayette, IN.
Hylmö, A. (2003). Women, men, and changing organizations: An organization culture examination of gendered experiences of telecommuting. In P. Buzzanell, H. Sterk, & L. Turner (Eds.), *Gendered approaches to applied communication* (pp. 47–68). Thousand Oaks, CA: Sage.
Hylmö, A., & Buzzanell, P. (2002). Telecommuting as viewed through cultural lenses: An empirical investigation of the discourses of utopia, identity, and mystery. *Communication Monographs, 69*, 329–356.
Iannello, K. (1992). *Decisions without hierarchy: Feminist interventions in organization theory and practice*. New York: Routledge.
Israel, B. (2002). *Bachelor girl*. New York: HarperCollins.
Ivarsson, S. (2001). *Kvinnors karriärväg mot chefsskap: Om könsrelaterade monster i karriärsutvecklingsprocessen*. Stockholm, Sweden: Arbetslivsinstitutet.
Janis, I. (1982). *Groupthink*. Dallas, TX: Houghton Mifflin.
Janss, S. (2001, March 12). Teleworking top 10: Questions to think about before you set up your teleworkers. *Network World*, 57.
Kanter, R. M. (1977). *Men and women of the corporation*. New York: Basic Books.
Kayany, J. M., Wotring, C. E., & Forrest, E. J. (1996). Relational control and interactive media choice in technology-mediated communication situations. *Human Communication Research, 22*, 399–421.
Kendall, L. (1999). Reconceptualizing "cyberspace": Methodological considerations for on-line research. In S. Jones (Ed.), *Doing internet research: Critical issues and methods for examining the net.* (pp. 57–74.) London: Sage.
Keough, C. M. (1998). The case of the aggrieved expatriate. *Management Communication Quarterly, 11*, 453–459.
Kerri, J. N. (1976). Studying voluntary associations as adaptive mechanisms: A review of anthropological perspectives. *Current Anthropology, 17*, 23–44.
Khaifa, M., & Davidson, R. (2000). Exploring the telecommuting paradox. *Communications of the ACM, 43*(3), 29–31.
Khatri, S. (2000, December). Where's the voice in remote access? Make telecommuting a cinch with service advances to workers' homes. *Communication News, 37*, 24.
Kompast, M., & Wagner, I. (1998). Telework: Managing spatial, temporal, and cultural boundaries. In P. J. Jackson & J. M. van der Wielen (Eds.), *Teleworking: International perspectives from telecommuting to virtual organisation* (pp. 95–117). London: Routledge.
Kraut, R. E., & Grambsch, P. (1987). Home-based white collar employment: Lesson from the 1980 census. *Social Forces, 66*, 410–426.
Kugelmass, J. (1995). *Telecommuting: A manager's guide to flexible work arrangements*. New York: Lexington Books.
Kunda, G. (1992). *Engineering culture*. Philadelphia: Temple University Press.
Kurland, N. B. & Bailey, D. E. (1999). Telework: The advantages and challenges of working here, there, anywhere, and anytime. *Organizational Dynamics, 28*(2), 53–68.

Langhoff, J. (1996). *The telecommuter's advisor: Working in the fast lane*. Newport, RI: Aegis.

Lee, J. (2001). Leader-member exchange, perceived organizational justice, and cooperative communication. *Management Communication Quarterly, 14,* 574–589

Loker, S. (2000). Interweaving home and work spheres: Gender and the Vermont knitters. In C. B. Hennon, S. Loker, & R. Walker (Eds.), *Gender and home-based employment* (pp. 189–212). Westport, CT: Auburn House.

Lont, C. (1988). Redwood Records: Principles and profit in women's music. In B. Bate & A. Taylor (Eds.), *Women communicating: Studies of women's talk* (pp. 233–250). Norwood, NJ: Ablex.

Maguire, M., & Mohtar, L. F. (1994). Performance and the celebration of a subaltern counterpublic. *Text and Performance Quarterly, 14,* 238–252.

Markham, A. N. (1998). *Life online: Researching real experience in virtual space*. Walnut Creek, CA: Altamira.

Martin, J. (1990). Rethinking feminist organizations. *Gender and Society, 4,* 182–206.

Martin, J. (1992). *Cultures in organizations: Three perspectives*. New York: Oxford University Press.

Martin, J. (1994). The organization of exclusion: Institutionalization of sex inequality, gendered faculty jobs and gendered knowledge in organizational theory and research. *Organization, 1,* 401–443.

Martin, P. Y., & Collinson, D. (2002). "Over the pond and across the water": Developing the field of gendered organizations. *Gender, Work, and Organization, 9,* 244–265.

Maruca, R. F. (1998, July-August). How do you manage an off-site team? *Harvard Business Review, 76,* 22–27.

Matheson, K. (1992). Women and computer technology. In M. Lea (Ed.), *Contexts of computer-mediated communication* (pp. 66–88). New York: Harvester Wheatsheaf.

Matei, S., Ball-Rokeach, S. J., Wilson, M. E., Gibbs, J., & Hoyt, E. G. (2001). Metamorphosis: A field research methodology for studying communication technology and community. *Electronic Journal of Communication, 11*(2), 1–34.

McGerty, L. J. (2000). "Nobody lives only in cyberspace": Gendered subjectivities and domestic use of the internet. *Cyberpsychology and Behavior, 3,* 895–899.

McLuhan, M. (1965). *Understanding media: The extensions of man*. New York: McGraw-Hill.

Meade, J. (1993). *Home, sweet office*. Princeton, NJ: Peterson's.

Meyerson, D. E. (1991). "Normal" ambiguity?: A glimpse of an organizational culture. In P. Frost, L. Moore, M. Louis, C. Lundberg, & J. Martin (Eds.), *Reframing organizational culture* (pp. 131–144). Newbury Park, CA: Sage.

Mills, A. J., & Murgatroyd, S. J. (1991). *Organizational rules: A framework for understanding organizational action*. Philadelphia: Open University Press.

Mirchandani, K. (1998a). No longer a struggle? Teleworkers' reconstruction of the work-nonwork boundary. In P. J. Jackson & J. M. van der Wielen (Eds.), *Teleworking: International perspectives from telecommuting to the virtual organisation* (pp. 118–135). London: Routledge.

Mirchandani, K. (1998b). Protecting the boundary: Teleworker insights on the expansive concept of "work." *Gender and Society, 12,* 168–187.

Mirchandani, K. (1999) Legitimizing work: Telework and the gendered reification of the work-nonwork dichotomy. *Canadian Review of Sociology and Anthropology, 36,* 87–101.

Mumby, D. K. (1996). Feminism, postmodernism, and organizational communication studies: A critical reading. *Management Communication Quarterly, 9,* 259–295.

Mumby, D. K. (2000). Communication, organization, and the public sphere: A feminist perspective. In P. M. Buzzanell (Ed.), *Rethinking organizational and managerial communication from feminist perspectives* (pp. 3–23). Thousand Oaks, CA: Sage.

Mumby, D. K., & Putnam, L. (1992). The politics of emotion: A feminist reading of bounded rationality. *Academy of Management Review, 17,* 465–486.

Mumby, D. K., & Stohl, C. (1998). Commentary: Feminist perspectives on organizational communication. *Management Communication Quarterly, 11,* 622–634.

Munro, R. (1999). The cultural performance of control. *Organization Studies, 20,* 619–40.

Murphy, J. (2001). Is telecommuting losing favor? *Risk and Insurance, 12*(2), p. 4.

Myburgh, S. (1998). Cyberspace: A new environment for women. *Women and Environments International, Vol 42–43*. Retrieved from http://80-Web6.epnet.com.proxy.ohiolink.edu:9099

National Foundation for Women Business Owners. (2000). Technology boosts growth in home-based businesses. Retrieved December 11, 2000, from http://www.nfwbo.org

Newsom, V. (2003). Contained empowerment: A study of online third wave feminisms. Unpublished manuscript.

Nilles, J. M. (1977). *The telecommunication transportation tradeoff?* New York: John Wiley.

Nilles, J. M. (1988). *Transportation Research, 22*, 301–317.

Nippert-Eng, C. E. (1996). *Home and work: Negotiating boundaries through everyday life*. Chicago: University of Chicago Press.

Odih, P. (1999). Gendered time in the age of deconstruction. *Time & Society, 8*, 9–38.

Olson, M. H., & Primps, S. B. (1984). Working at home with computers: Work and nonwork issues. *Journal of Social Issues, 40*, 97–112.

Orbe, M. P. (1998). An outsider within perspective to organizational communication: Explicating the communicative practices of co-cultural group members. *Management Communication Quarterly, 12*, 230–279.

Orbe, M. P., & Warren, K. T. (2000). Different standpoints, different realities: Race, gender, and perceptions of intercultural conflict. *Qualitative Research Reports in Communication, 1*, 51–57.

Padavic, I., & Reskin, B. (2002). *Women and men at work* (2nd ed.). Thousand Oaks, CA: Sage.

Paik, A. (2000, November 30). Working, but not in the office: Columbia firm gives state telecommuting program a try. *Washington Post* (Howard County Extra), p. M5.

Papa, M. J., Auwal, M. A., & Singhal, A. (1997). Organizing for social change within concertive control systems: Member identification, empowerment, and the masking of discipline. *Communication Monographs, 64*, 219–249.

Parker, P. S. (2001). African American women executives' leadership communication within dominant-culture organizations: (Re)conceptualizing notions of collaboration and instrumentality. *Management Communication Quarterly, 15*, 42–82.

Parr, J. (1999). Homeworkers in global perspective. *Feminist Studies, 25*, 227–235.

Perin, C. (1998). Work, space, and time on the threshold of the new economy. In P. Jackson & J. van der Wielen (Eds.), *Teleworking: International perspectives from telecommuting to the virtual organization* (pp. 40–55). London: Routledge.

Perlow, L. A. (1998). Boundary control: The social ordering of work and family time in a high-tech corporation. *Administrative Science Quarterly, 43*, 328–357.

Plant, S. (1995). The future looms: Weaving women and cybernetics. *Body and Society, 1*(4), 55–67.

Plant, S. (1996). On the matrix: Cyberfeminist simulations. In R. Shields (Ed.), *Cultures of internet: Virtual spaces, real histories, living bodies*. (pp. 184–195). London: Sage.

Powell, G. N. (1999). Reflections on the glass ceiling: Recent trends and future prospects. In G. N. Powell's (Ed.), *Handbook of gender and work*, (pp. 325–346). Thousand Oaks, CA: Sage.

Powell, G. N., & Graves, L. M. (2003). *Women and men in management*. (3rd ed.). Thousand Oaks, CA: Sage.

Powell, G. N., & Mainiero, L. A. (1999). Managerial decision making regarding alternative work alternatives. *Journal of Occupational and Organizational Psychology, 72*, 41–56.

Putnam, L. L., Phillips, N., & Chapman, P. (1996). Metaphors of communication and organization. In S. R. Clegg, H. Cynthia, & W. R. Nord (Eds.), *Handbook of Organization Studies* (pp. 375–408). Thousand Oaks, CA: Sage.

Qvartrop, L. (1998). From telework to networking: Definitions and trends. In P. Jackson & J. van der Wielen (Eds.), *Teleworking: International perspectives from telecommuting to the virtual organization* (pp. 21–33). London: Routledge.

Rakow, L. F., & Navarro, V. (1993). Remote mothering and the parallel shift: Women meet the cellular phone. *Critical Studies in Mass Communication, 10*, 144–157.

Rapoport, R., Bailyn, L., Fletcher, J., & Pruitt, B. H. (2002). *Beyond work-family balance: Advancing gender equity and workplace performance*. San Francisco: Jossey-Bass.

Reinelt, C. (1995). Moving onto the terrain of the state: The battered women's movement and the politics of engagement. In M. M. Ferree & P. Y. Martin (Eds.), *Feminist organizations: Harvest of the new women's movement.* Philadelphia: Temple University Press.

Rheingold, H. (1993). *The virtual community: Homesteading on the electronic frontier* (pp. 84–104). Reading, MA: Addison-Wesley.

Roberts, L. (2001a, April) The telework puzzle: Juggling the pieces of a successful telework program. *Home Office Computing, 19,* 90.

Roberts, L. (2001b, April). The remote promotion: Telework can help you attain your career goals. *Home Office Computing, 19,* 68.

Roberts, L. (2001c, April). Tele-resentment: Overcoming colleagues' envy when you're the teleworker. *Home Office Computing, 19,* 69.

Rose, K. (1996, February). The new workforce: Let's be flexible. *HR Focus,* p. 16.

Rothschild-Whitt, J. (1979). The collectivist organization: An alternative to rational-bureaucratic models. *American Sociological Review, 44,* 509–527.

Rothschild, J., & Whitt, J. A. (1986). Worker-owners as an emergent class: Effects of cooperative work on job satisfaction, alienation and stress. *Economic & Industrial Democracy, 7,* 297–317.

Russo, T. C. (1998). Organizational and professional identification: A case of newspaper journalists. *Management Communication Quarterly, 12,* 72–111.

Sahay, S. (1997). Implementation of information technology: A time-space perspective. *Organization Studies, 18,* 229–260.

Schepp, B. (1990). *The telecommuter's handbook.* Thousand Oaks, CA: Pharos Books.

Scott, C. R., & Timmerman, C. E. (1999). Communication technology use and multiple workplace identifications among organizational teleworkers with varied degrees of virtuality. *IEEE Transactions on Professional Communication, 42,* 240–260.

Scott, C. R., Connaughton, S. L., Diaz-Saenz, H. R., Maguire, K., Ramirez, R., Richardson, B., Shaw, S. P., & Morgan, D. (1999). The impacts of communication and multiple identifications on intent to leave: A multimethodological exploration. *Management Communication Quarterly, 12,* 400–435.

Shear, M. D. (2000, November 8). Area governments, firms to encourage telecommuting. *Washington Post* (Prince William County Extra), p. V1.

Sheley, E. (1996). Flexible work options: Beyond 9 to 5. *HR Magazine, 41,* 52–58.

Shotter, J. (1993). *Conversational realities: Constructing life through language.* Thousand Oaks, CA: Sage.

Silver, A. D. (1994). *Enterprising women: Lessons from 100 of the greatest entrepreneurs of our day.* New York: AMACOM.

Silver, S. D., Cohen, B. P., & Crutchfield, J. H. (1994). Status differentiation and information exchange in face-to-face and computer-mediated idea generation. *Social Psychology Quarterly, 57,* 108–123.

Siskos, C. (2001, February). Remote control. *Kiplinger's Personal Finance Magazine, 55,* 28.

Snizek, W. E. (1995). Virtual offices: Some neglected considerations. *Communications of the ACM,* 38(9), 15–17.

Sotirin, P. (2000). "All they do is bitch bitch bitch": Political and interactional features of women's officetalk. *Women and Language, 23,* 19–25.

Spain, D. (1994). *Gendered spaces.* Raleigh: University of North Carolina Press.

Spivak, G. C. (1995). Can the subaltern speak? In B. Ashcroft, G. Griffiths, & H. Tiffin (Eds.), *The postcolonial studies reader* (pp. 24–28). New York: Routledge.

Staggenborg, S. (1995). Can feminist organizations be effective? In M. M. Ferree & P. Y. Martin (Eds.), *Feminist organizations: Harvest of the new women's movement* (pp. 339–355). Philadelphia: Temple University Press.

Staples, D. S. (2001). A study of remote workers and their differences from non-remote workers. *Journal of End User Computing, 13,* 3–14.

Stier, H. & Lewin-Epstein, N. (2001). Welfare regimes, family-supportive policies, and women's employment along the life-course. *American Journal of Sociology, 106,* 1731–1760.

Stohl, C., & Cheney, G. (2001). Participatory processes/paradoxical practices: Communication and the dilemmas of organizational democracy. *Management Communication Quarterly, 14,* 349–407.

Sundström, E. (1999). Should mothers work? Age and attitude in Germany, Italy, and Sweden. *International Journal of Social Welfare, 8,* 193–205.

The telecommuting paradox: Heady growth or revolving door? (1998). TSI, Inc. Retrieved August 15, 2000, from http://www.telsuccess.com/ Telecommuting%20Paradox%20Heady%20Grwth%20or%20Revolving%20Door$798.htm

Trethewey, A. (1999). Disciplined bodies: Women's embodied identities at work. *Organization Studies, 20,* 423–450.

Umiker-Sebeok, J. (1996). Power and construction of gendered spaces. *International Review of Sociology, 6,* 389–403.

Van Maanen, J, & Barley, S. R. (1984). Occupational communities: Culture and control in organizations. *Research in Organizational Behavior, 6,* 287–365.

Vega, G., & Brennan, L. (2000). Isolation and technology: The human disconnect. *Journal of Organizational Change Management, 13,* 468–481.

Wanca-Thibault, M., & Thompkins, P. K. (1998). Speaking like a man (and a woman) about organizational communication: Feminization and feminism as a recognizable voice. *Management Communication Quarterly, 11,* 606–621.

Weijers, T., Meijer, R., & Spoelman, E. (1992, December). Telework remains 'made to measure': The large-scale introduction of telework in Netherlands. *Futures, 24,* 1048–1055.

Wiesenfeld, B. M., Raghuram, S., & Garud, R. (1998). Communication patterns as determinants of organizational identification in a virtual organization. *Journal of Computer Mediated Communication, 3*(4). Retrieved June 7, 2001, from http://jcmc.huji.ac.il/vol3/issue4/wiesenfeld.html

Wolf, F. R. (2001, April 12). "Telework" would ease the commute: If more employees worked from home using modern technology, roads would be less clogged, says Rep. Frank Wolf. *Washington Post,* p. T5.

Wolfe, S. (2001). Identifying best telecommuting candidate is a must. *Business Journal, 21*(6), 16.

CHAPTER CONTENTS

4   Meetings: Discursive Sites for Building and Fragmenting Community

KAREN TRACY
AARON DIMOCK
University of Colorado

Meetings are talk-saturated events in which people come together to tackle a variety of explicit goals and tacit concerns. They enable accomplishments of people's most valued ideals (e.g., democracy, voice); at the same time, meetings are also practices that are the frequent objects of derision and complaint. The review synthesizes and critiques descriptive and normative ideas about meetings, drawing on both academic and popular literature. After a definitional discussion of the term and a brief history of how meetings came to be, the chapter turns to its main focus: the routine and problematic practices of organizational work meetings and public meetings. Within each type, special attention is given to how meetings build and fracture community and communities. The conclusion argues why future communication research should foreground meetings and take them as objects of study—rather than, as has been the usual practice, treat them as noninteresting containers for other communication processes.

M eetings are undoubtedly the primary communicative practice that institutional groups use to accomplish important goals. Public hearings; teams in workplaces; school, city, and interorganizational councils; and grassroots movements all do work in meetings. It is only a slight exaggeration to say that meeting is what groups are all about. Through meetings groups solve and create problems, give information and misinformation, develop and rework policies, make and retool decisions, and while doing these focal activities build or fracture a sense of community among participants, and solidify or cause tension among the communities that comprise any particular group. Meetings are where groups celebrate and challenge institutionally important values; they are also sites in which people display their own power and resist the demands of others. The

AUTHORS' NOTE: The authors thank the Spring Semester 2003 participants of the University of Colorado's Communication Department graduate seminar (Meetings: Their Practices and Problems). Their lively and insightful discussion helped us frame issues in this chapter.

Correspondence: Karen Tracy, Department of Communication, UCB 270, University of Colorado, Boulder, CO 80309; email: Karen.Tracy@colorado.edu having of meetings is linked to some of society's most valued ideals—giving voice, fairness, democracy. At the same time, meetings are among everyone's favorite things to hate—occasions to be escaped, complained about, and derogated.

The purpose of this chapter is to review and synthesize what scholars know about communication in work and public meetings. In focusing on meetings rather than, for instance, decision making (Hirokawa & Poole, 1996), participatory democracy (Gastil, 1992), or bona fide groups (Frey, 2003), this chapter implicitly advances an argument as to how future scholarly work ought to shift its focus. A considerable amount of research has occurred in the meeting setting; however, that the occasion being studied is a meeting is usually backgrounded and treated as a descriptive detail in a study's setting. Our chapter inverts the usual focus: meetings as a gathering where people come together to talk is our focus. To build this review of meetings, work is examined in a variety of academic and popular traditions. Studies that asked a communication-relevant question in a meeting context, or theorized about a communicative practice that should be occurring in meetings were inspected. To each the current study asked: How does this article or book inform scholars' understanding of meetings? By the chapter's end, the advantage of foregrounding meetings in communication research should clearly emerge.

The chapter begins by sorting through some complexities in defining and categorizing meetings. Then, as a brief historical overview, the chapter traces how meetings came to be such a common societal practice. Next, attention is turned to the two categories of meetings that are the chapter's focus: organizational work meetings and public meetings. Within each category, the study identifies what has been taken for granted in prior theory and research, summarizes key conclusions within normative and descriptive traditions, and describes what is known about how meeting purposes are accomplished discursively. In considering discursive functions, the study devotes particular attention to the relational activities of building and fracturing community and communities. The conclusion gathers together argumentative threads, making clear what taking the meeting context seriously would entail and why future research should do so.

DEFINITIONAL ISSUES: WHAT COUNTS AS A MEETING?

What counts as a meeting? In ordinary usage, *meeting* has a broad meaning and a more focused one. This difference can be seen as the difference between using meeting as a verb and as a noun. Its verb form, *to meet*, means simply for people to come together. This coming together is done with purpose rather than accidentally, but just about any number of people for any kind of purpose can be described as doing the activity of meeting. In contrast, meeting as a noun is used more restrictively. Not all activities where people intentionally come together would be referred to as *a meeting*.

Schwartzman (1989), in one of the few books that provides a scholarly analysis explicitly focused on meetings, defined meetings as communicative events that

TABLE 1
Definitions of Meeting

Definition	Examples
People coming together intentionally for a variety of activities	• I'm **meeting** my sister for lunch.
	• The International Communication Association **meets** in May.
	• They're going **to meet** with a counselor to see if they can patch together their marriage.
	• My coworkers and I **met** for beers on Friday.
Three or more people assembling to address issues of a group's functioning	• At our weekly management **meeting**, we'll be deciding whether to change the process for job transfers.
	• A public **meeting** is scheduled next week to get input on where to site the homeless shelter.
	• My research team had an informal **meeting** to plan what each of us should do when we run the experiment.
	• At the city council **meeting**, numerous citizens spoke out against the proposed begging ordinance.

involve three or more people, who gather together to address issues related to the functioning of a group or its larger community. Not everyone agrees that a meeting requires at least three people—some see two as sufficient (e.g., Boden, 1995; Volkema & Niederman, 1995); however, only a small set of functions are considered a meeting. Table 1 illustrates each meaning.

This chapter focuses on the second meaning. Admittedly, there remains ambiguity about boundaries; specifying when a set of people talking together constitutes a group and determining what kinds of activities count as contributing to a group's functioning are by no means straightforward. In practice, however, meeting seems to be reserved for sets of people whose primary purpose in assembling is to (a) give and get information, (b) coordinate and plan future actions, or (c) deliberate, problem solve, and make decisions. Sets of people whose central purpose in gathering is to provide self-focused enrichment (e.g., book clubs), professional help, or peer-level social support are less likely to be referred to as conducting a meeting. In addition, while almost everyone would regard social and celebratory activities as contributing to a group's functioning, if these functions are the main activity—a party, an awards ceremony—people do not generally think of the occasion as a meeting.

Interestingly, while the giving and getting of information that occurs in workplace training is often regarded as a meeting (Volkema & Niederman, 1995), when training and education occur in other settings, such occasions are less likely to be labeled a meeting. The giving and getting of information that goes on in classrooms (Cook-Gumperz & Szymanski, 2001; Ford, 1999), colloquia (Grimshaw,

1989; Tracy, 1997), and advising sessions (Erickson & Shultz, 1982; He, 1995), as well as through a range of professional activities such as mediation (Folger & Jones, 1994; Greatbatch & Dingwall, 1999), medical rounds (Atkinson, 1995, 1999), or genetic counseling (Sarangi & Clarke, 2002), are usually seen as discrete communicative activities. When the participants in a gathering can be framed as professionals delivering a service to clients, or sets of people whose purpose in talking is for general edification rather than an immediate institutional goal, an occasion is unlikely to be seen as a meeting. Typically, gatherings that have their own commonly used names (e.g., classes, support groups, medical rounds) are not usually thought of as meetings in the narrower sense, although it is always possible to do so.

Meetings might best be thought of in terms of prototype theory (Rosch, Mervis, Gray, Johnson, & Boyce-Braem, 1976). Just as a robin is a more typical example of a bird than an ostrich, gatherings in which people come together in work or public settings to make decisions are a robin-kind of meeting. A gathering that begins as three school friends having lunch together but evolves without planning into a discussion about an upcoming joint project proposal is an ostrich-kind of meeting.

Having arrived at a rough working definition of meetings, a second question concerns their types: What would be the best way to categorize meetings? Degree of spontaneity seems to be one criterion. In a study of a mental health center, Schwartzman (1989) distinguished scheduled from unscheduled meetings; in another study that looks across a range of business settings, Boden (1994) separated formal and informal meetings. Formal meetings occur at pre-specified times and involve a chair and an agenda, whereas informal meetings occur among smaller sets of people without an appointed leader or written agenda. Another way that meetings have been categorized is in terms of foci and format. Volkema and Niederman (1995) categorized meetings into six types based on whether they have a single focus (e.g., brainstorming about a particular issue) or are multi-focused (e.g., announcements, reports, and then making a decision), and based on their format (e.g., hierarchical, organic, or a combination). Typologies have also been built from the ground up. Analyzing the meetings that comprised the Meetings at Work (MAP) Corpus, 15 hours of audio- or videotaped meetings collected at a large multinational airline company, Bilbow (2002) distinguished among (a) cross-departmental coordination meetings, (b) weekly department meetings, and (c) brainstorming meetings. In a study focused mostly on the strategic use of emotion in meetings in university settings, Bailey (1983) distinguished among meeting types based on their emotional style and management. Ad hoc committees, where people come together a few times to make a specific decision with relatively clear and agreed-upon criteria, differ from elite committees (selective sets of people put together for longer units of time to advise on a range of issues). Both of these types differ from arena committee, a meeting group comprised to insure that the range of interests in the larger institution are represented (e.g., a meeting of department chairs). Among these three types, arena committees engaged in the most heated and expressive behavior, whereas ad hoc committees exhibited the most rational demeanor.

The above systems for categorizing meetings are interesting and useful; at the same time, all can be seen as operating within a taken-for-granted frame that could be labeled organizational work meetings. Organizational work meetings differ in important ways from those that occur in public life between elected officials or experts of one type or another, and citizens. The divide between public meetings and organizational work meetings perhaps is the biggest one distinguishing among meeting types.

Public meetings differ from their organizational counterparts in three ways. First, who may attend a public meeting is relatively open-ended. McComas (2003), for instance, defined a public meeting as a *nonrestricted* gathering of three or more people who gather for various purposes (e.g., providing information, seeking input, discussing issues, solving problems, and developing recommendations). In contrast, organizational meetings usually have a person in charge who decides who will be allowed (or required) to attend a meeting. In that sense, organizational work meetings have restricted attendance rights. In fact, one commonplace piece of advice given to meeting planners in popular meeting manuals is to consider carefully who should be included or excluded from a meeting (e.g., Hindle, 1999; Timm, 1997). A second feature separating the two kinds of meetings is size. In general, public meetings tend to be much larger than organizational ones. In a survey of 35 groups that came from organizations ranging in size from 5-person to 4000, Volkema and Niederman (1995) found group meeting size to range from 4 to 56 with a mean size of 13 persons at meetings. A public meeting could be this small as when, for instance, a hearing or a regularly occurring council only attracts a handful of citizens, but public meetings are often large (at least 100). Ryfe (2002), in a study of 16 organizations, categorized groups as "small (less than 50 members), medium (50 to several hundred members), and large (entire communities of national publics)" (p. 362). Related to this second difference is a third one. Community and other kinds of public groups tend to use relatively formal participation and turn-taking practices such as parliamentary procedure, particularly as they get larger (see Ryfe, 2002); this contrasts with organizational groups' usage of, at most, moderately structured interaction (i.e., using an agenda), and quite often unstructured, ordinary conversational exchanges. In saying that community groups use parliamentary procedure, it is important to note that participants frequently do not use this set of procedures expertly (Weitzel & Geist, 1998). It is, however, the usual frame within which talk is conducted. In sum, unlimited attendance rights, a larger group size, and a participation format that has strong restrictions on speaking rights (e.g., strictly enforced topical requirements, speaking time limitations, and limited opportunities for certain parties to do follow-up) mean that public meetings face rather different communicative challenges than organizational meetings usually confront.

A HISTORY: HOW MEETINGS CAME INTO BEING

Gathering together in order to talk and to reach decisions about the common future has become an increasingly important means of social integration. As a means of bonding and distinction for the elite, the stylization of meeting behavior has replaced the stylization of eating and drinking. (van Vree, 1999, p. 5)

In a fascinating book Wilbert van Vree (1999) traced the history of meetings from the early Middle Ages to the present. Building upon Elias's (1994) argument in *The Civilizing Process*, van Vree showed how meetings, and rules of conduct that were a part of them, were key contributors to European countries' evolution toward less violent, more civilized societies. In fact, books offering guidelines about meeting behavior only began to be written when papal or monarchical pronouncements, swordfighter dueling, water torture tests of truth, and battles were no longer the preferred ways to settle conflict.

In the early Middle Ages, when men were primarily farmers, meetings served essentially military aims. A meeting would be held to finalize a plan to go to war. In these meetings, called *things*, participants voted with their feet. If they did not like the intended military action, they would absent themselves from a thing. In so doing, a member exempted self from the military decision the group was taking. To fail to attend a meeting, however, always carried some risk of punishment. As power came to be more centralized under monarchs, meetings became events— called by government officials or kings—in which attendees were required to be present and affirm the monarch's plan. It was not until near the end of the Middle Ages that the right to call meetings existed for anyone other than the monarch and his representatives. The emergence of meetings, as places where participants actually talked with each other to arrive at joint decisions, evolved at different times in the countries of Western Europe, with the Netherlands being among the first. The Netherlands's monarchs were relatively weak. In addition, the geography of the Netherlands confronted its citizens with a pressing need to coordinate water regulation and dikes across extended areas. Most likely for these two reasons, meetings, as we now conceive of them, originated in the Netherlands.

An important force in the emergence of the contemporary meeting genre was the Protestant Reformation. For the first time, rather than priests instructing what the Bible meant, lay people were being asked for their own thoughts. In these discussion-oriented, relatively egalitarian settings, rules began to emerge about meeting conduct. In particular, rules specified how participants were to regulate their emotional behavior. Typically read at the start of meetings, rules announced what people were to do, or more often, refrain from doing; they also specified what fines would be levied if participants broke rules. During these early Reformation times a meeting would routinely begin with announcements indicating that participants would be fined if they were caught sleeping, swearing, pulling knives, or throwing glasses. In these earlier times, meeting and eating were almost always co-occurring activities.

In the late 1700s parliamentary procedures were developed and first used extensively in Western Europe, North America, Australia, and Japan. "[F]rom approximately 1770 to 1870, national parliaments, parliamentary government and restricted voting rights emerged" (van Vree, 1999, p. 205). In these parliamentary settings, talking rather than fighting became the vehicle through which groups in society began to resolve differences. In general, the frequency of meetings increased as societies adopted and broadened their commitments to equality and democracy. It is undoubtedly the importance of these two ideals in 19th century American life that contributed to the frequency of meetings and led French traveler, Alexis de Tocqueville (1945) to be so amazed at the number of associational activities in the United States. At a practical level, then, doing democracy means having meetings. As van Vree (1999) wryly put it: "Democracy is the dream, meeting the actual practice." (p. 207)

In 1845 a clerk in the Massachusetts House of Representatives wrote the first meeting manual for legislative assemblies in the United States.[1] However, it was Major Henry Martin Robert, an engineering officer in the U.S. army, a man active in religious and civic groups, who wrote the manual that was to become the standard guide for meeting conduct for much of the 20th century. Drawing upon Congress as a model, *Robert's Rules of Order* sought to provide ordinary societal groups methods for organizing and conducting themselves. The rules gave guidelines describing the duty of officers and the meaning and names of ordinary motions. The rules also spelled out how motions could be objected to, amended, and debated. By 1997 the manual was on its ninth edition and had sold more than 4,450,000 copies (van Vree, 1999).

With the increasing internationalization of industry following World War II, the number of meetings in businesses and other work organizations began to increase dramatically. One oft-quoted statistic, from Mintzberg's (1973) study, estimated that over 60% of a manager's time is spent in meetings. In a recent survey of Dutch companies carried out while preparing his history, van Vree (1999) found that companies with fewer than 10 people spent at least 10% of their time preparing, executing, and concluding meetings while organizations with 500 or more people spent around 75% of their time on these activities.

Accompanying the growth in organizational meetings was a growing dissatisfaction with them. Meetings were routinely experienced as ineffective, unproductive, boring, and wasteful (Schwartzman, 1989). Soon psychology, communication, and business experts were stepping forward to advise on the problems with meetings. A large set of conference-meeting manuals appeared seeking teach people how to participate in and lead this increasingly pervasive form. In these new meeting manuals, the emphasis changed from teaching parliamentary procedure to teaching people decision-making procedures and how to understand and interact with others, particularly those judged to be difficult. Among the more successful books was then-speech professor, H. P. Zelko's *Successful Conference and Discussion Techniques*, published in 1957. Zelko's book was translated into multiple languages; in the Netherlands, it was reprinted 13 times in the period from 1963 to 1993 (van

Vree, 1999). In the 1970s and 1980s the number of published meeting manuals continued to grow. As of 1990 about 150 different manuals had appeared just in the United States and United Kingdom. (Later, this chapter looks at a small selection of current manuals.)

In their historical context, meetings clearly first emerged as a new form of social interaction and political cooperation that offered societies a more satisfying, inclusive, and peaceful way to coordinate and deal with differences among individuals and groups of people. Later, as communicative conduct routinely became more controlled (and such control was expected), meetings no longer were understood as the societal alternative to a duel or a dunking. In today's world, meetings are inescapable, no longer an option. Not only are they necessitated by the democratic ideals held by many societies and community groups, but they are a requirement of a work world that expects efforts among different departments and agencies to be coordinated, design and manufacturing of complex products and services to be accomplished quickly and well, and the selling of products to attend to global markets. With these transformations of work and public life, meetings have become an ordinary facet of living, a way people spend time with each other, sometimes satisfying, often times not, but not a choice. A world without meetings is unimaginable. Consider, now, how meetings are enacted, talked about, and criticized in organizational and public contexts.

ORGANIZATIONAL WORK MEETINGS

Work meetings come in many sizes and flavors. Consider just a few of the meetings that could be found occurring in a typical day at a school district's administration center.

• *Meeting A:* The superintendent and several other high-ranking administrators in a school district hold their weekly meeting with the president and vice president of the school board. Seated in the superintendent's office at his small conference table, the group is drinking coffee as the superintendent gives the board officers information about the past week's happenings; the group's task is to finalize the agenda for the upcoming public board meeting.

• *Meeting B:* A group of nine people, including eight middle and high school teachers and a district staff member, are concluding a series of monthly meetings that has had the task of revising the district's language arts curriculum. The documents (proposals) that the group has generated through its year-long meetings are scheduled to be presented at the next public board meeting for discussion and voting.

• *Meeting C:* An upset mother is involved in a meeting with her son's elementary school principal and the principal's immediate supervisor at the district office. Her son's history project was not allowed to be displayed because it was judged to have discriminatory material in it. She is angry, seeing it as unfair, and wants the district office to reprimand the principal for the decision.

• *Meeting D:* The council of middle school principals is having its regular monthly meeting. Twelve of the 14 members are present. After gaining approval of the previous month's minutes, accomplished with a number of person-directed teases and organizational in-jokes, the group is turning its attention to the first item of a rather lengthy agenda.

Meetings Versus Groups

Meetings such as the above are ubiquitous, the bread and butter of organizational life. Only in the last 10–15 years, however, have scholars begun to look seriously at them. The reasons for this inattention are many; one contributing factor is the dominant frame adopted in much research. By and large, communication scholars have treated the *group* as the focus and investigated features of general group functioning. Review essays (e.g., Bonita & Hollingshead, 1997; Frey, 1994a, 1994b, 1994c, 1996) and handbooks (Frey, 2003; Frey, Gouran, & Poole, 1999; Hirokawa & Poole, 1996) about the state of group communication research shows that decision making and problemsolving (Bormann, 1996; Gouran, 1991; Gouran, Hirokawa, & Leatham, 1993, Hirokawa & Salazar, 1999) as well as related activities such as argument-making (Meyers, 1997; Meyers & Brashers, 1998), information processing (Propp, 1999), and leadership (Pavitt, 1999) have been the paramount focus, albeit not the only focus. Other foci include relational issues in groups (Keyton, 1999), creativity (Jarboe, 1999), and nonverbal dimensions (Ketrow, 1999). For the most part, though, group research has been conducted in laboratory settings among sets of unrelated people who have assembled to do a research task. This research tradition has generated valuable insights into general group processes; however, it is difficult to know how and if the conclusions apply to actual meetings with their considerably more complicated task and relational histories.

Perhaps most useful for this focus on meetings is a review (Sunwolf & Seibold, 1999; see also Seibold & Krikorian, 1997) that identified and assessed a large array of procedures that have been developed to help groups manage four decision making activities. A first activity groups must deal with is structuring their group process and the group time. Procedures such as Robert's Rules of Order, a written agenda, or a discussion format (e.g., symposium or roundtable) help groups do this. A second function that most meeting groups must manage is determining the best way to frame and analyze their problems. Frequently used procedures such as reflective thinking, assigning a devil's advocate, and using the Delphi technique help groups with this, as do less commonly employed, more issue- or problem-specific procedures such as Program Evaluation and Review Techniques (PERT) or the use of focus groups. Practices to assist groups in framing and analyzing are by far the most developed kind of procedures. Sunwolf and Seibold (1999) identified 28 different ones in this category. A third challenge that groups face in meetings is generating ideas and options. Procedures such as brainstorming, buzz groups, and a lateral thinking approach all seek to help groups do this. Finally, there are a set of procedures that help groups come to agreement. Most basically, groups need to decide if they will make decisions by consensus or use some type of voting procedure. If a vote is to be taken, there has to be a clear decision rule (e.g., simple majority, plurality, or unanimity) and the way a vote is to taken (e.g., raising hands or calling out, secretly or openly, or round robin or simultaneously) needs to be agreed upon. In their review, Sunwolf and Seibold (1999) summarized the results of a vast number of comparative studies of different combinations of these procedures. How these conclusions should be extrapolated to groups having meetings, given the preponderance of results coming from laboratory studies, is difficult to determine.

Scholars criticize the dominance of the laboratory paradigm. The importance of studying existing groups, with all of their boundary conflicts and relational issues, has been well argued by Putnam and Stohl (Putnam, 1994; Putnam & Stohl, 1990, 1996; Stohl & Holmes, 1993; Stohl & Putnam, 1994, 2003). Indeed, communication researchers are increasingly studying actual existing groups—often labeled *bona fide groups* (Frey, 2003). Bona fide group studies include mountain-climbing groups (Houston, 2003), surgery teams (Lammers & Krikorian, 1997), youth programs (Howell, Brock & Hauser, 2003) and support groups on the internet (Alexander, Peterson, & Hollingshead, 2003), as well as meeting-oriented groups (Greenbaum & Query, 1999; Meier, 2003).

Under the bona fide group rubric are many interesting case studies (e.g., Frey, 1994c, 2003). There are, however, two reasons for not subsuming an interest in meetings within this frame. First, the label itself implicitly directs attention to the laboratory setting, placing it and the questions about communication that this setting has generated as the standard of comparison. Marking a group as a bona fide one rather than a laboratory one reinforces that studying groups outside the lab as unusual and in need of comment. This also makes experimental results the argumentative anchoring point. This implicit tethering is problematic, as the agenda for experimental research has been dictated by what is possible when researchers bring together strangers who have little investment in the task they are to do. Research on meetings moves attention away from the issue of whether it is better to study groups in the lab or in the world—treating the later as a given—and pursues a set of issues relevant to actual meetings. Second, the shape and content of communication in meetings, where talk about a group's functioning is the focal activity, is quite different than sites in which talk is secondary to another activity (e.g., surgery or mountain climbing). Bona fide group studies would not dispute this difference; however, it is not foregrounded. The meetings concept, in contrast, highlights that the research focus is upon a talk-saturated practice that occurs among people invested, at least to some degree, in their relationships and the task.

Consensus Versus Voting and Majority Rule

When the focus of attention shifts to actual institutional groups as they struggle how best to accomplish goals through meetings, a key issue becomes how to run a meeting: In particular, should consensus or majority rule be used to make decisions? The trade-offs in using these two decision-making approaches are relatively clear, although deciding in any particular meeting group whether the situation better matches the criteria that favor one rather than the other approach may not be so easy.

The 1970s in the United States was a time of social movements that involved frequent criticism of the status quo. Groups committed to social change sought to alter existing power structures and refashion workplaces and other institutions so they would be more responsive to people's needs. Part of the commitment of many social change organizations, in contrast to most other organizations at the time, was to function as participatory democracies. Within a participatory democracy framework, decisions were expected to be made (a) directly by all involved, rather than by representatives, (b) face-to-face, (c) through consensus rather than voting, and (d) the group was to be one in which all participants were equal. Behind these efforts lay a fervent idealism that Mansbridge (1973) described as the following:

> The belief that if an institution makes its members feel powerless or discourages them from participating in decisions, if it makes them unequal or allows inequalities of influence, if it makes people feel disrespected or forces them to conform to norms they don't believe in—then it is not worth their commitment. (p. 354)

Participatory democracy is a powerful and attractive ideal; however, making it work as a meeting practice is often difficult. A first and most obvious challenge is that it presupposes a relatively small group of no more than 15–20 people (Mansbridge, 1973). When institutional and community groups are bigger than this, which they often are, meetings become unwieldy—but this is not the only trouble. Consider the particulars of Helpline, a crisis center, and one of the best known extended case studies of a group using consensus methods (Mansbridge, 1980).

Begun in 1967 by two seminary students, it was a 41-person organization by 1973 when Mansbridge began her study. Helpline was an alternative organization committed to workplace democracy. Its members met frequently within their different work units (e.g., switchboard or emergency van) and as a larger group, making decisions by consensus. To decide by consensus requires a group to continue talking when there are conflicts, seeking to find solutions that everyone in the group can at least support, if not enthusiastically endorse. Helpline's frequent face-to-face meetings were crucial to the organization's sense of community and connectedness. Through talk and the use of consensus decision-making, the group and subgroups fostered senses of their units as committed to a common good and valuing all members' input. Consensus decision-making knits a group together and helps them achieve that much valued, but frequently elusive goal of being a real community. Consensus procedures, as Mansbridge (1980) puts it, give "legal support to the drive for harmony that appears in most face-to face groups." (p.164)

A drive to consensus with its accompanying concern for others, however, is not an unmitigated good, a fact that Janis (1982; see also Cline, 1994) makes apparent in his analysis of the advisory meetings that led to the Bay of Pigs invasion during the Kennedy administration. When meeting members become too concerned about achieving harmony and fearful of expressing dissent, the group may fall prey to the vividly-labeled problem of groupthink. Most organizational meetings are not making decisions that have the scope of impact seen in the Bay of Pigs; however, the problem is the same. A commitment to making decisions by consensus often leads in practice to the elimination of minority views. There is no way for a person to hold onto a minority position, yet let the group proceed with a decision without the member giving assent to the dominant view. Voting can keep alive a minority viewpoint on a situation. In addition, consensus decision making "generates imprecision. In order to reach unanimous agreement, groups formulate their collective decision so as to blur potential disagreement" (Mansbridge, 1980, p. 167).

Beside this hard-to-eliminate danger of consensus-seeking, there are three more prosaic disadvantages (Mansbridge, 1973). First, consensus decision making takes a lot of time. To listen to all members' views for all decisions before moving toward proposals is going to take more time than voting after short informational presentations. Too much time spent in meetings is, in fact, one pervasive complaint about them. Second, a commitment to consensus is likely to result in more emotion-filled meetings. People are connected to their ideas; speaking at length about why one favors one course of action rather than another is likely to enhance people's emotional states. Enhanced emotionality (i.e., involvement) may be part of increasing a sense of community among a group when an actual consensus is achieved, but is likely to contribute to persons' negative feelings (e.g., that their views were dismissed if agreement feels coerced). Finally, consensus methods run into trouble because equality never fully exists. Even in groups that eschew obvious markers of power and status, there will be members who have an expertise that is particularly valued, are more knowledgeable by dint of their longer involvement with a group, or are especially articulate and persuasive. All of these differences mean that equality of influence is virtually an unattainable ideal. Equality of respect, Mansbridge (1973, 1980) suggested, may be a better ideal to aim for.

Thus far, this chapter has highlighted the troubles with consensus decision making. This is not because voting and majority decision rule are better: they are not. Majority rule has equally, if not more, serious shortcomings. The shortcomings of majority rule, however, have been widely recognized in a variety of educational and public contexts (see Rawlins, 1984 for a history) as the ideals of participatory democracy have become increasingly popular in workplaces (Cheney, 1995; Cheney et al., 1998). At its base, majority rule can be alienating and unresponsive to people, fostering divisions among a larger group, and unimaginative in its generation of options. Notwithstanding these limitations, it will be the better option some of the time. Reasons to favor voting and majority rule over consensus (Rawlins, 1984; Wood, 1984) are that (a) a decision needs to be made quickly, either because of an emergency or because it does not deserve much meeting time; (b) the decision is more a matter of preference among options, rather than better and worse quality;

(c) there are real competing interests among members that carry little potential for reframing; (d) the decision will not require much in the way of member support once it is made; (e) the group is large; and (f) there is value in keeping visible that there is a minority viewpoint on an issue. This last point, in fact, is part of the logic undergirding the U.S. Supreme Court's decision making style.

A well-functioning organizational meeting, then, is likely to use both consensus and voting to make decisions, moving back and forth between procedures as the issue demands. One business meeting manual recommends asking members at the start of an agenda item to indicate how important that issue is to them. If a good number of people raise their hands, Streibel (2003) suggested that the issue be decided by consensus; if no one raises a hand, then the group should vote. In more formal groups, voting is often built into the meeting's rules so decision making procedure is not an item-by-item choice. Nonetheless, it is possible to use voting yet draw on a consensus philosophy (see Mansbridge's, 1980, analysis of the Vermont town hall meetings)—just as it may be possible for the official decision making procedure to be consensus while a group implements it in a majority rule fashion.

Technologies in Meetings

At their simplest, technologies are tools that help a group do its tasks. Written documents, such as agendas and minutes, are among the most common tools, as are chalkboards or whiteboards (Volekma & Niederman, 1995). Through an analysis of the talk at a set of meetings, and how the presumed points of consensus were represented in a PowerPoint presentation that was developed across meetings, Anderson (in press) showed how a task force in a high technology firm created and shaped what it had to say to the larger organization. The generation of documents in meetings is a key way the larger organization constructs a sense of its solidity— to see itself as a stable container for people and actions rather than as a constantly changing set of tasks, goals, and people.

Using particular technologies will impact meetings; exactly how is the question. The growth of so many new technologies has led to a co-occurring surge in research about their effects. Harrison and Falvey (2001) review theories about how new technologies can contribute to democracy, and assess how adequately these theories are explaining what is happening. More directly tied to organizational meetings is Scott's (1999) review of communication technology in small groups in which he considers how technologies such as email group decision support software (GDSS), and other implements (e.g., video, audio, and data-conferencing tools) are supporting teamwork. Not all technologies enable interaction in the ways developers tout. Videoconferencing, for example, has been adopted much more slowly than expected. Meier (2003) attributed this slowness to the disruption in turn-taking coordination that even partial-second time lags cause, as well as screen size that make facial cues, one of the advantages of visually-mediated interaction, rather than audio only, of not much use.

An important point about technologies is that they are not transparent. Aakhus (2001) interviewed and observed GDSS facilitators responsible for helping groups manage meetings around particularly important issues (e.g., crafting a mission statement). He found that facilitators oscillated between two contradictory views of communication in doing their work. One view treated their communication, and all of the technologies that they employed, as neutral, value-free tools to help groups accomplish their decisions. In that sense GDSS facilitators took a technical stance toward their activity. At the same time facilitators took a more design-oriented, persuasive stance toward what they were doing, seeing their job as shaping the group's communication so that everybody could buy into important decisions. Aakhus's work suggests that understanding of new technologies in meetings must take account of how technologies are embedded in and oriented to through participants' talk.

One realization that becomes apparent when looking at the talk of groups having real meetings is that key analytic concepts, such as decision, are difficult to observe. As Boden (1994) noted, decisions:

> in the typical sense discussed in business and academic settings, indeed often with many diagrams and much hand-waving—are frequently invisible. It is instead the *incremental process* of decision-making that is the observable feature of so many organizational settings. (p. 84)

Schwartzman (1989), in fact, goes so far as to argue that meetings are important in American culture "because they generate the *appearance* that reason and logical processes are guiding discussions and decisions, whereas they facilitate . . . relationship negotiations, struggle, and commentary" (p. 42).

Community Shaping and Identity Work Functions

"Meetings are valuable because they are not what they seem to be," commented Schwartzman (1989, p. 86). When conceived as activities of information-sharing, coordination, and decision making, meetings might be regarded as a somewhat problematic communicative form. If these functions are not the only or even the most important ones, then what else are meetings accomplishing?

First, and most prominently, meetings are the arena in which organizational and community groups constitute who they are. Through back-and-forth talk, as well as the exchanges that occur in a meeting's pre- and post-interaction spaces, participants negotiate who they are, both as individuals and as a group: "It is in meetings that we come to know ourselves and our social systems" (Schwartzman, 1989, p. 314). Eisenberg, Murphy, and Andrews (1998) evidenced this in their analysis of a university committee's meetings to search for a provost, Bullis (1991) in her study of meetings of the forest service, and Schwartzman (1989) in her extended case study of a mental health center.

At Midwest Community MHC, the site for Schwartzman's (1989) extended study of meetings, the organization lived through its meetings. People dated their participation in the organization by referring to key meetings, about which stories of people and memorable actions were regularly shared. Meetings quite often generated conflict, as well as more meetings. Conflicts gave participants a sense of excitement, involvement, and an opportunity to test the seriousness of the organization's ideals and commitments. To know itself as an alternative organization, Midwest needed a forum in which to live its ideals. Meetings provided that space.

Enactment of an organization's persona (i.e., institutional identity work) is important for all organizations, especially those who define themselves as alternatives. In a study of a hospice team's weekly meetings, Tracy and Naughton (2000, see also Naughton, 1996) found staff used small positive off-topic asides about patients and families (e.g., "she's such a dear") to display their commitment to not treating people as biological machines. That is, by talking about patients in personal, emotionally-responsive terms, staff made real their organization's status as an alternative medical care facility committed to holistic care.

It is also through small devices within talk that groups, as well as the individuals in them, constitute themselves as persons of particular nationalities (e.g., Bargiela-Chiappini & Harris, 1997a, 1997b; Poncini, 2002). Yamada (1990, 1992, 1997), for instance, showed how Japanese and Americans differ in their use of back channels (e.g., *uh huh, okay*), the sheer amount of talk a person does, how a remark is connected to others' remarks, and the way verbal reports are organized. All of these small choices, Yamada showed, are how American and Japanese bankers enact different ideals about being a reasonable professional in their weekly meetings. Americans' discourse choices in meetings enacted a self-assertive demeanor, whereas Japanese choices enacted an other-attentive stance.

Small talk and humor are two communicative practices to which Holmes and her colleagues (Holmes, 1999, 2000; Holmes, Marra, & Burns, 2001; Holmes & Stubbe, 2003a, 2003b) have given extensive attention in their analysis of meetings in government, academic, and private sector settings (also see Yedes, 1996). Centrally interested in issues of gender, these authors showed a complex pattern of similarities and differences among men and women in their meeting behavior. Chairs of meetings tended to do certain things such as begin and close meetings, summarize where a discussion is, and talk considerably more than other participants. For these kinds of communicative actions, a person's role (e.g., chair or non-chair) was more important than the person's gender. In other ways, however, meeting talk had a gender seasoning. For example, women leading a meeting where there had been dissension were likely to seek the views of former dissenters (e.g., "You comfortable with that?") before closing a topic.

Meetings that had a large percentage of women engaged in longer stretches of small talk before turning to a meeting's focal task and the content of the small talk was less impersonal than in majority-male meetings. In female dominant meetings, small talk leaked into the official discussion more frequently. Women were also more likely than men in these meetings to initiate humor sequences. Holmes & Stubbe (2003a) concluded:

[S]equences of jointly constructed humorous talk and amusing anecdotes were commonly interleaved with the business at hand during formal meetings and other discussions. Although strictly speaking "off-topic," such digressions were usually related in some way to the issue being discussed and performed important discourse management and affective functions. (p. 584)

In sum, the more women who were present at a meeting, the more common humor as an activity was among a group. On the other hand, when women led a mostly-male meeting, their use of humor (and small talk) was more restrained. Meeting behavior, then, appears to depend on the gender makeup of a meeting as much as a speaker's gender.

The basic expectation of what is to happen during a formal meeting is itself culturally variable (Pan, Scollon, & Scollon, 2002). For Chinese and other Asian groups, compared to Americans, formal meetings are less likely to be understood as the sites for decision making. Meetings, instead, are places to ratify a leader's proposed directions, whereas pre- and post-meeting gatherings are where much of the decision making actually occurs. Lower-ranking organizational members thus have an opportunity to influence the unfolding decision, but this influence is accomplished in other ways than through direct argument at a meeting. In premeeting activities for instance, a high ranking manager will usually consult certain others about when to initiate a meeting, where it should be and who is to come, how people are to be notified and by whom, how seats are to be arranged, and what is the official agenda. As Pan, Scollon, and Scollon (2002) noted: "[E]stablishing the agenda is already a significant portion of the process of making a decision" (p. 119). Postmeeting activities are also consequential. It is here that people gather to discuss what implementing a policy or a course of action really means; more than occasionally a decision made at a formal meeting can take a 180 degree turn as talk about how to implement it occurs.

Meetings, of course, are playgrounds for power games, where individuals and subgroups struggle to get more power and resist the moves of others. From the opening moves of setting a meeting time or deciding on a setting to identifying what is (or is not) to go on the agenda—from how decision items are to be worded to the arguments that are made pre-, during, and postmeeting—participants jockey to frame the situation in a way that favors their preferences. Sometimes this jockeying is highly overt, as occurred in the spat among the Waco city council about when to hold their council meetings (Barge & Keyton, 1994). Should the meetings be in the middle of the day, the at-the-time existing practice, or should they be changed to evening? On its surface this might seem too small an issue to generate such a big conflict. In this instance, the dispute was more than it appeared. The dispute was actually a power struggle between the city's ruling elite and the local townspeople. Having the meeting midday when few working citizens could attend was a way for the council to limit townspeople's influence. This spat was also a political fight between the newly-elected mayor, who treated the election as having a mandate to make unilateral time changes, and the majority of the council who though they had a right to have a say about the matter. Conflicts that occur at meetings are invariably accompanied by expression of feelings, although overt feeling forms may be avoided (Putnam, in press; Tracy, in press).

At other times, influence processes seem so natural that they are harder to see as power moves. This is especially likely to be the case when a dispute occurs between a party who has a high-status position and other parties with little status. The expert language of a psychologist that is taken by meeting members to outweigh the input of an ordinary teacher and parent on a committee charged with deciding if a child has a learning disability (Mehan, 2001), or the information-giving agenda frame adopted by the director of a school's parent-teacher association that makes important decisions invisible (Wodak, 1996), exemplify how individual power assertions can be naturalized.

Advice Manuals About Meetings

Books offering advice about leading or participating in meetings come in all shapes and sizes; all promise to aid readers in bringing order to this most disorderly of communicative genres. On their jackets, the books proclaim that they will "give readers the tools necessary to be dramatically improve the quality and efficiency of your meetings" (Micale, 2002), to provide "solutions for dealing with difficult or disruptive personalities at the meeting place" (Miller & Pincus, 1997) and to turn meetings that readers lead "from a roomful of clock-watching individuals into a collaboration of involved and enthusiastic partners" (Streibel, 2003). The titles of seven books selected from the shelves of bookstore chains and a nonspecialized local bookstore can be seen in Table 2.[2]

Advice manuals such as the above provide a window into North American cultural beliefs about meetings. Inspection of these seven books suggests the following: First, and most obviously, there is a strong presumption that meetings are troublesome, ineffective affairs that need fixing. This view is suggested by book titles and jacket copy, but is underscored in opening pages, which often cite disaster stories or jokes about meetings. Timm (1997), for instance, began by equating meetings with "dental surgery" and presents two jokes: (a) "A meeting brings together the unfit appointed by the unwilling to do the unnecessary" and (b) "When all was said and done, a lot was said but nothing was done." (p. 5)

Second, all of the manuals are organized around descriptions of problems and advice, although the quality and sophistication of different books' problem analysis and advice vary considerably. At one end (e.g., Streibel, 2003) are books that reflect much of the research about group decision making and problemsolving in an accessible, reader-friendly style that recognize the problem of making categorical pronouncements about what to do or avoid. At the other end (e.g., Hindle, 1999; Timm, 1997) are books, in this sample the shortest and smallest, that treat meeting problems as transparent and advice as not needing explication or reasons. Organized into lists of tips, the worst of the genre tells readers how to deal with problematic people or read emotional states through an eyebrow twitch or body

TABLE 2
Titles of Meeting Manuals

Title	Reference Citation
First Aid for Meetings	(Hawkins, 1997)
Effective Meeting Skills	(Haynes, 1997)
Managing Meetings	(Hindle, 1999)
Not Another Meeting: A Practical Guide for Facilitating Effective Meetings	(Micale, 2002)
Running a Meeting that Works	(Miller & Pincus, 1997)
The Manager's Guide to Effective Meetings	(Streibel, 2003)
How to Hold Successful Meetings	(Timm, 1997)

posture (Hindle, 1999). Interestingly, there is a tendency, although not in all manuals (e.g., Hawkins, 1997), to treat meeting problems as the equivalent of problematic people. Haynes (1997) told meeting leaders how to deal with a person who "tends to dominate the discussion," "is antagonistic or skeptical," or "starts another meeting with neighbors" (pp. 52–53) and Miller and Pincus (1997) guided readers how to deal with the "yakkers," "tyrants," or "squabblers." (pp. 75–78)

Third, the manuals take for granted an organizational work frame, and a North American one at that. If cultural differences are mentioned they are brief and usually linked to nonverbal behaviors (e.g., Miller & Pincus, 1997).There is little recognition that cultures differ with regard to what they take to be the purpose for having a meeting. That the important work of a meeting may be to use decision talk not to make a decision, but to affirm that the group is a harmonious community who shares a view of their future together, is completely ignored. That this type of relational goal, at least occasionally and perhaps more often, may be what North American meetings are about is also invisible in these meeting manuals.

Finally, scholars pay little attention to the relational and face concerns that are so important in shaping the way people actually talk in meetings (Holmes & Stubbe, 2003a, 2003b). One result of this is that the advice offered about communicative actions that address these concerns is particularly inconsistent. Consider, for example, the advice given about humor. In a section focused on boring meetings, Hawkins (1997) informed readers they should "[l]earn to include humor in . . . meetings. It can be as simple as starting out the meeting by asking participants to share something humorous that happened in their department or showing the latest Dilbert cartoon" (p. 109). In contrast, Streibel (2003) suggested meeting facilitators deal with people telling jokes by saying, "We appreciate a little humor, but we need all the time we have for the agenda," (p. 151) and Miller and Pincus (1997) cautioned meeting participants, "Don't embarrass yourself with bad humor . . . one person's joke is another person's insult." (p. 68)

All the manuals contain at least a few nuggets of helpful advice (e.g., explaining how to brainstorm); some of them have quite a few. At the same time, all are exacerbating what we see as the biggest problem with meetings: people's inappropriate expectations about what a good meeting will be. Meetings are not merely about making decisions and giving information; they are places where people live out who they are, work through relationships, and seek to influence current events for future purposes. These kinds of delicate, interpersonal goals take time to accomplish. Mansbridge (1973), in fact, counseled meeting participants to be prepared to spend a "lot of time on emotional issues" (p. 360). This time will be needed, she argued, "no matter how sane, well-balanced, intelligent, and dedicated to its members" a group is. Two questions future scholarly work on organizational meetings needs to address is: (a) How does talk at meetings actually weave task, identity, and community goals together? and (b) What are better and worse ways to pursue these multiple purposes? Consider, now, how the focus shifts when examining public meetings.

PUBLIC MEETINGS

The Significance of the Public in Public Meetings

Board President: Well, I think we need to talk about scheduling a public hearing about this.
Vice President: (Groan)
Board Member: Mike, do we really need to get into that now?
Superintendent: I think it's about time. I always thought we should have been having them all along.
Vice President: I know, Sandy, but it's just that these things always end up being a big waste of time. The people who come just have their own agendas and complaints to make, and—
Superintendent: It doesn't have to be that way.
Board Member: But it usually is. Mike's right, though; we have to have one. We need a definite proposal, though—before we start.
Superintendent: What's the point in having a meeting if we aren't going to take account of what they have to say?
Vice President: That's when all the yelling starts. Nobody wants *their* school to close, and nobody wants to listen to the facts.
Board President: With an issue like closing schools, we're in for a really heated discussion.
Vice President: That's an understatement. Do you remember what happened last time?
Board President: That's why we need to talk about what to do differently.

Across the United States, from community groups to local city councils and school boards, from state regulatory commissions to federal and national organizations, there are wide varieties of public meetings (Checkoway, 1981; Gastil,

1992; Webler, 1999) that both the public and meeting organizers approach with trepidation (McComas, 2001, 2003). Public meetings are a staple of American democracy, providing a vehicle for the public deliberation that is necessary for a democratic society to work (Gastil, 1992; Hicks 2002). At the same time, institutional organizers, the public, and researchers see these meetings as causes of frustration and apathy (Checkoway & Van Til, 1978; McComas, 2001, 2003). Public meetings may be fundamental to building community but they also play a part in destroying the bonds that unite publics (see Kemmis, 1990).

As with organizational work meetings, public meetings are not so much a distinct research area as a context for studying other issues. Nonetheless, two traditions—theorizing about public deliberation and research on public participation—help scholars understand meetings. For each, this chapter describes its contribution, as well as its limitation. It concludes by focusing on the small set of case studies of public meetings that have given attention to interaction in actual meetings.

As noted earlier, the fundamental difference between organizational and public meetings stems from the inclusion of the public as participants (even if they are participating as audience). To be sure, there is a certain level of publicness in any meeting, since voicing a concern to the group takes the issue out of a private (individual) context and places it in the community (the group). There are thus similarities and common concerns in public meetings and organizational ones. At the same time, the shift from a restricted to an unrestricted audience markedly changes the nature of the meeting and the discourse that takes place within it. McComas (2001) emphasized that being nonrestrictive means being open to any member of the public. This nonrestrictive element is taken for granted in definitions of public deliberation (e.g., Gastil, 1992), although the emphasis often shifts to representative ness of the citizenry involved (Slaton, 2001) or the inclusiveness of the participation (Roberts, 1997). In any case, the most important difference between the public and organizational meetings is the audience. What makes a public meeting public is the involvement of several audiences

The expansion of meetings into the public realm begs the question of just what it means for an issue to be public and, for that matter, what a public is. Publics theory (see Phillips, 1996, and Squires, 2002, for reviews) is a broad and deep research tradition in its own right; here only a brief sketch of three relevant concepts (i.e., the public, the public sphere, and public deliberation) relates to the current review of meetings. Theories of the public provide the foundation for understanding meeting participants; the public sphere is the context for meetings, and concepts about public deliberation have implications for meeting purposes and interaction patterns.

The publicness of public meetings is at once obvious and difficult to define. Although a common conceptual category in both research and common discourse, the term has inherent instability. In a debate between Hart and Downing (1992), Downing argued that the term *public* glosses over substantial differences between genders, races, classes, and other groups; referring to *the American public* is neither useful nor sensible. At the same time, Hart countered, there are themes in American life that transcend time and factions; the notion of the American public is meaningful. Furthermore, Hart argues, it is essential for a complete understanding of social discourses. A term like the public is obviously a generalization. In use it works to define a collective based on certain attributes rather than others (see Dimock, 2003; Hopkins, 1994; Sacks, 1995; Wieder, 1990). In this sense, then, both Hart and Downing are correct: The public is an essential concept for understanding discourse at the mass level, but if it is considered as corresponding to an actual population, it is a horribly inaccurate generalization. The concept's two sides make visible competing concerns about unity and diversity, a tension always present in public issues.

The public that attends (or attends to) a public meeting, though, is not necessarily the public that Hart and Downing (1992) are arguing about. Hauser (1999) provides a useful distinction between the public at large (i.e., the citizenry) and a public. In the public deliberation tradition, there is a focus on getting the citizenry to take an active role in political issues. A public, in Hauser's sense, is made up of those people with opinions on an issue who are seeking to influence its definition and outcome. A public in this sense refers to the people who, borrowing terminology from the organizational tradition, are the stakeholders. This public may not include everyone who could be involved in an issue, or even those who should be involved in an issue, but it demarcates those who are involved in the issue, either by attending meetings or by attending to news about the public meetings. Even within this more modest definition, a public will involve multiple communities of people with at least partially competing interests; it will be a body that needs to manage its unity and diversity.

According to Ryfe (2002, p. 369) "no public conversation can succeed without a minimal recognition of shared values." It is these shared values that allow community and a public orientation to an issue to develop. Civil society (which contains the public sphere) is "a network of associations independent of the state whose members, through social interactions that balance conflict with consensus, seek to regulate themselves in ways consistent with the valuation of difference" (Hauser, 1999, p. 21). It is the *valuation of difference* or the need to live and cooperate with others that requires democracy to function as a mode of governance for a "society of strangers" (Hauser & Benoit-Barne, 2002, p. 271). More simply put, when citizens participate in public meetings, they must negotiate the tension between unity, tying them to a public good and community values, and their own legitimate individual interests.

A public group's unity is fragile. As people argue about issues in terms of their own interests, they may eliminate the ground necessary for finding solutions to problems that tap into a common good (Eliasoph, 1998, 2000; Kemmis 1990). At the same time, excessive unity is also problematic. As Ryfe (2002) has noted, many pubic meetings might be better thought of factions or special interest groups rather than a public. By co-opting dissent (Keith, 2002a), excessive unity results in the *disease of cooperation* (Burke, 1962), a problem similar to the groupthink of organizational meetings. In the public sphere, excessive unity's main danger is that it may reinforce a faction's values at the expense of other communities' values. Mendelberg and Oleske (2000), for instance, compared racially homogenous and heterogeneous public meetings and found that the homogenous meeting adopted implicitly racist views in their discussion, whereas the racially diverse meeting was able to find a common ground that worked for the whole group. While both meetings led to decisions acceptable to those attending, only the heterogeneous meeting led to a decision that would be acceptable to the greater public.

Public theorists consider the public not just the name for a collectivity of people, but as referencing a distinctive sphere of discourse. The public sphere is where private individuals come together, freely as a public body to address issues of general concern (Habermas, 1989). While discourse may be made public in the sense of moving from a smaller to larger collective within an organizational meeting, meetings in the public sphere change the context of the discourse. Consider the case before the school board in the simulated exchange. The question of what schools to close in a budget crunch could be addressed as a technical question of finances and economics, a decision that could be made through an organizational work meeting. If this issue is brought before the public, however, the grounds of the argument need to shift: The decision is no longer merely a technical matter. Moving it to a public meeting transforms it into a practical political decision.

The type of argument appropriate between friends, colleagues, or public representatives is inherently different; and as Goodnight (1982) argued, the grounding of arguments should shift for these different relationships. In Perelman and Olbrechts-Tyteca's (1969) argumentation theory, the context of an argument determines what knowledge, values, and assumptions may be taken for granted, as well as what will constitute adequate proof and the appropriate interactional style of the deliberations. The need for such shifts is not always recognized. A common complaint, for instance, from the public is that hearings are too technical and adversarial (McComas, 2001; 2003). Ideally, deliberation in the public sphere would operate on the basis of common understandings and values, but this, like the tension between unity and diversity, is difficult to accomplish.

Most studies of actual deliberations show a lack of argumentative reasoning in public meetings (Eliasoph, 1998, 2000; Mansbridge, 1980; Price, 2000). This probably has multiple causes, but one factor is the larger culture's preference for objective information and the discomfort with decisions validated by argument (Toker, 2002). The assumption that information can solve all problems leads to overly technical presentations from experts which neither incorporate the views of the public nor seek to enlist public acceptance (Button & Mattson, 1999). The result of this information emphasis is that citizens feel they need to be highly knowledgeable to participate. As a result they turn over decision-making authority to political and technical experts (Button & Mattson, 1999; Ryfe, 2002), disengage from public deliberation (Eliasoph, 1998), and become dissatisfied with public meetings (McComas, 2003; Ryfe, 2002).

Different proposals about the ideal communicative style for interacting around public issues have been developed (see Button & Mattson, 1999; Pearce & Pearce, 2000; Pellizzoni, 2001). The key difference seems to be between a valuing of rationality and the boisterous disagreement that is associated with confrontation and debate (Ivie, 2002) versus favoring dialogue with its commitment to discussion and building of community (Pearce & Pearce, 2000). Scholars favoring the former see the agonism of conflict as fundamental to maintaining a democracy.

Another feature of the context of the public sphere that makes public meetings distinctive is the relevance of media. Just as meetings in organizations are influenced by hallway conversations before and after meetings, as well as written correspondence, public meetings are influenced by the media that report on and interpret them (Eliasoph, 1998; Gastil, 1992). By framing issues (Simon & Xenos, 2000) and dispersing information (Ostman & Parker, 1986/1987), the media shape the nature of public meetings. Public meetings are inescapably multilayered. Various outlets of the media represent what happens in public meetings, as well as shape discussion about the issues. Wahl-Jorgensen (2001), for instance, argued that print and television media tend to favor individual expression (person on the street or a particular public figure's opinions) over group-linked, collective stances. Through influencing discussion among the public at large, the media shape the discourses that occurs within public meetings. It is quite common, for example, for a citizen to begin a comment to a school board meeting with a reference to an article or editorial that appeared in the local newspaper.[3]

Public deliberation theorizing is based on counterfactual ideals, especially Habermas' (1989; also see Hauser, 1999) *ideal speech situation*, which requires (a) equal opportunity to speak, (b) equal opportunity to respond, (c) equal access to information, and (d) judgment based on warranted assent. It is questionable whether such a situation has existed, or even could exist. Gastil (1992), in fact, argued that what usually happens in public meetings is more an index of undemocratic discourse, than a demonstration of the ideals. Pervasive in public deliberation scholarship is the belief that public deliberation is necessary for democracy but seriously lacking in current society. There is a notable, nostalgic tendency in this line of work: an attempt to recall or reinvent a degree of citizen participation that presumably occurred in ancient Athens, past French coffeehouses, or "olde" New England town meetings (see Elisaoph, 2000; Hauser, 1999; Hauptmann, 2001, Slaton, 2001). As Schudson (1998) has demonstrated, all eras of political participation are marked by the ways they fail to achieve ideals. Assessing the place deliberative ideals should hold in meetings-focused work, such as this study proposes, require a careful look at the theoretical and *ideal-logical* footing of the deliberative tradition.

Public Deliberation

Democracy holds a lofty status in the American *civitas* and is intrinsically tied to the practice of public deliberation. More than a forum or process, public deliberation is a type of relationship between the citizen and the state in which the state is responsive to the vox populi, the will of the people. "[D]emocracy posits that broadly based participation will lead to laws and policies that are more inclusive and more just than measures enacted by monarchs and powerful elites" (Hauser, 1999, p. 5). Connections among democracy, public deliberation, and better decisions are routinely ma¹le or assumed by most authors writing about public deliberation (e.g., Hicks, 2002), whereas the real questions concern who or what is to blame for its lack and how to correct the current state of affairs (Gastil, 1992). This intellectual tradition tends to adopt the liberal view of public participation which developed in the social movements of the 1960s and 70s. Public deliberation scholars largely discount a competing tradition that argues for the reasonableness of citizens having more limited influence because the public is fickle and prone to creating factions (Hauptmann, 1999; Mattson, 2002; Morrow, 2000). It is important to recognize, though, that both traditions are alive and well (see Hart & Downing, 1992), although the former tends to eclipse the latter in academic circles.

Within theories of public deliberation, the issues of community and legitimacy have particular relevance for public meetings. Community entails a concern with the unity of sets of peoples and publics with conflicting interests. A concern for community leads to questions about how to achieve cooperative social action among people while maintaining the separation that allows them to hold independent, individual views (Hauser, 1999). Practically formulated, a commitment to community generates a concern to keep people seated at the table, as well as talking (Arendt, 1958; Kemmis, 1990). Community intersects and partly overlaps with a second concern: to establish legitimacy. An important question for many authors (e.g., Hauptmann, 1999) is the relationship between deliberation and the legitimate exercise of authority. In public meetings, communities either come together—perceiving the authority that was exercised as legitimate—or they do not.

To address these concerns, theorists have put forth necessary criteria for the deliberative process, often building upon or reworking Habermas's criteria for the ideal speech situation that was summarized above. Hicks (2002), for example, suggested that the promises of deliberative democracy are inclusion (the ability of all citizens to participate), equality (or the equal opportunity of all views), and reason (the promise of publicly acceptable reason for decisions). Gastil (1992) sees deliberative decisions as aiming at a *rationally motivated consensus* or a concern for the public's interest rather than private interest; equal participation rights; and a relational concern with mutually acknowledged autonomy, mutuality, and competence. In general, these normative models highlight reasoned deliberation, which is either assumed or asserted to lead to better decisions; a relationship of equality and common concern for a unifying good; and a participatory forum in which equal and reasoned discussion can occur.

In this tradition, there is a commitment to strengthening the place of deliberation in contemporary society, presuming, as Putnam (2000) has shown, that citizen involvement in civic life has declined alarmingly. Centers such as the Kettering

Foundation (see *Economist*, 1998) and the National Issues Forum (see O'Connell & McKenzie, 1995) seek to reconstruct the deliberative forums from earlier in the century, others try to regenerate a lost oratorical culture (see Sproule, 2002), and still others have turned to the Internet, seeking to understand its strengths and problems as a deliberative site (Dahlberg, 1998; Gastil, 2000; Harrison & Falvey, 2001; Keith, 2002b).

Co-occurring with passionate arguments about the importance of achieving the conditions for an engaged citizenry and civil society is the judgment that modern society is falling short. Scholars have viewed public deliberation as the bastion of unreasoned decisions (see Price, 2000), unfounded assertion and ad hominem attack (Barge & Keyton, 1994), citizen apathy and exclusion from participation (Eliasoph, 1998; Mansbridge, 1980), lack of trust and divergent interests (Hicks, 2002; Mattson, 2002), and discursive and rhetorical subterfuge (Gastil, 1992), as well as a host of other problems. When viewed through the lens of deliberative ideals, actual public meetings would be judged an unholy mess, a deliberative wasteland seriously endangering the accomplishment of democracy.

To understand public meetings, scholars need to understand the ideals that surround them, and the enactment of democracy is certainly an important one. Theorizing about deliberative democracy, however, is not the same as understanding defensible ideals for public meetings. Deliberation theorizing concerns itself with democratic principles and the idea of citizen participation in a usually taken-for-granted, American context. In addition, it approaches issues of good conduct in an abstract way (i.e., detached from actual interaction), which is problematic. As Dewey (1927) long ago argued: "Ideals and standards formed without regard to the means by which they are to be achieved and incarnated in the flesh are bound to be thin and wavering." (p. 141) An interest in meetings, in contrast, focuses on people coming together in particular situations for defined and usually multiple reasons. Meetings frequently involve deliberation, but they also involve sharing of information, conducting of administrative business, and a wide swath of personal and social goals. To build a reasonable ideal for public meetings requires accounting for the full range of activities that do and should concern meeting participants. Consider, now, what is to be seen when viewing public meetings from a public participation vantage point.

Public Participation

In contrast to the decontextualized idealism of public deliberation studies is public participation research that seeks to assess citizen and planners' viewpoints of one or another type of meetings. The meetings analyzed in the public participation tradition are most often those required for public health and safety reasons, currently mandated by U.S. law. Over the last 50 years, government bureaucracy has grown to affect more and more aspects of citizens' daily lives. As a result, there have been movements to gain rights for greater citizen involvement in existing agencies (N. Rosenbaum, 1978). At the federal level, the Administrative Procedure Act of 1946 was the first legislation to mandate public involvement in governmental activities. It took until the 1960s and 1970s, however, for public hearings to become commonplace occurrences. It was citizens' increasing distrust of government, as well as their increased involvement in political and civil rights, that brought about public meetings as commonplace activities (W. Rosenbaum, 1978). Moreover, as these new forms became more prominent, researchers began to study them, investigating what worked and why (Checkoway, 1981, Kasperson, 1986; McComas, 2003; Webler, 1999).

In the public participation tradition, meetings are considered as one type of a wide variety of participatory programs, others being opinion polls, surveys, and initiatives (Fiorino, 1990; Heberlein, 1976). Meetings themselves take a variety of forms and go by different names in different areas of research (McComas, 2001). The most common are those that go by the generic name of hearing or meeting (Fiorino, 1990; Heberlein, 1976), but there are also *planning cells* (Slaton, 2001), *citizen juries* for more technically oriented questions (Parker, 2000; Price, 2000; Slaton, 2001), organic, self-sustaining *planning groups* (Plein, Green, & Williams, 1998), as well as various other *citizen, community*, and *activist groups* (Eliasoph, 1998, 2000).

The varieties of public meetings largely reflect different ways meetings are expected to function relative to policy decisions. Most commonly, meetings presumably serve to disseminate or help participants acquire information, justify emerging policies, and, not as often as many see as desirable, involve the public in decision making regarding a policy (Checkoway, 1981; Roberts, 1997; Webler, 1999). Newer forms of meetings, such as citizen juries that take representatives from the public and give them information and time to consider technical issues, tend to give public participants a larger role in the decision-making process than some of these other formats (see Plein, Green, & Williams, 1998; Slaton, 2001), although critics (Price, 2000; Webler, 1999) see citizen juries as unduly guided by organizational concerns.

The public participation tradition, similar to the deliberative democracy one, has also been shaped by a normative impulse, but by and large (cf. Webler, 1999) this impulse has had a relatively applied, nontheoretically elaborated focus that promoted success as its key principle. The concern with success, an outcome often never defined explicitly, has led to a proliferation of standards (Chess & Purcell, 1999; McComas, 2003). At its simplest, successful public participation seems to mean a fair meeting process that produces a competent decision and satisfaction among the public (Webler, 1999). Whether a decision appears competent and the process fair, however, often depends on whether the scene is examined from the institutional planners' point of view or from that of citizens. Surprisingly, there is little evidence that participation in public meetings affects citizens' satisfaction with either policy outcomes or their assessment of a process's fairness (McComas, 2003).

Institutional representatives, whether elected officials or technical experts, are faced with the problem of constructing a policy that is practically useful and politically legitimate (Kasperson, 1986; McComas, 2001). This requires balancing the concerns of divergent public and private interests, which may or may not be represented at the public meetings that are held, and the institutions' other needs, limitations, and commitments. Many public institutions are required to have public meetings, with different agencies having varying legal requirements for their meetings (McComas, 2000; N. Rosenbaum, 1978; W. Rosenbaum, 1978). These differences lead to different practices regarding who is contacted for participation, when participation occurs, and what effect the participation has on the decision. Critics (Checkoway, 1981; McComas, 2001) tend to assume that institutional planners hold public meetings mainly because they are required to do so, and that their goal in the meeting is to persuade the public to approve what they have already decided to do. From this viewpoint, meetings provide the semblance of democratic legitimacy, but are actually used to legitimate decisions made without public input; they are devices to inoculate against strong antagonisms, allowing the public to let off steam.

As with organizational meetings, there tends to be an extensive practitioner literature giving advice to public officials about how to design and run meetings (Webler, 1999). In contrast to workplace meeting manuals, however, public meeting manuals are less easily available, with copies circulated only within a particular agency or buried in library files of government documents. In addition, there is a legalistic air to brochures, absent from their organizational counterparts. An example is the Nuclear Regulatory Commission's (*NRC public meetings,* 2002) 10-page brochure about its public meetings. The brochure began with an explanation of the NRC's commitments and how it sees public meetings:

> Public meetings play a significant role in enhancing public confidence in the Nuclear Regulatory Commission (NRC) and it's (sic) ability to carry out its mission—to protect public health and safety in commercial uses of nuclear energy. The NRC has long recognized the importance and value of public communication and involvement as a key cornerstone of strong, fair regulation of the nuclear industry. (p.1)

Following the opening comments, the brochure spelled out how announcements of public meetings will be made, as well as to whom, how far in advance and, given the September 11, 2001 attacks, the kinds of security that will be implemented at meetings. The heart of the brochure is an explanation of three categories of meetings, what their usual content is, and the public's participation rights at each type. A Level 1 meeting, for instance, allows members of the public only to observe; a Level 2 allows for citizens to speak at a designated point on the agenda; and a Level 3 allows citizens to be involved in extensive discussion. Of note, citizen involvement is the most restricted on particular decisions (Level 1) and most open on policy discussion and direction-setting untied to particular decisions (Level

3). In a section labeled "Special Circumstances," it was mentioned that a Level 1 meeting can be changed to a Level 2 or 3 if there is an unusually high public interest. This note is intriguing, as it suggests the mechanism through which the public actually gains a voice is to have a critical mass of citizens turning out at a meeting. It also suggests that whenever possible this government agency, and presumably others, works to treat meetings as sites where officials inform the public. The decision to frame an issue as giving information or making a decision is an important way organizational leaders exercise power. Issue framers do not have complete control over how an issue unfolds; however, its initial framing is undoubtedly consequential for what is most likely to happen.

The public participation tradition draws our attention to an important facet of many public meetings. Public meetings often involve two groups: (a) those people responsible for developing and framing issues, listening to the public, and making the final decision, and (b) those ordinary citizens who are sufficiently motivated to turn out at a meeting to enact their identity as a public. These two groups are by no means equal. The former haves professional expertise and/or political legitimacy, and it is they who will be praised and blamed for the content of a decision, as well as the process through which it was made. The latter, in contrast, have expressive rights about a meeting's issue, with the accompanying moral expectation that their expression will be heard and treated seriously.

The judgment that the public's views are usually not given sufficient weight seems a reasonable criticism of public meetings; however, to fault them for failing to ensure full equality does not. It is arguably right and fitting that certain parties in public meetings have more say over what happens than others do. A strict equality in participation and authority does not seem appropriate in many cases. Public meetings need to juggle political fairness to all segments of a community, professional and technical expertise, financial feasibility, and responsiveness to the public that expresses itself on any particular decision. Taking a close look at what officials and citizens actually say and do in public meetings as they struggle with the multiple concerns that do and should animate their conduct is necessary to develop a functional and morally defensible ideal for public meetings. As Eliasoph (1998) noted: "Just advocating 'participation' is not enough. The quality of dialogue within these civic groups matters, too." (p. 259)

Case Studies of Public Meetings

Research in the participation tradition highlights one kind of public meeting that, a government agency holds to secure citizen input before moving ahead on a specific proposed course of action. This, however, is but one kind of public meeting. Besides meetings that seek issue-specific input, are the routine and regularly occurring community meetings of city councils, town halls, and school boards, as well as meetings of social action groups as they plan how to address both public hearings and regularly scheduled community meetings. Existing case studies give insight into the difficulties and successes that participants in public meetings have had in achieving their multiple aims.

Eliasoph's (1998) study of an environmental activist group suggested that a key problem of public meetings is the impoverished discourse available for discussing political issues. On the one hand was a language of expertise—double negatives, passive voice verbs, and expressions replete with qualifiers. The language of experts, viewed with suspicion if used by anyone not in an official role, is a register of *neutral dead facts* and no emotion. On the other hand was a *mom* discourse in which citizens spoke emotionally about how some proposed decision would harm their children. Interestingly, a concern about the children was considered not being political. Notably absent from these public meetings was a public-spirited, political *we* discourse in which arguments could occur about what was best for the community. Invoking the community or collective good was presumed inappropriate, merely self-interest masquerading in the guise of beneficence; therefore, it became difficult to discuss what would be a desirable shared future for a community. In contrast to Elisasoph's pessimistic assessment of political change and how to talk it into existence is Brock and Howell's (1994) case study narrating how church and civic leaders in Detroit came together to combat gambling as a proposed answer to the city's economic woes. Less discursively detailed than Eliasoph, it nonetheless made visible how management of key moments was consequential.

Explored in Tracy and colleagues' studies of one western U.S. community's school board meetings is the significance of framing issues, problems, and activities. In one study, Tracy and Ashcraft (2001) examined a six-month discussion about a district's racial diversity and sexual orientation policy, considering how participants tacked back and forth between talking about document language and the policy. Discursive moves such as framing (and resisting the framing of) a proposed wording change as a matter of wordsmithing, mere technical editing, or inadvertent introduction of a policy change were ways the group navigated among strongly oppositional stances about the legitimacy of supporting gay students and staff, as well as its need to arrive at a district-level policy.

Meeting groups experiencing turmoil and conflict must decide how to label their difficulty. In another study, Tracy and Muller (2001) considered the limitations of this western U.S. community task force's labeling of its board meeting problems as poor communication, comparing it with what would be suggested if the meetings were viewed as lack of good argument (van Eemeren, Grootendorst, Jackson, & Jacobs, 1993), a moral conflict (Pearce & Littlejohn, 1997), or the usual discourse activities of people with different interests (Potter, 1996). Other studies of these school board meetings considered (a) how board candidates made arguments about other candidates' conduct without calling into question that they themselves were reasonable and respectful (Tracy, 1999); (b) how board members in the minority position problematized the majority coalition's decisions, as well as the reasonableness of re-electing them (Tracy & Standerfer, 2003); (c) the trade-offs between framing agenda items as issues to be argued versus problems to be solved, and why community boards will adopt a problem frame whenever possible (Craig & Tracy, 2003); (d) how accusation and defense were accomplished in meetings where one or more school board members were called upon to resign (Tracy, 2003); and (e) the different ways to understand why a father's complaint at a board meeting about the decision to pull his daughter's science project from the school fair could turn into a controversy eliciting national media attention (Tracy & McDaniel, forthcoming).

Finally, in Mansbridge's (1980) classic study of meetings in Selby (a small predominately working class Vermont town with a 500-person population), there emerged a tension that faced this town committed to free and open participation of all. Upon interviewing townspeople who were silent at meetings, most of whom were working class, she found people feared speaking in public, afraid that they would come across as foolish. In contrast, the professionals who had moved to Selby only a few years earlier had an ease with words, spoke out readily, and quickly became town leaders. Given Selby's belief in the freedom of all to speak, working class townspeople saw themselves as having had an equal opportunity to the newcomers. The ramifications of this were paradoxical: The townspeople's belief in openness "ironically closes any avenue of complaint and soothes the consciences of the privileged" (Mansbridge, 1980; p. 116). Even though an open process might not be fully realizable in practice, whether public meetings should be structured as direct or representative democracies is an interesting issue. Based on a study of town meetings in the New England states, Zimmerman (1999) argued that in small communities (of 25,000 or fewer people) that could use either direct or representative governance, there are advantages to continuing an open town meeting system. Open town meetings, Zimmerman argued, are a "leading symbol of grass-roots democracy." With small adjustments, such as building in a committee system in which people develop expertise and insuring the possibility of a protest referendum, the open town meeting, can remain a "lithe and tenacious institution" (p. 191). Two foci could benefit future study of public meetings: (a) developing practical ideals that take into account the full range of activities public meetings need to accomplish (e.g., maintaining unity but allowing for dissent), and (b) developing case studies that examine the problems and practices encountered as meeting groups attempt to achieve these ideals.

CONCLUSIONS

What would be gained in future research if communication scholars conceptualized what they were studying as meetings in addition to or, perhaps, instead of bona fide groups, problem-solving and decision making, deliberative democracy, or public participation? First, to frame an activity as a meeting legitimates and directs attention to a public or work group's multiple purposes. Meetings are a genre of activity in which multiple aims are the rule rather than the exception.

Thinking about something as a meeting leads to questions about how multiple purposes are put together on an occasion, or how multiple purposes could and should be put together for some category of meeting. This kind of question is vital.

Second, to frame an activity as a meeting reinforces the importance of looking at interaction. Meetings, by definition, are occasions of talk. Labeling an event as such keeps center stage questions that concern the content and style of how people communicate with each other, about each other, and the consequences of existing variations. A focus on interaction is not the only useful lens on meetings, but certainly it is one in which communication scholars should be leading contributors.

Third, theoretical vocabulary including meetings, participatory democracy, bona fide group, public participation, and group decision making enable and foreclose particular avenues of thinking. Admittedly, it is possible to move among these lexical frames and take advantage of the different kinds of inferences each sets in motion. As Dewey (1927) pointed out, however, habits (include verbal labeling habits?) direct thought along certain paths and away from others. Meetings, more than any of the other concepts, keeps prominent a sense that the activity being studied is situational and historically shaped, not primarily an abstract form with invariant features. In addition, meetings gives equal attention to the concerns of planners and attending folk, in contrast to a focus on public participation (planners) or deliberative democracy (attendees).

Finally, a focus on meetings permits a relatively easy yoking of descriptive and normative impulses, something communication research should be doing regularly. As a term, meetings is relatively descriptive, thereby encouraging the analysis of ordinary communicative sites that social scientists have excelled at. Descriptive terms have the advantage of clarifying what is to be observed rather than making whether it should be applied a problem, as normative terms like democracy or dialogue immediately do. At the same time, communication research needs to be contributing to society's reflection about how people ought to be conducting themselves in their dealings with each other. The term meetings reverberates with evaluation; it references a communicative activity inescapably bound up with cultural members' oughts, shoulds, complaints, and moments of praise. In that sense, a focus on meetings directs descriptive work into channels that simultaneously aid reflection and cultural critique.

Meetings are not merely the dreaded time wasters of our work day and the frustrations of our political lives, events to be escaped. They are the essential site for achieving multiple, often diffuse, and competing personal, community, and societal ideals. Meetings are where people define and do who they are as groups, organizations, and publics. Meetings are the interactional means through which people create, sustain, reform, and destroy unity (or division) among their immediate groups and their larger communities. It is time for communication scholars to give their very best observational and reflective energies to the study of meetings; our society needs it.

NOTES

1. Schudson (1998, see also Schwartzman, 1989) identified Thomas Jefferson as writing and publishing a manual for parliamentary practice when he was U.S. Vice President and President of the Senate (1801). Presuably earlier manuals, such as Jefferson's, were not easily available for groups other than the one it was written for.

2. This sample of seven books is, admittedly, a convenience sample.

3. This generalization is based on 33 months of observation of school board meetings in Boulder Valley School District, Colorado.

REFERENCES

Aakhus, M. (2001). Technocratic and design stances toward communication expertise: How GDSS facilitators understand their work. *Journal of Applied Communication Research, 29,* 341–371.

Alexander, S. C., Peterson, J. L., & Hollingshead, A. B. (2003). Help is at your keyboard: Support groups on the internet. In L. Frey (Ed.), *Group communication in context: Studies of bona fide groups* (pp. 309–334). Mahwah, NJ: Erlbaum.

Anderson, D. L. (in press). The textualizing functions of writing for organizational change. *Journal of Business & Technical Communication, 18.*

Arendt, H. (1958). *The human condition.* Chicago: University of Chicago Press.

Atkinson, M. (1995). *Medical talk and medical work.* London: Sage.

Atkinson, P. (1999). Medical discourse, evidentiality, and the construction of professional responsibility. In C. S. C. Roberts (Ed.), *Talk, work and institutional order: Discourse in medical, mediation and management settings* (pp. 75–108). Berlin: Mouton de Gruyter.

Bailey, F. G. (1983). *The tactical uses of passion.* Ithaca, NY: Cornell University Press.

Barge, J. K., & Keyton, J. (1994). Contextualizing power and social influence in groups. In L. R. Frey (Ed.), *Group communication in context: Studies of natural groups* (pp. 85–105). Hillsdale, NJ: Erlbaum.

Bargiela-Chiappini, F., & Harris, S. J. (1997a). *Managing language: The discourse of corporate meetings.* Amsterdam: John Benjamins.

Bargiela-Chiappini, F., & Harris, S. (Eds.). (1997b). *The languages of business: An international perspective.* Edinburgh, UK: Edinburgh University Press.

Bilbow, G. T. (2002). Commissive speech act use in intercultural meetings. *International Review of Applied Linguistics in Language Teaching, 40,* 287–308.

Boden, D. (1994). *The business of talk: Organization in action.* Cambridge, UK: Polity Press.

Boden, D. (1995). Agendas and arrangements: Everyday negotiations in meetings. In A. Firth (Ed.), *The discourse of negotiation: Studies of language in the workplace* (pp. 83–99). Oxford, UK: Pergamon.

Bonita, J. A., & Hollingshead, A. B. (1997). Participation in small groups. In B. R. Burelson (Ed.), *Communication yearbook 20* (pp. 227–261). Thousand Oaks, CA: Sage.

Bormann, E. G. (1996). Symbolic convergence and communication in group decision making. In R. Y. Hirokawa & M. S. Poole (Eds.), *Communication and group decision-making* (pp. 81–113). Thousand Oaks, CA: Sage.

Brock, B. L., & Howell, S. (1994). Leadership in the evolution of a community-based political action group. In L. R. Frey (Ed.), *Group communication in context: Studies of natural groups* (pp. 135–152). Hillsdale, NJ: Erlbaum.

Bullis, C. (1991). Communication practices of unobtrusive control: An observational study. *Communication Studies, 42,* 254–271.

Burke, K. (1962). *A grammar of motives and a rhetoric of motives.* New York: Meridian.

Button, M., & Mattson, K. (1999). Deliberative democracy in practice: Challenges and prospects for civic deliberation. *Polity, 31,* 609–637.

Checkoway, B. (1981). The politics of public hearings. *The Journal of Applied Behavioral Science, 17*, 566–582.

Checkoway, B., & Van Til, J. (1978). What do we know about citizen participation? A selective review of research. In S. Langton (Ed.), *Citizen participation in America: Essays on the state of the art* (pp. 25–42). Lexington, MA: Lexington Books.

Cheney, G. (1995). Democracy in the workplace: Theory and practice for the perspective of communication. *Journal of Applied Communication Research, 23*, 167–200.

Cheney, G., Straub, J., Speirs-Glebe, L., Stohl, C., Degooyer, J. D., & Whalen, S. (1998). Democracy, participation, and communication at work: A multidisciplinary review. In M. E. Roloff (Ed.), *Communication yearbook 21* (pp. 35–91). Thousand Oaks, CA: Sage.

Chess, C., & Purcell, K. (1999). Public participation and the environment: Do we know what works? *Environmental Science and Technology, 33*, 2685–2692.

Cline, R. J. W. (1994). Groupthink and the Watergate cover-up: The illusion of unanimity. In L. R. Frey (Ed.), *Group communication in context: Studies of natural groups* (pp. 199–223). Hillsdale, NJ: Erlbaum.

Cook-Gumperz, J., & Szymanski, M. (2001). Classroom "families": Cooperating or competing—Girls' and boys' interactional styles in a bilingual classroom. *Research on Language and Social Interaction, 34*, 107–130.

Craig, R. T., & Tracy, K. (2003). The "issue" in argumentation theory and practice. In F. H. van Eemeren, J. A. Blair, C. A. Willard, & A. F. S. Henkemans (Eds.), *Proceedings of the Fifth Conference of the International Society for the Study of Argumentation* (pp. 213–218). Amsterdam: SicSat.

Dahlberg, L. (1998). Cyberspace and the public sphere: Exploring the democratic potential of the net. *Convergence, 4*, 70–84.

Dewey, J. (1927). *The public and its problems*. New York: Henry Holt and Company.

Dimock, A. (2003). *Categorization in discourse: Developing the identity "juvenile offender."* Paper presented at the Rocky Mountain Communication Association, Boulder, CO.

Economist. (1998, July, 22). American democracy: Building the perfect citizen, p. 21.

Eisenberg, E. M., Murphy, A., & Andrews, L. (1998). Openness and decision-making in the search for a university provost. *Communication Monographs, 65*, 1–23.

Elias, N. (1994). *The civilizing process: The history of manners and state formation and civilization*. Oxford, UK: Oxford University Press.

Eliasoph, N. (1998). *Avoiding Politics: How Americans produce apathy in everyday life*. Cambridge, UK: Cambridge University Press.

Eliasoph, N. (2000). Where can Americans talk politics: Civil society, intimacy, and the case for deep citizenship. *Communication Review, 4*, 65–94.

Erickson, F., & Shultz, J. (1982). *The counselor as gatekeeper: Social interaction in interviews*. New York: Academic Press.

Fiorino, D. J. (1990). Citizen participation and environmental risk: A survey of institutional mechanisms. *Science, Technology, and Human Values, 15*, 226–243.

Folger, J., & Jones, T. (Eds.). (1994). *New directions in mediation*. Thousand Oaks, CA: Sage.

Ford, C. E. (1999). Collaborative construction of task activity: Coordinating multiple resources in a high school physics lab. *Research on Language and Social Interaction, 32*, 369–408.

Frey, L. R. (1994a). The naturalistic paradigm: Studying small groups in the postmodern era. *Small Group Research, 25*, 551–577.

Frey, L. R. (1994b). Introduction: Revitalizing the study of small group communication. *Communication Studies, 45*, 1–6.

Frey, L. R. (Ed.). (1994c). *Group communication in context: Studies of natural groups*. Hillsdale, NJ: Erlbaum.

Frey, L. R. (1996). Remembering and "re-membering": A history of theory and research on communication and group decision making. In R. Y. Hirokawa & M. S. Poole (Ed.), *Communication and group decision making* (2nd ed., pp. 19–51). Thousand Oaks, CA: Sage.

Frey, L. R. (2003). Group communication in context: Studying bona fide groups. In L. R. Frey (Ed.), *Group Communication in context: Studies of bona fide groups* (pp. 1–22). Mahwah, NJ: Erlbaum.

Frey, L. R., Gouran, D. S., & Poole, M. S. (Eds.). (1999). *The handbook of group communication research*. Thousand Oaks, CA: Sage.

Gastil, J. (1992). Undemocratic discourse: A review of theory and research on political discourse. *Discourse and Society*, 3, 469–500.

Gastil, J. (2000). Is face-to-face citizen deliberation a luxury of a necessity? *Political Communication*, 17, 357–361.

Goodnight, G. T. (1982). The personal, technical, and public spheres of argument. *Journal of the American Forensic Association*, 18, 214–227.

Gouran, D. S. (1991). Rational approaches to decision-making and problem-solving discussion. *Quarterly Journal of Speech*, 77, 343–358.

Gouran, D. S., Hirokawa, R. Y., & Leatham, G. B. (1993). The evolution and current status of the functional perspective on communication in decision-making and problem-solving groups. In S. A. Deetz (Ed.), *Communication yearbook 16* (pp. 573–600). Newbury Park, CA: Sage.

Greatbatch, D., & Dingwall, R. (1999). Professional neutralism in family mediation. In C. S. C. Roberts (Ed.), *Talk, work and institutional order: Discourse in medical, mediation and management settings* (pp. 271–292). Berlin: Mouton de Gruyter.

Greenbaum, H. H., & Query, J. L., Jr. (1999). Communication in organizational work groups: A review and analysis of natural work group studies. In L. Frey, D. Gouran, & M. S. Poole (Eds.), *The handbook of group communication* (pp. 539–564). Thousand Oaks, CA: Sage.

Grimshaw, A. D. (1989). *Collegial discourse: Professional conversation among peers*. Norwood, NJ: Ablex.

Habermas, J. (1989). The public sphere: An encyclopedia article. In S. E. Bonner & D. M. Kellner (Eds.), *Critical theory and society* (pp. 136–142). New York: Routledge.

Harrison, T., & Falvey, L. (2001). Democracy and new communication technologies. In W. B. Gudykunst (Ed.), *Communication Yearbook 25* (pp. 1–43). Mahwah, NJ: Erlbaum.

Hart, R., & Downing, J. D. H. (1992). Is there an American public?: An exchange of correspondence. *Critical Studies in Mass Communication*, 9, 201–215.

Hauptmann, E. (1999). Deliberation = legitimation = democracy. *Political Theory*, 27, 857–872.

Hauptmann, E. (2001). Can less be more? Leftist deliberative democrats' critique of participatory democracy. *Polity*, 33, 397–421.

Hauser, G. (1999). *Vernacular voices: The rhetoric of publics and public spheres*. Columbia: University of South Carolina Press.

Hauser, G., & Benoit-Barne, C. (2002). Reflections on rhetoric, deliberative democracy, civil society and trust. *Rhetoric and Public Affairs*, 5, 261–275.

Hawkins, C. (1997). *First aid for meetings: Quick fixes and major repairs for running effective meetings*. Wilsonville, OR: BookPartners.

Haynes, M. E. (1997). *Effective meeting skills* (Revised ed.). Menlo Park, CA: Crisp Learning.

He, A. W. (1995). Co-constructing institutional identities: The case of student counselees. *Research on Language and Social Interaction*, 28, 213–231.

Heberlein, T. A. (1976). Some observations on alternative mechanisms for public involvement: The hearing, public opinion poll, the workshop and the quasi-experiment. *Natural Resources Journal*, 16, 197–212.

Hicks, D. (2002). The promise(s) of deliberative democracy. *Rhetoric and Public Affairs*, 5, 223–260.

Hindle, T. (1999). *Managing meetings*. New York: D K Publishers.

Hirokawa, R. Y., & Poole, M. S. (1996). *Communication and group decision making* (2nd ed.). Thousand Oaks, CA: Sage.

Hirokawa, R. Y., & Salazar, A. J. (1999). Task-group communication and decision-making performance. In L. Frey, D. Gouran, & M. S. Poole (Eds.), *The handbook of group communication* (pp. 167–191). Thousand Oaks, CA: Sage.

Holmes, J. (1999). Women at work: Analyzing women's talk in New Zealand workplaces. *Australian Review of Applied Linguistics*, 22(2), 1–18.

Holmes, J. (2000). Politeness, power, and provocation: How humour functions. *Discourse Studies*, 2, 159–185.

Holmes, J., Marra, M., & Burns, L. (2001). Women's humor in the workplace. *Australian Journal of Communication*, 28, 83–108.

Holmes, J., & Stubbe, M. (2003a). "Feminine" workplaces: Stereotype and reality. In J. Holmes & M. Meyerhoff (Eds.), *The handbook of language and gender* (pp. 573–599). Oxford, UK: Blackwell.

Holmes, J., & Stubbe, M. (2003b). *Power and politeness in the workplace*. London: Pearson.

Hopkins, N. (1994). Young people arguing and thinking about the police; Qualitative data concerning the categorization of the police in a police-youth contact program. *Human Relations*, 41, 1409–1432.

Howell, S., Brock, B., & Hauser, E. (2003). A multicultural, intergenerational youth program: Creating and sustaining a youth community group. In L. R. Frey (Ed.), *Group communication in context: Studies of bona fide groups* (pp. 85–107). Mahwah, NJ: Erlbaum.

Houston, R. (2003). In the mask of thin air: Intragroup and intergroup communication during the Mt. Everest disaster. In L. R. Frey (Ed.), *Group communication in context: Studies of bona fide groups* (pp. 137–156). Mahwah, NJ: Erlbaum.

Ivie, R. L. (2002). Rhetorical deliberation and democratic politics in the here and now. *Rhetoric and Public Affairs*, 5, 277–285.

Janis, I. L. (1982). *Groupthink* (2nd ed.). Dallas: Houghton Mifflin.

Jarboe, S. (1999). Group communication and creativity processes. In L. Frey, D. Gouran & M. S. Poole (Eds.), *The handbook of group communication* (pp. 335–368). Thousand Oaks, CA: Sage.

Kasperson, R. E. (1986). Six propositions on public participation and their relevance for risk communication. *Risk Analysis*, 3, 275–281.

Keith, W. (2002a). Introduction: Cultural Resources for Deliberative Democracy. *Rhetoric and Public Affairs*, 5, 219–221.

Keith, W. (2002b). Democratic revival and the promise of cyberspace: Lessons from the forum movement. *Rhetoric and Public Affairs*, 5, 311–326.

Kemmis, D. (1990). *Community and the politics of place*. Norman: University of Oklahoma Press.

Ketrow, S. M. (1999). Nonverbal aspects of group communication. In L. Frey, D. Gouran, & M. S. Poole (Eds.), *The handbook of group communication* (pp. 251–287). Thousand Oaks, CA: Sage.

Keyton, J. (1999). Relational communication in groups. In L. Frey, D. Gouran, & M. S. Poole (Eds.), *The handbook of group communication* (pp. 192–222). Thousand Oaks, CA: Sage.

Lammers, J. C., & Krikorian, D. H. (1997). Theoretical extension and operationalization of the bona fide group construct with an application to surgical teams. *Journal of Applied Communication Research*, 25, 17–38.

Mansbridge, J. J. (1973). Time, emotion, and inequality: Three problems of participatory groups. *The Journal of Applied Behavioral Science*, 9, 351–368.

Mansbridge, J. (1980). *Beyond adversary democracy*. Chicago: University of Chicago Press.

Mattson, K. (2002). Do Americans really want deliberative democracy? *Rhetoric and Public Affairs*, 5, 327–329.

McComas, K. A. (2000). *Theory and practice of public meetings*. Ann Arbor: UMI Dissertation Services.

McComas, K. A. (2001). Theory and practice of public meetings. *Communication Theory*, 11, 36–55.

McComas, K. A. (2003). Citizen satisfaction with public meetings used for risk communication. *Journal of Applied Communication Research*, 31, 164–184.

Mehan, H. (2001). The construction of an LD student: A case study in the politics of representation. In M. Wetherell, S. Taylor, & S. J. Yates (Eds.), *Discourse theory and practice* (pp. 345–363). London: Sage.

Meier, C. (2003). Doing "groupness" in a spatially distributed work group: The case of videoconferences at Technics. In L. Frey (Ed.), *Group communication in context: Studies of bona fide groups* (pp. 367–397). Mahwah, NJ: Erlbaum.

Mendelberg, T., & Oleske, J. (2000). Race and public deliberation. *Political Communication*, 17, 169–191.

Meyers, R. A. (1997). Social influence and group argument. In L. R. Frey & J. K. Barge (Eds.), *Managing group life: Communicating in decision-making groups* (pp. 183–201). Boston: Houghton Mifflin.

Meyers, R. A., & Brashers, D. E. (1999). Influences processes in group interaction. In L. Frey, D. Gouran, & M. S. Poole (Eds.), *The handbook of group communication* (pp. 288–312). Thousand Oaks, CA: Sage.

Micale, F. A. (2002). *Not another meeting! A Practical guide for facilitating effective meetings.* Central Point, OR: Oasis Press.

Miller, R. F., & Pincus, M. (1997). *Running a meeting that works.* Hauppauge, NY: Barron's Educational Series.

Mintzberg, H. (1973). *The nature of managerial work.* New York: Harper & Row.

Morrow, T. S. (2000). Representation and political deliberation in the Massachusetts constitutional ratification debate. *Rhetoric and Public Affairs, 3,* 529–553.

NRC public meetings. (2002). Washington, DC: U.S. Regulatory Commission.

Naughton, J. M. (1996). *Discursively managing evaluation and acceptance in a hospice team meeting: A dilemma.* Ann Arbor: UMI Dissertation Services.

O'Connell, D. W., & McKenzie, R. H. (1995). Teaching the art of public deliberation - National Issues Forums in the classroom. *Political Science and Politics,* 230–232.

Ostman, R. E., & Parker, J. L. (1986/1987). A public's environmental information sources and evaluations of mass media. *Journal of Environmental Education,* 9–17.

Pan, Y., Scollon, S. W., & Scollon, R. (2002). *Professional communication in international settings.* Malden, MA . Blackwell.

Parker, M. (2000). Public deliberation and private choice in genetics and reproduction. *Journal of Medical Ethics, 26,* 160–165.

Pavitt, C. (1999). Theorizing about the group communication-leadership relationship: Input-process-output and functional models. In L. Frey, D. Gouran, & M. S. Poole (Eds.), *The handbook of group communication* (pp. 313–334). Thousand Oaks, CA: Sage.

Pearce, W. B., & Littlejohn, S. (1997). *Moral conflict: When social worlds collide.* Thousand Oaks, CA: Sage.

Pearce, W. B., & Pearce, K. A. (2000). Combining passions and abilities: Toward dialogic virtuosity. *Southern Communication Journal, 65,* 161–175.

Pellizzoni, L. (2001). The myth of the best argument: Power, deliberation and reason. *British Journal of Sociology, 52,* 59–86.

Perelman, C., & Olbrechts-Tyteca, L. (1969). *The New Rhetoric: A Treatise on Argumentation* (J. Wilkinson & P. Weaver, Trans.). Notre Dame, IN: University of Notre Dame Press.

Phillips, K. R. (1996). The spaces of public dissension: Reconsidering the public sphere. *Communication Monographs, 63,* 231–248.

Plein, L. C., Green, K. E., & Williams, D. G. (1998). Organic planning: A new approach to public participation in local governance. *The Social Science Journal, 35,* 509–523.

Poncini, G. (2002). Investigating discourse at business meetings with multicultural participation. *International Review of Applied Linguistics in Language Teaching, 40,* 345–373.

Potter, J. (1996). *Representing reality: Discourse, rhetoric and social construction.* London: Sage.

Price, D. (2000). Choices without reasons: Citizens' juries and policy evaluation. *Journal of Medical Ethics, 26,* 272–276.

Propp, K. M. (1999). Collective information processing in groups. In L. Frey, D. Gouran, & M. S. Poole (Eds.), *The handbook of group communication* (pp. 235–250). Thousand Oaks, CA: Sage.

Putnam, L. L. (1994). Revitalizing small group communication: Lessons learned from a bona fide group perspective. *Communication Studies, 41,* 248–265.

Putnam, L. L. (in press). Suppression through expression in the meta-talk about feelings in the organizational decision making in *After Mr. Sam.* In F. Cooren (Ed.), *Interacting and organizing: Analysis of a board meeting.* Mahwah, NJ: Erlbaum.

Putnam, L. L., & Stohl, C. (1990). Bona fide groups: A reconceptualization of groups in context. *Communication Studies, 41,* 248–265.

Putnam, L. L., & Stohl, C. (1996). Bona fide groups: An alternative perspective for communication and small group decision making. In R. Y. Hirokowa & M. S. Poole (Eds.), *Communication and group decision making* (pp. 147–178). Thousand Oaks, CA: Sage.

Putnam, R. (2000). *Bowling alone: The collapse and revival of American community.* New York: Touchstone.

Rawlins, W. K. (1984). Consensus in decision-making groups: A conceptual history. In J. M. Phillips & J. T. Wood (Eds.), *Emergent issues in human decision making* (pp. 19–39). Carbondale: Southern Illinois University Press.

Roberts, N. (1997). Public deliberation: An alternative approach to crafting policy and setting direction. *Public Administration Review, 57,* 124–132.

Rosch, E., Mervis, C., Gray, W., Johnson, D., & Boyce-Braem, P. (1976). Basic objects in natural categories. *Cognitive Psychology, 8,* 382–439.

Rosenbaum, N. M. (1978). Citizen participation and democratic theory. In S. Langton (Ed.), *Citizen participation in America: Essays on the state of the art* (pp. 43–54). Lexington, MA: Lexington Books.

Rosenbaum, W. A. (1978). Public involvement as reform and ritual: The development of federal participation programs. In S. Langton (Ed.), *Citizen participation in America: Essays on the state of the art* (pp. 81–96). Lexington, MA: Lexington Books.

Ryfe, D. M. (2002). The practice of deliberative democracy: A study of 16 deliberative organizations. *Political Communication, 19,* 359–377.

Sacks, H. (1995). *Lectures on Conversation.* Malden, MA: Blackwell.

Sarangi, S., & Clarke, A. (2002). Zones of expertise and the management of uncertainty in genetics risk communication. *Research on Language and Social Interaction, 35(2),* 139–171.

Schudson, M. (1998). *The good citizen.* New York: The Free Press.

Schwartzman, H. B. (1989). *The meeting: Gatherings in organizations and communities.* New York: Plenum Press.

Scott, C. R. (1999). Communication technology and group communication. In L. Frey, D. Gouran & M. S. Poole (Eds.), *The handbook of group communication* (pp. 432–473). Thousand Oaks, CA: Sage.

Seibold, D. R., & Krikorian, D. H. (1997). Planning and facilitating group meetings. In L. Frey & K. Barge (Eds.), *Managing group life* (pp. 270–305). Boston: Houghton Mifflin.

Simon, A., & Xenos, M. (2000). Media framing and effective deliberation. *Political Communication, 17,* 363–376.

Slaton, C. D. (2001). New models of citizen deliberation. *Futures, 33,* 357–360.

Sproule, J. M. (2002). Oratory, democracy, and the culture of participation. *Rhetoric and Public Affairs, 5,* 301–310.

Squires, C. R. (2002). Rethinking the Black public sphere: An alternative vocabulary for multiple public spheres. *Communication Theory, 12,* 446–468.

Stohl, C., & Holmes, M. E. (1993). A functional perspective for bona fide groups. In S. Deetz (Ed.), *Communication yearbook 16* (pp. 601–614). Newbury Park, CA: Sage.

Stohl, C., & Putnam, L. L. (1994). Group communication in context: Implications for the study of bona fide groups. In L. R. Frey (Ed.), *Group communication in context: Studies of natural groups* (pp. 285–292). Hillsdale, NJ: Erlbaum.

Stohl, C., & Putnam, L. L. (2003). Communication in bona fide groups: A retrospective and prospective account. In L. R. Frey (Ed.), *Group communication in context: Studies of bona fide groups* (pp. 399–414). Mahwah, NJ: Erlbaum.

Streibel, B. J. (2003). *The manager's guide to effective meetings.* New York: McGraw Hill.

Sunwolf & Seibold, D. R. (1999). The impact of formal procedures on group processes, members, and task outcomes. In L. Frey, D. Gouran, & M. S. Poole (Eds.), *The handbook of group communication* (pp. 395–431). Thousand Oaks, CA: Sage.

Timm, P. R. (1997). *How to hold successful meetings.* Franklin Lakes, NJ: Career Press.

Tocqueville, A. de (1945). *Democracy in America.* New York: Vintage.

Toker, C. W. (2002). Debating "what out to be": The comic frame in public moral argument. *Western Journal of Communication, 66,* 53–83.

Tracy, K. (1997). *Colloquium: Dilemmas of academic discourse.* Norwood, NJ: Ablex.

Tracy, K. (1999). The usefulness of platitudes in arguments about conduct. In. F. H. van Eemeren, J.A. Blair, & C. A. Willard (Eds.), *Proceedings of the fourth international conference of the international society for the study of argumentation* (pp. 799–803). Amsterdam: SICSAT.

Tracy, K. (2003). *Accusatory talk in sites of unitary democracy: Discursive practices and a group dilemma.* Paper presented at the annual conference of the International Communication Association, San Diego, CA.

Tracy, K. (in press). Feeling-limned talk: Conduct ideals in the Steinberg succession meeting. In F. Cooren (Ed.), *Interacting and Organizing: Analysis of a board meeting.* Mahwah, NJ: Erlbaum.

Tracy, K., & Ashcraft, C. (2001). Crafting policies about controversial values: How wording disputes manage a group dilemma. *Journal of Applied Communication Research, 29*, 297–316.

Tracy, K., & McDaniel, J. P. (Eds.). (in press). *Rhetoric, discourse, and ordinary democracy.* Tuscaloosa: University of Alabama. Press.

Tracy, K., & Muller, H. (2001). Diagnosing a school board's interactional trouble: Theorizing problem formulating. *Communication Theory, 11*, 84–104.

Tracy, K., & Naughton, J. M. (2000). Institutional identity-work: A better lens. In J. Coupland (Ed.), *Small Talk* (pp. 62–83). Harlow, UK: Pearson.

Tracy, K., & Standerfer, C. (2003). Selecting a school superintendent: Sensitivities in group deliberation. In L. Frey (Ed.), *Group communication in context: Studies of natural groups* (2nd ed., pp. 109–134). Mahwah, NJ: Erlbaum.

van Eemeren, F. H., Grootendorst, R., Jackson, S., & Jacobs, S. (1993). *Reconstructing argumentative discourse.* Tuscaloosa: University of Alabama Press.

van Vree, W. (1999). *Meetings, manners and civilization: The development of modern meeting behaviour.* London: Leicester University Press.

Volkema, R., & Niederman, F. (1995). Organizational meetings: Format and information requirements. *Small Group Research, 26*, 3–24.

Wahl-Jorgensen, K. (2001). Letters to the editor as a forum for public deliberation: modes of publicity and democratic debate. *Critical Studies in Media Communication, 18*, 303–320.

Webler, T. (1999). The craft and theory of public participation: A dialectical process. *Journal of Risk Research, 2*, 55–71.

Weitzel, A., & Geist, P. (1998). Parliamentary procedures in a community group: Communication and vigilant decision making. *Communication Monographs, 65*, 244–259.

Wieder, D. L. (1990). On being a recognizable Indian among Indians. In D. Carbough (Ed.), *Cultural communication and intercultural contact* (pp. 45–64). Hillsdale, NJ: Erlbaum.

Wodak, R. (1996). *Disorders of discourse.* London: Longman.

Wood, J. T. (1984). Alternative methods of group decision making: A comparative examination of consensus, negotiation and voting. In J. M. Phillips & J. T. Wood (Eds.), *Emergent issues in human decision making* (pp. 3–18). Carbondale: Southern Illinois University Press

Yamada, H. (1990). Topic management and turn distribution in business meetings: American versus Japanese strategies. *Text 10*, 271–295.

Yamada, H. (1992). *American and Japanese business discourse. A comparison of interactional styles.* Norwood, NJ: Ablex.

Yamada, H. (1997). Organisation in American and Japanese meetings: Task versus relationship. In F. Bargiela-Chiappini & S. Harris (Eds.), *The languages of business: An international perspective* (pp. 117–135). Edinburgh, UK: Edinburgh University Press.

Yedes, J. (1996). Playful teasing: Kiddin' on the square. *Discourse and Society, 7*, 417–438.

Zimmerman, J. F. (1999). *The New England town meeting: Democracy in action.* Westport, CT: Praeger.

CHAPTER CONTENTS

5   Transcending Tolerance: Pragmatism, Social Capital, and Community in Communication

JEFFREY ST. JOHN
GREGORY J. SHEPHERD
Ohio University

This article investigates tolerance in its application to communities as a form of social capital. We argue that, although the building and sustaining of communities is widely viewed to be aided by infusions of tolerance, contemporary characterizations of tolerance are in fact at loggerheads with the work of social capital. We would supplant tolerance with transcendence and seek thereby to reconceive communication within communities as a pragmatic mode of civic interaction effected between self and other, self and community, and community and community. To these ends, we draw from communication literatures on tolerance and social capital and from pragmatist schemas that envision communication within communities as representing transcendence, not tolerance.

The renascence of North American philosophical pragmatism has been serious, relatively recent, and voluminous. Since 1985, a flood of articles, monographs, and edited volumes have addressed the work of individual American philosophers such as Dewey, James, Peirce, and Rorty; a range of domestic problems both social and political in nature (public education and its reform foremost among them); and various strategic frameworks for resolving international dilemmas (Dickstein, 1998; Hardwick & Crosby, 1997; Mounce, 1997; H. Putnam, 1995; Rosenthal, Hausman, & Anderson 1999; West, 1989). Much of this work, written by and for academic specialists, has been technical, (constructively) narrow in scope, and mainly theoretical. Other efforts have reached for a broader audience of academic and lay intellectuals, most notably Menand's (2001) bestselling history of North American pragmatism, *The Metaphysical Club*.

Correspondence: Jeffrey St. John, School of Communication Studies, 9 Lasher Hall, Ohio University, Athens, OH 45701; email stjohn@ohio.edu

The new flowering of pragmatism, and its philosophical cousin, communitarianism, particularly as applied to practical questions about communication and community, is encouraging. Though the political commitments and material goals of thinkers as diverse as Fukuyama (1995, 2001), Etzioni (1993), Rorty (1982, 1991), and R. D. Putnam (1995, 2000) span a broad ideological spectrum, these theorists appear to share certain core concerns—concerns that echo those of the first "classical" pragmatist thinkers of the last century, most notably James, Dewey, and Mead. Contemporary versions of pragmatism advance a commitment to protecting a given community's health; a concern for political pluralism, or the rough secular equivalent of a civic ecumenicalism; and an explicit pledge to the forging of effective public action. Expressed metaphorically or plainly, implicitly or directly, these three commitments are among the central foci of the new theorizing in, about, and around pragmatism, as they were in classical expressions of that philosophy.

Health, pluralism, and action have consistently been building blocks of pragmatist theory and practice and have, thus, always required both a site of construction and a prime mover to do the work of theory building and civic implementation. In this essay, we argue that, although the three core concerns of classical pragmatism have migrated to, and been diffused among, contemporary pragmatisms—and therein received much theoretical attention—the site of their development has changed, but been left largely unexamined, even as the rhetorical force that once underlay these foundational foci has eroded. We argue that the discursive site of much current work in community building has shifted from a faith in transcendence to an insistence on tolerance, and that tolerance is now frequently wielded as a form of social capital in those community contexts.

To put our case bluntly, we believe this shift is wrongheaded and counterproductive. Well-intentioned but questionably theorized programs positing tolerance as the cornerstone of healthy, pluralistic, and action-oriented pragmatisms within communities serve little of the good that is intended of them. Where tolerance is lauded as a fertile ethical soil, we claim that its effects are fundamentally damaging to the health of communities. Where tolerance is conceived metaphorically as a conduit for infusions of the commonwealth or as a vessel for egalitarianism, we think it in fact stifles public discourse and thereby silences the very constituencies that the new generation of pragmatists most wish to emancipate. Lastly, where tolerance is held to actuate practical politics and constructive social change, we challenge such assertions and the assumptions about communication on which they appear to rest. As we will argue throughout this chapter, the practice of tolerance tends, albeit unintentionally, to reinscribe the political and social status quo (in a given community formation). It is, in this way, a fundamentally conservative embrace. Tolerance does not accomplish what its proponents claim it will because its effects for public actors are largely monologic, and thus run counter to the true aims of social capital, as the latter term is normatively applied in pragmatist programs. Tolerance invites expression, or declaration, rather than conversation, and so holds forth neither the expectation nor the accomplishment of real change. In a simple sense, the trouble with current treatments of community is that they have brought forward Dewey's and others' conceptions and concerns about *The Public and Its Problems* (Dewey, 1927), but have left behind their corresponding understanding of communication as being the miracle that allows for increasing freedom in the service of an ever-larger community (see Dewey, 1925, especially pp. 138–170).

The most serious underlying consequence of contemporary tolerance is that it fails to unite citizens. Conversely, it divides them. Tolerance is presently constructed and enacted in ways that assume a view of the other as permanently other, such that the gulf between selves is held to be unbridgeable. Within communities, efforts to overcome personal differences and unite for either a common cause or for the mere pleasures of congregation are discouraged under a strange rubric that defines good interaction as the absence of any interaction that might impinge upon self-oriented aims or desires. In other words, I would reach out to you if not for the fear that communing with you might interfere with the complete satisfaction of my own needs and wants. Governing all of this, in our view, are an unstated absence of genuine communication and, relatedly, an implied disbelief in the possibility of such communication. In practice, then, tolerance does not tolerate at all. It separates, individuates, and isolates, to the detriment of citizens and the communities in which they live.

In developing this thesis, we look first at the ways in which tolerance has been defined and applied in communication and community literature, across (principally) the past 2 decades. We devote particular attention to what tolerance putatively is in relation to what it is expected (or has been expected) to do to promote the advancement of pragmatist visions for revitalized communities and especially in its presumptive relationship to the formation of social capital. We then propose a return to the adoption of a metaphor of transcendence in the theorization and practice of communities. In so doing, we suggest that social capital is useful to the building of good communities only to the degree that it is wed to (i.e., conceptually consistent with) ideas of transcendence, and that such weddedness allows for a vision of community as fostering freedom and responsibility, social trust and productive change, and always in the aforementioned contexts of health, plurality, and action.

DEFINING TOLERANCE: FORBEARANCE

Formal definitions of tolerance have evolved significantly across time. *The Oxford English Dictionary (OED)* records appearances of tolerance in English as early as the 15th century. The primary meaning of the word as given in the *OED*, however, is not the one that likely springs to mind when one thinks of tolerance today. The first definition offered is in fact nearly the opposite of what one might expect. Tolerance is held to be "[t]he action or practice of enduring or sustaining pain or hardship; the power or capacity of enduring." We do not suspect that this characterization resonates with current uses or conceptions of the word. The second definition listed gets us somewhat closer to the general, contemporary sense of the word. Here tolerance is "[t]he action of allowing; license, permission granted by an authority." Even here, however, we would ask: Does a person in today's culture really think of tolerance in terms of an authority that grants permission to a citizen or group to speak or act? For many reasons, the answer is likely to be no. We suspect that only in the third definition does one hit upon a genuinely familiar characterization. Here, tolerance is "[t]he action or practice of tolerating; toleration; the disposition to be patient with or indulgent to the opinions or practices of others," in the explicit sense of representing a "freedom from bigotry or undue severity in judging the conduct of others." It is, in the end, a "forbearance" or "catholicity of spirit." In this last and, for our contemporaries, probably most palatable definition, tolerance means that one person not only allows another to say or think what he or she will, but does so in a painstakingly nonjudgmental way. Tolerance in this context is essentially defensive, inert, and noninterventionist. Tolerating someone else's speech or action entails doing nothing to interfere with either one. It is, counterintuitively, a vigorously active passivity.

The *OED* dates the earliest use of this third definition of tolerance to 1765, appropriately coinciding with the acts of British Parliament that provoked the colonial uprising and subsequent revolution in America, namely, the Stamp Act, requiring taxes to be paid by colonists directly to England, and the Quartering Act, requiring colonists to house and feed British troops. These established the first liberal, pluralistic nation-state. There has since long been an association between the difficulties of establishing a community built on the primacy of persons and their natural rights and the perceived need for tolerance as a kind of forbearance. There has been a strong tendency in U.S. culture to define freedom as liberation from the dictates of others (cf. Bellah, Madsen, Sullivan, Sidler, & Tipton, 1985, p. 24). As Dewey (1927) put it in his analysis of the rise of the democratic state:

> Freedom presented itself as an end in itself, though it signified in fact liberation from oppression and tradition. Since it was necessary, upon the intellectual side, to find justification for the movements of revolt, and since established authority was upon the side of institutional life, the natural recourse was appeal to some inalienable sacred authority resident in the protesting individuals. . . . The revolt against old and limiting associations was converted, intellectually, into the doctrine of independence of any and all associations. (pp. 86–87)

This doctrine of independence, or what Tocqueville coined *individualism* in his observations of America in the 1830s (see Arieli, 1964), is, of course, itself problematic for the establishment and maintenance of community. Here is both the theoretical and practical rub of the tenuous relation between tolerance and community. On one hand, the challenge of enacting Locke's (later, Jefferson's) liberal pluralism is one of holding together a functioning society of strangers, people unrelated by ties of blood, religion, race, ethnicity, or tradition. Such a society of strangers seems to demand considerable forbearance, or tolerance. On the other hand, being free of all others and their dictates, being independent of any and all associations, vitiates community ties and makes the experience of real society rare. This is the paradox that moved earlier pragmatist theorists James, Dewey, and Mead to invoke a metaphor of transcendence over and against one of mere tolerance. We will return to this move later in the chapter, in the context of showing how reigning definitions of tolerance thwart communities at nearly every turn and typically result in an empty kind of stasis, one that is antithetical to all that community is so widely believed to entail. In the following section, we review relatively recent literatures in communication that have relied on a metaphor of tolerance and explain its contemporary popularity.

TOLERANCE IN COMMUNICATION LITERATURES

Communication research deploys tolerance in a variety of ways and contexts. It has been studied in public opinion research on political tolerance (Bobo & Licari, 1989; Mueller, 1988); as a threshold term having measurable implications for the behavior of social actors (Glastra & Kats, 1993); as a threshold term having positive or negative psychological effects on subjects' perceptions in ambiguous situations (Ilardo, 1973); and as a dispositional factor influencing the application of information technologies (Baker & Ward, 2002; Harrison & Falvey, 2001). The studies cited above have generally looked at tolerance as a biochemical or psychosocial phenomenon whose origins and implications are primarily genetic or conditioned.

In a very different vein, communication scholars and political philosophers have recently looked at tolerance in the context of a major subfield within communication: the area(s) of civics, community, democracy, or democratic deliberation, in conjunction with questions about power, gender, culture, and social relations. Researchers have explored individual citizens' participation in communities (Hindman, 1998; Jeffres, Atkin, & Neuendorf, 2002); community involvement writ large (Rothenbuhler, Mullen, DeLaurell, & Rue, 1996); interpersonal or community-oriented dialogue in various settings (Penman, 1996; Simpson, 1995; Zoller, 2000); and pluralism in civic/communal contexts (Hindman, Littlefield, Preston, & Neumann, 1999). Tolerance has also featured prominently in rhetorical analyses of the critical dimensions of culture (Hamilton, 1998); in a study of the fostering of community in the classroom and in classroom pedagogy (McKerrow, 1998); and in the public construction of personal identity and social boundaries (Dollar & Zimmers, 1998).

Though these scholars and others mining similar ground differ as widely in their conclusions as they do in their initial hypotheses, the implied or overt importance of tolerance is manifest across the range of their inquiries. Simpson's (1995) ethnographic investigation of Tampa, Florida's decaying Ybor City neighborhood, for instance, chronicled the array of cultural and ethnic groups whose social and economic interplay made the area so unique. Even as the activist

descendants of the neighborhood's founders struggled with modernization and assimilation into the American middle class, they looked back warmly upon their
cultural heritage and fought to preserve it. Part of that effort toward preservation
lay in their recognizing that Ybor City's embrace of a diverse population was what
most endeared it to the people who inhabited it. Not surprisingly, tolerance is taken
to be key to the maintenance of this community.

The struggle against cultural assimilation detailed in Simpson's study and the
role tolerance presumably plays in such a struggle have become major themes in
our communal consciousness. Oberdiek (2001) typified the faithful, whose fulfillment is thought to lie in "[d]eveloping tolerant attitudes, acquiring the virtue of
tolerance, and encouraging tolerant practices radiates outward, making it possible
for most members of pluralist, multicultural societies to live flourishing lives" (p.
173). Given the implications of such expressions of faith, however, the "melting
pot" metaphor favored by urban progressives of the 18th and early 19th century,
including the classical pragmatist thinkers, has undergone severe critique in the
past few decades (see Leeds-Hurwitz, 2002, for a recent discussion; but see Joppke
& Morawska, 2003, for a recent collection suggesting a turn away from
multiculturalism and a return to assimilation). In the main, there has been a move
to preserve differences: The teeter-totter of pluralism and unity has for some time
been tilting the way of the many rather than the one. Bellah et al.'s *Habits of the
Heart* (1985) was a popular early warning of this tilt; Putnam's *Bowling Alone*
(2000) is an even more popular recent alert. The fear of cultural assimilation that
now seems common makes tolerance, where tolerance means tolerance of difference, a very attractive term and accompanying practice. This constellation of problems provides some accounting for the popularity of tolerance as a solution for
community ills, especially in North America.

There is, however, a second and in some ways more compelling account. Attendant to the fear of cultural assimilation is a deep-seated fear of psychological appropriation: the fear of losing one's self to another or of being overwhelmed by
another. This fear of seeing one's individuality subsumed has led to a critique of
community itself. Young (1990) put it plainly: "The ideal of community presumes
subjects can understand one another as they understand themselves. It thus denies
the difference between subjects" (p. 302). This fear, in turn, rests upon an assumption of a given, essential self (see Shepherd, 2001a, for a brief account of the rise
of the individual in modernity), a sense of self that the early pragmatists tried hard
to counter.

Mead (1934), in particular, offered a theory of individuation that is social and
constructionist: "[A]ll selves are constituted by or in terms of the social process,
and are individual reflections of it" (p. 201). Selves arise in social interaction.
Difference, or individuation, is an accomplishment of communication, not a fixed
mental state. This pragmatist position is given current voice in the wide-ranging
work of Habermas and is nicely summarized by Benhabib (1992):

The "I" becomes an "I" only among a "we," in a community of speech and action. Individuation does not precede association; rather it is the kinds of associations which we inhabit that define the kinds of individuals we will become. (p. 71)

In this view, communication is the process through which individuals are made and communities realized.

Communication, as an idea and practice, assumes the role of creator or generator in this theory. It is, in Dewey's (1925) memorable phrase, "a wonder by the side of which transubstantiation pales" (p. 138), "a natural bridge that joins the gap between existence and essence" (p. 139). Communication is what allows for the transcendence of selves, assuring, in direct contrast to the implications of (contemporary) tolerance, that selves are never fixed. In the following sections we highlight some of the negative consequences, in both theory and practice, of adopting a metaphor of tolerance over one of transcendence.

THE TROUBLE WITH TOLERANCE

Communities and Citizens in Association

The decision to embrace tolerance over other concepts has had direct repercussions for the viability of communication in communities. This is true, in part, because real-world efforts to implement prosocial (or multicultural) policies, especially in emergent liberal democracies, abound in both theoretical and applied contexts. For example, UNESCO has produced a series of instructional booklets aimed at educating people how to teach one another to be tolerant in multicultural and cross-cultural arenas. In a related context, noninterventionist political platforms, foreign and domestic, are now routinely founded on a framework of tolerance, that is, let each nation do as it will, provided that none interferes with the interests of the other.

As de Chaine (2002) observed in a recent essay about the international medical relief organization, Doctors Without Borders:

[T]he global "we" now spans geography and socioeconomic class; we have the capacity to imagine entire identities and entire worlds. [Doctors Without Borders'] discourse in this way capitalizes on the play of the imagination: its constituency, whether unwittingly or deliberately, works to harness the forces . . . of the global we. (p. 366)

As such, de Chaine warns, we must be vigilant in protecting social formations that encourage healthy communities, whether local or global, and must scrutinize material conditions that potentially threaten those communities. He writes: "The discursive landscape of our globalized world evinces the fact that we have entered into an 'altogether new condition of neighborliness' in which persons, money, commodities, and information circulate in uneven flows of power" (p. 366).

Neighborliness of this kind has, in a sense, always been a measure of the good community in pragmatist theory. In 1916, Dewey proposed two criteria for distinguishing good from bad communities: First, "how numerous and varied are the interests which are consciously shared?" (p. 83), and second, "how full and free is the interplay with other forms of association?" (p. 83). Good communities encourage interplay with other communities, recognizing that there is nothing essential or fixed about community borders. Full and free interplay between communities may, in fact, lead to the blurring of the old boundaries, the forging of new solidarities, and an expanded sense of the community (cf. Rorty, 1989, 1998; see Smiley, 1992, for a contemporary pragmatist consideration of the complexities of defining community boundaries). For us, the interplay that good communities allow suggests something much more than just tolerance. Indeed, we fear that too much talk of tolerance carries the danger of reifying community borders.

We want to be careful and clear here. Do we fault the efforts of UNESCO, Doctors Without Borders, or other programs or organizations like them? Of course not; their goals are inspiring and their efforts are courageous. We do call to account, however, implicit assumptions about the role of tolerance in achieving the aims of such humanitarian and prosocial efforts. How can a global we coalesce within a philosophical-communicative model that holds, as one of its central tenets, the belief that persons may best come together only by working assiduously to leave one another alone? How can UNESCO simultaneously teach both its noninterventionist platform, that is, do not bother me and I will not bother you, and pursue increased social and communal interaction? It seems to us that the two philosophical streams here not only fail to merge, but in fact flow in opposite directions. Summoning Buber, we would argue that the ostensible twin aims of contemporary tolerance, an increase in citizens' sense of community and a decrease in citizens' actual social interaction, are fundamentally irreconcilable and surely incompatible with a pragmatist program. We explore this irreconcilability at various junctures throughout the remainder of the essay.

The attempt to mix philosophical apples and oranges has not been the only perceived solution to the problem of tolerance. On the other end of the spectrum, the rejection of tolerance (again, as the term is currently defined) may be seen in North American public schools' zero tolerance policies, which vigorously punish speech or action that deviates from a rigidly enforced code of student conduct. Elsewhere, tolerance is invoked to varying degrees under the banner of human rights, religious diversity, economic parity, the eradication of sexual discrimination, freedom of scientific inquiry, and a host of other interests—often paradoxically—within a philosophical program that calls for the sanction or censure of any person or organization that refuses to accept or endorse that program's cause. These versions of tolerance thereby often implicitly advocate intolerance of those persons or groups deemed insufficiently tolerant.

In another paradox, of course, a tolerant person cannot force an intolerant one toward toleration because to exert discursive or physical coercion in the name of tolerance would itself constitute intolerance of the most abject kind. It is here that the unexpectedly pernicious effects of contemporary tolerance are exposed in their full unsightliness, because it is here that wanting to be tolerant by refusing to tolerate any form of (perceived) intolerance becomes true intolerance of a highly virulent strain. Recall our earlier invoking of Habermas. His various discussions of the importance of a community's arts of association all hinge on the same factor: citizens' range of freedom to come together to associate, to speak, act, eat, dance, vote, marry, celebrate, eulogize, compete, or worship, voluntarily in public places. These arts of association are, pointedly, social capital in action: They are lived instantiations of the fuel that makes the engine of community run. In the presence of a conceptually impoverished tolerance, though, there can be no arts of association, and so no community. As Habermas (1962/1989) observed, in what is still the finest historical account of community formation in incipient Western liberal-democratic nation-states, people doing things together is sine qua non for the life of any community.

His argument focuses partly on the alchemy of community interactions over and against the roles of the state and the media, roles that are often debilitating for communities. On the one hand, Habermas warned, individual citizens' desires to affiliate themselves with the state or the media— at the expense of the community— reduces public discourse to a sham symbolism. Community *transactions,* as he termed them, are:

> stylized into a show. Publicity [or, efficacious public speech and action] loses its critical function in favor of a staged display; even arguments are transmuted into symbols to which again one cannot respond by arguing but only by identifying with them. (p. 206)

These words are Habermas', but the fundamental concerns that they reflect are Burke's and Dewey's as well. A community whose citizens do not enliven and strengthen it with their physical, discursive, moral, political, and spiritual presence is no community at all; it is a puppeteered collective of unassociated persons whose sense of community has been prepackaged for them by the media, the state, or both.

On the other hand, a sentimental, nostalgic, or revisionist feeling for a community's revival or restoration may prove just as dangerous as no feeling for that community at all. Simply wanting community without thinking about what is wanted, or why, or to what ends, is naive and accomplishes little in and of itself. It is also damaging to citizens' sense of their community as a politically viable entity. Bake sales and church bazaars are well and good, but they are not enough in the face of external and internal contingencies like crime, budget crises, and zoning controversies. Habermas (1962/1989) sized up this problem quite astutely, observing that:

> The extent to which the public sphere as a sphere of ongoing [community] participation in a
> rational-critical debate concerning public authority is measured by the degree to which it has
> become a genuine . . . task for parties to generate periodically something like a public sphere to
> begin with. (p. 211)

In other words, arousing fellow-feeling by striking up the band in the public park
once a year does little for a community in the long term, nor, Habermas implied,
should it be expected to.

Both of these Habermasian problems display, in full canvas, the trouble with
tolerance. In the first scenario, citizens bypass community, drawn instead to the
fickle and ultimately nonassociative flame of media or state. In the second scenario, community is an odd kind of wish fulfillment, a harkening for what one
never had. The question begged in both cases is: Where is tolerance? Why have
these citizens failed or refused to apply tolerance squarely and confidently in the
face of their community's problems? If tolerance is thought to reside inextricably
these days in community, what is it about tolerance, or more precisely, about
tolerance's effect(s) on community, that makes citizens prefer an empty symbolism or a false revivalism to the prospects of real community? Our answer, again, is
that contemporary applications of tolerance make real community of the sort
Habermas claims citizens are most drawn to impossible to achieve. The paradoxes
of tolerance's intolerance, and the concomitant, paralyzing effect of its silent call
for an aggressively inert passivity, are sharply drawn. What is most desired is thrown
out because what is least desired cannot be conceptually or pragmatically detached
from it; the promise of the former is squandered by dint of its fidelity to the latter.

Tolerating, Thinking, and Acting

Tinder (1976) addressed the problem of tolerance in a seminal study of the
subject. He described in lucid terms a fundamental paradox besetting the very idea
of tolerance. Tinder stressed that:

> [w]e should remember that for the most part tolerance has been practiced by people who felt
> morally bound to be intolerant. People have usually been intolerant not because they defected
> from their principles but because they adhered to them. Defending tolerance thus is not merely
> a matter of calling to mind a few propositions so obviously true that no reasonable person could
> dispute them. It may well be that, as a value, tolerance is more open to doubt than is peace,
> economic security for everyone, or any other widely accepted ideal of our time. (p. 7)

The immediate and inescapable problem confronting tolerance here is that if
followed or observed, its practitioners significantly tie their own hands. It would
be very difficult to function as a community-oriented pragmatist while also sub-
scribing to, and practicing, tolerance as defined by the *OED*'s third entry (as discussed earlier).

In a recent essay on how the pragmatic tradition envisions community, Bernstein (1998) stressed that a properly conceived community must contain within itself a capacity for critique—of the self, of the whole, and of others. In reviewing Peirce's notion of what counts as a community, Bernstein asked: "Why is this notion of community so important?" He answered his own query as follows:

> It is [important] because each of us is conditioned by the prejudgments and the prejudices that have shaped us—prejudices that are at once enabling, but which can also prevent us from knowing what is real; prejudices responsible for the "vagaries of you and me." Individually, we cannot hope to escape from these prejudices, *but in a critical community it is possible to transcend our individual biases* (Bernstein 1998, 142–143, emphasis added).

The contrast here is clear. A community must prove willing to criticize itself and others if it wishes to escape charges of manifesting a form of prejudice. In Bernstein's view, prejudice is escaped by one's speaking and thinking critically. His formulation is quickly upended, however, if one's sense of what constitutes a healthy community is founded on contemporary definitions of tolerance. To be critical is to discriminate, in the most positive sense of that term. It is to make distinctions between better and worse resources, better and worse conditions, better and worse agendas, and better and worse decisions. Critical thinking is not inert, not passive, and above all not noninterventionist. A good part of the work of communities, then, is found in people speaking and acting assertively and constructively in the promotion of what they think is best for themselves and their communities. On this logic, not to do what one believes is right is an anticommunal error of omission, a disservice to one's fellow citizens, a ranking of a self-styled apathy over the willingness to act even in the face of potential disagreement or discord.

We return now to tolerance as popularly defined. The critical theorist Marcuse (1965), in his famous polemic *Repressive Tolerance,* lucidly outlined its pitfalls. In that essay, Marcuse developed a powerful argument about the ways in which silently oppressive majoritarian politics in liberal-democratic states (like the United States) are enforced culturally under the ironical banner of tolerance. We live in an individualistic society, Marcuse contended, one whose citizens pride themselves on their countless social and political freedoms. Yet the version of tolerance that has come to prominence since the end of World War II is one that represses individual freedoms at every turn by distancing citizens from one another. The result is nonsensical but marvelously effective from the perspective of statist interests. Citizens become isolated from one another; the social and communal bonds they might otherwise have formed for grassroots organizing or civil protest weaken or disappear altogether; each citizen turns individually for guidance and direction to the only other coherent cultural structure remaining: the state. This sequence, of course, drains older definitions of tolerance of all meaning. "When tolerance mainly serves the protection and preservation of a repressive society, [and] when it serves to neutralize opposition and to render men immune against other and better forms of life," Marcuse (1965) argued, "then tolerance has been perverted" (p. 111). In the end, "what is proclaimed as tolerance today . . . is in many of its most effective manifestations serving the cause of oppression" (p. 81).

It may be seen as a stretch for us to accuse tolerance of producing oppressive effects on this scale. On the other hand, the confusion over how tolerance is defined does reveal something about the term's implications for the health of communities, a point that can be illustrated by contrasting Marcuse's definition above with Vogt's (1997) characterization of tolerance in a recent book on tolerance and public education. Vogt explained:

> Most simply, tolerance is putting up with something one does not like. . . . [T]olerance often involves support for the rights and liberties of others, others whom one dislikes, disapproves of, disagrees with, finds threatening, or toward whom one has some other negative attitude. It follows from this definition that the opposite of tolerance is not prejudice, as is often assumed. Rather, the opposite of tolerance is discrimination, that is, taking action against people one dislikes or with whom one disagrees. Tolerance, by contrast, involves refraining from acting against people about whom one feels negatively. Tolerance generally requires self-control. (p. xxiv)

Marcuse's and Vogt's definitions anchor opposite poles of thought about tolerance. For the former, tolerance is dangerous precisely insofar as it limits direct agitation for change at moments when some person or party objects to the form or content of that agitation (or, the intended change). For the latter, tolerance works only if and when persons or organizations avoid doing or saying anything that does or could offend or hamper another person or organization. We think the dissonance between these two views, putatively grounded in the same governing term, could not be more striking.

We see two practical repercussions issuing from Vogt's definition of tolerance. First, by treating tolerance as an antonym of discrimination, Vogt leaves little room for any pragmatic action. If, as he views it, tolerance is mostly about not acting out against someone whose words or deeds one dislikes or disagrees with, then tolerance is necessarily almost functionless. In keeping with a tolerant stance, one does not act toward others at all. Second, and relatedly, we ask what kind of productive relations among citizens in a community remain possible under this definition of tolerance. How can persons come together to strengthen and deepen their social and civic ties if their principal aim is a kind of self-interested detachment from the needs or goals of their fellow citizens? Vogt appears to elevate nondisturbance of the self, for every self in a community, at the expense of any serious communion with others. Tolerance, though, cannot serve as a working form of social capital under this arrangement, nor would any legitimate version of community be workable under it.

R. D. Putnam (1995, 2000) has argued for the need for greater, wider, and more frequent social interaction among families, friends, and neighbors and has demonstrated empirically how social and communal ties weaken when such interaction wanes. Coleman (1988) argued that the presence of certain societal structures that make possible social interaction may prompt the increase of such interaction. Etzioni (1993) has argued that with strong rights come strong responsibilities, or that persons owe specific kinds of service to their communities. None of these arguments or its program(s) for communal change will be fulfilled so long as one person's action may be permanently checked by accusations of intolerance. In what follows, we discuss the work of social capital and make a case for its incompatibility with tolerance as the latter term is used in contemporary theorizing.

THE INADEQUACY OF TOLERANCE AS A FORM OF SOCIAL CAPITAL

Social Capital

Coleman (1988) has characterized social capital as a twofold system or process, one that is "defined by its function," not by its content (p. 98). Social capital "is not a single entity, but a variety of different entities, with two elements in common: They all consist of some aspect of social structures, and they facilitate certain actions of actors . . . within the stucture[s]" (p. 98). Social capital is not a good or service or any other measurable resource or product fostered within a social system. It is, rather, a framework of potentiality, a set of conditions that actualize communal goods. In a manner similar to Habermas' lifeworld, social capital "inheres in the structure of relations between actors and among actors. It is not lodged either in the actors themselves or in physical implements of production" (p. 98).

Responding to and augmenting Coleman's formulation, R. D. Putnam (1995) emphasized social capital's effects on communities. In a key passage, he summarized the benefits of communities' promotion of increased social capital. R. D. Putnam (1995) asserted that:

> [L]ife is easier in a community blessed with a substantial stock of social capital. In the first place, networks of civic engagement foster sturdy norms of generalized reciprocity and encourage the emergence of social trust. Such networks facilitate coordination and communication, amplify reputations, and thus allow dilemmas of collective action to be resolved. When economic and political negotiation is embedded in dense networks of social interaction, incentives for opportunism are reduced. At the same time, networks of civic engagement embody past success at collaboration, which can serve as a cultural template for future collaborations. Finally, dense networks of interaction probably broaden the participants' sense of self, developing the "I" into a "we," or (in the language of rational-choice theorists) enhancing the participants' "taste" for collective benefits (p. 67).

R. D. Putnam's discussion of "dense networks" is important to us for two reasons. First, we agree with his assessment that the presence of social capital in communities encourages continued density of social networks and reproduces itself as yet more social capital. We would additionally claim that tolerance is antithetical to the development of these networks, because the presence of a discursive and material force that can kill discussion by sheer fiat precludes possibilities for social density. An example illustrates the problem we encounter here. If I charge my city councilwoman with intolerance of the views of others, I will have likely placed her in an extraordinarily difficult position. She could not very well reply that yes, she is intolerant of my view. Her doing so would surely be politically suicidal. She could, instead, say that no, she is not intolerant, but she would then be left in the equally thorny position of having to explain how she could reject my viewpoint and yet still think of herself as a practitioner of tolerance. Her only real solution would be to adopt a strict policy of never saying or doing anything in response to, or (especially) in contradistinction to, what anyone else has said or done, and to make a weirdly adolescent countercharge of intolerance ("I am not intolerant. You are!"). This would likely lead either to a peaceful paralysis, one in which neither side says anything at all, or a mean-spirited partisanship in which both sides assume their differences so deep-seated as to be almost completely overdetermined. The latter would obviate the need for any dialogue and produce instead alternating monologues peppered with charges and countercharges of intolerance.

An implausible scenario? We do not think so. We should stress, however, that we do not view Putnam's dense networks simplistically as cohorts or collectivities of completely like-minded persons, nor do we think that R. D. Putnam holds this view. Rather, our position is informed by Rothenbuhler's (2001) characterization of community as "a container of differences" (p. 169), that is, an accomplishment of communication. As we see it, good deliberation is robust deliberation; it draws its vigor from the productive friction of disagreement. Conversely, in a fully tolerant community, vigorous public deliberation cannot be sustained for long because constructively open disagreement is structurally intolerable. Our point is that density does not equal unanimity and should not be perceived as being defeated or compromised by the absence of unanimity. To our way of thinking, the councilwoman is to be lauded for standing her ground and speaking her mind. What is served by her forcible silencing, other than the contradictory mandates of tolerance?

A second point about dense networks is also important. They help turn an "I" into a "we." This point should be extended to include the idea that the work of I-to-we transformation occurs in civic or public talk between the two parties. As Levinas (1961) has argued, "[t]o approach the Other in conversation is to welcome his expression [and] . . . [i]t is therefore to *receive* the Other beyond the capacity of the I" (p. 51, emphasis in the original). Specifically, the tie between the I and the we is language, and it is best understood, Levinas argued, through a metaphor of transcendence. He wrote:

> We shall try to show that the relation between the [self] and the other—upon which we seem to impose such extraordinary conditions—is language. For language accomplishes a *relation* such

that the terms are [limited by the new relationship], such that the other, despite the [new] relationship with the [self], remains transcendent to the same. (1961, p. 39, emphasis in the original)

The we of a community, then, does not entail a ceding of either one's selfhood or one's political views. That is precisely, as Shepherd (2001a, 2001b) put it, what communication allows, the simultaneous experiencing of self and other. Citizens within a community remain (individuated) persons, but they join together to act constructively in the service of the whole. The community they create transcends the power and influence of the individual citizen, yet neither compromises nor subsumes that citizen's standing as a singular person.

Putting together these two strands of R. D. Putnam's argument, we believe we are met with a model of social capital that cannot be adequately fueled by contemporary versions of tolerance. This is true, in large part, because social capital, unlike tolerance, rests ultimately on a foundation of social trust. Without it, all decision making and indeed all communal life itself becomes a zero-sum game in which any choice that does not reflect my individual interests is perceived to be intolerant of my needs. Any ontological push toward a social-communal us is thus held to entail, necessarily, my being something less than a fully self-determining me.

Transcending Tolerance

The touchstone of social capital is the principle of generalized reciprocity, I'll do this for you now, without expecting anything immediately in return and perhaps without even knowing you, confident that down the road you or someone else will return the favor. (R. D. Putnam, 2000, p. 134)

Generalized reciprocity, in turn, requires considerable social trust, "a 'standing decision' to give most people—even those whom one does not know from direct experience—the benefit of the doubt" (Rahn & Transue, 1998, p. 545). One way to summarize our concern with the glorification of tolerance we find in much of the community literature is to note that tolerating another does not require much, if any, actual trust in that other. Good communities evince an abundance of social trust, and so must preach and practice something much more than a nominal tolerance. It is difficult to overstate the import of this point. As Fukuyama (1995) convincingly showed, "a nation's well-being, as well as its ability to compete, is conditioned by a single, pervasive cultural characteristic: the level of trust inherent in the society" (p. 7). Following the classical pragmatist teachings of James, Dewey, Mead, and others, we envision the something more than mere tolerance that is necessary to the establishment of trust to be the idea and experience of communication, or transcendence.

Democratic communities are often tough places in which to reside because of a perceived incommensurability between freedom and responsibility, individual goals and social goods, the want of liberty and the attraction of unity. Bellah et al. (1985) offer a pithy summary of our shared discomfort. In contemporary America, they observed, the "freedom to be left alone is a freedom that implies being alone" (p. 23). Of course, few of us really want to be alone, or at least for very long. What then to do?

Pragmatists of the past century theorized their way out of this dilemma by refusing to accept the dichotomy of the psychological and the sociological. This refusal was captured in James's elegant oxymoron of the "pluralistic universe." Mead spent the better part of his academic life working out the relationship between self and society so as to ensure that neither of them could be found guilty of detracting from the other. Mead and his long-time friend Dewey turned to communication as the construct that would allow citizens and communities to enhance one another. Mead's "goal was not to eliminate difference but to somehow maintain it in a larger whole, a whole that for Mead develops in part through enhanced opportunities for communication" (Aboulafia, 1995, p. 182). Dewey (1927) tied the essence of humanity itself to this magical experience: "To learn to be human is to develop through the give-and-take of communication an effective sense of being an individually distinctive member of a community" (p. 154). For these classical pragmatists, as for us, communication dissolves the tired dichotomy and resolves the old dilemma such that it is possible to live "in service of a freedom which is cooperative and a cooperation which is voluntary" (Dewey, 1939/1989, p. 133). This position is voiced in Habermas's work as well. In his introduction to a collection of Habermas's essays, Hohengarten (1992) summarized our shared view succinctly: "Communication unites diverse forms of life without canceling their diversity" (p. xv).

In some ways, it is easy to tout the metaphysical, philosophical, and theoretical advantages of transcendence as opposed to tolerance when it comes to building and maintaining good communities, but harder to provide evidence of its enactment. Leeds-Hurwitz (2002) has recently done so in her compelling study of intercultural weddings. Leeds-Hurwitz shows how some couples are able to do more than tolerate each other's cultural practices; some couples manage to integrate traditions in complex ways that create entirely new, and so transcendent, social modes. These couples demonstrate the making of democratic communities at the site of the most basic unit of analysis—the dyad. They enact the hermeneutic/dialogic possibility envisioned by Gadamer (1989), whereby persons overcome their own particularity to reach an understanding. "To reach an understanding in a dialogue is not merely a matter of putting oneself forward and asserting one's own point of view, but [of] being transformed into a communion in which we do not remain what we were" (p. 379).

Another way to summarize the potential benefits of transcendence is to note that if we take communication to be the transcending of the gaps between self and other (cf. Peters, 1994, 1999), then this goal rightly entails transcending the self, or overcoming the self. The onus of civic responsibility here falls on each human self, which must escape itself by reaching out to an other or others. If, however, communication is held to be merely tolerance, as understood in today's culture, then the self's objective devolves to a resentful acceptance of the political and social presence of others. Again, we do not believe that real communion among a community's citizens can be fostered within this latter arrangement.

Transcendence overcomes the impasse of tolerance by actively promoting the thing that tolerance is most keen to avoid: interaction between persons, even in moments when they disagree; and further still, even in moments when they passionately disagree. In the worst-case scenario, citizens who categorically disagree about abortion or a zoning policy or a candidate for public office can still foster good grounds for interaction—in other words, social capital—by meeting and talking through their disagreements. In the best-case scenario, citizens bridge political and social gaps and form new relationships that in turn nurture the deeper soil of the community. Instead of shielding humans from messy but ultimately constructive human contact, as tolerance does, transcendence invites that contact, acknowledging its necessity and recognizing the potential community gains that lie on the far side of civic discourse.

Metaphors of transcendence promulgate an attitude of (positively) bearing with. The sense here is not that of gritting one's teeth while another stokes the fire of an opposing viewpoint. Conversely, it is a coming alongside, a walking together in a manner that privileges the fundamental humanity of one's fellow citizens above lesser considerations of political or cultural dissonance. Instead of leading with the self, in spear-like fashion, the citizen leads with a desire to seek the health of the community itself, keeping what that community in fact is, a gathering of human beings, foremost in mind.

In a very real sense, following Shepherd (2001a), we take community to be an interpersonal accomplishment of communication and find support for this view in the recent work of Johnson (2002). Johnson posed a question central to what we have argued here. She asked, in essence: What is community good for? Her answer: for finding practical solutions to interpersonal problems. We would extend her answer only by noting that in solving those problems, the interests of a strong and vital community are served as well. Recall our description above about the worst-case scenario: that persons would completely disagree. Even that outcome, Johnson (2002) observed, is better than their having never come together to express their views in the first place. She concluded that:

> [Persons have] reported that agreeing to disagree was the most common solution to public issue arguments. This could be especially true if these arguments served the function of routine, everyday talk or [of] transmitting knowledge. Therefore, such pragmatic outcomes as solving the argument might not be as important in public issue arguments. (p. 102)

Johnson's caveat underscores the value of knowing what serves well (or does not) as social capital, even as it veers from the course of claims about the need for a pragmatic transcending of tolerance.

CONCLUSION

The contrast between tolerance and transcendence as governing metaphors for theorizing and practicing community building is stark in at least one regard. As a young man, James despaired over realizing the fundamental isolation of every person from every other person (see Shepherd, 2001b, for an account of James's despondence and recovery). He sank into a deep depression, believing he could never incorporate others into himself. On the brink of suicide, James willed himself out of this crisis of mind and spirit by making what came to be his famous leap of faith. In essence, James willed himself to believe in the possibility of transcendence: in the possibility of overcoming his severed self and meeting others as he jumped into the social world. Contrast this with what seems to be a widespread contemporary metaphysical worry, that of losing one's self to an other or others. Whereas James feared never connecting with others, and overcame that fear by asserting faith in the possibility of communication, citizens today fear being deindividuated by social associations, and so erect a barrier of disbelief in the very possibility of connection or communication. This contrast is, we think, critical to understanding the problem of community that has received so much attention across the past 20 years. It is also key to understanding the inseparability of communication and community.

If, as the Greek dramatist Aeschylus claimed in *Prometheus Bound*, tyranny's disease is "to trust no friends" (trans. 1980), then democracy's need must be to have faith even in strangers. Social trust is necessary to the development of social capital, which in turn is required of good communities. All of this, we believe, hinges not upon the unengaged tolerance of others, but upon the willful transcendence of selves into the lives of others, where self and other do not lose what they are, yet become something more— healthier, pluralistic, and active—through the experience of community.

REFERENCES

Aboulafia, M. (1995). George Herbert Mead and the many voices of universality. In L. Langsdorf & A. R. Smith (Eds.), *Recovering pragmatism's voice: The classical tradition, Rorty, and the philosophy of communication* (pp. 179–194). Albany: State University of New York Press.

Arieli, Y. (1964). *Individualism and nationalism in American ideology.* Cambridge, MA: Harvard University Press.

Baker, P. M. A., & Ward, A. C. (2002). Bridging temporal and spatial "gaps": The role of information and information technologies in defining communities. *Information Communication & Society, 5,* 207–224.

Bellah, R. N., Madsen, R., Sullivan, W. M., Sidler, A., & Tipton, S. M. (1985). *Habits of the heart: Individualism and commitment in American life.* New York: Harper & Row.

Benhabib, S. (1992). *Situating the self.* New York: Routledge.

Bernstein, R. J. (1998) Community in the pragmatic tradition. In M. Dickstein (Ed.), *The revival of pragmatism: New essays on social thought, law, and culture* (pp. 141–156). Durham, NC: Duke University.

Bobo, L., & Licari, F. C. (1989). Education and political tolerance: Testing the effects of cognitive sophistication and target group affect. *Public Opinion Quarterly, 53,* 285–308.

Coleman, J. S. (1988). Social capital in the creation of human capital. *American Journal of Sociology, 94,* 95–120.

deChaine, R. (2002). Humanitarian space and the social imaginary: Médecins Sans Frontières/Doctors Without Borders and the rhetoric of global community. *Journal of Communication Inquiry, 26,* 354–369.

Dewey, J. (1916). *Democracy and education.* New York: Free Press.

Dewey, J. (1925). *Experience and nature.* Chicago: Open Court.

Dewey, J. (1927). *The public and its problems.* New York: Holt.

Dewey, J. (1939/1989). *Freedom and culture.* Buffalo, NY: Prometheus Books

Dickstein, M. (Ed.). (1998). *The revival of pragmatism: New essays on social thought, law, and culture.* Durham, NC: Duke University Press.

Dollar, N. J., & Zimmers, B. G. (1998). Social identity and communicative boundaries: An analysis of youth adult street speakers in a U.S. American community. *Communication Research, 25,* 596–617.

Etzioni, A. (1993). *The spirit of community: The reinvention of American society.* New York: Simon & Schuster.

Fukuyama, F. (1995). *Trust.* New York: Free Press.

Fukuyama, F. (2001). Social capital, civil society and development. *Third World Quarterly, 22,* 7–20.

Gadamer, H. G. (1989). *Truth and method* (2nd rev. ed.). New York: Crossroad.

Glastra, F., & Kats, E. (1993). The filmic construction of tolerance: Representations of interethnic relations in educational films. *European Journal of Communication, 8,* 345–363.

Habermas, J. (1989). *The structural transformation of the public sphere: An inquiry into a category of bourgeois society* (T. Berger, Trans.). Cambridge, MA: MIT Press. (Original work published 1962)

Hamilton, J. (1998). Migrant space, migrant community: Williams, Bakhtin, and cultural analysis. *Communication Review, 2,* 395–431.

Hardwick, C. D., & Crosby, D. A. (Eds.). (1997). *Pragmatism, neo-pragmatism, and religion: Conversations with Richard Rorty.* New York: Peter Lang.

Harrison, T. M., & Falvey, L. (2001). Democracy and new communication technologies. In W. B. Gudykunst (Ed.), *Communication yearbook 25* (pp. 1–43). Mahwah, NJ: Erlbaum.

Hindman, D. B. (1998). Community, democracy, and neighborhood news. *Journal of Communication, 48*(2), 27–39.

Hindman, D. B., Littlefield, R., Preston, A., & Neumann, D. (1999). Structural pluralism, ethnic pluralism, and community newspapers. *Journalism & Mass Communcation Quarterly, 76,* 250–263.

Hohengarten, M. W. (1992). Translator's introduction. In J. Habermas, *Postmetaphysical thinking: Philosophical essays* (pp. vii–xx). Cambridge, MA: MIT Press.

Ilardo, J. A. (1973). Ambiguity tolerance and disordered communication: Therapeutic aspects. *Journal of Communication, 23,* 371–391.

Jeffres, L. W., Atkin, D., & Neuendorf, K. A. (2002). A model linking community activity and communication with political attitudes and involvement in neighborhoods. *Political Communication, 19,* 387–421.

Johnson, A. J. (2002). Beliefs about arguing: A comparison of public issue and personal issue arguments. *Communication Reports, 15,* 99–111.

Joppke, C., & Morawska, E. (2003). *Toward assimilation and citizenship: Immigrants in liberal nation-states.* New York: Macmillan.

Leeds-Hurwitz, W. (2002). *Wedding as text: Communicating cultural identities through ritual.* Mahwah, NJ: Erlbaum.

Levinas, E. (1961). *Totality and infinity* (A. Lingis, Trans.). Pittsburgh, PA: Duquesne University Press.

Marcuse, H. (1965). Repressive tolerance. In R. P. Wolff, B. Moore, Jr., & H. Marcuse, *A critique of pure tolerance* (pp. 81–123). Boston: Beacon.

McKerrow, R. E. (1998). Rhetoric and the construction of a deliberative community. *Southern Communication Journal, 63*, 350–356.

Mead, G. H. (1934). *Mind, self, and society.* Chicago: University of Chicago Press.

Menand, L. (2001). *The metaphysical club.* New York: Farrar, Straus, & Giroux.

Mounce, H. O. (1997). *The two pragmatisms: From Peirce to Rorty.* New York & London: Routledge.

Mueller, J. (1988). Trends in political tolerance. *Public Opinion Quarterly, 52*, 1–25.

Oberdiek, H. (2001). *Tolerance: Between forbearance and acceptance.* Lanham, MD: Rowman & Littlefield.

Oxford English Dictionary (2nd ed., Vol. 11). (1970). Oxford, UK: Clarendon Press.

Penman, R. (1996). Imagining conversation and community. *Australian Journal of Communication, 23*, 16–23.

Peters, J. D. (1994). The gaps of which communication is made. *Critical Studies in Mass Communication, 11*, 117–140.

Peters, J. D. (1999). *Speaking into the air: A history of the idea of communication.* Chicago: University of Chicago Press.

Putnam, H. (1995). *Pragmatism: An open question.* Cambridge, MA: Blackwell Publishers.

Putnam, R. D. (1995). Bowling alone: America's declining social capital. *Journal of Democracy, 6*, 65–78.

Putnam, R. D. (2000). *Bowling alone: The collapse and revival of American community.* New York: Simon & Schuster.

Rahn, W. M., & Transue, J. E. (1998). Social trust and value change: The decline of social capital in American youth, 1976–1995. *Political Psychology, 19*, 545–565.

Rorty, R. (1982). *Consequences of pragmatism: Essays 1972–1980.* Minneapolis: University of Minnesota Press.

Rorty, R. (1989). *Contingency, irony, and solidarity.* Cambridge, UK: Cambridge University Press.

Rorty, R. (1991). *Objectivity, relativism, and truth: Vol. 1: Philosophical papers.* Cambridge, UK: Cambridge University Press.

Rorty, R. (1998). *Truth and progress: Vol. 3: Philosophical papers.* Cambridge, UK: Cambridge University Press.

Rosenthal, S. B., Hausman, C. R. & Anderson, D. R. (1999). *Classical American pragmatism: Its contemporary vitality.* Urbana: University of Ilinois Press.

Rothenbuhler, E. W. (2001). Revising communication research for working on community. In G. J. Shepherd & E. W. Rothenbuhler (Eds.), *Communication and community* (pp. 159–179). Mahwah, NJ: Erlbaum.

Rothenbuhler, E. W., Mullen, L. J., DeLaurell, R., & Ryu, C. R. (1996). Communication, community attachment, and involvement. *Journalism & Mass Communication Quarterly, 73*, 445–466.

Shepherd, G. J. (2001a). Community as the interpersonal accomplishment of communication. In G. J. Shepherd & E. W. Rothenbuhler, *Communication and community* (pp. 25–35). Mahwah, NJ: Erlbaum.

Shepherd, G. J. (2001b). Pragmatism and tragedy, communication and hope: A summary story. In D. K. Perry (Ed.), *American pragmatism and communication research* (pp. 241–254). Mahwah, NJ: Erlbaum.

Simpson, T. A. (1995). Communication, conflict, and community in an urban industrial ruin. *Communication Research, 22*, 700–719.

Smiley, M. (1992). *Moral responsibility and the boundaries of community: Power and accountability from a pragmatic point of view.* Chicago: University of Chicago Press.

Tinder, G. (1976). *Tolerance: Toward a new civility.* Amherst: University of Massachusetts Press.

Vogt, W. P. (1997). *Tolerance and education: Learning to live with diversity and difference.* Thousand Oaks, CA: Sage.

West, C. (1989). *The American evasion of philosophy: A genealogy of pragmatism.* Madison: University of Wisconsin Press.

Young, I. M. (1990). The ideal of community and the politics of difference. In L. J. Nicholson (Ed.), *Feminism/postmodernism* (pp. 300–323). New York: Routledge.

Zoller, H. M. (2000). "A place you haven't visited before": Creating the conditions for community dialogue. *Southern Communication Journal, 65,* 191–207.

CHAPTER CONTENTS

6 Ideal Collaboration: A Conceptual Framework of Community Collaboration

RENEE GUARRIELLO HEATH
LAWRENCE R. FREY
University of Colorado at Boulder

Collaboration has become a central feature of organizational and community landscapes in recent years. Although the concept of collaboration has received much scholarly attention, *community collaboration* has not been adequately considered and conceptualized as a unique and important form of collaboration. This chapter first offers a conceptual framework for understanding community collaboration that emerges from principles and concepts articulated by the *bona fide group perspective* and the *systems perspective*. The 12-cell matrix, produced by combining the four constituents of community collaborations identified from a bona fide group perspective (individual representatives, collaboration groups, organizational stakeholders, and the communities within which collaborations are embedded) with the three major categories from the systems perspective (inputs/antecedents, throughputs/processes, and outputs), provides the basis for reviewing what is known from the extant literature about successful or ideal community collaboration and what remains to be known. The framework, thus, serves the heuristic purpose of conceptualizing collaboration, organizing the relevant literature, and suggesting directions for future research, especially about the constitutive role that communication plays in community collaborations.

C ollaboration is more than a popular buzzword dropped casually into organizational discourse, and more than the jargon used to describe joint software projects in the technology industry. In most communities today, it is a necessity for groups, organizations, and institutions to work together collaboratively to confront complex issues. A quick perusal of current events taking

AUTHORS' NOTE: The authors would like to thank Jessica MacDonald, Timothy Kuhn, and Randal Ford for their helpful suggestions that shaped this chapter.

Correspondence: Renee Guarriello Heath, University of Colorado at Boulder, Department of Communication, 270 UCB, Boulder, CO 80309-0270; email: Renee.Heath@colorado.edu place throughout the United States illustrates the prevalence and need for *community collaboration*. In Moraine Valley, Nevada, two organizations joined forces with the Moraine Valley Community College to improve the safety of college campus buildings. The collaboration was recognized by the American Federation of Teachers (AFT)-Saturn/United Auto Workers (UAW) Partnership Award, which acknowledges outstanding alliances "based on trust, teamwork, shared decision-making, training, accountability, quality and the ability to survive conflict and change" (U.S. Newswire, 2002). In Milwaukee, Wisconsin, the Private Industry Council, a private, nonprofit organization, was invited to join the state's Labor Department to work with religious and community groups to improve local unemployment conditions, a model of collaboration the partners hope will be replicated across the country (Dresang, 2002). In Redondo Beach, California, the AIDS Healthcare Foundation, the nation's largest provider of HIV and AIDS medical care, and a local service provider collaborated to create a new medical clinic (McDermott, 2002). Where collaboration is not yet happening, community leaders are alerting their constituents about the need for it. Community leaders in Charleston, South Carolina, for example, have pleaded for community collaboration as the key to improving local public education and confronting other complex and difficult community issues. The need for and value of collaboration was articulated in the comments made by one involved community member: "Only through collaboration on a regional strategy can we maximize our limited financial resources and harness the ingenuity of our people to produce the quantum leaps we need" (McDermott, 2002).

The topic of community collaboration is not only important from the pragmatic perspective of the sheer number of collaborations taking place, it can also help communication scholars to understand the theoretic (and pragmatic) implications of what Mumby and Stohl (1996) called the "problematic of organization-society" (p. 54). To these scholars, organizations are conceptually "recognized as embedded in a cultural/societal context that affects and is affected by internal organizational action," but are routinely treated as "separate and distinct from society" (p. 65). By blurring the boundaries between organizations and society, community collaborations serve as an important site for shedding light on the communicative processes of organizing in context. Moreover, community collaborations expand the focus on organizing beyond the traditional workplace context and boundaries; studying them, thus, has the potential to demonstrate what the communication discipline can contribute to the very social issues that community collaborations often try to address.

Given the theoretical and practical significance of collaboration, it is no wonder that, in the last decade, scholars have turned their attention to understanding this phenomenon. A number of general principles and characteristics of collaboration have been advanced, as will be shown, and case studies of collaboration have been documented; however, to date, there have been, as far as we know, no systematic attempts to document and synthesize the available scholarly literature on community collaboration. The purpose of this essay is to fill that gap by advancing a conceptual framework for understanding community collaboration that articulates central concepts and categories that can be used to organize the extant research, reveal the role that communication plays in community collaboration, and set agendas for future research.

This chapter begins by defining the concept of collaboration, in general, and community collaboration, more specifically. It then articulates a conceptual framework for understanding community collaboration that combines elements of two conceptual/theoretical perspectives that are particularly appropriate for understanding this phenomenon: the bona fide group perspective and the systems perspective. Next, this chapter reviews the extant literature on collaboration in light of the categories comprising the conceptual framework, focusing in particular on what the research reveals about ideal community collaboration (i.e., those characteristics that have been theorized or shown to be associated with successful community collaboration). The chapter concludes by discussing how this conceptual framework contributes to an understanding of communication and community and offering suggestions for future research.

DEFINING COMMUNITY COLLABORATION

Collaboration historically emerged within the context of for-profit organizations as a new way of organizing workers to accomplish tasks. Appley and Winder (1977) saw collaboration as an important alternative to hierarchical ways of organizing in light of the significant transitions that were taking place in the workplace during the 1970s. Approaching it from a psychological perspective, they defined collaboration (in this case, intraorganizational collaborations between different units within the same organization) as

a relational system in which: 1) individuals in a group share mutual aspirations and a common conceptual framework; 2) the interactions among individuals are characterized by "justice as fairness"; and 3) these aspirations and conceptualizations are characterized by each individual's *consciousness* of his/her motives toward the other; by a *caring* or concern for the other; and by commitment to work with the other over time provided that this commitment is a matter of *choice*. (p. 281)

Appley and Winder viewed this type of relational system "as a value system upon which new solutions can be framed" (p. 280) and, thus, believed that organizations would increasingly turn to intraorganizational collaboration.

The concept of collaboration was first introduced in the 1960s (see Trist, 1989); however, not until the late 1980s and early 1990s, when interorganizational collaborations emerged, did scholars seriously focus attention on understanding collaboration. Gray and Wood (Gray, 1989; Gray & Wood, 1991; Wood & Gray, 1991) offered seminal perspectives on interorganizational collaboration, viewing it as composed of interdependent stakeholders having a shared goal and working on mutual problem solving in a nonhierarchical structure, to the extent that is possible in an organizational context.

Since that time, scholars have generally moved toward consensus on some crucial elements that should be included in any definition of collaboration. As Keyton and Stallworth (2003) explained, "Nearly all definitions identify a collaboration as a temporarily formed group with representatives from many other primary organizations" (p. 236). Stohl and Walker's (2002) definition is representative, viewing collaboration as "involving autonomous stakeholders with varying capabilities, and including resources, knowledge and expertise which is directed toward individual goals and mutually accountable innovative ends" (p. 240).

Scholars also generally agree on some central characteristics of successful collaborations. In summarizing the available literature, Stallworth (1998) identified four elements that are viewed as essential to the success of a collaboration: (a) shared goal, (b) member interdependence, (c) equal input of participants, and (d) shared decision making.

Scholars have identified these characteristics and elements; however, given the view of collaboration as a temporary or short-term work group, the extant literature primarily emerges from and applies to collaborations between business organizations rather than to community collaborations. Community collaborations represent a distinct type of collaboration, in part, because they focus on issues at the local level and problems that usually demand long-term social change (e.g., health care and juvenile crime); hence, community collaborations contrast sharply with short-term collaborations designed to develop new products and services offered by for-profit organizations. Community collaborations, consequently, more often require a stable collaboration structure that may live on in some form for years or even become permanently institutionalized into a community. Community collaborations may also differ from the voluntary participation that typically characterizes other types of collaborations (Gray & Wood, 1991), as government bodies frequently mandate some aspect of the membership of community collaborations (Keyton & Stallworth, 2003).

A focus on community collaboration also calls increased attention to the processes that should characterize a collaboration. Marshall (1995), for instance, argued that collaboration should be a "principle-based process of working together that produces trust, integrity and breakthrough results by building true consensus, ownership and alignment in all aspects of other ways to think about collaboration" (p. 15). Haskins, Liedtka, and Rosenblum (1998) viewed collaboration as an ethic that moves teams beyond a transactional or task-oriented aim to one that is relational: "At the core of . . . collaboration is a set of moral values and principles that is rooted in a desire to serve and manage" (p. 34). Chrislip and Larson (1994) approached collaboration as a community model of civic leadership, highlighting processes such as shared responsibility and authority:

> [Collaboration] is a mutually beneficial relationship between two or more parties who work toward common goals by sharing responsibility, authority, and accountability for achieving results. Collaboration is more than simply sharing knowledge and information (communication) and more than a relationship that helps each party achieve its own goals (cooperation and coordination). The purpose of collaboration is to create a shared vision and joint strategies to address concerns that go beyond the purview of any particular party. (p. 5)

At the heart of these collaborative principles and processes, whether in community or business-based collaborations, is communication. Lawrence, Hardy, and Phillips (2002) claimed that "collaboration is a cooperative, interorganizational relationship that is negotiated in an ongoing communicative process" (p. 282). Kuhn (1998) claimed that "collaboration always involves the coordination and control of action through the use of symbols" (p. 1) and Keyton and Stallworth (2003) explained that the essential elements of collaboration—shared goal, member interdependence, equal input of participants, and shared decision making—are "products of the reflexive relationship between the communication of collaboration members and the development of the collaboration's culture and operating procedures" (p. 240). A number of studies have verified the significant influence of communication on collaboration effectiveness (see, e.g., Stegelin & Jones, 1991; Taber, Walsh, & Cooke, 1979; Yon, Mickelson, & Carlton-LaNey, 1993).

Communication scholars are thus in a unique position to illuminate the central principles and processes that enable collaboration, in general, and on which community collaboration, in particular, is based. With little initial infrastructure, such as office buildings and full-time staff persons (Stohl & Walker, 2002), community collaborations rely heavily on meeting processes and informal networking to organize and thereby centralize communicative practices in their organizing. In addition, the commitment of community collaborations to social change at local levels is often driven by deeper principles that are explicitly espoused in mission and vision statements (although the influence of such statements on actual behavior is debatable). Indeed, community collaboration is an alternative model of communication to traditional civic decision-making modes (Hogue, 1993).

Scholars have developed various definitions for the term collaboration, identified some of its salient characteristics, and recommended processes that collaborations should use; however, they have not focused enough attention on community collaboration as a distinct and unique type of collaboration. In part, this is because "collaboration theory has not yet come to terms with analysis at the societal level" (Pasquero, 1991, p. 55). Scholars, instead, have concentrated on studying collaborations between for-profit organizations that do not directly involve community members or are not designed to solve community needs per se (e.g., the collaboration of Boeing Corporation with companies in Japan and other countries to design the 767 aircraft, as studied by Hladik, 1988). Pasquero, thus, concluded that "collaboration theory frameworks must therefore be extended to include societal-level variables" (p. 55).

A focus on community collaborations extends the study of collaboration to the societal level by focusing on those collaborations that involve members of a local community and/or are designed to meet the needs of a local community. Community is an enduring concept with a rich history (see Depew & Peters, 2001); however, it is also a highly contested term with multiple meanings (see Adelman & Frey, 1997). This chapter uses the term in a fairly traditional sense to refer to the people and places that constitute a locale (see Young, 1995) that has particular needs that the type of collaboration we are discussing is designed to meet. Accordingly, this chapter offers the following definition of community collaboration:

> *Community collaboration* is composed of a group of autonomous stakeholders with varying capabilities (including resources, knowledge, and expertise) that are directed toward mutually accountable, typically innovative ends, producing long-term social change at a local level in a cooperative, relatively nonhierarchical relationship that is negotiated in an ongoing communicative and principled process.

A CONCEPTUAL PERSPECTIVE FOR UNDERSTANDING COMMUNITY COLLABORATION

Gray and Wood (1991) contended that collaboration has typically been studied from six conceptual-theoretical perspectives: resource dependence theory, corporate social performance theory-institutional economics theory, strategic management theory-social ecology theory, microeconomics theory, institutional theory-negotiated order theory, and political theory. Resource dependence theory seeks to understand the relationship between the impetus for collaboration and the interdependence of stakeholders' organizational resources. Corporate social performance theory asks what role business should play as a social institution and is combined with institutional economics theory, which focuses on how social and institutional legitimacy are defined and achieved. Strategic management theory "depicts a focal organization charting independent courses of action to gain competitive advantage" (Gray & Wood, 1991, p. 9) and is combined with social ecology theory, which emphasizes a collective approach to solving problems. Microeconomics theory is concerned with organizations achieving efficient "transactions" with other organizations (Gray & Wood, p. 10). Institutional theory's central premise is that "organizations seek to achieve legitimacy from institutional actors by structurally adjusting to institutional influences" (Gray & Wood, p. 10) and can be combined with negotiated order theory, which "focuses on the symbolic and perceptional aspects of interorganizational relationships, particularly on the evolution of shared understandings among stakeholders" (Gray & Wood, p. 10). Political theory "is inherently a relational theory for which key questions include, Who has access to power and resources? and Who does and does not benefit from various distributions of power and resources?" (Gray & Wood, p. 11).

None of these perspectives, however, approaches collaboration (which, as previously explained, is a type of group) from a group perspective. Moreover, although some of these theories (e.g., institutional/negotiated order theory) are compatible with a communication approach, none of these perspectives per se "provide[s] much insight into the process of collaboration—that is, how members communicate to enact or engage in collaborative activity" (Keyton & Stallworth, 2003, p. 239). A number of group communication perspectives could potentially be brought to bear to explain community collaborations; however, given that collaboration is a type of group that is part of a larger context or system, two conceptual/theoretical perspectives rooted in the contextual study of groups as systems—the *bona fide group perspective* and the *systems perspective*—are particularly useful for understanding community collaboration. The bona fide group perspective is especially helpful for understanding the constituents composing a collaboration; the systems perspective is particularly helpful for understanding the processual or developmental nature of a collaboration.

The bona fide group (BFG) perspective is a relatively new perspective (Poole [1999] called it and other recent conceptual developments in the study of groups, such as the naturalistic paradigm, an agenda-setting perspective, in contrast to general theories of group communication, such as functional theory) that offers an alternative to the traditional container model of groups that focuses solely on internal group processes (see Frey, 2003; Putnam & Stohl, 1990, 1996; Stohl & Putnam, 1994). Specifically, the BFG perspective argues that bona fide groups are characterized by permeable and fluid boundaries, unstable and ambiguous borders, and interdependence with relevant contexts. *Permeable boundaries* acknowledges that groups are characterized by "(a) multiple group memberships and conflicting role identities, (b) representative roles, (c) fluctuations in membership, and (d) group identity formation" (Putnam & Stohl, 1996, p. 150); *unstable and ambiguous borders* signify that "groups continually change, redefine, and renegotiate their borders to alter their identities and embedded context" (Stohl & Putnam, 1994, p. 291); and *interdependence with relevant contexts* focuses on "(a) intergroup communication, (b) coordinated actions among groups, (c) negotiation of jurisdiction or autonomy, and (d) interpretations or frames for making sense of intergroup relationships" (Putnam & Stohl, 1996, p. 153). Keyton and Stallworth (2003) believed that these characteristics are particularly applicable to collaborations:

> Four characteristics—(a) members from various organizations addressing a shared problem, (b) the potential imbalance of power, (c) divided membership loyalty, and (d) rotating organizational representation—place collaborations within the bona fide group perspective and its emphasis on permeable boundaries, shifting borders, and the effects of a group's contexts on its internal processes. (p. 239)

Stohl and Walker (2002) recently used the BFG perspective to develop a Bona Fide Group Collaboration Model (BFGCM). The model places equal emphasis on

(a) environmental exigencies that affect a collaboration and (b) internal collaboration communication processes. In addition, the BFGCM underscores that collaborations lack formal hierarchical structures and are distinguished from other groups by their composition, being composed of people representing different organizations and community groups. The model is especially useful in recognizing that dialectical tensions often exist among the goals of individual collaboration members, the collaborating group, and collaboration members' stakeholder organizations. In doing so, the BFGCM directs attention not only to the individual collaboration participants and to the internal collaboration group processes but also to the organizational stakeholders represented in a collaboration. The BFGCM model, thus, identifies three primary constituents of a collaboration: (a) individual collaboration representatives, (b) the collaboration group itself, and (c) stakeholders represented in the collaboration. To this group of constituents this chapter adds (d) the community in which the collaboration is embedded and for which a community collaboration, in particular, is designed to serve.

Systems theory is a well-developed perspective that has been widely applied to understand the interconnectivity of related elements bound together in a meaningful manner; indeed, Mabry (1999) argued that the term *systems* is "*the* dominant metaphor for describing virtually every major component of daily life . . . for example, the solar system, ecosystem, political system, management system, family system, and the autoimmune system" (p. 71). It is no surprise, then, that the systems perspective is one of the dominant paradigms used to describe and explain small groups (see Gouran, 1997), especially communication in small groups, for "a core assumption of systems theorizing is that *communication* is the observable phenomenon binding together constituent components of systemic entities. . . . Thus, group members (or sets of groups) are joined together as a social system through their communication" (Mabry, 1999, p. 72).

There are many important assumptions and principles that characterize the systems perspective (and are applicable to community collaborations, such as collaborations as open systems; see Keyton & Stallworth, 2003). Nonetheless, much of the theorizing about systems has centered on their process or developmental nature, with a number of constructs referencing the important relationship between the development of a system and the environments within which it is embedded (e.g., *morphostasis*, "system-environment interaction that stimulates a system to repeat a course of action or continue along a particular goal path," and *morphogenesis*, "the ability of a system to modify its goals, behavioral processes, and structure through interaction with its environment"; Mabry, 1999, p. 77). Within the context of small groups as systems, scholars have focused on three broad categories that describe in general terms the development of a group system: inputs, throughputs, and outputs. As applied to collaboration, *inputs* are antecedents that precede and potentially structure the interaction that occurs in a collaboration group; relevant input variables include members (e.g., their needs and skills), the physical environment within which a collaboration group meets (e.g., room setting), and the resources available to a collaboration group (e.g., time and funds).

Throughputs are the processes in which a collaboration group engages as members interact (e.g., communication processes enacted and decision-making procedures employed). *Outputs* are the outcomes that result from the interactions of a collaboration group (e.g., decisions made and effects on the local community). Gray and Wood (1991) used these general categories of inputs, throughputs, and outputs in their analysis of collaboration literature, arguing that these categories were "essential to understanding collaborative alliances" (p. 13; see also Cohen & Mankin, 1999).

Together, the systems perspective and the bona fide group perspective (especially as articulated in the BFGCM) provide useful perspectives for an integrated understanding of the antecedents, processes, and outcomes of a community collaboration from an internal and external perspective, as seen from the points of view of the individual representatives of a collaboration, the collaboration group, the organizational stakeholders involved in the collaboration, and the community within which the collaboration is embedded and that it is attempting to serve. Accordingly, the three general categories of the systems perspective constitute the rows of the conceptual framework advanced here and the four constituents of a collaboration identified by the BFGCM (including the one we added) constitute the columns of the framework (see Table 1). The chapter now examines the available literature on collaboration within the categories of this conceptual framework, explaining what the theory and research reveals about the relevant input, throughput, and output characteristics for individual collaboration members, the collaboration group, participating collaboration stakeholder organizations, and the community within which a collaboration is embedded that are associated with a successful community collaboration. The findings reviewed in the various cells are not mutually exclusive and could be potentially categorized into multiple cells of the framework. As an example, "collaborative competence" (as explained below) can be potentially seen as an antecedent to collaboration or as an outcome that results from having experienced the collaborative process. When appropriate, explanations of the choices made in placing findings into a particular cell accompany the table.

The focus is on collaboration in the ideal form because the ideal has proven historically useful in understanding and evaluating complex organizational types. Weber's (1947) seminal theories of social and economic organizations were developed with ideal forms in mind, and Rothschild-Whitt (1979) outlined collectivist-democratic organizations in an ideal form that feminist scholars continue to use today as a yardstick when assessing organizations. Ideal forms have also proven useful for illuminating other types of contexts, events, and activities, such as Habermas's (1970a, 1970b, 1984) conception of the *ideal speech situation* on which society should be modeled. The focus, therefore, is on *ideal collaboration* as a heuristic tool for understanding what the literature reveals about the principles and practices of successful community collaboration.

The literature reviewed comes from a wide range of scholarly disciplines, for collaboration, in one form or another, has been studied by many different scholars, including those in public management, health care, education, and technology.

TABLE 1
A Conceptual Framework of Ideal Community Collaboration

	Antecedents of ideal collaboration	Processes of ideal collaboration	Outcomes of ideal collaboration
Individual Representative	Traits: **cognitive complexity** (ability to integrate complex goals of collaboration) (Kline et al., 1990) and **self-monitoring** (awareness of communication behaviors) (Ellis & Cronshaw, 1992); **predisposition to engage in collaborative conflict management** (e.g. extrovert on MBTI) (Kilmann & Thomas, 1977) **Collaborative competence/ethic**, including ability to trust others, values processes such as consensus, flat hierarchy, and shared power—things that are not easily trainable (Barrett, 1995; Haskins et al., 1998; Mintzberg et al., 1996; Welch, 2000) **Power to make decisions** (Heath & Sias, 1999; Marshall, 1995) **Committed to long-term engagement** with the collaborative group (Lange, 2003)	**Understands and takes part in participative processes** (Haskins et al., 1998; Heath & Sias, 1999; Innes & Booher, 1999) **Enacts dialogic processes** (Barrett, 1995; Medved et al., 2001; Zoller, 2000) **Attentive to/willingness to spend time on communication processes and structures** (time spent talking about) (Barrett, 1995) **Manages ongoing dialectical tensions** (e.g., organizational versus collaborative group's goals) (Jones & Bodtker, 1998; McKinney, 2001; Medved et al., 2001) **Displays organizational agendas** (Jones & Bodtker, 1998; Keyton & Stallworth, 2002) **Participates in informal networking and communication processes outside of formal settings** (Rumsey et al.,1998)	**Increased self-efficacy** (Heath & Sias, 1999; Selsky, 1991) **Greater appreciation for participative processes** (Haskins et al., 1998) **Greater collaborative communication competence** (Barrett, 1995) **Identification with group goals and processes—culture of group** (Tompkins & Cheney, 1983) **Greater understanding of complexities/boundaries of other organizations** (Innes & Booher, 1999) **Increased knowledge/better informed about partners, partners' organizations, and community** (Innes & Booher, 1999) **Greater trust of other individuals and organizations** (Innes & Booher, 1999; Jones & Bodtker, 1998) **Increased political power** (Heath & Sias, 1999; Manev & Stevenson, 2001; Thomann & Strickland, 1992) **Satisfaction with group processes and outcomes** (Bennis & Biederman, 1997)
Collaborative Group	**Flat hierarchy** (Gray, 1989; Keyton & Stallworth, 2003; Mintzberg et al., 1996) **Nonhierarchical convener or facilitator** (Provan & Milward, 1995; Sanders, 2001) **Ability to meet face-to-face occasionally** (Mintzberg et al., 1996) **Physical structures reflecting egalitarian environment** (e.g., roundtable seating) (Pasquero, 1991) **Appropriate time allotted to communication processes** (e.g., meetings) (Barrett, 1995)	**Communication focuses on group mission** (Gray & Wood, 1991; Heath & Sias, 1999; Sanders, 2001) Group **"legitimizes conversations about organizational vision"** (Barrett, 1995) **Culture "fosters dialogue" and direction** (Barrett, 1995; Jones & Bodtker, 1998; Zoller, 2000) **Narrative helps to socialize changing representatives** (Mumby, 1987) **Communication processes reflect egalitarian values** (e.g., uses rotating structures for responsibilities) (Cheney, 1983; Heath & Sias, 1999; Jones & Bodtker, 1998; Keyton & Stallworth, 2003) **Limits use of hierarchical structures** (e.g., executive committees) (Heath & Sias, 1999) **Communication processes are designed to represent various constituencies** (e.g., open to new members or visitors) (Barrett, 1995; Lange, 2002; Zoller, 2000) **Communication enhanced by media technologies** (Kasper-Fuehrer & Ashkanasy, 2001; Walther, 1997)	**Accomplish of group goals** (e.g., fiscal and/or philanthropic (Innes & Booher, 1999) **Consensus decision making** (Marshall, 1995; Zoller, 2000) **Increased creativity and innovation** (Agranoff & McGuire, 2001; Bennis & Biederman, 1997; Innes & Booher, 1999; Lawrence et al., 2002; Montgomery, 1997) **Increased political power as a collaboration** (Innes & Booher, 1999) **Increased recognition or legitimacy by communities** (Lawrence et al., 2002)

TABLE 1 (continued)

A Conceptual Framework of Ideal Community Collaboration

	Antecedents of ideal collaboration	*Processes of ideal collaboration*	*Outcomes of ideal collaboration*
Stakeholder Organizations	**Organizational need** (e.g., fiscal or public relations) **and/or organizational desire** (e.g., philanthropic related to goal) (Agranoff & McGuire, 2001; Gray, 1989; Logsdon, 1991; Powell et al., 1996) **Organizational leaders' ability to entrust decision-making power** (Agranoff & McGuire, 1998; Chrislip & Larson, 1994) **Organizational leaders' ability to share a common goal** (e.g., not in danger of losing clients) (Gray & Wood, 1991; Keyton & Stallworth, 2002; Logsdon, 1991; Provan & Milward, 1995) **Organizational leaders' ability to commit resources** (Gray, 1989; Sanders, 2001; Wood & Gray, 1991) **Organizational leaders' ability to be flexible to radical structural changes** (Agranoff & McGuire, 2001) **Organizational leadership fosters a question-legitimizing culture** (Barrett, 1995)	**Organizational leaders display commitment to process of collaborating in their community** (e.g., commitment to display organizational agenda and respect for dialectics) (Bond & Keys, 1993; Chrislip & Larson, 1994) **Culture allows for "arenas of accessibility"** (Barrett, 1995) **Organizational leaders share ongoing information and resources with their individual collaboration representatives** (Bond & Keys, 1993; Mintzberg et al., 1996)	**Stronger links with other organizations** (Powell et al., 1996) **Organizational leaders' greater understanding of other organizations' processes and boundaries** (Lawrence et al., 2002) **Decreased competitiveness of organization with potential partners** (Jones & Bodtker, 1998; Lawrence et al., 2002) Increased political power of organization (Lawrence et al., 2002) **Organizational leaders' increased collaborative communication competence** (Simonin, 1997) **Organizational leaders' increased willingness to participate in other collaborations** (Innes & Booher, 1999; Simonin, 1997)
Collaborating Community	**Embrace nontraditional public policy** (Chrislip & Larson, 1994; Pasquero, 1991) **Provides a neutral legitimizing entity for the collaboration** (Chrislip & Larson, 1994; Gray, 1989; Pasquero, 1991) **Interdependent need transcends stakeholders' needs and is rooted in a larger community need** (Chrislip & Larson, 1994; Gray, 1989; Heath & Sias, 1999; Medved et al., 2001) **Provides boundary spanners, leaders, and conveners** (Bond & Keys, 1993; Chrislip & Larson, 1994; Gray, 1989; Zoller, 2000) **Boundary spanners, leaders, and conveners initiate the communicative groundwork for collaboration** (Chrislip & Larson, 1994; Moseley, 2001)	**Experiences and celebrates small successes with the collaboration** (Zoller, 2000) **Facilitates the sharing of information between the collaboration and the greater community** (Gray 1989) **Ratifies the consensus of the collaboration through legislative action** (Gray, 1989) **Oversees the implementation of decisions and projects brought forth by the collaboration** (Gray 1989; Moseley, 2001)	**New community leaders** (Chrislip & Larson, 1994) **New institutions** (Innes & Booher, 1999; Lawrence et al., 2002; Thompson, 2003) **New civic culture, including norms, heuristics, and discourses** (Chrislip & Larson, 1994; Innes & Booher, 1999; Moseley, 2001) **Ability to mobilize new collaborations** (Chrislip & Larson, 1994; Innes & Booher, 1999) Community (Chrislip & Larson, 1994)

Given its interest in communication and collaboration, this study first privileged communication scholarship by identifying, via the search engines of *COMABSTRACTS* and *Communication Abstracts*, any literature using the key word *collaboration* in a deductive investigation. Initially, fewer than 50 articles and chapters were found, dating back to 1973. An additional search, using the same search engines employing the word *community* when combined with the words community and/or collaboration, revealed no matches.[1] Further searches explored collaboration literature using the search engines *Infotrac* and *First Search Gold*. Whenever literature was discovered, the references were checked for additional sources, which were then acquired inductively. This resulted in a total of more than 130 sources that were reviewed, 50 of which were particularly germane to this essay. The literature reviewed is not completely exhaustive of cross-disciplinary research; however, it is representative of the literature on communication and collaboration.

THEORY AND RESEARCH FINDINGS REGARDING
IDEAL COMMUNITY COLLABORATION

Individual Representatives in Community Collaboration

Individual participants, the constituents who comprise a collaborative group (i.e., those who actually sit at the table), serve as representatives for their stakeholder groups and organizations in a community collaboration. Most likely, individuals participate in a community collaboration as a collateral duty to their job in the stakeholder organization they are representing. Their participation involves a commitment to attend meetings, participate on committees, and assist on projects that will further the goals of the collaborative group, as well as to act as the primarily liaison for their stakeholder organization. They are thus responsible for both furthering the goals of their stakeholder organization and the goals of the collaborative group. The following review documents those characteristics that have been found concerning antecedents, communication processes, and outcomes for individual collaboration participants.

Antecedents for individual collaboration representatives. What are the preconditions for individual representatives involved in an ideal community collaboration? Previous research suggests that individual representatives should possess specific traits and dispositions, have a general collaborative competence or hold a collaborative ethic, have decision-making power, and be committed to long-term engagement in the collaboration.

An important consideration of individuals involved in a collaborative process is their *traits* and/or *predispositions* toward collaborating. For example, *cognitive complexity*, the tendency to exhibit conceptual differentiation and integration, has been identified as a trait that affects group processes (Kline, Hennen-Floyd, & Farrell, 1990), and it is especially important for integrating the multilayered goals of collaboration. As another example, *self-monitoring*, the ability to be aware of one's communicative behavior (Ellis & Cronshaw, 1992), may be necessary for the type of awareness that constitutes competence in collaboration. It is also difficult to conceptualize an individual's predisposition toward collaborating without including Kilmann and Thomas's (1977) seminal work on conflict management styles, specifically their notion of a *collaborative conflict management style*, identified as an individual's tendency to choose win-win solutions in conflict situations. Kilmann and Thomas asserted that extroverts, those who are outgoing (as identified on the Meyers Briggs Type Indicator; MBTI), are predisposed to a collaborative conflict management style.

Most relevant to this discussion of individual collaboration representatives is Barrett's (1995) idea of *collaborative competence*, an appropriate level of competence that is needed to be an effective collaborator, both as an individual collaboration member and as a representative of a stakeholder group or organization. At the individual level, Barrett included as part of collaborative competence the need to "hold a disrespect for hierarchy and other boundaries to inclusion and involvement" (p. 46). He emphasized the importance of collaboration participants' cognizance of hierarchical distinctions, such as titles, roles, and rewards, and the role such distinctions may play in limiting participation in a collaboration group. If participants recognize these things as undermining flat power structures, they will be less likely to engage in behaviors that reassert hierarchical positions. The significance of maintaining a flat hierarchy in a collaboration is discussed later in this chapter; for now, the point is that individuals hold attitudes about these matters, which, in turn, potentially affect the collaborative process.

Other authors refer to a *collaborative ethic* that includes an individual's ability to trust others and value processes such as consensus and sharing power (Haskins, Liedtka, & Rosenblum, 1998; Mintzberg, Jorgensen, Dougherty, & Westley, 1996). However, Welch (2000), in emphasizing the ambiguous character of a collaborative ethic, argued that it involves those things that are not easily trainable, raising the question of whether predispositions associated with being a good collaborator can be learned.

Some scholars (e.g., Marshall, 1995) believe that a precondition for successful collaboration is an *individual's power to make decisions*. If the persons representing stakeholder groups and organizations are limited in their ability to make decisions during the collaborative group process, the process itself is likely to become stymied. In a community collaboration that tackled juvenile delinquency issues, Heath and Sias (1999) found that participating individuals explicitly referred to each other as *decision makers* and were specifically invited to collaborate based on the positions of power they held in their respective organizations. A collaboration may suffer unnecessary bureaucratic delays in decision-making processes if the representatives around the table lack the authority to commit needed resources and to make appropriate decisions. Recognizing the significance of individual decision-making power, thus, has important implications for choosing who should represent a stakeholder in community collaboration.

Finally, individuals participating in a collaborative effort, especially community collaboration, must understand and be willing to commit to long-term engagement. Recall that the current national events awarding, announcing, and calling for collaboration are communities tackling large-scale issues (e.g., safety, medical care, and crime), ongoing problems that will not go away in the short term. Hence, individual representatives who join such community collaborations ideally have some understanding of the commitment they must make and the effect they will have on the group should they depart before the collaboration has reached its goals. Lange's (2003) case study of an environmental collaboration provides a poignant example of the complexity of the individual's role as a representative of a constituency and how his or her commitment to a collaboration can alter and be altered. He described one collaborating participant's journey from initially participating as an individual stakeholder representative to later maintaining membership as an unaffiliated participant after parting ways officially with the original stakeholder partner he represented because of decisions made by the collaboration group. In this case, the individual representative and the stakeholder organization held incongruent ideologies that were resolved with the individual maintaining a relationship with the collaboration, whereas the stakeholder organization did not. As a result, committing to a collaboration is not a simple obligation and may even result in testing the established ideologies traditionally held by individuals and/or stakeholders.

In each of the above cases, the traits and predispositions identified describe what best facilitates collaboration at an individual level prior to participating in a collaboration. Some of these individual-level skills identified, however, may be gained during the process of collaboration; for instance, the development of collaborative competence may also be an outcome for individuals participating in collaboration.

Individual representatives and collaboration processes. Collaboration processes refer to the interaction that individual representatives should engage in to facilitate ideal collaboration. The relevant literature points to giving critical attention to group processes, employing participative and dialogic processes, managing dialectical tensions, sharing organizational agendas, and participating in informal networks. The individual representative throughout the duration of his or her participation performs these inherently communicative processes that are the central activity of collaborating.

The notion that individual representatives ideally share organizational power surfaces frequently in the literature on collaboration. Specifically, communication scholars are interested in how shared power in collaborations is accomplished communicatively. Many collaborations make a commitment to using consensus and/or democratic voting procedures (Haskins et al., 1998; Heath & Sias, 1999; Innes & Booher, 1999); consequently, individual collaboration members must understand and take part in participative processes. This notion is complicated by the fact that participative processes may be foreign to the cultural practices of the organizations individuals represent. Heath and Sias's (1999) study, for instance, described an interview with a vice president in the banking industry who participated in the juvenile delinquency community collaboration but whose military training and hierarchical management practices at the bank left him astounded by the time-consuming processes used to make decisions in the collaboration.

Participative processes in community collaboration are centered in the use of dialogue. As Isaacs (1999) posited, "Dialogue is a conversation in which people think together in relationship. Thinking together implies that you no longer take your own position as final" (p. 19). Barrett's (1995) commitment to dialogic processes as a part of his description of collaborative competence stresses the need for individuals to understand the value of and *enact dialogic processes*, which suggests the need for collaboration members to *pay attention to communication processes*. Preserving dialogue, however, is not easy, as Zoller (2000) found in her study of a collaboration, in which dialogic processes were enacted at the expense of accomplishing community goals, suggesting the importance of striking a balance between collaboration goals and processes.

Other authors note the difficulty of *managing ongoing dialectical tensions* between individual representatives' participation in a collaboration and their responsibilities to their constituent stakeholder organizations (Jones & Bodtker, 1998; McKinney, 2001; Medved et al., 2001). Dialectical tensions manifest themselves, for instance, in differences between organizational goals and collaboration processes. With respect to goals, individuals have to balance their organization's motivation for participating with the larger goals of the collaboration group. Lange (2001) identified this phenomenon as the "stakeholder paradox" (p. 203). Sometimes, dichotomies appear out of an absence of trust, as in Jones and Bodtker's (1998) case study, using a theory of paradox, of an international partnership, where participants were initially not willing to let go of their organization's agendas and turf for the greater good of the collaboration. The authors cautioned against hasty solutions and pointed out that one method for managing goal dialectics is for collaboration members to explicitly and honestly *share organizational agendas* (see also Keyton & Stallworth, 2003).

Sharing organizational agendas may be premature in the absence of trust among collaboration members; however, it still may be worth the risk for some members and promote the development of such trust. For example, a nonprofit organization may be reluctant to share resources with collaboration members that are specifically restricted by state or federal grant money, but by openly sharing these concerns and constraints, other collaboration members are less likely to see the organization as acting competitively. Frequently, a motivation for community collaboration is to reduce agency overlap (especially if it is mandated by the government), but this is sometimes seen as a threat to organizations' turf. Sharing potential threats and sensitizing partners to the survival realities of their organization, however, decreases competition and increases collaboration. At other times, the tensions are process oriented, as in the frustration expressed by the vice president of banking described in Heath and Sias's (1999) research, where his own organizational practices were at odds with the style of practice used in the collaboration in which he participated. Successfully managing these dialectics requires skill on the part of individual collaborators.

Finally, collaboration processes necessitate participating in informal networking. Rumsey, Fulk, and Monge (1998) examined the relationship between various motives to join an interorganizational alliance and the likelihood of forming informal networking relationships. Among many propositions, they predicted that "reciprocity-motivated organizations . . . will foster multiplex linkages (interpersonal communication, semantic and trust) with . . . potential and actual alliance members" (p. 23). Collaborations lack solid infrastructures, as illuminated by the BFG perspective; therefore, it is impossible to imagine that all relevant business is conducted around the collaboration meeting table.

Outcomes for individual collaboration members. Individuals have much to gain from participating in a collaborative group, as indicated by the lengthy list of outcomes in Table 1. Research shows that individual representatives gain increased efficacy in collaborating, greater appreciation for participative processes, greater collaborative communication competence, identification with group goals and the culture of the collaborative group, greater understanding of the complexities and boundaries of other organizations, increased knowledge of partner organizations and the community, greater trust of other individuals and organizations, increased political power, and satisfaction with group processes and outcomes. Researchers often attribute outcomes to the collaborative group as a whole; however, the outcomes referenced here result in increased knowledge or skill on the part of the individual collaboration representatives and are, thus, accordingly categorized as individual-level outcomes. Other researchers may argue that the collaborative group itself achieves these outcomes, but for the sake of consistency, this study does not situate such intrapersonal changes outside of the individual. An argument for doing so is beyond the scope of this essay and risks confusing the concepts that the current study attempts to make clear through this framework.

Scholars have found that participation in a collaboration leads to an *increased self-efficacy* on the part of individuals regarding their perceived ability to participate in collaboration. Heath and Sias (1999) found a consistent theme of pride in collaborating expressed by the participants interviewed in their study, and Selsky (1991) noted an extraordinary belief in collaboration resulting from experience with it. Coupled with collaborative efficacy following a collaborative experience is a greater appreciation for participative processes. As Haskins et al. (1998) explained, "Such attitudes are the fruit of a collaborative ethic that predates and supersedes the tenure and authorship of any one person" (p. 42). They implied that a collaborative ethic is composed of a commitment to participation and retreat from individualistic values, such as single authorship. Participating individuals also benefit from *greater collaborative competence* demonstrated, for instance, by an individual's increased commitment to dialogue. Barrett (1995) developed his notion of collaborative competence as the "power of dialogue to transform systems" (p. 46), arguing that:

> The belief in the importance of dialogue reflects in a sense of hope, a belief that through inter-
> action new ideas will emerge. Accordingly, by embracing and partaking in the processes that
> are assumed natural to collaboration, the individual gains "collaborative competence." (p. 46)

As individual members gain self-efficacy, appreciation for collaborative processes, and collaborative competence, they are likely to emerge from a collaboration identifying more closely with the collaboration group's goals. According to
Tompkins and Cheney (1983), a decision maker identifies with an organization
when he or she desires to choose the alternative that best promotes the perceived
interests of that organization. Accordingly, when individuals engage successfully
in consensus decision making, or make a decision that benefits the greater collaboration, even at the expense of their own organization, they come to identify with
the collaboration's group goals and culture.

Perhaps more concretely, individuals gain a greater understanding of the complexities and boundaries of other organizations and increased knowledge about
their partners and the communities involved. Innes and Booher (1999) claimed
that "shared problem frames" are a first-order effect (p. 419), meaning that one of
the more direct results of collaboration is that individuals come to see their
organization's goals in the context of the greater collaboration.[2] In sharing problem frames, collaborators share their boundaries and help each other to gain a
mutual understanding of one another's capabilities and goals and, thereby, arrive
at a mutual goal, telling a community story.

In an ideal collaboration, individuals will also gain a greater trust of other individuals and organizations. Some scholars see this as a natural result of using consensus processes (Innes & Booher, 1999). Jones and Bodtker (1998) narrated a
story of trust in their case study of an international collaboration in South Africa,
carefully pointing out that disclosure does not necessarily lead to trust. Nevertheless, they showed how trust between two organizations that initially clung to their
turf was eventually gained through the process of collaboration. Of course, the
timeline for gaining trust may differ greatly among community collaborations. In
Jones and Bodtker's case, the collaborating parties had to overcome a history of
race conflicts and other political issues of authority. Individuals in collaborations
with less political history may find that trust develops more quickly. Although
trust may be seen as an outcome at all levels and domains of collaboration, it is
ultimately something that an individual feels toward others.

Another potential beneficial outcome for individual collaborators is *increased
political power*. For example, Thomann and Strickland (1992) discussed recipro-
cal/rational strategies in collaborative organizations; specifically, they talked about
"trading on past favors for future rewards, exchange tactics, [and] 'coalition building'" (p. 27). Although their research is limited to organizations that adopt a collaborative work style within the organization, similar outcomes result for individuals involved in community collaborations. Individuals may form alliances with
partners in which they support each other on decisions that are more meaningful to

one or the other party; Heath and Sias (1999) identified this tactic as "barter and negotiate" (p. 366). These alliances may also flow over into business arrangements that take place outside the milieu of the collaboration, with individuals enjoying increased political power in their community. In addition, network research has linked boundary spanning with increases in personal influence that may possibly "have helped upper-level managers rise to their positions" (Manev & Stevenson, 2001, p. 198). It is conceivable that individuals gain valuable information about other relevant organizations and the community that makes their position in their own organization more vital.

Finally, as would be expected, individuals should emerge from an ideal collaboration with a sense of satisfaction with the group processes and outcomes. Bennis and Biederman (1997) implied that, in fact, it would not be collaboration if the parties involved were unsatisfied: "In true collaboration, almost everyone emerges with a sense of ownership" (p. 28). This outcome is consistent with the processes that are typically identified with collaboration, such as consensus, which is sometimes viewed as both process and outcome.

The Collaborative Group in Community Collaboration

The second constituent group identified in this essay, the collaborative group, is composed of the individual representatives and operates at the interorganizational domain referred to by Gray and Wood (1991). Community collaborative groups are likely to be more heterogeneous that other interorganizational groups, such as for-profit alliances, due to the nature of the problems community collaborations address. Common throughout the literature on community collaboration, such groups are composed of diverse individuals who are, for example, from government offices and nonprofit organizations, or simply private citizens, and may not hold a bottom-line stake in participating but may be motivated to participate for altruistic reasons or mandated to participate. In addition, consistent with the BFG perspective, the composition of a community collaboration group is likely to undergo many changes over the course of its long-term existence as individual representatives leave the group for reasons such as advancement or termination from their position in the stakeholder organization. Community collaboration groups are also different from other interorganizational collaborations in terms of their responsibility for making decisions that have civic implications.

The current study notes antecedent conditions that are ideally in place for a group to collaborate, highlights processes that should characterize a collaborative group, and identifies outcomes that are specific to the collaborative group. Constructs placed in these sections are best understood as belonging to the interorganizational domain. For example, although a nonhierarchical convener is listed as a necessary antecedent of the collaborative group, some may see the convener as a stakeholder (the organizational stakeholder domain). This study places the convener here because this is the domain that requires and eventually benefits from the efforts of a convener. The convener is also examined later in relationship to the community.

Antecedents for collaborative groups. What ideally needs to be in place in a collaborative group prior to engaging in collaborative processes? Based on the available literature, a flat hierarchy, a nonhierarchical convener or facilitator, the ability to meet face-to-face, physical structures that reflect an egalitarian environment, and appropriate time for communication processes emerge as central features that prepare a group for collaboration. These features do not belong to any one individual of the collaboration but instead are characteristic of the group as a collective.

Having a *flat hierarchy* is such an integral precondition to community collaboration that it is written into most definitions of collaboration. The idea of a horizontal hierarchy in interorganizational relationships is not a new concept; Leblebici and Whetten (1984) examined the phenomenon nearly 20 years ago and, today, it remains a central phenomenon in collaboration studies. Mintzberg et al. (1996) argued that "power imbalances between participants appears to be one of the chief sources of failure of interorganizational collaboration" (p. 65). Gray (1989) has written widely about collaboration as sharing power, and, more recently, Keyton and Stallworth (2003) focused on the ideal of shared power in collaborations.

Another structural precondition to successful community collaboration is the presence of a *nonhierarchical convener/facilitator.* Sanders (2001), for instance, cited the lack of a coordinator (facilitator) as a problem in her study of school community collaborations. The convener is typically a representative person of one of the participating stakeholder organizations who initiates the collaboration and takes some responsibility for organizing it; for example, the convener may act as a fiscal agent to the collaboration. The task of the convener is to maintain a nonhierarchical relationship with the collaborating stakeholder organizations, which is difficult given that the convening person may bear additional responsibilities, such as funneling grant money for the collaboration through his/her organization's accounting system. Provan and Milward (1995) claimed that centralized integration and coordination is necessary for successful collaboration; they also referred to a coordinating agency as being necessary to fulfill this role. Research, however, has not yet established whether coordination need be the responsibility of an organization or an individual member.

More recent literature has focused on the ability of technology to enhance collaboration; however, there is still a case to be made for a collaborative group to *meet face-to-face*, at least occasionally. Mintzberg et al. (1996), referring specifically to collaboration in the era of new technologies, claimed that "face-to-face collaboration is a richer medium [than mediated collaboration] because it allows for nonverbal communication, facilitating the delicate process of integrating ideas and energies" (p. 63).

Not only does the communication channel matter, but *physical structures in a collaborative group ideally reflect an egalitarian environment.* An interesting illustration of this principle is the study of the National Roundtable, a collaborative project involving the Canadian government (Pasquero, 1991). It is instructive that the project adopted a metaphor of an equalizing structure, a roundtable, to name itself. The metaphor facilitates collaboration by eliminating the perceived hierarchy of the head of the table. The metaphor can thus be taken quite literally as good advice to collaborating groups.

Finally, the emphasis on participative processes means that collaboration members need to be prepared for the length of time it takes to honor everyone's input and to reach consensus. Scholars frequently talk about these processes as taking longer than traditional decision-making processes (Barrett, 1995). Accordingly, the collaborative group must *set aside appropriate time needed to engage in the group communication processes just described.*

Communication processes in collaboration groups. Most relevant processes happen within the context of the collaborative group, often around a meeting table, although the informal network of communication outside the formal meeting context cannot be underestimated. The constructs identified here belong specifically to a collaborative group; they could easily be formally adopted by a group as guidelines for doing business, as some popular and scholarly literature suggests that groups should do (e.g., Harrington-Mackin, 1994). Accordingly, they are best thought of as group-level phenomena.

Collaborative group processes include explicit communication about the mission of the group and legitimizing conversation about its vision. The culture of an ideal collaborative group fosters dialogue, employs narrative to socialize new individuals, and has discourse and other structures that reflect egalitarian values. Collaborative group processes limit the use of hierarchical structures and, instead, employ ones that share power such as rotating structures. The communication processes practiced by collaborative groups, such as dialogue and consensus decision making, attempt to honor the viewpoints of their members' various constituencies. Finally, collaborative groups use technology to enrich their communication.

The literature on collaboration frequently focuses on the importance of a shared vision or mission in a collaborative group (Gray & Wood, 1991). In addition, collaborative groups have been found to spend significant time communicating about their mission; because individual members have various reasons for collaborating, frequent conversation about their group goal prevents them from straying from the big picture. This is presumably amplified in community collaborations when contrasted with other types because of their heterogeneous composition.

Communication frequently addresses the focus of the collaboration group's mission, thus creating a sustainable story about its purpose. Sanders (2001) emphasized the importance of goal identification in her study of collaborative partnerships between schools and their communities. Similarly, Heath and Sias (1999) found that the members of the collaborative group in their case study spent a significant amount of time talking both formally and informally about their mission. In contrast to organizations that do not support organizational members spending time on process issues, collaborative group members devote time legitimizing conversations about their group's vision and direction. Barrett (1995) claimed that "by legitimizing conversations about organizational vision and direction, they [collaborators] allow for joint discovery" (p. 46). The assumption here is that collaborations should not consider it to be a waste of time to revisit their vision or direction. In fact, these conversations are to be encouraged. Barrett specifically referred to for-profit organizations that function collaboratively, but his point is especially applicable to community collaborations in that to achieve innovation and creativity, collaboration members need to be free to continue talking and dreaming about their collective vision. These communicative practices must be owned by the group to ensure the success of a community collaboration.

In addition, the *culture of a collaborative group fosters dialogue* (Barrett, 1995). Zoller's (2000) work demonstrated what happens when equal attention is not paid to both fostering dialogue and delimiting it in a collaboration, as dialogue must inevitably lead to community action. In her study, the conveners emphasized dialogue at the expense of creating a shared vision that would enable participants to set goals; in the end, participants felt as though they were spinning their wheels in dialogue. At the other end of the continuum, Jones and Bodtker (1998) found that "the negotiation of group identity was impeded by members who were unwilling to voice their ideas in public, or even in private" (p. 365), but also cautioned that openness does not necessarily build trust. Accordingly, trust cannot be overlooked as the key to creating a culture that fosters dialogue and collaboration (Agranoff & McGuire, 2001).

At the same time, narrative helps to socialize changing representatives. Mumby (1987) claimed that "organization members tell stories to other members or to outsiders to show how their organization is different from any other" (p. 120). In long-term community collaborative groups, where individual members are likely to change more frequently than stakeholders, narrative is used to orient new and old participants to the goals and mission of the collaborative group. Heath and Sias (1999) noted that testimonials given by beneficiaries of community collaboration worked to emphasize the collaborative group's purpose and thereby reinforced participants' commitment to their mission.

Conceptualizing the communication processes of a collaborative group calls attention to the notion that communication processes must reflect egalitarian values. Jones and Bodtker (1998) found that "the attempt to invoke authority was counterproductive. It resulted in a false, public consensus that made visible the degree of internal dissensus operating" (p. 367). Collaborative groups should, thus, be mindful of discourse and other processes that decrease shared authority of the group. For example, an emphasis on *we* (rather than *I*) language can help to lessen authority and foster members' identification with the collaborative group (Cheney, 1983). Structures such as executive committees, which are often formed to organize the messy nature of volunteer groups, as well as to alleviate the burden the collaboration creates as a collateral duty for its members, create a layer of authority. Consequently, collaborative groups must carefully weigh the benefits of using such structures against the costs of jeopardizing the shared power structure (Heath & Sias, 1999). In essence, collaboration groups should limit use of hierarchical structures whenever possible. Other processes that reflect egalitarian values are rotating structures used for sharing responsibilities; for example, some collaborations rotate a chairperson position, who works closely with a facilitator to plan agendas for the meetings (Heath & Sias, 1999; Keyton & Stallworth, 2003), or the location of meetings is rotated, giving all participants and organizations a chance to host the collaborative group.

Regardless of the specific structures and processes employed by a collaborative group, communication processes are designed to represent various constituencies (Zoller, 2000). For example, meetings are open to new members or visitors, not held in private and inaccessible locations. Barrett (1995) also called for collaborations to promote the articulation of multiple perspectives (for exemplars of collaborative groups honoring multiple voices and perspectives, see Lange, 2003; Zoller, 2000). At the same time, seemingly egalitarian communicative practices, such as consensus, can undermine the efforts to include representatives from various constituencies. Promoting the articulation of multiple perspectives often conflicts with employing participative processes; for example, it can be very difficult to come to consensus with a large number of constituents. These values and processes are not meant to undermine each other; they should simply be understood as a dialectic working in a delicate balance that deserves equal attention.

Finally, communication enhanced by media technologies, such as email, can potentially facilitate collaboration processes. Indeed, a growing body of literature examines the relationship between collaboration and virtual organizations (Kasper-Fuehrer & Ashkanasay, 2001). There is a practicality in using media technologies. As Walther (1997) stated about his study of computer-mediated collaboration:

> Pragmatically, this research shows that decisions about CMC [computer-mediated communication] need not be related to a choice about whether to use it or not, or what the inherent social risks and benefits of using CMC must be where it is the most practical means of communication. (p. 360)

Most collaborations involve busy individuals who cannot meet frequently; therefore, communication in a collaboration needs to be simultaneously efficient and effective. Moreover, Kasper-Fuehrer and Ashkanasay (2001) found that trust among group members can be enhanced through communication technologies, further making the case for using technology as a tool to assist communication processes in community collaboration.

Outcomes for collaborative groups. Outcomes specific to collaborative groups are those that the group owns or can put its name on. They are most easily identified with the group at the interorganizational domain. Most collaborative groups are working toward specific outcomes outlined in their mission; therefore, the most significant outcomes a collaborative group will accomplish are those related to their goals, whether philanthropic or fiscal. Other outcomes that ideally result for a collaborative group include achieving consensus on issues, increased creativity or innovation, increased political power as a collaboration, and increased recognition or legitimacy by various communities.

Innes and Booher (1999) claimed that "high-quality agreements" are the result of collaboration (p. 419). Indeed, there is a general belief on the part of stakeholders that a collaboration will lead to the accomplishment of group goals, a view that is reinforced in the identified advantages of collaboration that promise innovation, creativity, and better decisions. Two process-oriented outcomes that are often achieved as collaboration groups work to accomplish the larger goals are that consensus is reached on decisions and creativity is increased.

Consensus is often viewed as part of the definition of collaboration itself (Marshall, 1995), and most collaborations embrace some form of *consensus decision making*; however, some scholars have cautioned against seeing consensus as a necessary goal of collaboration. For example, Zoller (2000) pointed out that consensus can come at the expense of including a wide range of participants' voices. In consensus decision making, conflicts are embraced and dialogue moves collaboration members toward agreement, which is difficult with large numbers of participants. Collaborators may, thus, consider the completion of the consensus process to be a great accomplishment. In the process, members learn more about each others' goals, visions, and fears, and trust is likely to have been established.

Studies of collaboration and interorganizational relationships have also found that creativity and innovation increase. For instance, collaboration was viewed as vital to increasing knowledge and innovation in links among government, academia, and industry in a Canadian study of a research-motivated collaboration (Montgomery, 1997). Innes and Booher (1999) identified one of the potential outcomes of collaboration as "innovative strategies" (p. 419), and Agranoff and McGuire (2001) called such an outcome *synergy*. Finally, Lawrence et al. (2002) found that "intense interorganizational relationships are more likely to lead to learning and innovation" (p. 289). Bennis and Biederman (1997) attributed this phenomenon, in part, to a sense of ownership on behalf of participants, visionary leadership that gets out of the way of smart and creative people, and access to a variety of resources.

Other outcomes of collaboration serve to strengthen the collaboration group. For instance, collaborative groups gain increased political power as a collaboration. This is a significant outcome for community collaborations that will leverage their power to further their social goals. Indeed, Innes and Booher (1999) claimed that an important outcome of collaboration was "political capital: ability to work together for agreed ends" (p. 419). Increased recognition or legitimacy by communities is also identified as an outcome of collaboration according to the findings of Lawrence et al.'s (2002) study of *proto-institutions*, collaborations that were transitioning to institutions in their communities. By placing such an outcome in this cell, the current study highlights a collaborative group as a beneficiary of institutional status, which grants the group longevity, funding, and structure to tackle a defined social problem. Later, the institutionalizing of collaborations is examined as a reciprocal beneficial outcome for the community.

Stakeholder Organizations in Community Collaboration

Frequently, individual representatives and organizational stakeholders involved in a collaboration have been lumped together as one and the same. Viewing a stakeholder as "one who is affected by or affects a particular problem or issue" (Chrislip & Larson, 1994 p. 65) does not distinguish the individual representative from the stakeholder organization, yet it is clear that individual representatives can have different goals, motivations, and outcomes for participating in collaboration than the stakeholder organizations they represent (Lange, 2001, 2003; Moseley, 2001). Indeed, one of the reasons collaboration is so complex is because of the relationships individual representatives have with their stakeholder organizations. Regardless of the aptitudes, skills, or efforts of individual representatives in a collaborative group, there are certain commitments that must come from stakeholder organizations for the individual representative and, consequently, for the collaborative group to succeed.

Gray and Wood (1991) referred to research centered around stakeholder issues as being focused on the organizational domain. Accordingly, this study separates individual representatives and stakeholder organizations as different constituent groups of collaboration, and determines what is ideally needed from stakeholder organizations prior to committing to and for the duration of a collaboration, as well as specific outcomes that result from their participation. Many of these constructs are attributed to the leadership group within stakeholder organizations because of those individuals' decision-making responsibility. The leadership of a stakeholder organization, however, is not to be confused with individual representatives who belong to a collaborative group; they may or may not be one and the same. In the cases described below, leaders act for their stakeholder organization; hence, although attributes are associated with individual leaders, this study clearly situates them within the organizational domain. Below is an examination of the antecedents, processes, and outcomes specific to this constituent group.

Antecedents for stakeholder organizations. The available literature suggests a number of preconditions that should exist for stakeholder organizations for a collaboration to be successful. The leadership of stakeholder organizations first, and most importantly perhaps, must recognize a need or impetus to participate in a collaboration. In addition, the various leaders of stakeholder organizations must have the ability to entrust decision-making power and share goals with the other participating organizations and to devote available resources to achieve the collaboration's mission. Finally, the leaders of stakeholder organizations must be flexible with respect to radical structural changes, and they must foster norms that legitimize the right to question decision-making processes and decisions made within their own organization.

First, stakeholder organizations must have a need or desire to participate in a collaboration. Resource dependency theory explains this need or desire for collaboration from a fiscal standpoint: Organizations need the resources that other organizations have to meet a greater goal than any organization could accomplish alone. Community collaboration, however, is not bound by bottom-line goals; hence, a variety of stakeholders with many different needs and desires often participate in a community collaboration, greatly increasing the complexity of the composition of such a collaboration. For example, a private, for-profit business may participate for philanthropic reasons, whereas a government organization may be mandated to participate. In this scenario, the former fulfills a need to contribute to the community, whereas the latter participates out of a need to sustain funding. Powell, Koput, and Smith-Doerr (1996) claimed that "firms turn to collaboration to acquire resources and skills they cannot produce internally" (p. 118). Agranoff and McGuire (2001), explaining why organizations not bounded by any authority (e.g., not on the same payroll) would come together voluntarily, said that "trust, common purpose, mutual dependency and resource availability" are some reasons for doing so (p. 311). In fact, organizational need may be essential to maintaining the integrity of a collaboration because need sustains power balances. Logsdon (1991) claimed that "stakes and perceived interdependence with other parties are critical elements for assessing whether or not organizations will consider cross-sectoral collaboration" (p. 34). In other words, organizations may be more willing to collaborate if they view themselves and the other participating organizations as needing something from one another—that is, if there are interdependent (Gray, 1989).

Scholars recognize that networks and collaborations call for a new type of manager who is "no longer dependent on command and control mechanisms of hierarchy" (Agranoff & McGuire, 1998, p. 81). Stakeholder organizational leaders therefore must have the ability to entrust decision-making power with their individual collaboration representatives and the other participating stakeholder organizations (Chrislip & Larson, 1994). Not only are they willing to allow individual representatives to make decisions in the collaborative group on behalf of the organization, but stakeholder organizations must also have the communicative structural capability, such as direct lines between the individual representatives and organizational leadership, to do so. For example, if bureaucratic processes within an organization hamstring quick decision making, that organization is in less of a position to collaborate. Especially in community collaborations, where nonprofit organizations frequently participate, participating organizations are sometimes stymied by grant or credential requirements that limit their flexibility to collaborate.

Leaders of stakeholder organizations must have the ability to share a common goal with other collaborating organizations. Many scholars emphasize the importance of stakeholders sharing a vision or goal (see, e.g., Gray & Wood, 1991; Keyton & Stallworth, 2003; Logsdon, 1991). As Provan and Milward (1995) explained:

> In public and not-for profit sector, where public interest is at stake, network outcomes are especially salient, and the rationale for organizations cooperating to accomplish system goals rather than organizational ends is often stronger than in the private sector. (p. 3)

Realistically, however, organizations have to weigh whether they are in danger of losing grant money or clients if they choose to participate in a collaboration. Often, community collaboration is mandated or encouraged to prevent the replication of services; this requires organizations to find meaningful goals to replace their missions when duplication is eliminated.

Stakeholder organizational leaders must have the ability to commit resources. The main reason organizations are invited to participate in a collaboration is because they have certain resources to offer (Sanders, 2001); as previously mentioned, much has been written about resources and collaboration (see Gray, 1989; Wood & Gray, 1991). Resources may come in the form of physical structures, such as schools housing collaborative programs in their buildings; monetary funds; or the symbolic status that a participating organization brings that enhances the likelihood of the collaborative group being awarded competitive grants. Two points about the relationship between resources and collaboration stakeholders are particularly important: (a) A lack of resources serves as an impetus for collaboration, and (b) stakeholders' ability to allocate what resources they have is fundamental.

Leaders of stakeholder organizations must be flexible with respect to radical structural changes. As Agranoff and McGuire (2001) claimed:

> The ability to manage networks is related to the internal support and cooperation of the manager's primary organization. [Network participants] should have the cooperation of [their parent organizations and leaders] as a means to more confidently engage in networking and achieve the strategic purpose at hand. (p. 300)

Inferred from their claim is the importance of the stakeholder organizations' leaders giving collaboration members the freedom to engage in strategy within the collaboration. The need for strategy may come in the face of change experienced by the collaborative group. For example, community collaborations are made up of stakeholders from nonprofit and other organizations that depend on legislated funds; consequently, grants can run out and legislatures can choose not to fund programs, ultimately leaving the funding base of a collaboration unstable. In such a case, leaders of stakeholder organizations must be flexible and anticipate change.

Finally, for the individual representative to feel comfortable in a collaborative group, the stakeholder organization ideally fosters a question-legitimizing culture that "legitimizes members' right to question and provoke at all levels of organizational activity" (Barrett, 1995, p. 46). Accordingly, individual representatives must feel comfortable challenging their organization's commitments to collaboration whenever needed and have the freedom to participate in honest dialogue with organizational leaders about, for instance, conflicting goals between the organization and the collaborative group.

Communication processes for stakeholder organizations. Just as individual representatives of the collaborative group participate in specific communication processes throughout the duration of the collaboration, a number of interactive processes are experienced by and within collaboration stakeholder organizations. They require the leaders of stakeholder organizations to display their commitment to the processes of collaborating, create arenas of accessibility, provide ongoing information to their individual representatives, and share ongoing resources with the collaboration.

Organizational leaders must display a commitment to the process of collaborating in their communities (Chrislip & Larson, 1994). Bond and Keys (1993) found that organizational cultures that promote appreciation for collaborative values, such as mutual respect and interdependence, are critical to collaboration. Included in this commitment is the willingness to share organizational agendas. As previously mentioned, in the nonprofit arena, organizations are frequently stymied by grant restrictions or legislative mandates. Through the process of sharing both constraints and goals for their organizations, collaborating partners can build trust instead of creating an impression of unwillingness to commit funding or time to the process. Individual collaboration representatives ultimately share these agendas; however, agenda sharing must be promoted at the organizational level.

Barrett (1995) emphasized the importance of participating organizations' culture allowing for "arenas of accessibility" (p. 46). These arenas, by which he meant forums and opportunities, keep communication channels open for individual representatives to provide constant feedback to their stakeholder organization. In addition, a culture that facilitates organizational leaders sharing ongoing information and resources with their individual collaboration representative allows for arenas of accessibility to be enacted. Bond and Keys (1993) claimed that organizations must support boundary spanners, "people who can permeate otherwise rigid boundaries around another subgroup and thereby, begin to create some bridges .... They are people who travel comfortably between groups" (p. 44). They further posited that, in the process of supporting boundary spanners, organizations must empower them to collaborate as an essential element to keeping power balances within the collaborative group in check. Organizational leaders, by sharing information and resources with their individual representative, ultimately demonstrate support and commitment to the collaboration and, of course, to meeting the greater community goal. Mintzberg et al. (1996) emphasized the importance of the stakeholder organizational leaders' commitment to the collaborative effort, calling it "back home commitment building" (p. 66).

Outcomes for stakeholder organizations. Other than the obvious accomplishment of meeting their own organizational needs, why do organizations participate in community collaboration, especially when it can be such a difficult process? Through participation in a community collaboration, stakeholder organizations ideally achieve a number of beneficial outcomes. Specifically, they can develop stronger links with other organizations, greater understanding of other organizations' boundaries and processes, decreased competition with collaborative partners, and increased political power as an organization. Leaders of stakeholder organizations can also increase their collaborative competence and willingness to participate in other collaborations.

Stakeholder organizations achieve stronger links with other organizations. Powell, Koput, and Smith-Doerr (1996), writing about interorganizational collaboration, argued that "biotech firms grow by being connected to benefit-rich networks" (p. 139). Participating in an interorganizational collaboration offers the benefit of developing deeper connections with each participating organization. Because every organization has an interorganizational relationship with each collaboration partner, participating in a collaboration can strengthen other interorganizational relationships outside of the collaboration, further facilitating the meeting of stakeholder organizational goals. For example, a relationship between two government organizational stakeholders may blossom as a result of getting to know each other through the collaboration, ultimately allowing for dyadic interorganizational collaboration on other issues important to those two organizations. This phenomenon was reported by the vice president of a community college regarding her newfound relationship to the police chief in Heath and Sias's (1999) study.

The strengthening of relationships with other organizations is bound to happen when stakeholder organizational leaders gain greater understanding of other organizations' processes and boundaries. As a result of dialogic communication in collaboration groups, and increased trust among collaboration members, participating members learn about each other and that information is, in turn, shared with the leadership of their stakeholder organization. For these reasons, stakeholder organizations experience decreased competitiveness with potential partners. Jones and Bodtker's (1998) study demonstrated the gradual diminishing of such turf issues for, as trust was built, participating organizations worried less about hiding their agendas and holding onto their turf. Lawrence et al. (2002) also found that "bilateral information flows" allowed stakeholder organizations to "learn about their competitor" at the same time that it allowed them to share their own expertise (p. 288).

Stakeholder organizations ideally have increased political power as an organization as a result of participating in a collaboration. Lawrence et al. (2002) observed that a stakeholder organization emerged as a community leader as a result of its participation in a collaboration. As they explained, "These practices then diffused beyond the specific coalition to establish Mere et Enfant's [a collaborating partner] status as the legitimate regional expert on nutritional matters was due to the highly embedded nature of the collaboration" (p. 288).

Finally, some outcomes of collaboration are specific to skills or attitudes learned by stakeholder organizational leaders, such as greater collaborative communication competence. If particular processes are in place, such as a culture that creates a reciprocal communication between stakeholder organizational leaders and their individual representatives, leaders have the potential to grow in their understanding and skills of collaborative processes. Such growth will inspire organizational leaders to participate in other collaborations. Simonin (1997), studying strategic alliances, referred to this phenomena as "collaborative know-how" (p. 1154), coupling it with collaborative experience as a necessary union for successful future collaborating partnerships. Innes and Booher (1999) found that new collaborations are a result of positive consensus-building experiences in previous collaborations; therefore, successful collaboration is bound to spawn more collaboration.

The Collaborating Community

The final constituent group examined in this essay, the collaborating community, is best understood as the interorganizational context in which individual representatives, the collaborative group, and stakeholder citizens, groups, and organizations operate and in which the collaboration is embedded. A few examples of community collaborations included in this paper include the Applegate Partnership, an environmentally focused land management council (Lange, 2001, 2003; Moseley, 2001), the Healthy Cities/Healthy Communities project launched by the World Health Organization with the purpose of moving communities to collaborate on health issues (Zoller, 2000), and the Drug Dealer Eviction Program (DDEP) a five-organization collaboration in Memphis, Tennessee (Keyton & Stallworth, 2003). These collaborations illustrate the embedded nature of community collaboration to the wider community. In each case, the collaboration was composed of key public entities in the community, as well as a variety of interested non-profits, citizens, and organizations that had a stake in the outcome. The goals of these community collaborative groups are inherent to the goals of the community (e.g., a healthy environment, healthy community, and lower drug use and crime rates).

Community collaboration, as previously explained, diverges from for-profit interorganizational collaboration for various reasons that warrant its scholarly distinction, including its diversity of stakeholders represented, long-term nature, institutionalizing effects left on the host community, dependency on alternative funding sources, and public accountability captured in its power to replace traditional decision-making models, such as authority-based positions, elected councils, and elected representatives. Here, we provide a review of what is known about communities that host collaborative groups. Scholars have identified specific commitments and actions that communities ideally partake in before and throughout the duration of the collaboration, as well as the resulting outcomes for host communities.

Antecedents for the collaborating community. Some of the literature has tracked the community as the context for interorganizational collaboration. Following the systems perspective, this study examines antecedents described for communities that host interorganizational collaboration. These are communities that are open to nontraditional public policy, have legitimizing governments that sanction the collaborative process, are composed of organizations with interdependent needs (internally or externally driven issues), and provide host boundary spanners, leaders, and/or conveners who initiate and engage in the communication background work prior to formally organizing a collaboration. These antecedents are not exclusive to the community and may be repeated at other levels of collaboration; however, their presence facilitates collaboration in communities.

Pasquero (1991) noted a *paradigmatic shift* in thinking from adversarial to collaborative modes in environmental protection policy in her study of a Canadian environmental collaboration, demonstrating a need for communities to embrace nontraditional public policy. Chrislip and Larson (1994) also documented numerous cases in which communities embraced alternative rather than traditional methods to solving social problems. At times, community leaders may participate directly in the collaboration. At other times, those leaders are less involved but openly sanction the work produced by collaborative groups, revealing an openness to nontraditional mechanisms for forming public policies. Similarly, a community must provide a neutral legitimizing entity for a collaboration, sometimes operating as the convener (Gray, 1989; Pasquero, 1991). There must, ultimately, be the presence of a sanctioning body. Embracing nontraditional public policy speaks to a community's predisposition to accept collaboration as way of solving problems; however, there must be a context for which the work of the collaboration is legitimized or implementation processes will later fall short (Chrislip & Larson, 1994).

Interdependent need as an impetus to collaboration was previously mentioned in the current discussion of stakeholder antecedents. In community collaboration, this interdependent need transcends stakeholders' needs and is rooted in a larger community need (Chrislip & Larson, 1994; Gray, 1989). This phenomenon is unique to community collaborations as opposed to alliances formed for profit-oriented endeavors, where bottom-line–oriented motivations may be the presiding impetus for participating stakeholders. Medved et al. (2001) found that a community need can be internally driven by members of the community or brought to the attention of the community in what they called *externally driven issues*. In their case study, a health issue was brought to the community from an outside facilitating organization. Whereas in noncommunity-centered interorganizational collaboration, individual stakeholder needs may be the primary motivator for participating in collaboration, in community interorganizational relationships, social needs are shared and provide a strong force for participating in collaboration. For example, juvenile crime issues affect the entire community at some level, whether physical, emotional, or financial. An issue such as juvenile crime can motivate vary diverse partners, as seen by Heath and Sias (1999), where private businesses participated alongside schools and justice officials. In other words, the need for collaboration belongs to the entire community, as well as to the collaborating participants.

Communities hosting collaboration provide boundary spanners, leaders, and conveners. Previously, this study mentioned empowering boundary spanners as an essential process performed by stakeholder organizations throughout their participation in a collaboration. Boundary spanning, however, may also take place before the collaboration is born on behalf of interested citizens, long before stakeholder organizations commit to the collaboration. Chrislip and Larson (1994) focused on the importance of leadership in community collaboration and documented the formation of the American Leadership Forum (ALF), whose purpose they described as one that "identifies and brings together leaders from different sectors of the community and prepares them to work on significant issues" (p. 49). Gray (1989) also discussed the importance of training leaders to collaborate and added the role of a convener as another significant function to collaboration:

The inspiration to collaborate may come from the convener or from one of the stakeholders, but it is up to the convening organization [or person] to invite and/or persuade other stakeholders to participate. . . . The convener may or may not be a stakeholder in the problem . . . [but] need[s] to appreciate the potential value of collaborating. (pp. 70–72)

A common denominator to each of these roles is that the person(s) or organization(s) that serves as a boundary spanner, leader, or convener of collaboration is first and foremost a member of the community. Indeed, these persons or organizations belong more appropriately to the community than to the collaborative group because they may or may not continue as a member of the collaborating group, yet their support is essential. It is the community that must produce these key roles. Even in the case where collaboration has been encouraged by outside (community) sources, scholars are clear that for trust to flourish, there need to be community members who serve in these roles in some capacity, whether official or unofficial (Chrislip & Larson, 1994; Zoller, 2000).

Boundary spanners, leaders, and conveners initiate the communication groundwork that sparks the formalizing of a community collaboration. In many case studies documenting community collaboration, the convener spent a considerable amount of time, often personal time, engaged in discussions with key community members long before the collaboration was initiated. These discussions laid the groundwork for establishing a common vision later adapted by the collaborative group. For instance, in the Applegate Partnership, an environmental collaboration in southern Oregon, the convener spent months meeting with potential stakeholders, sometimes hosting backyard barbecues, sometimes as an unannounced visitor to local officials (Moseley, 2001; for other examples, see Chrislip & Larson, 1994). Conveners were mentioned previously as an antecedent to a collaborative group; however, the role of the convener to the group is different than that needed in the community, although the convener is often one and the same person(s) or organization(s). That person or organization's relationship to the group at the interorganizational level is that of a nonhierarchical presence that provides ongoing support to this specific group. The convener's relationship to the community, the context in which the interorganizational relationships are embedded, is as an instigator. Conveners start the process of collaborating from scratch and may spend months or years networking in the community before a specific collaborative group is organized. A convener specific to the community level of collaboration may not continue in this role with the collaborative group once the groundwork is laid.

Communication processes in the collaborating community. The collaborating community is communicatively linked to the collaborative group in a number of ways, but what role does the community play during collaboration? Scholarship identifies useful communication processes that take place within a community context that facilitate collaboration among stakeholders with regard to the experience and celebration of small successes, facilitation of sharing information between the collaborative group and the rest of the community, ratification of the consensus through legislative action, and implementation of decisions and projects brought forth by the collaborative group. These processes include the collaborative group; nevertheless, they require the community to participate as a vital interactant.

Zoller (2000) suggested the importance of the experience and celebration of small successes in sustaining community collaboration. As she explained: "These small projects may help participants envision the relationship between the collaboration of community stakeholders and 'real' outcomes for the community" (p. 202). In other words, the community at large will be more likely to support collaborations if the community experiences and celebrates concrete successes with the collaboration. This means that the community must be the recipient of information regarding the progress of the collaboration and part of any celebrations of that progress. This point supports Gray's (1989) early claim that local officials need to facilitate the sharing of information, in this case, between the collaborative group and the rest of the community. This facilitation may result in communities providing forums for collaborative groups to communicate with the community, and vice versa. Gray (1989) also claimed that local officials need to ratify the consensus achieved in the collaboration through legislative action and oversee the implementation of decisions and projects brought forth by the collaborative group. Through these processes, leadership in the community legitimates the collaboration by accepting, promoting, and implementing, when appropriate, the decisions and innovations created through the collaboration. Ratification and implementation could be viewed as end-processes of community collaboration, but it is more likely in long-term community collaboration that these processes occur throughout the duration of the collaboration. Most importantly, given their absence, the collaboration is not likely to be sustained. Moseley (2001) found that support by key government agencies was crucial to the continuation of collaborative efforts in the Applegate Partnership. When a change of leadership occurred at the Bureau of Land Management, more traditional forms of management were pursued and the culture of the community regressed to what she deemed a "'pay later' approach by minimizing public involvement and asking for feedback when planning was already well underway," resulting in "legal appeals" and "community uproar" (Moseley, 2001, p. 110).

Outcomes for collaborating communities. Finally, communities are the benefactors of positive outcomes that result from the ideal community collaboration. Previous literature claims that new leaders, institutions, and cultures result from collaboration. Collaboration also leads to additional collaboration and is sometimes responsible for creating a sense of community, making community itself an outcome of community collaboration.

Chrislip and Larson (1994) found that collaboration created new leaders for the community to the extent that new persons ran for public office based on their experience with collaboration. As they explained, "The most extraordinary and unexpected result of successful collaboration is that people are empowered and energized by their engagement in collaborative projects" (p. 116). The result is that the community benefits from new and energized leadership.

Innes and Booher (1999) identified *new institutions* as an indirect effect of consensus building in coalitions. This is consistent with Lawrence et al.'s (2002) study of proto-institutions, examining cases of collaborative groups that became institutionalized into the community. As a result, the community is the beneficiary as long-term collaborations morph into community institutions that address specific social problems. Such is the case with the Best Summer Education Learning and Fun program in Skagit County, Washington, which began in 1991 as a collaborative project among two school districts, the county, a half-dozen other nonprofit organizations, and interested citizens in an effort to reach at-risk children during the summers. Today, it includes all seven school districts in the county, has served thousands of children over the past 13 years, and has been replicated by other counties. Its mission now includes after-school programs for children and local politicians frequently run on the platform that they will continue to support it (Margaret Thompson, personal communication, June 30, 2003).

New norms, heuristics, and discourses are claimed to be outcomes of community coalitions (Innes & Booher, 1999). This is supported by Chrislip and Larson's (1994) assertion that collaboration changes "the way communities 'do business' on public issues. . . . Advocacy changes to engagement, hostility to civility, confrontation to conversation and separation to community. A *new civic culture* [italics added] is created" (p. 119). Moseley (2001) demonstrated this cultural shift taking place in the early years of the Oregon environmental collaboration, the Applegate Partnership: "In effect, the partnership helped agencies realize they would 'pay now' with up-front participation and innovation or 'pay later' with time-consuming appeals, court cases and civil disobedience" (p. 108).

The ability to mobilize new collaborations is another outcome of adopting a new way of doing business or a new culture in the community and new relationships with other community partners (Chrislip & Larson, 1994; Innes & Booher, 1999). Collaborating communities hence produce multiple collaborations.

Finally, Chrislip and Larson (1994) best articulated the reciprocal relationship between collaborations and their communities by suggesting that community itself is an outcome of collaboration. As they claimed, "Empowerment and community are created when these successful efforts engage citizens constructively to address issues and problems they care about" (p. 123). Communities become solidified through the processes of collaboration; citizens and organizations become owners of and are empowered to address their community's problems.

CONCLUSION

Collaboration has become a central feature of the community landscape, given the significant problems communities face. Chrislip and Larson (1994) wrote a decade ago that "communities must look inward for the incentive and capacity to change is a lesson learned painfully over the past thirty years" (p. xiii). They saw a pressing need for communities to organize, taking local control of the important social issues confronting them so as to build the capacity to deal with them. The current political climate, which encourages local decision making and problem solving, also provides an impetus for communities to act. It is no wonder, then, that community groups and organizations have turned to collaboration to solve the problems they face, a trend that certainly can be expected to grow.

Given the impact of collaboration on groups, organizations, and communities, it is also not surprising that scholars have turned their attention to studying it. The study of community collaboration, however, is in its infancy, as scholars have focused their attention primarily on collaborations within and between for-profit organizations. The importance of community collaboration, coupled with the lack of focus by the academy on this particular type of collaboration, provided the impetus for this study. The resulting chapter, thus, first constructed a definition of community collaboration to distinguish it from other types of collaborations. It then proposed a conceptual framework for understanding community collaboration and used the categories of that framework to review the literature relevant to understanding successful, or ideal, community collaboration. The literature synthesized spans many disciplines (e.g., communication, public network management, and education) and types of collaborations (e.g., intraorganizational, interorganizational, and community). The intended result is a conceptual framework and review of the relevant literature that provides a summary of what scholars currently know and serves as a starting point for proposing potential directions for future research with respect to (a) collaboration, (b) community collaboration, and (c) communication in community collaboration.

First, the conceptual framework provides a heuristic tool that organizes major contributions that can be the potential building blocks of a tentative theory of collaboration. As this review demonstrates, there has been a wealth of scholarship examining collaboration. This literature, however, cries out for organization and synthesis, as it exists all over the academic terrain, from the work on strategic business alliances to studies of interdisciplinary health teams—with little attempt to pull it together in a meaningful manner. The result is a set of disparate research findings that do not produce an integrated understanding of collaboration. Previous attempts to organize the literature have tended to be discipline specific (such as reviews of collaboration in education or in public network management; see, respectively, Welch, 2000; Oliver & Ebers, 1998) rather than synthesizing literature across disciplines to create a broad understanding of collaboration. Those attempts have also not fully identified all of the central players and processes that characterize collaboration to create a deep understanding of collaboration. Cohen and Mankin (1999), for instance, used a systems model to understand collaboration but they did not focus on how antecedents, processes, and outcomes applied to the different constituents of a collaboration. Even when scholars have taken such collaboration constituents into account, they have not properly differentiated between, for instance, individual representatives and organizational stakeholders, and most have ignored the context within which a collaboration is embedded and the fact that collaboration is a group phenomenon. The 12-cell conceptual framework offered here identifies both the constituents involved in a collaboration, as articulated by the BFG perspective, and what researchers know about these constituents as viewed through the general categories of the systems perspective. The result is a conceptual framework that offers both a broad and a deep understanding of collaboration.

There is, however, much that still needs to be done by scholars to understand the relationships between the inputs, throughputs, and outputs with regard to the four constituents of collaboration members, the collaborative group, stakeholder organizations, and the community in which a collaboration is embedded. The extant literature reveals much about each category of the systems model for each constituent, but less is known about the relationships between these categories and constituents. Much is still unknown about how processes (column 2) change when specific inputs (column 1) are not in place, relationships between the processes identified and the specific outcomes of a collaboration (column 3), or how the outcomes experienced influence the antecedents for subsequent collaborations. In essence, each column of the conceptual framework (indeed, each cell) has tended to be treated, as the BFG perspective would argue, as a separate container; consequently, more study of the relationships between these columns (and cells) is needed.

Second, the previous literature has not adequately distinguished interorganizational collaboration from community collaboration. This is unfortunate for, as this review suggests, there is a growing body of literature that warrants recognizing this type of collaboration as a distinct form. Community collaboration has important characteristics that transcend the boundaries of organizations and that are not present in studies that focus solely on interorganizational collaboration. As pointed out, scholars previously have viewed collaborations as temporary work groups, but community collaborations more typically occur over a relatively long period of time. Whether the characteristics that lead to successful collaboration are the same for short- and long-term collaborations, or for for-profit and community collaborations, remains to be seen. There probably are important differences; as one example, members' commitment to a collaboration is probably more influential in affecting the success of a long-term collaboration than a short-term one. Researchers, thus, need to know whether the findings obtained about for-profit intraorganizational and interorganizational collaborations also apply to community collaborations.

A focus on community collaboration does demand that a collaborative group, its representative members, and the stakeholder organizations involved not be treated as some type of container divorced from its relevant contexts but, instead, in line with the BFG perspective, that these constituents should be studied as embedded within a community context that both influences these constituents and, in turn, is influenced by them. Such a perspective suggests the need for studies examining the reciprocal effects between the internal and external aspects of community collaboration. Such studies would go a long way toward meeting Mumby and Stohl's (1996) critique of traditional organizational studies in which organizations are treated as "separate and distinct from society" (p. 65). The BFG perspective is particularly useful for suggesting starting points for examining the relationship between the internal and external aspects of community collaboration. For instance, the BFG perspective argues that people are members of multiple groups and that these multiple memberships potentially influence people's behavior in any particular group and lead them to engage in boundary-spanning activities. Consequently, scholars might focus on how people's multiple roles as an individual, organizational stakeholder representative, and community member influence their behavior in a collaborative group, what happens when these roles are in conflict, or how collaboration members serve as boundary spanners for a collaboration group and for the community at large. The interdependence of a group with its relevant contexts also calls into question, from the BFG perspective, a collaborative group's negotiation of its jurisdiction or autonomy, as well as coordinated actions among the relevant groups involved in a collaboration. What happens when community leaders or members do not agree with the work being done by a collaboration, such as in Lange's (2003) study of an environmental collaboration, in which a stakeholder organization was at odds with a collaboration (and its representative collaboration member) and subsequently withdrew and became an opposing force in the community? What processes (column 2) might a collaboration group enact to manage such a dilemma? Given the ideal characteristics of community collaboration, what happens when these characteristics do not live up to the ideal?

Community collaboration also highlights some particularly important processes and practices that are not examined very well in the traditional literature on interorganizational collaboration. For example, community collaboration amplifies concerns such as representation and voice. These issues may be apparent in other forms of interorganizational collaboration; however, they become especially foregrounded in the context of a community collaboration seeking to solve a social problem. For example, shared power has a historical place in collaboration theory, with stakeholders, as well as individual representatives, striving to avoid hierarchy in a collaboration. In community collaboration, however, shared power becomes important for other reasons; if a collaboration is not characterized by shared power, the outcomes of that collaboration cannot represent all of its participants. In turn, if the collaboration is charged with making recommendations to civic leaders or implementing community programs, the implications of not being representative threaten notions of fairness in civic problem solving (Coggins, 2001). In that sense, community collaboration offers a potential new civic model of leadership (see Chrislip & Larson, 1994) and, hence, the close examination of community collaborations can help to shed light on the social construction of civic life, as well as to document the history of particular communities and predict their abilities to tackle further social issues.

Scholars also know little about the actual effects that community collaborations have on their communities. Chrislip and Larson (1994) claimed that "the most important result to come out of successful collaboration initiatives is a revolutionary change in the culture of a community" (p. 119), but such claims demand empirical evidence, evidence that will need to be collected over a longitudinal period of time to understand how communities achieve outcomes from collaboration (column 3).

Third, the most important contribution of this conceptual framework is toward understanding the role of communication in community collaboration. This conceptual framework calls specific attention to the importance of communication processes and practices for successful collaboration, making evident the contribution that communication scholars can make to understanding community collaboration. The study of collaboration has tended to be dominated by management and education scholars, neither of whom privileges communication processes and practices in understanding collaboration. This study argues for the importance of including the mediating effects of throughput processes in the more traditional input-output model of collaboration that has dominated the literature.

As this synthesis of the literature shows, communication is an important tool used by successful collaborations, in the sense that collaborative groups, for instance, employ certain communication structures (e.g., roundtable seating) and channels (e.g., media technologies) that facilitate the process of successful collaboration. There is, of course, much that still needs to be known about the communicative practices that do and should characterize community collaborations. Such understanding is complicated by the fact that community collaborations, in comparison to their for-profit interorganizational counterparts, typically are more heterogeneous in terms of membership, often composed of a mix of representatives from public, private, nonprofit, and for-profit organizations. The group literature reveals that the communicative practices of heterogeneous groups are often more complex and more difficult than those demonstrated in homogeneous groups (see, e.g., Kirchmeyer, 1993; Kirchmeyer & Cohen, 1992; Ruhe & Eatman, 1977; Triandis, 1960; Triandis, Hall, & Ewen, 1965; Vaid-Raizada, 1985); scholars should expect the same to be true for community collaboration in comparison to many other forms of collaboration.

Communication, however, is more than a tool used by collaborations: It is constitutive of community collaboration. Communication scholars, using theories of paradox and dialectics, have been at the forefront of explaining the reflexive and reciprocal relationship between communication and collaboration. As that work has shown, communication is infused into our understanding of what it means to collaborate. The current model, thus, illuminates the importance of both microlevel communicative practices (e.g., sharing agendas or mission statements) that facilitate collaboration and macrolevel communication processes (e.g., dialogue and consensus) by which collaboration is created and sustained.

Focusing on communication as the sine qua non of collaboration will, hopefully, eventually lead to a communication-oriented theory of collaboration. Such a theory would be in line with other communication approaches to organizational theorizing, such as Kuhn and Ashcraft's (2003) call for a communicative theory of the firm, in which the term *collaboration* could easily be substituted for the term *firm* or *organization* and the previously named theories associated with collaboration, such as resource dependency theory, could be criticized for the same lack in organizational theorizing indicated in the passage below:

> Scholarship on the communicative constitution of organization supplies a strong foundation on which to construct a communicative theory of the firm, for it informs issues central to theory of the firm, crafting a novel position on the ontology of organization. First, it develops the role of emergent meaning construction by bringing into relief specific discursive processes fundamental to the (re)production of organization. It also articulates a communicative rationale for the existence and maintenance of firms and their boundaries, premised on the firm as a text-object that is necessary to enable and constrain collection action. In such ways, the communication-as -constitutive literature takes organiz*ing* seriously and begins to furnish the "microfoundations" lacked by such theories as the RBV, while also illuminating mechanisms that connect [resource-based view] situated interaction to institutionalized systems. (pp. 41–42)

The constitutive view enables scholars to examine microfoundations such as the consequences of employing specific discursive strategies. Deetz and Simpson (in press) asserted that the type of concepts invoked have multiple meanings to individuals. For example, they wrote of the word *dialogue* that "the coupling of high expectations with an ill-defined and murky concept . . . increase [sic] the likelihood of disappointments, stagnation, and entrenchment of polarized positions that do not bear out the dialogic promise" (p. 17). Future researchers, hence, may want to use this study's conceptual framework as a starting point for examining how multiple interpretations of communication processes, such as dialogue and consensus (column 2), become negotiated as a community engages in collaborative problem solving.

In closing, there is still much that needs to be known about community collaboration. Given the significance of collaboration to communities and the central role that communication plays in collaboration, community collaboration provides an important site for understanding the more general relationship between communication and community building. Ideally, the conceptual framework offered here provides an impetus for creating a community of communication scholars who will devote more attention to community collaboration.

NOTES

1. Not revealed through academic search engines, and not highlighted in our framework due to their practitioner-focused nature, some community collaboration materials are accessible in online forms (see, e.g., National Network for Collaboration; http://crs.uvm.edu/nnco/).

2. Based on the study of 13 cases of social-problem–oriented groups specifically engaged in consensus building, Innes and Booher (1999) found outcomes that fit in three categories: First-order effects are direct and instantly identifiable at the end of the project, such as a high-quality agreement between collaborating partners; second-order effects "show up while the project is underway but outside the boundaries of the project or even after it is completed" (p. 419), such as participants' "changes

in perceptions" (p. 419); and third-order effects may not be obvious for an extended period of time, as in the creation of "new institutions" (p. 419).

REFERENCES

Adelman, M. B., & Frey, L. R. (1997). *The fragile community: Living together with AIDS.* Mahwah, NJ: Erlbaum.

Agranoff, R., & McGuire, M. (1998). Multinetwork management: Collaboration and the hollow state in local economic policy. *Journal of Public Administration Research and Theory, 8,* 7–93.

Agranoff, R., & McGuire, M. (2001). Big questions in public network management research. *Journal of Public Administration Research and Theory, 11,* 295–334.

Appley, D. G., & Winder, A. E. (1977). An evolving definition of collaboration and some implications from the world of work. *Journal of Applied Behavior Science, 13,* 279–291.

Barrett, F. J. (1995). Creating appreciative learning cultures. *Organizational Dynamics, 24,* 36–49.

Bennis, W., & Biederman, P. W. (1997). *Organizing genius: The secrets of creative collaboration.* Reading, MA: Addison-Wesley.

Bond, M. A., & Keys, C. B. (1993). Empowerment, diversity and collaboration: Promoting synergy on community boards. *American Journal of Community Psychology, 21,* 37–58.

Cheney, G. (1983). The rhetoric of identification and the study of organizational communication. *Quarterly Journal of Speech, 69,* 143–158.

Chrislip, D. D., & Larson, C. E. (1994). *Collaborative leadership: How citizens and civic leaders can make a difference.* San Francisco: Jossey-Bass.

Coggins, G. C. (2001). Of Californicators, quislings, and crazies: Some perils of devolved collaboration. In P. Brick, D. Snow, & S. Van de Wetering (Eds.), *Across the great divide: Explorations in collaborative conversation and the American West* (pp. 163–171). Washington, DC: Island Press.

Cohen, S. G., & Mankin, D. (1999). Collaboration in the virtual organization. In C. L. Cooper & D. M. Rousseau (Eds.), *Trends in organizational behavior* (pp. 105–120). London: Wiley.

Deetz, S., & Simpson, J. (in press). Critical organizational dialogue: Open formation and the demand of "otherness." In R. Anderson, L. Baxter, & K. Cissna (Eds.), *Dialogic approaches to communication.* Thousand Oaks, CA: Sage.

Depew, D., & Peters, J. D. (2001). Community and communication: The conceptual background. In G. J. Shepherd & E. W. Rothenbuhler (Eds.), *Communication and community* (pp. 3–21). Mahwah, NJ: Erlbaum.

Dresang, J. (2002, October 8). Metro area tapped as test site for federal faith-based work project. *Milwaukee Journal Sentinel,* p. 3. Retrieved November 25, 2002, from www.jsonline.com/bym.news/oct 02/86100.asp

Ellis, R. J., & Cronshaw, S. F. (1992). Self-monitoring and leader emergence. *Small Group Research, 23,* 114–115.

Frey, L. R. (2003). Group communication in context: Studying bona fide groups. In L. R. Frey (Ed.), *Group communication in context: Studies of bona fide groups* (2nd ed., pp. 1–20). Mahwah, NJ: Erlbaum.

Gouran, D. S. (1997). Communication in groups: The emergence and evolution of a field of study. In L. R. Frey (Ed.), D. S. Gouran, & M. S. Poole (Assoc. Eds.), *The handbook of group communication theory and research* (pp. 3–36). Thousand Oaks, CA: Sage.

Gray, B. (1989). *Collaborating: Finding common group for multi-party problems.* San Francisco: Jossey-Bass.

Gray, B., & Wood, D. J. (1991). Collaborative alliances: Moving from practice to theory. *Journal of Applied Behavior Science, 27,* 3–22.

Habermas, J. (1970a). Toward a theory of communicative competence. *Inquiry, 13,* 360–375.

Habermas, J. (1970b). Toward a theory of communicative competence. In H. P. Dreitzel (Ed.), *Recent sociology 2* (pp. 114–148). London: Collier-Macmillan.

Habermas, J. (1984). *The theory of communicative action: Vol. 1. Reason and the rationalization of society* (T. McCarthy, Trans.). Boston: Beacon Press.

Harrington-Mackin, H. (1994). *The team building tool kit: Tips, tactics, and rules for effective working teams.* New York: American Management Association.

Haskins, M., Liedtka, J., & Rosenblum, J. (1998). Beyond teams: Toward an ethic of collaboration. *Organizational Dynamics, 26*(4), 38–64.

Heath, R., & Sias, P. (1999). Communicating spirit in a collaborative alliance. *Journal of Applied Communication Research, 27,* 356–376.

Hladik, K. F. (1988). R&D and international joint ventures. In F. J. Contractor & P. Lorange (Eds.), *Cooperative strategies in international business* (pp. 187–203). Lexington, MA: Lexington Books.

Hogue, T. (1993). *Community based collaboration: Community wellness manual.* Retrieved September 1, 2003 from www.crs.uvm.edu/nnco/collab/wellness.html

Innes, J., & Booher, D. E. (1999). Consensus building and complex adaptive systems: A framework for evaluating collaborative planning. *Journal of American Planning Association, 65,* 412–423.

Isaacs, W. (1999). *Dialogue and the art of thinking together: A pioneering approach to communicating in business and in life.* New York: Currency.

Jones, T. S., & Bodtker, A. (1998). A dialectical analysis of a social justice process: International collaboration in South Africa. *Journal of Applied Communication Research, 26,* 357–373.

Kasper-Fuehrer, E. C., & Ashkanasay, N. M. (2001). Communicating trustworthiness and building trust in interorganizational virtual organizations. *Journal of Management, 27,* 235–257.

Keyton, J., & Stallworth, V. (2003). On the verge of collaboration: Interaction processes versus group outcomes. In L. R. Frey (Ed.), *Group communication in context: Studies of bona fide groups* (2nd ed., pp. 235–260). Mahwah, NJ: Erlbaum.

Kilmann, R., & Thomas, K. (1977). Developing a forced-choice measure of conflict-handling behavior: The "MODE" instrument. *Educational and Psychological Measurement, 37,* 309–327.

Kirchmeyer, C. (1993). Multicultural task groups: An account of the low contribution levels of minorities. *Small Group Research, 24,* 127–148.

Kirchmeyer, C., & Cohen, A. (1992). Multicultural groups: Their performance and reactions with constructive conflict. *Group & Organization Management, 17,* 153–170.

Kline, S. L., Hennen-Floyd, C. L., & Farrell, K. M. (1990). Cognitive complexity and verbal response mode use in discussion. *Communication Quarterly, 38,* 350–360.

Kuhn, T. (1998, November). *Dynamic processes and emergent structures: A parallel distributing processing model of communication networks.* Paper presented at the annual conference of the National Communication Association, New York, NY.

Kuhn, T., & Ashcraft, K. L. (2003). Corporate scandal and the theory of the firm: Formulating the contributions of organizational communication studies. *Management Communication Quarterly, 17,* 20–57.

Lange, J. (2001). Exploring paradox in environmental collaborations. In P. Brick, D. Snow, & S. Van de Wetering (Eds.), *Across the great divide: Explorations in collaborative conversation and the American West* (pp. 200–209). Washington, DC: Island Press.

Lange, J. (2003). Environmental collaboration and constituency communication. In L. R. Frey (Ed.), *Group communication in context: Studies of bona fide groups* (2nd ed., pp. 209–234). Mahwah, NJ: Erlbaum.

Lawrence, T. B., Hardy, C., & Phillips, N. (2002). Institutional effects of interorganizational collaboration: The emergence of proto-institutions. *Academy of Management Journal, 45,* 281–290.

Leblebici, H., & Whetten, D. A. (1984). The concept of horizontal hierarchy and the organization of interorganizational networks: A comparative analysis. *Social Networks, 6,* 31–58.

Logsdon, J. M. (1991). Interests and interdependence in the formation of social problem-solving collaborations. *Journal of Applied Behavioral Science, 27,* 23–37.

Mabry, E. A. (1999). The systems metaphor in group communication. In L. R. Frey, D. S. Gouran, & M. S. Poole (Assoc. Eds.), *The handbook of group communication theory and research* (pp. 71–91). Thousand Oaks, CA: Sage.

Manev, I. M., & Stevenson, W. B. (2001). Balancing ties: Boundary spanning and influence in the organization's extended network of communication. *Journal of Business Communication, 38,* 183–222.

Marshall, E. M. (1995, June). The collaborative workplace. *Management Review,* pp. 13–17.

McDermott, J. P. (2002, June 28). Region should work harder on community issues, Charleston, SC, official says. *Post and Courier,* p. B9. Retrieved November 10, 2002, from www.charleston.net

McKinney, M. J. (2001) What do we mean by consensus? Some defining principles. In P. Brick, D. Snow, & S. Van de Wetering (Eds.), *Across the great divide: Explorations in collaborative conversation and the American West* (pp. 200–209). Washington DC: Island Press.

Medved, C. E., Morrison, K., Dearing, J. W., Larson, S., Cline, G., & Brummans, B. (2001). Tensions in community health improvement initiatives: Communication and collaboration in a managed care environment. *Journal of Applied Communication Research, 29,* 137–152.

Mintzberg, H., Jorgensen, J., Dougherty, D., & Westley, F. (1996, Spring). Some surprising things about collaboration—knowing how people connect makes it work better. *Organizational Dynamics,* pp. 60–71.

Montgomery, M. J. (1997). Providing links among government, academia, and industry: The role of CISTI in scholarly communication. *Canadian Journal of Communication, 22*(3/4), 1–8.

Moseley, C. (2001). The Applegate Partnership: Innovation in crisis. In P. Brick, D. Snow, & S. Van de Wetering (Eds.), *Across the great divide: Explorations in collaborative conversation and the American West* (pp. 102–111). Washington, DC: Island Press.

Mumby, D. K. (1987). The political function of narrative in organizations. *Communication Monographs, 54,* 113–127.

Mumby, D. K., & Stohl, C. (1996). Disciplining organizational communication studies. *Management Communication Quarterly, 10,* 50–72.

Oliver, A. L., & Ebers, M. (1998) Networking network studies: An analysis of conceptual configurations in the study of inter-organizational relationships. *Organization Studies, 19,* 549–583.

Pasquero, J. (1991). Supraorganizational collaborations: The Canadian environmental experiment. *Journal of Applied Behavioral Science, 27,* 38–64.

Poole, M. S. (1999). Group communication theory. In L. R. Frey, D. S. Gouran, & M. S. Poole (Eds.), *The handbook of group communication theory and research* (pp. 37–70). Thousand Oaks, CA: Sage.

Powell, W. W., Koput, K. W., & Smith-Doerr, L. (1996). Interorganizational collaboration and the locus of innovation: Networks of learning in biotechnology. *Administrative Science Quarterly, 41,* 116–145.

Provan, K. G., & Milward, H. B. (1995). A preliminary theory of interorganizational effectiveness: A comparative study of four community mental health systems. *Administrative Science Quarterly, 40,* 1–33.

Putnam, L. L., & Stohl, C. (1990). Bona fide groups: A reconceptualization of groups in context. *Communication Studies, 41,* 248–265.

Putnam, L. L., & Stohl, C. (1996). Bona fide groups: An alternative perspective for communication and small group decision making. In R. Y. Hirokawa & M. S. Poole (Eds.), *Communication and group decision making* (2nd ed., pp. 147–178). Thousand Oaks, CA: Sage.

Rothschild-Whitt, J. (1979). The collectivist organization: An alternative to rational-bureaucratic models. *American Sociological Review, 44,* 509–527.

Ruhe, J., & Eatman, J. (1977). Effects of racial composition on small work groups. *Small Group Behavior, 8,* 479–486.

Rumsey, S., Fulk, J., & Monge, P. (1998, November). *Communication network models for the development and management of interorganizational alliance processes.* Paper presented at the annual conference of the National Communication Association, New York, NY.

Sanders, M. G. (2001). The role of "community" in comprehensive school, family and community partnership programs. *Elementary School Journal, 102,* 19–37.

Selsky, J. W. (1991). Lessons in community development: An activist approach to simulating interorganizational collaboration. *Journal of Applied Behavioral Science, 27,* 91–115.

Simonin, B. (1997). The importance of collaborative know-how: An empirical test of the learning organization. *Academy of Management Journal, 40,* 1150–1174.

Stallworth, V. (1998). *Building a model of interorganizational nonprofit collaboration.* Unpublished master's thesis, University of Memphis, TN.

Stegelin, D. A., & Jones, S. D. (1991). Components of early childhood interagency collaboration: Results of a statewide survey. *Early Education and Development, 2,* 54–67.

Stohl, C., & Putnam, L. L. (1994). Group communication in context: Implications for the study of bona fide groups. In L. R. Frey (Ed.), *Group communication in context: Studies of natural groups* (pp. 284–292). Hillsdale, NJ: Erlbaum.

Stohl, C., & Walker, K. (2002). A bona fide perspective for the future of groups: Understanding collaborating groups. In L. R. Frey (Ed.), *New directions in group communication* (pp. 237–252). Thousand Oaks, CA: Sage.

Taber, T. D., Walsh, J. T., & Cooke, R. A. (1979). Developing a community-based program for reducing the social impact of a plant closing. *Journal of Applied Behavioral Science, 15,* 144–155.

Thomann, A., & Strickland, D. E. (1992). Managing collaborative organizations in the 90s. *Industrial Management, 34*(4), 26–29.

Tompkins, P., & Cheney, G. (1983). Account analysis in organizations: Decision making and identification. In L. L. Putnam & M. E. Pacanowsky (Eds.), *Communication and organizations: An interpretive approach* (pp. 123–146). Beverly Hills, CA: Sage.

Triandis, H. C. (1960). Cognitive similarity and communication in a dyad. *Human Relations, 13,* 175–183.

Triandis, H. C., Hall, E. R., & Ewen, R. B. (1965). Member heterogeneity and dyadic creativity. *Human Relations, 18,* 33–35.

Trist, E. (1989). Foreword. In B. Gray, *Collaborating: Finding common group for multi-party problems* (pp. xiii–xvi). San Francisco: Jossey-Bass.

U.S. Newswire. (2002, July 18). *Joint labor-management partnerships committed to quality and cooperation honed with AFT-Saturn/UAW partnership award.* Retrieved November 25, 2002, from http://www.releases.usnewswire.comGetRelease.asp?id=108-07182002

Vaid-Raizada, V. K. (1985). Management of interethnic conflict in an Indian manufacturing organization. *Psychological Reports, 56,* 731–738.

Walther, J. (1997). Group and interpersonal effects in international computer-mediated collaboration. *Human Communication Research, 23,* 342–369.

Weber, M. (1947). *The theory of social and economic organizations* (A. M. Henderson & T. Parsons, Trans.). New York: Oxford University Press.

Welch, M. (2000). Practitioners' perspectives of collaboration: A social validation and factor analysis. *Journal of Education and Psychological Consultation, 11,* 357–379.

Wood, D. J., & Gray, B. (1991). Toward a comprehensive theory of collaboration. *Journal of Applied Behavioral Science, 27,* 139–162.

Yon, A., Mickelson, R. A., & Carlton-LaNey, I. (1993). A child's place: Developing interagency collaboration on behalf of homeless children. *Education and Urban Society, 25,* 410–423.

Young, I. M. (1995). The ideal community and the politics of difference. In P. A. Weiss & M. Friedman (Eds.), *Feminism and community* (pp. 233–257). Philadelphia: Temple University Press.

Zoller, H. M. (2000). "A place you haven't visited before": Creating the conditions for community dialogue. *Southern Communication Journal, 65,* 191–207.

CHAPTER CONTENTS

7   "Community" as a Foundation for Public Relations Theory and Practice

KIRK HALLAHAN
Colorado State University

This essay argues that community serves as a viable theoretical foundation for the development of public relations theory and practice. Four arguments are set forth, based on (a) the pervasiveness of the community idea and ideal in everyday life and contemporary scholarship, (b) conceptual limitations rooted in the widely accepted focus on publics in public relations, (c) the emerging recognition of community-related theories in public relations scholarship, and (d) the strength of community building as a philosophy to drive public relations practice.

Our theory is that public relations is better defined and practiced as the active attempt to restore and maintain a sense of community. (Kruckeberg & Starck, 1988, p. xi)

[P]ublic relations must begin to think of our publics and our organizations in the sense of community. (Wilson, 1996, p. 74)

Recent observations that community represents the essence of public relations underscore the need for public relations theorists to reexamine critically many of the central concepts and assumptions that comprise public relations theory and practice.

For 8 decades, public relations practitioners since Bernays (1923) have talked about "the public" and "publics." Researchers, however, have devoted little theoretical attention to the idea of publics (Botan & Soto, 1998) or alternative frameworks in which to analyze public relations (Toth & Heath, 1992).

Despite the ubiquity of the public construct, a strong argument can be made for positioning community as the conceptual centerpiece for examining and practicing public relations. Indeed, the field might be better called "community relations." Making that case, however, requires going beyond limited conceptualizations to examine the community construct broadly.

Correspondence: Kirk Hallahan, Department of Journalism and Technical Communication, Colorado State University, C-225 Clark, Fort Collins, CO 80525; email: Kirk.hallahan@colostate.edu

Communication Yearbook 28, pp. 233–279

Following a brief review of the community construct, this chapter argues that there are separate pragmatic, theoretical, and philosophical reasons that community could serve as a viable and useful foundation for the development of public relations theory and practice. The pragmatic argument revolves around the resonating nature of the community construct itself, which has received increased attention among communication and other scholars. The theoretical argument is that community is a broader and richer concept compared to publics, the accepted focus of most public relations theory-building. At the same time, public relations scholars have recognized a variety of new theoretical approaches to the study of public relations that dovetail with the community concept. Finally, the philosophical argument contends that, as Kruckeberg and Starck (1988) suggested, public relations should be looked upon as a process of building and preserving communities—versus the adversarial (and often reactionary) reconciliation of organizational and public goals.

DEFINING COMMUNITY

Community is one of the murkiest concepts in the social sciences and humanities. Its Latin root is the same as that for communication, common, and commune: *communis*. The term *community* dates from the 14th century in its Middle English and French forms. A cursory look at one dictionary finds 11 meanings.

J. Grunig and Hunt (1984) pointed to the multiplicity of meanings associated with the term. The text authors suggest community can be thought of either as a locality or as a nongeographic grouping of interest, such as the scientific community or the business community. They explained:

> Nearly all community relations programs are designed for the first kind of community. The second definition of community is essentially the definition we have given to a public—a group with a common problem or interest, regardless of geographic location. (p. 286)

Elsewhere, J. Grunig (1989a) observed that communities can be classified according to the number and variety of publics found within them. By this analysis, a *pluralistic community* includes more than one public.

Burke (1999) argued that the goal of the community relations function in public relations should be for organizations to become the "neighbors of choice." This requires building relationships; establishing practices and procedures that anticipate and respond to community expectations, concerns, and issues; and focusing on support programs that respond to community concerns and strengthen the quality of community life. Lundborg (1950) noted that traditionally the *community public* has been considered the most "tangible and visible public" (p. 3) for organizations because its members are in close proximity to an organization's operations and often become customers, employees, and investors. The importance of geographic community publics often is less obvious than the impact of these other groups, which engage in direct economic exchanges with the organization. Nevertheless, community publics are important because they provide other needed resources (e.g., natural, physical, human, or political) required for an organization's success. Banks (1995) pointed out that traditional community relations has received less attention in recent years. Similarly, although community relations remains a critical part of the public relations practice, community relations receives comparatively little theoretical attention from scholars (e.g., Tichenor, Donohue, & Olien, 1977). Most recent articles have focused on case studies (e.g., Henry, 1993; Mitchell & Schnyder, 1989; Tilson & Stacks, 1997).

Alternative Views of Community

A wide range of definitions and characteristics of community can be found in the sociology and anthropology literature (Chekki, 1989). Mendelbaum (1972) for example stated, "A man's community is, quite simply, the set of people, roles, and places with whom he communicates." For purposes of the present argument, a useful distinction is to think of these definitions on a continuum from purely geographic communities to purely symbolic communities.

Geographic communities are what many individuals consider the traditional meaning of the term. Sociologists' interest in geographic community can be traced to Tönnies' (1887/1988) distinction between *gemeinschaft* (i.e., localized rural folk life or community, characterized by strong interpersonal relationships and tradition-based regulation of behavior) and *gesellschaft* (i.e., complex urban life or society, characterized by estranged relationships and rules-based regulation of behavior).

Among the first academics to focus on community was philosopher Josiah Royce (1908, 1913, 1916), who celebrated the democratic ideal of a plurality of diverse people who maintained their individuality but engaged in a common cause of creating a "Great Community." Royce defined loyalty as devotion to one's community. He contended happiness could be achieved by individuals and social groups if they identified with the common will of the community (Rawlins & Stoker, 2001; Stoker & Rawlins, n.d.).

Community-as-a-locality also provided the basis for much of the early research in American sociology, notably the work of sociologists at the University of Chicago from the 1890s through the 1930s. Burgess, Park, Quandt, and others focused on the community theme (e.g., Kruckeberg & Starck, 1988). Burgess (1973) contended that an individual might belong to many social groups, but could not belong to more than one geographic community. Park and his colleagues (Park, 1952; Park, Burgess, & McKenzie, 1925/1967) pioneered ethnographic field work in the neighborhoods of Chicago and conceptualized a community as the aggregation of people as well as the various social institutions (e.g., churches, social service agencies, and media) that allowed neighborhoods to operate as self-contained villages within larger urban settings.

Even though geographic and structural approaches to community have practical value, later scholars found the Chicago School's approach theoretically inadequate. Subsequent community research steadily has shifted away from a geographic focus to emphasize cultural aspects. Stacey (1974; see also Carey, 1989) summed up the difficulty of any territorially based definition, short of a global one, by noting spatial boundaries have been eliminated through communications and transportation.

Symbolic Communities. Cohen (1985) called for the antithesis of the geographic-based definition of community when he suggested that all communities are symbolic and socially constructed. Drawing on constructionist ideas that provide for multiple social realities (Berger & Luckmann, 1967), Cohen argued that a community exists exclusively in people's minds and is rooted in its symbolic constituents, without regard to place. Just as arterial roads often define the perimeter of a neighborhood, psychic boundaries exist that represent the lines of demarcation for a community. Cohen suggested these socially constructed boundaries enclose elements considered to be more like one another than they are different. He observed:

> Community . . . is a boundary-expressing symbol. As a symbol, it is held in common by its members, but its meaning varies with its members' unique orientations to it. In the face of this variability of meaning, community has to be kept alive through the manipulation of symbols. The reality and efficacy of the community's boundary—and therefore, of the community itself—depends on its symbolic construction and embellishment. (p. 15)

In order to understand community, Cohen stressed the necessity of capturing the experiences of its members. If the members of a community come to feel they have less in common with one another than they do with members of another community, the integrity of the community becomes impugned.

Various other sociologists following the demise of the Chicago School have placed increased emphasis on the cultural dimensions of community. Hillery (1955), in a classic literature review, suggested that community, in fact, involves a territorial variable (place), a sociological variable (social interaction), and a psychocultural variable (a commonality of ties). Later, Effrat (1974) suggested three slightly different categories of community: as solidarity institutions, as a form of primary interaction, and as institutionally distinct groups. Bell and Newby (1974) identified a broader list of elements present in most definitions of community: social interaction based on geographic area, self-sufficiency, common life, consciousness of a kind, and possession of common ends, norms, and means. Minar and Greer (1969) suggested that communities "express our vague yearnings for a communality of desire, a commune with those around us, an extension of the bond of kin and friendship to all of those who share a common fate" (p. xi). Poplin (1972) focused on such groups as *moral communities*, which he suggested incorporated a sense of identification, a commonality of goals, involvement, and wholeness.

For many cultural theorists, a key issue involves how community relates to an individual's personal identity (Byker & Anderson, 1975; Cheney, 1991; Sandel, 1982). MacIntyre (1981, 1988) argued that our self-identities are intertwined with our membership in various communities. Indeed, understanding social reality can be achieved only within socially embedded traditions of thought through shared practices (e.g., Leeper & Leeper, 2001). MacIntyre's ideas are consistent with Carey's (1989) call for a ritualistic model of communication.

As suggested here, defining community in symbolic terms shifts the paradigm from a primarily structural-functional approach to primarily a cultural perspective. This approach to community is not altogether new, but can be traced back to Durkheim's (1893/1933) distinction between *mechanical solidarity* and *organic community*. For further discussion of the symbolic nature of communities, see Anderson (1991) and Hunter (1972).

A careful reading of Chicago School writers suggests the importance of culture. Burgess (1973) pointed out that an individual is not a member of a community because he or she lives in it, but to the extent that she or he participates in the common life of the community. Park (1938) emphasized the cultural ties that bind a community and how people participate in a common memory. He wrote: "[C]ommunal society rises out of the need of individuals to survive as individuals because they are important to one another" (p. 94), compared to the family, which thrives primarily to preserve the species (e.g., Bellah, Madsen, Sullivan, Swidler, & Tipton, 1985; Park, Burgess, & McKenzie, 1925/1967). Similarly, Dewey (1927), an early member of the Chicago School, emphasized that communal life was moral, which he defined as being sustained emotionally, intellectually, and consciously.

PERVASIVENESS OF THE COMMUNITY IDEA AND IDEAL

This essay began by suggesting four bases upon which community might serve as a superior construct for public relations theory/practice. The first argument centers on the pervasiveness of the community concept.

Pragmatically, as a concept for the practice of public relations, community links the field to an idea and an ideal that is widely and positively accepted in the everyday world. Community strikes a resonating chord among many individuals, particularly contrasted with sterile alternatives such as market, publics, or audiences. Many people want to feel they are part of a community. Similarly, the community construct has received increased attention from scholars in recent years, which allows public relations scholars to integrate their research with other threads of contemporary research in the social sciences and humanities.

Community as a Theme in American Culture

Central to the issue of community is the tension between the ideals of individualism and collectivity that characterize much of Western (and especially American) thought. As a people, Americans cherish individual freedom, but at the same time yearn to be part of something larger. Bellah and his colleagues (1985) cogently sum up this struggle in their seminal study on American individualism and commitment:

> [I]f the language of the self-reliant individual is the first language of American moral life, the languages of tradition and commitment to communities . . . are the "second languages" that most Americans know as well, which they use when the language of the radically separate self does not seem adequate. (p. 154)

Peck, founder of the Foundation for Community Encouragement, a consulting firm in Ridgefield, CT, popularized the idea of community building during the 1990s in two popular, best-selling books (1987, 1993). Peck defined a community as a

> group of two or more people who have been able to accept and transcend their differences regardless of the diversity of their backgrounds (social, spiritual, educational, ethnic, economic, political, etc.). This allows them to communicate effectively and openly and to work together toward goals identified as being for their common good. (Foundation for Community Encouragement, n.d., p. 1)

Peck launched a broader community movement in the U.S. in which Shaffer and Anundsen (1993) and Whitmayer (1993) stressed many of the same ideas. Gardner (1996) argued that the feeling of being a part of a community is integral to individualism; the loss of a community sense can be evidenced in a loss of meaning, a sense of powerlessness, and the diminution of individual responsibility and commitment (Community = relationships, 1997). A more narrowly focused approach was the *communitarian* movement, which called for a new social and public order based upon a society composed of small, cooperative, partially collectivized communities. Communitarian Etzioni (1991, 1993) invoked an "I and We" paradigm to suggest that both individualism and community have a basic moral standing in American society; neither is secondary nor derivative. The "I" stands for the individual while the "We" signifies the social, cultural, political, and historical forces that shape the collective factor—the community (1991, p. 137).

Community thus is robust idea, which Day and Murdoch (1993) explained "just will not lay down" (p. 83). Nisbet (1953) has argued that Americans remain on a "quest for community" and that the problem of community lost and community regained is "the towering moral problems of the age" (p. 27). Naisbitt (1982) pointed to community involvement, within the broader framework of the self-help movement, as a major megatrend of 1980s (see also Toch, 1965). More recently, Naisbitt and Aburdene (1990) suggested that the 1990s heralded the demise of institutions and the triumph of the individual. Individuals, however, do not remain alone, they contend: "Stripped down to the individual, one can build community, the free association of individuals" (p. 324).

The community theme continues as a dominant part of America's political and social rhetoric. The first recorded reference can be traced to Winthrop's imploring of Pilgrim settlers to work together while en route to the New World aboard the *Arbella* in 1630 (Wilson, 1968, p. 1). Today, the same message is heard in everyday political rhetoric (Clinton, 1996; Shaffer & Anundsen, 1993).

Community as a Scholarly Interest

Brenkman (1992) traced the rise of individualism, and the corresponding decline of community, as concepts addressed by intellectuals during the late 18th and 19th centuries. He observed that the decline in interest in community corresponded with the rise of capital markets, the polis (i.e., nation-state), and the family—the institutions that captured the attention of Hegel and Marx, and later Freud. Chatterjee (1990) explained that community was a premodern concept and argued that the "narrative of community" was systematically absorbed into other institutions. This transformation occurred at the same time that the idea of the mass society evolved (Williams, 1967).

Early 19th century American letters similarly focused on the virtues of individualism, witnessed by the writings of such authors as Emerson, Garrison, Thoreau, Hawthorne, Melville, and others. Wilson (1968) contended that, after the American Civil War, there was a almost wholesale rejection of the transcendental individual in favor of an emphasis on the idea of community and related topics, such as politics, intellectual inquiry, morality, nature, and genetics (Quandt, 1970).

As an intellectual idea today, community crosses a broad spectrum of American and European thought. The concept continues to interest researchers in the modern tradition. Interest in the idea also has been boosted by postmodernism, religious existentialism, neo-Marxism, post-Freudian psychotherapy, sociological interactionism, and poststructuralism. The community concept flourishes as topics of intellectual interest in such broad areas as history (Calhoun, 1980; Wuthnow, 1989), philosophy (King, 2001; Moon, 1993; Plant, 1974), political science (Anderson, 1991; Wolfe, 1970), consumer behavior (Fischer & Gainer, 1995; Gainer & Fischer, 1994; Prensky & Wright-Isak, 1997; Thompson & Holt, 1996), business ethics (Post, 2000), and urban studies (Little, 2000; McKnight, 1994).

In speech communication, *speech community* is used to describe groups and their boundaries in ethnographic and cross-cultural studies (Hymes, 1974). Duncan (1962/1985) referred to symbolization as taking the form of community or social dramas, and Gadamer (1975/1989, p. 446) described communication, which he defined as the coming to an understanding, as "the life process through which a community of life is lived out" and that "[a]ll kinds of human community life are forms of linguistic community." Goffman (1959) used the same community-based drama motif. Hardt (1975) equated communication as both a theory and method of community. Most recently, Ball-Rokeach, Kim, and Matei (2001) have sparked new interest in interpersonal ties and the creation of the *storytelling neighborhood.*

Organizational theorists and organizational communication researchers have similarly embraced the notion of community in a broad range of contexts, including *learning communities* (Gozdz, 2000), *moral communities* (Milley, 2002), and *workforce communities* (Cairncross, 2002). Boone (2001) identified five kinds of communities that can be found within the modern organization. These are communities of practice, purpose, interest, learning, and support.

Ouchi (1979) referred to *clans* within organizations and industries and stressed the importance of traditions, shared values and beliefs, and trust. What were once considered differences in management styles between organizations are more commonly attributed to differences in organizational cultures (Harris, 1990; Pepper, 1995). The introduction of new technologies, in particular, heightened interest in the community metaphor among organizations (Beamish, 2001; Gattiker, 2001; Komito, 1998; Wasko & Faraj 2000; Wasko & Mosco, 1992). Organizational communities have been conceptualized in terms of *alliances* and *cooperative communities* (Tapscott, Ticoll, & Lowy, 2000), *networked economies* (Liebowitz, 2002), and *integrated networks* (Contractor & Eisenberg, 1990; Hampton & Wellman, 2001; Wellman, Salaff, Dimitrova, Garton, Gulia, & Haythornthwaite, 1996). Technology has restructured organizational forms and functions (DeSanctis & Fulk, 1999; Fulk & Steinfield, 1990) and formed the basis for the *knowledge management* function in organizations (Shand, 1999). Meanwhile, organizational communicators have acknowledged the importance of *community meaning* as a foundation for organizational narratives (Kelly & Zak, 1999).

In mass communication, researchers have recognized the value of research conducted at the community level. This research tradition can trace its roots to Park, and has focused principally on the role of media in creating community ties and measurement of community involvement (e.g., Barlow, 1988; Bogart & Orenstein, 1965; Carter & Clarke, 1963; Christians & Hammond, 1986; Doolittle & MacDonald, 1978; Edelstein & Larson, 1960; Finnegan & Viswanath, 1988; Friedland, 2001; Haring, 1972; Jankowski, 1982; Janowitz, 1952; Jeffres & Dobos, 1988; Jeffres, Dobos, & Lee, 1988; Jeffres, Dobos, & Sweeney, 1987; McLeod et al., 2000; Overduin, 1986; Rothenbuhler, 1991; Shah, McLeod, &Yoon, 2001; Stamm, 1985, 1988, 2001; Stamm & Fortini-Campbell, 1983; Stamm & Guest, 1991; Stamm & Weis, 1986; Steiner, 1988; Stone, 1977; Viswanath, Finnegan, Rooney, & Potter, 1990). Other research has focused on the role of media in community conflict (Olien, Donohue & Tichenor, 1984; Tichenor, Donohue, & Olien, 1980) and the consequences of *community knowledge gaps* (Donohue, Tichenor, & Olien, 1986; Gaziano, 1988; Tichenor, Donohue & Olien, 1970; Viswanath, Kosicki, Park, & Fredin, 1993). Most recently, the *civic* or *public journalism movement* focused on community in examining news practices and processing (Albers, 1994; Anderson, Dardenne & Killenberg, 1994; Gibbs, 1994; Merritt, 1995; Merritt & Rosen, 1995; Rosen & Merritt, 1994, Schudson, 1978).

The increased emphasis on community has been spurred on by the continuing growth of cultural and critical studies, in which community plays a central role in

theory development by emphasizing dependency and relationships using macro-
and meso-level approaches. The primary means by which community has been
employed by cultural studies scholars has been through the idea of *interpretive
communities* to describe groups of audiences that develop their own meanings for
what is read, viewed, or heard (Cheney, 1982; Fish, 1980; Fontain, 1988; Frentz &
Rushkin, 1999; Hebdige, 1979; Lindlof, 1988; Lindlof & Meyer, 1987; Littlejohn,
2002; Nightengale, 1986; Radway, 1984; Steiner, 1988). One study, for example,
identified the local bookstore as a vital institution around which people search for
community (Miller, 1999).

The community concept has also been a focal point for writers concerned with
the deleterious consequences of technology on social relationships (Gergen, 1991;
Kirby, 1989; Meyrowitz, 1985a, 1985b; Mosco, 1998; Phelan, 1988). The literature is replete with community-related references, such as *global village* (McLuhan,
1964), *smart communities* (Jung, 1998), *switched-on communities* (Williams, 1982),
telecommunity (Toffler, 1971, 1982), *pseudocommunity* (Beniger, 1987), and *virtual community* (Hegel & Armstrong, 1997; "Information highway," 1994; Jones,
1995; Quarterman, 1993; Rheingold, 1993; Schwartz, 1995; Watson, 1997; Wright,
1998, 2001). Technology has been both lauded for making possible community
information services (Slack & Williams, 2000) and criticized for transforming societal processes and social structure (Calabrese, 1991, 2001; Grossman, 2001), for
the disruption of political unity and structures (Carey, 1998; Shaw & Hamm, 1997),
and for the creation of a "digital divide" (Logos & Jung, 2001).

Critical scholars invoke community when calling for needed changes in the
power relationships in society (e.g., Ashcraft, 2001; Vrooman, 2002). Drawing on
writers such as Foucault (1980), who argued that culture emerges out of a struggle
between desire and power, the agendas of feminist and neo-Marxist scholars seek
to establish new forms of community as alternatives to extant bureaucracies in
society (Davis & Puckett, 1992). Central to this critical approach to community
are the ideas of solidarity and empowerment created by alternative discourses
(Haber, 1994) that can lead to unity or fragmentation (Hogan, 1998). Community
particularly resonates with activists representing gay and lesbian, African American, Native American, feminist, and other marginalized groups in society engaged
in struggles over place, identity, or political voice.

COMMUNITY AND THEORETICAL LIMITS OF THE PUBLIC CONSTRUCT

Public relations practitioners and theorists have only recently begun to address
community in the nongeographic senses described above. Instead of community,
the field has relied almost exclusively on the closely related concept of public as a
conceptual framework in which to address public relations activities. A strong argument can be made that public is overly narrow in meaning and excessively mechanistic to be useful in today's modern practice.

The Concepts of Public Versus Community

The origins of the public concept can be traced to the mid-18th century when courtiers to Louis XV and Louis XVI were dispatched to listen to the thoughts of successful businessmen and influential political leaders in the salons of Paris (Herbst & Beniger, 1994). Ironically, this original use of the term public actually meant the small and closely knit community composed of France's elites. More recently, the term public regained attention in the 1920s with the recognition of the importance of public opinion (Lippmann, 1922, 1925) and the concomitant emergence of public relations (Bernays, 1923).

When used in the context of public opinion, public connotes the general public or the population of an entire nation-state or other political unit. This provided the context in which Bernays (1923) coined the term *public relations counsel*. Importantly, conceptualizations of public and public opinion have changed significantly over time (Herbst, 1995; Herbst & Beniger, 1995; Peters, 1995). Participation in public life (which was then distinct from the realm of one's private life) was considered a cornerstone of citizenship in ancient Greece (Arendt, 1998). That democratic ideal was carried forward into the 18th century with the idea that the middle class was engaged in a robust discussion of citizen concerns. Habermas (1962/ 1989) described this arena or network of discussion as the *bourgeois public sphere*, situated between what he termed the *private realm* and *sphere of public authority* in society. People came together in this public sphere "to engage in a debate over the general rules governing relations in the basically privatized but publicly relevant sphere of commodity exchange and social labor" (p. 27). These streams of conversation then coalesced into public opinion. Habermas lamented that the nature and quality of the debates once carried out in towns, clubs, and newspapers have been irreversibly transformed with the advent of mass media, particularly with the rise of modern advertising and public relations. His argument paralleled Lippmann's (1925) contention that the people have disengaged from public discussion and provided the basis for what Mayhew (1997) termed the new public, where professional communication specialties dominate discourse and thus undermine the ties between citizens. As described by Habermas, the very existence and dimensions of this robust arena of discussion have been challenged by scholars (e.g., Robbins, 1995; Woodward, 1975).

From an organizational perspective, public can be generalized to mean all persons not directly associated with an organization. This is the reflective approach of European public relations theorists and practitioners who are more public oriented in their approach to the public relations practice than their organization-oriented American counterparts (Ruler, Vercic, Bütschi, & Flodin, 2000). European theorists have special concern for the implications of organizational behavior toward and in the public sphere. Ruler & Vercic (2002a, p. 4), for example, cited Ronneberger and Röhl's (1992) argument that public relations is to be measured by the quality and quantity of the public sphere it coproduces through its activities, particularly those that contribute to the free flow of information. Similarly, participation in the public sphere highlights the use of legitimacy and legitimization as one of the central concepts in European public relations (e.g., Jensen, 1997). In part, this can be traced to the strong European commitment to the ethical principle of publicness that can be traced to Kant (1795/1983; Splichal, 1999).

The limitations of addressing the entire population of a society have been recognized by theorists and practitioners alike, particularly in an era in which interest in many topics are in narrow niches of the population and audience segmentation has become widely adopted as a communication strategy. Today, public relations practitioners use public loosely as a synonym for a variety of constructs, including communities, audiences, markets, and segments. Recently, most theorizing in public relations has defined publics narrowly. Grunig and Hunt (1984), for example, suggested that a public is a "loosely structured system whose members detect the same problem or issue, interact either face-to-face or through mediated channels, and behave as though they were the one body" (p. 144). Their definition drew heavily upon philosopher John Dewey and sociologist Herbert Blumer.

Dewey (1927) defined a public as a group of people that (a) faces a similar problem, (b) recognizes the problem exists, and (c) organizes to do something about it. He explained: "Indirect, extensive, enduring and serious consequences of conjoint and interacting behavior call a public into existence having a common interest in controlling those consequences" (p. 126). Blumer (1946/1960) similarly described a public as a group of people who (a) have confronted an issue, (b) are divided in their ideas about to how to meet the issue, and (c) engage i discussion over the issue. Significantly, Blumer (1946/1960) contended that a public is a spontaneous grouping that lacks (a) prescribed traditions or cultural patterns, (b) any form of pre-established organization or fixed status roles, and (c) any "we-feeling" (pp. 46–47) or consciousness of identity among members.

From these classical sociological definitions, a public can be described narrowly as an ephemeral, limited-purpose social coalition that is created through discussion related to particular issues in which members have a self-interest. Members are willing to cooperate, to form coalitions, and to share power as long as mutual goals are served.

By contrast, community is broader concept. A community can be defined as any group that shares common interests developed through common experience. Table 1 contrasts key differences between a public and a community.

Unlike a public, a community is not organized around a specific issue and need not constitute itself through direct issue-specific discussion (Mason, 1993). A community can be a preexisting collectivity concerned with a broad range of interests. Members' goals might be apolitical and involve nothing more than sustenance (e.g,, preservation, enrichment, or enjoyment). The goal of many public relations programs, for example, is to promote products and services that people believe contribute to the quality of their lives. Organizations thus strive to relate to people as they pursue their private lives—not their public lives (Arendt, 1958/1998; Habermas (1962/1989). Even though Dewey (1927) chided such

TABLE 1

Comparison of Public and Community Concepts

Focus of group	Public	Community
	Issues	*Interests*
Power orientation	Generally political	Often apolitical
Goal	Change	Sustenance
History	Limited to time since organized; often ephemeral because of group's limited focus/purpose	Often long and rich because well-established
Linkages within group	Common goal; discussion about issue; activist activities	Culture (beliefs, values, ritual, traditions, artifacts, language), discursive activities, participation, shared identity
Composition	Generally considered to be organizations, composed of individuals	Individuals and institutions
Organizational recognition	Difficult to locate until group makes concerns known	Easier to locate and to become familiar with interests
Organizational involvement	Often reactive, mostly mandated or provoked by the group	Ideally proactive
Organizational communication	Continuum of responses from accommodation to advocacy; negotiation	Ingratiation (involvement, nurture, organizing)
Relationships of concepts	Most publics form out of communities.	A limited-purpose public often later evolves into a community, but the group's focus usually broadens beyond a single issue.

instinct-induced activities related to consumption and amusement as only distracting people's attention from public matters (Aronowitz, 1995), topics such as cereal, bank services, or motorcycles are relevant and worthwhile because they relate to the activities in which real-world organizations engage as producers of goods or the provider of services. When controversies arise and topics such as child nutrition, financial privacy, or highway safety enter the arena of public discussion as issues, the focus of public relations activities shifts. Then one of several public relations specialties might be employed, such as *issues management* or *community/government relations*.

A comparison of the origins of the two concepts illustrates significant differences. The term public as used in much public relations theory today is grounded in political economy, systems theory, and social exchange theory. Public defines a group solely from the perspective of its relationship to a particular organization and an issue. A public is a group that must be reckoned with by the organization whose goals might be incompatible with that public. An organization's involvement with these publics is often reactive, rather than proactive. Such responses are thought to be arrayed along a continuum from pure accommodation to pure advocacy (Dozier, L. Grunig, & J. Grunig, 1995) and often involve negotiation.

Community, on the other hand, embodies both social scientific and humanistic approaches and recognizes that self-identifying communities exist without regard to their relationship to any particular organization or problem. Communities can thrive based on social, cultural, and economic interests as well as general political interests unrelated to any particular problem. Importantly, members often can readily identify themselves as members of a particular community. By contrast, few people willingly identify themselves as members of a public.

As a broader concept than publics, communities are the units from which issues-based publics emerge. For a public to emerge, it is necessary for members of the community to be able to interact and to share a set of common beliefs, values, and symbols. Indeed, communities shape the factors that might influence the formation of issues-based publics. In his nested model for segmentation for information campaigns, J. Grunig (1989a) acknowledged communities as the social structure that most closely encircles a public. In turn, publics that do not dissolve following the successful resolution of a problem but often persevere by becoming a community. Notably, however, the scope of the group's interests inevitably expands.

Limitations of the Public Construct for Public Relations Practice

A closer reading of Dewey and Blumer shows that both authors recognized the importance of communities. For Dewey (1927), publics were not the ideal form of social organization for solving societal problems; in fact, he lamented the existence of too many competing publics. Dewey's goal was the transformation of society into a Great Community. Dewey later wrote that communication was, at the same time, instrumental in enabling people to live in a world with things that have meaning and final in the sense of providing for a "sharing in the objects precious to a community, sharing whereby meanings are enhanced, deepened and solidified in the sense of communion" (Dewey, 1929, p. 159; Bybee, 1999). In a similar vein, Blumer (1969) recognized the importance of a common culture, which was referred to as community by his mentor, Mead. Blumer wrote:

> The participants involved in the formation of [a] new joint action always bring to that formation the world of objects, the set of meanings and the schemes of interpretation they already possess. . . . One is on treacherous and empirically invalid ground if [one] thinks that any given form of joint action can be sliced from its historical linkage, as if its makeup and character arose out of the air through spontaneous generation instead of growing out of what went before. (p. 20)

Significantly, a public need not be composed of members from a single community (J. Grunig, 1989a). Indeed, coalitions represent members of different interest groups who come together on a particular topic. As the number of different communities increases, it becomes increasingly difficult to find a common ground of understanding beyord the single subject that brings members of a public together.

From a practical viewpoint, the public construct also poses difficult problems for practitioners. First, to be conceptually consistent, the use of the term public in public relations suggests that the field is effectively limited to dealing with groups actually organized around an issue. Such is not the case. J. Grunig's (1975, 1978) typology of publics illustrates the problem when he suggests that publics can include active, aware, and latent publics, as well as nonpublics (defined as a group not potentially affected by an organization). Public relations directed to a nonpublic seems nonsensical.

Second, publics are not the only social organizations involved in the recognition of issues today. Besides the grassroots individual organizers envisioned by Dewey and Blumer, issues today are initiated by already organized special interest groups, political parties, public interest research groups, and various community development corporations (Hallahan, 2001). As Lippmann (1925) noted, citizens in modern society can easily become a phantom public that is perfectly content to turn over the resolution of problems to these experts. By comparison, the notion of community accommodates the fact that formal organizations and institutions are important threads in the fabric of society that must be recognized by organizations.

Third, a public can be the target of public relations efforts but only after the group is formed and can be located. Absent the ability to locate specific groups of active publics, many proactive public relations programs are directed, in fact, to communities of stakeholders, which can be defined as individuals who can influence or are influenced by an organization's actions. Due to their ephemeral nature, publics in the early stages of emergence are difficult to locate, whereas communities are more well-established and actually are the groups that organizations can monitor.

Finally, the field's focus on publics, as so narrowly defined, fails to provide insights about how to communicate effectively with publics because cultural understanding of the group is not addressed. J. Grunig's (1976, 1983) situational theory of publics, for example, provided useful direction for predicting the likelihood that individuals will become active in a particular situation or on particular issue (high problem recognition, high involvement, and low constraint recognition), but provides few clues for developing responses. By contrast, community clearly recognizes that groups that already exist share a culture and have already engaged in a variety of discursive activities that provide clues for how an organization might relate to them.

Alternative Theorizing About Publics

Public relations researchers have recognized the limitations in the traditional treatment of publics. In particular, they have argued that contemporary public relations theory is strongly biased by its organization-centered, structural–functional perspective. Implicit in the traditional definition of public is the idea that an organization must strive to manage or control publics to its advantage, or at least to the mutual benefit of both the organization and the publics upon which the organization depends on for its success or failure (Cutlip, Center, & Broom, 1999). This organization-based focus has relegated publics to a secondary position in public relations theory (Karlberg, 1996; Leitch & Neilson, 2001; Moffitt, 1994).

Various authors have called for a reconceptualization of the publics construct. Hallahan (2000a, 2000b, 2001) has argued that not all groups to which public relations efforts are directed are necessarily focused on issues, and that too much attention has been paid to activists, despite their potential impact on organizations. He pointed to the importance of *inactive publics*, which comprise the majority of the public at large. He defined inactive publics as people with low knowledge and low involvement in a particular topic (Hallahan, 1999a). Inactive publics are somewhat akin to what Blumer (1960/1946) termed a *mass*, but often take on characteristics of a community.

Moffitt (1994, 2001) called for replacement of the term public altogether with a segmentation scheme that focused on *public positions*. Her collapse model of corporate image identified from the larger population particular opinions, attitudes, or behaviors that are shared by all members across the entire population. The concept of publics as segments of people is replaced with a more precise and detailed view of public positions as shared knowledge, attitudes, and behaviors within a population (community).

Other writers have sought to shift the definition of a public from a structural-functional management perspective to a communication-based perspective. For example, Vasquez (1994) argued that organization-public relationships are better defined as linkages between an organization and publics. Drawing upon Borman's symbolic convergence theory, Vasquez contended that a public might be defined as individuals who have created, raised, and sustained a group consciousness around a situation where each person participated in creating a shared symbolic reality. Later Vasquez and Taylor (2001) identified Vasquez's *homo narrans* perspective as one of four alternative conceptualizations of public. Other perspectives were based on theories of mass society, situational issues, and agenda-building. Vasquez's emphasis on symbolic reality closely aligns with rhetorical theories about interpretive communities.

Leitch and Neilson (2001) similarly attempted to redefine the notion of a public and called for a publics-centered approach to public relations. Drawing upon Habermas (1962/1989), they distinguished between the public and private domains and between *system organizations* and *lifeworld organizations*. A system organization operates according to the logic of strategic or instrumental rationality. Examples include corporations created to generate profits. By contrast, a lifeworld organization is rooted in communicative action, such as a grassroots social movement. Similarly, the relationships between publics and these two types of organizations differ based upon competing discourses and the differential access to power enjoyed by these organizations. The objective of public relations in a traditional system organization is to maximize public support or minimize objections to organizational actions. By contrast, relationships between lifeworld organizations and publics are often more reflexive and complementary. Leitch and Neilsen defined a public in terms that are strikingly similar to that of a community: a group of people who develop their own identities and representations of their collective interests. People play multiple roles as members of multiple publics, but these roles are sometimes conflicting and require individuals to negotiate their own identities and priorities (e.g., Cheney & Christensen, 2001).

Chay-Nemeth (2001) argued for an alternative conceptualization of publics as a political space or site in which material resources and discourses are appropriated and exchanged among participants to effect social and political change or to maintain the status quo. In an archaeological study of participants in the HIV/AIDS debate in Thailand, the author framed a typology of participants whom she identified as circumscribed, co-opted, critical, and circumventing publics. In order to understand fully a public, she argued that it is necessary to understand the level of a public's resource dependency, discursive connectivity, and legitimacy.

Jones (2002) also called for the reconceptualization of publics and opined that the rise of a risk-based society had led to the emergence of new communicatively powerful publics and the movement of politics into subpolitical arenas dominated by activists and NGOs (nongovernment organizations). Jones observed:

> Current conceptualisations of public within public relations remain remarkably simplistic and reflect the managerial and normative traditional prevalent in the discipline. Most notably they tend to impose a rational-managerial logic onto publics. This neglects to consider the internal dynamics of public[s by] assuming that they are composed of information-processing individuals who react to organisationally defined issues, and fails to incorporate the idea that publics might form without organizational action. (p. 50)

Jones defined the presence of two or more publics as a community. He noted, "These communities are built and sustained through issue-based discourse" (p. 50). He contended that public relations thus is fundamentally involved in the exchange of identities and in shared discourse and meanings. Jones argued that publics converge around a common way of communicating and that "[p]ublics form communities of shared meaning, where issues become the interest" (p. 56).

Finally, Botan (1993a) drew upon the rhetorical approach to community when he suggested that "public relations addresses its communications to . . . interpretive communities, which we call publics" (p. 73). Botan and Soto (1998) also challenged the prevailing view that publics are entities created in reaction to problems or issues. Following the linguistic tradition of Charles Peirce (versus Ferdinand Saussure), and incorporating ideas of Bormann and Eco, Botan and Soto argued that publics ought to be understood primarily as self-actuated and interactive social entities with complex values and internal dynamics who interpret and share the meanings of signs. The interpretations are virtually endless (unlimited semiosis) and contextual. Importantly, publics are created through a chain of interpretations that occur in a community. Whereas Vasquez (1994) stated that a public is composed of "individuals who have created, raised, and sustained a group consciousness around the problematic event or issue" (p. 271) in the past, Botan and Soto (1998) contended that a public should be conceived as "ongoing process of agreement upon an interpretation" (p. 38). As a result, there is no point in time in which the public is finally or definitely constituted.

From the foregoing discussion, it is clear that the field's traditional conceptualization of public is under challenge. To define public as all of the citizens within a society is of marginal value to organizations because relatively few organizations or topics are truly of broad interest to all citizens. This effectively limits the utility of conceptualizing public relations as being engaged in discussion in a single public sphere. Although researchers such as J. Grunig (1983; Grunig & Hunt, 1984) have focused on public as a group organized around an issue (created out of discussions about a problem), many public relations efforts are directed toward audiences, stakeholders, or constituencies for whom no problem exists. A simple commonality of interests suffices.

The term community provides a potentially useful alternative. A community can be any subset of a society or social system (and in limited circumstances, the whole society) in which members are drawn together by common interests. More importantly, those common interests are constituted in common symbols (Cohen, 1985), common discursive activities, and common identities (Botan, 1993a; Jones 2002). A community provides the arena in which people communicate. Unlike an ephemeral public that emerges around a particular issue and then dissolves, a community can be located, and its interests, values, history, power, and political structure understood.

EMERGING COMMUNITY-RELATED THEORIES IN PUBLIC RELATIONS

For more than a decade, public relations theorists have been engaged in a paradigm struggle both to define the practice and find alternative ways to study public relations. Kuhn (1970) popularized the concept when he defined a paradigm as a collection of beliefs shared by scientists about how problems are to be understood and studied. Toth and Heath (1992) defined the paradigm struggle in public relations as pitting traditional organization-centered research that draws upon systems theory against alternative perspectives that use rhetorical theory and critical theory. This struggle is reflected in the alternative approaches to the public construct outlined in the previous section. The debate has been carried forward in other calls for new directions for public relations theory (Botan, 1993b; Dozier & Lauzen, 2000; Karlberg, 1996).

Public Relations and Restoration of Community

Kruckeberg and Starck (1988) are credited as being the first to argue that public relations ought to be conceptualized as the active attempt to restore and maintain a sense of community. The Iowa researchers drew heavily upon theorizing by members of the Chicago School of Social Thought. Despite criticisms that their argument sought to return to a romanticized (perhaps nonexistent) past and failed to cohere theoretically or practically (e.g., Cheney & Christensen, 2001, p. 174), the authors have sustained their argument through the years (Kruckeberg, 1998a, 1998b). They argue that the problem is even more urgent today because of the institutional power of corporations (Kruckeberg, 2001; Starck & Kruckeberg, 2001).

Kruckeberg & Starck (1988) contended that a community emphasis in public relations places a premium on a caring attitude toward others:

> It is a humane and altruistic function, but one based on sound and pragmatic philosophy. It is a role, to a very great extent, of nonmanipulation. Too, it is a role that, if practiced as espoused here, should result in a more human and mutually supportive society. (p. 117)

Kruckeberg and Starck (1988; Kruckeberg, 1998a) outlined their vision of a community-oriented practice as one in which public relations practitioners do eight things: (a) make community members concscious of their common interests, (b) overcome alienation, (c) use technology to create community in the same way Dewey called for the use of schools, (d) promote leisure-time activities, (e) engage in consummatory (self-fulfilling) communication that can be enjoyed for its own sake, (f) lead in charitable works, (g) help communities share aesthetic experience, religious ideas, personal values, and sentiments, and (h) foster personal relationships.

Other public relations scholars have offered similar support for the community concept. The two most explicit arguments involve *strategic cooperative communities* and *communitarianism*.

Strategic Cooperative Communities

Wilson (1994, 1996, 2000, 2001, 2002; Wilson & McNiven, 2001, Wilson & Stoker, 2000) followed Kruckeberg and Starck by arguing that positive community relations is a means for corporations to foster positive relationships. Wilson's notion of strategic cooperative communities suggests that an organization's core values in such efforts should focus on the importance of people, safety, health and the environment, service and participation (care, concern, and loyalty), and respect.

Wilson (1996) argued that building community requires corporations to possess five characteristics: (a) long-range vision, (b) a sincere commitment to community service, not just profit, (c) organizational values that emphasize the importance of people (including trust, respect, and human dignity), (d) cooperative problem solving and empowerment, and (e) a relationship-building approach to public relations. Wilson rejected notions of social responsibility that are justified based upon bottom-line, economic benefits. Instead, Wilson (1994) argued that community must be based on genuine cooperation. Social responsibility ought better to be understood under a communitarian framework that emphasizes "the interdependent relationship and role of business as a participant in [communities] that consist of a variety of actors, individual and organizational, all cooperating for a common good that that extends far beyond solely financial factors" (Wilson, 2001, p. 522).

Such an approach would reject the exploitation identified in some corporate community relations programs. Rawlins and Stoker, two of Wilson's colleagues, departed from Kruckeberg and Stark (1988) and drew upon the philosophy of Royce (1916) to argue that organizations have contributed to the loss of community by becoming detached through callous exploitation of communities. They argued genuine community requires organizations to (a) adopt ideal ends that connect to the values and ideals of the community, (b) seek moral attachment to the community by enabling neighbors and organizational members to achieve the ideals and purposes inherent in the genuine community, (c) promote autonomy and independence among community members, and (d) show loyalty to the community and be willing to sacrifice self-interests to promote the ideals and values of the community (Rawlins & Stoker, 2001; Stoker & Rawlins, n.d.).

Communitarianism

Theorists other than Wilson have pointed to communitarianism (Etzioni, 1991, 1993) as a potentially useful ethical framework for public relations. K. Leeper (1996) focused on the issues of quality, social responsibility, and stewardship. Leeper cited the cases of the Tylenol recall in 1982 and the Exxon Valdez mishap in 1989 as contrasting examples of exercising and not exercising communitarian ethics.

Culbertson and Chen (1997) similarly outlined six tenets of communitarianism pertinent to public relations (italics in original):

1. Whether a behavior is right or wrong depends in large part on its positive contribution to *commitment to* and *quality of relationships.*

2. Community requires a sense of interconnectedness and *social cohesion.*

3. Identification of—and humble but firm commitment to—*core values and beliefs are essential* to a sense of community.

4. People who claim *rights* must be willing to balance them with *responsibility.*

5. Community requires that all citizens have a feeling of *empowerment*—of involvement in making and implementing decisions that bear on their lives.

6. Community requires a *broadening of one's social world*—one's array of significant others—so as to reduce fragmentation and enhance breadth of perspective.

R. Leeper (2001) extended the argument to suggest that communitarianism, as a particular community-based approach, could serve as a metatheory for the practice of public relations in the context of research about practitioners' role and communication symmetry (see next section). Communitarianism, he said, also has implications for publics, corporate social responsibility, and ethics. Later, Leeper and Leeper (2001) argued that the development of community might stand as the end goal for public relations if the field is to be considered a professional practice as outlined by philosopher Alasdair MacIntyre.

Even though these three threads of theory explicitly term community as a foundation for public relations theory and research, a wider range of other recent theorizing draws heavily upon closely related concepts.

Symmetric, Dialogic, and Transactional Approaches to Community

Public relations has been characterized for decades as using information or persuasion to influence people's beliefs, attitudes, or actions (Miller, 1989). Such influence efforts are still legitimate and remain an integral part of public relations practice today; however, public relations theorists have recognized that public relations provides a conduit through which communication exchanges can and should occur between an organization and others.

J. Grunig (1976, 1992, 2001; Grunig & Hunt, 1984; L. Grunig, J. Grunig, & D. Dozier, 2002) proposed one of the most widely researched and debated models in public relations when he suggested that public relations can be practiced alternatively or in combination as press agentry, public information, two-way asymmetric communication (scientific persuasion), or two-way symmetrical communication. J. Grunig and colleagues argued that public relations is ideally practiced as two-way symmetrical communication in which organizations and publics are equally engaged and equally empowered to exchange ideas, and organizations are willingly responsive to the needs, concerns, and interests of others. J. Grunig and his colleagues do not explicitly state that two-way symmetrical communication is an effort to foster community; however, other researchers believe that is the case. Karlberg (1996) wrote, "By reformulating public relations as an ethical and effective force for resolving conflict and enhancing community, J. Grunig and his colleagues have provided a new theoretical framework within which public relations research can be reshaped and redirected" (p. 271).

As an alternative to communication symmetry, several theorists have invoked notions of dialogue—a foundational concept in community—as a potential basis for public relations theory. Pearson (1989a, 1989b) argued dialogue and reciprocity were central to public relations ethics and outlined rules for engaging in ethical dialogue. Van Es and Meijlink (2000) point to Pearson as well as White and Mazur (1993) as illustrations of a distinct dialogic turn in direction in theorizing about public relations ethics, compared to pragmatic ethics. Kersten (1994), however, argued to make the assumption that symmetric communication is more ethical is both unrealistic and potentially dangerous because of the inherent imbalance in power relationships between organizations and individuals.

Botan (1993a, 1997) similarly advocated for dialogue in his efforts to redefine publics and argued that dialogue effectively elevates publics to the level of an organization (Leicht & Neilson, 2001). Kent and Taylor (1998) drew heavily upon

Botan to contend that dialogue is a product, rather than process, that stems out of relationships. Later Kent and Taylor (2002) identified five overarching tenets of dialogism: mutuality (collaboration, spirit of equality), propinquity (immediacy of presence, temporal flow, engagement), empathy (supportiveness, communal orientation, confirmation), relational risk (vulnerability, unanticipated consequences, strange otherness), and commitment (genuineness, commitment to conversation, commitment to interpretation). Of the requisite communal orientation, the authors argued: "Dialogue presupposes a communal orientation among interactants, whether they are individuals, organizations or publics" (p. 27). Importantly, these ideals apply to both interpersonal and mediated communication, and are particularly applicable to Web communications (Kent & Taylor, 1998; Kent, Taylor, & White 2003; Taylor, Kent, & White, 2001).

Woodward (1996, 2000) argued that the symmetrical communication model's emphasis on dialogue fits within a broader transactional model of communication. Drawing on Dewey, as well as the notion of community building, Woodward (2000) asserted that the transactional philosophy is more comprehensive than mere balance or the bidirectionality of communication between entities. Instead of dyadic processes of cause and effect or the linear flows of information, the transactional view is triadic and focuses on the encompassing medium or milieu as a third element of all communication. Using language that is striking similar to the ritualistic model of communication (Carey, 1989), Woodward (2000) explained:

> Dyadic, sender-receiver models emphasize transmissions and their effects, whereas the triadic transactional view draws attention to how shared worlds of knowledge are created. Successful communicators collaborate in shaping communicative environments based on mutuality; the aim is to contribute language, values and experiences that that partners can share. (p. 258)

Indeed, the transactional perspective recognizes communities as the milieu in which communication takes place.

Community-related Orientations as Professional Values

In 1999, a panel at the International Communication Association's annual conference examined the core values of public relations for the new millenium. In that session, J. Grunig (2000) cited collectivism, societal corporatism, and collaboration as core professional values—all of which resonate with the notion of community. J. Grunig maintained that organizations should promote the value of collectivism despite the fact that many organizations and the cultures in which they operate are fiercely individualistic. He also argued that the practice should help build democracy based on societal corporatism, where government (and other organizations) openly and publicly build collaborative relationships with special interest groups they affect or are affected by. Societal corporatism differs from pure corporatism, which limits access to government and other entities only to others with close-knit relations. Societal corporatism also can be contrasted with pluralism, which encourages open, fierce competition. J. Grunig suggested that true community and his principles of public relations Excellence are more likely to develop in a societal corporatism system (J. Grunig, personal communication, October 24, 2002).

J. Grunig's (1989b) notions about collaboration built on his earlier theorizing contrasting asymmetric with symmetric worldviews. He identified seven presuppositions that made up an asymmetrical worldview among practitioners and organizations: internal orientation, closed systems, an emphasis on efficiency and control, conservatism, tradition, and central authority. By contrast he identified these characteristics of a symmetrical worldview: interdependence, open system, moving equilibrium, equity, autonomy, innovation, decentralization, responsibility, conflict resolution, and interest group liberalism (Deatherage & Hazelton, 1998). A symmetric worldview clearly is consistent with a community perspective.

Relationship Building

A recent major avenue for public relations theorizing has called for renewed emphasis on identifying the antecedents, processes, and consequences of organizational-public relationships (Broom, Casey, & Ritchey, 1997; J. Grunig & Huang, 2000; Hon & Grunig, 1999). Drawing on a proposition by Ferguson (1984), J. Grunig spearheaded research involving five organizations that focused on identifying and analyzing six benchmark measures of relationship quality (Hon & Grunig, 1999; J. Grunig & Huang, 2000). These measures included trustworthiness, commitment, satisfaction, control mutuality, exchange relationships, and communal relationships.

J. Grunig and colleagues adapted theorizing by Clark and Mills (1993) to suggest that public relations strives to create communal relationships versus mere exchange relationships. Hon and Grunig (1999) explained:

> In a communal relationship, both parties provide benefits to the others because they are concerned about the welfare of the other—even when they get nothing in return. The role of public relations is to convince management that it also needs communal relationships . . . as well as exchange relationships with customers. (p. 22)

Hon and Grunig created a 7-item scale for measuring communal relationships.

1. *This organization does not especially enjoy giving others aid. (Reversed)
2. *This organization is very concerned with the welfare of people like me.
3. *I feel that this organization takes advantage of people who are vulnerable. (Reversed)
4. *I think that this organization succeeds by stepping on other people. (Reversed)
5. **This organization helps people like me without expecting anything in return.
6. I don't consider this is to be a particularly helpful organization. (Reversed)
7. I feel that this organization tries to get the upper hand. (Reversed)
* Items in four-item shortened scale (Cronbach's alpha = .80) **Item added in a five-item scale (Cronbach's alpha = .83). For seven-item scale, Cronbach's alpha = .86. (Hon & Grunig, 1999, pp. 30, 40).

Importantly, communal relationships are not altogether altruistic; the authors argued that individuals have been shown to achieve greater outcomes in communal relationships with families, friends, and acquaintances. They described the existence of a communal relationship as the "purest indicator" of success in relationship building (Hon & Grunig, 1999, p. 22).

Separately, Ledingham and Bruning (1998, 2000, 2001; Bruning, 2002) launched a research agenda to measure organization-public relationships among both consumers and citizens. From a list of 17 potential dimensions, they distilled five dimensions of a relationship that were particularly good predictors for future relationships (i.e., whether people intended to stay in or to leave a relationship). Their findings were consistent among banking customers, telephone company customers, and citizens in a small community: The presence of a felt relationship was important for retention. Four of the items they used examined individuals' perceptions of organizations in the context of the community:

Trust: I feel I can trust (company name) to do what it says it will do.
Investment: (Company name) is the kind of company that invests in the community.
Commitment: I think (company name) is committed to making my community a better place to live.
Involvement: I am aware (company name) is involved in my community.
Openness: (Company name) shares its plans for the future with the company.

Critical and Postmodern Views of Public Relations

Researchers similarly have posed broader questions about who practices public relations and how it is practiced. This trend has brought renewed interest in the community actors engaged in public relations activities as well as the role of the professional practitioner as a community representative.

Karlberg (1996) argued that public relations research has placed too much emphasis on instrumental or administrative studies and ignored critical investigations. He contended that even research that emphasized community and communications symmetry viewed public relations as an instrument of commerce or of the state. He called for greater attention to how citizens and public interest groups engage in public relations initiatives—and the problems and limitations that confront them in doing so. Dozier and Lauzen (2000) picked up on Karlberg's contention and called for a redefinition of the intellectual domain of public relations research, particularly to study activism as an important part of the public relations process. Along these same lines, in outlining an integrative model of issues dynamics, Hallahan (2001) suggested that understanding issues activation was just as important as examining organizational responses.

Holtzhausen (2000, 2002; Holtzhausen & Voto, 2002) similarly has called for public relations researchers to recognize the biases inherent in the field's roots in modernism, including the field's historical complicity with capitalism. Holtzhausen used postmodern theory to argue that public relations is an organizational function fundamentally involved in change. "This understanding of public relations takes it out of organizations and into communities and transforms public relations into a discipline of immediate and just action" (Holtzhausen, 2000, p. 110). Holtzhausen contended public relations is inherently political and recast the role of the postmodern public relations practitioner as one of an organizational activist who represents the interests of both the organization and others important to an organization. She questioned many premises found in the landmark Excellence research underwritten by the International Association of Business Communicators. That 17-year project concluded—among other things—that to be effective, public relations practitioners must be aligned with the dominant coalitions within organizations (Dozier, L. Grunig, & J. Grunig, 1995; J. Grunig, 1992; L. Grunig, J. Grunig, & Dozier, 2002). Holtzhausen and Voto (2002) argued that public relations is more than an organizational practice and ought to be examined as a social, cultural, and political phenomenon.

Cultural Perspectives

Public relations researchers have increasingly recognized the importance of culture—characteristics shared by people in a community or an organization—as an important factor in effective public relations (Banks, 1995; Elwood, 1995; L. Grunig, 1995; Heath, 1992, 1994; MacManus, 2000; Mickey, 1995; Molleda, 2001; Sriramesh, 1996; Sriramesh, J. Grunig, & Buffington, 1992; Sriramesh & White, 1992; Taylor, 2000). Culture entails the beliefs and values, rituals and traditions, and language and artifacts that effectively constitute a community.

The authors of the IABC Excellence study suggested that certain public relations principles are generic and can be applied globally; however, other researchers have pointed to important differences in the way that public relations is and ought to be practiced based upon national or regional cultures (Culbertson & Chen, 1996). Drawing upon the comparative framework outlined by Hofstede (1984, 1991), for example, Sriramesh & White (1992) suggested that adherence to Excellence principles is more likely in cultures characterized by low levels of individualism, low power distance relationships, low masculinity, and low uncertainty avoidance. Huang (2000, 2001) similarly pointed out that many of the assumptions underlying public relations in the West are based on individualism, whereas different assumptions based on collectivism must be applied in the Far East. Leichty and Warner (2001) similarly argued that at least five different cultural biases can predominate the discussion of values in a society: fatalism, egalitarianism, hierarchy, autonomous individualism, and competitive individualism. These topoi must be considered depending upon the community.

Organizational cultures and communities also have been recognized as important variables that can influence public relations practice (MacManus, 2000; Sriramesh, J. Grunig, & Buffington, 1992). Sriramesh, J. Grunig, & Dozier (1996) showed a participatory (versus authoritarian) organizational culture can nurture public relations excellence. Drawing upon ideas reminiscent of cultural approaches to community, Everett (1990) described organizational culture as a cognitive system based on the group's experience and shared among members. He called for examining organizations as sociocultural systems (i.e., communities) using ethnoecological research.

Emerging Technologies

The advent of new technology has required public relations researchers to reexamine communication practices. Badaracco (1998) suggested the Internet provides the potential for the development of a true sense of community. The potential effect is to provide more equalized exchanges (Heath, 1998) and to rebalance power inequities (Coombs, 1998a, 1998b). Hearit (1999), based on his case study of the Intel Pentium chip controversy in 1994, argued that publics can be constituted online communities and can have a tangible effect on companies in a crisis.

The emergence of the community concept as a means to describing the linkages between participants in discussion groups and other forms of online communications led Cozier and Witmer (2001), using structuration theory, to argue that new technologies can create new publics. They call for the analysis of online communities and for the reconceptualization of organizations as systems composed of reproduced practices. In an empirical test of this idea, Stein (2001) found that employees believe establishing community in the workplace is important and that technologies can be an important part of that process. Interestingly, Stein found that employees had a greater sense of a virtual community at the departmental level, compared to either the regional or organization-wide levels.

Application of the community construct also can be seen in two communications specialties often associated with public relations.

Risk Communication

Research about risk is a cross-disciplinary field that focuses both on the communication of important information to individuals as well as groups who might be affected by hazards. Risk communication originally relied upon expert spokespersons to disseminate news and information. Heath and colleagues explain, however, that the old, linear paradigm has been replaced by a new democratic approach that emphasizes dialogue, conflict resolution, consensus building, and relationship development among affected parties (Heath, Bradshaw, & Lee, 2002). Professional risk communicators have adopted risk democracy models that include both local emergency planning committees and community advisory panels (also known as community advisory panels). Both structures play a pivotal role in both establishing policy and disseminating information within jurisdictions and the communities they serve.

Health Communications

In a similar vein, public health communication models today involve the proactive promotion of health and disease prevention (versus treatment of illness or injury) and calls for the active participation, representation, and empowerment of community members rather than passive compliance by individuals at risk (Kar & Alcalay, 2001). Many traditional public health campaigns continue to be focused on geographic communities (Finnegan, Bracht, & Viswanath, 1989; Flora, Maccoby, & Farquhar, 1989; Hornick, 2002; Mittelmark et al., 1986; Nash & Farquhar, 1980; Weenig, 1993). Community-level campaigns, however, have also focused on ethnic and other subcommunities and on the importance of combining mediated communications with interpersonal efforts also known as social marketing. These efforts include health coalitions and partnerships composed of health care professionals and other care givers in a community (Braithwaite, Taylor, & Austin, 2000). Such efforts have focused on assessing community readiness (Oetting, Donnermeyer, Plested, Edwards, Kelly, & Beauvais, 1995) and striven to change behaviors and help people avoid risks through community preparedness and health-organizing activities in both urban and rural settings (Bracht, 1999, 2001). Most recently, health communicators have recognized the important potential contribution of the Internet in creating community among at-risk populations as well as their social support groups (Rice & Katz, 2001).

Other Approaches

Several other streams of research in public relations mesh easily with the community construct. For example, Springston and Keyton (2001; Springston, Keyton, Leichty, & Metzger, 1992) incorporated community orientation versus self-orientation as one of three dimensions in their model of public relations field dynamics. Borrowing from other applications in economics and political science, Hazelton and Kennan (2000) argued that the creation of social capital (a property of a community) is an alternative measure of public relationships and can be an important outcome of corporate communication. Broadly summarized, social capital theory suggests that the vitality and viability of society is enhanced by the quantity and quality of social (community) interaction, involvement, and participation (e.g., Putnam, 2000; Scheufele & Shah, 1999).

COMMUNITY BUILDING AS AN IDEAL IN PUBLIC RELATIONS

Against this backdrop, a final argument for the adoption of community as a foundation for public relations is a philosophical one that addresses what public relations should strive to achieve as a professional practice. As a concept that resonates with American culture, community building appeals to many practitioners who want to engage in meaningful work that makes a constructive contribution to society.

As Hutton (1999) observed, public relations suffers from a clear and compelling explanation of its purpose as a field. Various metaphors have been proposed (e.g., Ewen, 1996; Harlow, 1977; Hutton 1999). Pioneer practitioner Lee once likened his role to that of being a physician to corporate bodies. Later, practitioners were compared to attorneys who represent clients in the court of public opinion. In truth, such analogies to established professions are self-serving and smack of efforts to manage and manipulate.

The Concept of Community Building

Community building involves the integration of people and the organizations they create into a functional collectivity that strives toward common or compatible goals. Drawing upon the rhetorical and cultural elements discussed previously, community building can involve a variety of informational, persuasive, relational, or discursive approaches (Ruler & Vercic, 2002b) that create understanding—manifested in shared beliefs and values, rituals and traditions, and symbols and artifacts.

Researchers who have focused on community (Culbertson & Chen, 1997; Kruckeberg & Stark, 1988; Leeper & Leeper, 2001; Wilson, 1994, 1996) clearly see building community as a practical outcome to be achieved in public relations practice. Other scholars have called for practitioners to engage in community building (Banks, 1995; Hallahan, 1996; Neff, 1998; Vasquez, 1998). St. John (1998), a practitioner and writer in the field, pointed to the role of public relations in constructing community in the early American West and argued that the concept is equally relevant today. Meanwhile, the late Patrick Jackson, one of the field's most prominent practitioner-strategists and editor of the *pr reporter* newsletter, advocated community-building as a model for the practice ("Authentic communication," 1996; "Building community," 1997; "Community = relationships," 1997; Miller, 1995).

Community building implies that public relations is a proactive (versus reactive) endeavor that focuses on the positive and functional rather than the negative and dysfunctional. Community building also redirects public relations' focus away from its institutional focus and slavish emphasis on achieving organizational goals (Dozier & Lauzen, 2000; Holtzhausen, 2000; Karlberg, 1996) to address community citizenship. Community building provides a framework that can be used by both established (system) organizations and emerging (lifeworld) social movements or causes. Community building squares with the definition that public relations establishes and maintains mutually beneficial relationships on which an organization's or cause's success or failure depends (Cutlip, Center, & Broom, 1999). This shift also moves public relations away from an emphasis on control—what Bernays (1955) called the *engineering of consent*—to the two fundamental functions that public relations performs: providing counsel about community interests and facilitating communication. In short, community building is a broader and nobler metaphor that practitioners can rally around.

Three Dimensions of Community Building

Several of the explicit calls for community as a framework for public relations (Kruckeberg & Starck, 1988; K. Leeper, 1994, 1996; Wilson, 1994) are grounded in the need for organizations to act responsibly and ethically. A community-oriented approach to public relations especially appeals to practitioners who seek to improve the practice's performance. Banks (1995) summarized the argument well:

> [I]f Kruckeberg and Starck's idea is modified by recognizing that all communications from institutions in fact constitute forms of community (both desirable and undesirable), then the objection to their communitarian purpose can be overcome. By this I mean that organizations must recognize that their long-term ability to survive depends on fostering an attitude of social responsibility that nurtures socially healthy communities among their various publics. This observation, by which organizations see their well-being as intimately bound to the well-being of their publics, is not obvious in the short term; however, over long periods of time the convergence of interests between institutions and their relevant publics is unavoidable, and communities, whether positive and supportive or debilitating, are created and maintained. The fundamental goal of public relations, then, is to communicate in ways that nurture the development of positive and supportive communities, communities of which their institutions see themselves as members. (pp. 20–21)

The need for a greater emphasis on organizational social responsibility has been the subject of extensive discussion within public relations (e.g., Daugherty, 2001). Similarly, normative standards for responsible and ethical communications are the underlying premises of the IABC-supported Excellence studies (J. Grunig, 1992; L. Grunig, J. Grunig, & Dozier, 2002). If it is assumed that an organization is a part of one or more communities, and that community membership includes both rights and responsibilities, then the obligation of organizations to act in a socially responsible manner becomes readily apparent. In a similar way, extensive debate has ensued about ethical behavior by both organizational and public relations managers (e.g., Curtin & Boynton, 2001; Day, Dong, & Robins, 2001; Haas, 1998/2001; Holtzhausen, 2000; Kersten, 1994, Komisarjevsky, 2002; R. Leeper, 1996). If managers also recognize their organization's or cause's role in a community and that their personal loyalties belong to both their organization and to their communities, the framework for ethical decision making become more readily evident. An emphasis on community and community building thus suggests an effective way to improve public relations practice.

What is involved in building a community from the perspective of an organization or cause? Hallahan (1996) identified three distinct forms of community building activities: *community involvement*, *community nurturing*, and *community organizing*.

Community involvement entails public relations representatives facilitating an organization or cause's participation in an already-existing community. This is the traditional boundary-spanning task performed by community relations specialists (Burke, 1999). By becoming involved, practitioners and their organizations or causes can demonstrate legitimacy and the compatibility of their beliefs and values with others (Jensen, 2000). In so doing, community-involved organizations shed their bureaucratic fronts and don the personae of social actors (Heath, 1994).

Involvement involves socially responsible gestures (such as attendance at community events) and open and ethical communications, whether face-to-face or through media. Involvement can include promotional communications designed to inform community members about what the organization offers or to enhance an organization's reputation among community members. More importantly, involvement also includes participation in discussions and dialogue—where organizations and community members are both active speakers and listeners. Additionally, community involvement or engagement, as suggested here, makes no assumptions or normative judgments about communication symmetry (J. Grunig, 1983), the merits of advocacy versus accommodation (Dozier, L. Grunig, & J. Grunig, 1995; Murphy, 1991), or discourse ethics (Haas, 1998/2001, R. Leeper, 1996). Instead, ethical community involvement merely suggests community members have the right to voice their concerns and to be heard. Conversely, those to whom those concerns are directed enjoy the right and responsibility to listen and to respond.

Community nurturing involves fostering the economic, political, social, and cultural vitality of communities in which people and organizations or causes are members—beyond mere involvement expected of an organization as one of many community members. The importance of community nurturing within organizations has been expressed by forward-thinking business managers (Klein & Izzo, 1998; Manning, Curtis, & McMillen, 1996). Chappell (1994), for example, contended that a company is a community—in which values once associated with paternalism and team-building flourish and are fostered under as the aegis of community.

Many organizations nurture communities inside and outside of their organizational boundaries by serving as community sponsors, particularly in cases of communities of workers or customers. Examples range from Little League and fan clubs to employee work improvement teams. Sponsors can provide infrastructure and support systems, underwrite events, and supply information. Many of the community-building ideas suggested by Kruckeberg and Starck (1998; Starck & Kruckeberg, 2001) are examples of community nurturing. This aspect of traditional community relations is familiar to many businesses that engage in volunteerism (Leeper, 1998) and philanthropy (Kelly, 1998). Many for-profit organizations believe they have an obligation to give back to the communities they serve, although some economists and business people argue to the contrary (e.g., Dunlap, 1996; Friedman, 1970). Some organization managers say philanthropy simply makes good business sense or is a quid pro quo—a form of enlightened self-interest. Legitimate community building, however, suggests such generosity is valuable because it is genuine and benefits everyone—and avoids exploitation (Rawlins & Stoker, 2001). Community organizing involves the grassroots forging of new communities among disparate individuals with common interests. This describes the formation of many clubs, associations, and societies. To the extent that this approach is rooted in social problems, community organizing resembles the formation of a public or a social movement (Hallahan, 2001). In reality, community organizing can take place at a variety of levels. For example, community organizing might involve the application of public relations to support national development (Van Leuven, 1996; Van Leuven & Pratt, 1996) and thus involve participatory communications (Jacobson & Servaes, 1999; Servaes, Jacobson, & White, 1996). Alternatively, community organizing might involve the use of public relations strategies and tactics to improve economic or social conditions in a particular neighborhood or for members of a particular minority group (Bender, 1978; Biklen, 1983; Brager, Specht, & Torczyner, 1987; Gittell & Vidal, 1998; Jeffres & Dobos, 1984; Rivera & Erlich, 1992; Rubin & Rubin, 1997; Schoenberg & Anderson, 1995).

Communities are constantly organizing and reorganizing, and employ public relations strategies and tactics in doing so. One concern is that such turmoil will result in community fragmentation. Change is inevitable; chaos theory suggests that upheaval will return to a natural state of normalcy (Murphy, 1996). To minimize fragmentation requires organizations or causes to strive to maintain and strengthen community ties.

In summary, the specific roles and activities of public relations professionals differ in each of these three dimensions of community building. In community involvement, public relations workers are agent representatives of an organization or cause and active participants in community conversations and activities. In community nurture, public relations professionals act as facilitators, orchestrators of rituals and events, producers of information, and coordinators of volunteer and philanthropic efforts. In community organizing, the roles are as recruiters and advocates. The overarching metaphor that encompasses all of these is community builder.

Community as an Ideal

This vision of community building extends the meaning of community in a way that might seem idealistic or even naïve. Indeed community itself has been labeled a tragic ideal (Tinder, 1980), nostalgic (Bernasconi, 1993; Cheney & Christensen, 2001), illusionary (Scherer, 1972), or absurdly utopian (Bellah et al., 1985). Similar criticisms have been lodged at concepts such as two-way symmetrical communication (e.g., L. Grunig, J. Grunig, & Dozier, 2002).

In today's increasing complex environment, public relations needs a strong ideal if the field is to reach its full potential as contributor to society. Kruckeberg (1998a) observed, "[T]he greatest challenge for 21st century public relations practitioners will be the identification of organizational values and their reconciliation with societal values within the context of a quickly and seemingly chaotic syncretizing popular culture" (p. 3).

To what degree must true community be achieved in order to be a viable concept in public relations? Scholars differ about what is required for true community. Shaffer and Anundsen (1993) differentiated between functional communities and conscious communities. A functional community is one in which members support the physical well-being of the group so that members are productive and social order can be maintained. Rorty (1989, 1991), a prominent social theorist, argued this approach is sufficient. He stressed that a community exists when members share enough of the same beliefs and values for each to resolve disagreements through fruitful conversation. By contrast, a conscious community goes beyond mere functionality—but how far is not clear. Shaffer and Amundsen (1993) suggested that a conscious community emphasizes personal needs for expression, growth, and transformation. Mason (1993) argued that in a community members must also demonstrate genuine mutual concern and avoid the systematic exploitation of others. Similarly, Stevenson (1995) suggested that a community requires members to demonstrate an interest, a moral capacity, and empathy for others.

Overall, it might not be necessary to attain conscious community status for the idea of community to be useful in public relations. Indeed, it might be sufficient to create functioning communities that communicate effectively. Importantly, the creation of community does not require all members of a community to think alike. Postmodernism recognizes dissensus (Holtzhausen, 2000). Differences within communities are useful. Zarefsky (1995) suggested that community and diversity are complementary, dialectical terms. Pursuing either alone is destructive and unnecessary. He observed, "The common focus on the same story is a bond of community; the contest among alternative readings promotes diversity" (p. 7).

Friedman (1983) made a parallel distinction between two types of communities. A community of affinity is based on likemindedness—or what people think they have in common, such as race, sex, religion, nationality—or a common formula or creed. As he suggested, this idea is particularly powerful for those who feel oppressed. At the same time, he believed a community of affinity is a false community because members feel secure only because they are afraid of conflict and opposition. By contrast, Friedman proposed a community of otherness, wherein people find themselves in a common situation that they approach in different ways, and that discovery calls them out as individuals. There are just as many points of view as there are people in a community of otherness, without a polarization of communication.

Polarization was the concern of philosopher Martin Buber, whose I-Thou distinction focused on how individuals must strike a careful balance between the interest of self and the interest of others. Buber suggested that we must walk along a narrow ridge between the interests of self and the interests of others (e.g., Arnett, 1986). Palmer (1992, p. 25) made a similar distinction between competition (as represented in game theory; Murphy, 1989) and communal conflict (i.e., a public encounter in which the whole group can win by growing). Indeed, healthy conflict is possible only within the context of supportive community.

CONCLUSION

This chapter presented four arguments that support the idea that community is a potentially useful foundation for theory building about and for the practice of public relations.

First, at the pragmatic level, a focus on community links public relations to a widely accepted and valued idea in society—a concept that is receiving continuing attention in academe.

Second, at the theoretical level, community is a rich and versatile construct, and therefore a more useful construct than public—a concept that severely constricts theorizing and defies application in public relations.

Third, considerable momentum has developed among public relations researchers to use concepts closely related to community in studying the field. Besides explicit calls for a community-based focus, researchers now address community indirectly under the aegis of symmetrical, dialogic, and transactional communications; collaboration, collectivism, and social corporatism; and relationship management. Other researchers are tapping into critical, postmodern, and cultural research traditions that already have embraced the community notion. Still other researchers are applying community-based concepts to Internet, risk, and health communication.

Finally, at the philosophical level, this paper has argued that community building cogently summarizes what many practitioners envision that public relations ought to be—a proactive (nonreactive) effort to bring people together through involvement, nurturing, and organizing. This notion particularly resonates with Americans, but perhaps to a more limited degree elsewhere in the world where community is less recognized culturally.

By suggesting community as a foundation for public relations theory and practice, this essay further extends the call for public relations theorists and practitioners to examine alternative perspectives and domains for pubic relations practice (Dozier & Lauzen, 2000; L. Grunig, 1992, p. 77; Karlberg, 1996). Unlikely as it is that community relations will usurp public relations as a unifying descriptor of the field, it is worthwhile to note that communication management has become the predominant term used to describe the function in Europe (Ruler & Vercic, 2002b, 2003; Vercic, van Ruler, Bütschi, & Flodin), and that the majority of Fortune 500 firms use terms other than public relations, (such as corporate communication and public affairs) to label the pubic relations function.

A focus on community reorients the field to examine how organizations fit into the large scheme of society, but also recognizes that organizations themselves are constituted of communities and subcommunities within them. Internal stakeholder groups are probably one of the best cases where community can be applied. In building an organization, managers create communities, which are measured in terms of the quality of relationships among participants.

Community offers the potential for organizations to become more socially responsible by heightening awareness of the greater whole of which the organization is a part. Community shifts the organizational emphasis from the cold treatment of impersonal, often adversarial publics, to a warmer, more enlightened emphasis on collaboration and cooperation with others.

Importantly, this shift does not presume naively that organizations automatically will act more responsibly, ethically, or humanely in dealing with others.

Indeed, the prospect remains that organizations can still exercise undue advantage or power (Kersten, 1994) to exploit community members for the organization's self-interest (Rawlins & Stoker, 2001; Trujillo, 1992). Indeed, community—like persuasion or information—can be misused as a mechanism of control (Gossett & Tompkins, 2001). Yet the idea of integrating organizational goals and activities with the needs, concerns, and interests of people is the very essence of public relations and creating community.

REFERENCES

Albers, R. R. (1994, September). Going public: "Public journalism" unites some publics and newsrooms in a controversial mission. *Presstime, 16*(8). 28–30.

Anderson, B. (1991). *Imagined communities: Reflection on the origin and spread of nationalism* (Rev. ed). London: Verso.

Anderson, R., Dardenne, R., & Killenberg, G. M. (1994). *The conversation of journalism: Communication, community and the news.* Westport, CT: Praeger.

Arendt, H. (1998). *The human condition* (2nd ed.). Chicago: University of Chicago Press. (Original work published 1958)

Arnett, R. C. (1986). *Communication and community: Implications of Martin Buber's dialog.* Carbondale: Southern Illinois University Press.

Aronowitz, S. (1995). Is a democracy possible? The decline of the public in the American debate. In B. Robbins (Ed.), *The phantom public sphere* (pp. 75–92). Minneapolis: University of Minnesota Press.

Ashcraft, K. L. (2001). Feminist organizing and the construction of alternative community. In G.J. Shepherd & E.W. Rothenbul er (Eds.), *Communication and community* (pp. 79–110). Mahwah, NJ: Erlbaum.

Authentic communication method builds team & bottom line (1996, February 26), *pr reporter, 39*(9), 1.

Badaracco, C. (1998). The transparent corporation and organized community. *Public Relations Review, 23,* 265–272.

Ball-Rokeach, S. J., Kim, Y., & Matei, S. (2001). Storytelling neighborhood: Paths to belonging in diverse urban environments. *Communication Research, 28,* 392–428.

Banks, S. D. (1995). *Multicultural public relations: A socio-interpretive approach.* Thousand Oaks, CA: Sage.

Barlow, W. (1988). Community radio in the U.S.: The struggle for a democratic medium. *Media, Culture and Society, 10,* 81–106.

Bell, C., & Newby, H. (1974). *The sociology of community.* London: Cass.

Bellah, R. N., Madsen, R., Sullivan, W. M., Swidler, A., & Tipton, S. M. (1985). *Habits of the heart: Individualism and commitment in American life.* New York: Harper & Row.

Beamish, A. (2001). Creating communities of practice: Using information technology for learning and communication in automobile dealerships. *Journal of Planning Literature, 16,* 80–163.

Bender, T. (1978). *Community and social change in America.* New Brunswick, NJ: Rutgers University Press.

Beniger, J. R. (1987). Personalization of mass media and the growth of pseudo-community. *Communication Research, 14,* 352–371.

Berger, P. L., & Luckmann, T. (1967). *The social construction of reality.* Garden City, NY: Doubleday.

Bernasconi, R. (1993). On deconstructing nostalgia for community within the West: The debate between Nancy and Blanchot. *Research in Phenomenology, 23,* 3–32.

Bernays, E. L. (1923). *Crystallizing public opinion.* New York: Liveright.

Bernays, E. L. (1955). *The engineering of consent.* Norman: University of Oklahoma Press.

Biklen, D. P. (1983). *Community organizing. Theory and practice.* Englewood Cliffs, NJ: Prentice Hall.

Blumer, H. (1960). The mass, the public and public opinion. In M. J. Janowitz (Ed.), *Reader in public opinion and communication* (2nd ed., pp. 40–50). New York: Macmillan.

Blumer, H. (1969). *Symbolic interactionism: Perspective and method.* Berkeley: University of California Press.

Bogart, L., & Orenstein, F. E. (1965). Mass media and community identity in a interurban setting. *Journalism Quarterly, 42,* 105–128.

Boone, M. E. (2001). *Managing interactively.* New York: McGraw-Hill.

Botan, C. H. (1993a). A human nature approach to image and ethics in international public relations. *Journal of Public Relations Research, 5,* 71–81.

Botan, C. H. (1993b). Introduction to the paradigm struggle in public relations. *Public Relations Review, 19,* 107–110.

Botan, C. H. (1997). Ethics in strategic communication campaigns: The case for a new approach to public relations. *Journal of Business Communication, 34,* 188–202.

Botan, C. H., & Soto, F. (1998). A semiotic approach to the internal functioning of publics: Implications for strategic communication and public relations. *Public Relations Review, 24,* 21–44.

Bracht, N. (Ed.). (1999). *Health promotion at the community level. New advances* (2nd ed.). Thousand Oaks, CA: Sage.

Bracht, N. (2001). Community partnership strategies in health campaigns. In R. E. Rice & C. K. Atkins (Eds.), *Public communication campaigns* (3rd ed., pp. 323–342). Thousand Oaks, CA: Sage.

Brager, G., Specht, H., & Torczyner, J. L. (1987). *Community organizing.* New York: Columbia University Press.

Braithwaite, R. L., Taylor, S. E., & Austin, J. N. (2000). *Building health coalitions in the Black community.* Thousand Oaks, CA: Sage.

Brenkman, J. (1992). Family, community, polis: The Freudian structure of feeling. *New Literary History, 23,* 923–954.

Broom, G. M., Casey, S., & Ritchey, J. (1997). Toward a concept and theory of organization-public relationships, *Journal of Public Relations Research, 9,* 83–98.

Bruning, S. D. (2002). Relationship building as a retention strategy: Linking relationship attitude and satisfaction evaluations to behavioral outcomes. *Public Relations Review, 28,* 39–48.

Building community: 10 essential elements & steps toward solutions (1997, June 23). *pr reporter, 35*(8), 1–2.

Burgess, E. W. (1973). *On community, family, and delinquency: Selected writings.* (L. S. Cottrell, A. Hunter, & J. F. Short, Eds.). Chicago: University of Chicago Press.

Burke, E. M. (1999). *Corporate community relations: The principle of the neighbor of choice.* Westport, CT: Praeger.

Bybee, C. (1999). Can democracy survive in the post-factual age? A return to the Lippmann-Dewey debate about the politics of news. *Journalism & Communication Monographs, 1*(1), 27–66.

Byker, D., & Anderson, L. J. (1975). *Communication as identification: An introductory view.* New York: Harper & Row.

Cairncross, F. (2002). New ways to build a fragmented workforce into a cultural community. *Journal of Organizational Excellence, 21*(3), 31–42.

Calabrese, A. (1991). The periphery in the center: The information age and the "good life" in rural America. *Gazette, 48,* 105–128.

Calabrese, A. (2001). Why localism? Communication technology and the shifting scale of political community. In G. J. Shepherd & E. W. Rothenbuhler (Eds.), *Communication and community* (pp. 251–270). Mahwah, NJ: Erlbaum.

Calhoun, C. J. (1980). Community: Toward a viable conceptualization for comparative research. *Social History, 5,* 105–129.

Carey, J. W. (1989). *Communication as culture.* New York: Routledge.

Carey, J. W. (1998). The internet and the end of the national communication system: Uncertain predictions of an uncertain future. *Journalism & Mass Communication Quarterly, 75,* 28–34.

Carter, R. E., Jr., & Clarke, P. (1963). Suburbanites, city residents and local news. *Journalism Quarterly, 40,* 548–558.

Chappell, T. (1994). *The soul of a business: Managing for profit and the common good.* New York: Bantam.

Chatterjee, P. (1990). A response to Taylor's invocation of civil society. *Working Papers and Proceedings of the Center for Psychosocial Studies, 31,* 1–17.

Chay-Nemeth, C. (2001) Revisiting publics: A critical archaeology of publics in the Thai HIV/AIDS issue. *Journal of Public Relations Research, 13,* 127–162.

Chekki, D. (1989). Some dimensions of community: An overview. In D. Chekki (Ed.), *Dimensions of community: A research handbook* (pp. 3–14). New York: Garland.

Cheney, D. (1982). Communication and community. *Communication, 7,* 1–32.

Cheney, G. (1991). *Rhetoric in an organizational society: Managing multiple identities.* Columbia: University of South Carolina Press.

Cheney, G., & Christensen, L. T. (2001). Public relations as contested terrain: A critical response. In R. L. Heath (Ed.), *Handbook of public relations* (pp. 167–182). Thousand Oaks, CA: Sage.

Christians, C. G., & Hammond, L. (1986). Social justice and a community information utility. *Communication, 9,* 127–149.

Clark, M. S., & Mills, J. (1993). The difference between communal and exchange relationships: What it is and is not. *Personality and Social Psychology Bulletin, 19,* 684–691.

Clinton, H. R. (1996). *It takes a village and other lessons children teach us.* New York: Simon & Schuster.

Cohen, A. P. (1985). *The symbolic construction of community.* New York: Tavistock (Routledge).

Community = relationships to nth power, a major motivator (1997, April 27). *pr reporter, 40*(16), 1–2.

Contractor, N. S., & Eisenberg, E. M. (1990). Communication networks and new media in organizations. In J. Fulk & C. Steinfield (Eds.), *Organizations and communication technology* (pp. 143–172). Thousand Oaks, CA: Sage.

Coombs, W. T. (1998a, November). *The development of internet communities: The role of public relations.* Paper presented to Public Relations Division, National Communication Association, New York.

Coombs, W. T. (1998b). The internet as potential equalizer: New leverage for confronting social irresponsibility. *Public Relations Review, 24,* 289–305.

Cozier, Z. R., & Witmer, D. M. (2001). The development of a structuration analysis of new publics in an electronic environment. In R. L. Heath (Ed.), *Handbook of public relations* (pp. 615–624). Thousand Oaks, CA: Sage.

Culbertson, H. M., & Chen, N. (1996). Communitarianism: A foundation for communication symmetry. *Public Relations Quarterly, 42*(2), 36–41.

Curtin, P. A., & Boynton, L. A. (2001). Ethics in public relations: Theory and practice. In R. L. Heath (Ed.), *Handbook of public relations* (pp. 411–422). Thousand Oaks, CA: Sage.

Cutlip, S. M., Center, A. H., & Broom, G. M. (1999). *Effective public relations* (8th ed.). Englewood Cliffs, NJ: Prentice Hall.

Daugherty, E. (2001). Public relations and social responsibility. In R. L. Heath (Ed.), *Handbook of public relations* (pp. 389–403). Thousand Oaks, CA: Sage.

Davis, D. K., & Puckett, T. F. N. (1992). Mass entertainment and community: Toward a culture-centered paradigm for mass communication research. In S. A. Deetz (Ed.), *Communication yearbook 15* (pp. 3–34). Newbury Park, CA: Sage.

Day, G., & Murdoch, J. (1993). Locality and community: Coming to terms with place. *Sociological Review, 41,* 82–11.

Day, K. D., Dong, Q., & Robins, C. (2001). Public relations ethics: An overview and discussion of issues for the 21st century. In R. L. Heath (Ed.), *Handbook of public relations* (pp. 403–410). Thousand Oak, CA: Sage.

Deatherage, C. P., & Hazelton, V. (1998). Effects of organizational worldviews on the practice of public relations: A test of the theory of public relations excellence. *Journal of Public Relations Research, 10,* 57–71.

DeSanctis, G., & Fulk, J. (Eds.). (1999). *Shaping organizational form: Communication, connection and community.* Thousand Oaks, CA: Sage.

Dewey, J. (1927). *The public and its problems*. Athens, OH: Swallow Press.

Dewey, J. (1929). *Experience and nature*. New York: Norton.

Donohue, G. A., Tichenor, P. J., & Olien, C. N. (1986). Metro daily pullback and knowledge gaps within and between communities. *Communication Research, 13*, 453–471.

Doolittle, R. J., & MacDonald, D. (1978). Communication and a sense of community in a metropolitan neighborhood: A factor analytic examination. *Communication Quarterly, 26*, 2–7.

Dozier, D. M., Grunig, L. A., & Grunig, J. E. (1995). *Manager's guide to excellence in public relations and communication management*. Mahwah, NJ: Erlbaum.

Dozier, D. M., & Lauzen, M. M. (2000). Liberating the intellectual domain from the practice: Public relations, activism and the role of the scholar. *Journal of Public Relations Research, 13*, 3–22.

Duncan, H. (1985). *Communication and social order*. New Brunswick, NJ: Transaction. (Original work published 1962)

Dunlap, A. (1996). *Mean business: How I save bad companies and make good companies great*. New York: Random House.

Durkheim, E. (1933). *The division of labor in society*. (G. Simpson., Trans.). New York: Free Press. (Original work published 1893)

Edelstein, A., & Larson, O. N. (1960). The weekly press' contribution to the sense of urban community. *Journalism Quarterly, 37*, 489–498.

Effrat, M. P. (1974). *The community: Approaches and applications*. New York: Free Press.

Elwood, W. N. (Ed.). (1995). *Public relations inquiry as rhetorical criticism: Case studies of corporate discourse and social influence*. Westport, CT: Praeger.

Everett, J. L. (1990). Organizational culture and ethnoecology in public relations theory and practice. *Public Relations Research Annual, 2*, 235–251.

Etzioni, A. (1991) *The responsive society*. San Francisco: Jossey-Bass.

Etzioni, A. (1993). *The spirit of community: Rights, responsibilities and the communitarian agenda*. New York: Crown.

Ewen, S. (1996). *PR! A social history of spin*. New York: Basic Books.

Ferguson, M. A. (1984, August). Building theory in public relations: Interorganizational relationships. Paper presented to the annual conference of the Association for Education in Journalism and Mass Communication, Gainesville, FL.

Finnegan, J. R., Jr., Bracht, N., & Viswanath, K. (1989). Community power and leadership analysis in lifestyle campaigns. In C.T. Salmon (Ed.), *Information campaigns: Balancing social values and social change* (pp. 54–84). Newbury Park, CA: Sage.

Finnegan, J. R., Jr., & Visawanath, K. (1988). Community ties and use of cable TV and newspapers in a midwest suburb. *Journalism Quarterly, 65*, 456–463.

Fischer, E., & Gainer, B. (1995). Community and consumer behavior (Working paper). Ontario, Canada: York University.

Fish, S. (1980). *Is there a text in this class?* Cambridge, MA: Harvard University Press.

Flora, J. A., Maccoby, N., & Farquhar, J. W. (1989). Communication campaigns to prevent cardiovascular disease: The Stanford community studies. In R. E. Rice & C. K. Atkin (Eds.), *Public communication campaigns* (2nd ed., pp. 233–252). Newbury Park, CA: Sage.

Fontain, S. (1988). The unfinished story of the interpretive community. *Rhetoric Review, 7*, 86–96.

Foucault, M. (1980). *Power/knowledge*. New York: Pantheon.

Foundation for Community Encouragement (n.d.). *Community described*. [Brochure]. Ridgefield, CT: Author.

Frentz, T. S., & Rushkin, J. H. Courting community in contemporary culture. In. T. Rosteck (Ed.), *At the intersection: Cultural studies and rhetorical studies* (pp. 313–344). New York: Guilford.

Friedland, L. A. (2001). Communication, community and democracy: Toward a theory of the communicatively integrated community. *Communication Research, 28*, 358–391.

Friedman, M. (1970, September). The social responsibility of business is to increase its profits. *New York Times Magazine*, p. 146.

Friedman, M. S. (1983). The community of affinity versus the community of otherness. In *The confirmation of otherness: Family, community and society* (pp. 133–151). New York: Pilgrim Press.

Fulk, J., & Steinfield, S. (1990). *Organizations and communication technology*. Newbury Park, CA: Sage.

Gadamer, H. G. (1989). *Truth and method* (2nd rev. ed.). (J. Weinsheimer & D. G. Marshall, Trans.). New York: Crossroad. (Original work published 1975)

Gainer, B., & Fischer, E.(1994). Community and consumption. *Advances in Consumer Research, 21*, 137.

Gardner, J. W. (1996). *Building community*. Washington, DC: Independent Sector.

Gattiker, U. E. (2001). *The internet as a diverse community, cultural, organization, and political issues*. Mahwah, NJ: Erlbaum.

Gaziano, C. (1988). Community knowledge gaps. *Critical Studies in Mass Communication, 5*, 351–357.

Gergen, K. J.(1991). *The saturated self: Dilemmas of identity in contemporary life*. New York: Basic Books.

Gibbs, C. (1994, Fall-Winter). A vision for Richmond: Communities, communications and connectedness. *Huck Boyd National Center for Community Media Review*, 17–19.

Gittell, R. J., & Vidal, A. (1998). *Community organizing: Building social capital as a development strategy*. Thousand Oaks, CA: Sage.

Goffman, E. (1959). *The presentation of self in everyday life*. New York: Anchor Books.

Gossett, L. M., & Tompkins, P. K. (2001). Community as a means of organizational control. In G. J. Shepherd & E. W. Rothenbuhler (Eds.), *Commuication and community* (pp. 111–134). Mahwah, NJ: Erlbaum.

Gozdz, K. (2000). Toward transpersonal learning communities in business. *American Behavioral Scientist, 43*, 1262–1285.

Grossman, W. M. (2001). *From anarchy to power: The net comes of age*. New York: New York University Press.

Grunig, J. E. (1975). Some consistent types of employee publics. *Public Relations Review, 1*(4), 17–36.

Grunig, J. E. (1976). Organizations and public relations: Testing a communication theory. *Journalism Monographs*, 46.

Grunig, J. E. (1978). Defining publics in public relations: The case of a suburban hospital. *Journalism Quarterly, 55*, 109–118.

Grunig, J. E. (1983). Communication behaviors and attitudes of environmental publics: Two studies. *Journalism Monographs*, 81.

Grunig, J. E. (1989a). Publics, audiences and market segments: Segmentation principles for campaigns. In C. T. Salmon (Ed.), *Information campaigns: Balancing social values and social change* (pp. 199–228). Newbury Park, CA: Sage.

Grunig, J. E. (1989b). Symmetrical presuppositions as a framework for public relations theory. In C. H. Botan & V. Hazelton (Eds.), *Public relations theory* (pp. 17–44). Hillsdale, NJ: Erlbaum.

Grunig, J. E. (1992). Communication, public relations and effective public relations: An overview of the book. In J. E. Grunig (Ed.), *Excellence in public relations and communication management* (pp. 1–28). Hillsdale, NJ: Erlbaum.

Grunig, J. E. (2000). Collectivism, collaboration and societal corporatism as core professional values in public relations. *Journal of Public Relations Research, 12*, 23–48.

Grunig, J. E. (2001). Two-way symmetrical public relations: Past, present and future. In R. L. Heath (Ed.), *Handbook of public relations* (pp. 11–30). Thousand Oaks, CA: Sage.

Grunig, J. E., & Huang, Y. (2000). From organizational effectiveness to relationship indicators: Antecedents of relationships, public relations strategies and relationship outcomes. In J. A. Ledingham & S. D. Bruning (Eds.), *Relationship management: A relational approach to the study and practice of public relations* (pp. 23–54). Mahwah, NJ: Erlbaum.

Grunig, J. E., & Hunt, T. (1984). *Managing public relations*. Fort Worth, TX: Holt, Rinehart, & Winston.

Grunig, L. A. (1992). Toward the philosophy of public relations. In E. L. Toth & R. L. Heath (Eds.), *Rhetorical and critical approaches to public relations* (pp. 65–92). Hillsdale, NJ: Erlbaum.

Grunig, L. A. (1995). The consequences of culture for public relations: The case of women in the foreign service. *Journal of Public Relations Research, 7*, 139–161.

Grunig, L. A., Grunig, J. E., & Dozier, D. (2002). *Excellent public relations and effective organizations*. Mahwah, NJ: Erlbaum.

Haas, T. (2001). Public relations between universality and particularity: Toward a moral-philosophical conception of public relations ethics. In R. L. Heath (Ed.), *Handbook of public relations* (pp. 423–434). Thousand Oaks, CA: Sage. (Original work published 1998)

Haber, H. F. (1994). *Beyond postmodern politics: Lyotard, Rorty, Foucault.* New York: Routledge.

Habermas, J. (1989). *The transformation of the public sphere: An inquiry into a category of bourgeois society.* (T. Burger, Trans.). Cambridge, MA: MIT Press. (Original work published 1962)

Hallahan, K. (1996, August). "Community" as the foundation for public relations theory and research. Paper presented to the annual conference of the Association for Education in Journalism and Mass Communication, Anaheim, CA.

Hallahan, K. (2000a). Inactive publics: The forgotten publics in public relations. *Public Relations Review, 26,* 499–515.

Hallahan, K. (2000b). Enhancing the motivation, ability and opportunity of publics to process public relations messages, *Public Relations Review, 26,* 463–480.

Hallahan, K. (2001). The dynamics of issues activation and response: An issues processes model. *Journal of Public Relations Research, 13,* 27–59.

Hampton, K., & Wellman, B. (2001). Long distance community in the network society. *American Behavioral Scientist, 45,* 476–495.

Hardt, H. (1975). Communication as theory and method of community. *Communication, 2,* 81–92.

Haring, A. (1972). Communication and change in community development. *Journalism Quarterly, 49,* 512–518, 530.

Harlow, R. (1977). Public relations definitions through the years. *Public Relations Review, 3,* 49–63.

Harris, T. E. (1990). Organizational cultures: An examination of the role of communication. In S. Thomas (Ed.), *Studies in communication* (Vol. 4, pp. 143–155). Norwood, NJ: Ablex.

Hazelton, V., & Kennan, W. (2000). Relationships as social capital: Reconceptualizing the bottom line for public relations. *Corporate Communication: An International Journal, 5*(2), 81–86.

Hearit, K. (1999). Newsgroups, activists, publics and corporate apologia: The case of Intel and its Pentium chip. *Public Relations Review, 26,* 291–308.

Heath, R. L. (1992). The wrangle in the market place; A rhetorical perspective on public relations. In E. L. Toth & R. L. Heath (Eds.), *Rhetorical and critical approaches to public relations* (pp. 17–36). Hillsdale, NJ: Erlbaum.

Heath, R. L. (1994). *Management of corporate communication. From interpersonal contacts to external affairs.* Hillsdale, NJ: Erlbaum.

Heath, R. L. (1998). New communication technologies: An issues management point of view. *Public Relations Review, 24,* 273–288.

Heath, R. L., Bradshaw, J., & Lee, J. (2002). Community relationship building: Local leadership in the risk communication infrastructure. *Journal of Public Relations Research, 14,* 317–353.

Hebdige, D. (1979). *Subculture: The meaning of style.* New York: Metheun.

Hegel, J., III, & Armstrong, A. G. (1997). *Net gain. Expanding markets through virtual communities.* Boston: Harvard Business School Press.

Henry, P. W., Jr. (1993). A billion dollars worth of publicity: New Orleans and the 1988 Republican national convention. *Public Relations Review, 19,* 213–218.

Herbst, S. (1995). On the disappearance of groups: 19th and Early 20th-century conceptions of public opinion. In T. L. Glaser & C. T. Salmon (Eds.), *Public opinion and the communication of consent* (pp. 89–104). New York: Guilford.

Herbst, S., & Beniger, J. R. (1994). The changing infrastructure of public opinion. In J. S. Ettema & D. C. Whitney (Eds.), *Audiencemaking: How the media create the audience* (pp. 95–114). Thousand Oaks, CA: Sage.

Hillery, G. A., Jr., (1955). Definitions of community: Areas of agreement. *Rural Sociology, 20,* 111–123.

Hofstede, G. (1984). *Culture's consequences: International differences in work-related values* (abridged ed.). Newbury Park, CA: Sage.

Hofstede, G. (1991). *Cultures and organizations: Software of the mind.* London: McGraw-Hill.

Hogan, J. M. (1998). *Rhetoric and community: Studies in unity and fragmentation.* Columbia: University of South Carolina Press.

Holtzhausen, D. (2000). Postmodern values in public relations. *Journal of Public Relations Research*, *12*, 93–114.

Holtzhausen, D. (2002). Towards a postmodern research agenda for public relations. *Public Relations Review*, *28*, 251–264.

Holtzhausen, D., & Voto, R. (2002). Resistance from the margins: The postmodern public relations practitioner as organizational activist. *Journal of Public Relations Research*, *14*, 57–84.

Hon, L., & Grunig, J. E. (1999). *Guidelines for measuring relationships in public relations*. Gainesville, FL: Institute for Public Relations.

Hornick, R. C. (Ed.). (2002). *Public health communication: Evidence for behavior change.* Mahwah, NJ: Erlbaum.

Hunter, A. (1972). *Symbolic communities*. University of Chicago Press.

Huang, Y. (2000, June). Cultural aspects of organization-public relationships. Paper presented to the annual conference of the International Communication Association, Acapulco, Mexico.

Huang, Y. (2001). OPRA—A cross cultural, multiple-item scale for measuring organization-public relationships. *Journal of Public Relations Research*, *13*, 61–90.

Hutton, J. G. (1999). The definition, dimensions and domain of public relations. *Public Relations Review*, *25*, 199–214.

Hymes, D. (1974). *Foundations in sociolinguistics: An ethnographic approach*. Philadelphia: University of Pennsylvania Press.

Information highway enables people to forge relationships and create their own communities (1994, August 1). *Purview* (no. 368), 1. [Supplement to *pr reporter*.]

Jacobson, T., & Servaes, J. (Eds.). (1999). *Theoretical approaches to participatory communication*. Cresskill, NJ: Hampton Press.

Jankowski, N. (1982). Community television: A tool for community action? *Communication*, *7*, 33–58.

Janowitz, M. B. (1952). *The community press in an urban setting: The social elements of urbanism.* Chicago: University of Chicago Press.

Jeffres, L. W., & Dobos, J. (1988). Communication and neighborhood mobilization. *Urban Affairs Quarterly*, *20*, 97–112.

Jeffres, L. W., Dobos, J., & Lee, J. (1988). Media use and community ties. *Journalism Quarterly*, *65*, 575–581.

Jeffres, L.W., Dobos, J., & Sweeney, M. (1987). Communication and commitment to community. *Communication Research*, *14*, 619–643.

Jensen, I. (1997). Legitimacy and strategy of different companies: A perspective of external and internal public relations. In D. Ross, T. MacManus, & D. Vercic (Eds.), *Perspectives on public relations research: An international perspective* (pp. 255–246). London: International Thomson Business Press.

Jones, R. (2002). Challenges to the notion of publics in public relations: Implications of the risk society for the discipline. *Public Relations Review*, *28*, 49–62.

Jones, S. G. (1995). Understanding community in the information age. In S. G. Jones (Ed.), *Cybersociety. Computer mediated-communication and community* (pp. 1–17). Thousand Oaks, CA: Sage.

Jung, J. C. (1998). Smart communities: Digitally inclined and content rich. *New Telecom Quarterly*, *6*, 19–26.

Kant, I. (1983). To perpetual peace. In *Immanuel Kant: Perpetual peace and other essays* (pp. 104–144). Cambridge, UK: Hacker. (Original work published 1795)

Kar, S. B., & Alcalay, R. (Eds.). (2001). *Health communication. A multicultural approach*. Thousand Oaks, CA: Sage.

Karlberg, M. (1996). Remembering the public in public relations research: From theoretical to operational symmetry. *Journal of Public Relations Research*, *8*, 263–278.

Kelly, C., & Zak, M. (1999). Narrativity and professional communication: Folktales and community meaning. *Journal of Business and Technical Communication*, *13*, 297–317.

Kelly, K. S. (1998). *Effective fund-raising management*. Mahwah, NJ: Erlbaum.

Kent, M. L., & Taylor, M. (1998). Building dialogic relationships through the World Wide Web. *Public Relations Review*, *24*, 321–334.

Kent, M. L., & Taylor, M. (2002). Toward a dialogic theory of public relations. *Public Relations Review, 28,* 21–38.

Kent, M. L., Taylor, M., & White, W. J. (2003). The relationship between Web site design and organizational responsiveness to stakeholders. *Public Relations Review, 29,* 63–77.

Kersten, A. (1994). The ethics and ideology of public relations: A critical examination of American theory and practice. In W. Armbrecht & U. Zabel (Eds.), *Normative aspekte der public relations* (pp. 109–130). Opladen, Germany: Westdeucher Verlag.

King, R. J. H. (2001). Virtue and community in business ethics: A critical assessment of Solomon's Aristotelian approach to social responsibility. *Journal of Social Philosophy, 32,* 487–499.

Kirby A. (1989). A sense of place. *Critical Studies in Mass Communication, 6,* 322–326.

Klein, E., & Izzo, J. B. (1998). *Awakening corporate soul: Four paths to unleash the power of people at work.* Lion's Bay, B.C., Canada: Fairwinds Press.

Komisarjevsky, C. (2002, October). *Integrity: The final frontier. Vernon C. Schranz distinguished lecture in public relations.* [Brochure]. Muncie, IN: Ball State University.

Komito, L. (1998). The net as a foraging society: Flexible communities. *Information Society, 14,* 97–106.

Kruckeberg, D. (1998a, November). *Public relations and its education: 21st century challenges in definition, role and function.* Paper presented to the annual conference of the National Communication Association, New York.

Kruckeberg, D. (1998b, November). *A revisitation of the concept of community in public relations practice in the 21st century.* Paper presented to the annual conference of the National Communication Association, New York.

Kruckeberg, D. (2001, May). *Public relations and community: A theoretical construct for the 21st century.* Paper presented to the annual conference of the International Communication Association, Washington, DC.

Kruckeberg, D., & Starck, K. (1988). *Public relations and community: A reconstructed theory.* New York: Praeger.

Kuhn, T. S. (1970). *The structure of scientific revolutions* (2nd ed.). Chicago: University of Chicago Press.

Ledingham, J. A., & Bruning, S. D. (1998). Relationship management in public relations: Dimensions of an organization-public relationship. *Public Relations Review, 24,* 55–65.

Ledingham, J. A., & Bruning, S. D. (2000). Introduction: Background and current trends in the study of relationship management. In J. A. Ledingham & S. D. Bruning (Eds.), *Relationship management: A relational approach to the study and practice of public relations* (pp. xi-xvii). Mahwah, NJ: Erlbaum.

Ledingham, J. A. & Bruning, S. D. (2001). Managing community relationships to maximize mutual benefit: Doing well by doing good. In R. L. Heath (Ed.), *Handbook of public relations* (pp. 527–534). Thousand Oaks, CA: Sage.

Leeper, K. A. (1994, November). *When a newcomer intrudes: The public relations of (re)building community.* Paper presented to Speech Communication Association, New Orleans, LA.

Leeper, K. A. (1996). Public relations: Ethics and communitarianism: A preliminary investigation, *Public Relations Review, 22,* 163–180.

Leeper, K. A. (1998). *Building the volunteer community in the non-profit organization: A new approach for a new century.* Paper presented to the annual conference of the National Communication Association, New York.

Leeper, R. V. (1996). Moral objectivity, Jürgen Habermas's discourse ethics and public relations. *Public Relations Review, 22,* 133–152.

Leeper, R. V. (2001). In search of a metatheory for public relations: The argument for communitarianism. In R.L. Heath (Ed.), *Handbook of public relations* (pp. 93–104). Thousand Oaks, CA: Sage.

Leeper, R. V., & Leeper, K. A. (2001). Public relations as "practice": Applying the theory of Alasdair MacIntyre. *Public Relations Review, 27,* 461–474.

Leichty, G., & Warner, E. (2001). Cultural topoi: Implications for public relations. In R. L. Heath (Ed.), *Handbook of public relations* (pp. 61–74). Thousand Oaks, CA: Sage.

Leitch, S., & Neilson, D. (2001). Bringing publics into public relations: New theoretical frameworks for the practice. In R. L. Heath (Ed.), *Handbook of public relations* (pp. 127–138). Thousand Oaks, CA: Sage.

Liebowitz, S. (2002). *Re-thinking the network economy.* New York: AMACOM.

Lindlof, T. R. (1988). Media audiences as interpretive communities. In J. A. Anderson (Ed.), *Communication Yearbook 11* (pp. 81–107). Newbury Park, CA: Sage.

Lindlof, T. R., & Meyer, T. P. (1987). Mediated communication as ways of seeing, acting and constructing culture: The tools and foundations of qualitative research. In T. R. Lindlof (Ed.), *Natural audiences: Qualitative research of media uses and effect* (pp. 1–32). Norwood, NJ: Ablex.

Lippmann, W. (1922). *Public opinion.* New York: Macmillan.

Lippmann, W. (1925). *The phantom public.* New York: Harcourt Brace.

Little, S. E. (2000). Networks and neighborhoods: Household, community and sovereignty in the global economy. *Urban Studies, 37,* 1813–1825.

Littlejohn, S. W. (2002). *Theories of human communication* (7th ed.). Belmont, CA: Wadsworth.

Logos, W., & Jung, J. (2001). Exploring the digital divide: Internet connectedness and age. *Communication Research, 28,* 536–562.

Lundborg, L. (1950). *Public relations and the local community.* New York: Harper.

MacIntyre, A. (1981). *After virtue: A study in moral theory.* South Bend, IN: University of Notre Dame Press.

MacIntyre, A. (1988). *Whose justice? Which rationality?* London: Duckworth.

MacManus, T. (2000). Public relations: The cultural dimension. In D. Moss, D. Vercic, & G. Warnaby (Eds.), *Perspectives on public relations research* (pp. 159–178). London: Routledge.

Manning, G., Curtis, K., & McMillen, S. (1996). *Building community: The human side of work.* Cincinnati, OH: Thomas Executive Press.

Mason, A. (1993). Liberalism and the value of community. *Canadian Journal of Philosophy, 23,* 215–240.

Mayhew, L. H. (1997). *The new public. Professional communication and the means of social influence.* New York: Cambridge University Press.

McKnight, J. L. (1994). Redefining community. *Social Policy, 23,* 56–62.

McLeod, J. M., Scheufele, D. A., Hicks, J., Kwak, N., Zhang, W., & Holbert, R. L. (2000, August). Communicating community: The role of mass and interpersonal communication in promoting complexity of individuals' understanding of community. Paper presented to the annual conference of the Association for Education in Journalism and Mass Communication, New Orleans, LA.

McLuhan, M. (1964). *Understanding media. The extensions of man.* New York: McGraw-Hill.

Mendelbaum, S. J. (1972). *Community and communications.* New York: Norton.

Merritt, D.(1995). *Public journalism and public life: Why telling the news is not enough.* Hillsdale, NJ: Erlbaum.

Merritt, D., & Rosen, J. (1995, April). Imagining public journalism: An editor and scholar reflect on the of an idea. Bloomington, IN: Roy W. Howard Public Lecture in Journalism and Mass Communication Research, 5.

Meyrowitz, J. (1985a). The generalized elsewhere. *Critical Studies in Mass Communication, 6,* 326–334.

Meyrowitz, J. (1985b). *No sense of place: The impact of electronic media on social behavior.* New York: Oxford University Press.

Mickey, T. J. (1995). *Sociodrama: An interpretive theory for the practice of public relations.* Lanham, NY: University Press of America.

Miller, E. (1995, March 20). Community building = community. Is public relations ready for this challenge? *pr reporter, 33*(4), 1.

Miller, G. R. (1989). Persuasion and public relations: Two "Ps" in a pod. In C. H. Botan & V. Hazelton, Jr. (Eds.), *Public relations theory* (pp. 45–66). Hillsdale, NJ: Erlbaum.

Miller, L. J. (1999). Shopping for community: The transformation of the bookstore into a vital community institution. *Media, Culture & Society, 21,* 385–407.

Milley, P. (2002). Imagining good organizations: Moral orders or moral communities. *Educational Management & Administration, 30*(1), 47–64.

Minar, D. W., & Greer, S. (1969). *The concept of community: Readings with interpretations.* Chicago: Aldine.

Mitchell, C. C., & Schnyder, C. J. (1989). Public relations for Appalachia: Berea Mountain life and work. *Journalism Quarterly, 66,* 974–978.

Mittelmark, M. B., Luepker, R. V., Jacobs, D. R., Bracht, N. F., Carlaw, R., Crow, R. S., et. al. (1986). Community-wide prevention of cardiovascular disease: Education strategies of the Minnesota Heart Health Program. *Preventive Medicine, 15,* 661–672.

Moffitt, M. A. (1994). Collapsing the concepts of "public" and "image" into a new theory. *Public Relations Review, 20,* 159–170.

Moffitt, M. A. (2001). Using the collapse model of corporate image for campaign message design. In R. L. Heath (Ed.), *Handbook of public relations* (pp. 347–355). Thousand Oaks, CA: Sage.

Molleda, J. C. (2001). International paradigms: The Latin American school of public relations. *Journalism Studies, 2,* 513–530.

Moon, J. D. (1993). *Constructing community: Moral pluralism and tragic conflicts.* Princeton, NJ: Princeton University Press.

Mosco, V. (1998). Myth-ing links: Power and community in the information highway. *Information Society, 14,* 57–62.

Murphy, P. (1989). Game theory as a paradigm for the public relations process. In C. H. Botan & V. Hazelton, Jr. (Eds.), *Public relations theory* (pp. 173–192). Hillsdale, NJ: Erlbaum.

Murphy, P. (1991). The limits of symmetry: A game theory approach to symmetric and asymmetric public relations. *Public Relations Research Annual, 3,* 115–131.

Murphy, P. (1996). Chaos theory as a model for managing issues and crises. *Public Relations Review, 22,* 95–114.

Naisbitt, J. (1982). *Megatrends.* New York: Warner Books.

Naisbitt, J., & Aburdene, P. (1990). *Megatrends 2000.* New York: Avon.

Nash, J. D., & Farquhar, J. W. (1980). Applications of behavioral medicine to disease prevention in a total community setting: A review of the three community study. In J. M. Ferguson & C. B. Taylor (Eds.), *The comprehensive handbook of behavioral medicine* (pp. 313–325). New York: Spectrum.

Neff, B. D. (1998). *Building multicultural communities: A key boundary spanning function for public relations.* Paper presented to Public Relations Division, National Communication Association, New York.

Nightengale, V. (1986). Community as audience—audience as community. *Australian Journal of Communication, 9/10,* 31–41.

Nisbet, R. A. (1953). *The quest for community.* New York: Oxford University Press.

Oetting, E. R., Donnermeyer, J. F., Pledsted, B. A., Edwards, R.W., Kelly, K., & Beauvais, F. (1995). Assessing community readiness for prevention. *International Journal of Addictions, 30,* 659–683.

Olien, C. N., Donohue, G. A., & Tichenor, P. J. (1984, September). Media and stages of social conflict. *Journalism Monographs,* 90.

Ouchi, W. G. (1979). A conceptual framework for the design of organizational control mechanisms. *Management Science, 25,* 833–848.

Overduin, H. (1986). News judgment and the community, connection in the technological limbo of videotex. *Communication, 9,* 127–149.

Palmer, P. J. (1992, September/October). Community, conflict and ways of knowing. *Change, 24,* 22–26.

Park, R. E.(1938). Reflections on communication and culture. *American Journal of Sociology, 44,* 187–205.

Park, R. E. (1952). *Human communities: The city and human ecology.* Glencoe, IL: Free Press.

Park, R. E., Burgess, E. W., & McKenzie, M. C. (1967). *The city.* Chicago: University of Chicago Press. (Original work published 1925)

Pearson, R. (1989a). Beyond ethical relativism in pubic relations: Coordination, rules and the idea of communicative symmetry. *Public Relations Research Annual, 1,* 67–87.

Pearson, R. (1989b). Business ethics as communication ethics: Public relations practice and the idea of dialogue. In C. H. Botan & V. Hazelton (Eds.), *Public relations theory* (pp. 111–131). Hillsdale, NJ: Erlbaum.

Peck, M. S. (1987). *The different drum.* New York: Simon & Schuster.

Peck, M. S. (1993). *A world waiting to be born: Civility rediscovered.* New York: Bantam.

Pepper, G. (1995). *Communicating in organizations: A cultural approach.* New York: McGraw-Hill.

Peters, J. D. (1995). Historical tensions in the concept of public opinion. In T. L. Glaser & C. T. Salmon (Eds.), *Public opinion and the communication of consent* (pp. 3–32). New York: Guilford.

Phelan, J. M. (1988). Communing in isolation. *Critical Studies in Mass Communication, 5,* 347–351.

Plant, R. (1974). *Community and ideology: An essay on applied social philosophy.* Boston: Routledge & Kogan Poge.

Poplin, D. E. (1972). *Communities: A survey of theories and methods of research.* New York: Macmillan.

Post, J. E. (2000). Moving from geographic to virtual communities: Global corporate citizenship in a dot.com world. *Business and Society Review, 105,* 27–46.

Prensky, D., & Wright-Isak, C. (1997). Advertising, values and the consumption community. In L. Kahle & L. Chiagouris (Eds.), *Values, lifestyles and psychographics* (pp. 69–81). Mahwah, NJ: Erlbaum.

Putnam, R. D. (2000). *Bowling alone: The collapse and revival of American community.* New York: Simon & Schuster.

Quandt, J. (1970). *From the small town to the great community: The social thought of progressive intellectuals.* New Brunswick, NJ: Rutgers University Press.

Quarterman, J. S. (1993). The global matrix of minds. In L. Harasim (Ed.), *Global networks* (pp. 35–56). Cambridge, MA: MIT Press.

Radway, J. A. (1984). *Reading the romance: Women, patriarchy and popular literature.* Chapel Hill: University of North Carolina Press.

Rawlins, B., & Stoker, K. (2001, November). *The prostitution of community relations: When morally detached organizations exploit their communities for economic gratification.* Paper presented to the annual conference of the Association for Education in Journalism and Mass Communciation, Southwest Symposium, Tulsa, OK.

Rheingold, H. (1993). *The virtual community.* New York: HarperPerennial.

Rice, R. E., & Katz, J. E. (Eds.). (2001). *The internet and health communciation. Experience and expectations.* Thousand Oaks, CA: Sage.

Rivera, F. G. & Erlich, J. L. (1992). *Community organizing in a diverse society.* Boston: Allyn & Bacon.

Robbins, B. (Ed.). (1995). *The phantom public sphere.* Minneapolis: University of Minnesota Press.

Ronneberger, F., & Röhl, M. (1992). *Theorie der public relations ein entwurf* [Public relations theory, and outline]. Opladen, Germany: Westdeutscher Verlag.

Rorty, R. (1989). *Contingency, irony and solidarity.* Cambridge, UK: Cambridge University Press.

Rorty, R. (1991). Solidarity and objectivity. In *Objectivity, relativism and truth* (Vol. 1). Cambridge, UK: Cambridge University Press.

Rosen, J., & Merritt, D., Jr. (1994). *Public journalism: Theory and practice.* Dayton, OH: Kettering Foundation.

Rothenbuhler, E. W. (1991). The process of community involvement. *Communication Monographs, 58,* 63–78.

Royce, J. (1908). *Race questions, provincialism and other American problems.* New York: Macmillan.

Royce, J. (1913). *The problem of Christianity.* New York: Macmillan.

Royce, J. (1916). *The hope of the great community.* New York: Macmillan.

Rubin, H. J., & Rubin, I. S . (1997). *Community organizing and development.* Boston: Allyn & Bacon.

Ruler, B. van, & Vercic, D. (2002a). *The Bled manifesto on public relations.* Ljubljana, Slovenia: Pristop.

Ruler, B. van, & Vercic, D. (2002b). 21st century communication management: The people, the organization. In P. Simcic Bronn & R. Wiig (Eds.), *Corporate communication: A strategic approach to building reputation* (pp. 277–294). Oslo, Norway: Gyldendal Akademisk.

Ruler, B. van, & Vercic, D. (2003, May). *Reflective communication management: A public view on public relations.* Paper presented to the annual conference of International Communication Association, San Diego, CA.

Ruler, B. van, Vercic, D., Bütschi, G., & Flodin, B. (2000). *The European body of knowledge on public relations/communication management. The Report of the Delphi Research Project 2000.* Ghent/Ljubljana: European Association for Public Relations Education and Research.

Sandel, M. (1982). *Liberalism and the limits of justice.* Cambridge, UK: Cambridge University Press.

Scheufele, D. A., & Shah, D. V. (1999, August). *Opinion leadership and social capital.* Paper presented to the annual conference of Association for Education in Journalism and Mass Communication, New Orleans, LA.

Scherer, J. (1972). *Contemporary community: Sociological illusion or reality?* London: Tavistock.

Schoenberg, G. T., & Anderson, J. A. (1995). Social action media studies: Foundational arguments and common premises. *Communication Theory, 5,* 93–116.

Schudson, M. (1978). The ideal of conversation in the study of mass media. *Communication Research, 5,* 320–329.

Schwartz, E. (1995, Winter). Looking for community on the Internet. *National Civil Review, 84*(1), 37–41.

Servaes, J., Jacobson, T., & White, S. A. (1996). *Participatory communication for social change.* New Delhi, India: Sage.

Shaffer, C., & Anundsen, K. (1993). *Creating community anywhere: Finding support and connection in a fragmented world.* New York: Tarcher/Perigee.

Shah, D. V., McLeod, J. M., & Yoon, S. (2001). Communication, context and community. An exploration of print, broadcast, and Internet influences. *Communication Research, 28,* 464–506.

Shand, D. (1999, June). Making community. *Knowledge Management,* 65–70.

Shaw, D. L., & Hamm, B. L. (1997). Agendas for public union or for private communities? How individuals are using media to reshape American society. In M. McCombs, D. L. Shaw, & D. Weaver (Eds.), *Communication and democracy. Exploring the intellectual frontiers in agenda-setting theory* (pp. 209–230). Mahwah, NJ: Erlbaum.

Slack, R. S., & Williams, R. A. (2000). The dialectics of place and space. *New Media & Society, 2,* 313–334.

Splichal, S. (1999). *Public opinion: Developments and controversies in the twentieth century.* Lanham, MD: Rowman & Littlefield.

Springston, J. K., & Keyton, J. (2001). Public relations field dynamics. In R. L. Heath (Ed.), *Handbook of public relations* (pp. 115–126). Thousand Oaks, CA: Sage.

Springston, J. K., Keyton, J., Leichty, G. B., & Metzger, J. (1992). Field dynamics and public relations theory: Toward the management of multiple publics. *Journal of Public Relations Research, 4,* 81–100.

Sriramesh, K. (1996). Power, distance and public relations: An ethnographic study of southern Indian organizations. In H. M. Culberton & N. Chen (Eds.), *International public relations: A comparative analysis* (pp. 171–190). Mahwah, NJ: Erlbaum.

Sriramesh, K., Grunig, J. E., & Buffington, J. (1992). Corporate culture and public relations. In J. E. Grunig (Ed.), *Excellence in public relations and communication management* (pp. 577–596). Hillsdale, NJ: Erlbaum.

Sriramesh, K., Grunig, J. E., & Dozier, D. M. (1996). Observation and measurement of two dimensions of organizational culture and their relationship to public relations. *Journal of Public Relations Research, 8,* 229–262.

Sriramesh, K., & White, J. (1992). Societal culture and public relations. In J. E. Grunig (Ed.), *Excellence in public relations and communication management* (pp. 597–614). Hillsdale, NJ: Erlbaum.

St. John, B., III. (1998). Public relations as community building: Then and now. *Public Relations Quarterly, 43*(1), 34–40.

Stacey, M. (1974). The myth of community studies. In C. Bell & H. Newby (Eds.), *The sociology of community* (pp. 13–26). London: William Clowes.

Stamm, K. R. (1985). *Newspaper use and community ties: Toward a dynamic theory.* Norwood, NJ: Ablex.

Stamm, K. R. (1988). Community ties and media use. *Critical Studies in Mass Communication, 5,* 357–361.

Stamm, K. R. (2001). Of what use civic journalism: Do newspapers really make a difference in community participation? In G. J. Shepherd & E. W. Rothenbuler (Eds.), *Communication and community* (pp. 217–234). Mahwah, NJ: Erlbaum.

Stamm, K. R., & Fortini-Campbell, L. (1983). The relationship of community ties to newspaper use. *Journalism Monographs, 84.*

Stamm, K. R., & Guest, A. M. (1991). Communication and community integration: An analysis of the communication behavior of newcomers. *Journalism Quarterly, 68,* 644–657.

Stamm, K. R., & Weis, R. (1986). The newspaper and community integration. A study of ties to a local church community. *Communication Research, 13,* 125–137.

Starck, K., & Kruckeberg, D. (2001). Public relations and community: A reconstructed theory revisited. In R. L. Heath (Ed.), *Handbook of public relations* (pp. 51–60). Thousand Oaks, CA: Sage.

Stein, A. (2001, May). Connecting the dots: Exploring the relationship between employee communications and community. Paper presented to the annual conference of the International Communication Association, Washington, DC.

Steiner, L. (1988). Oppositional decoding as an act of resistance. *Critical Studies in Mass Communication, 5,* 1–15.

Stevenson, N. (1995). *Understanding media cultures. Social theory and mass communication.* Thousand Oaks, CA: Sage.

Stoker, K., & Rawlins, B. (n.d.). *Ethical characteristics of community and community building* (Working paper). Provo, UT: Brigham Young University.

Stone, G. C. (1977). Community commitment: A predictive theory of daily newspaper circulation. *Journalism Quarterly, 53,* 509–514.

Tapscott, D., Ticoll, D. & Lowy, A. (2000). *Digital capital.* Boston: Harvard Business School Press.

Taylor, M. (2000). Cross cultural variance as a challenge to public relations: A case study of the Coca-Cola scare in Europe. *Public Relations Review, 26,* 277–294.

Taylor, M., Kent, M. L., & White, W. J. (2001). How activist organizations are using the Internet to build relationships. *Public Relations Review 27,* 263–284.

Thompson, C. J., & Holt, D. B. (1996). Communities and consumption: Research on consumer strategies for constructing communal relationships in a postmodern world. *Advances in Consumer Research, 23,* 204–205.

Tichenor, P. J., Donohue, G. A., & Olien, C. N. (1970). Mass media flow and differential growth of knowledge. *Public Opinion Quarterly, 34,* 159–170.

Tichenor, P. J., Donohue, G. A., & Olien, C. N. (1977). Community research and evaluating community relations. *Public Relations Review, 3,* 96–109.

Tichenor, P. J., Donohue, G. A., & Olien, C. N. (1980). *Community conflict and the press.* Beverly Hills, CA: Sage.

Tilson, D. J., & Stacks, D. W. (1997). To know us is to love us: The public relations campaign to sell a "business-tourist-friendly" Miami. *Public Relations Review, 23,* 95–116

Tinder, G. E. (1980). *Community: reflections on a tragic ideal.* Baton Rouge: Louisiana State University Press.

Toch, H. (1965). *The social psychology of social movements.* Indianapolis, IN: Bobbs-Merrill.

Toffler, A. (1971). *Future shock.* New York: Bantam Books.

Toffler, A. (1982). *The third wave.* New York: Bantam Books.

Tönnies, F. (1988). *Community & society [Gemeinschaft and gesellschaft].* (C. P. Loomis, Trans. & Ed.). Rutgers, NJ: Transaction. (Original work published 1887)

Toth, E. L., & Heath, R. L. (Eds.). (1992). *Rhetorical and critical approaches to public relations.* Hillsdale, NJ: Erlbaum.

Trujillo, N. (1992). White knights, poker games, and the invasion of the carpetbaggers: Interpreting the sale of a professional sports franchise. In E. L. Toth & R. L. Heath (Eds.), *Rhetorical and critical approaches to public relations* (pp. 257–278). Hillsdale, NJ: Erlbaum.

van Es, R., & Meijlink, T. L. (2000). The dialogical turn of public relation ethics. *Journal of Business Ethics, 27,* 69–77.

Van Leuven, J. (1996). Public relations in South East Asia from nation-building campaigns to regional interdependence. In H. M. Culbertson & N. Chen (Eds.), *International public relations: A comparative analysis* (pp. 207–222). Mahwah, NJ: Erlbaum.

Van Leuven, J. K., & Pratt, C. B. (1996). Public relations' role: Realities in Asia and Africa South of the Sahara. In H. M. Culberton &. N. Chen (Eds.), *International public relations: A comparative analysis* (pp. 93–106). Mahwah, NJ: Erlbaum.

Vasquez, G. M. (1994). A homo narrans paradigm for public relations: Combining Bormann's symbolic convergence theory and Grunig's situation theory of publics. *Journal of Public Relations Research, 5,* 201–216.

Vasquez, G. M. (1998, November). *Public relations and community building for a new century.* Paper presented to the annual conference of the National Communication Association, New York.

Vasquez, G. M., & Taylor, M. (2001). Research perspectives on "the public." In R. L. Heath (Ed.), *Handbook of public relations* (pp. 139–154). Thousand Oaks, CA: Sage.

Vercic, D., van Ruler, B., Bütschi, G., & Flodin, B. (2001). On the definition of public relations: A European view. *Public Relations Review, 27,* 373–378.

Viswanath, K., Finnegan, J. R., Jr., Rooney, R., & Potter, J. (1990). Community ties in a rural midwest community and the use of newspapers and cable TV. *Journalism Quarterly, 67,* 899–911.

Viswanath, K., Kosicki, G., Park, E., & Fredin, E. (1993). Community involvement, community boundedness and knowledge gaps. Paper presented to the conference of the Midwest Association for Public Opinion Research, Chicago.

Vrooman, S. S. (2002). Flamethrowers, slashers and witches: Gendered communication in a virtual community. *Qualitative Research Reports in Communication, 2,* 33–41.

Wasko, J., & Mosco, V. (Eds.). (1992). *Democratic communications in the information age.* Norwood, NJ: Ablex.

Wasko, M. W., & Faraj, S. (2000). It is what one does: Why people participate and help others in electronic communities of practice. *Strategic Information Systems, 9,* 155–173.

Watson, N. (1997). Why we argue about virtual community: A case study of the phish.net fan community. In S. G. Jones (Ed.), *Virtual culture: Identity and communication in cybersociety* (pp. 102–132). Thousand Oaks, CA: Sage.

Wellman, B., Salaff, J., Dimitrova, D., Garton, L., Gulia, M., & Haythornthwaite, C. (1996). Computer networks as social networks: Collaborative work, telework and virtual community. *American Review of Sociology, 22,* 213–238.

Weenig, M. (1993). The strength of weak and strong communication ties in a community information program. *Journal of Applied Social Psychology, 23,* 1712–1722.

White, J., & Mazur, L. (1995). *Strategic communication management: Making public relations work.* London: Addison-Wesley.

Whitmayer, C. (1993). *In the company of others: Making community in the modern world.* New York: Tarcher/Perigee.

Williams, F. (1982). *The communications revolution.* Beverly Hills, CA: Sage.

Williams, R. (1967). *Culture and society.* London: Chatto & Windrus.

Wilson, L. J. (1994). The return to gemeinschaft: Toward a theory of public relations and community relations as relationship building. In A. F. Alkhafaji (Ed.), *Business research yearbook: Global business perspectives* (Vol. 1, pp. 135–141). Lanham, MD: University Press of America.

Wilson, L. J. (1996). Strategic cooperative communities: A synthesis of strategic, issue management, and relationship building approaches in public relations. In H. M. Culbertson & N. Chen (Eds.), *International public relations: A comparative analysis* (pp. 67–80). Mahwah, NJ: Erlbaum.

Wilson, L. J. (2000). Building employee and community relationships through volunteerism: A case study. In J. A. Ledingham & S. D. Bruning (Eds.), *Public relations as relationship management: A relational approach to the study of public relations* (pp. 137–144). Mahwah, NJ: Erlbaum.

Wilson, L. J. (2001). Relationships within communities: Public relations in the new century. In R. L. Heath (Ed.), *Handbook of public relations* (pp. 521–526). Thousand Oaks, CA: Sage.

Wilson, L. J. (2002, March). Constructing a socially-responsible organization: A preliminary comparison of corporate community involvement in two study communities. Paper presented to the conference of the Public Relations Society of America Educators Academy, Miami, FL.

Wilson, L. J., & McNiven, M. D. (2001, May). Corporate social responsibility: Good business or true citizenship in strategic cooperative communities. Paper presented to the annual conference of the International Communication Association, Washington, DC.

Wilson, L. J., & Stoker, K. (2000, June). Building strategic cooperative communities: A communitarian perspective of organization-public relationships. Paper presented to Public Relations Division, International Communication Association, Acapulco, Mexico.

Wilson, R. J. (1968). *In quest of community. Social philosophy in the United States, 1860–1920*. New York: John Wiley.

Wright, D. K. (1998). *Corporate communications policy concerning the Internet: A survey of the nation's senior-level corporate public relations officers*. Gainesville, FL: Institute for Public Relations.

Wright, D. K. (2001). *The magic communication machine. Examining the Internet's impact on public relations, journalism and the public*. Gainesville, FL: Institute for Public Relations.

Wolfe, A. (1970). Conditions of community: The case of Old Westbury College. In P. Green & S. Levinson (Eds.), *Power and community: Dissenting essays in political science* (pp. 195–222). New York: Vintage.

Woodward, M. C. (1975). In search of "the public": A rhetorical alternative. *Quarterly Journal of Speech, 61*, 235–249.

Woodward, W. D. (1996). Triadic communication as transactional participation. *Critical Studies in Mass Communication, 13*, 155–174.

Woodward, W. D. (2000). Transactional philosophy as a basis for dialogue in public relations. *Journal of Public Relations Research, 12*, 255–275.

Wuthnow, R. (1989). *Communities of discourse. Ideology and social structure in the Reformation, the Enlightenment and European socialism*. Cambridge, MA: Harvard University Press.

Zarefsky, D. (1995, November 17). *The roots of American community: Carroll C. Arnold distinguished lecture presented at the annual convention of the Speech Communication Association, San Antonio, TX*. [Brochure]. Boston: Allyn & Bacon.

CHAPTER CONTENTS

8 Visual Images of Community: Implications for Communication Research

LAWRENCE J. MULLEN
University of Nevada Las Vegas

This chapter gathers a body of literature from fields that examine communities visually. Works from anthropology, sociology, and documentary photography are brought together to show how such work is relevant to communication studies and, more specifically, to the study of communication and community. The literature is organized into four categories along two dimensions: small scope and large scope as well as gemeinschaft and gesellschaft (small-scope/gemeinschaft, large-scope/gemeinschaft, small-scope/gesellschaft, and large-scope/gesellschaft). This typology is examined for its theoretical qualities and the implications it has for the study of visual images. The second part of the essay examines the visual study of community within the communication field with emphasis on theoretical, methodological, and ethical issues as well as issues pertaining to photographic truth. Visual research methods have the potential to change the way communication and community inquiry are conducted and the way communication and community phenomena are understood.

G ombrich (1982) stated that it is "important to clarify the potentialities of the image in communication, to ask what it can and what it cannot do better than spoken or written language" (p. 137). At the time, he believed that the amount of attention devoted to understanding visual communication was disappointingly small. Since then, the study of visual images in communication has been a growing area of interest. The various visual communication interest groups, commissions, and divisions in the field's associations, journals such as *Visual Communication, Visual Communication Quarterly, Journal of Visual Communication and Image Representation, Journal of Visual Literacy*, and the spate of current books on visual communication and related topics (Barry, 1997; Berger, 1998; Hoffman, 1998; Horn, 1998; Lester, 2003; McQuade & McQuade, 2000; Messaris, 1994, 1997; Morgan & Welton, 1992; Sturken & Cartwright, 2001;

Correspondence: Lawrence J. Mullen, Hank Greenspun School of Communication, University of Nevada Las Vegas, 4505 Maryland Parkway, Box 455007, Las Vegas, NV 89154-5007; email: mullen@ccmail.nevada.edu

Communication Yearbook 28, pp. 281–313

Tufte, 1990, 1997; Zelizer, 1998, 2001; Zettl, 1999) provide evidence for this development.

This essay contributes to this area of research in two ways. First, it creates a typology for organizing visual images of communities. Through categorization and examination of visual methods and photographic data, this analysis of the extant work on community imagery assumes that visual images provide a dimension to our understanding of community that is unlike research data typically used in the communication studies field. Second, it discusses the issues related to the use of visual methods for the communicative study of community. This discussion is meant to support the argument that visual methods not only change the way we understand community, they change the way communication research is conducted and disseminated.

The analysis relies primarily on the work of social documentary photographers and filmmakers, visual sociologists, and visual anthropologists, but the subjects covered are persistent foci in communication and community research. The findings of these bodies of work inform the study of communication and community because they examine such things as cultural change, human interaction, and relationships of various types. Assorted contextual factors that influence who people are and how they interact socially, politically, economically, and communicatively also intersect these areas of study.

Community is defined here by the very techniques of visual analysis. Visual methods require the perception of something resulting in an exposure to a photosensitive surface (digital, chemical, retinal), or in the case of videotape, a magnetic surface. As a result, community is a physical manifestation of some sort. If community is defined in abstract (invisible) terms, then those abstractions need a physical (visible) referent. According to this requirement, visual studies tend to conceptualize community in terms of people and places (i.e., as places where people live and do things).

Research on community as a visual construct takes varied forms. The scope of the communities that have been studied visually is wide-ranging. *The Family of Man* (Steichen, 1955), for example, showed the commonalities of people around the world, or as Steichen wrote in the introduction, "It was conceived as a mirror of the universal elements and emotions in the everydayness of life—as a mirror of the essential oneness of mankind [sic] throughout the world" (¶ 2). This photographic work saw the world population as an extended community.[1] It is one of the few photographic works to define community as such a large, all-encompassing entity. Other visual studies define community in smaller scope such as a country, region, or people (Ewald, 1985; Holdt, 1985; Leigh, 2000; Michaud & Michaud, 2002; Stryker & Wood, 1973); a state or an area of a state (Harper, 1987a; Williams, 2000); a village (Adra, 1998; Bateson & Mead, 1942); a city (Natali, 1972; Schwartz, 1998; Smith, 1984; Tice, 1972); a section of a city (Owens, 1973; Snyder, 1970); a neighborhood (Birenbaum-Carmeli, 1998; Duneier, 1999; Suchar, 1993; van der Does, Edelaar, Goostens, Liefting, & van Mierlo, 1992); or smaller ken such as Jackson's (1977) study of an Arkansas state prison.

For the purposes of this study, the literature is partitioned into four categories along two dimensions. One dimension is based on the scope of the community in question. As mentioned above, some studies examine communities in large scope, anything from a country to a big city. Small-scope studies, on the other hand, look at rural villages, towns, associations, neighborhoods, and small groups of various types. The other dimension, embraced by the communication and community field, is one in which communities have been sociologically observed: gemeinschaft and gesellschaft (Tönnies, 1988).

Gemeinschaft is the traditional sense of community. It describes a type of social relation based on "consensus of wills, resting on harmony, and developed by folkways, mores, and religion" (Simonson, 1996, p. 325). It is connected with a past, disappearing way of life. In contrast, gesellschaft is characterized by independent, self-interested people bound by contract, and connected to an emerging modern order shot through with feelings of anomie. The four categories, then, are:

1. Small-scope community as gemeinschaft. These studies encompass a traditional sense of community within a small geographic region like a village.

2. Large-scope community as gemeinschaft. There are a number of studies that examine the potential for community to form across a large region.

3. Small-scope community as gesellschaft. Studies in this category examine how the traditional sense of community in small geographic regions has broken down and approaches gesellschaft.

4. Large-scope community as gesellschaft. Such studies tend to focus on the effects of urbanization and modernization in the large city setting, but they occasionally examine larger regions as well.

The logic behind sorting the studies along a two-by-two polar-type design is rooted in the belief that the bipolar continuum "is a vital notion in the comparative analysis of social phenomena. The types establish the . . . standards by means of which the processes of change or intermediate structural forms can be comprehended from the perspective of the continuum" (Loomis & McKinney, 1988, p. 12). It is in this heuristic sense that the typologies of gemeinschaft and gesellschaft, and large- and small-scope communities, are important to this endeavor. But more than that, they play a role in the communication process. Casmir (1994) tells us that

> any system of inquiry requires some form of categorization and labeling, as well as an explanation of how and why we used these particular approaches. Communicating requires common terms, common language, and a logical explanation for why we came up with the idea in the first place. (p. 21)[2]

Within each category are the various visual images of communities. What do images contribute to our understanding of communities? As forms of communication, visual representations tell us something about the processes of community change and stability within each category. They carry messages with meanings about a place and its people, and they offer a way to understand reality that differs from verbal and numerical (statistical) explication of social phenomena. After categorizing the images with the four dimensions outlined above, these ideas are discussed in more detail.

VISUALIZING SMALL-SCOPE COMMUNITIES AS GEMEINSCHAFT

"The predominant symbol, metaphor, and model for the logic of real community in America remains the rural agrarian small town" (Robertson, 1980, p. 223), and research on community focuses primarily on centralized, local collectivities where gemeinschaft is likely to be manifested and possibly threatened by modernization or urbanization. A concern seen throughout the visual literature is with the preservation of a disappearing way of life.

Toward the end of the 19th century, "interest in social customs led some photographers to capture on glass plate and film indigenous peoples and folk customs that were in danger of extinction" (Rosenblum, 1989, pp. 347–348). Efforts in Spain and France, for example, were undertaken for a variety of reasons. Some wanted to preserve ancient customs for future generations; some saw urbanization overtaking old folkways and wanted to have some record of vanishing customs and costumes. The images tended to "romanticize handwork and folk mannerisms while seldom suggesting the difficulties and boredom of provincial life" (p. 348). Photographers in the United States were also attempting to preserve vanishing folkways. Between 1895 and 1910, projects by Curtis, Moon, the Flahertys, and Vroman "were designed to play up the positive aspects of tribal life, in particular the sense of community and the oneness of the individual Native American with nature" (p. 348; e.g., Aperture, 1972; Davis, 1985; Lyman, 1982; Webb & Weinstein, 1973). The portraits and arranged group scenes of Southwestern Indians and the close-ups of cheerful Inuit people composed by the Flaherty's reflect a "desire to make their subjects appear palatable to white Americans with strong ethnocentric biases" (Rosenblum, 1989, pp. 348–349).

> As pioneers in the documentary film in the United States in the early 1920s, the Flahertys became known for their ability to give dramatic form to mundane events, and among the 1,500 or so still photographs they made of the Inuit there are works that seem arranged and posed to accord with a concept of their subjects as heroic and energetic peoples. (p. 349)

Like other studies of vanishing cultures, the plot of their movie, *Nanook of the North* (Flaherty, 1922), hinted at that old cliche about the noble savage being pushed towards a civilization that will destroy him (e.g., Barker, 1993; Cheung, 1996; Coles & Harris, 1978). Others did not entirely romanticize their subjects. Vroman, for example, did not "obscure the hardships shaping Indian society of his time. In true documentary fashion, he used the photographs in slide lectures and publications in order to awaken white Americans to the plight of the Native American" (Rosenblum, 1989, p. 349).

In this category of community imagery, anthropological research on primitive communities is prototypical. Many anthropological studies include photographs, but for some the visualization of the people and their culture is central. The seminal work in this area was conducted by Malinowski (1922, 1926, 1927, 1929, 1935). His photo-ethnographic work with the people of the Trobriand Islands has been written about extensively (Coote, 1993; Edwards, 1992; Samian, 1995; Wright, 1991, 1993, 1994; Young, 1998). Despite the importance of imagery and the claim that he achieved a "'maximal symbiosis' between written description and visual representation" (Young, 1998, p. 5), photographs primarily supported the written text.

It was not until Bateson and Mead's (1942) research that photography assumed a dominant role in anthropological research. Since then, very few "have matched the analytic sophistication of Mead and Bateson's pioneering work" (Harper, 1989, p. 85). As they described in the introduction of their book, *Balinese Character*, they used photographs to help overcome some of the shortcomings associated with attempts to describe other cultures with the stylings of another language. The result epitomizes what visual communication can do that verbal communication cannot. Some words, phrases, ideas, behaviors, and feelings are difficult, if not impossible, to describe and verbally translate across cultures. Goffman (1979) said that images can be used when there is "insufficient literary skill to summon up [thoughts] through words alone" (p. 25) and that "verbal glosses can serve as a means to direct the eye to what is to be seen, instead of having to serve as a full rendition of what is at issue" (p. 25).

It was their hope, through the use of photographs, to portray a wholeness to the analysis of the behaviors of the Balinese and their culture. The subject matter of their study ranged from an overview of a typical village community (with the camera recording spatial relationships better than the written word) to other aspects of community life such as cockfighting, sharing and social organization, industrialization, and various rituals such as funerals, marriage, and birthdays. These early anthropological works greatly influenced visual anthropology research that came after it. The influence permeates, for example, Gardner and Heider's (1968) book on a Dani village in a remote area of New Guinea, which resulted in several projects: two books, a feature-length motion picture (*Dead Birds*, Gardner, 1963), and two doctoral dissertations.

In an innovative approach, Berger and Mohr (1967) used a case study method to visually examine an entire rural community. Their pioneering study of an English country doctor used narrative text with accompanying photographs of the doctor, his patients, and the surrounding landscape to tell the story of a poor, rural countryside in England. Likewise, Harper's (1987a) study showed how one person "fits into the 'web of group life'" (p. 1) and how this person's work "was part of a functioning rural neighborhood" (p. 10). Perhaps it is only with rural and small communities that an individual can be a case study for an entire community. Studies in which a single person is used to portray an entire community are relatively rare; however, the study of the traditional sense of community as manifested in poor, rural areas is a recurring theme in this category (e.g., Pierce, 1996).

In this category, one finds some of the seminal work in community visualization. The anthropological work of Malinowski, the Flahertys, and Bateson and Mead as well as the photojournalistic work that attempted to preserve indigenous ways of life laid the foundation for the visual study of community and communication.

VISUALIZING LARGE-SCOPE COMMUNITIES AS GEMEINSCHAFT

As important as research on neighborhoods, towns, local institutions, workplaces, or similar close-knit clusters of people is, it is not the only way to conceptualize community. As a concept, community may also form around larger regions in which a sense of community is, by definition, fragmented and sometimes held together by only the most tenuous of bonds (Cuba, 1987; Cuba & Hummon, 1993; Rothenbuhler & Mullen, 1996). These larger geographies are particularly interesting because only a fraction of the people in a large territory can know one another, and it is principally through communication media and public culture that they can develop any sense of community (Rothenbuhler, 1988a). The territory, its people, and its meaning as a community must be represented by maps, censuses, polls, histories, news, stories (of heroes and other folk legends), museums, and ceremonies (Anderson, 1983; Cohen, 1985; Dayan & Katz, 1988; DeLaurell, 1993; Durkheim, 1912/1965; Halbwachs, 1950/1980; Hummon, 1988; Katz & Dayan, 1986; Rothenbuhler, 1988b, 1989; Shils, 1975).

Studies examining large-scope, gemeinschaft communities include the photographic research on the Andean Highlands Indians (Collier & Buitrón, 1949) and the Maya descendants, the Zinacantecos, of southeastern Mexico (Cancian, 1974). This research goes back to P. H. Emerson's photographic images of 19th-century East Anglia (Newhall, 1975), William P. Frith's paintings of British Victorian society (Herrmann, 2000), and even as early as Pieter Bruegel's paintings of peasant society of the 16th century (Kavaler, 1999; Orenstein, 2001; Roberts-Jones & Roberts-Jones, 2002; Stechnow & Bruegel, 1990; Sullivan, 1994) to find portrayals of larger society as a cohesive whole in the visual media.

The intention of some of these works is not academic study, yet the images resonate with widely held ideas associated with communication and community research. Emerson's photographs of rural life in late Victorian-era England and Bruegel's paintings, for example, were intended as art, but they also depict community life.

Emerson was one of the first photographers to photograph in society rather than in the studio. His images are of specific class-bound locations or activities: eel fishermen at work, village cottages, details of working-class life such as fish processing or sail making, and the leisure activities of the bourgeoisie such as sailing matches and snipe hunting. (Harper, 1989, p. 83)

In America, some of the more well-known examples include the nostalgic and mythic imagery of Norman Rockwell (Bauer, 1996; Buechner, 1972; Rockwell,

1988) and the Farm Security Administration's images of the Great Depression (Anderson, 1940; Stryker & Wood, 1973).

A few studies examine the visual nature of community life in a state or large area of a state. Adelman (1972) documented life in rural Wilcox County in Alabama. Coles and Harris (1973) studied the elderly Spanish-speaking people of New Mexico, primarily in the area north of Albuquerque. Ganzel (1984) looked at the American Midwest, Leigh (2000) studied the South, and Williams (2000) examined the contrasting aspects of work in Texas. The tenuous bond created by bringing a group of images together in a bound volume makes it appear as though the authors attempted to portray a sense of community writ large.

Cities, in general, present a problem in classification. Some studies portray communal cohesiveness and others depict the divisiveness of city life. Regardless, cities remain a popular topic of visual research. Even the popular media have explored the issues surrounding city life and the community experience, as did HBO's *A City on Fire: The Story of the '68 Detroit Tigers* (2002). This documentary told the story of Detroit's turbulent racial problems of the late 1960s and how a baseball team brought the city together, if only for a brief time. Schwartz's (1998) study of the impact of the Super Bowl on the St. Paul/Minneapolis area also fits this category.

Perhaps no city has been as visually documented as New York City (Abbott, 1939; Feininger, 1978; Hunstein, 1962; Lehnartz, 1969; Lightfoot, 1981). In fact, a whole cottage industry has been built on the photo-documentation of life in and around New York City (e.g., catalogue of works at Dover Publications). This body of work is primarily historically descriptive and, although other interpretations are possible, one could say that the images depict the city as gemeinschaft, but multiple readings are always a possibility when visual images are used to communicate the meaning of a place.

The polysemic nature of the image is discussed in more detail below, but in general, a diversity of community imagery and meaning characterizes this category. Some of the images included in this category are borderline cases (i.e., they were difficult to classify in terms of gemeinschaft or gesellschaft). Large-scope communities require some sort of mediation for any sense of community to be communicated across significant distances—visual images play an important role in defining a large community.

VISUALIZING SMALL-SCOPE COMMUNITIES AS GESELLSCHAFT

A large body of research on American communities has examined the decline of traditional community, or the transition from gemeinschaft to gesellschaft in small towns, villages, and associations of various sorts. Of concern are the patterns of this transition, the influence of change on the relationships between people, the ways in which they interrelate with each other, their work, and other facets of life. The anomic tendencies of gesellschaft are, for example, portrayed in Clark's (1971) photographs of a community of drug addicts in Tulsa, Oklahoma. Also anomic is

Jackson's (1977) study of prison life at the Cummins prison farm in Grady, Arkansas. Active and loud, the densely populated prison is "nonetheless a terribly lonely place" (Jackson, 1977, p. 17).

Other studies in this category come in many forms. An American Legion Post was the nexus for studying the changing social and cultural dynamics of everyday life in a community in rural northeastern Iowa (Schwartz, 1989). In the face of declining involvement with the association, Schwartz documented the community's activities, or lack thereof. Similarly, Lyon's (1969) *The Destruction of Lower Manhattan* focused, as it sounds, on the decline of a community that had been around since the Civil War. Some parts of the area had been in commercial use since 1812, yet modern society had no use for the community, except to level it and start anew. The Washington Street produce market was a bustling business area during those early days. Later, restaurants and other commercial ventures took over the street-level parts of the buildings, and the upper floors were rented out. At the time of Lyon's photographic venture, the last of the loft-occupying tenants were being evicted. The only inhabitants of the community remained the homeless, urban explorers, and demolition workers. His images are primarily of the community's space, the buildings, street configurations, building interiors, and various architectural qualities, but there are several shots of demolition crew workers and sundry other people. It is an examination of the final stage of a community's demise.[3]

Anomie and communal disintegration are also seen in several other photographic works. Copeland's (1969) *People's Park* documented the social upheaval surrounding a communal park in Berkeley, California, in the 1960s. Snyder's (1970) *Haymarket* took a reminiscent visual journey to the market area of Boston that no longer exists. Her photographs foretold the ultimate demise of the place. Davidson's (1970) study of a community in East Harlem, New York, also depicted the anomic tendencies of gesellschaft. Owens's (1973) study of suburban life in Livermore, California, is an interesting study because it does not, at first, appear to side one way or another on the dimension of gemeinschaft or gesellschaft. The images and the text, however, depict a general sense of anomie and disjuncture among the suburban residents: "You assume the mask of suburbia for outward appearances and yet no one knows what you really do" (Owens, 1973, caption, unnumbered). Though more concerned with sociological method, Margolis (1994) examined archival images of Colorado coal mining camps where people lived in constant, sometimes violent, struggle with management. Anomie and the fated struggle to maintain old ways of life have also been visually examined in the lives of the well-off (e.g., Estrin, 1979; Suchar, 1993).

As with rubberneckers at a car wreck, people feel an almost undeniable need to see a community in struggle or in a dilapidated state. Besides documentation, another function of photographs may be to satisfy this need. As with small gemeinschaft communities, the visual portrayal of a small gesellschaft community in several of the above cases relied on the photographers being intimately connected to the place they are photographing. The difference may, arguably, lie in the photographer's origins. Researchers come from outside the community to study its gemeinschaft qualities, whereas photographers from within a community photograph the community's gesellschaft qualities. In other words, in many of the studies in this category, the photographer lived or had lived in the community he or she photographed. Owens (1973) lived in the community he studied; Snyder (1970) worked in the Haymarket district before she started taking photographs; and Clark (1971) was a drug addict himself and lived with the community he later photographed. One can only speculate what this means, but one possibility might be linked to the nature of gesellschaft itself. Gesellschaft communities may not be open or easily revealed to an outsider. The independent, self-interested nature of such communities may shut out others who wish to understand them visually. Many assume that only people who have belonged to the community can photograph it in a meaningful way.

VISUALIZING LARGE-SCOPE COMMUNITIES AS GESELLSCHAFT

Early work in the United States by Riis (1890, 1892) and Hine (see Gutman, 1967; Rosenblum, Rosenblum, & Trachtenberg, 1977) visually documented the plight of the poor, neglected, and abused. Not only were Riis and Hine documenting these social ills, they were also providing information about the communal living conditions of industrial society and the effects of a nefarious gesellschaft. What was life like for the less fortunate? How did they live and work? Riis's answers came in his images of tenement life in New York City. Hine's pictures more broadly illustrated the conditions in which people worked. More famous for his photographic work of child labor, Hine took on American industrialism as it manifested itself in cities along the Eastern seaboard, Chicago, and places in Mississippi, Oklahoma, Texas, Tennessee, and West Virginia (e.g., Guimond, 1991).

Truth, objectivity, and bias are concepts tied to the style of documentary photography that Riis and Hine pioneered. The concept of truth and its relation to photographic images are discussed later in this chapter; briefly stated, the study of community, whether sociologically, anthropologically, or communicatively based, usually adheres to the ideals of truth. There are times, however, when there is a less-than-objective purpose in mind. Riis's (1900) study of the poor community, for example, had the purpose of exposing subhuman living conditions and denouncing rich absentee landlords of New York City.

Riis and Hine had distinctive approaches to photography that were not clearly defined until the 1930s (Rosenblum, 1989). It was at this time that

> photography historian Beaumont Newhall noted that while the social documentary photographer is neither a mere recorder nor an "artist for art's sake, his reports are often brilliant technically and highly artistic"—that is, documentary images involve imagination and art in that they imbue fact with feeling. (p. 341)

There is a commitment to the betterment of the human condition, exposing fraud and moral wrongs, often with a sense of passion.

One of the earliest works in this vein was Federic Thrasher's (1936) systematic documentation of 1,313 gangs in Chicago. The photos are not the central part of the study, but they are informative and provide the reader with a visual reference that goes beyond the text to give a better sense of the time, setting, clothes, and physical expressions of the gang members. Later that decade, James Agee and Walker Evans's (1939) work, *Let Us Now Praise Famous Men*, examined life in the poverty-stricken rural South through its documentation of the lives of three families. Reproduced through the courtesy of the Farm Security Administration, United States Department of Agriculture, the captionless photographs depicted the people, their homes, and other details of itinerant farm life in and around the years of the Great Depression.

The 1950s' sense of declining community in large scope was captured by Robert Frank (1958). His work, *The Americans*, displayed people at lunch counters, each looking straight ahead, nearly touching, yet ignoring their neighbors. It shows symbols of American culture such as patriotic statues isolated in the middle of concrete parking lots—certainly a commentary (if not analysis of) social or moral disintegration in American culture (Harper, 1989).

A previous section of this chapter looked at cities as gemeinschaft, or being cohesive with a traditional sense of community. Cities are classified here as gesellschaft, and perhaps this is the most practical way to conceptualize the sense of community in the city. Robertson (1980) agreed when he wrote:

> [L]ife in the modern city or its suburbs is, for most, a sharp contrast to the ideal, to the myth of the peaceful, neighborly, unified, cooperative *real* community, the *American* small-town community. . . . For the majority of Americans who live in cities, the images and symbols of community are fragmented. (p. 224)

The quintessential work in the genre of city as gesellschaft was Eugene Atget's images of Paris (Abbot, 1979; Adam, 2001; Szarkowski & Hambourg, 1981, 1982, 1984, 1985; Trottenberg, 1963). He was one of the first to visually document city life and his photographs served at least two purposes. First, he offered his photographs to artists and craftsman to serve as studies for their work. Second, and more importantly for the task at hand, he began systematically documenting what was known as "Old Paris" before the government began rebuilding and renovating the city. He led the way in documenting the changing social conditions in an urban setting. In effect, he documented a changing way of life: from gemeinschaft to gesellschaft, from old folkways to modern ways of life in Paris at the end of the 19th century. Since Atget, few works have been as methodical, but there are studies that portray a declining sense of citywide community (e.g., Stummer, 1994; Tice, 1972).

With the intention of engendering social change, W. Eugene Smith and Aileen M. Smith (1975) photographed the struggle of the poor fisher folks of the city of

Minamata, Japan, against a chemical company, Chisso, which was poisoning the waters they fished. Here Smith and Smith captured how a work of photographic documentation can, in a very real way, light the fires of social change. They documented the subsequent health problems and complexities surrounding the conflict. They approached the problems associated with truth and photographic documentation by stating up front that their effort was not objective. In this way they believed that they could best document the events and move the viewers of their images to act on the social injustice perpetrated on this community. Despite the images of a community working together to fight a large company, this study is classified here because of the overall sense of damage done to the community and seen through the images of broken human bodies caused by ingesting the chemical pollutants as well as the general sense that the community was depleted even after winning its fight against the company.

Like the small-scope/gemeinschaft category, this category contains pioneering work that visually depicts communities. The works of Riis (1890, 1892, 1900) and Hine (Guimond, 1991; Gutman, 1967; Rosenblum et al., 1977) laid the framework for future muckraking photojournalists. Atget, Frank, and Thrasher were also seminal in terms of social documentation of large-scale communities. In general, this category of community imagery seemed to draw together important and sometimes multivolume works. One might surmise that large communities lend themselves to such tomes. Perhaps large communities, which naturally engender frayed communal bonds, necessitate the use of social artifacts such as photographs to provide some sense of community. Whatever the reason, this category contains some significant work relevant to the study of communication and community.

THEORETICAL IDEAS ABOUT THE CATEGORIES
AND VISUAL IMAGES

What does the categorizing scheme say about the use of visual images to portray communal life? As a heuristic device, the taxonomy is but one way to organize images of community. It could be thought of as "a way of looking rather than a reproduction of reality" (Littlejohn, 2002, p. 32). It is a step in the direction of understanding the meaning of visual images of communities, but it is admittedly tentative and qualified. The images, as with reality, can be interpreted in a variety of ways. Other bipolar typologies such as Emile Durkheim's (1933) mechanical and organic solidarity, Robert Redfield's (1947) folk-urban continuum, and Howard Paul Becker's (1968) sacred and secular society's might have substituted for Tönnies's (1988) gemeinschaft and gesellschaft binary, or the large-scope and small-scope continuum. Future researchers should explore these alternative categorization schemes. In terms of theoretical development, the scheme used for this study enables an understanding of the relationships among visual images, communication, and community.

Moreover, any scheme chosen to categorize visual images of community might be as tenuous, (at times) ambiguous, and open as the one used here—not because the categories are unclear or incorrectly contrived, but because visual images, like all symbolic modes of communication, are multidimensional and polysemic. This serves to highlight the "limitations of our perceptual, descriptive, and explanatory capabilities" (p. 16), especially when it comes to visual imagery and their associated methods (Casmir, 1994). Visual images, in other words, cause researchers problems when it comes to categorization. This, however, should not discourage any attempt to understand them as social phenomena.

In terms of the photographic techniques used to portray community, the visual images are, in a sense, categorically interchangeable (i.e., the same types of visual techniques or aesthetic design can be found across the categories).[4] Are dark, shadowy images used primarily for portraying the anomic tendencies of gesellschaft? Although the technique was a characteristic of some images classified as gesellschaft, one can also find dark imagery in the gemeinschaft categories. Pictorial or textual codes (Chaplin, 1994) or any aesthetic technique or style (Dondis, 1973) might play a role in the way the images are interpreted and classified. Dark, shadowy images might connote a sense of anomie. On the other hand, a very brightly lit image can portray a sense of sterility in the environment, making it, in a sense, look like an uninhabitable place. A shallow depth of field can be used to portray a sense of shallowness to life, or a lack of focus beyond the subject's immediate environment. Close-up images depict a sense of emotion and identification between the person photographed and the viewer, but what this says in terms of classification along the gemeinschaft-gesellschaft or small-scope–large-scope dimension is ambiguous. It is difficult, then, to draw well-defined lines of meaning based on these aesthetic factors because they cut across the categories of gemeinschaft and gesellschaft, as well as large and small communities.

Representational content can play a categorizing role. A collection of images of a decrepit city, with pictures of people looking unhappy, might be classified in the large-scope/gesellschaft category, but the reason for their unhappiness would need to be determined. Unhappiness may be connected with a ritual that helps define the community in a traditional gemeinschaft way. A photographer's intent, though not always clear (or necessary) in the categorizing process, can play a role in one's categorical decision making as well. Through the images, the photographer chooses to communicate based on a project's overall goal that the viewer/interpreter forms his or her meanings of the community. The photographer may, for example, explicitly attempt to portray the aesthetic look of destruction and anomie (gesellschaft) or preserve traditional images of the old ways (gemeinschaft). Such explicit information can help the categorizing decision, but it is not the primary determinant.

Messaris (1992) argued that knowing what images mean can only be ascertained when we investigate how people, places, and actions within the images are positioned relative to the viewer. He outlined three roles that visual images play: They can elicit emotions by simulating the appearance of a real object (i.e., this is a real place that has the properties of a community); they serve as visual proof that something really did happen (i.e., the events depicted really happened in this community); and they can establish an implicit link between the thing that is represented in the picture and some other image (i.e., the picture may relate to a mental image the viewer has of the community, or one photograph may depict a community at one time and an adjacent photograph shows the community at a later time—in the sense of historical change—thus giving the viewer a chance to compare the images (see Chung, 2002). Messaris (1997) argued that "these three functions of . . . images stem from underlying, fundamental characteristics of visual communication—characteristics that define the essential nature of images and distinguish them from the other modes of human communication" (p. vii).

Like any communicative message, pictures can be described in terms of either semantic or syntactic properties. Semantic analysis focuses on the elements of a particular mode of communication (e.g., images and words) and their meanings. Syntactic analysis examines the interrelationships among the elements as they combine to form larger units of meaning.

The semantic properties of visual messages (or any message) are the particular concern of fields such as semiotics, the study of signs and their associated signifiers and signified. Simply stated, the various schools of thought in the field of semiotics offer systematic ways to examine the semantic properties of images (e.g., Barthes, 1972; Clarke, 1987; Eco, 1979; Hervey, 1982; Krampen, Oehler, Posner, Sebeok, & von Uexküll, 1987; Lacan, 1977; Wiener, 1966). The literature is somewhat less methodical and less developed when it comes to the syntactic aspects of images. As Messaris (1997) indicated, "There is a lack of explicit means for identifying other ways in which images might be related to each other" (p. x). Verbal communication has words and sentence structures (a propositional syntax) that allow one to make clear the kinds of connections being proposed in a statement. Visual images have no such syntax. "Whereas spatial and temporal connections can be presented quite explicitly through images, visual communication does not have an explicit syntax for expressing analogies, contrasts, causal claims, and other kinds of propositions" (p. xi). As a result, images can take on a life of their own and influence various aspects of life itself.[5] As representations of a community, photographs and various other forms of visual imagery do not merely

> reflect their sources but refashion them . . . so that they are quite separate from, and other than, those sources. Further, "representation" can be understood as articulating and contributing to social processes. Social processes determine the representation but are consequently influenced and altered by it. Thus, representations articulate not only visual . . . codes and conventions but also the social practices and forces which underlie them, with which we interpret the world. (Chaplin, 1994, p. 1)

Not only are gemeinschaft and gesellschaft, as well as large-scope and small-scope communities, analytical categories used for this analysis, but they are also social processes that influence the images within each category.[6] Moreover, the images influence the social processes as well (in the sense that images affect perceptions, behaviors, attitudes, beliefs, and opinions toward community).[7]

This sort of circular thinking—in which the community influences the photographic images, which in turn influence the community—is part and parcel of the constitutive role of theory in social life as discussed by Craig (1993): "Theory, on this view, influences how people in society think and talk about their own activities and thereby shapes those activities and the emergent social structures produced and reproduced by them" (p. 30). Such a theory, however, runs counter to scientific forms of explanation in which

> a theory that actively shapes the very phenomena it purportedly explains is essentially untestable and thus irreparably unscientific. Any observations that might be adduced to test predictions derived from such a theory are hopelessly contaminated, and the logic of explanation falls into a vicious circle. (p. 30)

The most logical way out of this dilemma, as Craig expressed it, is to "embrace the constitutive potential of theory and to take due responsibility for its consequences" (p. 31). This means that the conventional aspects of explanation, prediction, and control become theoretically inadequate, which opens the possibility for aesthetic, moral, and political values for theories that become integral components of an engaged social practice.

The constitutive relationship between visual images and the things they represent is evident in other fields such as medical diagnostics, surveillance, astronomy, physics, and other domains of knowledge.[8] As with these fields, visual imagery used in communication research will affect the approach taken to understand the relationship between communication and community. Visual methods change the way one does communication research. Just the act of conceptualizing communities as visual constructs, as was done in the above literature review, brought together disparate, but related bodies of knowledge in a new and different way. There were some problems and discrepancies in the categorization scheme, but that is an aspect of the problematic nature of visual images themselves.

The second part of this essay goes into more detail on the problems associated with visual images as research data and addresses the issues concerning the relationship between visual images and communication and community research. How do the techniques of visual analysis influence communication research?

VISUAL METHODS AND COMMUNICATION
AND COMMUNITY RESEARCH

Despite the increased interest in visual communication, the use of visual methods and photographic data remains largely marginalized in the communication field.[9] To understand why, one might reexamine the social scientific roots of the discipline and ask: What if Marx and Engels (Engels, 1968; Marx & Engels, 1965;

Marx, 1967), for example, had used photography in their analyses of the working class and capitalism? What if Durkheim (1951), who gave very explicit and vivid descriptions of the collective and individual states of anomie, had used photographic evidence? Would their research have benefited? The work of the early social documentary photographers, at least in part, leads one to answer yes. The photographic work of Hine and Riis, for example, showed the conditions of the working class, urban squalor, the working conditions of children and other subjects that are part and parcel of the theories of Marx, Engels, and Durkheim.

The community studies tradition of the 1930 and 1940s, upon which the study of communication and community is largely based, might also have used visual methods, but did not. The Lynds's (1929, 1937) studies of Muncie, Indiana, may have been enriched by photographic documentation of work, neighborhood development, or the house interiors of different social classes. The research tradition developed at the University of Chicago also did not include photographic methods, thus casting the original definition of community research in terms that excluded a meaningful visual component. By the end of World War II,

> survey methods and other approaches that distanced the researcher from the subject had come to dominate American sociology. The research program of sociology became the examination of statistical patterns among variables rather than the description of social life woven so convincingly into the earlier community studies and fieldwork traditions. (Harper, 1989, p. 85)

Even though the contemporary restudy of Muncie included still photographs and five films (Caplow, Bahr, Chadwick, Hill, & Williamson, 1982), community studies do not make use of visual documentation, especially in the domain of communication studies. Frank's photographic essay of America in the 1950s "had a profound effect on how Americans have looked at themselves" (Harper, 1989, p. 83), but most of his and similar work have been lost on communication researchers. Deep with meaning, his work visually chronicled the culture of a people in the decade of the 1950s, yet no measure of its credibility is available to communication researchers.

The discipline tends to marginalize the use of visual data, and so there is a lack of knowledge about the criteria that make a good photographic analysis, the ways photography is used theoretically to make useful observations, or the relevant variables:

> The camera is merely a means through which an informed vision can be made concrete. Unfortunately (depending on your point of view), we do not train our students to use this technology, aside from a small number of courses and workshops. (Harper, 1989, p. 87)

Consequently, the field remains largely unprepared to evaluate photographic research. For these reasons it is difficult to establish one's academic reputation using visual techniques. One's peers are less able to judge critically research based on visual data than they are able to evaluate more conventional research. Indeed, the "concept of 'visual data' has never really been thoroughly explicated" (Emmison & Smith, 2000, p. 3; e.g., Rose, 2001).

A recurring issue associated with the use of images as research data, and another reason why visual techniques are not used more often, revolve around the related ideas of truth, reality, and meaning:

> One should be able to say that a photograph in effect can provide us with an objective, veridical version—an "actual picture of" socially important aspects of what is in fact out there. . . . However, these conclusions . . . fail to tell us why there should be so much doubt and concern among students as to what in fact photographs do represent. (Goffman, 1979, p. 12; see also Pinney, 1992)

Those who make the claim that a photograph portrays reality suggest that an image shows what actually existed in front of a camera for the moment necessary to make an exposure, and that the image is of something that would have occurred in the ordinary course of events regardless of the photographer's presence. They also suggest that the image portrays some essential feature of the phenomenon, that some fundamental quality was captured, or that the photograph shows what is ordinarily hidden from view and the photographer revealed it for us to see. That a picture truly portrays someone, an event, or a place is, however, uncertain at best (Becker, 1974, 1986). There are incidents in the area of documentary photography that begin to erode truth claims. Allegedly candid photos have been later found to have been posed (e.g., Scherer, 1975). Another form of erosion to truth claims is more insidious because it places the whole idea of reality in question. Could someone else photograph the same people, place, or event and produce a different statement of social reality? The answer is necessarily yes. There are infinite ways to alter an image through exposure time, camera angle, framing, and other forms of composition, not to mention the type of digital manipulation that can occur with today's cameras and computer software (for related ideas, see Newton, 2000; Schwartz, 1999). Some of the problems related to photographic truth might be solved with a better use of theory and method.

Theory

> The work of social documentary photographers suffers . . . from its failure to use explicit theories, such as might be found in social science. . . . The theories photographers rely on are, not surprisingly, lay theories, the commonplace of everyday life in the intellectual and artistic circles they move in. . . . They use the ideas and attitudes that are making the rounds in order to organize their own seeing . . . photographs of Harlem residents tend to revolve around such ideas as 'Look how these people suffer' and 'Look how noble these people are in the face of their suffering. . . . It is not that these things are incorrect or that for any reason they should not be said. But they are not sufficiently complex to sustain the weight of a real exploration of society, which will inevitably show that things are more complicated. (Becker, 1986, pp. 243–244)

Training in communication studies, which presumably fills the head with theories, will not necessarily improve the theoretical content of one's photographs. Theory does not automatically shape what one creates, but works only when it is deliberately put to work and consciously brought into play.

Becker (1986) examined how traditional research, which relies on verbal and numerical data and the conceptualization and operationalization of concepts, differs from research relying on visual data. Traditionally, the deductive approach to research starts with a general, abstract idea and moves to specific observable phenomena in the form of indicators, indices, or embodiments of some sort. Photographers, conversely, work along inductive lines, moving from specific images to general ideas. It is as though photographers strive for a cumulative effect through their images: They might display an image of a person in a rumpled suit and tie, then his wife in a dirty, torn burlap dress, then the unsmiling, shoeless children, then their rough-shod home with barren wood floor and walls, and then the family working in the field. Cumulatively, such images say something about a life of poverty in the rural American South of the 1930s (e.g., Agee & Evans, 1939).

An inductive approach is important to photographic research. Take the concept of community involvement, a concept central to communication and community research, which has been conceived as a cognitive and active interaction between self and community (e.g., Rothenbuhler, Mullen, DeLaurell, & Ryu, 1996). It implies that someone thinks about community affairs, stays caught up with the news, and interacts with other people in the community on issues, problems, and sundry other activities. Does this concept have a visual counterpart? No single image could embody all that this concept means; however, if one were to collect several images of communal interaction—such as attendance at a county meeting, going to church, attendance at a Boy Scout meeting, reading a newspaper—all of these images might begin to portray visually the idea that there is a sense of community established through these various community-based activities (i.e., the activities that involve a person with the community).

Obviously, not every research idea needs to be connected to a visual image to be useful or valid. Some researchers say that a basic problem of empirical research is finding observable indicators in real life to measure a concept whose meaning has been defined. A sizable literature discusses the logic by which the two can be defensibly linked. As the example of community involvement suggests, something else is at work here: The basic imagery we intuitively supply to fill out the meaning of an abstract concept is operationally defined. Becker (1986) argued that the logic by which we connect concepts and indicators to imagery, or the procedures by which we develop that imagery explicitly and connect it defensibly to concepts and indicators, is seldom considered. Considering the processes by which photographic imagery arises may help us understand what is involved. These processes are considered presently.

The imagery underlying a communication research concept implies, if not stated explicitly, a picture of people acting together. It may picture them engaged in an everyday form of social interaction, or lend a more mechanistic vision in which people are conceptualized as members of an aggregate rather than an interactive group. In both cases, the concept and its indicators evoke an image of social life even when the language of operational definitions is used.

> The fidelity of that imagery to the realities of social life is, as Herbert Blumer (1969) has emphasized, an important issue in assessing the utility of a concept. . . . We can easily judge for ourselves how well the abstract concept and the empirical indicators mesh with the imagery. Where the underlying imagery is left implicit, the reader invents his own and the critical assessment of that relationship tends not to occur. (Becker, 1986, p. 263)

With the tendency to discuss concepts in purely verbal and logical ways, divorced from empirical reality, there is a lack of dispute over the meaning of theoretical concepts. Photographic research does not have this problem. Photographers, in fact, work in the opposite direction, finding concepts that express the important elements of the image they produce. The inability to express explicit concepts and theories can hamper the development of photographic analysis—Messaris (1994) made similar arguments about what pictures can and cannot do—but over time good photographers refine what they create. They may photograph people, places, and events again and again in order to clarify their ideas. They approach this task visually by "stripping away extraneous elements so that the statement the image makes communicates its substance efficiently and emphatically to the viewer" (Becker, 1986, p. 264).

Method

Visual research of communities also suffers from methodological shortcomings. In his study of community disintegration, Lyon (1969) wrote:

> While I photograph in a quasi-systematic way, the successful pictures must fall where they will. I have to have an adequate picture of at least some of the buildings, that is pictures of their exterior, something of the inside, some details from the inside, a photograph showing where it stood in relation to the others, and a picture of it during demolition. But to do this for every building on the block is impossible. The fact is that most of the buildings are very similar. (p. 6)

Another photographer stated another haphazard methodological approach:

> My daily routine took me into the homes of hundreds of families and into contact with the social life of three suburban communities. . . . To me nothing seemed familiar, yet everything was very, very familiar. At first I suffered from culture shock. I wanted to photograph everything, thousands of pictures. Then slowly I began to put my thoughts and feelings together and to document Americans in Suburbia. It took two years. (Owens, 1973, ¶ 10).

The methodological problem these examples illustrate is the idea of sampling. Sampling relates to the generalizability of an image or images. If the visual data were gathered at some other time, from another angle, at a different shutter speed, with more or less saturated colors, or with more depth of field, would the results change significantly? Unlike communication scientists, who apply research methods to enhance the possibility of a generalizable sample,

> photographers are seldom concerned with quantitative generalizations, or with covering some theoretical map adequately. But they often present their material in a way that suggests they believe that what they show us applies to a far wider area and population than the one they have covered, that were we to look at a different part of the same whole, we would see more of the same. (Becker, 1986, p. 253)

A field researcher, not using photography, may use crude time-sampling devices in which he or she will check up on an individual or place in a given time interval over a day, week, or year. Some may attach themselves to an individual and follow them around to record their routine in detail so as not to leave anything out of the analysis. They may ask those to suggest others for them to study. Then, as they become more aware of categories or situations that deserve attention, they can systematically choose some to observe or observe them all. Field researchers record everything they see and hear while making these observations. Those using visual methods may utilize similar methods, but as Becker (1986) mentioned, "They would need to observe some discipline equivalent to incorporating everything into field notes, for a photographer's data do not exist unless they expose some film" (p. 253). Becker also suggests that the photographer might adopt the convention of exposing at least one roll of film over an appropriate time frame, which would depend on the subject they were observing. This helps avoid the tendency of waiting until something interesting happens. Such a method also helps to increase the chance that things that do not yet fit the researcher's understanding of the subject nevertheless get into the record. One might develop other ways to interfere with the tendency to shoot only that which is interesting (see Collier, 1974). Adopting a theory is a good way to overcome this problem. Theory itself is a sampling device, specifying what must be incorporated into a full description and directing the photographer to things intuition and visual sense might not call to his or her attention.

Following some of these procedures might, as Becker (1986) warned, "produce a lot of dull pictures, but so do most procedures; exciting and informative photographs are always hard to come by" (p. 253). Nevertheless, snapping what seems to be interesting is the usual method of choice for photographers. What this leads to is the production of the same type of picture in a variety of settings because, as Becker says, "their notion of what is visually interesting has become divorced from the social reality they are working in" (p. 254). A systematic method helps to break this tendency.

"For photographers, 'framing'—choosing what will go inside the bright line of the viewfinder—is one of the key decisions" (Becker, 1986, p. 264). Everything cannot be included in a study, no matter the method. Some aspects of a community will be photographed and studied and others will not. How would Riis's documentation of the urban poor been affected had he included pictures of the landlords who profited from the rent collected from the rundown, non-maintained buildings in which people lived? He might have made a more condemning indictment of the whole system.

Something will, however, always lie beyond the frame. The photographer may choose to invoke the reality that lies beyond the frame, or not, simply by the chosen way to frame what is included. In other words, a picture can be self-contained, or include things that extend beyond the frame. For example, in photographing a person, one can include the whole person, or cut the person off at the waist to suggest going beyond the frame to a world beyond what is pictured. Further, part of the person's setting—such as home or workplace—might be made visible within the frame to show the context in which the person lives and works. The ability to suggest that there is a reality beyond the frame is one characteristic of visual methods that tends not to be the case in traditional social science research. In most traditional forms of research the preference is to broach only that which is scientifically examined. Implicit in the traditional methods of researchers is a built-in ignorance of things that lie beyond the frame,

> ignoring even what they do know by casual observation or in some other informal way. Instead of building such partial knowledge into their analyses, they rely on time-honored verbal formulae (e.g., "all other things being equal") to limit and frame their analyses. (Becker, 1986, pp. 266–267)

As part of the rhetoric of contemporary science, this may lead to defensible statements, but little more.

Other methodological questions concern the idea of reactivity. The issues surrounding reactivity involve the question of whether the sample of behavior observed and recorded accurately reflects how people ordinarily act or how they respond to the observer's presence and activities? Addressing this question involves the art of being unobtrusive. How does the photographer get the people being observed to largely ignore her or him? As Becker (1986) tells us, how this is done is not explicitly known and deserves investigation. Here are some ways one might achieve unobtrusiveness:

1. Recording people or events in an unfamiliar public space may, at times, make being unobtrusive easier. There are instances in which a camera may actually validate a person's right to use it (e.g., as a tourist, a member of a group recording a scene for specific purposes, or a member of the media).

2. There are some situations in which the person being observed is engaged in an activity of such importance that they cannot change their behavior for the benefit of the photographer even if they want to.

Reactivity depends on the freedom of those observed to respond to the observer's (or photographer's) presence. If they are enmeshed in the constraints of the social structure in which they carry on their normal activities, they will have to carry on as they ordinarily do for whatever reason causes them to do that ordinarily. . . . They may be well aware that they are being observed or photographed, but not be free to change what they do. (Becker, 1986, pp. 255–258)

Becker gives the example of a woman reprimanding a child on a playground with a photographer practically on top of them, "but the child was kicking and screaming and, though she had no idea who he was, she felt she had no choice but to deal with the child despite the unwelcome recording going on" (p. 258).

3. If the photographer can convince the observed person or people that the photographs he or she is taking will not be used to harm them— and maintain a line of communication regarding what the investigator is doing, and why certain things need to be photographed, while asking for feedback about photographs already taken and other matters—then the observed person or group may choose to ignore the photographer.

4. With time, the photographer may blend in and become part of the observed person's natural environment.

5. A final possibility is to encourage reactivity and make it the basis of the exploration of people and events. The photographs then become a record of the relationship between the observed and the observer. The reaction of the people to being photographed becomes the focus of the analysis.

The problem of reactivity comes up in all sorts of research designs. One of the problems with survey research, for example, is that people are asked for their opinions of things about which they may have had no opinion until the questionnaire arrives. It is also a chief element in studies of experimenter bias.

A final methodological issue concerns the concept of research style. Although it is changing somewhat in recent years with the acceptance of such methods as auto-ethnography, style, in traditionally accepted research design and writing, is one of impersonality. One is taught to separate oneself from one's research in order to make it more objective or less biased. In many of the photographic works reviewed here, impersonality is not a characteristic. Such work often borders on the level of art or is art; photographers of such work accept the responsibility for the personally expressive component of their work. "Accepting that status allows them the quasi-mystical retreat from analyzing the social components of their work and the emphasis on intuitive inarticulateness" (Becker, 1986, p. 268). This type of stylistic treatment is evident in the FSA work of Walker Evans and the respect with which he chose to portray the rural poor (e.g., Agee & Evans, 1939). One might see an impersonal side to traditional, verbal research through the use of adjectives, rhetorical tropes such as irony, or through the ways in which comparative work is done (what one chooses to compare a research subject to can add a personal statement to the work).

Some photographers avoid the variety of theoretical and methodological issues by not making the claim of truth or objectivity (e.g., Smith & Smith, 1975). Rather the only truth in their image is how the phenomenon "felt" to them. This makes the photograph what Becker (1986) calls "the visual analogue of something like a lyric poem," with truth lying in the honest rendering of the photographer's feelings and responses.

The various theoretical and methodological issues associated with visual research attempt to address the issues of truth, reality, and meaning in a photograph. However, a photograph's ability to "blur truth and fiction is one of its most compelling qualities" (Simon, 2003, p. 37). Schwartz (1998) declared that "the simple notion that photographs offer a mirror of reality has been shelved by most scholars and replaced by a more complex view of photographic communication" (p. 3). Visual meaning emerges in the course of social interaction (e.g., Byers, 1966, and Sekula, 1975, for early articulations of this argument). An interaction between the photographer, the subject, and the circumstances surrounding the taking of the photograph shape the final picture (Prins, 2002, takes a political angle on this point). Once the picture is disseminated, those who see it engage in an act of interpretation. The image offers a range of meanings that the viewer negotiates through the filter of life experience.

Moreover, there are a host of contextual factors involved with the production of photographic meaning. This includes the institutional setting and its associated codes and conventions to which photographers and viewers respond (Musello, 1980; Rosenblum, 1978; Schwartz, 1986, 1992). "Photojournalism, fine arts photography, and snapshot photography, for example, have all generated a distinctive set of practices and expectations governing the social production of meaning" (Schwartz, 1998, p. 3; also see Chalfen, 1987; Perlmutter, 1998, 1999). The various forces, such as potential profitability, within the mass market also influence what gets photographed and ultimately disseminated to the public. These are among a variety of factors associated with truth and generalizability one must contend with when considering the use of visual data for academic research.

Ethical and Legal Issues

Ethical and legal issues offer yet more reasons for the marginalization of visual methods in communication research. Such research is often dependent on the subjects' informed consent and guarantee of anonymity to protect subjects from harm, protect the researcher against legal action (e.g., libel or invasion of privacy), and generally maintain high ethical standards. Consent waiver forms are one way to avoid legal action, although their usefulness has been questioned (e.g., Krages, 2001, for related legal issues). In any sort of research investigation it is fair to say that the people studied probably do not know what they are getting into. They may give their consent, but it is not always informed. Usually there are methods in survey research and experiments to maintain the anonymity of the subjects, so this is generally not an issue. With photographic methods of data collection, the problems associated with anonymity are obvious—people, things, and places in the photograph are identifiable. This is the strength of the method and should not be sacrificed for ethical considerations. As a result, photographers have taken a hard line regarding informed consent: "[P]eople can and should take care of their own interests, and once the investigator has honestly described his intentions he has fulfilled his obligations" (Becker, 1986, p. 260).

The strength of the method may, in fact, not depend on identification of the person, place, or thing specifically, "since the implicit argument is that what you see is characteristic of a large class," so the people are, in effect, anonymous (Becker, 1986, p. 260). Most photographic studies of a community do not specifically identify individuals by name, but rather by type or in some other generic way. For example, in their study of the Balinese, Bateson and Mead (1942) captioned images with phrases such as, "Man holding a cock" (p. 140) or "A father with his son" (p. 184). In general there seems to be little purpose in identifying people by name, but some studies use the first names of subjects as Harper (1987a) did in his study of a Northern New York community: "Willie and Skip attach the radiator cover they have just cut to size" (p. 87). Turner's (1970) study of Detroit not only named people but provided their approximate addresses as well.

In contrast, there is a whole class of people who are public figures and expect to be photographed. The ethics associated with subject anonymity are of little concern in these cases. These people epitomize the ethical rationale mention above: "[P]erfectly capable of defending their own interests, they accept their photographic burden as one of the costs of being a public figure, whether they like it or not" (Becker, 1986, p. 260).

Those using photographic methods may try to maintain friendly relations with the people they photograph because it discourages any negative repercussions from the research. Too often, though, a researcher will rely on the fact that this is a large, differentiated society in which it is relatively unlikely that anyone will see the photograph of him or her in a book, research article, or exhibit.

Community Research as a Visual Communication Endeavor

Now that the theoretical, methodological, and ethical issues of photographic research have been covered, one might ponder why the communication discipline should use visual methods to study community. Research-wise, these methods are problematic, but photographs and visual images of various types are natural communication phenomena. There is an abundance of communication research that examines images from various media (e.g., television, newspapers, magazines, and new media) under the rubrics of mass media, journalism, and visual communication. The interpersonal study of nonverbal facial displays and other gestures constitute other subspecialties for research. Even the rhetorical assessment of style and delivery is not exclusively a verbal construct. Therefore, as with the fields of sociology and anthropology, the study of community as a visual construct should fall squarely within the communication field.

There are several reasons why communication researchers might use visual methods and visual data to study community. As a research tool, photographs and other visual recording methods can be used to "produce a record of information that would be too fleeting or complicated to remember or to describe in writing" (Harper, 1989, p. 88). As research tools, photographs can be applied to many settings and situations in which one studies communication and community. The nuances of people interacting, public presentations of self, and relations between people and their material environment are legitimate topics of research using visual data and methods. For example, aerial photography has been used to show housing patterns, farming conditions, and field conditions in an agricultural community (Harper, 1987b, 1997). Others have used photographs to study the social interaction in urban public areas (Whyte, 1980).

Change can be measured by rephotographing the same or similar social phenomena over isolated moments in time. This requires patience with a longitudinal study or access to a photographic archive or collection from an earlier era (e.g. Chung, 2002). Rieger (1987) documented the social changes in communities of Michigan's Upper Peninsula by photographing the exact same setting over 10–15-year periods. The prosperous community in his first images becomes a deserted town in later images with industries closed and churches converted to residential uses. The devolution of the community was shown to be quite rapid. This technique can also be done on film, as it was with *Nanook Revisited* (Massrote, 1990). The filmmaker revisited Inukjiak, the Inuit village where Flaherty (1922) filmed *Nanook of the North*. The film examined the realities behind the groundbreaking documentary and the changes since it was made almost 70 years before. As Harper (1989) described, this method produces striking results. Capturing changes in a community's environment or the unfolding of the lives of groups and institutions in different historical periods and circumstances, this method does what no other can. It is important not to assume that one comprehends only by seeing; however, it is fair to say that viewers of such images get a different sort of meaning from which they may build inferences of social phenomena than does a reader of verbal text.

The process of communal interaction over time and the long-term changes that happen in a community tell a story of the community. This can be done with still photography, as with the Smiths' (1975) work on *Minimata* (see above), but in some cases film or video is better for detailing the processual nature of community life.[10] Flaherty's (1922) *Nanook of the North*, Conally and Anderson's (1988) *Joe Leahy's Neighbors*, Owen's (1990) *Man Without Pigs*, Jonathan Stack's (1996) *Harlem Diary*, and Mark Freeman's (1997) *Weaving the Future* are a few examples.

Goffman (1979) also offered reasons to use pictures as data for research. One advantage to working with photographs is that pictures are now relatively easy and inexpensive to make and reproduce. A collection allows for easy arranging and rearranging, which makes for a good aid for uncovering patterns and finding examples. Another benefit is that competency in understanding visual images is society-wide.

It is also possible for a communication researcher to come along later, subject the images that someone else has used for some nonresearch purpose to analysis (either in relation to the first author's work or in relation to some other project), and make a legitimate claim that it is an exercise that constitutes visual communication research of a community. This is where a wealth of research possibilities lies in the study of communication and community, and some have taken advantage of this opportunity (e.g., Adams, 2000; Berlier, 1999a; Cheung, 1996; DeLaurell, 1993; Flanagan, 1999; Margolis, 1994).

There are links between visual anthropology and communication that are important for justifying the use of visual images to study community in the communication discipline. For example, visual anthropology and communication share concerns in the theoretical areas of phenomenology, functionalism, structuralism, and postmodernism. Other overlaps occur with the general concerns in the study of the human experience and the ethnographic method. Visual anthropology and communication research share concerns about cultural issues involving the political awareness of our research, which recognizes the colonial or neo-colonial underpinnings of the relationship between a researcher and his or her subject, as well as the subject's right and ability to enter into a discourse about the construction of their lives.

The study of visual images, in and of itself, does not always make an appropriate topic for communication research. Nor does the mere use of images in a study of a community qualify the study as communication and community research. The images may merely be used as illustrations. The study of the visual aspects of community should only be considered visual communication research if it is informed by the concerns and underpinnings of communication more generally. If communication research, defined very crudely, is an exercise in the interpretation of symbolic forms that seek to understand the meaning, thought, interactions, and relationships amonh people, groups, cultures, and the content of shared message and message systems, then visual studies must engage this, or some part of it, if they wish to be taken seriously as communication research.

NOTES

1. *The Family of Man*, as an exhibit and in book form, has attracted many critics and researchers. Barthes (1972), for example, critiqued the mythic qualities of the work. Berlier (1999b) offered a historical/critical analysis.

2. Admittedly, the logic behind the categorization scheme is superficially explained here, but it is discussed in more detail below.

3. I detail this study somewhat more than others primarily because of the extreme form of Gesellschaft that it documents. It depicts a community literally in the throes of its final stage of demise, its physical dismantling.

4. Hall (1997) was instructive here:

It is worth emphasizing that there is no single or "correct" answer to the question, "What does this image mean?". . . . Since there is no law which can guarantee that things will have "one, true meaning," or that meanings won't change over time, work in this area is bound to be interpretive—a debate between, not who is "right" and who is "wrong," but between equally plausible, though sometimes competing and contesting, meanings and interpretations. (p. 9)

5. Cassirer (1946) could have included photographic images when he stated:

[M]yth, art, language and science appear as symbols; not in the sense of mere figures which refer to some given reality by means of suggestion and allegorical renderings, but in the sense of forces each of which produces and posits a world of its own. In these realms the spirit exhibits itself in that inwardly determined dialectic by virtue of which alone there is any reality, any organized and definite Being at all. Thus the special symbolic forms are not imitations, but *organs* of reality, since it is solely by their agency that anything real becomes an object for intellectual apprehension, and as such is made visible to us. The question as to what reality is apart from these forms, and what are its independent attributes, becomes irrelevant here. For the mind, only that can be visible which has some definite form; but every form of existence has its source in some peculiar way of seeing. (p. 8)

As one might imagine, these ideas also have implications for the relationship between photographic imagery and truth, which is discussed in another part of this essay.

6. Examining images of a community in the categorical manner as was done here, in a way, distorts the process of community. A community is constantly changing, some more than others. However, typing communities distorts their ever-changing characteristics (e.g., Becker, 1998).

7. Here is some anecdotal evidence on this point: I recently had the privilege to meet environmental activist Lois Gibbs and hear her talk (February 16, 2003, in Salt Lake City, Utah, at the annual meeting of the Western States Speech Communication Association). She is known primarily for her efforts in battling the chemical companies and government over a toxic chemical dump at Love Canal in Niagra Falls, New York. What is relevant to this study is her description of how images of the community's children were able to change political attitudes toward the neighborhood surrounding Love Canal. The images, in part, brought to light the injustice of the corporations and government toward the community; thus support was gained for her cause and the people of the Love Canal area received the funds they needed to move away from the poisonous water, soil, and air in the community. It is a story in which the demise of the community, structurally, was needed in order to save the people who lived there. The community became, essentially, a modern-day ghost town.

8. What I am referring to here is that the ways these fields use images and the techniques to reproduce images have changed the research done in these fields; indeed, the fields have changed because of the way they use images. For example, in medical diagnosis images from new technologies such as magnetic resonance imagery (MRI), positron emissions tomography (PET scan), and computerized axial tomography (CAT scan) have changed the way doctors and medical technicians look at and into the body. In the area of surveillance, techniques in satellite surveillance and video cameras have contributed important changes in this controversial field. In astronomy, the Hubble telescope has changed the way we understand the universe. In physics, new powerful electron microscopes have changed the way we understand the structure of the atom.

9. Sociologists have made similar claims regarding the marginalization of visual techniques in their field (e.g., Caulfield, 1996; Harper, 1996).

10. This review discusses the visual documentation of community as if still photography had always been the primary mode of investigation. In fact, film—the moving image—was the primary medium for documenting society up until about the 1960s (Banks, 1998). "In the first half of the century it was film's recording and documentary qualities that were chiefly (but not exclusively) valued by anthropologists" (p. 9; see also Ruby, 2000). Film could document concrete human activity that could be incorporated into formalist modes of analysis, but it could not add much to the understanding of more abstract formal systems (e.g., in kinship analysis).

In the 1960s, attention turned from film as a tool of science to film as a tool of experience. The "pseudo-experiential representational quality of film" (Banks, 1998, p. 10) anticipated the phenomenological emphasis in written ethnography by a decade or two. "Now film was to be valued for giving some insight into the experience of being a participant in another culture, permitting largely Euro-American audience to see life through the eyes of non-European others" (p. 10). In fact, some experiments went so far as to train subjects in the use of film equipment and allow them to represent themselves. Such was the case with Worth and Adair's *The Navajos Film Themselves* in 1972 (e.g., Worth & Adair, 1997).

The Worth and Adair (1972) effort was an anomaly in the area of visual ethnography. With few exceptions, film was used to do something to another. In other words, ethnographic film produced using 16mm cameras placed the ethnographer in the active role while the subject remained passive. Besides altering their behavior for the camera, or not behaving at all, the subjects had little or no control over the way their lives were constructed by the medium and the filmmakers. Such was the case with a film on a northern Inuit community in Flaherty's (1922) *Nanook of the North*. Being one of the earliest of its kind, the film was a watershed in the style of ethnographic film. Only later was it revealed how much manipulation had taken place to dramatize the lives of the native people.

REFERENCES

Abbot, B. (1939). *New York in the thirties*. New York: Dover.

Abbot, B. (1979). *The world of Atget*. New York: Paragon Books.

Adam, H. C. (Ed.). (2001). *Eugene Atget's Paris*. New York: Taschen.

Adams, N. L. (2000). *Lure of the past, promise for the future: A study of community*. Unpublished doctoral dissertation, Fielding Institute, Santa Barbara, CA.

Adelman, B. (1972). *Down home*. New York: McGraw-Hill.

Adra, N. (1998). Dance and glance: Visualizing tribal identity in highland Yemen. *Visual Anthropology*, *11*(1–2), 55–102.

Agee, J., & Evans, W. (1939). *Let us now praise famous men*. Boston: Houghton Mifflin.

Anderson, B. (1983). *Imagined communities: Reflections on the origin and spread of nationalism*. London: Verso.

Anderson, S. (1940). *Home town: Photographs by the Farm Security photographers*. New York: Alliance.

Aperture (Ed). (1972). *The North American Indians: A selection of photographs by Edward S. Curtis*. New York: Aperture.

Banks, M. (1998). Visual anthropology: Image, object and interpretation. In J. Prosser (Ed.), *Image-based research: A sourcebook for qualitative researchers*. London: Falmer Press.

Barker, J. H. (1993). *Always getting ready, Upterrlainarluta: Yup'ik Eskimo subsistence in Southwest Alaska*. Seattle: University of Washington Press.

Barry, A. M. S. (1997). *Visual intelligence: Perception, image, and manipulation in visual communication*. New York: State University of New York Press.

Barthes, R. (1972). *Mythologies*. New York: Hill & Wang.

Bateson, G., & Mead, M. (1942). *Balinese character: A photographic analysis*. New York: New York Academy of Sciences.

Bauer, F. (1996). *Norman Rockwell's faith of America*. New York: Artabras.

Becker, H. P. (1968). *Through values to social interpretation: Essays on social contexts, actions, types, and prospects*. New York: Greenwood Press.

Becker, H. S. (1974). Photography and sociology. *Studies in the anthropology of visual communication*, *1*, 3–26.

Becker, H. S. (1986). *Doing things together: Selected papers*. Evanston, IL: Northwestern University Press.

Becker, H. S. (1998). *Tricks of the trade: How to think about your research while you're doing it*. Chicago: University of Chicago Press.

Berger, A. A. (1998). *Seeing is believing: An introduction to visual communication* (2nd ed.). Mountain View, CA: Mayfield.

Berger, J., & Mohr, J. (1967). *The fortunate man: The story of a country doctor.* New York: Holt, Rinehart & Winston.

Berlier, M. (1999a). *Picturing ourselves: Photographs of Belgian Americans in northeastern Wisconsin, 1888–1950.* Unpublished doctoral dissertation, University of Iowa, Iowa City.

Berlier, M. (1999b). The family of man: Readings of an exhibition. In B. Brennen & H. Hardt (Eds.), *Picturing the past: Media, history, and photography* (pp. 206–241). Urbana: University of Illinois Press.

Birenbaum-Carmeli, D. (1998). Residential integration and its constructed reflection: An Israeli case study. *Visual Anthropology, 11*(3), 175–190.

Buechner, T. S. (1972). *Norman Rockwell: A sixty year retrospective.* New York: Harry N. Abrams.

Byers, P. (1966). Cameras don't take pictures. *Columbia University Forum, 9,* 27–31.

Cancian, F. (1974). *Another place: Photographs of a Maya community.* San Francisco: Scrimshaw Press.

Caplow, T., Bahr, H. M., Chadwick, B. A., Hill, R., & Williamson, M. H. (1982). *Middletown families: Fifty years of change and community.* Minneapolis: University of Minnesota Press.

Casmir, F. L. (1994). The role of theory and theory building. In F. L. Casmir (Ed.), *Building communication theories: A socio/cultural approach* (pp. 7–45). Hillsdale, NJ: Erlbaum.

Cassirer, E. (1946). *Language and myth.* London: Harper.

Caulfield, J. (1996). Visual sociology and sociological vision, revisited. *American Sociologist, 27*(3), 56–68.

Chalfen, R. (1987). *Snapshot versions of life.* Bowling Green, OH: Bowling Green State University Popular Press.

Chaplin, E. (1994). *Sociology and visual representation.* New York: Routledge.

Cheung, S. (1996). Change of Ainu images in Japan: A reflexive study of pre-war and post-war photoimages of Ainu. *Visual Anthropology, 9*(1), 1–24.

Chung, S. K. (2002). *Las Vegas: Then and now.* San Diego: Thunder Bay Press.

Clark, L. (1971). *Tulsa.* New York: Rapoport.

Clarke, D. S. (1987). *Principles of semiotic.* London: Routledge & Kegan Paul.

Cohen, A. P. (1985). *The symbolic construction of community.* London: Tavistock.

Coles, R., & Harris, A. (1973). *The old ones of New Mexico.* Albuquerque: University of New Mexico Press.

Coles, R., & Harris, A. (1978). *The last and first Eskimos.* Boston: New York Graphic Society.

Collier, J., Jr. (1974). *Visual anthropology: Photography as a research method.* New York: Holt, Rinehart, & Winston.

Collier, J., Jr., & Buitrón, A. (1949). *The awakening valley.* Chicago: University of Chicago Press.

Conally, B., & Anderson, R. (Directors). (1988). *Joe Leahy's neighbors.* [Videorecording]. (Available from Documentary Educational Resources at http://www.der.org).

Coote, J. (1993). Malinowski the photographer. *Journal of the Anthropological Society of Oxford, 24*(1), 66–69.

Copeland, A. (Ed.). (1969). *People's park.* New York: Ballantine Books.

Craig, R. T. (1993). Why are there so many communication theories? *Journal of Communication, 43,* 26–33.

Cuba, L. (1987). *Identity and community on the Alaska frontier.* Philadelphia: Temple University Press.

Cuba, L., & Hummon, D. M. (1993). A place to call home: Identification with dwelling, community, and region. *Sociological Quarterly, 34,* 111–131.

Davidson, B. (1970). *East 100th street.* Cambridge, MA: Harvard University Press.

Davis, B. A. (1985). *Edward S. Curtis: The life and times of a shadow catcher.* San Francisco: Chronicle Books.

Dayan, D., & Katz, E. (1988). Articulating consensus: The ritual and rhetoric of media events. In J. C. Alexander, (Ed.), *Durkhemian sociology: Cultural studies* (pp. 161–186). Cambridge, UK: Cambridge University Press.

DeLaurell, R. (1993). *Cartographic representations of community as communication: A case study of the Amana Colonies*. Unpublished doctoral dissertation, University of Iowa, Iowa City, IA.

Dondis, D. A. (1973). *A primer of visual literacy*. Cambridge, MA: MIT Press.

Duneier, M. (1999). *Sidewalk*. New York: Farrar, Straus, & Giroux.

Durkheim, É. (1933). *The division of labor in society*. Glencoe, IL: Free Press. (Original work published 1893)

Durkheim, É. (1951). *Suicide: A study in sociology*. Glencoe, IL: Free Press. (Original work published 1897)

Durkheim, É. (1965). *The elementary forms of the religious life*. New York: Free Press. (Original work published 1912)

Eco, U. (1979). *A theory of semiotics*. Bloomington: Indiana University Press.

Edwards, E. (1992). Jenness and Malinowski: Fieldwork and photographs. *Journal of the Anthropological Society of Oxford, 23*(1), 89–93.

Emmison, M., & Smith, P. (2000). *Researching the visual: Images, objects, contexts and interactions in social and cultural inquiry*. Thousand Oaks, CA: Sage.

Engels, F. (1968). *The condition of the working class in England*. Stanford, CA: Stanford University Press. (Original work published 1886)

Estrin, M. L. (1979). *To the manor born*. Boston: New York Graphic Society.

Ewald, W. (1985). *Portraits and dreams: Photographs and stories by children of the Appalachians*. New York: Writers & Readers.

Feininger, A. (1978). *New York in the forties*. New York: Dover.

Flaherty, R. (Director). (1922). *Nanook of the north* [Film]. United States: Kino Video.

Flanagan, K. (1999). *Casting shadows now and then: The use of photography in the observation and analysis of social change in Digby County, Nova Scotia*. Unpublished doctoral dissertation, University of Toronto, Toronto, Canada.

Frank, R. (1958). *The Americans*. Paris: Robert Delpire.

Freeman, M. (Director). (1997). *Weaving the future*. [Videorecording]. Retrieved from Documentary Educational Resources at http://www.der.org

Ganzel, B. (1984). *Dust bowl descent*. Lincoln: University of Nebraska Press.

Gardner, R. (Director). (1963). *Dead birds*. [Film]. (Available from the Film Study Center at Harvard at http://www.filmstudycenter.org).

Gardner, R., & Heider, K. G. (1968). *Gardens of war: Life and death in the New Guinea Stone Age*. New York: Random House.

Gibbs, L. (2003, February). *Love canal: 25 years later—what we have learned*. [Keynote Address]. General keynote session conducted at the 74th annual conference of the Western States Communication Association, Salt Lake City, UT.

Goffman, E. (1979). *Gender advertisements*. Cambridge, MA: Harvard University Press.

Gombrich, E. H. (1982). *The image and the eye: Further studies in the psychology of pictorial representation*. London: Phaidon Press.

Guimond, J. (1991). *American photography and the American dream*. Chapel Hill: University of North Carolina Press.

Gutman, J. M. (1967). *Lewis W. Hine and the American social conscience*. New York: Walker.

Halbwachs, M. (1980). *The collective memory*. New York: Harper & Row. (Original work published 1950).

Hall, S. (1997). Introduction. In S. Hall (Ed.), *Representation: Cultural representations and signifying practices* (pp. 1–12). London: Sage.

Harper, D. (1987a). *Working knowledge: Skill and community in a small shop*. Chicago: University of Chicago Press.

Harper, D. (1987b, July). *Aerial photographs as social landscapes*. Paper presented at the meeting of the International Visual Sociology Association, Omaha, NE.

Harper, D. (1989). Visual sociology: Expanding sociological vision. In G. Blank, J. L. McCartney, & E. Brent (Eds.), *New technology in sociology* (pp. 81–97). New Brunswick, NJ: Transaction.

Harper, D. (1996). Seeing sociology. *American Sociologist, 27*(3), 69–78.

Harper, D. (1997). Visualizing structure: Reading surfaces of social life. *Qualitative Sociology, 20*(1): 57–77.

HBO Sports (Executive Producer). (2002, July 11). *A city on fire: The story of the '68 Detroit Tigers* [Television broadcast]. New York: Home Box Office.

Herrmann, L. (2000) *Nineteenth century British painting.* London: Giles de la Mare.

Hervey, S. (1982). *Semiotic perspectives.* London: Allen & Unwin.

Hoffman, D. D. (1998). *Visual intelligence: How we create what we see.* New York: Norton.

Holdt, J. (1985). *American pictures.* Copenhagen, Denmark: American Pictures Foundation.

Horn, R. E. (1998). *Visual language: Global communication for the 21st century.* Bainbridge Island, WA: MacroVU.

Hummon, D. M. (1988). Tourist worlds: Tourist advertising, ritual, and American culture. *Sociological Review, 29,* 179–202.

Hunstein, D. (1962). *New York.* London: Spring Books.

Jackson, B. (1977). *Killing time: Life in the Arkansas penitentiary.* Ithaca, NY: Cornell University Press.

Katz, E., & Dayan, D. (1986). Contests, conquests, coronations: On media events and their heroes. In C. F. Grauman & S. Moscovici (Eds.), *Changing conceptions of leadership* (pp. 135–144). New York: Springer-Verlag.

Kavaler, E. M. (1999). *Pieter Bruegel: Parables of order and enterprise.* Cambridge, UK: Cambridge University Press.

Krages, B. P. (2001). *Legal handbook for photographers: The rights and liabilities of making images.* Buffalo, NY: Amherst Media.

Krampen, M., Oehler, K., Posner, R., Sebeok, T. A., & von Uexküll, T. (1987). *Classics of semiotics.* New York: Plenum Press.

Lacan, J. (1977). The agency of the letter in the unconscious or reason since Freud. In A. Sheridan (Trans.), *Écrits: A selection.* London: Tavistock.

Lehnartz, K. (1969). *New York in the sixties.* New York: Dover.

Leigh, J. (2000). *The land I'm bound to.* New York: Norton.

Lester, P. M. (2003). *Visual communication: Images with messages* (3rd ed.). Belmont, CA: Wadsworth.

Lightfoot, F. S., (Ed.). (1981). *Nineteenth-century New York in rare photographic views.* New York: Dover.

Littlejohn, S. W. (2002). *Theories of human communication.* Belmont, CA: Wadsworth.

Loomis, C. P., & McKinney, J. C. (1988). Introduction: Tönnies and his relation to sociology. In F. Tönnies, *Community and society: (Gemeinschaft und gesellschaft;* pp. 12–29). New Brunswick, NJ: Transaction Books. (Original Work Published in 1957).

Lyman, C. M. (1982). *The vanishing race and other illusions: Photographs of Indians by Edward S. Curtis.* New York: Pantheon Books.

Lynd, R. S., & Lynd, H. M. (1929). *Middletown: A study in modern American culture.* New York: Harcourt Brace.

Lynd, R. S., & Lynd, H. M. (1937). *Middletown in transition: A study in cultural conflicts.* New York: Harcourt Brace.

Lyon, D. (1969). *The destruction of lower Manhattan.* Toronto, Canada: Macmillan.

Malinowski, B. (1922). *Argonauts of the Western Pacific: An account of native enterprise and adventure in the archipelagoes of Melanesian New Guinea.* London: Routledge.

Malinowski, B. (1926). *Crime and custom in savage society.* New York: Harcourt Brace.

Malinowski, B. (1927). *Sex and repression in savage society.* London: Routledge.

Malinowski, B. (1929). *The sexual life of savages in North-western Melanesia: An ethnographic account of courtship, marriage, and family life among the natives of the Trobriand Islands, British New Guinea.* London: Routledge.

Malinowski, B. (1935). *Coral gardens and their magic: A study of the methods of tilling the soil and of agricultural rites in the Trobriand Islands.* New York: American Book.

Margolis, E. (1994). Images in struggle: Photographs of Colorado coal camps. *Visual Sociology*, 9(1), 4–26.

Marx, K. (1967). *A critical analysis of capitalist production*. New York: International Publishers. (Original work published 1889).

Marx, K., & Engels, F. (1965). *The German ideology* (C. J. Arthur, Trans.). London: Lawrence & Wishart. (Original work published 1846).

Massrote, C. (Director). (1990). *Nanook revisited*. [Videorecording]. (Available from Films for the Humanities at http://www.films.com).

McQuade, D., & McQuade, C. (2000). *Seeing & writing*. Boston: Bedford/St. Martin's.

Messaris, P. (1992). Visual "manipulation": Visual means of affecting responses to images. *Communication*, 13, 181–195.

Messaris, P. (1994). *Visual literacy: Image, mind, & reality*. Boulder, CO: Westview Press.

Messaris, P. (1997). *Visual persuasion: The role of images in advertising*. Thousand Oaks, CA: Sage.

Michaud, R., & Michaud, S. (2002). *Afghanistan: The land that was*. New York: Harry N. Abrams.

Morgan, J., & Welton, P. (1992). *See what I mean? An introduction to visual communication* (2nd ed.). London: Edward Arnold.

Musello, C. (1980). Studying the home mode: An exploration of family photography and visual communication. *Studies in Visual Communication*, 6(1), 23–42.

Natali, E. (1972). *New American people*. Hastings-on-Hudson, NY: Morgan & Morgan.

Newhall, N. (1975). *P. H. Emerson: The fight for photography as a fine art*. New York: Aperture.

Newton, J. H. (2000). *The burden of visual truth: The role of photojournalism in mediating reality*. Mahwah, NJ: Erlbaum.

Orenstein, N. M. (Ed.). (2001). *Pieter Bruegel: Drawings and prints*. New Haven, CT: Yale University Press.

Owen, C. (Director). (1990). *Man without pigs*. [Videorecording]. (Available from Documentary Educational Resources at http://www.der.org).

Owens, B. (1973). *Suburbia*. San Francisco: Straight Arrow Books.

Perlmutter, D. D. (1998). *Photojournalism and foreign policy: Icons of outrage in international crisis*. Westport, CT: Praeger.

Perlmutter, D. D. (1999). *Visions of war: Picturing warfare from the stone age to the cyber age*. New York: St. Martin's Press.

Pierce, O. (1996). *Up river: The story of a Maine fishing community*. Hanover, NH: University of New England Press.

Pinney, C. (1992). The parallel histories of anthropology and photography. In E. Edwards (Ed.), *Anthropology and photography* (pp. 74–95). New Haven, CT: Yale University Press.

Prins, H. E. L., (2002). Visual media and the primitivist perplex: Colonial fantasies, indigenous imagination, and advocacy in North America. In F. D. Ginsburg, L. Abu-Lughod, & B. Larkin (Eds.), *Media worlds: Anthropology on new terrain* (pp. 58–74). Berkeley: University of California Press.

Redfield, R. (1947). The folk society. *American Journal of Sociology, 52*, 295.

Rieger, J. (1987, July). *Photographic approaches to the documentation of social change*. Paper presented at the meeting of the International Visual Sociology Association, Omaha, NE.

Riis, J. A. (1890). *How the other half lives: Studies among the tenements of New York*. New York: Scribner. (Reprinted edition with added photographs. New York: Dover Press, 1971).

Riis, J. A. (1971). *The children of the poor*. New York: Arno Press. (Original work published 1892)

Riis, J. A. (1900). *A ten years' war: An account of the battle with the slum in New York*. New York: Freeport.

Roberts-Jones, P., & Roberts-Jones, F. (2002). *Pieter Bruegel*. New York Harry N. Abrams.

Robertson, J. O. (1980). *American myth American reality*. New York: Hill & Wang.

Rockwell, T. (1988). *The best of Norman Rockwell*. Philadelphia: Courage Books.

Rose, G. (2001). *Visual methodologies: An introduction to the interpretation of visual materials*. London: Sage.

Rosenblum, B. (1978). Style as social process. *American Sociological Review, 43*, 422–438.

Rosenblum, N. (1989). *A world history of photography.* New York: Abbeville Press.

Rosenblum, W., Rosenblum, N., & Trachtenberg, A. (1977). *America and Lewis Hine.* Millerton, NY: Aperture.

Rothenbuhler, E. W. (1988a). Live broadcasting, media events, telecommunication, and social form. In D. R. Maines & C. Couch (Eds.), *Information, communication, and social structure* (pp. 231–243). Springfield, IL: Charles C. Thomas.

Rothenbuhler, E. W. (1988b). The living room celebration of the Olympic games. *Journal of Communication, 38*(4), 61–81.

Rothenbuhler, E. W. (1989). Values and symbols in public orientations to the Olympic media event. *Critical Studies in Mass Communication, 6*, 138–157.

Rothenbuhler, E. W., & Mullen, L. J. (1996). *Do you think of yourself as an Iowan? State of residence as place of attachment.* Iowa City: University of Iowa Press.

Rothenbuhler, E. W., Mullen, L. J., DeLaurell, R., & Ryu, C. R. (1996). Communication, community attachment, and involvement. *Journalism and Mass Communication Quarterly, 73*(2), 445–466.

Ruby, J. (2000). *Picturing culture: Explorations of film & anthropology.* Chicago: University of Chicago Press.

Samian, É. (1995). Bronislaw Malinowski et la photographie anthroplogique. [Bronislaw Malinowski and anthropological photography. Ethnography.] *L'Ethnographie, 91*(2), 107–130.

Scherer, J. C. (1975). You can't believe your eyes: Inaccuracies in photographs of North American Indians. *Studies in the Anthropology of Visual Communication, 2*, 67–86.

Schwartz, D. (1986). Camera clubs and fine art photography: The social construction of an elite code. *Urban Life, 15*(2), 165–195.

Schwartz, D. (1989). Legion post 189: Continuity and change in a rural community. *Visual Anthropology, 2*(2), 103–133.

Schwartz, D. (1992). To tell the truth: Codes of objectivity in photojournalism. *Communication, 13*(2), 95–109.

Schwartz, D. (1998). *Contesting the Super Bowl.* New York: Routledge.

Schwartz, D. (1999). Objective representation: Photographs as facts. In B. Brennen, & H. Hardt (Eds.), *Picturing the past: Media, history, and photography* (pp. 158–181). Urbana: University of Illinois Press.

Sekula, A. (1975). On the invention of photographic meaning. *Artforum, 13*(5), 36–45.

Shils, E. A. (1975). *Center and periphery: Essay in macrosociology.* Chicago: University of Chicago Press.

Simon, T. (2003, January 26). Freedom row. *New York Times Magazine*, 32–37.

Simonson, P. (1996). Dreams of democratic togetherness: Communication hope from Cooley to Katz. *Critical Studies in Mass Communication, 13*(4), 324–342.

Smith, M. P. (1984). *Spirit world: Pattern in the expressive folk culture of African-American New Orleans.* Gretna, LA: Pelican.

Smith, W. E., & Smith A. M. (1975). *Minamata.* New York: Holt, Rinehart, & Winston.

Snyder, W. (1970). *Haymarket.* Cambridge, MA: MIT Press.

Stack, J. (Producer/Director). (1996). *Harlem diary: Nine voices of resilience.* (Available from Discovery Communications, Inc., Bethesda, MD 20814).

Stechnow, W., & Bruegel, P. (1990). *Pieter Bruegel: The elder.* (Masters of art series). Boston: Harry N. Abrams.

Steichen, E. (1955). *The family of man.* New York: Museum of Modern Art.

Stryker, R. E., & Wood, N. (1973). *In this proud land: America 1935–1943 as seen in the FSA photographs.* Greenwich, CT: New York Graphic Society.

Stummer, H. M. (1994). *No easy walk: Newark, 1980–1993.* Philadelphia: Temple University Press.

Sturken, M., & Cartwright, L. (2001). *Practices of looking: An introduction to visual culture.* New York: Oxford University Press.

Suchar, C. S. (1993). The Jordaan: Community change and gentrification in Amsterdam. *Visual Sociology*, *8*(1), 41–51.

Sullivan, M. A. (1994). *Bruegel's peasants: Art and audience in the northern Renaissance.* Cambridge, UK: Cambridge University Press.

Szarkowski, J., & Hambourg, M. M. (1981). *The work of Atget. Vol. I: Old France.* New York: Museum of Modern Art.

Szarkowski, J., & Hambourg, M. M. (1982). *The work of Atget. Vol. II: The art of Old Paris.* New York: Museum of Modern Art.

Szarkowski, J., & Hambourg, M. M. (1984). *The work of Atget. Vol. III: The ancient regime.* New York: Museum of Modern Art.

Szarkowski, J., & Hambourg, M. M. (1985). *The work of Atget. Vol. IV: Modern times.* New York: Museum of Modern Art.

Thrasher, F. M. (1936). *The gang: A study of 1,313 gangs in Chicago.* Chicago: University of Chicago Press.

Tice, G. A. (1972). *Paterson.* New Brunswick, NJ: Rutgers University Press.

Tönnies, F. (1988). *Community and society (Gemeinschaft und Gesellschaft).* New Brunswick: Transaction. (Original work published 1957)

Trottenberg, A. D. (Ed.). (1963). *A vision of Paris: The photographs of Eugène Atget; The words of Marcel Proust.* New York: Macmillan.

Tufte, E. R. (1990). *Envisioning information.* Cheshire, CT: Graphics Press.

Tufte, E. R. (1997). *Visual explanations: Images and quantities, evidence and narrative.* Cheshire, CT: Graphics Press.

Turner, A. S. (1970). *Photographs of the Detroit people.* Detroit, MI: Alwyn Scott Turner.

van der Does, P., Edelaar, S., Gooskens, I., Liefting, M., & van Mierlo, M. (1992). Reading images: A study of a Dutch neighborhood. *Visual Sociology*, *7*(1), 4–67.

Webb, W., & Weinstein, R. A. (1973). *Dwellers at the source: Southwestern Indian photographs by A. C. Vroman, 1895–1904.* New York: Grossman.

Whyte, W. H. (1980). *The social life of small urban spaces.* New York: Conservation Foundation.

Wiener, P. P., (Ed.). (1966). *Charles S. Peirce: Selected writings.* New York: Dover.

Williams, R. (2000). *Working hands.* College Station: Texas A&M University Press.

Worth, S., & Adair, J. (Directors). (1972). *Navajos film themselves.* [Film]. (Available on videotape from the Museum of Modern Art Film Library, New York).

Worth, S., & Adair, J. (1997). *Through Navajo eyes: An exploration in film communication and anthropology.* Albuquerque: University of New Mexico Press.

Wright, T. (1991). The fieldwork photographs of Jenness and Malinowski and the beginnings of modern anthropology. *Journal of the Anthropological Society of Oxford*, *22*(1), 41.

Wright, T. (1993). Malinowski and the imponderabilia of art and photography. *Journal of the Anthropological Society of Oxford*, *24*(2), 164–165.

Wright, T. (1994). The anthropologist as artist: Malinowski's Trobriand photographs. *European imagery and colonial history in the Pacific: Nijmegen studies in development and cultural change*, *19*, 116–130.

Young, M. W. (1998). *Malinowski's Kiriwina: Fieldwork photography 1915–1918.* Chicago: University of Chicago Press.

Zelizer, B. (1998). *Remembering to forget: Holocaust memory through the camera's eye.* Chicago: University of Chicago Press.

Zelizer, B. (Ed.). (2001). *Visual culture and the Holocaust.* New Brunswick, NJ: Rutgers University Press.

Zettl, H. (1999). *Sight, sound, motion: Applied media aesthetics* (3rd ed.). Belmont, CA: Wadsworth.

CHAPTER CONTENTS

9 Personal Mediated Communication and the Concept of Community in Theory and Practice

JAMES E. KATZ
RONALD E. RICE
SOPHIA ACORD
KIKU DASGUPTA
KALPANA DAVID
Rutgers University

This chapter has three purposes: first, to review theoretical and practical aspects of the concept of community that may be relevant to a better understanding of relationships between mediated communication and community; second, to explore how personal mediated communication may be affecting the creation, processes, and fates of communities; and third, to consider how the power of mediated communication technologies might alter traditional theories of communities. The chapter begins with a review of the concept of community, discussing positive and negative perspectives on the relationship between mediated communication and community. Then the chapter examines mediated communications, especially the Internet and mobile phone technology, and their potential impact on social relationships within communities. Next, the chapter considers the prospect of virtual mobile communication-based communities becoming an effective source of social capital. Interwoven with these considerations are suggestions for modifications in traditional community theory-building in light of these new technologies. Mobiles are a special focus because so much of the world's population are using them and the number of users and the extent of their use are expected to continue to grow rapidly.

C ommunity as an intellectual construct and as a component of social life has long commanded interest among social scientists and philosophers in general, and communication scholars in particular, as the other chapters in this volume amply demonstrate. Here we wish to highlight how mediated technologies have affected, and are likely to affect, our notions and experiences of

AUTHORS' NOTE: We thank Joshua Meyrowitz, Mark Poster, and Robert Putnam for their extremely helpful comments on earlier drafts.

Correspondence: James E. Katz, School of Communication, Information, and Library Studies, Rutgers, The State University of New Jersey, 4 Huntington Street, New Brunswick, New Jersey 08901-1071; email: jimkatz@scils.rutgers.edu

Communication Yearbook 28, pp. 315–371

community. Our focus is not mass media such as radio, newspapers, and TV, but rather mediated personal communication technology. By mediated personal communication technology, we refer especially to the mobile phone and the Internet, but also include in our definition (though cannot say much about them in our analysis) Personal Digital Assistants (PDAs) and civilian band (CB) and similar radio technology. All these are individual-to-individual or individual-to-group technologies, as opposed to mass media, which can be thought of as organization-to-mass communication technologies. The mediated communication perspective has much to offer because, for instance, mobile phones now outnumber TV sets, and Internet usage has become a major activity for millions around the globe. Even those who are illiterate find themselves relying on mobile phones for important communication, especially in developing countries (Katz & Aakhus, 2002).

Mobile phones have become ubiquitous in many societies, especially among the young, and in several areas such as Finland, Hong Kong, and Taiwan, there are more active handsets than there are people. Understandably, the mobile phone has become an important part of many social networks, which are comprised of kin, friends, and workmates (Katz, 2001; Ling 2001). At the same time, conventional communicative practices have been eroded due to the extensive use of mobile phones. Use of public space and responses to others in one's vicinity clearly seem to have been affected by mobile phone usage. De Gournay (2002) claimed conventional codes of conduct regarding communicative behavior in public spaces are fast disappearing owing to the seemingly random use of mobile phones. On a larger scale, Katz and Aakhus (2002) held that the mobile phone reflects a broader sociological effect involving aspirations to perpetual contact with family, friends, people of potential interest, and information sources. At the very least, as suggested above, even mobiles are part of a larger set of new communication technologies that interplay with various human communication needs generally and human community in particular. With this perspective on the changing format of interpersonal communication, we turn to the theoretical construct of community so that we will then have a foundation upon which to examine mediated communication's potential consequences to community as praxis and as lived experience.

THE CONCEPT OF COMMUNITY

Definitions of Community

Denotatively and connotatively, community has been used to characterize participants in aboriginal villages (Morgan, 1942), tight-knit urban neighborhoods (Gans, 1962), members of a specific industry such as butchers (Wenger, 1998), as well as more exotic settings such as string theory researchers, eBay's global auctions, and computer programming teams (Rheingold, 2000). Despite the plethora of uses, some careful attention has been directed towards analyzing the term's meaning.

Arensberg and Kimball (1965) identified three elements to the concept: environment, social form, and patterned behavior. Sanders (1966) argued for four: a place to live, a spatial unit, a way of life, and a social system. Effrat (1974) said that communities can be analyzed at the levels of distinct residential groups, solidarity institutions, and interactions of interpersonal and informal relations. Looking at the concept from an historical perspective, Poplin (1979) found three phases: first, as a territorial definition; second, as a unit of social organization; and, more recently, as a set of psycho-cultural bonds. Several scholars have tried crosscutting analysis. Hillery's 1982 comprehensive analysis of 94 definitions of community yielded the three most frequently invoked elements: social interaction, common ties, and physical colocation. More recently, Jones (1995) found that the majority of constructs rely on social involvement and interaction; in essence, community is a social system.

Meyrowitz (1985, 1989) has argued that communities can be viewed in a context that is both upward to institutions and downward to social roles. He analyzed social roles and identities in terms of information systems that are comprised of patterns of access to social information, determined by the mix of physical settings, media, and mental constructs. Regarding mental constructs, he extended Mead's notion of the *generalized other* to the *mediated generalized other*. He described how people gain a sense of who they are in part by imagining how others, both live and mediated, view them. Additionally, he anticipated much discussion of virtual life by advancing the notion of the *generalized elsewhere*, wherein one imagines how distant others imagine one's own city and general environment. In this way, he added the important element of media and mediation to the theoretical development of community.

Turning from the definitional to the analytical, in this section we would argue that the construct might be usefully discussed along several dimensions or axes. First, we will briefly review the idealized utopia of community and then present common theoretical conception of this utopian community as a lost or unrealized entity. Theorists have often compared real communities, those one might actually have experienced, to potentially realizable ones on either a physical or a virtual plane. To depict these elements, we will propose an analytic matrix and suggest the extent to which various definitive characteristics overlap. Finally, we will juxtapose several authors' analyses to compare potential aspects of physical and virtual communities. In this context, as we will show, those who see community life as sadly diminished in the contemporary world often rely on social capital (to be defined) to rejuvenate the idealized conception of community.

IDEALIZED VISIONS OF COMMUNITY

Many theorists conceive of community as a moral entity that transforms the individual through group pressure (Calhoun, 1980; Nisbet, 1966; Poplin, 1979;

Sclove, 1995). As Cobb (1996) noted, community allows the individual to transcend himself and find partnership with humanity. Classical philosophers such as Kant, June, Rousseau, Hegel, and Locke underscore the moral component of community relative to the innate attributes of humankind. As we will show, these idealized conceptions of community also inform current arguments about the nature of community.

Kant held that community, which he dubbed "The Kingdom of Ends," was an inherently moral force that would ultimately be able to save humankind from itself. All would be treated with respect, and as worthy in their own right, rather than as means to selfish ends. Such a community would be based on dynamic reciprocity and responsibility and, though it was not conceived of such at the time, would be the fountainhead of social capital, a concept that will be discussed later.

Jung introduced the notion of the *collective unconscious*, namely that there is a set of universal symbols, responses, and mental conditions that all human beings share. Even though we are unaware of any credible evidence that anything approaching this complex but unseen innate world exists, the conceit of a joint cultural inheritance, manifested through the psyche, remains a compelling one for many scholars. This idea forms the basis for many definitions of physical community, notably that physical community is based on intrinsic, natural solidarity among people (Schmalenbach, 1977). This idea of community as being hardwired, rather than created, is the essence of the spontaneous, natural, and traditional community.

The French romantic philosopher Rousseau saw community deriving from the vast interior reality of the human life cycle. In its natural primitive state, community exuded great concern and altruism, and evil was the result only of the corrupting influence of civilization. In contrast to community, Rousseau viewed social life as the result of corrosive associations, the distorted views that arise when social tools are provided for aggregations of individuals to pursue their egocentric means.[1] In fact, Rousseau's conception of the *general will* expressed a community's common interests and values, which transcend the different wills of individuality. In coming together to recognize their common will, a group of individuals is revealed as a community. Many proponents of virtual community argue that this common will is the basis of communities of interest that form online (Rheingold, 2000; Slevin, 2000; Stone, 1991). Interestingly, some have earlier claimed that prior mediated communication technologies (e.g., rural and party line telephones, ham radio, and CB radio) gave rise to communities (as discussed in Katz, 1999). However, proponents of physical community argue that this common will can exist only with reference to locality and face-to-face (F2F) interaction, and must permanently subsume all other personal interests (Morgan, 1942; Tönnies, 1957).

For Locke, the power of community was in humanity, as a natural right or state, and thus humans would pursue innately moral lives in natural justice without the invasion of civil society. As with Rousseau, this distinction between natural community and civil society prefigures Tönnies's distinction between gemeinschaft and gesellschaft. This distinction is often applied to physical communities and virtual communities, as the former are viewed as whole, positive entities (König, 1968), the latter are seen as impersonal illusions of community (Kolko & Reid, 1998). As with Rousseau's general will, Locke introduced the *social contract* to explain how men and women come together for the common good. The social contract shows that people coming together in community can accomplish far more than any aggregate of individual action. Again, this prefigures notions of social capital through spontaneous and voluntary participation (Coleman, 1986). Nevertheless, viewing the community as having a greater existence than the individual lends substance to critics' claims that social networks erode community by elevating individuals' interests above those of the community (Jacobs, 1961).[2] Hegel saw community as the basic cell from which society evolves, like many others (Arensberg & Kimball, 1965; Edwards & Jones, 1976; Jacobs, 1961; König, 1968; Morgan, 1942; Park, 1952). Like Kant, Hegel views community as a necessarily ethical environment, shaping a national culture (like Coleman, 1954; Etzioni, 2001; Morgan, 1942; Schmalenbach, 1977; Tönnies, 1957). The most useful of Hegel's constructions for us here is his view of dialectics. For Hegel, each sociohistorical situation could be seen as having its own internal logic as well as a dialectical relationship with earlier periods. Building on Hegel, we may see communities in the same light: Modernity met physical needs, but fractionated previously vital social ties in the physical community; this brought about its antithesis in the virtual community. Even though this may lead to its own antithesis, as suggested by Jacobs (1961) and others in urban renewal movements, this may also lead to an ultimate synthesis, such as is suggested by Katz and Rice, with their model of Syntopia (Katz & Rice, 2002). (As to their neologism Syntopia, Katz & Rice hold that people build multidimensional sets of relationships and develop them online and off, with smooth integration across relationships and media.) Other theorists are also attempting to find a synthesis of the two worlds (Castells, 2000; Etzioni, 2001; Giddens, 1994; Poster, 2001, 1995; Sennett, 1971; Slevin, 2000; Walls, 1993).

Habermas (1989) has made repeated attempts to devise schemata that would integrate the antipodal elements of the private and the public continuum and mesh these with an understanding of communication and political processes. To the extent he achieved this, Habermas has been as cited widely as he has been difficult to interpret, and his thoughts have evolved over the decades. Here we can pin him down by saying that he conceived of the public sphere as a space independent of government and partisan interests and dedicated to rational, inclusive, and general debate. To be more specific, the public sphere is intrinsically private, as it is formed by private people coming together as a public. It is, in other words, a vehicle for enhanced democracy, but of a form not yet experienced by mortals.

In essence, the intimacy and subjectivity emanating from the private sphere have prevented public authority from taking control of the entire public sphere. As a result, Habermas envisioned a separation between the sphere of the state and public authority vis-à-vis the public sphere of society. The true public sphere thus remains private in the sense that it responds to the citizens and not to authority.

Within the public sphere then, there is the realm of letters, markets of culture, and political realm; these of course are all public places where private citizens interact.

The political realm in the public sphere is pivotal because it represents this appropriation of public authority by private citizens. Habermas found that the private citizens make certain matters (e.g., authoritative, church, and court) topics of common and hence public concern. In other words, the sociocultural product hence becomes a private commodity and object of general and democratic discussion. The political realm functions entirely through discourse, as people discuss these common concerns and reach agreement. As a result, the necessity for this consensus is that the public realm both be entirely inclusive and offer universal access (Habermas, 1989). Accordingly, the public sphere for political discourse finds a consensus over what is necessary for the lives of all, a kind of negotiated general will. It is this focus on consensus and necessity that constituted the very publicity of public authority and state organs that now have to answer to the public opinion of private consensus.

Habermas further pointed out that this notion of the public was actually generated through the same shift that produced political discourse. In other words, the public sphere was created under conditions identical to those when the artistic endeavor became democratized (previously patronized, in the original sense of the word), and the concept of audience developed (where previously the audience for "professional" musicians was not public, but rather had consisted of the commissioned musicians playing only for private courts and rich families). Again, we see that the public realm necessarily appropriates a limited commodity from the public authority and turns it into a public (social) good. Habermas, in a bow to Hegel, wrote that indeed the public sphere represents the subjection of domination to reason, through a democratic appropriation (not revolution).

Originally, Habermas modeled the public sphere using two fictitious roles played by private individuals: the role of the property owner and the role of the human being. In this model, as the role of private property and the bourgeois declined, people had autonomy only in their sense as human beings. They therefore used the political realm of the public sphere to establish decency and privacy based on simply being a human being.

At this point, Habermas highlighted the notion of solidarity as an essential ingredient in moral community formation. By solidarity he referred to a general concern on the part of each citizen for the well-being of others and the general integrity of the community and sphere of shared life. Solidarity is created by the political discourse in the public realm, as publicity is able to bridge politics and morality (similarly to Kant; Habermas, 1989).

Unfortunately, Habermas felt that the public sphere is increasingly separating from the private realm. Consequently, political discourse, so important to forming solidarity and moral community, is ceasing to be exclusively part of the private domain. Political discourses in the public realm, such as the press, have become commercialized, and public consumer services (e.g., advertising) have taken the place of private men and women of letters who previously (supposedly) were rationally debating the common good and forming a bulwark against excessive public authority.

Even though Habermas provided an excellent framework to view the separation of community from authority, as well as visualize the ways in which community forms spontaneously and self-regulates, Poster (2001) appropriately pointed out some limitations. Poster maintained that Habermas viewed the public sphere as an idealized Greek agora: It is logocentric and not dependent on the space and time deferrals of print. Rather, any mediation in the public sphere is unnatural and precludes reasoned discussion. As we will see in the next section, however, the national identity that brings people together in the public sphere is itself mediated. Public authority must rely on the press to communicate with the public. There can be no ideal agora. Hence, the Internet remains incomplete and partial as a potential proxy for the agora, despite the fact that Habermas proposed that it can be a new source of solidarity.

In short, the idealized conceptions of community, drawn from philosophical analysis, form the backdrop of contemporary views of technology and modern social relations. Despite their impressive historical pedigrees, these visions of community as regimes of sentiment or as innately just are idealized and utopian (Suttles, 1972). The resulting contradiction between the ideal community as a sought-after but unattainable vision, and its sense that it existed to some degree at a prior time, yield a continually reemerging theme of the lost community. "Paradise lost" remains as popular and pervasive in recent contemporary social theory as it had been for prior generations of theoreticians (and theologians).

COMMUNITY OR SOCIETY

The *Oxford Dictionary of the Social Sciences* observes that definitions of community almost exclusively privilege localized attributes relative to universal or cosmopolitan ones. They esteem aspects such as boundedness, affective ties, face-to-face contact, openness to those who are inside the community (at the tacit cost of excluding those who are outside), and other values typically associated with traditional agrarian ways of life. These necessarily contrast the ideals of community with other forms of social organization that encompass impersonal relations and larger numbers of mobile and often unknown participants. This latter form may be thought of as society, which can also stand in for modernism's impact and infringement upon the traditional community, or in brief, life under industrialization. As a result of a global master trend to move away from agrarianism and local isolation and toward industrialization and communication, the ever-diminishing local world helps create the perception that community is an endangered mode of social organization and interaction. An understandable impulse for nostalgia and overseers' selective recall can quickly give rise to a sense that real-life community is fast disappearing. We will examine this notion before exploring alternative (and positive) theories of postmodern prospect for community.

In this context, a leading exponent of the perennial analytical/critical device of a lost golden-pastoral age has been Tönnies (1957). He characterized the transition from community to society as dynamism between gemeinschaft and gesellschaft. Gemeinschaft represents real, organic, intimate, and private life, folk beliefs, kinship and friendship relations; in a sense, it was the rural village. Prominent processes were the common will, which created and enforced consensus. In contrast, gesellschaft is the immense instrumental structure, the public world that one goes out into from the home and hearth. It encompasses commodification, in the Marxist and Benthamite senses. Everything, from social ties to labor, and from sentiment to body parts, is treated as a means to an end (*zwecksrationalitat*), with little regard for the ends themselves (Veblen, 1934). This progression is often compared to Durkheim's concept of mechanical and organic solidarity (i.e., association through sameness versus association through difference, see his *The Division of Labor in Society* (1893/1984). Society's exploitation of the individual is, in both cases, detrimental to a sense of traditional community or gemeinschaft. The intimate, natural basis of human life is swept away forever in the modernist rush of technology, which not only alienates individuals from each other, but also from their species being. For Tönnies, there is no community in or after society.

Marx is not examined in this analytical landscape; however, his influence on Tönnies and other social philosophers is inescapable. According to Marx and Engels (1975) money is the alienated ability of mankind. Money, in having an exchange value, alienates workers from the goods that they are producing. Additionally, the competitive sphere of wage-labor alienates a person from other people. As humans are by nature social beings, whose essence is that of production, their isolation from their work and peers alienates each individual from herself or himself. Thus, all hope of community in society is lost.

A conundrum arises: Relatively few participants in modern life report feeling isolated. Hence, the question naturally arises as to how critical theorists are able to integrate inconvenient facts with their elegant efforts. A clever dodge has been that people are really alienated, but they just do not know it. Different theories can account for it, of course: In Marxist terms, it is called false consciousness; in Freudian terms, repression. Anderson (1983), for his part, responded that current social organizations are neither real nor communal, but rather are *imagined communities*. That is, our traditional communities have become so large and dispersed, that the collective social bond must be imagined and created in the mind of each of its participants, rather than directly experienced through direct contact. Our conceptions of a community must be imagined because we conceive of them as sovereign, limited, and having a horizontal equality among members. In real life, however, communities are constantly challenged, have only arbitrarily chosen boundaries, and hierarchical structures. Thus, real community grounded in intimate, personal contact and concrete issues of integration has vanished, replaced by a mental construct. Poster (2001) agreed that the nation is a historical construct, but said as soon as we realize this we will cease to be threatened by its disappearance. It is important to realize, according to Poster, that all that is virtual is actually real, once we understand the imaginary component inherent in all psychic phenomena.

Nancy (1991) also found that all of the essential attributes of physical community are merely mythical supports, produced to create and sustain power in the political community. In reality, there is no natural identity; the formation of a community identity instead serves to obscure the real political powers that shape community. For Nancy, the only thing we really share is "being in common" (1991, p. 6). The mere existence of community is determined from our simply being in a common place, space, and time. Nancy's real community is thus the absence of community: a collection of fragmented identities that all point to one another (Poster, 1995). In a similar theory, Suttles (1972) saw the formation of a master identity as an illusion of sentiment that creates a defended community. For Anderson, Nancy, and Suttles, the common identity and sameness ties of the community are social constructions, which obscure (or compensate for) our real, physical coexistence.

Following Merton (1946), Beniger (1987) argued for a second way in which what we think of as real community is in fact tromp d'oeil. Our social forms have transformed from interpersonal communities to systems of mass communication. From here, they have progressed to a further level: *pseudocommunity*. Pseudo-community provides an ersatz simulation of the high levels of intimacy that supposedly mark real, physical communities. Sincerity, a strong indicator of intimacy, is artificially constructed by the mass media or other propagandists, such as governments and corporations, or mass mailing advertisers who can make the most automated factory-produced entreaty exquisitely personalized, down to a friendly cursive signature. As Habermas (1989) argued, the public sphere is beginning to override private functions; the fabricated sincerity, seen by Beniger, fools us into thinking that we are indeed in real communities. In reality, we are living in pseudo-communities.

Beniger's essay is of course derivative of Merton's powerful work on *pseudo-gemeinschaft* (1946). By this term, Merton referred to "the feigning of personal concern with the other fellow in order to manipulate him the better" (1946, p. 142). This fooling effect is achieved by appeals to sincerity and genuineness, as well as through computerized databases and printing representations of individual creation. As a result, the acting out of rudimentary affectionate ties of community through, for instance, neighborhood pride or antilitter campaigns, does not produce real community. Rather, this produces a false sense of strong traditional communality without any base of physical interaction to accompany the subjective feeling.

The above critics portray a world that has exhausted the reservoirs required for community, as defined by its local and sentimental existence. They also reinforce the point that the communities that may be perceived as concrete ties and structures, and thus physically real, are actually virtual, immaterial, and created by social work and technologies of communication, and thus constantly subject to immediate negation or obliteration (Garfinkel, 1967).

PHYSICAL VERSUS VIRTUAL COMMUNITIES

Just as Tönnies viewed community and society as distinct forms, it is also easy to consider physical and virtual communities as mutually exclusive forms of social organization. More analytical traction may be possible if, instead of treating each social form as if it objectively and separately existed, the *virtual community* and the *physical community* are considered ideal types (in a Weberian understanding), each possessing certain general characteristics.

Physical community, as its name denotes, can exist only by virtue of physical colocation in space. On the far end of this definition are the ecologists, who, like Park (1952), view community as solely physical and not social at all. Community thus has a biological definition: It is a "population group defined by the space that it occupies" (Park, 1952, p. 182).

This emphasis on a physical basis for community has been prevalent throughout the 20th century. As Arensberg and Kimball (1965) asserted, every community occupies its own physical setting and is spatially surrounded by others. Although many consider the sense of belonging to be important to forming a community, the basic physicality of community formation has to do only with a group of people who exercise local autonomy in meeting their needs in a specific locality (Edwards & Jones, 1976). Other theorists also include physical locality as necessary for community (Jacobs, 1961; König, 1968; Park, 1952; Tönnies, 1957).

The members of the physical community live in mutual interdependence and solidarity. Their social ties are thus marked by universal, residential solidarity; unplanned stability (spontaneous creation); and sentimental ties (Suttles, 1972). Like gemeinschaft, physical community is based on people's natural association through sameness and by exclusion of otherness.

Drawing the discussion of physical community together, we can cluster several lines of thought. Table 1 shows selected theorists and, in reference to our discussion here, highlights in one quadrant the attributes they identify with physical community.

A few millennia ago, thinkers such as Plato and social movements such as the Essenes sought alternative forms of social organization. This search continues today as both social organizational and technological conditions change. With the rise of computer-mediated technology, there has been a concomitant desire to find a new, fulfilling form within cyberspace, also known as the virtual community (Baym, 1997; Stone, 1991). The term originally referred to communities that were mediated through electronic communication technologies. Although Rheingold (1993) and other popularizers of the term were speaking of virtual communities as existing purely online, such as through multiuser domains (MUD), Internet relay chats (IRC), bulletin board systems (BBS), or other online forums and chat

TABLE 1.
Characteristics of Physical Communities

Characteristic	Proponent(s)
Borders/wholeness/exclusion of others	(Kolko & Reid, 1998; Meyrowitz, 1997; Sanders, 1966)/(König, 1968)/(Etzioni, 2001; Jacobs, 1961)
Crisscrossing, interpersonal bonds	(Morgan, 1942; Poplin, 1979; Tönnies, 1957; Walls, 1993)
Face-to-face communication	(Beniger, 1987)
High social influence on human action	(Beniger, 1987; Calhoun, 1980)
Information driven	(Meyrowitz, 1985, 1989)
Intimacy ties/sentiment	(Etzioni, 2001; Kolko & Reid, 1998; Maffesoli, 1996; Merton, 1946; Morgan, 1942; Sclove, 1995; Tönnies, 1957)
Involuntary participation of members	(Ahlbrandt, 1984)
Organization/civic engagement	(Calhoun, 1980; Cobb, 1996; Edwards & Jones, 1976; Etzioni, 2001; König, 1968; Putnam, 2000)
Requires embodied selves	(Kolko & Reid, 1998; Nisbet, 1966)
Small in size	(Beniger, 1987; Coleman, 1954; Morgan, 1942)
Stability/sustained interaction among members	(Coleman, 1986; Sclove, 1995)
Trust/sincerity	(Giddens, 1994; Merton, 1946)
Common:	
Background and memory	(Bellah et al., 1985; Dirksen & Smit, 2002; Morgan, 1942)
Equality	(Nisbet, 1966)
Identity	(Cobb, 1996; Etzioni, 2001; Sennett, 1971; Suttles, 1972; Wenger, 1998)
Needs	(Edwards & Jones, 1976; Morgan, 1942)
Sameness	(Jacobs, 1961; Sennett, 1971)
Values	(Morgan, 1942; Schmalenbach, 1977; Tönnies, 1957)

memberships, virtual communities are also sustained through personal communication technologies such as mobile phones, text messaging, and email devices. Virtual communities merit consideration as communities because of the term's definition, although they are independent of geospatial location. That is, they have been denoted as "large groups of individuals [who] may be linked together to share information, ideas, feelings, and desires" (Calhoun, 2002).

The virtual community, in juxtaposition to the concept of physical community, is represented by intimate secondary relationships, specialized relationships, weaker ties, and homogeneity by interest (Wellman & Gulia, 1999). Rather than being locally isolated from the seeming oppression of society, as is the case of physical communities, the virtual community looks out to society as an enhancement of affective and social ties. As Wellman observed, community becomes "a metaphor for the primary ties outside of households that provide us with larger social systems" (1988a). Gesellschaft and public society, therefore, need not entail the end of community. The virtual community can create and preserve ties among people who are physically separate (Stone, 1991).

The virtual community sees the physical community of proximity as potentially repressive, as it ignores despatialized interests (Rice, 1987; Wellman, 1971). Instead, virtual communities attempt to break through some of the boundaries of race, gender, ethnicity, and geographic location established in physical communities (Katz & Rice, 2002). Depending on the politics of the observer, virtual communities may be celebrated as ways that individuals can express their identities and beliefs in a manner that is true to their internal self, or condemned as systems through which individuals are cut adrift from cardinal values that allow them to engage in unfortunate and even dangerous and evil practices. Thus, the encouragement of White Power or homosexual teen dating services may be seen as either community benefits or liabilities of the Internet (Katz, 1998). Ultimately, virtual communities are based on shared social practices and interests whereas physical communities are based on shared social and physical boundaries.

Poster (2001) held that the "salient trait of the virtual is community" (p. 131). He was not talking about "helmet-and-glove computer-generated worlds, but rather IRCs, chatrooms, MUDs, and other forms of communication over electronic mediums." Virtuality itself then refers simply to "all electronically mediated exchanges of symbols, images, and sound, so that a second world is constituted over and against the 'real' world of sensory proximity" (Poster, 2001, p. 131). The only thing virtual about virtual community is that it provides simultaneity without physical presence.

As a result of this point of view, most of the ways analysts distinguish virtual communities from physical ones are merely reversed statements of physicality. That is, they are communities without physical limitations. There are also some novel aspects. Table 2 is an inventory of claims about virtual community. Part A are those that are the nonphysical items of traditional community, and part B are ones that to us appear as novel claims of virtual communities. Exponents of the particular characteristic are also listed alongside the items. Table 2 implies that physical and virtual communities are clearly distinguishable and are treated so by some theorists (Baym, 1995; Beniger, 1987; Carey, 1993); thus, we consider them as ends of a continuum.

Notions of space and place are important when considering virtual community. Aakhus pointed out: "[O]ur sense of place is negotiated regardless of our physical presence" (2003, p. 39). It is easy to fall prey to the assumptions of virtual life so that one loses sight of the physical reality in which users must actually operate

TABLE 2.
Characteristics of Virtual Community

Characteristic	Proponent(s)
Part A. Additional characteristics of communities when they exist online	
Absence of institutional authority	(Steinmueller, 2002; Sternberg, 2001)
Based in information exchange	(Carey, 1993; Steinmueller, 2002; Walls, 1993)
Characterized by links more so than relationships	(Steinmueller, 2002)
Common interest	(Wellman, 1971, Wellman & Gulia, 1999)
Emerge from technology	(Rheingold, 2000)
Reconfiguring the nature of physical communities	(Meyrowitz, 1985, 1989, 1997)
Self-organized	(Dirksen & Smit, 2002; Katz & Rice, 2002)
Voluntary participation by members	(Ahlbrandt, 1984; Steinmueller, 2002)
Part B. Novel characteristics of virtual community	
Common beliefs and practices	(Coleman, 1954; Etzioni, 2001; Morgan, 1942) —(Stone, 1991)
Common purpose	(Putnam, 1993; Slevin, 2000; Tönnies, 1957; Wenger, 1998)—(Baym, 1995; Rheingold, 2000)
Group-specific meanings/norms	(Putnam, 1993)—(Baym, 1995)
Informal conversation	(Coleman, 1986)—(Rheingold, 2000)
Interpersonal bonds	(Etzioni, 2001)—(Baym, 1995)
Mediated "generalized other"	(Meyrowitz, 1985, 1997)
Reciprocity	(Giddens, 1994; Putnam, 1993) —(Wellman & Gulia, 1999)
Sense of belonging/community feeling	(Anderson, 1983; Morgan, 1942; Tönnies, 1957) —(Dirksen & Smit, 2002; Wellman, 2001)
Spontaneous formation	(Morgan, 1942; Suttles, 1972) —(Rheingold, 2000; Katz & Rice, 2002)
Supported by meaningful communication	(Poster, 2001; Sanders, 1966) —(Turkle, 1995; Walls, 1993; Wenger, 1998)

NOTE: In Part B, the first analyst(s) under each characteristic refers to those who emphasized that characteristic in physical community, and the proponent(s) of the character in a virtual context comes after a dash.

(Wynn & Katz, 1997). This is perhaps a mistake to which Turkle and Stone fell prey: Analysts become so enraptured with the idea of virtual community that we forget that the action is actually happening somewhere: someone typing on a keyboard, someone talking on a phone, someone in a studio speaking into a camera. Ultimately, as Terkenli (1995) argued, humans occupy a space and use symbols to transform it into a place.

In essence, then, the differences between physical and virtual communities cannot be based on constructions and place, but rather must focus on the existence of totally embodied, physical and social presence and simultaneous meeting in space and time. This difference of interpretation is especially important when we return to our notion of Syntopia as we integrate the effects of personal communication technology into our models of community.

RELATIONSHIP OF COMMUNITY TYPES AND THEORISTS

To display the interrelationships among ideal types and theorists, a matrix may be a helpful analytical device. In Figure 1, the x-axis represents the virtual-physical dimension of the community concept. The left end of the x-coordinate represents the purely spatial, geographic, and locality-based conception of community (physical proximity, small size, embodied individuals, face-to-face communication, and kinship groups). The right end of the x-coordinate represents the concept of community operating without physical location (by means of technologically mediated communication devices). It is marked by lack of necessary colocation or the immediate prospect of physical contact, and membership that tends to be large and fragmented with unstructured social ties. Those in the middle are a mix of the two types.

As commented above, the concept of physical place alone is insufficient to distinguish between the theorists' conceptions of physical and virtual communities. Hence, Figure 1 adds a y-axis to represent the dimension of emotional commitment that characterizes the ideal types. The upper y-axis includes the extreme individually centered attributes of the virtual community, such as personal development, voluntary association, private relations, and association by interest. The lower portion of the y-axis depicts public and group focus. These concern issues such as community development, professional association, public relations, political causes, social capital, or even virtual neighborhoods. They share an emphasis on belonging in space. Again, mixed types appear toward the middle of the axis.

This analytic tool exhibits the theorists in multidimensional relationships to the objective and subjective aspects of community. It shows, for instance, the ways in which a theorist may proclaim traditional, physical community to be the only real community, but then associate the physical base with subjective attributes common to virtual communities. In other words, by showing the spread of theorists across this matrix we can argue that community need not be lost with technological mediation and may even be aided by it. Further, significant ties of community are not necessarily bound either to physicality or technological mediation, and physical community may be highly exclusionary and constrained.

Each quadrant allows one of four ideal types of community, each briefly described; the theorists relevant to social capital and distance issues are discussed later and not included on this matrix.

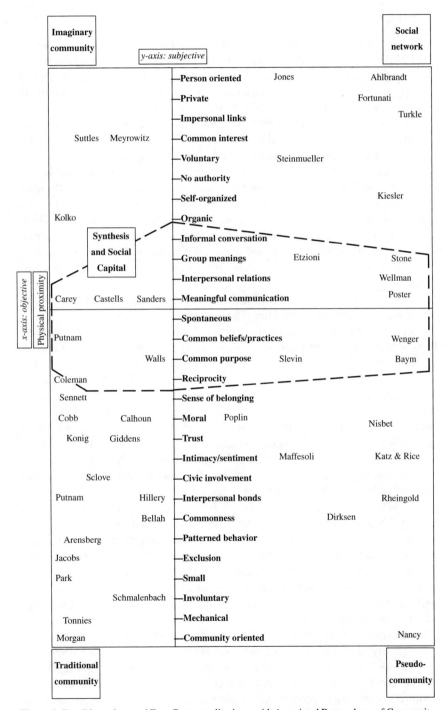

Figure 1. Two Dimensions and Four Conceptualizations, with Associated Researchers, of Community

Traditional Community

Those theorists in the lower left quadrant favor the traditional conception of community, as represented by residential areas and villages. This is perhaps what most people think of when they use the term physical community. Community is strongly grounded in physical space and consists of conservative ties of sentiment, codependency, and a moral sense of belonging. As König (1968) argued, community is the basic form of social life. It is a complete whole, encompassing all social relationships, a pure totality of life.

Social critics fault advocates of virtual communities because they see such communities as bleeding off commitment to the more important real life, physical community. Indeed, they have argued that only physicality can produce the interpersonal congruence, or sameness, through which members turn inwards to the group to focus on each other and by necessity exclude outsiders (Jacobs, 1961). Likewise, a community of people must have a common purpose, but this purpose must also be founded in a local initiative. Ultimately, in this view, community cannot be achieved without the colocated space in which to found and nourish this connection.

The patterned behavior of traditional communities is often linked to a sense of strong intimacy and sentimental ties. The sentimentality attached to the local community is the reason why the small, traditional community remains the idealized form of human social organization. Morgan argued that community is "an association of individuals and families that, out of inclination, habit, custom, and mutual interest, act in concert as a unit in meeting their needs" (1942, p. 20). Nevertheless, these needs are common needs of the community as a whole. The traditionalist conception of community thus does not endorse the therapeutic conception of community, which sees social life as an arrangement to fulfill the needs of the individual (Bellah, Madsen, Sullivan, Swidler, & Tipton, 1985). This distinction applies to later, social networks. Rather, Morgan emphasized that community must be spontaneously created, requiring intimate firsthand acquaintance and community feeling in which individual interests are subsumed.

For Bellah et al. (1985), this intimacy is fundamentally linked to a common identity. Their development of the term *community of memory* represents the common history and identity of a people. It is essential to the definition of community as an all-inclusive whole of interdependence, participation, and shared practices. Too much freedom yields not the personal fulfillment from which one can reenter the community, but instead a sense of arbitrariness, tentativeness, and anomie (Slater, 1970). Rather, as Terkenli (1995) believed, one's identity can only be found by a return to the original community.

Similarly to Terkenli, Sclove saw the local community as the important base for commonality, shared ethical principles, and moral agency required for democratic foundations. In this regard, he wrote that local communities provide distinctive and inescapable physical and moral interdependencies that arise at the local level, territorial grounding of political jurisdiction, and the distinctive quality of mutual understanding, learning, and personal growth that can take place through sustained, contextually situated, face to face discourse and interaction (Sclove, 1995, p. 40).

Sclove further held that virtual communities cannot replace real communities without a careful examination of their nonfocal dimensions. The human warmth, stability, and coherence so necessary in community is lost with electronically-mediated communication. In fact, it is impossible to escape the fact that one's body is locally situated, so any interaction in a virtual community is necessarily also embodied.

With this ideal of traditional community, it is little wonder that many scholars have been highly critical of technology and virtual communities and seen them as inherently opposed to real community values and systems. Putnam argued in *Bowling Alone* (2000) that TV draws people away from their initial environment and alienates them from their copresent families and peers. Suburban sprawl is seen as the real enemy here, as it causes people to leave their local community for both work and leisure time, leading to a 40% reduction in group involvement on the local level. Nevertheless, as to the Internet, Putnam himself asserted he is "agnostic"—that is, it is not necessarily so that the Internet (or any other mediated technology, such as the telephone or TV) has these effects. He held that it is the way people use the technology, not the technology itself, that is the problem (personal communication, August 22, 2003). Hence, the Internet could be used to displace or erode social capital and networks or strengthen and reinforce the sense of community. The work of Katz and Rice (2002) confirmed this, in that they found that Internet use overall does not appear to have deleterious consequences on social capital and even appears beneficial to it.

Social Network

Theorists favor the sociopersonal network conception of community (see the upper right quadrant). This conception is most similar to the common definition of virtual community, as it is sustained by personal communication technologies and cyberspace and deviates widely in its social implications from the traditional community.

Wellman claimed that the definition of community has transformed from a spatial basis to a base of social networks (1999). Community has never been the pastoral myth or ideal type. Instead, as noted earlier, community ties have long been geographically dispersed, specialized, and connected by telecommunications and transportation technologies. As a result, we must cease to mourn for community life, as the idealized version never existed, and begin to think of the personal community, every individual's social network. Only in this way can we see computer-mediated technology as a panacea for, rather than an exacerbation of, the loss of community. Thus, community describes relations that provide a sense of belonging, not a group in physical proximity. In other words, "[W]e haven't lost community . . . it is just liberated from the traditional boundaries of the neighborhood and the kinship group" (Wellman, 1993, online).

With Wellman's social network, community relations have been moved to the private sphere, rather than the public sphere. (Mobile phones may contradict Wellman's social network ideas: Whereas the Internet might make us bring our public communities to our homes, mobiles allow us to take our private communities into the public sphere of action; we will address that later). The essence of the community is one of networked individualism, in which we all choose our own communities, rather than be fitted with others into them involuntarily (Rice, 1987; Wellman, 2001). This is similar to Ahlbrandt's "community of limited liability," which also implies voluntary relations, weaker social ties, and an individual-centered existence (1984, p. 2). Within the community of limited liability, attachment is a function of residents' economic and social investments in a community. Whereas the traditional community required the suppression of the individual for the common good, the social network elevates the individual as the peak and root of his own community. Community is no longer a localized phenomenon of interpersonal links that all cross, but an individual network of informal links that fits into a larger social structure (Wellman, 1988b). In other words, we are social on a larger scale than the physical community allows (Hiltz & Turoff, 1995; Rice, 1987).

Nonetheless, there do seem to be clear cognitive and social bounds as to how large a community can grow. Moreover, there are paradoxes that stem from these kinds of network growth. Meyrowitz (1997) emphasized: "[T]here is a limit to the number of people with whom one can feel truly connected. Electronic media, therefore, foster a broader, but also a shallower sense of 'us.'" (p. 66). In the same article, he also described the resulting macrolevel homogenization of identities that is, ironically, accompanied by microlevel fragmentation within traditional communities and families. Hence, he imagined the effects of personal mediated communication as weakening senses of local belongingness and physical community even as they increase delocalized levels of social capital (as defined by Putnam).

Cellular or, more generally, mobile communication is an important part of the individual basis of the social network. In contrast to traditional societies, which exert morality through common will and purpose, the voluntary nature of cellular communication places individual interest before that of the community—though it can also develop and activate communities much faster than can physical communities (see Rheingold, 2002). As mobile phone users ignore their physical peers and communicate with their distant social ties, mobile phones are typically an impediment to society's moral project as unified whole and totality. This is precisely the point made by Gergen in his project on *Technology, Self, and the Moral* (Gergen, 2003). Fortunati (2002) likewise raised this concern regarding intimacy. Instead of having intimate relations with our entire community, we have intimate relations with our social network. Intimacy is not a general sentiment, but rather a guarded function.

Whereas the traditional community requires a whole, embodied self, the social network lends itself to fragmentation. (Mary Douglas's *Natural Symbols*, 1970, unfolded the idea that the body is a model for bounded systems. If our social networks are fragmented and boundless, then our bodies and selves must be as well.)

Turkle's discursive analysis of the technological interface fostered a conception of identity and the self as multiple. Just as Stone (1991) argued that virtual communities create a duality of person, Turkle argued that they offer us infinite divisions of the self. Wellman and Gulia noted that our personal communities are engaged in widespread social networks (1999), and Turkle added that these points of engagement can be accessed simultaneously through multiple windows on a computer. Similarly, Fortunati observed that some Italian women carry separate mobile phones for communicating with the husband and with the lover (2002). Technology sustains a conception of community as multiple and personal, in contrast to the stable identity and limited set of possibilities provided by face-to-face, physical communities. Indeed, communication technologies in general, but computer-based ones in particular, allow the "saturation of self," whereby a person can engage in all one's various possible identities, rather than be bounded by the traditional, single-location identity (Gergen, 1991).

For Stone, the virtual community is in cyberspace. It is a "passage point for collections of common beliefs and practices that united those who were physically separate" (1991, p. 85). Likewise, Baym believes that communities are based on coming together to share a common interest (1997). In her research on the USENET group r.a.t.s (rec.arts.tv.soaps; threaded postings about soap operas) Baym concluded that communities develop understood conventions, rather than objective patterns of organization. Even though they might not bear ties of sentiment or intimacy, virtual communities are fostered by forms of expression with group-specific meanings, specific identities, interpersonal relationships, and behavioral norms linked to the purpose of the group (Baym, 1995).

Early speculations concerning the way of life online were generally utopian in the extreme. There was much discussion of hacker ethos and other ways in which the social life in the virtual world would operate along new lines. Early reports supported this notion and many believed that a new dawn of utopian egalitarianism was at hand, and many were persuaded by such a hopeful portrait (Laurel, 2001). Such reports, in retrospect, were premature at best. Most evidence now points to the striking parallels between the way norms are created and enforced online and off. (See Sternberg, 2001, for an analysis of how virtual communities evolve toward regulating behavior similarly to face-to-face ones. Particularly striking in her analysis are the parallels in terms of how people govern transactions with strangers.)

An important difference between the two worlds is the degree of latitude one has in choosing communication partners and venues. In contrast to the involuntary nature of physical proximity, Steinmueller focused on the importance of voluntary association in defining virtual communities. He conceived that virtual communities exist when it is possible for a group of individuals to voluntarily interact and meet in cyberspace (Steinmueller, 2002). These social networks could be considered communities of intention.

Ultimately, Poster suggested that there is too much pessimism in predictions about the impact of the Internet and other electronic communications on community. It is true that the Internet will indeed determine the fate of groups in our world, but it will affect them only as they are currently constituted (Poster, 2001). The Internet is characterized as a threat to "general types of practice that are characterized as human," such as face-to-face communication, but everything that comes between human presence does not detract from the human condition, and it is a mistake to see it that way (Poster, 2001, p. 4). Rather, we must embrace the innovation of the Internet. Although mediated life does not and will never equal real life, mediated life is here to stay and is thus real for us as social actors. In sum, Poster stated that "one can expect . . . the birth of a monster, of a human-machine assemblage whose encounters may be feared as those of an alien but who surely will be yet another incarnation of ourselves" (2001, p. 128).

Pseudocommunity

The lower right quadrant represents those theorists who view community by its subjectively traditional connotations, yet do not require it to have a physical locality. These definitions of community resemble Merton's and Beniger's pseudocommunity. They might also represent the communities of ethnic or interest groups dispersed in society (Effrat, 1974). In other words, they imitate many of the mental, social, and interpersonal conceptions of traditional community, but have no stable geographic base. These socially constructed spaces are thus imitations (or, as their strong advocates claim, instantiations) of Gemeinschaft, sustained through exterior means.

For Rheingold, there was no question that community can exist through the use of Internet technologies. This community has nothing to do with our common conceptions of virtual communities. Rather, Rheingold defined community by the collective good; it is indeed a matter of emotions (2000). The collective good it fosters is information and knowledge sharing. It arises spontaneously, actually creating itself (2002). In this regard, it has a group memory preserved by computers. Virtual communities are not exclusive of relationships, but rather entail a many-to-many communication. As Rheingold explained, mobile phones create a self-conscious community (2002). They are based on everyone receiving similar information through their personal communication technologies. Like Anderson's definition of an imagined community, Rheingold construed person-to-person technologies of virtual communities as resulting in a horizontal community. If this is not true, which is what Poster found, then Rheingold's democratic and glorious virtual community is a mere simulacrum (2001). Rheingold is positioned under the context of pseudocommunity, because he interpreted virtual communities in terms of his conceptions of real, physical ones.

Like Rheingold, Nisbet (1966) held that the important concepts of community transcend locality and physical boundaries. For him, community is an innately moral concept, fused with intimacy. Community must conceive of the wholeness of man, and not simply one of his many roles. Nisbet thus shares many of the connotations of traditional community. However, whereas the traditional theorists link these sentiments to geographic community, Nisbet argued that they come from elsewhere and are independent of this limitation.

As with the pseudocommunity, Dirksen and Smit (2002) remarked that virtual communities engage in a great deal of the practices endorsed by idealists. Community is formed mentally and not physically, like imagined communities, but they emphasize the sense of belonging and having something in common. Community is created by people's attachment to it and being in it. Like traditional communities, the virtual community is spontaneous. This spontaneity, however, is actually a false sense of achievement, as it also requires sporadic and direct intervention to sustain the community, or at least reduce somewhat its potential ephemerality (Rice, 1987).

Imagined Community

The upper left quadrant deals with conceptions of community that share many of the industrial, modern subjective characteristics of virtual communities, yet still link community to a spatial location. These definitions resemble Anderson's imagined community, or perhaps modern neighborhoods (Effrat, 1974). These communities have a local base, but ultimately create their own reality through the autonomous and interest-laden ties common to the virtual community. It is necessary to unearth the created identities and essences in order to discover the root of the community in local life. Even in postmodern relationships, distinguished by fragmented identities and multiplicity (Gergen, 1991), geographical embedding is fundamental to forming a functional community (Kolko & Reid, 1998). If we fragment space, we fragment ourselves, and thus prevent effective, embodied community (Meyrowitz, 1985). Virtual expression is rooted in an embodied identity, which requires geographical situation (Kolko & Reid, 1998).

Poster (2001), although not promoting a theory of imagined community, did offer an excellent framework for understanding how it is easy to fall into the trap of theorizing the imagined community. As he presented it, the introduction of the nation-state required people to change their local, kinship identification and related instead to a less geographically immediate, but still intensely identified nation-state. The media played a huge part in this transition, and thus print was responsible for extracting the citizen from the face-to-face community. This transformation had a side effect on the individual: The individual necessarily had to emerge as an autonomous creature in order to connect successfully with the nation, which then bonded itself to the citizen through the text. With the decline of the nation-state in global importance, due to the general cultural globalization supported by the Internet and communication technologies, the citizen of the nation- state has furthered this individuation and become simply a person, who joins with others in virtual communities. Thus, this is exactly why the imagined community is one in which geography remains important, but it is inhabited by postmodern, disjointed individuals who imagine their communion.

Finally, in the wake of modernization, territorial groups struggle to build neighborhoods and communities of locality in order to build their own collective representations (Suttles, 1972). This local community is not naturally based on sentimentality, but rather is a symbol of what its members want to be. In other words, Suttles (1972) sees how the physical, face-to-face nature of the local community works to create an imagined community of sentiment, based on its opposition to outsiders.

Having examined these various models of community using quadrants, it is now time to explore how new, often mobile, mediated communication technologies affects community formation, development, and survival.

HOW MEDIATED COMMUNICATION INTERACTS WITH COMMUNITY

Working upon the foundation that every community is mediated to some extent, this section's central goal is to examine how extreme forms of virtuality and mediated communication, especially mobile phones, might affect theoretical constructions of community.

Transformation of the Community Concept

The community matrix, and its subsequent breakdown into quadrants, were meant to illustrate the overlapping theoretical tendencies of physical and virtual communities. Now that we have offered a broad, theoretical grasp on the concept of community, it is time to deflate the commonly perceived real/virtual dialectic of community. Like Wellman and Gulia (1999), Poster viewed what is currently perceived to be the loss of local community due to computers to be instead the continuation of a pre-existing process of liberating "the mind from the force of hierarchical relations" (Poster, 2001, p. 108). As he concluded, "we have a current tendency to bemoan the loss of community" due to computers, but would we feel the same way about it if the man were reading a book? (2001, p. 108). In order to overcome this dichotomy, Poster said it is necessary to replace Anderson's term "imagined" with the term "mediated." It is not that we are engaged in hyperreal, illusory communities of our own creation, but rather, that our real communities are now mediated through technology (per above, on a continuum from none to completely). Ultimately, Poster argued that it is media and print that make possible the public sphere; they do not detract from it as noted earlier by Habermas. As a result, the idealization of Habermas's homogenous public sphere of symmetrical relations and reason is denied by electronic mediation, and thus is not of any service to further analysis (Poster, 2001).

Other theorists believe that we need a concrete synthesis of virtual and physical communities in order to truly inhabit our experiences. Castells (2000) held that experience is related to place, and we thus need a bridge between physical and virtual places in order to unify our experience. Virtual communities deal only in fragmented individuals when they are opposed to real life.

Still others believe that only in bridging the dialectic can we hope to construct good communities in the present and future. For Etzioni (2001), the best communities are hybrids of physical and virtual communities. Likewise, Walls (1993), Etzioni (2001), and Katz and Rice (2002) viewed the ideal community as virtual communities enhancing physical communities. In addition, Slevin (2000) asked us to recognize that individuals are intelligent agents and are consciously looking to create meaning and new forms of human association online. The importance here is to cease the divide of virtual and physical cultures, allowing for a progression, rather than abandonment, of the notion of community. The concept of social capital is, thus, fundamental in examining the ways in which mediated communication, and cell phones in particular, provide this bridge.

Social Capital

Coleman, who originated the term social capital, defined it as a common set of expectations, a set of shared values, and a sense of trust among people (1986, p. 306). Social capital is based on the fact that trust will allow a community to accomplish more with their physical and mental capacities than can individuals alone. Coleman (1988) thus had a very individualistic interpretation of social capital, as it is a social function that individuals can use to achieve their own interests. In a more social interpretation, Bourdieu (1986) saw social capital as provided to members of actual social systems.

Putnam has described social capital as "networks, norms, and social trust that facilitate coordination and cooperation for mutual benefit" (2000, p. 66). More specifically, he has said:

> Social capital is simply social networks plus the norms of reciprocity and trustworthiness that arise from them. Period. There's nothing in that definition that requires FTF [face-to-face], although as an empirical matter FTF is probably correlated with density of ties and with degree of reciprocity. (personal communication, August 22, 2003)

Colleagues of Putnam have inquired deeply into his definition to find that it has two components: social contact and civic engagement (Wellman & Quan-Haase, in press). To this double definition, Quan-Haase, Wellman, Witte, and Hampton (2002) added a third component: a feeling of community, the attitudinal side of social capital. Its essential yardstick is sentiment, which refers to an individual's emotional attachment to a community (Bolan, 1997). Ultimately, social capital in this view is best sustained by simple community involvement.

It is easy to see how this common definition of social capital favors the traditional community. It promotes face-to-face contact, physical reciprocity, and intimate social trust. We have seen, however, that even virtual communities share in social capital, as they celebrate their ability to promote widespread community involvement and interaction in virtual space. More fundamentally, Wellman's open social network integrates trust on a wider scale that is not limited to a defended community. This concept of community allows trust, and social capital, to be fostered on a larger scale, rather than as a private commodity. Thus, large-scale communities of interest can be activated for specific events in ways simply not possible through physical communities, limited in space and time and bound to known others (Katz & Rice, 2002).

Additionally, social capital can also explain the imagined community and pseudocommunity. Suttles (1972) believes that the local community is necessarily a defended community in order to preserve its social capital. The sentimentality of the natural community may be simply a way to store and guard social capital. Against whom is the community guarding itself? The answer is people and other communities it does not trust. People imagine themselves as an intimate, physical community simply because they fear interaction with a larger network.

In Beniger's pseudocommunity (1987), these ties of trust and intimacy are not imagined, but rather are fostered by impersonal agents; thus, social capital itself is imitated. An example of this is seen when an Internet user provides an email address and cell number to a website, and thus receives spam mail and phone solicitors, who cater their advertisements to a user's recorded interests and habits, thus purporting to be helpful. The pseudocommunity is "pseudo" because this social capital is not present in interpersonal communion and active involvement, but merely fabricated for its conversion into economic capital (Merton, 1946).

Ultimately, those attributes of community that are shared by physical and virtual communities (near the middle of the dimensional axis of Figure 2) tend to involve the highest amounts of social capital. As a result, it is these attributes that will come into play in the next section.

AREAS OF INTEREST: COMMUNITY BUILDING AND COMMUNITY REDUCING

The concrete application of social capital to virtuality and mobile phones explains the ways in which mediated communication can be said to both strengthen and harm concepts of community. This section will examine the ways in which mediated communication affects community, as well as how community considerations affect the use of mediated communication. In order to do so, it will focus on various components of social capital, breaking them down into the positive and negative roles of mediated communication.

Interactions in the Physical Sphere

Advantage: Mediated communication extends real communities. Wellman and Gulia (1999) criticized Rheingold's glorification of virtual community precisely because he views the Internet as a separate reality. Rheingold did note that although his virtual community of interest, the WELL (Whole Earth 'Lectronic Link), fosters relationships both online and offline, he perceived them as distinct environments. In contrast, Wellman and Gulia (1999) sought to transform the conception of community to unify these realities. Rather than abandon the notion of community in today's world, they chose to look at how it has evolved into the social network. In "Net Surfers Don't Ride Alone" (1999), they noted the important fact that community is not a zero sum game. An increase in virtual social relations does not entail a decrease in real-life relationships. Rather, the Internet can supplement and extend community relations. For example, text messaging can be used to coordinate face-to-face meetings. Overall, Katz and Rice (2002) summarized this view asserting that individuals with a greater sense of belonging are more likely to surf the Internet, according to a 1995 national survey that has been followed up in subsequent years.

Mediated communication thus allows us to reach out to more people, but also to reinforce and reassemble community relations (Etzioni, 2001). Social network theory provided the basis for Blanchard and Horan (2000), when they concluded that social capital is enhanced when virtual communities develop around and extend physical communities. The functions of virtual communities to foster communities of interest, information spread, and equality of status all work to enhance social capital, despite their lack of direct physical orientation.

If the Internet and other communication technologies actually do increase social capital, then they will be accompanied by a rise in offline contact, civic engagement, and a sense of community, and the other traditional forms of social capital formulated by Coleman and Bordieu. Indeed, Katz and Rice (2002) found exactly that: Internet users (compared to nonusers) were more likely to be politically involved (both offline and, of course, online), to be involved in community organizations, and to communicate with friends and family. In a 1996 survey, they found that although Internet use does not predict voting behavior, neither does it diminish offline political behavior. Instead, between 10% and 25% of Internet users participate in some political/civic activity online and the amount of use is proportional with this activity. Later, in a 2000 survey, they found that 28% of Internet users belonged to a community organization, versus only 14.2% of nonusers (this distinction did not apply to religious or leisure organizations).

This position of Katz and Rice (2002) supported the transformists' position that the best communities combine physical proximity and mediated communication. We may think, then, of mediated communities as a supplement to physical communities rather than as complete substitutes. Figallo (1995), for example, conceptualized the Internet as a link between regionally based electronic communities and as an information resource for those communities. Ultimately, Katz and Rice (2002) saw no decline in community involvement due to the Internet; age, education, and income remain much stronger predictors of community involvement. They believed instead that the Internet encourages the yearning for information and association evident in further examples, and thus social capital is increased through Internet use.

The San Francisco-based WELL and the New York East Coast Hang Out (ECHO) (Horn, 1998) public conferencing and email systems are exemplars of integrated online and physical community. Horn's (1998) account of ECHO, the New York-based virtual salon, showed how online communities can reinforce and complement, even create and foster, physical communities and interest in local culture. As with the WELL in Berkeley, ECHO participants get together at different New York settings for social gatherings, and conversation and relations blend together their online and offline lives. Slack and Williams (2000) studied the Craigmillar Community Information Service (CCIS), developed for a town outside of Edinburgh where many civilians are poor and underemployed. Before the CCIS, Craigmillar exhibited no sense of community feeling, no motivation to socialize, and offered no social or cultural activities. By means of the CCIS, however, "Craigmillar has . . . doped a strategy of self-presentation that counters external representations and which works by being grounded in the highly spatialized notion of a tightly knit community" (p. 322). Quan-Haase, Wellman, Witte, & Hampton (2001) found, in their study of a leading-edge, broadband-wired suburb near Toronto called Netville, that online users are more active neighbors (knowing about 25 neighbors) than are nonusers (about 8), and their contacts range more widely throughout the neighborhood. Hampton (2000) found increased social network, social capital, and local community involvement associated with the Netville online infrastructure. From a community action perspective, the system allowed Netville members to react to the local housing developer about housing problem, though faster organizing, and a greater number of active members. This allowed them to achieve greater concessions from the developer and blocked a second development.

Similarly, the Big Sky Telegraph network in Montana, begun in 1988, connected the teachers, students, families, and communities of dispersed small schools throughout Montana (Uncapher, 1999). The residents of the Jervay low-income public housing development in Wilmington, NC (mostly African American women) used the Internet as a tool to support their collective action of resisting proposed demolition and reconstruction of the development by housing authority officials (Mele, 1999). Shapiro and Leone (1999) described the effectiveness of a supplemental community network in Blacksburg, Virginia, where over 60% of the citizens participate. Parents and teachers communicated online and citizens participated in surveys regarding municipal government. While much attention is paid to the exotic and social aspects of online communities, they also represent consequential social policy issues, such as supporting neighborhood and community relations, local school systems, and public access to government services and information (Doheny-Farina, 1998), especially health information and services (Rice & Katz, 2001).

Despite the fact that mainstream communication scholars have, until recently, generally ignored mobile phones, there has nonetheless developed a small but robust set of studies that suggest how mobile communication technology has been modifying the web of social relations. The bulk of research seems to support the notion that mobiles improve relationships. Although these conclusions are plausible, numerous methodological questions that remain unanswered prevent a firm conclusion in this regard. Among the studies are:

1. A 2000 national random sample survey (Rice & Katz, 2003) found that only about 1 in 7 respondents reported that mobiles had caused problems in their primary relationship, and a much larger proportion thought that mobile phones improved their relationships.

2. Palen, Salzman, and Young (2001) concluded that 19 new mobile phone users found themselves more accessible to their social network; much communication was affect-oriented and psychologically pleasurable.

3. Oksman and colleagues at the Finnish University of Tampere have shown that mobile communication practices have become central to the construction and maintenance of teens' (and preteens') social networks (Oksman & Rautiainen, 2002)

4. Henderson, Taylor, and Thomson's (2002) studies in the United Kingdom and Northern Ireland demonstrated that mobile phones affect young people's sociality. They describe sociality as a practice that contributes to the securing of social capital, or resources based on connections and group membership. First, phones operated as commodities within a material economy and second, phones operated as a medium for social capital.

5. Blinkoff and Blinkoff (2002) claimed, based on ethnographic research of 160 mobile users in six countries (U.S., Italy, Sweden, Brazil, Australia, and China), that mobile devices are primarily a relationship tool. A consistent element in the mobile user stories he collected was that people see the mobile as a way to maintain relationships in a rewarding manner. This need was particularly important, he found, due to the perceived growing complexity of daily life.

Studies such as the one by Katz (1999) suggest that the mobile phone strengthens the user's existing social ties. Elliott (2003) studied the use of mobile phones by networks of New York cab drivers. She concluded that "days and nights spent in dozens of cabs, where conversations were recorded and translated, have revealed a spectacular alternate work of words beamed from cellphones to invisible audiences around the city and planet" (2003, p. A1). The cab itself, of course, is an interesting social convergence of the public and private, and now cab drivers maintain and develop their professional, ethnic, and social networks while driving strangers around town. One particularly interesting mediated community: "the group of Sherpa drivers who went to the same high school in Nepal and now debate, on a cell phone family plan, the Maoist guerrilla occupation of their hometown" (p. A1). This invisible communication network also provides much more immediate and practical social capital for the cabby community: business location, traffic and weather conditions, and maintenance contact with the family during long hours, sometimes simply to reassure the spouse that they have not been robbed or attacked. The mediated community support seems to be more valuable than in prior years when, cabby lore has it, there was much more conversation between driver and passenger—another possible indicator of the overall decline in social capital.

Disadvantage: Mediated communication disrupts real communities. Even though the above cab example showed how mediated communication has the potential to correct and counteract the general decline in social capital, there is evidence that it often works in an equal y negative way. Mediated communication may strengthen participation in one's community of choice, but often at the expense of the physical community at hand. To continue the preceding example, Elliott (2003) noted that cab drivers can become distracted, confused, or embarrassed when passengers talk, often loudly, on their cell phones on topics ranging from business deals to sexual exploits.

In response, there is a general dystopic concern that mediated communications, especially Internet use, lead to a decline in physical involvement in community (Baudrillard, 1983; Beniger, 1987; Calhoun, 1986; Gergen, 1991; Kiesler, Siegel, & McGuire 1984; Turkle, 1996). Moreover, Stoll (1995), Noll (1997), and Nie (2001) viewed the Internet as specifically taking away interactions in real-life communities, which are necessarily more meaningful than virtual communities (cited in Katz & Rice, 2002). Likewise, Shapiro & Leone (1999) viewed online interactions as indirectly proportional to offline interactions, working in the context of community as zero sum game. Katz and Rice (2002) further expounded on additional disruptions caused by the Internet, such as addiction, dependencies, violence, hate groups, and stalking.

As a result of this pessimistic perspective, many researchers have observed how the relation of individuals and space has changed as a result of mobile communication devices. Fortunati (2002) claimed that individuals now have the possibility of choosing more easily between the physical space and the psychological space of the intimacy of their social network. One has the possibility of choosing between public space (streets, bus stops) and private space (friends one decides to call using mobile phone). She concluded that when an individual uses the mobile phone in a public space, he or she is only half-present. The individual is present in body but not in the attention, mind, and senses.

Palen, Salzman, and Young (2001) commented on the conflict of social spaces. They were attempted to answer why the public use of a mobile phone is so offensive to some people: Talking on a mobile phone in a public place is in part a matter of a conflict of social spaces in which people assume different faces. When a call is received via the mobile, the individual needs to figure out what face takes precedence. When a mobile phone user is on the phone, the individual is simultaneously in two spaces: the physical space and the virtual space of the mobile communication. Choosing to be behaviorally present in a different space from one's physical location may be perceived as inconsiderate by those in the physical space. What is apparent to the public is that the face one presents on the phone is different from the face assumed just before the phone call. Fortunati (2000) argued that mobile phones have facilitated a preference for interacting with those who are distant as opposed to those who are in the immediate vicinity and hence leads to a withdrawal from experiencing public sites. This can be observed in most public settings such as a train station or a bus stop in which people engrossed in a mobile phone conversation are most often unmindful of their surroundings. An effect of mobile phones is to privatize communication, isolating the mobile user socially from the public world where he or she is physically located, while also imposing that private communication (usually just one half of it, except in the increasingly distressing context of mobile walkie-talkies) onto the public realm (Fortunati, 2002; Rice & Katz, 2003). Far from being invisible connectors (Chayko, 2002), phones, especially mobile phones, are very visible entities and can be extremely intrusive when used in a shared space.

The physical and sensory space of both mobile phone users and others within sight and hearing is often violated by a mobile phone call (Rice & Katz, 2003). The user cannot continue with the task at hand when he or she receives a call. Even if the individual chooses not to accept the call, the ringing still causes a disruption of the current activity (such as in a classroom or movie theatre). Outcomes such as these led Morse (1998) to conclude that electronic communications disrupt community and undermine face-to-face relations. Licoppe and Heurtin (2002) found that people refrained from using their mobile phones in bars and restaurants but didn't think twice about using them on the street or at a bus stop. This could be perhaps because in an enclosed setting, everything is magnified and one tends to feel part of a smaller group engaged in similar activities. However, on the street, there is a lot of space and each one is engaged in different activities. Rice and Katz (2003) reported that a national survey showed that by far the most unacceptable mobile discourtesy was when automobile drivers were using their mobile phones, presumably because the consequences of this may be highly significant and damaging to many others in public spaces.

People have devised many methods of dealing with these constant interruptions. Most often people just turn off their mobile phones when they do not wish to be disturbed. At other times, people hurry through a phone call or step out of a setting, such as a queue, to take the call (Licoppe & Heurtin, 2002). When a mobile phone rings in a public setting, it gets everyone's attention. People not only check their own phones, but also look to see whose phone it is. When the call is answered, people tend to look away or stare at nothing in particular. They look anywhere except at the person who is engaged in a mobile phone call. When a person chooses not to answer the phone, there are also reactions—most often, people offer an inquiring look. This discussion of conflicts of space is a perfect illustration of how our considerations of community impact our attitudes towards mediated communication, and mobile phones in particular.

Community Composition

Advantage: Mediated communication develops heterogeneous communities. What Van Dijk (1999) called an organic community (comprised of face-to-face interactions) is made up of a relatively homogeneous group of people because they have several interests in common, whereas a virtual community is relatively heterogeneous because only one interest links the participants in that community (though, of course, they may participate in multiple communities, each with its own focused interest). What might appear as online communities are really people who share some (usually single) category, whether it is a special interest or an easily generalized identity, not people bound across multiple activities or social differences (Jones, 1999). As a result, his reasoning followed, a physical (organic) community has a better chance of building and maintaining its own culture and identity than does a virtual community. Virtual and mediated communities, however, also work to overcome exclusionary barriers of race, gender, ethnicity, class, and sexual orientation that are often pervasive in the physical sphere. An analysis of the nearly 3,000 respondents to the 2000 General Social Survey data by Robinson at the University of Maryland (Young, 1996) found that Internet users are more likely to be socially tolerant and accept a wider diversity of opinions and social identities. Mediated communication and virtuality require one to exit a local sphere of comfort and engage in a wider scope of community formation with many more variables at hand.

Even though social conflicts in mediated communities are inescapable, they act as physical communities do to enhance their social cohesion by responding to controversies and differences in community-building ways. Only "all-powerful love" and dedication keeps the virtual community together, just as in the idealized physical community (Rheingold, 2000, p. 41).

As stated earlier, Morgan (1942) observed that real communities are based on coming together for the common good, something greater than each individual, and not on meeting individual needs through offering services in a heterogeneous environment. To the contrary, Rheingold (2000) has shown that virtual communities indeed are formed around the basis of a common good. For example, both Putnam (1993) and Rheingold (2000) viewed the public or common good as a key expression and reservoir of social capital. In this regard, the common good, although not subsuming all other personal interests, does indeed seem to drive community participants towards an organic unity.

Social capital is marked by equality of community relations. Poster (2001) noted that although new technology does not cancel out traces of face-to-face power relations virtual communities do exhibit a decrease in hierarchies of race, class, age, status, and gender. As a result, these more heterogeneous communities exhibit social capital, resisting inequalities in modern society. They function as Habermas's proposed public sphere, without actually being so or intending it (see Katz & Rice, 2001, for further statistics on Internet use as increasing involvement and tolerance).

Sennett and Giddens both discovered opportunities for the transformation of community in nontechnological ways, although they are strong proponents of the traditional community. In *The Fall of the Public Man*, Sennett (1977, 1995) echoed Tönnies in bemoaning the loss of Gemeinschaft and the true collective being. He noted that community is inherently anticity and is instead a reactive withdrawal from society as a territorial barricade within the city. On the other hand, in *The*

Uses of Disorder, Sennett emphasized that a community is "a social group in which men believe that they share something together . . . a common identity" (1971, p. 31). Community is thus an act of will and not experience. This draws obvious parallels to the imagined community, discussed above. Even though Sennett missed the we feeling of community, he also realized that in expelling deviants who vary from the sameness of gemeinschaft, we are alienating ourselves from our species being. The solution instead is to find a community of otherness, much like Durkheim's organic solidarity. Likewise, Giddens (1994) called for an interreliance and communion through difference. This acceptance of the community as a mixed salad, rather than melting pot, is threatening to traditional identity-based societies, such as France (Poster, 2001). In doing so, it is important to create a new sense of place where people can discover a purpose for their lives and cope with the global economy (state of disorder). Neither Sennett nor Giddens were willing to forgo space as a base for community, but they were willing to see community outside of gemeinschaft.

Disadvantage: Mediated communication supports exclusionary, homogenous communities. Tepper (1997) noted that in order to enforce community standards and cohesions virtual communities can also apply exclusion. Just like real communities, boundary demarcation can be important to virtual community identity as well. One way this happens is through trolling, as a USENET community's information managers and some members ostracize an outsider's post by replying to it with flaming or harsh language. Tepper remarked that people also seek to maintain private communities in public space. Rheingold (1993) noted that community is not a conflict-free environment and thus, that the occasional flaming, gossip, or argument that occurs in virtual communities can enhance, rather than detract, from the feeling of community. Indeed, some USENET groups specifically advocate and practice the art of flaming as their main purpose. Although mediated communication and virtuality can provide an outlet for certain repressed margins of society, they also foster exclusionary tactics.

As a result of these claims, Gurak (1997) pointed out that virtual communities work to squash opposing viewpoints and exaggerate their own claims. Likewise, Sunstein (2001) pointed out that participation in virtual communities online brings about the creation of a more egoistic individual, who takes comfort in his ability to live without confronting opposing views. In addition, Calhoun (1986, p. 389) believed that the compartmentalization of communities of interest runs directly counter to Habermas' public sphere. These considerations led Katz and Rice (2002) to muse that unfettered communication may not necessarily foster health and socially beneficial communities. Nonetheless, even among these homogeneous communities, these technologies' ability to create easy communication and shared information remains a vital common good and ingredient of Putnam's (2000) social capital.

Size

Advantage: Mediated communication increases contacts in the social network. As social capital is proportional to the quality or effectiveness of a community, a corollary would be that size ipso facto exerts a powerful influence on its creation and use. Indeed, the concept of positive network externality posits that social capital, such as the value of belonging to a network or community, grows much more rapidly than the number of participants (*N*), because it is the total number of possible relationships (*N* times *N*-1) that generates potential resources (see Katz & Rice, 2002; Rice, 1982, 1990).

Disadvantage: Mediated communication increases social distance, reducing social capital. On the other hand, Coleman (1986) claimed that social capital decreases when communities become quite large because, due to the permutation of interaction partners, individuals can defect from a group (in game-theoretic terms), capturing for themselves the benefits without having to bear the cost of reciprocation.[3] Small communities that exert high social pressure are rich in social capital. In addition, Calhoun (1980) held that community cannot be defined purely by members' location in a common locality or members' abstract sense of belonging together. Rather, his concept of community examined the ways in which members actually change their actions based on their relations to their community.

Commenting on social capital and education, Coleman and Hoffer (1987) recognized that community more strongly influences educational success than do variations in schools. The wholeness and integrity of the local community therefore must be preserved in order to enhance the social capital of its members, a greater public good.

Spontaneous, Voluntary, and Frequent Communication

Advantage: Mediated communication creates local, spontaneous bulwark of community association. Putnam (1993, 2000) noted that social capital fosters spontaneous, voluntary cooperation due to the forms of reciprocity, norms, and networks of civil engagement inherent in social capital. Putnam observed:

> Some technologies (e.g., the telephone) seem in practice to be used primarily to reinforce close, FTF ties. (Except for phone sex, people don't normally make new friends on the telephone.) The internet can certainly be used to reinforce close ties. . . . However, some aspects of internet technology can also be used in principle to reinforce weak ties (e.g., among long-lost school classmates). What I'm most skeptical about is the idea (now less common, of course) that the internet would create "virtual communities" entirely untethered from any FTF links.

> E-mail seems to me an unmitigated positive for social capital in the sense I defined it, and is probably very good for both strong ties and weak ties. . . . I don't know about instant messaging, although a student of mine did a preliminary study that suggested it was much better for maintaining strong ties (and ties that were rooted in FTF ties) than for creating new weak ties. (He tried using instant messaging to contact strangers and found that far fewer than one percent responded favorably.) I'm less sure about internet-based gaming or chat rooms. I don't see any reason in principle to think that mobile phones will have a different sort of impact than immobile phones, which was (I take it from Claude Fisher's work) mostly positive, but not transformative. I'm skeptical about broad generalizations about technology's impact, since different technologies are likely to have different effects. However, one broad trend over the last 100 years . . . has been the use of technology to privatize and individualize entertainment (TV, of course, but also recorded music and all the other elements in the modern "home entertainment

center"). I would not argue that all the effects of that master trend have been evil—I definitely do not like being or being thought to be a cultural grouch—but I do think that the privatization of leisure time is a very real and powerful trend that has thinned our social connections with other people. (Personal communication, August 22, 2003)

As these remarks suggest, Putnam's theorizing about social capital is readily applicable to mobile phones, as reciprocity norms are found in peoples' tendency to return calls and text messages, as well as informal dinner invitations over the mobile. We can also see networks of voluntary, spontaneous civil engagement in the ever-evolving field of mobile phone etiquette. At the same time, concerns about the loss of public civility in the pursuit of private pleasures, as implied in Putnam's comment above, certainly seem to hold true concerning mobile phone use (Katz, 2003; Rice & Katz, 2003).

Shareware also exemplifies reciprocity in virtual communities (Stone, 1998), as does participation within and across computer-mediated conference groups (Rice, 1982). Further, Turkle claimed that MUD Object Oriented (MOO) and MUDs "honor people's desires to connect and not to be lonely, and to form community" (in Bollier, 1995, p. 27). Overall, Poster (2001) noted that the Internet is a general economy of sharing that is not specific to barter or commodity exchange, but rather returns to the primordial social act.

Coleman (1986) noted the basis of affectual community is frequent informal communication. This is exactly the essence of the cellular, virtual community. Mobile phones provide an ideal case for this region of overlap, because the mobile phone call is less disembodied than other forms of computer-mediated communication technologies. The mobile phone includes the voice (and, recently, a video image and/or personal ring tones). This added sense of personality allows the mobile phone to connect different social networks and create a sense of belonging (Johnsen, 2003). The informal and perpetual nature of the mobile phone, its perpetual presence (Gergen, 2003; Katz & Aakhus, 2002), allows constant gift reciprocity and gossip that nurture social ties. Johnsen (2003) construed the Internet, at least the noncommercial sites, as primarily a gift economy involving participants in ongoing relations, rather than a site for commodity transactions among self-interested, independent actors. Givers gain self-efficacy in online relationships and prestige as informed sources, the information gifts become public goods shared by (i.e., cannot be kept from) all other members of the distribution list, newsgroup or Web forum, and the economies of scale derived from having many participants typically generate positive network externalities. We can see that mobile phones are not stand-alone technologies, but rather are integrated in the larger domain of social networks.

In fact, some argue that it is the frequency and continuity of conversation flow via mobile phones, not the content itself, that guarantees strength of relation (Licoppe, 2003). Likewise, Rheingold (2002) stated that text messaging is often more effective than a phone call in coordinating people and maintaining regular, daily contact. Perhaps text messaging also avoids all the tricky boundary work that happens when you are in a public place and having a private mobile phone conversation. One can text message in front of the world without disclosing any one-sided conversations or imposing one's privacy on the public. It is thus a more private technology, potentially, than the mobile phone (Rice & Katz, 2003).

Likewise, Fortunati (2002) described mobile phones as a device that lets one contact somebody of his or her intimate circle in order to activate the feeling of familiarity when in an environment perceived to be extraneous. She explained that mobile is used by people to strengthen communicative immediacy with their social networks when faced with the lack of informative immediacy of the place. She concluded that people are more interested in chosen sociality rather than chance sociality.

The frequency of mediated communication also helps to retain important social ties of community. Fischer (1982, p. 176) also found that local ties were not more intimate or crucial than distant ones; people kept distant associates in their networks because they were crucial or intimate. Frequency of contact as a cause for intimacy was not supported clearly and it could indeed be, as suggested by Fischer (1982), that frequency of contact is a consequence as opposed to a cause of closeness.

Disadvantage: Mediated communication relies on voluntary participation, neglecting involuntary association. Voluntary and spontaneous cooperation are tied together by the notion of social capital; however, they do imply an inherent contradiction. Many theorists hold that communities cannot be ordered into existence; they must arise spontaneously. This makes it especially problematic to determine the basis for community feeling online, as it is, in some sense, self-created. Mediated communication offers few possibilities to become involuntarily involved in community formation. In fact, in those few cases in which mediated communication does surpass our intentions, perhaps when a mobile phone picks up another's wavelength, or we mistakenly subscribe to an online newsletter, we become frustrated by our involvement in another community.

The intentionality inherent in mediated communication allows for the relaxed form of non-task-based communication that fosters face-to-face feelings of intimacy. Fortunati (2002), however, noted that mobile phones can at the same time frustrate communication, as people use them for short, information-eliciting conversations, or conversely, as an occupational mechanism while bored. Do we perhaps construct our feelings of spontaneous intimacy and attempts at informal conversation based on our desire to have a voluntary choice in our community formation?

Unfortunately, the information overload that results from mediated communication, as well as the general feeling that we are isolated when not plugged in, leads to what has been called the New Economy Depression Syndrome, or NEDS (Soto, 2003). Even though this is a variant on an old theme, the problem seems to be growing as gadgetry proliferates.

Interpersonal Bonds and Network Formation

Advantage: Mediated communication creates strong and widespread interpersonal ties. Wellman and Quan-Haase (in press) supported this idea as they see social capital increased through the use of information technologies, which connect distant and local communities and thus increase interpersonal bonds. Wellman viewed the Internet as very different from the television: It is less individually immersive and more actively and socially engaging. Likewise, Poster (2001) saw broadcast media as rigidly determined, whereas the Internet offers avenues for action and interpretation. In increasing social interaction and civic involvement, Wellman (like Katz & Rice, 2002) conceptualized the Internet and other virtual communities as increasing social capital. Ultimately, for Wellman and Gulia (1999), it was the very fears of virtual community that so trouble commentators that revealed just how important online connections are becoming. Turkle disputed the argument that Internet communities promote only secondary relationships. For example, she provided the example of one SeniorNet member who received dozens of calls and cards from her cyber friends as she lay dying in the hospital (in Bollier, 1995). Overall, there is a considerable body of scholars who, like Shapiro & Leone (1999), believe that the existence of virtual communities online reflects the desire for a more connected way of living.

Cyberspace involvement can create alternative communities that are as valuable and useful as our familiar, physically located communities (Preece, 2000; Rheingold, 1993; Sudweeks, McLaughlin, & Rafaeli, 1998). The weak ties that online communities enable may provide better and different kinds of resources than strong, familial ties. For example, online communities of patients with various kinds of terminal or serious illnesses can supply both the anonymity and objectivity that patients cannot or may not receive from family and friends, who may try to protect the patient by not providing complete feedback, or who may feel neither comfortable nor experienced enough to provide insight about the patient's condition (Rice & Katz, 2001). The Internet's potential to support such communities is largely due to a combination of several factors: increased bandwidth, continuous access, wireless portability, anonymity globalized connectivity, and personalization (such as collaborative filtering and content associated by shared users, individual email profiles and Web portals, and online communities of interests).

Calhoun (1986) took the position that the Internet encourages indirect relations with people, which although less meaningful, are nonetheless productive and work to enhance real-life relations. Granovetter (1973) argued that an innovation to be diffused can reach a larger number of people and traverse greater social distance when passed through weak ties as opposed to strong ties. Fischer (1982) argued that local ties, which are viewed as being superior to spatially dispersed ties, are in fact superior only by virtue of the fact that they are cheaper. He contended that distance is a cost of a social interaction like any other cost. Alternative ties are becoming cheaper through rapid transportation and new technologies such as mobile phones and the Internet. People are forming relationships across greater distances for relevant purposes based on the type of community to which they belong. This chapter, however, does not contend that one has to be the member of only one community. The more communities one is a part of, the more time is invested in keeping the ties alive.

A study conducted by Kim (2002) in Korea showed that Korean youth felt the need to be a part of the social network and felt that this could be achieved by being in touch with one another at any time and any place. People must be members of multiple groups, as these groups are formed on selective basis such as hometown, family name, or school attended. It would be fair to say that multiple groups would take up greater involvement via the mobile phone if being the member of one such group demanded time and energy (Kim, 2002). This is in agreement with Granovetter's (1973) hypothesis that if the tie between two individuals is strong, then the likelihood of these individuals knowing an overlapping number of people in a larger social milieu is more likely than if they had a weak tie.

The effect that a mobile phone will have on ties depends also on what kind of tie is being studied. Weak ties between women may have different characteristics from weak ties between men, or between adults and adolescents. The tie could also be between a superior and a subordinate at work, or between extroverts and introverts. It is not merely involvement with a group or a set of groups but also the fact that the mobile phone helps to establish bonds over space and time. It could be argued that long-lasting, bond-nurturing home phone calls could establish strong ties and that short goal-oriented phone calls establish weak ties. It is not, however, the length of the phone call alone that has an impact on the nature of the bond. A series of brief phone calls could also strengthen weak ties and establish and strengthen strong ties. For example, a mother who calls her teenager to find out where he or she is makes a brief, goal-oriented call, and yet this strengthens the trust that she shares with her child.

Disadvantage: Mediated communication ignores local ties and interactions. How does this newfound mobility affect social capital? Magdol and Bessel (2003) noted that social capital theory requires physical proximity and residential stability as prerequisites for a good community. In their study, they found that the availability of emotional and financial support was not affected by mobility distance, but that tangible favors and companionship were. As kin exchanges are affected by distance, nonkin exchanges increase, suggesting the replacement of kin by closer, nonkin in the social network. Social capital thus decreases as weak ties replace former strong, kinship-based ones (Magdol & Bessel, 2003). In contrast, Wellman and Hampton (2001b) noted that distance affects friend ties much more than kin ties. One's friends tend to be localized, which enhances the physical proximity requirement of social capital, but not the residential stability requirement that involves maintaining the same close ties with one's relatives through one's life. Likewise, online ties are likely to be more ephemeral, less sustainable, and easily excitable, compared to physical community relations (Jones, 1999; Rice, 1987; Shapiro & Leone, 1999).

Even though mobile devices assist in strengthening the individual's social network, some researchers claim that mobile devices are not used by individuals to expand their networks. Geser (2003), for example, claimed that mobile phones may support tendencies towards social closure rather than tendencies to open up. In other words, mobile phones can easily be used to shield one from making new acquaintances. People can escape into the narrower realm of highly familiar, predictable, and self-controlled social relationships. As a result, although the chances of interacting with strangers can be reduced, circles of established friendships can be deepened.

This is supported further by the fact that mobile phone numbers are usually communicated to a narrow circle of self-chosen friends and acquaintances so that no calls from unpredictable new sources have to be expected. People do not generally divulge their mobile telephone number except to people with whom they have very close relationships, or strong ties, as Granovetter defined it. The mobile phone thus creates a message to other people, who are accepted members of a particular individual's close circle of friends or family (Licoppe & Heurtin, 2002). This is not just a matter of trust but also of exclusivity. As Fortunati (2002) conceived of it, chance socialness is reduced. This theme is explored at length in Ling (in press), who describes the process as walled gardens. Ling envisions the net effect of strengthening the emotional content and thus the robustness of within-group social linkages, at the expense of more far-flung and cross-group or out-group networks.

Ling (2003) discussed how mobile phones can affect social capital at various levels. Mobile phones can be used in a particular social network such as a circle of friends to maintain a sense of connectedness (e.g., in terms of location or current news). He distinguished between this and emotionally based interaction, in which coordination is not the focus as much as interaction. The distinction could then be stretched to mobile conversations that strengthen weak ties and strong ties. He also stated that the coordinating talk can result in distancing one's self from people in the immediate vicinity or, as it was earlier defined, people who share a public space. It can be hypothesized then that strengthening weak ties through mobile phone usage almost eliminates possible ties with those in one's shared physical space. If one starts ignoring members of society who are copresent, becaue one is a member of another virtual community connected through the mobile phone, there could be some extensive negative ramifications, including the reduction in feelings of social integration, if not necessarily any reduction in social capital (Katz, 2003b).

Mediated communication can thus work to promote exclusion on a physical basis. For Wellman and Gulia (1999), the effect of distance on community produces geographically dispersed, specialized ties that are connected by telecommunications. Community becomes transformed into a personal-based, social network. Actual local communities then become loosely bound and sparsely knit (2001). As a result, neighborhoods have not disappeared. Wellman noted, however, that we have responded to the loose social network by engaging in selective neighboring, much like the community of limited liability. In response to this perceived social and physical distance, local neighborhoods work to increase services and reinforce security and a general sense of belonging (Wellman, 1988a).

Meaningful Communication, Trust, and Intimacy

Advantage: Mediated communication supports the effectual base of community. Here, the role of communication in sustaining any kind of community plays a pivotal role. As Poster (2001) observed, we imagine our virtual communities as real. The inverse must also be true. In this way, the role of communication as meaningful and value-based in virtual communities also works to construct real communities. Sanders further stated that community is "a system of social interaction and communication," and the two are interchangeable (1966, p. 347). What physical communities do through face-to-face communication to maintain their identity, virtual communities do through mediated communication. They are one and the same.

Strong community ties are linked to intimacy, voluntary involvement, frequency of communication, feelings of companionship, knowing each other in multiple contexts, enduring ties, mutual ties, having one's needs met, and shared social characteristics (Wellman & Gulia, 1999). Virtual communities and online environments deliver all of these, some argue, except emotional expression, intimacy, and multiple contexts. Ultimately, however, people base intimacy on shared interests and not shared social characteristics, such as in real-life communities. Wellman and Gulia noted that relational development takes longer online due to the lower bandwidth, its asychronicity, and the lack of physical cues; however, intimacy is not precluded. Walther (1996) indeed showed that mediated relational development could achieve levels of face-to-face relational development given sufficient time. Straus (1997) and Walther (1996) went so far as to claim that computer-mediated communication is as or more personal than face-to-face interactions. In addition, A. D. Smith (1999) noted that the physical distance and anonymity actually gives users support for intimacy in their relations. Unlike physical communities, the anonymity of online communities actually makes people more willing to help each other (Wellman & Gulia, 1999). This led Uslaner (2000) to claim that Internet use gradually produces environs of trust for its users.

On the other hand, Steinmueller (2002) claimed that virtual communities exhibit the full range of human emotion. One way that this seeming paradox is possible is through the employment of emoticons and emoting. Emoticons are an important way that the emotional embodied individual feels a sense of online community, despite narrow broadband (Baym, 1997; Curtis, 1996). Likewise, emoting is a replacement for real-life nonverbal behavior (Curtis, 1996; Kollock & Smith, 1999; Rheingold, 2000). High bandwidth also allows the addition of avatars and real-time video and audio streaming, which enhances community in realistic ways (Kollock & Smith, 1999). Kodama (2001) asserted that VideoNet technology actually provides the empathy and solidarity necessary for community formation and found in face-to-face communication. These emotional expressions on the Internet make it possible to understand the development of affectual communities online. The affectual community often links to a common memory and identity. Just as Bellah et al. (1985) spoke of the community of memory as being key to community identity and sentiment formation, personal Web pages allow people to share in their own communities of memory (Hozic, 2001). Additionally, online health support communities can exhibit high and consistent degrees of empathy for others (Preece & Ghozati, 2001). In the importance of virtual communication as substituting for physical social interaction, we can see the fundamental element of how virtual communities resemble physical communities in their formations of sentiment and community feeling.

For Wilbur (2000), a sense of virtual community requires a space of communication shared with others and an immersive connection with others (through which we create our own simulation of community in our heads, similar to the imagined community). Likewise, Baym (1995) perceived the shared norms of communicative practice as being the resource that brings everyone together to share in the meaning-making of a community. For example, online senses of social or shared interest distance can be measured in what Kendall (2003) calls "e-distance." Here, the distance from one place or one personal Web page to another is the number of clicks that it takes to get to them. One- and two-click e-distance imply a strong sense of community and cooperation among the actors creating and using those Web pages, just as Wellman's social network functions in real life.

The vastly increased ability to share information and reduce e-distance is a crucial factor in community formation. Jones (1999) emphasized that new media facilitate increased choice: The information highway will allow us to "forge our own places from among the many that exist, not by creating new places but by simply choosing from the menu of those available" (p. 220). For example, the Cultural Access Group's (2001) study of ethnic differences among online users reported that 59% of their African American and 73% of their Hispanic respondents reported that the Internet keeps them connected to their ethnic community, and find that the content on African American (79%) or Hispanic (69%) Web sites is meaningful to them. The link between online involvement and diversity may go even deeper than manifestations of particular groups of users.

Community is not built into residential life, but rather into the value-laden access of other people, the ability of moral and trustworthy communication (Etzioni, 2001). This expression of social capital as meaningful communication parallels Rheingold (1993), for whom knowledge sharing is a form and resource of social capital. Developments of trust are essential to determining meaningful communication, and trust is also a key component of social capital (Giddens, 1994). An example of trust building in a virtual community is the reputation system critiqued by Baym (1997). Members of online soap opera communities, as well as other virtual communities such as eBay, have the ability to rate other members and their posts according to their work and value, thus providing a trustworthiness database for all to see.

Cerulo (1997), somewhat rejecting Beniger's (1987) critique of the pseudo-community created by digital mass media, argued that we need to reconceptualize community due to the rise of new communication technologies, based on evidence about social interaction and social bonding (see also Rice, 1987) in settings such as parasocial interaction with mediated personalities, call-in radio shows, and emotional support in online discussion groups. Systems such as the Internet can "sustain forms of ongoing and improvisational group life where interactions cannot easily or routinely be face-to-face—including among members of discredited groups marginalized from public spheres" (Mukerji & Simon, 1998, p. 261).

Disadvantage: Mediated communication builds pseudocommunities. The idea of distance and physical community can also work to explain the pseudocommunity. As noted earlier, virtual communities still work around references to real-life images of space (Kollock & Smith, 1999; Stone, 1991). We require these images to create our affectual and emotional attachments to virtual communities. However, Rice (1987) and Shapiro and Lenone (1999) pointed out that virtual communities and the ties found within them are ephemeral, less sustainable, and much more easily excitable than in physical communities.

Just as with the pseudocommunity, Jeffres, Atkin, and Neuendorf (2002) noted that the distance of small communities from the center city is proportional to their dependence on the media versus their interpersonal influence in the political arena. The pseudocommunity emerges again to be one created by the media, which exploits the distance of its members and their yearning for small community. This is problematic, as Wright (2000) noted that city populations are dropping due to the resurgence of the suburban, small town: In 1970, 25% of Americans lived in cities, compared with 21% in 1990.

In *Bowling Alone* (2000) Putnam maintained, as seen above, that social capital is the glue that holds a livable society together. Without it, communities suffer: Crime rates balloon, social services wither, and people become depressed or sick or even die. With its ability to provide both one-way information and two-way communication, the Internet and mobile communication technologies provide an interesting potential. Putnam was equivocal and allowed for future improvements; however, he concluded that mediated communication inhibits interpersonal collaboration and trust (Putnam, 2000, p. 176).

Even though our communities are no longer our neighborhoods or our geographic locations, we create them instead in the social circles we come to inhabit (Fuentes, 2000). Perhaps, this all comes down to the fact that the further one gets away from the traditional community and home, the more one misses it (Fuentes, 2000; Terkenli, 1995). Mediated communities are thus not seen as real communities, but rather our imagined ways to deal with the social consequences of our chosen life paths. If we tend to imagine our virtual communities in terms of our idealized physical communities, those few aspects of virtual community that deviate from this mold may show the potential for a real transformation and synthesis of the community concept.

Distance

Advantage: Mediated communication keeps communities alive over distances. Communication technologies and the Internet are lauded for their ability to make distance irrelevant (Fuentes, 2000; M. J. Smith, 1999; Walmsley, 2000). It is in fact the virtual reduction of the friction of distance that Walmsley (2000) viewed as helping strengthen physical communities. In this context, Katz and Rice (2002) found that the social communities of Internet users are more dispersed than those of nonusers. In addition, Internet users are more likely to make long-distance telephone calls, according to their 1995 survey. The Internet is thus correlated, rather than causal, of breakdowns in physical community.

The mobile phone may be central in re-establishing the norms of community. Deriving from the works of Aronson (1971), Poole (1981), Fischer (1982), and Katz (1999), one can argue that the wire-line telephone is an ideal tool because it counteracts social distance and reinforces local ties. The work of Fischer and Katz is but the tip of a substantial body of literature on the telephone that, in all cases with which we are familiar, shows that the telephone is indeed a tremendously powerful stimulant, preserver, and enhancer of community. Pertinent examples beyond those just mentioned above include Dimmick, Jaspreet, and Patterson (1994), Fortunati (1993), Rakow (1991), and Umble (1992). It is plausible to anticipate that the mobile phone would extend these communal benefits.

Disadvantage: Mediated communication inflames the negative effects of distance on community. The traditionalists would presumably argue that distance (included mediated interaction) leads to community fragmentation and dissolution. Distance constrains communication, something necessary and important for all communities (Wellman & Hampton, 2001b). Communities dominated by mediated technology cannot be a source of real community (Baudrillard, 1983; Beniger, 1987; Gergen, 1991; Turkle, 1996). The use of online systems to communicate with more distant others may reduce the vitality and integration of physical communities (Calhoun, 1986).

Proponents of physical communities note that physical and social distance ruptures community fabric (Crow, Allen, & Summers, 2002). There are also positive relationships between emotional closeness and physical proximity, duration and emotional closeness, and face-to-face interaction and proximity (Adams, 1985). Physical distance determines our passive contacts, and thus proximity is a major determinant for relations in homogenous, high-interaction communities (Darke & Darke, 1969). The good physical neighbor is thus one who is warm and inviting, but can respect your privacy—one who maintains "friendly distance" (Crow et al., 2002).

As a result, Putnam (2000) conceived of suburban sprawl and the resulting increased distance from centralized foci of interaction as problematic for social capital and community formation. One might argue from this that all forms of mobility in fact undermine civic engagement and social capital, as communities that experience rapid turnover are overall less integrated.

If physical distance negatively affects the traditional community by turning it into a social network, what effect does distance have on the latter? Mobility distance is a predictor of network distance, according to Magdol (2000). People who move longer distances from their community have more dispersed networks, whereas local movers have more proximate networks. In his study of sentiment and moving, Bolan (1997) found that people who devoted more time to a move, moved for housing needs or stayed in the same census level experienced higher levels of community attachment. (In other words, these people experienced duration, necessity, and commonality in their local community, all components of the traditional community). Moreover, one measure of the social distance between any two people is the minimum number of steps in the network needed to go from one to the other (White, 2003). Clusters of one-to-one ties thus illustrate a strong sense of community. As noted above, mediated communication involves building widespread and diverse networks, not associating only with common or nearby groups of people.

Speed

Advantage: Choices between synchronous and asynchronous interactions allow mediated communication to imitate face-to-face communities. The face-to-face norm of constant, informal interaction contributes to the sense of community among online groups. Quan-Haase, Wellman, Witte, and Hampton (2002) noted that frequent email users have a greater sense of online community. In fact, rapid delivery email directly enhances community, according to Nie (2001). Likewise, LaRose, Eastin, and Gregg (2001) claimed that Internet use, especially email, creates more social support for its users, leading to a reduction in stress and feelings of isolation.

Real-time chatting is likewise strongly associated with a feeling of community, much more so than asynchronous forms of communication (Quan-Haase et al., 2002). Quan-Haase et al. additionally noted that frequent online communication with friends gives people a strong sense of online community, whereas online communication with kin is thought of as merely a good device to maintain ties. Real-time chatting is also lauded by Rheingold (2000) in his treatment of text messaging. MUDs, IRCs, and other chatrooms, which are predominant in the literature of virtual community, are marked by real-time chat (Curtis, 1996; Kollock & Smith, 1999; Stone, 1998). As Turkle (1995) agreed, virtual communities exist only among their members when they are logged in; the real-time nature of community ceases at the point of logging off. Absent the development of social capital as an enduring potential resource, the same could be argued for physical communities. Proponents of real-life communities argue that the random encounter is a key step in community building. Likewise, the turnover of players in a MUD during the day allows for a freshness of encounter and a similar phenomenon (Curtis, 1996). Informal communication, real-time interaction, speed, emotion, exclusion, conflict, and randomness represent ways in which the community-building components of virtual community reflect those in the physical community.

Speed indeed seems to influence sentiments of community feeling. Broadband is the single most powerful statistical predictor of the time devoted to Internet use. Broadband users are also more likely than dial-up users to feel that the Internet has had a positive connection on their community of family (71% vs. 58%) and friends (76% vs. 68%). Wellman and Hampton (2001b) also noted that high-speed networks allow people to enhance their social relations, especially their distant ones. According to Rheingold (2002), broadband will see its ultimate achievement in wireless technology, as physical locality is completely eliminated (i.e., one does not even need to be in a particular physical location to access connectivity to online resources and communities).

In his list of requirements for community, Etzioni (2001) found that among other things, communities require interactive broadcasting, access, and cooling-off mechanisms. Computer-mediated communication approximates this well through its ability to reach more people, availability of email and bulletin-board style feedback, and the small delays built into email programs and other "Are you sure now?" messages that precede information dissemination online. Other theorists have noted that asynchronous communication does not disrupt community, but rather enhances it in different ways (Baym, 1997; M. J. Smith, 1999). Curtis (1996) noted that the delays in conversation, due to bandwidth and typing, allow multiple, overlapping threads of discourse in any one conversation, as well as the ability to talk with many people simultaneously.

Disadvantage: Speed issues cause mediated communication to frustrate face-to-face community. Noll (1997) and Stoll (1995) held that face-to-face communication provides a depth of communication and speed of feedback that is basic to forming community and sentiment ties. In contrast, they portrayed computer-mediated communication as task-focused, depersonalized, filled with psychological distance, and lacking social cues. Additionally, as Wellman and Gulia (1999) stated, there is a constant worry that the reduced bandwidth of the Internet and communication technologies will undermine the supportive community because it can lead to misinterpretations of words and actions, as well as impede immediate conversational repair.

Constructions of Time and the Self

Advantage: Mediated communication contributes to a new construction of the self. Wellman (2001) maintained that the adoption of a distributed social network is one way to counteract the loss of community idea. Turkle and Stone have pointed out that mediated communications and virtual communities lead to fractured and fragmented selves, which they view as positive because it opens up many new groups in which to participate. The saturated self-concept (Gergen, 1991) is another way in which we deal with the fragmentation of self idea.

Maffesoli (1996) adopted the term *neo-tribes* to explain the relationship between the individual and mass communication/society. In the face of the unification of authority in mass society, our individualism is defined by our individual interactions with different groups. Neo-tribes are defined as "instantaneous conversions" (p. 76): They are unstable, self-defined communities marked by fluidity and dispersal. The neo-tribe is an excellent metaphor to show how our selves can be multifaceted, without being accompanied by social isolation.

Another useful metaphor is the invisible mouse developed by Katz and Rice (2002). Just as Adam Smith's invisible hand explained the way that self-motivated individualistic action contributed to the well-being of the common good, the invisible mouse explains how individuals acting in self-interest online and using mediated communications actually produce notions of social altruism and community. They cite self-help groups, mentoring programs, genealogy services, class reunion sites, affirmation groups, ethic and political groups, charitable activities, and other virtual networks as examples of this phenomenon. The Internet thus "neither directly creates nor diminishes social capital . . . but social capital is created as a by-product of people motivated by their own interests" (p. 199). Collective interaction far outweighs the development of introspection resulting from individual information seeking.

Mobile phones also can help users create identity. Sending text messages and talking on the mobile phone gives users an opportunity to be a part of a social network and this communication becomes a part of a daily routine in which the user is continually sending a stream of signals to the surroundings (Johnsen, 2003). In his ethnographic study of Norwegian teenagers, Johnsen (2003) found that the mobile phone gives a young user the ability to confirm her social status and be a part of a social network. He stated that she indulges in small talk and feeds the network gossip as and when the situation arises and stressed the fact that the content is not as important as the fact that communication occurs. His study found that even a third person who was mentioned in a mobile phone conversation was part of the same social network and inferred that the phone worked to strengthen these existent ties instead of isolating certain members of the group (see also work by Skog, 2002, on identify formation and mobile phones).

Many researchers have attempted to examine how the relation of individuals and time has changed with the spread of the mobile. With respect to social coordination with others, researchers Ling and Yttri (2002) noted that mobile phones soften time. In other words, mobile users tend to feel comfortable about refining schedules via mobile phones when coordinating to meet up with others as they approach an agreed-upon time. Schedules are constantly negotiable according to the changing situation, thereby causing the prearranged structure of everyday life to become more obscure. Zernicke (2003) also reported several studies that indicate that being late is becoming more acceptable than it used to be. After interviewing numerous mobile-using teenagers in Tokyo, Rheingold (2002) concluded that for this group, as long as everybody is reachable by SMS (short messaging service, or text messaging), being late is not an issue.

Disadvantage: Mediated communication works to fragment and isolate the self. Some researchers have focused on how mobiles reduce individuals' self-reliance, which in turn erodes their ability to react adaptively to unpredictable encounters. Geser (2003), for instance, claimed that mobile phones can cause individuals to become less prone to develop certain social competencies. This is because of the constant availability of external communication partners (as sources of opinion and advice) as mobile phones enable people to retain primary social relationships over distance. This affects people's self-reliance, making them unable to operate alone and leaving them dependent on the mobile phone as a source of assistance and advice. Witness, for example, increasing numbers of people using their cell phones while shopping in grocery stores or video rental shops, asking their family or partners what they should get.

In terms of the mobile phone as the device for filling unoccupied stretches of time, some people in Tokyo (Moseley, 2002) expressed concerns about how the mobile phone is used to avoid being alone with one's thoughts. In Japan, the traditional ways of killing time (e.g., reading books, comics, or newspapers) are losing out to mobile phones. Fortunati (2002) showed how the use of mobile phones has encouraged more productive use of time. For example, time spent in traffic, in waiting lines at the post office, and other situations where we usually consider time to be wasted is used to communicate with others via the mobile phone. Overall, our dependence on the cell phone leads us to consider time without the phone as time in social isolation.

As a result, Peters and Hulme (2002) stated that people consider the mobile phone to be an extension of the self. The loss of a mobile phone would be comparable to physical disintegration. Moseley (2002) commented on how people go out without their mobile phones and feel as if there is something missing: "A human with a mobile in the pocket is appreciably different from the human without one" (Moseley, 2002, p. 37). Although people are "increasingly developing skills they wouldn't have had before—for example, the ability to operate in two contexts at once" (Moseley, 2002, p. 37), each individual may be losing the skills to interact with his or her own self.

Similar to these complaints pertaining to cell phones, Kraut et al. (1998) reported that Internet use actually reduced personal network size and strength, as well as caused overall depression in its users. They found that the Internet worked to replace strong social ties with weak online ties, thus reducing meaningful relations. His research, however, has been criticized sharply as being based on modest effects being found in a few elements of a small convenience sample. Apropos of these criticisms, his subsequent analysis of additional data from the sample (Kraut et al., 2002) found that to whatever extent these effects may have existed in the first place, they were no longer present in the original sample.

Social Control

Advantage: Mediated communication allows flexible forms of social control. Poster (2001) maintained that one of the most important attributes of mediated communication is that it is underdetermined, versus fixed forms of print and broadcast media. We learned above from Merton and Beniger's pseudocommunity that fixed media have the ability to exert high forms of social control over the individual. In contrast, Poster noted that with mediated technologies, such as the Internet, individuals become real agents who are capable of resisting the world around them. Mediated communications are open to practice and are not closed to interpretation, thus allowing flexibility in identity, presence, and avoidance of strict social control.

Palen et al. (2001) came up with a list of factors that may impact the usage of a mobile phone, such as the mobility of one's profession, the availability of other communications media at home or at the workplace, the number of roles one assumes (e.g., wife, mother, manager), the degree of integration across roles, degree of personal responsibility, schedules of other people in the home, degree of resource sharing, and additional factors such as agility. Taking note of these factors, Fortunati (2002) asserted that the mobile phone strengthens social control over others. She observed that women are more likely than men to phone to give their location and hypothesized that this could stem from factors such as a woman being compliant with the needs of men and children to know where she is, thus making herself reachable. Based on in-depth interviews, Fortunati (2002) found that some people chose to call others on their mobile phone, although they knew their home or office number, as a means of exercising a form of control by shifting the center of communications gravity in their favor. Similarly, parents often give cell phones to their teenagers in order to keep track of them.

The counterargument persists that people have the choice of answering the phone based on who is calling. A person may call one's mobile phone, but one does not have to take the call. That is an exercise of power and being in control of the situation, experienced at an individual level. Likewise, Katz (1999) and Wynn and Katz (2000) argued that use of the mobile phone for intimate calls helps defend and develop young people's sense of autonomy and identity and allows them to escape the social control of others.

In addition, the greater incursions of freedom through mediated communication are reminiscent of the ideal community. The ideal community, as noted, is symbolized by the horizontal nature of social ties. Likewise, online interactions and their feeling of community are amplified by their ability to bypass authority and experience horizontal equality, as well as devise their own rules. This perception is related to the notion that people feel that they are in a community when they perceive total freedom to set up their own way of life within it (Rheingold, 1993). This is consonant with Jones's (1995) definition of community in which its members are totally free to act within them (cf. Wynn & Katz, 1997). Similarly, Curtis (1996) explained that the ability to interact with many people, or simply one person, in a MUD, as well as move around within it, is key to its sense of community. Finally, M. J. Smith (1999) stated that the potential audience existing online, as well as the all of ways of reaching them in a many-to-many form of communication, allows every person to access the larger community.

Disadvantage: Mediated communication can be easily manipulated, allowing for deceit. Studies have shown that parental control over telecommunication resources becomes a process of constant negotiation between the parents and children (Ling & Helmerson, 2000). Ling and Yttri (2002) found that youth devise various strategies to avoid being monitored by parents through mobile phones. Palen et al. (2001) found that the duration of incoming calls was longer than outgoing calls, although the average number of outgoing calls was larger than incoming calls. They hypothesized that this could be due to the user's lack of control over an incoming call or because the user may not have revealed that he or she was using a mobile device, in the hopes of remaining ambiguous about the location. This is something that teenagers are likely to do especially when the mobile phone is used as a device for exercising parental control.

Mobile phone usage affects users' perceptions of time and space, as noted above. The person who places a call or receives one on their mobile phone may not be able to assign either a social or a geographical identity to the other (Licoppe & Heurtin, 2002). This offers room for deception at various levels, and the location of the individual, especially in the case of teenagers trying to avoid detection by their parents, is likely to be common.

SUMMARY AND CONCLUSION

In this chapter, the concept of community has been analyzed along two dimensions, yielding four ideal types. Each of these types has implications for the way in which people are expected to perceive themselves, as well as interact with group members and outsiders. Each type suggests the consequences for the viability and quality of community in light of the proliferation of new personal mediated technology, such as the Internet and the mobile phone.

After this analysis, we highlighted studies of virtuality and the mobile phone that showed how these devices are being used, and how they might be expected to affect community and social capital formation. We commented that, in earlier eras, social ties were based on what Durkheim (1984) termed mechanical solidarity and were contingent on spatial proximity. More recently, relationships have become organic (again, in Durkheim's term), because ties are based more on common ideas, interests, and occupations. With the popularization of mediated technologies such as the Internet and mobile phones, the trend seems to be accelerating. Finally, we considered plausible impacts on community from a variety of points of view. Most of these potential impacts were based on empirical studies of the mobile phone.

In light of this discussion, we advance some prerequisites for establishing ties in the putative mediated communities. These are (a) the existence of mobile phones and Internet functions (or their equivalent) as mediators of (b) people who have similar psychological or value orientations, or at a minimum a resonance of common ideas, and (c) a real or virtual place in which the interaction can occur.

Our analyses have implications for communication praxis. One is that the pessimists have overlooked many positives conferred by mediated communication. Rather than indulging in self-serving hand-wringing over the seemingly continual eroding of physical community and social capital, cynics may find it more useful to look at how the fundamental attributes of social capital are alive and well in virtual communities, and what might be done to foster them. Moreover, theorists of virtuality might benefit from a broader understanding of what is termed social capital. This might necessitate a conceptual transformation in their work.

The new mediated communication technologies—especially the mobile phone, it could be argued—will advance the dream of fulfilled individuals operating within their respective communities, which in turn tolerate other communities. This latter development would help bring about the millenarian ideal of community, so often praised in the works of writers discussed above. The evidence is scant in support of this view.

More plausibly, it seems that the new mediated communication technologies will mean that it is no longer feasible to set as a social objective the pursuit of the hoary and oft-praised physically based utopia. Instead we should turn to examine ways in which mediated communication can itself be part of a positive social environment. Even though we have used the term "real life" in contrast with "virtual" communities to illustrate differences of theoretical interpretation throughout this chapter, it is in a growing portion of the world, developed and developing, a distinction without a difference. That is, it is no longer a necessarily meaningful distinction in the conduct of one's life or in the way one perceives the world (Katz, 2003a). Mediated communication is inherently part of real life in today's world. This trend shows only signs of growing. Ultimately, we need an operational synthesis of virtual and physical communities in order to have fulfilling, embodied experiences all of the time. It may well be that mobile phones embody this synthesis. In this way, they would be a link to the virtual and mobile, located in a physical setting.

In conclusion, there are some plausible reasons why mediated personal technology, such as the mobile phone, can help support and even create the smaller, more intimate communities assumed to have existed in the pastoral world of our ancestors. Mobile phones could also offer wider, more quickly assembled, if shorter lasting, communities of activism. Further, they could produce richer interior lives and provide a bulwark against the homogenizing and commoditized mass societies that have for so long been critiqued by scholars.

On the other hand, such communities might come at substantial cost. Ling (2003) used the term "walled garden" to denote the rich interior world available only to members of the mobile phone user's social network. The obvious implication, of course, is that the wall, while protecting those on the inside, seals out others. This would be the privatization of the social sphere. This analogy, if applied to the physical plane, suggests the experience of traversing a middle-class area of a city in a traditional society. There are the faceless, hostile streets for the public with lush, protected atriums for those with the right keys. If his analogy is correct, the lesson is apparent.

There is also the necessity of considering the question of the extent these technologies can sustain and enrich the social experience of using public space. Part of the answer is that, like the real-life venue of Putnam's bowling leagues (Putnam, 2000) or the meeting halls of Lipset's labor unions (Lipset, Coleman, & Trow, 1977), the mobile phone can give groups the setting needed to promote casual social contact, democracy, and social capital.

At the same time, and perhaps even as a necessity, these devices will also make our public places a colder, more hostile environment, with many more intrusions of other people's community interactions into our own public and private communities. The centrally planned, centrally implemented vision of broad national communities that were the hallmarks of the Progressive Era seem even more distant than they were a half century ago when, in the depth of the Great Depression, they exercised so much appeal over public intellectuals.

Nevertheless, before we become too consumed with the promised benefits of community, it is also prudent to consider the benefits of the opposite, namely privacy and private life for the cultivation of individuality and liberty. That is, we must pause to consider the benefits of isolation and independence even if purchased at the price of loneliness and anomie. This counterpoint is an important consideration. As those who have lived under communism know, privacy is an important element in protecting the individual from the state, which is precisely why the state so viciously attacks it. The tight-knit community offers a warm berth to those who conform. At the same time, it can also destroy those who are perceived to violate the will of the collective, however that will is determined.

Perhaps the liberating power given to the individual by the copper-wired telephone and the Internet will be further advanced by the mobile phone. This would probably come at the further expense of community. Ultimately, it is the values of people within social networks, what they want and how they wish to live, not the preordained technological capabilities of electronic networks, that will determine just how communal our future lives will be. Even though value formations are not independent of the ambient technology, we would be ill-advised to expect those technologies to achieve for us the desirable world that we moderns have thus far, unaided, not been able to achieve for ourselves.

NOTES

1. This distinction between community and association will be seen later in Tönnies's often-invoked distinction between community and society, which forms the basis of Morgan's 1942 development of a community of sentiment.
2. Wellman & Hampton (2001a), however, asserted that the critics have it wrong.
3. The story appears different with mediated social networks (see Rice, 1982; Katz & Rice, 2002.)

REFERENCES

Aakhus, M.A. (2003). Understanding information and communication technology and infrastructure in everyday life. In J. E. Katz (Ed.), *Machines that become us: The social context of personal communication* (pp. 27–42) New Brunswick, NJ: Transaction.

Adams, R. G. (1985). Emotional closeness and physical distance between friends: Implications for elderly women living in age-segregated and age-integrated settings. *International Journal of Aging and Human Development, 22*, 55–76.

Ahlbrandt, R., Jr. (1984). *Neighborhoods, people, and community.* New York: Plenum Press.

Anderson, B. (1983). *Imagined communities.* London: Verso.

Arensberg, C. M. & Kimball, S. T. (1965). *Culture and community.* New York: Harcourt, Brace, & World.

Aronson, S. (1971). The sociology of the telephone. *International Journal of Comparative Sociology, 12*(3), 153–167.

Baudrillard, J. (1983). *Simulations* (P. Foss, P. Patton, & P. Beitchman, Trans.). New York: Semiotext(e).

Baym, N. K. (1995). Emergence of community in computer mediated communication. In S. G. Jones (Ed.), *Cybersociety: Computer mediated communication and community* (pp. 138–163). Thousand Oaks, CA: Sage.

Baym, N. K. (1997). Interpreting soap operas and creating community. In S. Kiesler (Ed.), *Culture of the Internet.* (pp.103–120). Mahwah, NJ: Erlbaum.

Bellah, R. N., Madsen, R., Sullivan, W., Swidler, A., & Tipton, S. (1985). *Habits of the heart: Individualism and commitment in American life.* Berkeley: University of California Press.

Beniger, J. R. (1987). The personalization of mass media and the growth of pseudo-community. *Communication Research, 14*, 352–371.

Blanchard, A., & Horan, T. (2000). Virtual community and social capital. In G. D. Garson (Ed.), *Social dimensions of information technologies* (pp. 6–22). Hershey, PA: Idea Group.

Blinkoff, R., & Blinkoff, B. (2000, December). *Wireless opportunities: A global ethnographic study* [ethnographic report]. Baltimore: Context-Based Research Group.

Bolan, M. (1997). The mobility experience and neighborhood attachment. *Demography, 34*, 225–237.

Bollier, D. (Ed.). (1995). *The future of community and personal identity in the coming electronic culture.* Washington, DC: Aspen Institute.

Bourdieu, P. (1986). The forms of capital (R. Nice, Trans.). In J. G. Richardson (Ed.), *Handbook of theory and research for the sociology of education* (pp. 241–258). New York: Greenwood Press.

Calhoun, C. J. (1980). Community: Towards a variable conceptualization for computer research. *Social History, 5,* 105-129.

Calhoun, C. J. (1986). Computer technology, large-scale societal integration and the local community. *Urban Affairs Quarterly, 22,* 329–349.

Calhoun, C. J. (2002). Virtual community. In C. J. Calhoun (Ed.), *Dictionary of the social sciences.* Oxford, UK: Oxford University Press. Retrieved June 26, 2003, from http://www.oxfordreference.com/views/ENTRY.htmlsubview=Main&entry=t104.001764

Carey, J. W. (1993). Everything that rises must diverge. In Philip Guard (Ed.), *Agendas: New directions in communications research* (pp. 171–184). Westport, CT: Greenwood Press.

Castells, M. (2000). *The information age. Vol. I: Rise of the network society.* Malden, MA: Blackwell.

Cerulo, K. (1997). Reframing sociological concepts for a brave new (virtual?) world. *Sociological Inquiry, 67*(1), 48–58.

Chayko, M. (2002). *Connecting: How we form social bonds and communities in the Internet age.* Albany: State University of New York Press.

Cobb, J. B., Jr. (1996). Defining normative community. In W. Vitek & W. Jackson (Eds.), *Rooted in the land* (pp. 185-194). New Haven, CT: Yale University Press.

Coleman, J. S. (1954). *Community conflict.* New York: Free Press.

Coleman, J. S. (1986). *Individual interests and collective action.* Cambridge, UK: Cambridge University Press.

Coleman, J. S. (1988). Social capital in the creation of human capital. *American Journal of Sociology, 94,* 95–120.

Coleman, J. S., & Hoffer, T. (1987). *Public and private high schools: The impact of communities.* New York: Basic Books.

Crow, G., Allan, G., & Summers, M. (2002). Neither busybodies nor nobodies: Managing proximity and distance in neighborly relations. *Sociology, 36,* 127–145.

Cultural Access Group. (2001). *Ethnicity in the electronic age: Looking at the Internet through multicultural lens.* Los Angeles: Access Worldwide Communications.

Curtis, P. (1996). MUDDING: Social phenomenon in text-based virtual realities. In S. Kiesler (Ed.), *Culture of the Internet* (pp. 121–142). Mahwah, NJ: Erlbaum.

Darke, J., & Darke, R. (1969). *Physical and social factors in neighbourhood relations.* London: Center for Environmental Studies.

De Gournay, C. (2002). Pretence of intimacy in France. In J. E. Katz & M. Aakhus (Eds.), *Perpetual contact: Mobile communication, private talk, public performance* (pp. 193–205). Cambridge, UK: Cambridge University Press.

Dimmick, J. W., Jaspreet, S., & Patterson, S. J. (1994). The gratifications of the household telephone: Sociability, instrumentality, and reassurance. *Communication Research, 21*, 643–663.

Dirksen, V., & Smit, B. (2002). Exploring the common ground of virtual communities. In J. Kisielnicki (Ed.), *Modern organizations in virtual community*. Hershey, PA: IRM.

Doheny-Farina, S. (1998). *The wired neighborhood*. New Haven, CT: Yale University Press.

Douglas, M. (1970). *Natural symbols: Explorations in cosmology*. New York: Pantheon Books.

Durkheim, E. (1984). *The division of labor in society*. New York: Free Press. (Original work published 1893)

Edwards, A. D., & Jones, D. G. (1976). *Community and community development*. The Hague: Mouton.

Effrat, M. P. (Ed.). (1974). *The community: Approaches and applications*. London: Free Press.

Elliott, A. (2003, July 17). Talking to me? No, the cabby's on his cell. *New York Times*, pp. A1, B85.

Etzioni, A. (2001). *The monochrome society*. Princeton, NJ: Princeton University Press.

Figallo, C. (1995). The WELL: A regionally based on-line community on the Internet. In B. Kahin, & J. Keller (Eds.), *Public access to the Internet* (pp. 49–61). Cambridge, MA: MIT Press.

Fischer, C. R. (1982). *To dwell among friends*. Chicago: University of Chicago Press.

Fortunati, L. (1993). *Gli italiani al telefono*. Milano, Italy: Angeli.

Fortunati, L. (2000, June 16). *The mobile phone: New social categories and relationships*. Paper presented at the seminar, Sosiale konsekvenser av mobiltelefoni, organized by Telenor, Oslo, Norway.

Fortunati, L. (2002). Italy: Stereotypes, true and false. In J. E. Katz & M. Aakhus (Eds.), *Perpetual contact: Mobile communication, private talk, public performance* (pp. 42–62). Cambridge, UK: Cambridge University Press.

Fuentes, A. (2000). Won't you be my neighbor? *American Demographics, 22*(6), 60–62.

Gans, H. J. (1962). *The urban villagers: Group and class in the life of Italian-Americans*. New York: Free Press.

Garfinkel, H. (1967). *Studies in ethnomethodology*. Englewood Cliffs, NJ: Prentice Hall.

Gergen, K. J. (1991). *The saturated self: Dilemmas of identity in contemporary life*. New York: HarperCollins.

Gergen, K. J. (2003, April 24). *Self and community in the new floating worlds*. Presentation at the Mobile Communication and Social and Political Effects Conference, Budapest, Hungary.

Geser, H. (2003). *Towards a sociological theory of the mobile phone*. Release 2.1. September, 2003. Retrieved on October 27, 2003, from http://socio.ch/mobile/t_geserl.htm#8

Giddens, A. (1994). *Beyond left and right: The future of radical politics*. Stanford, CA: Stanford University Press.

Granovetter, M. S. (1973). The strength of weak ties. *American Journal of Sociology, 78*, 1360–1380.

Gurak, L. (1997). *Persuasion and privacy in cyberspace: The online protests over Lotus MarketPlace and the Clipper Chip*. New Haven, CT: Yale University Press.

Habermas, J. (1989). *The structural transformation of the public sphere*. Cambridge, MA: MIT Press.

Hampton, K. (2000, October). *Grieving for a lost network: Collective action in a wired suburb*. Cambridge, MA: MIT Department of Urban Studies & Planning.

Henderson, S., Taylor, R., & Thomson, R. (2002). In touch: Young people, communication and technology. *Information, Communication and Society, 5*, 494–512.

Hillery, G. A., Jr. (1982). *A research odyssey: Developing and testing a community theory*. New Brunswick, NJ: Transaction.

Hiltz, S. R., & Turoff, M. (1995). *Network nation* (Rev.). Cambridge, MA: MIT Press.

Horn, S. (1998). *Cyberville: Clicks, culture, and the creation of an online town*. New York: Warner Books.

Hozic, A. (2001). Hello my name is: Articulating loneliness in a digital diaspora. *Afterimage, 28*(4), 21–22.

Jacobs, J. (1961). *Death and life of great American cities*. New York: Random House.

Jeffres, L. W., Atkin, D., & Neuendorf, K. A. (2002). A model linking community activity and communication with political attitudes and involvement in neighborhoods. *Political Communication, 35*, 487–521.

Johnsen, T. E. (2003). Social context of mobile phone use of Norwegian teens. In J. E. Katz (Ed.), *Machines that become us* (pp. 144–167). New Brunswick, NJ: Transaction.

Jones, S. G. (1995). Understanding community in the information age. In S. G. Jones (Ed.), *Cybersociety: Computer mediated communication and community* (pp. 12–29). Thousand Oaks, CA: Sage.

Jones, S. G. (1999). Understanding community in the information age. In P. Mayer (Ed.), *Computer media and communication* (pp. 219–240). New York: Oxford University Press.

Katz, J. E. (1998). Struggle in Cyberspace: Fact and friction on the World Wide Web. *Annals of the American Academy of Political and Social Science, 556,* 194–200.

Katz, J. E. (1999). *Connections: Social and cultural studies of the telephone in American life.* New Brunswick, NJ: Transaction.

Katz, J. E. (2001). The telephone. In *The international encyclopedia of social science* (2nd ed.), *Vol. 23,* (pp. 15558-15565). Amsterdam: Elsevier.

Katz, J. E. (2003a). *Machines that become us: The social context of personal communication.* New Brunswick, NJ: Transaction.

Katz, J. E. (2003b). *A nation of ghosts?* Presentation at the Mobile Communication and Social and Political Effects Conference, Budapest, Hungary.

Katz, J. E., & Aakhus, M. (2002). Apparatgeist. In J. E. Katz & M. Aakhus (Eds.), *Perpetual contact: Mobile communication, private talk, public performance* (pp. 287–317). Cambridge, UK: Cambridge University Press.

Katz, J. E., & Rice, R. E. (2002). *Social consequences of Internet use: Access, involvement and interaction.* Cambridge, MA: MIT Press.

Kendall, J. E. (2003, March). E-distance and the theatre of South Jersey. *Decision Line,* 13–15.

Kiesler, S., Siegel, J., & McGuire, T. W. (1984). Social psychological aspects of computer mediated communication. *American Psychologist, 39,* 1123–1134.

Kim, S. D. (2002). Korea: Personal meanings. In J. E. Katz & M. Aakhus (Eds.), *Perpetual contact: Mobile communication, private talk, public performance* (pp. 63–79). Cambridge, UK: Cambridge University Press.

Kodama, M. (2001). New regional community creation: Medical and educational applications through video-based information networks. *Systems Research and Behavioral Science, 18*(3), 225–240.

Kolko, B., & Reid, E. (1998). Dissolution and fragmentation: Problems in online communities. In S. G. Jones (Ed.), *Cybersociety 2.0* (pp. 217–228). Thousand Oaks, CA: Sage.

Kollock, P., & Smith, M. A. (1999). Communities in cyberspace. In P. Kollock & M. A. Smith (Eds.), *Communities in cyberspace* (pp. 3–25). London: Routledge.

König, R. (1968). *The community.* (E. Fitzgerald, Trans.). New York: Schocken Books.

Kraut, R. E., Kiesler, S., Boneva, B., Cummings, J., Helgeson, V., & Crawford, A. (2002). Internet paradox revisited. *Journal of Social Issues, 58,* 49–74.

Kraut, R. E., Lundmark, V., Patterson, M., Kiesler, S., Mukhopadhyay, T., & Scherlis, M. (1998). Internet paradox: A social technology that reduces social involvement and psychological well-being? *American Psychologist, 53,* 1017–1031.

LaRose, R., Eastin, M., & Gregg, J. (2001). Reformulating the Internet paradox: Social cognitive explanations of Internet use and depression. *Journal of Online Behavior, 1*(2). Retrieved July 7, 2001, from http://www.behavior.net/JOB/v1n1/paradox.html

Laurel, B. (2001). *Utopian entrepreneur.* Cambridge, MA: MIT Press.

Licoppe, C. (2003). Two modes of maintaining interpersonal relations through telephone: From the domestic to the mobile phone. In J. E. Katz (Ed.), *Machines that become us* (pp. 56–89). New Brunswick, NJ: Transaction.

Licoppe, C., & Heurtin, J. (2002). France: Preserving the image. In J. E. Katz & M. Aakhus (Eds.), *Perpetual contact: Mobile communication, private talk, public performance* (pp. 94–109). Cambridge, UK: Cambridge University Press.

Ling, R. (in press). *The mobile connection: The cell phone's impact on society.* San Francisco: Morgan Kaufman.

Ling, R. (2003). Mobile telephony, mobility, and the coordination of everyday life. In J. E. Katz, (Ed.), *Machines that become us: The social context of personal communication* (pp. 127–39). New Brunswick, NJ: Transaction.

Ling, R., & Helmerson, P. (2000, June 16). *It must be necessary, it has to cover a need: The adoption of mobile telephony among pre-adolescents and adolescents.* Paper presented at the seminar Sosiale Konsekvenser av Mobiletelefoni, organized by Telenor, Oslo, Norway.

Ling, R., & Yttri, B. (2002). Hyper-coordination via mobile phone in Norway. In J. E. Katz & M. Aakhus (Eds.), *Perpetual contact: Mobile communication, private talk, public performance* (pp. 129–59). Cambridge, UK: Cambridge University Press.

Lipset, S. M., Coleman, J., & Trow, M. A. (1977). *Union democracy: The internal politics of the International Typographical Union.* New York: Simon & Schuster.

Maffesoli, M. (1996). *Ordinary knowledge.* Cambridge, UK: Polity Press.

Magdol, L. (2000). The people you know: The impact of residential mobility on mothers' social network ties. *Journal of Social and Personal Relationships, 17*(2), 183–204.

Magdol, L., & Bessel, D. R. (2003). Social capital, social currency, and portable assets: The impact of residential mobility on exchanges of social support. *Personal Relationships, 10*(2), 149–169.

Marx, K., & Engels, F. (1975) *Economic and Philosophical Manuscripts.* New York: International Publishers. (Original work published 1844)

Mele, C. (1999). Cyberspace and disadvantaged communities: The Internet as a tool for collective action. In M. A. Smith & P. Kollock (Eds.), *Communities in cyberspace* (pp. 290–310). London: Routledge.

Merton, R. K. (1946). *Mass persuasion: Social psychology of the war bond drive.* New York: Harper.

Meyrowitz, J. (1985). *No sense of place: The impact of electronic media on social behavior.* New York: Oxford University Press.

Meyrowitz, J. (1989). The generalized elsewhere. *Critical Studies in Mass Communication, 6*(3), 326-334.

Meyrowitz, J. (1997). Shifting worlds of strangers: Medium theory and changes in "them" vs. "us." *Sociological Inquiry, 67*(1), 59–71.

Morgan, A. E. (1942). *The small community: Foundation of democratic life.* Beallsville, OH: Raven Rocks Press.

Morse, M. (1998). *Virtualities: Television, Media Art, and Cyberculture I.* Bloomington: Indiana University Press.

Moseley, L. (2002, May 6). Digital culture: Rise of the thumb kids. *Newsweek,* 37–38.

Mukerji, C., & Simon, B. (1998). Out of the limelight: Discredited communities and informal communication on the Internet. *Sociological Inquiry, 68,* 258–273.

Nancy, J.-L. (1991). *The inoperative community.* (P. Connor, Ed. & Trans.). Minneapolis: University of Minnesota Press.

Nie, N. H. (2001). Sociability, interpersonal relations, and the Internet. *American Behavioral Scientist, 45*(3), 420–435.

Nisbet, R. A. (1966). *The sociological tradition.* New York: Basic Books.

Noll, A. M. (1997). *Highway of dreams: A critical view along the information superhighway.* Mahwah, NJ: Erlbaum.

Oksman, V., & Rautiainen, P. (2002). Perhaps it is a body part: How the mobile phone became an organic part of the everyday lives of Finnish children and adolescents. In J. E. Katz (Ed.), *Machines that become us* (pp. 293–310). New Brunswick, NJ: Transaction.

Palen, L., Salzman, M., & Youngs, E. (2001). Discovery and integration of mobile communications in everyday life. *Personal and Ubiquitous Computing, 5,* 109–122.

Park, R. E. (1952). *Human communities: The city and human ecology.* New York: Free Press.

Peters, S., & Hulme, M. (2002, April 10–12). *Rethinking networks: Identities and connectivity in the global age.* Presentation at Absent Presence: Localities, Globalities and Method Workshop, Helsinki, Finland.

Poole, I. de Sola. (1981). *Technologies of freedom.* Cambridge, MA: MIT Press.

Poplin, D. E. (1979). *Communities: A survey of theories and methods of research.* New York: Macmillan.

Poster, M. (1995). *Postmodern virtualities: In the second media age.* Cambridge, UK: Polity Press. Retrieved June 28, 2003, from http://www.humanities.uci.edu/mposter/writings/Internet.html

Poster, M. (2001). *What's the matter with the Internet?* Minneapolis: University of Minnesota Press.

Preece, J. (2000). *Online communities: Designing usability, supporting sociability.* Chichester, UK: Wiley.

Preece, J., & Ghozati, K. (2001). Experiencing empathy online. In R. E. Rice & J. E. Katz (Eds.), *The Internet and health communication* (pp. 237–260). Thousand Oaks, CA: Sage.

Putnam, R. D. (1993). *Making democracy work: Civic traditions in modern Italy.* Princeton, NJ: Princeton University Press.

Putnam, R. D. (2000). *Bowling alone: The collapse and revival of the American community.* New York: Simon & Schuster.

Quan-Haase, A., Wellman, B., Witte, J., & Hampton, K. (2001). Does the Internet incease, decrease, or supplement social capital? Social networks, participation, and community commitment. *American Behavioral Scientist, 45,* 436–455.

Quan-Haase, A., Wellman, B., Witte, J., & Hampton, K. (2002). Capitalizing on the Internet: Social contact, civic engagement, and sense of community. In B. Wellman & C. Haythornwaite (Eds.), *Internet and everyday life* (pp. 291–324). London: Blackwell.

Rakow, L. F. (1991). *Gender on the line: Women, the telephone, and community life.* Urbana: University of Illinois Press.

Rheingold, H. (1993). *The virtual community: Homesteading on the electronic frontier.* Reading, MA: Addison Wesley.

Rheingold, H. (2000). *The virtual community: Homesteading on the electronic frontier* (2nd ed.). Cambridge, MA: MIT Press.

Rheingold, H. (2002). *Smart mobs.* Cambridge, UK: Perseus.

Rice, R. E. (1982). Communication networking in computer-conferencing systems: A longitudinal study of group roles and system structure. In M. Burgoon (Ed.), *Communication yearbook 6* (pp. 925–944). Beverly Hills, CA: Sage.

Rice, R. E. (1987). New patterns of social structure in an information society. In J. Schement & L. Lievrouw (Eds.), *Competing visions, complex realities: Social aspects of the information society* (pp. 107–120). Norwood, NJ: Ablex.

Rice, R. E. (1990). Computer-mediated communication system network data: Theoretical concerns and empirical examples. *International Journal of Man-Machine Studies, 32,* 627–647.

Rice, R. E., & Katz, J. E. (Eds.). (2001). *The Internet and health communication.* Thousand Oaks, CA: Sage.

Rice, R . E., & Katz, J. E. (2003). Mobile discourtesy: National survey results on episodes of convergent public and private spheres. In K. Nyíri (Ed.), *Mobile democracy: Essays on society, self and politics.* Vienna: Passagen Verlag.

Sanders, I. T. (1966). *The community: An introduction to a social system* (2nd ed). New York: Roland Press.

Schmalenbach, H. (1977). *Herman Schmalenbach on society and experience: Selected papers.* (G.Lüschen & G. P. Stone, Eds. & Trans.). Chicago: University of Chicago Press.

Sclove, R. E. (1995). *Democracy and technology.* New York: Guilford.

Sennett, R. (1971). *The uses of disorder: Personal identity and city life.* New York: Vintage.

Sennett, R. (1977). *The fall of public man.* New York: Knopf.

Sennett, R. (1995). Community becomes uncivilized. In P. Kasinitz (Ed.), *Metropolis: Center and symbol of our times* (pp. 226–249). New York: New York University Press.

Shapiro, A., & Leone, R. (1999). *The control revolution: How the Internet is putting individuals in charge and changing the world we know.* New York: Public Affairs/Century Foundation.

Skog, B. (2002). Mobiles and the Norwegian teen. In J. E. Katz & M. Aakhus (Eds.), *Perpetual contact: Mobile communication, private talk, public performance* (pp. 255–273). Cambridge, UK: Cambridge University Press.

Slack, R. S., & Williams, R. A. (2000). The dialectics of place and space: On community in the "information age." *New Media and Society, 2,* 313–334.

Slater, P. E. (1970). *The pursuit of loneliness: American culture at the breaking point.* Boston: Beacon.

Slevin, J. (2000). *Internet and society*. Cambridge, UK: Polity Press.

Smith, A. D. (1999). Problems of conflict management in virtual communities. In P. Kollock & M. A. Smith (Eds.), *Communities in cyberspace* (pp.134–163). London: Routledge.

Smith, M. J. (1999). Strands in the Web: Community-building strategies in online fanzines. *Journal of Popular Culture, 33*(2), 87–99.

Soto, M. (2003, August 8). Too much technology diminishes work relationships, author says. *Seattle Times*. Retrieved October 9, 2003, from: http://seattletimes.nwsource.com/html/businesstechnology/2001436284_neds08.html

Steinmueller, W. E. (2002). Virtual communities and the new economy. In R. Mansell (Ed.), *Inside the communication revolution* (pp. 21–54). Oxford, UK: Oxford University Press.

Stoll, C. (1995). *Silicon snake oil: Second thoughts on the information highway*. New York: Doubleday.

Stone, A. R. (1991). Will the real body please stand up?: Boundary stories about virtual cultures. In M. Benedikt (Ed.), *Cyberspace: First steps* (pp. 81–118). Cambridge, MA: MIT Press.

Stone, A. R. (1998). *The war of desire and technology at the close of the mechanical age*. Cambridge, MA: MIT Press.

Sternberg, J. (2001). Misbehavior in cyber places: The regulation of online conduct in virtual communities on the Internet (Doctoral dissertation, New York University, 2001). *Dissertation Abstracts International, 62*, 2277.

Straus, S. (1997). Technology, group process, and group outcomes: Testing the connections in computer-mediated and face-to-face groups. *Human-Computer Interaction, 12*, 227–266.

Sudweeks, F., McLaughlin, M., & Rafaeli, S. (Eds.). (1998). *Network and netplay: Virtual groups on the Internet*. Cambridge, MA: MIT Press.

Sunstein, C. (2001). *Republic.com*. Princeton, NJ: Princeton University Press.

Suttles, G. D. (1972). *The social construction of community*. Chicago: University of Chicago Press.

Tepper, M. (1997). Usenet community and the cultural politics of information. In D. Purter (Ed.), *Internet culture* (pp. 39–54), New York: Routledge.

Terkenli, T. S. (1995). Home as a region. *Geographical Review, 85*, 324–334.

Tönnies, F. (1957). *Civilization and society: Gemeinschaft and Gesellschaft*. (C. P. Loomis, Trans.). East Lansing: Michigan State Press.

Turkle, S. (1995). *Life on the screen: Identity in the age of the Internet*. New York: Simon & Schuster.

Turkle, S. (1996). Virtuality and its discontents: Searching for community in cyberspace. *American Prospect, 26*, 50–57.

Umble, D. Z. (1992). *The Amish and the telephone: Resistance and reconstruction*. Baltimore: Johns Hopkins University Press.

Uncapher, W. (1999). Electronic homesteading on the rural frontier: Big Sky Telegraph and its community. In M. A. Smith & P. Kollock (Eds.), *Communities in cyberspace* (pp. 264–289). London: Routledge.

Uslaner, E. (2000, April). *Trust, civic engagement, and the Internet*. Paper presented at the Joint Sessions of the European Consortium for Political Research, University of Grenoble, Switzerland. Retrieved Summer 2001 from http://www.pewInternet.org/papers/paper.asp?paper=5

Van Dijk, J. (1999). *The network society: Social aspects of new media*. (L. Spoorenberg, Trans.) Thousand Oaks, CA: Sage.

Veblen, T. (1934). *Theory of the leisure class*. New York: Modern Library.

Walls, J. (1993). Global networking for local development. In L. M. Harasim (Ed.), *Global networks: Computers and international communication* (pp. 153–166). Cambridge,MA: MIT Press.

Walmsley, D. J. (2000). Community, place, and cyberspace. *Australian Geographer, 31*(1), 5–19.

Walther, J. (1996). Computer-mediated communication: Impersonal, interpersonal, and hyperpersonal interaction. *Communication Research, 23*, 3–43.

Wellman, B. (1971). Who needs neighborhoods? In A. Powell (Ed.), *The city: Attacking modern myths* (pp. 94–100). Toronto, Canada: McClelland & Stewart.

Wellman, B. (1988a). The community question re-evaluated. In M. P. Smith (Ed.), *Power, Community, and the City* (pp. 81–107). New Brunswick, NJ: Transaction Books. Retrieved June 29, 2003, from http://www.chass.utoronto.ca/~wellman/publications/index.html

Wellman, B. (1988b). Networks as personal communities. In B. Wellman & S. D. Berkowitz (Eds.), *Social structures: A network analysis* (pp. 130–184). Cambridge, UK: Cambridge University Press. Retrieved June 29, 2003, from http://www.chass.utoronto.ca/~wellman/publications/index.html

Wellman, B. (1993). *An egocentric network tale: Comment on Bien et al. Social Networks, 15*, 423–436. Retrieved June 29, 2003, from http://www.chass.utoronto.ca/~wellman/publications/index.html

Wellman, B. (2001). *The persistence and transformation of community: From neighbourhood groups to social networks.* Report to the Law Commission of Canada. 101 pp. Retrieved June 29, 2003, from http://www.chass.utoronto.ca/~wellman/publications/index.html

Wellman, B., & Gulia, M. (1999). Net surfers don't ride alone: Virtual community as community. In B. Wellman (Ed.), *Networks in the global village* (pp. 331–367). Boulder, CO: Westview Press. Retrieved June 29, 2003, from http://www.chass.utoronto.ca/~wellman/publications/index.html

Wellman, B., & Hampton, K. (2001a). Long-distance community in network society: Contact and support beyond Netville. *American Behavioral Scientist, 45*, 477–96. Retrieved June 29, 2003, from http://www.chass.utoronto.ca/~wellman/publications/index.html

Wellman, B., & Hampton, K. (2001b). Does the Internet increase, decrease, or supplement social capital? Sociability, interpersonal relations, and the Internet. *American Behavioral Scientist, 45*, 436–455.

Wellman, B., & Quan-Haase, A. (in press). How does the Internet affect social capital? In M. Huysman & V. Wulf (Eds.), *IT and social capital.* Retrieved June 29, 2003, from http://www.chass.utoronto.ca/~wellman/publications/index.html

Wenger, E. (1998). *Communities of practice: Learning, meaning, and identity.* Cambridge, UK: Cambridge University Press.

White, D. R. (2003). Ties, weak and strong. In K. Cristensen & D. Levinson (Eds.), *Encyclopedia of community.* Thousand Oaks, CA: Sage. Retrieved July 28, 2003, from http://eclectic.ss.uci.edu/~drwhite/6WWWVIT.html

Wilbur, S. P. (2000). Archaeology of cyberspace. In D. Bell & B. M. Kennedy (Eds.), *The cybercultures reader* (pp. 45–55). London: Routledge.

Wright, J. D. (2000). Small towns, mass society, and the 21st Century. *Society, 38*, 3–10.

Wynn, E., & Katz, J. E. (1997). Hyperbole over cyberspace: Self-presentation in Internet home pages and discourse. *Information Society, 13*(4), 297–329.

Wynn, E., & Katz, J. E. (2000). Teens on the telephone. *Info, 2*, 401–419.

Young, K. (1996, August 15). *Internet addiction: The emergence of a new clinical disorder.* Paper presented at the 104th annual meeting of the American Psychological Association, Toronto, Canada.

Zernicke, K. (2003, October 26). Calling in late. *New York Times*, section 9, pp. ST1, ST11.

CHAPTER CONTENTS

10 Communication in the Community of Sport: The Process of Enacting, (Re)Producing, Consuming, and Organizing Sport

JEFFREY W. KASSING
Arizona State University West
ANDREW C. BILLINGS
Clemson University
ROBERT S. BROWN
Ashland University
KELBY K. HALONE
University of Tennessee
KRISTEN HARRISON
University of Illinois
BOB KRIZEK
Saint Louis University
LINDSEY J. MEÂN
Manchester Metropolitan University
PAUL D. TURMAN
University of Northern Iowa

The community of sport is a pervasive, influential, complex, and restricted community comprised not only of participants such as coaches, athletes, and referees, but also of spectators at both live and mediated sporting events. Additionally, sports media, amateur and professional sports organizations, sport governing bodies, and fan clubs occupy terrain in the community of sport. We maintain that membership and participation in the community of sport are communicatively accomplished and maintained and that communication functions to constitute and give meaning to the experience of sport. For this reason we assert that the community of sport represents a communicatively rich locale that warrants the attention of communication scholars. Accordingly, we set out to explore the intersection of communication and sport within this chapter. Drawing on literature from the field of communication studies as well as from associated fields we discuss how members in the community of sport communicatively enact, (re)produce, consume, and organize sport. In each of these respective areas we discuss and highlight applicable work, recognize limitations in the current literature, and provide directions for future research. Integrating these areas serves to illustrate the multiplicity of ways in which communication informs and shapes the experience of sport.

Correspondence: Jeffrey W. Kassing, Department of Communication Studies, Arizona State University West, PO Box 37100, Phoenix, AZ 85069; email: jkassing@asu.edu

Communication Yearbook 28, pp. 373–409

Although the actual performance of sport is a physical activity, communi cation in, around, and about sport influences both the physical perfor mance of athletes and the social construction of the sporting experience. Whether it be coaches instructing athletes, spectators viewing a game via mass media, or a sports organization crafting a public campaign to develop support for a local sports franchise, communication is not only fundamental, but arguably con- stitutive to the experience of sport. For this reason the community of sport repre- sents a rich locale for communicative exploration and stands as a community that is in fact co-created and sustained communicatively. It is through communication that participants (e.g., coaches, athletes, trainers, and referees), spectators (i.e., at actual sporting events and via mediated channels), sports organizations (e.g., pro- fessional and amateur sports franchises, sports governing bodies, and fan clubs) and sports media combine in complex and intertwined ways to comprise the com- munity of sport. Communication is the vehicle by which community members participate in the enactment, (re)production, consumption, and organizing of sport. These overlapping communicative activities serve to signal membership in or ex- clusion from the community of sport, to bond members of that community, and to facilitate members' experiences of sport.

Before examining the particular communicative facets of the community of sport, it is necessary to discuss some important characteristics of this community. First, involvement in the community of sport is restricted and enhanced by social characteristics (e.g., culture, age, and gender). Consider, for example, that soccer is the largest supported sport on a global level but remains relegated to minor status in comparison to the big four sports (i.e., American football, baseball, bas- ketball, and hockey) in the United States (Delgado, 1997). The popularity of youth soccer is nonetheless formidable in the United States, and the U.S. national women's soccer team has won several World Cup championships. These contrasting per- spectives reveal that exposure to, access to, and interest and participation in sport vary with regard to culture, age, and gender. Thus, we recognize that experiences in the community of sport are bound by these demographics.

Second, the community of sport is complex and multilayered. Members are often involved in sport in multiple ways, at various levels, and to varying degrees. Consider for example the parent-coach-fan. Recent work by communication scholars highlights the complex and multiple identities that members of the community of sport enact concurrently and how those roles influence one another and shape the experience of sport for both parents and children (Kassing & Meân, 2001; Meân, Kassing, Gebhard, & Burkhart, 2002). In addition, identities constructed and roles enacted within the community of sport are also powerfully and reciprocally linked to other prominent discourses, identities, and social practices (Brown, 1998; Maingueneau, 1999; Messner, 1988; Shapiro, 1989). Thus, we recognize that mem- bership in the community of sport reflects and shapes multiple identities in com- plex, interwoven, and mutually influential ways (Brown, 1998; Duquin, 1982; Messner, 1988; Sugden & Tomlinson, 1994).

Third, the community of sport is influential. This is evident in the work of communication scholars who have examined the influence of media representations and social portrayals of particular athletes such as Nolan Ryan (Trujillo, 1991), George Foreman (Engen, 1995), Billie Jean King (Nelson, 1984), and Magic Johnson (Brown, Baranowski, Kulig, Stephenson, & Perry, 1996; Wanta & Elliott, 1995). It is also evident in work that explores how communication about sport functions to promote social and cultural values. For example, scholars have discussed how the presentation of particular sporting events such as the Super Bowl and the Olympic Games functions to strengthen existing social structures (Real, 1975; Real & Mechikoff, 1992), specific ideologies (Farrell, 1989), particular political agendas (Eastman, Brown, & Kovatch, 1996; Riggs, Eastman, & Golobic, 1993), and certain cultural values (Rothenbuhler, 1988, 1989). Moreover, scholars have considered how televised sports in general act to socialize viewers to conservative political values (Prisuta, 1979) and to value systems that serve an industrial society (Whitson, 1984). Collectively these works illustrate that members of a sport community are subject to, participate in, and co-construct wide-ranging and potentially significant incidents of social influence.

Fourth, the community of sport is pervasive. In many aspects of our social lives sports are no longer limited to media presentations of actual sport activities or reports of sport performances (Kinkema & Harris, 1998). Now sport becomes represented in other venues such as film (Aden, 1994, 1995), advertising (McDermott, Hocking, Johnson, & Atkin, 1989), and politics (Bineham, 1991; Fiddick, 1989; Scodari, 1993). Moreover, intertextual linkages, sport metaphors, and sporting discourse have pervaded everyday talk and are now readily apparent in the language practices of society at large (Shapiro, 1989). The infiltration of talk about sport into nonsport contexts supports the notion that sport, like religion and science (Maingueneau, 1999), is a pervasive foundational discourse (Meân, 2001).

The restrictedness, complexity, influence, and pervasiveness of the community of sport occur communicatively. The community of sport thus stands as an ideal site for exploring communication. It is the intention in this chapter to identify and organize the communicative practices within the community of sport. Accordingly, the reviewed literature pertinent to communication in the community of sport is drawn from three bodies of literature: (a) literature from the field of communication studies, (b) literature produced by communication scholars but published in other disciplines' journals, and (c) literature published by scholars working in other disciplines (e.g., sport psychology, sport sociology, and marketing) that is relevant to the discussion. This review will bring together and centralize literature from across associated disciplines that attend to communication within the community of sport. Collecting and centralizing this literature will facilitate subsequent efforts to recognize and conceptualize the communicative nature of sport and will foster the development of communication and sport as a viable context of study within the field of communication studies.

This exploration of communication within the community of sport examines how members of the community of sport communicatively enact, (re)produce, consume, and organize sport. The chapter therefore is organized around four general areas of focus (which are not proposed to be mutually exclusive): (a) communication and enacting sport, (b) communication and (re)producing sport, (c) communication and consuming sport, and (d) communication and organizing sport. Accordingly, communication and enacting sport can be broadly construed as communication within and around the actual performance of sport. This includes communication between teammates as well as between coaches and athletes, but also includes notions of how communication about sport and sport participation serve as important socializing forces that shape participant, spectator, and fan identity. Communication and (re)producing sport involves primarily media and other productive sources' portrayals and presentations of sport. Communication and consuming sport captures the impact and outcomes associated with media presentations of sport by focusing on how spectators, fans, and viewers are affected by and use sport media. Finally, communication and organizing sport centers around the communication generated by sports organizations (e.g., sport franchises, sport personalities, governing bodies, and fan clubs) and the implications that organizing sport generates with regard to messages created for audiences that are internal and external to sports organizations.

The proposed distinctions are designed to provide a structure for organizing previous work in the area, recognizing limitations in the current body of work, and offering suggestions for future research. To that end there is literature reviewed in each of the respective areas, limitations noted in previous work, and suggestions offered for future research. Even though they are necessary and helpful for conceptual and organizational purposes, the suggested focus areas are not discrete. Rather they overlap and possess permeable boundaries. Work in the various areas informs work in the other respective areas. Moreover, the experience of members in the community of sport traverses these permeable boundaries in numerous and complicated ways. To varying degrees, in complex and complicated ways, and through subtle and overt means, a community of sport members thus experiences and constitutes sport by communicatively enacting, (re)producing, consuming, and organizing sport.

COMMUNICATION AND ENACTING SPORT

Enactment is concerned with everyday practices and habits of language. This section considers not only the direct impact of communication on performance, interpersonal interaction, and identity, but also how communication functions to shape the prevailing ideologies, discourses, and beliefs about the way things are done and about what is natural. What is communicated explicitly and implicitly in the process of enacting sport can influence the behavior, beliefs, and prevailing discourses observed within sport, as well as wider society (Shapiro, 1989; Van

Dijk, 1993). Sport can be characterized by unique interpersonal interactions between parents and youth athletes, between teammates, between coaches and athletes, as well as with and between fans. However, these interactions take place within a context or discourse that articulates a powerful set of values and beliefs about how people do sport and who can do sport. Thus, communication about sport holds implications for the ways participants enact being a coach, an athlete, a parent, or a fan. Similarly there are implications for gender, ethnicity, and sexuality (such as inclusion or exclusion, performance evaluation, and expectations) that are especially significant given the wide-ranging psychological benefits of sports participation (Duquin, 1982) and its foundational influence on culture and identities (Creedon, 1998; Dunning, 1999; Messner, 1988). The upcoming section considers communication and the enactment of sport with regard to (a) sport socialization; (b) aggression, competition, and winning; (c) coach, athlete, and teammate interactions; and (d) the enactment of gender, ethnicity, and sexuality.

Sport Socialization

Much of the sport socialization literature has developed from social learning theory (Bandura, 1986), which views interaction with others as an effective method for internalizing appropriate and expected behavior. Sport socialization research demonstrates that sport represents a medium by which children learn and develop desirable social behaviors (McGuire & Cook, 1985; Roberts, Treasure, & Hall, 1994). It is implicit in sport socialization research that communication is necessary for connecting sporting actions and events to desired social behaviors. Parents (and society in general) tend to perceive sport as an opportunity for children to acquire skills, to develop their character and confidence, and to learn valuable lessons about winning and losing. For this to occur, however, communication about sporting events and activities must be present. It is through this type of communication that sporting behaviors become imbued with meaning. The enactment of sport in this regard concerns translating sporting acts and events into moral and social lessons.

More recent approaches focus on how communicative processes construct identities and understandings of events and action to fit with normative forms of behavior, values, and beliefs. Both perspectives emphasize an on-going process involving athletes' exposure to sport (e.g., the act of engagement in sport as participant and spectator, interacting with other athletes, following rules and procedures developed for the sport) and what is traditionally viewed as the reinforcement that is received from others (e.g., role models, peers, parents, coaches). The literature supports the notion that the social meaning of sport is continually constructed (i.e., produced and reproduced) through interactions and enactments in the social world in ways that influence understandings, identities, sport participation, and dropout rates (Horne, Tomlinson, & Whannel, 1999; Kassing & Barber, 2000). Considerable research in this area explores the powerful influence parents have on young children's initial and continued participation in sport (Fishwick & Greendorfer, 1987; Woolger & Power, 1993).

Certainly, parental communication involvement on the sidelines, at practice, or during competitive games is increasingly acknowledged as potentially problematic. Parents are becoming increasingly overinvolved and overinstructive. In fact, research reveals that coaches perceive parents as potentially threatening to coaching staffs and as potentially damaging to their children's performance (Duncan, 1997). Additionally, evidence suggests that overinvolved parents create additional pressures that youth athletes find difficult to escape (Thornton, 1991). The problems stem from a number of sources, but two stand out as particularly noteworthy. First, the overwhelming emphasis that is placed on sport as a focus of family and social life creates problems (Thornton, 1991). Second, the parental relationship with the child becomes focused on the parents' goal orientation, rather than the child's interests and orientations (Roberts et al., 1994). Youth athletes have reported that this persistent emphasis on winning and the competitive elements of sport undermine their pleasure in sport participation and directly affect their decisions to drop out of sports (Meân et al., 2002; Orlick & Botterill, 1975). Recent research supports the notion that the motives pursued and roles enacted at youth sporting events are bound up in the identities that parents, fans, and coaches construct through sport, including acts of aggression, success, and failure (Kassing & Meân, 2001). It has therefore become increasingly common for parents to be excluded or segregated from their children during training and practice sessions. In some instances parents are expected to sign noninterference contracts that include agreements that they will not approach or speak with coaches during practices or games. The continually evolving communicative climate constituted at youth sporting events and the subsequent impact upon sport socialization warrants the continued attention of communication scholars.

Aggression, Competition, and Winning

Aggression, competitiveness, the route to success, and the magnitude of winning and losing are just a few of the significant and familiar facets of how sport is communicatively enacted. Literature from a range of academic disciplines acknowledges that sport communicates a number of powerful social messages and behaviors that in turn influence wider discourses and cultural practices. Professional and adult sports are contexts of sanctioned violence (Jansen & Sabo, 1994) in which winning at all costs and (abusively) expressive coach and fan behavior have become accepted, and to a large extent, expected (Brown, 1998; Knoppers, 1989, 1992). These enactments can be seen in sport itself, but also are evident in the widely adopted and familiar sporting metaphors, idioms, and intertextual references that demonstrate the significant figurability of sport in society and its links to competition and war (Shapiro, 1989). Unfortunately such enactments are increasingly being seen in action on and off the field of youth sports.

Recent statistical accounts indicate that children involved in youth sports find themselves the focus of increasing incidents of pressure and abuse from parents, coaches, and fans (Lord, 2000; Wong, 2001). In addition, dramatic anecdotes further illustrate the problem. For example, on July 5, 2000, the father of a 10-year-old boy fatally beat another hockey player's father over a disagreement about body checking. A week earlier, a disgruntled parent-coach in Florida broke the jaw of a 13-year-old umpire, and in 1999 a Virginia mother slapped a 14-year-old official when she disagreed with a call (Butterfield, 2000). The apparently inappropriate levels of aggression, competitiveness, and overinvolvement described above appear related to the ways in which it has become culturally and communicatively normative to do sport. These practices appear to have spilled over into youth settings not simply through wider discourses and influences, but as coaches, parents, and fans communicatively enact their own sporting ambitions and identities in highly competitive and aggressive ways (Kassing & Meân, 2001).

Coach, Athlete, and Teammate Interactions

Coaching, instruction, and team development are clearly communicative activities, but the large body of literature in associate fields treating these subjects (e.g., sport psychology, sport sociology) does not regularly emphasize the communicative aspects of these phenomena. However, the communicative implications evident in this work are readily apparent. For example, Dwyer and Fischer (1990) discovered that athletes were more satisfied when they perceived their coaches to be well trained and skilled at instruction. Clearly training and instruction involve communication. Indeed, when coaches received social support training, athletes rated their coaches more favorably, reported having more fun, and reported that they liked their teammates more regardless of win-loss record (Smith, Smoll, & Barnett, 1995).

Coaching feedback stands as one clearly overt communicative facet of the coach-athlete relationship. The type, amount, and timeliness of feedback that coaches provide appear to influence athletes' motivation, self-confidence, and satisfaction (Black & Weiss, 1992; Sinclair & Vealey, 1989; Smith & Smoll, 1990; Weiss & Friedrichs, 1986). Whereas some findings indicate that coaches prefer prosocial forms of providing feedback, other findings demonstrate that coaches enact less supportive means of providing feedback. For example, coaches rated reward statements and encouraging self-talk as effective forms of providing feedback (Gould, Hodge, Peterson, & Giannini, 1989), but appeared to remain primarily subject-oriented rather than human-relations–oriented and tended to engage in less responsive coaching tactics as competition increased (Liukkonen, Laakso, & Telama, 1996). Further evidence has suggested that coaches resort to threatening punishment when faced with substandard performance (Miles & Greenberg, 1993). This is problematic in light of findings that suggest athletes respond more favorably to coaches who are reinforcing and encouraging and negatively to coaches who are less supportive (Smith & Smoll, 1990).

Research conducted within the field of communication studies reveals that male athletes who perceived their coaches to be comparably more verbally and physically aggressive reported being less satisfied with their coaches, reported less team success in terms of win-loss percentage, and reported less sportsmanship behavior

(Kassing & Infante, 1999). These findings suggest that coaches' communication styles directly influence how athletes behave athletically and socially. The influence of coaches' communicative practices during the enactment of sport is important because there is a predominant perception that the best form of coaching involves an authoritative and dominant style associated with traditional masculine sporting values (Knoppers, 1989, 1992). This idea also is reflected in discrimination against women coaches (Thorngren, 1990) despite increasing acknowledgment from professional sports organizations (e.g., U.S. Women's Sports Foundation) that there is no right or single way to coach.

Another developing body of literature in the field considers the communicative and educational potential of the coach-athlete relationship. Parrott and Duggan (1999), for example, found that coaches were instrumental in increasing athletes' self-efficacy toward health training through coaches' promotion of sun protection for their athletes. Turman (2003a) suggested that coaches' levels of experience and the time in the season influences athletes' preferences for and perceptions of their coaches' instructional strategies. These findings highlight the communicative potential of the coach-athlete relationship to serve as an educational agent.

As with the other communicative relationships that constitute the sport experience (e.g., coach-athlete, parent-athlete), there is evidence to indicate that communication among teammates influences the enactment of sport. In particular findings suggest that interpersonal attraction and communication ability directly influence team cohesion (Lefebvre & Cunningham, 1977) and performance for both interacting (e.g., sports requiring direct interaction from players during competition, such as football and basketball) and coacting (e.g., sports where team performance is based on the sum of individual performances, such as golf and wrestling) teams (Di Berardinis, Barwind, Flaningam, & Jenkins, 1983). More recent work reveals that poor group interaction and communication (e.g., ineffective communication about roles or inappropriate feedback about performance) emerged as the strongest predictors of players' stress and satisfaction (Campbell & Jones, 2002).

Communication among teammates also appears to be tied closely to interactions with coaches. Turman (2003b) found that college athletes' team cohesion levels were deterred when coaches embarrassed and ridiculed players or when coaches demonstrated inequity by showing favoritism to individual athletes or units. Conversely, team cohesion levels increased when coaches praised and teased athletes, utilized team prayer, and showed dedication to the sport. Heath (1991) described how team cohesion was continually fostered through the development of a collective knowledge that was cultivated and encouraged by the coach. These examples illustrate how communicative enactment of sport between and among teammates contributes to the experience of and satisfaction derived from sport.

Enacting Identity: Gender, Ethnicity, and Sexuality

Sport is a powerful cultural institution that acts as a highly significant site for identity construction and enactment (including resistance) across local, national, and global boundaries (Brown, 1998; Messner, 1988; O'Donnell, 1994). Sport is strongly associated with masculinity and masculine identities and it is the cultural practice that, arguably, most prominently demarcates men and women (Horne et al., 1999). When examining the communicative influence of sport, Maltz and Borker (1982) argued that games are influential in dividing individuals into a gender communication culture (masculine or feminine). They observed that because children's games tended to be sex segregated during adolescence, boys (e.g., playing football, basketball, or baseball) and girls (e.g., playing house, school, or library) learned different appreciations for when, why, and with whom they should interact. Recognizing the implications of this work, Wood (1996) argued that the nature and type of games that boys and girls play create differences in listening styles, topics of talk, conversation maintenance, and conflict resolution. Not only does involvement in games produce different communicative practices, but it also holds implications for gendered identities. For example, Chase and Drummer (1992) found that sport was a minor variable in predicting social status for girls and that girls identified sport as their least favorite activity in which to participate.

The traditional, continued, and routine segregation of males and females in sport socialization and participation provides support for the argument that sport serves as a primary site of enactment for White male hegemony via the prizing of masculinity and heterosexuality (Creedon, 1998), the active resistance to the inclusion of women (Duncan & Messner, 1998), and the persistent othering of women, ethnicity, and homosexuality (Dunning, 1999). In addition to structural and functional social segregation, positioning or framing social categories as the other cognitively functions to define the standard (Lakoff, 1987). Thus, maintaining males as the athletic prototype requires that women be positioned as the other (Kane, 1995). Scholars have suggested that the increasing significance of sport for masculinity occurs in light of widespread and consistent challenges to male hegemony in other spheres (Duncan & Messner, 1998), which is heightened by the increasing numbers of women participating in sport, particularly in traditionally male sports (Meân, 2001; Snyder & Spreitzer, 1989). The fierce heterosexualization of successful women athletes, the (re)production of the fear of lesbianism, and the positioning of lesbian athletes as outside the normal sphere of athletic achievement are all facets of this enactment (Lenskyj, 1986).

The enactment of these discourses and values can be identified at a number of levels discussed in subsequent sections, including the media (e.g., through commentary and technical production values) and sports organizations (e.g., regulators and leagues). It is, however, not just at these levels that ideologies are enacted, but also within the talk, texts, and action of all people who do sport. It is in the sports bars and locker rooms and on the playing fields that the ideologies of sport are played out, enacted, and maintained as part of everyday talk and discursive practices (Meân Patterson, 2003). In fact, the deployment of intertextual links to mobilize discourses that frame and position as well as include and exclude typically achieved by minimal references or single words, such as references to stereotypical features (O'Donnell, 1994). Recent research illustrates how women

athletes' enactment of normative (masculinized) practices and behaviors associated with a specific sport can be undermined and othered through the gendered
nature of routine decisions, explanations, and narratives provided by officials during games (Meân, 2001). Such evidence demonstrates the power in everyday enactment to protect underlying identities from inappropriate enactors (such as
women) and to exclude othered participants through motivated but not necessarily
cognizant (mis)interpretation based on social categories rather than actual performance.

The enactment of otherness and the routine construction and exclusion of category membership and identities around gender, sexuality, ethnicity, and nationality occur in everyday talk; it is apparent, however, that the rhetorical and discursive aspects of other texts, such as public debates and commentaries, inform this
type of enactment. Examining these texts enables us to address some of the underlying ideas communicated by sport. For example, the traditional lack of African
American quarterbacks in American football reflected ideas about suitability for
strategic positions (Harris, 1993), ideas that remain powerful and pervasive in other
strategic areas such as coaching. The continued failure to place African-Ameri-
cans in strategic positions, such as coaching, and the arguments justifying or deny-
ing the racism implicit in such decisions reflects the enactment of racist ideas as
embodied in the practice of sport (Hopkins, Reicher, & Levine, 1997). Equally, the
enactment of racist ideas and discourses within training and coaching practices
can be responsible for failure to facilitate the development of strategic thinking
and particular skills necessary for minority athletes to move into key influential
athletic roles. Similarly, the comparatively lesser performance of women compared to men has been argued to be a function of different coaching techniques and
expectations communicated to women based on the belief that women can never
perform as well as men and that coaching women is second rate (Knoppers, 1989).
This is an issue central to current debates about whether Title IX should continue
to be applied to sport in the face of criticism that it deprives men of sporting opportunities to provide for underserving women. In fact, in February 2003, the U.S.
Commission on Opportunity in Athletics recommended and endorsed changes to
the Department of Education requiring women and girls to prove their interest in
sport to achieve participation and sponsorship. In this instance enactment entails
debating a sport policy and the outcome of this enactment communicates and reaffirms the notion that only men are truly interested in sport and should be privileged
regarding access to sport.

Criticism and Directions for Future Research

Along with the initial explorations into the enactment of sport discussed here, a
number of possibilities for future research exist. First, further exploration is necessary to determine the ways in which and the extent to which involvement in the
community of sport serves to develop communication skills, both competitive and
social, and personal and social identities. A number of questions persist concerning how communication characteristics (e.g., argumentativeness, communicator

style, approach to conflict, and self-disclosure) and social identities (e.g., masculinity/femininity) are influenced by involvement with sport and vice versa. Research examining these issues would serve to help determine the intricacies of interconnection that exist between sport and human communication.

Second, it would be valuable to obtain a stronger representation of how members in the community of sport (e.g., parents, coaches, and teammates) communicatively foster or deter sport participation. There is a strong rationale for continuing to promote physical activity in young people (regardless of whether it occurs in organized or unorganized sports) that is linked closely to the established health benefits derived from sport participation (Anderssen & Wold, 1992). Adolescents are at a period where the development of values and norms concerning health-related behaviors will determine their likelihood for engaging in physical activity as adults. Sport socialization offers a number of opportunities for both family and health communication researchers to discover the communicative practices, functions, and roles members of the community of sport draw upon to encourage and shape children's sport experiences.

Third, examination of coach-athlete interaction warrants additional communication research from an instructional perspective. Over the past 3 decades there has been a tremendous growth in the area of organized youth sports. Research suggests that 26 million children (approximately 54% of children between the ages of 6 and 17 in the United States) played on an organized team (Seefeldt & Ewing, 2000). These young athletes were instructed by an estimated 3.5 million coaches, most of whom have little to no instructional background (Seefeldt, 1999). With such numbers, instructional scholars in particular and communication scholars in general should be doing more to investigate the coach-athlete relationship as a communicatively intense extension of the teacher-student relationship. The parallel between coaching behaviors and instructional activity suggests a need to continue examining athletics as an instructional setting. Instructional communication has limitless potential for examination of relationships between coaching and communication behaviors (e.g., immediacy, affective learning, teacher caring, power, and verbal aggressiveness) as a way to offer insight concerning the coaching process. It is well accepted that learning does not end once students leave the classroom and that athletics serve as an alternative instructional environment that warrants additional attention (Heath & McLaughlin, 1994). Topics to be addressed in this line of work would include (a) how coaches communicatively enhance or deter learning; (b) which life skills are fostered in athletics and howcoaches communicatively promote/deter the development of such skills; and (c) what assumptions and attitudes with regard to race, gender, and sexuality coaches communicate and how these are enacted within the context of sport by both coaches and athletes. These are just some of the ideas that could be addressed by continuing to explore the instructional capacity apparent in the community of sport.

Finally, more work is needed that examines the construction of sport in relation to talk, rhetoric, identities, and the performance of sport. These approaches offer insight into participation and exclusion, performance and motivation, and the

increased aggression and violence linked to sport. Given the increasing significance of sport for identities (Duncan & Messner, 1998) and wider cultural practices (Sklair, 1991), there is great value in further research focusing on how talk
and other communicative practices in and around sport function to enact and construct gendered, racialized, and sexualized identities. A further advantage of such
research is that it would offer insight for and progress in unpacking the ways in
which policies attached to sport are practiced, put into action, and justified and
defended. Work of this type would elucidate how the deployment of ideas, beliefs,
and actions among community of sport members occurs in the everyday communicative practice of enacting sport across individual, organizational, social, and
cultural levels.

COMMUNICATION AND (RE)PRODUCING SPORT

The one communication channel that frequently and directly enables participants to have immediate contact to and a symbolic connection with the sporting
community is the media. Even though the research characterizing this respective
domain of sport is far from replete, scholars have generally begun to devote attention toward how the media have influenced intergroup boundaries within the community of sport with respect to issues of (a) gender (e.g., Billings, Halone, &
Denham, 2002), (b) race (e.g., Billings & Eastman, 2002), and (c) nationality (e.g.,
Knoppers & Anthonissen, 2001). What follows is a selective yet representative
overview of communication research that has been systematically developed among
these three distinct and related avenues of inquiry. Each helps us understand the
ways in which media serve to (re)produce representatives, participants, and members in the community of sport.

Characterizations of Gender

Scholars exploring the community of sport have been interested in examining
how female athletes, and their respective sports, have encountered various intergroup obstacles throughout the historical evolution of sport (Birrell & Rintala,
1984; Theberge, 2000). Stephenson (2002) reported that female athletes have been
portrayed throughout the media in novel yet perplexing ways. Communication
scholars have begun to examine how the media may be (in)directly contributing to
such media paradoxes (Halone, 2003; Shugart, 2003). Three general avenues
through which scholars have considered gender and (re)production of sport include (a) media exposure, (b) on-air broadcast commentary, and (c) production
and promotion considerations.

Media exposure. Scholars have begun to comparatively examine the degree to
which women's sports receive media attention and exposure. For example, Eastman
and Billings (2000) found that leading televised sports programs devoted only 5–
7% of their coverage to female athletes. Similarly, research examining Olympic

telecasts throughout the 1990s consistently revealed that male athletic events were shown more frequently to viewers than female athletic events (Billings, Eastman, & Newton, 1998; Eastman & Billings, 1999; Eastman & Otteson, 1994; Higgs & Weiler, 1994; Tuggle & Owen, 1999). With regard to the content of media presentations of female athletes, Tuggle and Owen (1999) concluded that television coverage of the 1996 Olympic games almost exclusively featured those events that were physically attractive to the viewer (e.g., women's gymnastics, diving, and sprinting). Similarly, findings indicate that, although people thought the success of the 1999 Women's World Cup team was the primary reason for the increased coverage, in actuality the attractiveness of the team as a feminine phenomenon prompted its media promotion (Christopherson, Janning, & McConnell, 2002).

In addition, these same patterns of media attention and exposure are apparent in other mediated formats. For example, examinations of *Sports Illustrated* and *Sports Illustrated for Women* indicate that women athletes compared to male athletes were highly underrepresented in articles and photographs (Daddario, 1992; Fink & Kensicki, 2002). Moreover, when such representations of female athletes would surface, they often presented women athletes in nonsport situations (e.g., model-like poses) or in historically feminine sports (e.g., figure skating). These findings illustrate how the amount and type of media coverage may contribute to (re)producing intergroup issues surrounding men's and women's athletics.

On-air broadcast commentary. Scholars have examined the demeanor of sports broadcasters with respect to how their commentary practices, and the broadcast content, may interactively contribute to the (re)production of intergroup distinctions within the community of sport. Research findings suggest that broadcasters have demonstrated a tendency to refer to female athletes as girls, while referring to male athletes as men (Koivula, 1999; Messner, Duncan, & Jensen, 1993). Research examining the broadcasts of successive Olympic Games revealed that references were made about the attractive features of certain female athletes and not others whose appearance did not prompt such commentary and that broadcaster's made more than twice as many comments about the strength of male vs. female athletes (Eastman & Billings, 1999). Similarly, content analyses of championship and regular season collegiate basketball games indicated that commentary content degraded and trivialized female athletes (Duncan & Hasbrook, 1988), characterized female athletes as slow (Eastman & Billings, 2001), and suggested that female athletes were not ready for heightened competition (Eastman & Billings, 2000). Conversely, descriptions such as "Kryptonite," "savior," and "messiah" were used to typify the activity of male athletes (Eastman & Billings, 2000, p. 208).

Additional research indicated that commentators, in comparison to comments made about male athletes, provided significantly fewer accounts of female athlete's physicality and athleticism and significantly more accounts of female athletes' background, personality, and looks/appearance (Billings et al., 2002). The on-air commentary communicatively advanced across broadcasters and sporting events further reveals how intergroup distinctions arise as a result of the (re)production of men's and women's representations within the community of sport.

Production and promotion considerations. Intergroup gendered differences also appear with respect to the production and promotion of men and women's sporting events. Hallmark and Armstrong's (1999) analysis of the National Collegiate Athletic Association (NCAA) men's and women's basketball championships (1991–1995) found that the women's championship game employed fewer cameras and graphics than did the men's championship game. They concluded that differential production decisions could mediate public perceptions about the value and significance of NCAA women's championship games. Messner, Duncan, and Wachs's (1996) critical analysis argued that the men's Final Four was promoted by the media to be a must see event while the women's games were largely construed by the media to be a nonevent. They lamented that endorsing such mediated practices serves to perpetuate processes of hegemonic masculinity and financial gain for television networks, while preserving dominant power structures in the domain of intercollegiate athletics. These findings and criticism prompt questions regarding the role and function that production and promotion considerations play in perpetuating mediated accounts of athletic performance.

Characterizations of Race

This section considers how mediated exposure to, and audience experiences with, athletes of various races facilitate intergroup assumptions about the nature of sport and athletic performance (Davis & Harris, 1998; Edwards, 1969). Although scholarly accounts surrounding this issue abound, they are far from complete (Dewar, 1993; Entine, 2000; Harris, 1993). Three race-related knowledge claims have traditionally surfaced throughout the interdisciplinary literature addressing race within the community of sport. These claims, emergent from the (re)production of sport, position community of sport members in particular ways.

The three race-related knowledge claims that have been perpetuated through the (re)production of sport concern contentions of athletes' capability. The first claim pertains to athletic intelligence. Historically, White athletes have allegedly been superior to their Black counterparts with respect to their athletic intelligence (Birrell, 1989; McCarthy & Jones, 1997). The (re)production of this knowledge claim was evident in Rada's (1996) examination of broadcast coverage of professional football games. The analysis revealed that announcers tended to emphasize the cognitive qualities of White athletes and the physical qualities of Black athletes.

The second claim pertains to athletic performance, particularly allegations that Black athletes are born athletes whereas White athletes must achieve athletic excellence through hard work (Staples & Jones, 1985; Whannel, 1992). The (re)production of this claim can be seen in work that examines commentary produced during the Olympic Games and the collegiate basketball season (Billings & Eastman, 2002; Eastman & Billings, 2001). Billings and Eastman (2002) found in their examination of 2000 Sydney Summer Olympics that the success of White athletes was attributed to their commitment, whereas the success of Black athletes was attributed to their innate athletic ability. Similarly, Eastman and Billings's (2001) content analysis of on-air coverage of regular season collegiate basketball games revealed that Black athletes were revered for their athleticism, quickness, and power, whereas White athletes were acknowledged for their intelligence and their hard work.

The third claim pertains to athletic leadership. White athletes have, historically, laid claim to their alleged natural ability to lead their team (e.g., being the point guard in basketball, the quarterback in football, or the pitcher in baseball) over that of Black athletes (Wonsek, 1992). The (re)production of this knowledge claim was recently questioned in research conducted by Denham, Billings, and Halone (2002). In their examination of the broadcast commentary provided during the 2000 NCAA Men's and Women's Final Four championship games, they found that Black athletes, across all athletic contests, continued to be praised for their athleticism and their physicality, but also garnered a greater number of accounts regarding their intelligence and their ability to lead. Moreover, this trend held for the (re)production of both men's and women's games. Such findings possibly represent a changing cultural impression of the nature of Black collegiate athletic performance and a move away from the historical knowledge claims communicatively (re)produced for and about members of the community of sport.

Characterizations of Nationality

Whereas the previous two areas of (re)production of sport have focused on domestic intergroup issues, a slowly growing body of communication research has begun to focus on how the media, however indirectly, foster intergroup impressions and distinctions within the community of sport at the international level. For example, Larson and Rivenburgh (1991) found in their comparative analysis of three national telecasts during the 1988 Seoul Olympics Opening Ceremony that differential preferences existed with regard to how Australia, Great Britain, and the United States covered the event. In a related study of international athletic events, findings indicated that few biases against Black athletes surfaced; however, national biases did appear to manifest themselves in the mediated portrayals of Asian and Hispanic athletes (Sabo, Jansen, Tate, Duncan, & Leggett, 1996). Finally, a series of studies have illustrated that a U.S. nationalistic broadcasting bias surfaces in U.S. Olympic telecasts (Billings & Eastman, 2002; Eastman & Billings, 1999). This was demonstrated in the disproportionate presentation of American athletes particularly with regard to medal-winning performances. These examples demonstrate that the (re)production of sport also holds implications for characterizations of and reactions to nationality.

Criticism and Directions for Future Research

The above review, and its attendant implications, begin to provide communication scholars with a preliminary base for understanding how mediated messages play a direct, explicit, and formative role in the (re)production and facilitation of intergroup issues related to gender, race, and nationality. The above findings prompt a host of communication-related questions for future empirical consideration. First, the examination of media content prompts further investigation into how the framing of sporting events establishes an intergroup agenda within the community of sport. Agenda setting would appear to be one candidate framework to account for such empirical findings, given the subtle nature with which such intergroup boundaries become constructed throughout the spectacle of televised sporting telecasts. Tankard (2001) has argued that media framing is a prospectively more robust framework to account for issues of media bias, as it moves beyond dichotomous forms of thinking (e.g., positive versus negative) and looks at how those definitional issues and features of selection, emphasis, and exclusion ultimately function. Adopting such perspectives could lend to our further understanding of how communication and sport connect to (re)present participants within the community of sport.

Second, the continued examination of media content also prompts a consideration of those dynamics and (re)presentations that become cultivated (Gerbner, Gross, Morgan, & Signorielli, 1986) through announcer (Hansen, 1999) and spectator (Duncan & Brummett, 1989; Gantz & Wenner, 1995; Sargent, Zillmann, & Weaver, 1998) participation in such processes. One theoretical assumption on which cultivation theory rests is that prolonged exposure to television will alter viewers' perceptions of society, making heavy television viewers more likely than light viewers to construct a reality that closely matches what is mediated on television (Gerbner et al., 1986). As illustrated previously, the (re)production of sport involves the presentation of accounts of gendered activity, characterizations of various ethnicities, and representations of certain nationalities, all of which potentially stand to be cultivated into a particular reality for community of sport members. The processes by which those members of the community of sport who engage in various forms of mediated sporting activity cultivate such realities can be understood more clearly when we consider the degree to which such messages are being processed and subsequently discussed (Katz & Lazarsfeld, 1955). Exploring these considerations should prompt continued opportunities to empirically assess the potential impact of communication and the (re)production of sport.

Additionally, it is evident from the review of literature addressing communication and (re)producing sport that scholars working in this area favor content analysis. This methodological technique has increased our understanding of media (re)presentations of the community of sport considerably. However, there are inherent limits in what media content analyses can articulate. That is, such analyses simply tell us about the degree to which varying (re)presentations portray and are presented to the community of sport. From them it emerges that particular agendas are at work in reporting and (re)presenting sport and that subsequent effects may be apparent from the consumption of sport, which will be discussed in the upcoming section. Additional and complementary frameworks of analysis, such as those noted in the preceding paragraphs, would prove beneficial in future efforts to understand the interconnectedness between the (re)production of sport and the subsequent consumption and enactment of sport.

COMMUNICATION AND CONSUMING SPORT

Sports audiences comprise a considerable portion of the community of sport. Moreover, sport audiences are among the largest in the world. More than a third of all programming on network television is sports-related, and half of the 10 most viewed U.S. television programs of all time were sporting events (Nielsen Media Research, 1998). No arena is vast enough to hold millions of people, but through television they can join together as a single virtual audience to witness athletic contests from the Super Bowl to World Cup Soccer to the Olympics (Bryant & Raney, 2000). Considering live events, television, Internet, newspapers, and other media, opportunities for sports consumption abound. Accordingly, a growing body of research is exploring the ways sports fans use sports media, and the effects sports media have on audience members. This section summarizes some of the most prominent research on communication and consuming sport, paying particular attention to the effects produced by and experienced within the community of sport. In particular this section focuses on (a) the processes of consumption, (b) consumption within the family and the larger community, and (c) the effects of sports consumption.

Processes of Consumption

People consume sports and sports-related commodities for a variety of reasons, some of which are linked with the political economy of sports corporations, and some of which derive from specific features of the sports genre and personal characteristics of its audience members. To understand the political economy of sports consumerism, it is helpful to draw upon Meehan's (1993) notion of the consumerist caste, that segment of the population that possesses the money to buy the products that sports corporations are attempting to sell. Although advertisements for sports-related products may appear to appeal to a universal audience, they are in fact aimed at the consumerist caste. Communities of consumers outside the consumerist caste are excluded from the corporation's message. This exclusion does not occur overtly; however, heavy advertising aimed at the consumerist caste can spill over into these marginalized communities, causing them to desire commodities that they cannot afford. In an essay critiquing the Nike corporation, Stabile (2000) pointed out that "for media industries, audiences are commodities that are sold or delivered to advertisers" (p. 191). She argued that Nike's use of African Americans in its advertisements, particularly those with a basketball theme (Cole & Hribar, 1995), was intended to sell to middle-class White consumers both an urbanized style of sports gear and the image of Nike itself as a pro-Black corporation, not to support African Americans in any meaningful way. Yet African Americans respond to Nike's advertisements. Indeed, at the time of the 1990 Chicago boycott of Nike products, African Americans accounted for 30% of Nike's annual sales (Woodard, 1990). Critical scholars have argued that such marketing encourages lower income African Americans to overspend on luxury commodities they cannot afford, which can lead to materialistic depression (Caution, 1984) or even criminal activity such as theft of high-status, sports-related property like shoes and team apparel (Stabile, 2000).

Sports consumption occurs for reasons other than corporate manipulation, however. Characteristics of the sports genre itself and of the consuming audience both determine consumption. Sports genres are highly engaging because they feature multiple elements that heighten the entertainment experience. Sports provide thrills and suspense and offer spectators the opportunity to exercise empathy toward loved athletes and teams and antipathy toward hated athletes and teams (Bryant & Raney, 2000). The disposition theory of sportsfanship suggests that people derive pleasure from witnessing the success of liked others and the failure of disliked others (Zillmann, Bryant, & Sapolsky, 1989). Sporting contests provide an ideal arena for communicating one's affiliation. It would seem, then, that fans would avoid exposure to games that their favored teams were likely to lose, but research shows that the perception of risk actually increases enjoyment (Sargent et al., 1998). Furthermore, brutal athletic contests may appeal to viewers' sense of morbid curiosity (Zillmann & Bryant, 1994). Sports media, moreover, offer all of this in the comfort of the audience member's home, with companions of his or her choosing.

Although sports fans within the community of sport are diverse, certain individual characteristics predispose some audience members to be heavier consumers than others. Men tend to pay more attention to sports news than women (Perse, 1992) and attribute their sports fanship to personal interest based on a history of playing sports coupled with the desire to keep up-to-date on sports information (Dietz-Uhler, Harrick, End, & Jacquemotte, 2000).

Interpersonal and small-group communication for many men may revolve around the sharing of such information. Women, in contrast, report that they view and attend sporting events to spend time with friends and family (Dietz-Uhler et al., 2000). Moreover, cultural affiliation is a major motivation behind African Americans' consumption of sport (Armstrong, 2002). In addition to gender and race, individual difference variables such as loyalty, word-of-mouth communication, and willingness to pay steep prices increase consumers' investment in sports, especially live sports (Hightower, Brady, & Baker, 2002). Beyond these basic demographic variables, a more complex series of factors influence the uses and effects of sports consumption. These factors affect community of sport members within their families and local communities.

Consumption Within Families and Communities

Researchers have explored consumption practices within both marriages and families (Gantz & Wenner, 1991; Wann, Lane, Duncan, & Goodson, 1998; Way & Gillman, 2000). Gantz and Wenner (1991), for example, found that husbands and wives have markedly different relationships with sports media. Results indicated that husbands were more fan-like (i.e., more emotionally invested in each game and its outcome), whereas wives were more likely to report watching sports for companionship. Further, Wann et al. (1998) found that married fans or fans with children were more likely than others to report consuming sports in order to spend time with family. Thus, sports coviewing may serve a familial relationship-enhancing function for spouses, parents, and children. Although the stereotype holds that fathers and sons bond over discussions of sport, Way and Gillman (2000) reported that daughters also cement their relationships with their fathers by consuming and communicating about sport. These examples denote some of the consumption patterns apparent within marriages and families.

At the community level, sports consumption serves to broadcast and confirm social and civic identities. Indeed, the tendency among sports fans to bask in the reflected glory of their favored teams by wearing team apparel after winning games (Cialdini et al., 1976) suggests that it is important to sports fans to communicate their affiliations. In a case study of sport consumerism and cultural identity in Northern Ireland, McGinley, Kremer, Trew, and Ogle (1998) found that sports fans negotiated their fanship in such a way that they were able to share a Northern Irish identity while maintaining the separate identities of their respective communities. Sports consumerism and membership in the community of sport thus allows members of distinct communities to shift identities to maximize their civic pride and to communicate their affiliation on multiple levels. Stabile (2000) argued that the Nike Corporation capitalized on this desire for a malleable identity with an advertising campaign that featured people of different ages, races, and genders all stating, "I am Tiger Woods."

Effects of Sports Consumption

Regardless of why people consume live sports and sports media, they most certainly will be affected by the athletic contests they witness. These effects, in turn, are likely to influence further consumption. Most of the research exploring the effects of sports spectatorship within the community of sport falls under the research tradition of media effects. Media effects research draws heavily upon theory and methods from the fields of communication, psychology, sociology, and even medicine. The studies summarized here represent some of the more prominent sports spectatorship research in these fields that relates directly to communication and the consumption of sport.

The literature on sports media effects supplies evidence that sports media exposure can produce changes in attitudes and beliefs, behaviors, and even hormones. Hirt, Zillmann, Erickson, and Kennedy (1992) investigated the costs and benefits of allegiance to specific sports teams and found that the fans of winning teams reported increases in self-esteem and predicted that they would succeed when performing various mental, physical, and social tasks. In contrast, fans of losing teams predicted relative failure for themselves. When both sets of fans were asked to perform the tasks, however, there were no differences. In more recent work Harrison and Fredrickson (2003) found that exposure to lean athletes increased adolescent Anglo girls' tendencies to objectify their own bodies, whereas exposure to nonlean athletes decreased this tendency slightly. In contrast, adolescent girls of color reported the opposite pattern. These studies demonstrate that exposure to athletes and their performance resonated with audience members to the extent that their attitudes and beliefs about themselves were temporarily altered. Additionally, investigators have considered the impressions sports fan develop about the athletes themselves. For example, Frank and Gilovich (1988) demonstrated through a series of experiments that athletes in black uniforms were perceived as more aggressive by both fans and referees than athletes wearing other colors.

Aggressive behavior in mediated sports is an issue not only among athletes, but among fans as well. In spite of the argument that spectatorship of violent sports should produce a cathartic effect, thus reducing aggressive impulses in audience members (Lorenz, 1963), studies show that actual effects are in the direction of increased aggression. Arms, Russell, and Sandilands (1979) found that exposure to aggressive sports contests (professional wrestling and ice hockey) resulted in increased aggression among college students, whereas exposure to nonaggressive sports contests (swimming) had no such effect. Similarly, Celozzi, Kazelskis, and Gutsch (1981) reported that male high school students who viewed a hockey video were subsequently more aggressive than those who had only discussed hockey or those who neither viewed nor discussed it. Moreover, these effects were strongest for viewers who were the most aggressive at the outset of the study. Presumably, violent sports give audiences the opportunity to model aggressive behavior and the cues for priming aggressive thoughts, feelings, and behavioral impulses. Trait aggression has been associated with sports fanship (Wann, Shelton, Smith, & Walker, 2002). Therefore, much of the aggressive behavior occurring at live sporting events may be disinhibition of aggression among those who are already more inclined to behave violently.

There are many theoretical explanations for increased aggression during or following exposure to sports, including but not limited to modeling of aggressive behavior (Arms et al., 1979), disinhibition of aggression and diffusion of responsibility in a crowd (Bandura, Underwood, & Fromson, 1975), and excitation transfer (Zillmann, Johnson, & Day, 2000), but any discussion of the behavior of fans would be incomplete without mention of alcohol. In a recent study Nelson and Wechsler (2003) found that sports fans were heavier drinkers and experienced more social problems than nonfans. Moreover, the number of sports fans at a university or college was positively correlated with binge-drinking rates and secondhand effects of heavy drinking (e.g., assault, disrupted studying, and date rape). Thus, the effects derived from the combination of sports, aggression, and alcohol affected not only sports fans, but also their immediate social communities.

Attitudes, beliefs, and behaviors are not the only variables affected by sports consumption. One of the most intriguing outcomes of sports spectatorship concerns the effects of a team's win or loss on fans' hormones, testosterone in particular. Physiological outcomes of media exposure are often excluded from discussions of communication processes and effects because they are noncognitive. It is, however, important to include investigations of such outcomes in summaries of sports media effects because the sports genre itself is inherently rooted in the physiological. The research on the effects of sports spectatorship on testosterone suggests that the outcome of a favored team's performance may communicate a message to fans about their own status as potential contenders. For instance, Bernhardt, Dabbs, Fielden, and Lutter (1998) measured saliva testosterone levels in male sports fans before and after exposure to a live college basketball game and a televised World Cup soccer match. For both events, testosterone levels rose in the fans whose team had won and dropped in the fans whose team had lost. Because higher testosterone levels increase the likelihood of domination in subsequent physical contests (Bernhardt et al., 1998), watching one's team win may, in the short term at least, make a fan feel and behave more like a winner.

Criticism and Directions for Future Research

The studies summarized here are relevant to processes and effects of communication at multiple levels (i.e., mass, interpersonal, and intrapersonal) yet a large proportion of them were published outside the field of communication. We maintain that the sports consumption processes and effects outlined here are communicative phenomena, and as such, further investigation and elaboration of these phenomena should be included in communication journals. Moreover, the processes occurring at each of these levels have, for the most part, been studied separately. Mass communication research has focused either on the political economy of sports consumerism or on the psychological or physiological effects of exposure. Interpersonal communication research has focused on the incorporation of sports into familial or small-group relationship practices. Research relevant to intrapersonal communication (i.e., studies investigating how sports play into individuals' self-perceptions and personal identity) is scattered throughout multiple disciplines. Given the conceptual interconnectedness of these communicative processes, and the fact that the self is nestled within one's family, culture, and nation, it seems clear that the most fruitful future research efforts will acknowledge the means by which the community of sport traverses and connects these various audiences in complex and meaningful ways. Gantz and Wenner (1991), for instance, merged mass communication processes with interpersonal processes in their investigation of couples' use of sports media within the community of marriage. Further research should explore how mass communication uses and effects operate within other communities, be they familial, peer-based, gender-based, recreational, geographical, civic, cultural, or national. Researchers must be open to merging mass, interpersonal, small group, and intercultural theory and methods to answer questions about consumption in the community of sport.

The studies summarized here represent some of the more prominent areas of research on consumption within the community of sport, but there is much ground to be covered. Regarding uses and gratifications of sports consumerism, some key questions remain unanswered. How does one characterize the nontraditional sports media user (e.g., the married woman who loves professional football)? What uses and gratifications does the nontraditional sports media user obtain from sports media? Moreover, how do different racial, economic, cultural, or social subcultures use sports media to meet different needs? As Stabile (2000) argued, corporations have long manipulated members of these subcultures into meeting corporate needs, but how have these subcultures creatively subverted corporate attempts at manipulation to meet their own needs? Finally, how are sports media used creatively to meet new needs and provide new gratifications (e.g., fantasy leagues)? All of these questions need to be addressed to obtain an accurate picture of the interactivity between sports consumption and community.

Regarding effects, the main limitation of the research done to date is that it focuses almost exclusively on male audiences and male athletes. Female consumers as members of the community of sport have been overlooked, especially in research on aggression as an outcome of spectatorship. Equally important is the issue of race. Content analyses summarized earlier in this chapter point to the implications of sports commentary for racial stereotyping. What are the effects of exposure to such commentary on sports consumers of different racial or ethnic backgrounds? How do they process this information within the framework of their various (e.g., personal, racial, gender, social, geographical, national) identities? Bernhardt et al. (1998), in their article on sports spectatorship and testosterone, briefly alluded to the staunch nationalism of World Cup soccer fans (i.e., a national community) but elected to confine their assessment to the individual and his saliva testosterone level. They ignored the opportunity to explore the broader implications with regard to membership and membership classes within the community of sport. Research on sports consumption will fail to progress much further until researchers are willing to expand common conceptual and methodological assumptions about the community of sport (e.g., predominantly male consumers) and until we are able to recognize and assess the interconnected and interdependent nature of membership in the community of sport.

COMMUNICATION AND ORGANIZING SPORT

Within the community of sport the process of organizing rests primarily with sports organizations such as teams, governing agencies, fans clubs, players' unions, and their stakeholders. As with any other formal collective, the sports organization engages in both internal and external communication, two distinct yet related activities. As such, this section considers how previous literature elucidates the ways in which sports organizations function communicatively via internal and external message exchange to organize the sporting experience. The focus now turns to how a sports organization can either engage in organizing itself externally or internally, and how these practices in turn shape people's experiences in the community of sport.

Organizing Externally—Communication Emanating
From a Sports Organization

Sports organizations communicate with external audiences in multiple ways, including marketing, public relations, brand imaging, and merchandising. For example, Midrigal (2001) and McDaniel (1999) considered consumer behavior, marketing communication, and corporate sponsorship of sports. Perhaps more directly related to the communication of sports organizations themselves, Sutton (1987) examined the marketing plans for sports organizations and Fortunato (2000) studied the public relations and media strategies of the National Basketball Association (NBA). Also in relation to the NBA, Andrews (1999) looked at the significance of the NBA as a marketing organization at the core of the sporting landscape in the United States. Similarly, Bremmer and Kesselring (1993) examined the relationship between advertising and university athletic success.

Whereas some scholars have examined issues such as brand imaging and various marketing tools with regard to external communication (Gwinner & Eaton, 1999; Sutton, Irwin, & Gladden, 1998), others have focused on the challenges to and impact of sports marketing. Garcia (1995), for example, compared the dilemmas of sports merchandising and marketing in major and small market franchises, and Burnett, Menon, and Smart (1993) examined various demographics of sports participants and spectators in order to predict their marketability for corporate America. Irwin, Zwick, and Sutton's (1999) research took a slightly different tack by identifying the indicators of a sport franchise's marketing success, and Yiannakis (1991) assumed yet another approach to marketing by presenting a social science perspective on training the sport marketer. Finally, Mullin, Hardy, and Sutton (2000) published a comprehensive review of the various aspects, including communication, of sports marketing.

In addition to the literature on marketing, advertising, and media and public relations efforts of sports organizations, various scholars have examined the economic impact of the marketing and merchandising effects of sports organizations. For example, Crompton (1995), Baade (1996), and Coates and Humphreys (1999) have investigated the economic impact of sport franchises and their marketing efforts. Nunn and Rosentraub (1997) used a case study approach to argue for the need for regional cooperation in regard to many issues (including marketing) to reduce public sector fiscal risks and the subsidies given to teams by sponsoring cities. In addition, scholars have examined the economic discourse surrounding issues involved in building new stadiums and arenas to support local sports organizations. For example, Brown and Paul (2002) conducted a comprehensive review of the public ballot measures for funding new sports facilities, and Anderson (1997) analyzed the negotiations behind the Baltimore Colts relocation to Indianapolis. Finally, Boyd (2000) chronicled the rise in corporate naming of stadiums arguing that sacrificing the commemorative name of a sports venue for a paid corporate name altered the identity statements of memory places and abbreviated the narrative of a city and its team.

The majority of research on external communication from sports organizations considers public relations, marketing campaigns, and aspects of the economics of sports; however, there is occasional work that explores how individual members of the organization speak externally. Take, for example, the work of Staffo (1989), who explored the relationship between sports coaches and the news media. More work of this nature—work that considers when and how individual members (e.g., coaches, players, general managers) of sporting organizations engage external audiences—is needed.

In addition to encouraging more research that focuses on individual organizational stakeholders' attempts to engage external audiences, there should be more research with critical urges in the spirit of Boyd's (2000) work on corporate naming. The community of sport does not exist in a vacuum and, therefore, researchers should read sports organizations' efforts to influence external audiences within the context(s) and texts in which they are created. These contexts include various economic and power relationships such as the ever-expanding association between media organizations and sports organizations. Unfortunately, there currently appears to be research only somewhat tangential to these issues. For example, McChesney (1999) only briefly visited the topic of sport franchises and other sport endeavors when discussing the effects of the new global media conglomerates. McChesney critically argued that highly concentrated media ownership has affected or could affect workers, advertisers, and consumers in a number of negative ways. Likewise, Rowe, Lawrence, Miller, and McKay (1994) assumed a critical cultural approach in their examination of the interrelatedness of politics, economics, and cultural dynamics of sports and how these affect local, regional, national, and international social life. Despite a certain amount of overlap here with regard to (re)producing sport, it is appropriate in a discussion of organizing sport to encourage more communication scholars to examine the external discourses of organizations within the economic structures and hierarchical power relationships in which they exist. The new media conglomerates are a major component of these economic structures (McChesney, 1999).

Organizing Internally—Communication Between and Among Stakeholders Within a Sports Organization

Organizations and their members communicate with a variety of internal audiences and in various ways. Much of the research regarding internal organizational communication involves, just as it does in the nonsports organizational literature, superiors and subordinates (coaches and athletes) and peers (teammates). As such, some of the research terrain covered below overlaps with literature and concepts discussed in the communication and enacting sport section of this chapter.

A majority of the scholarly research concerning communication between and among stakeholders of sports organizations is being accomplished in other disciplines, most notably the area of sport psychology. These scholars have paid particular attention to the topics of group cohesion and leadership or the intersection of the two; some have a strong communication component. For example, Hanrahan and Gallois (1993) examined the relationship between social interactions and group dynamics. Westre and Weiss (1991) found that higher levels of instruction behaviors, positive feedback, and democratic style were associated with higher levels of cohesion in athletic teams. Shields, Gardner, Bredemeier, and Bistro (1997) examined the relationship between leadership behaviors and team cohesion in natural groups (i.e., baseball and softball teams). Other topics related to communication in this area include seeing interpersonal relationships through self-disclosure and the Johari Window (Horine, 1990); the relationship of coach-athlete compatibility to coaching behaviors (Kenow & Williams, 1999); leader-member exchange processes between players and coaches (Case, 1999); mentoring female athletes (Lough, 2001); transformational leadership in coaching (Armstrong, 2001; Charbonneau, Barling, & Kelloway, 2001); and authoritarian and democratic leadership styles (Pratt & Eitzen, 1989). For an extensive review of the sport psychology literature, including leadership behaviors and their affect on group cohesion, see Singer, Hausenblas, and Janelle (2001).

In addition to the sport psychology literature on leadership behaviors and group dynamics, researchers in the areas of small group and sociology of sport also study elements of communication in sports organizations. For example, Turman (2001) examined athletes' preferences and perceptions and coaches' perceptions of leadership styles across time; in another article, Turman found team cohesion levels to be directly influenced by interaction with the head coach (2003b). Sullivan and Feltz (2001) studied the effects of conflict on team cohesion, whereas Zacharatos, Barling, and Kelloway (2000) looked at transformational leadership behaviors in relation to high school athletic teams. Jimerson (2001) analyzed messages and bonding behaviors in locker rooms, and Jacobs and Singell (1993) examined the effects of baseball managers' behaviors on won-loss records. These examples are not intended to be exhaustive, but rather to highlight the instrumental role communication occupies within the community of sport with regard to organizing principles such as group cohesion, leadership, and conflict.

To date, there are a minimal number of manuscripts within the discipline of communication studies that examine sport from an internal organizing perspective. This literature would include any work that studies the communication between and among the stakeholders of a sports organization or articles that unpack the meaning of a sports organization. Examples of the former are Turman's work cited above and Kassing and Infante's (1999) study of aggressive communication in the coach-athlete dyad. Also, one should include in this category Hawkins and Tolzin's (2002) examination of the leadership behaviors of members of a minor league baseball team. These authors concluded that such behaviors represented an analogue for leadership in postmodern organizations. As an example of research that unpacks the meaning of a sports organization, we turn to Rybacki and Rybacki (1995), who examined the sport of vintage car racing by reading it against a backdrop of the Burkean concepts of frame and form.

The remainder of the scholarly work in the field of communication centering on the community of sport belongs primarily to Nick Trujillo. Trujillo (1992) examined the communicative actions and interactions of employees who worked for the Texas Rangers, a major league baseball franchise. He followed that piece of ethnographic research with two related articles. The first focused on baseball parks as organizational sites (Trujillo & Krizek, 1994). The second featured a discussion of an interview Trujillo conducted with George W. Bush (Trujillo, 2000). At the time Bush was the owner of the Texas Rangers and discussed with Trujillo his day-to-day organizational activities and various topics relevant to management and communication. Beyond these articles there is little to identify with regard to communication and the internal organizing of sport.

Criticism and Directions for Future Research

The intersection of communication, organizations, and sport merits three main criticisms. First, a bias exists in the subdiscipline of organizational communication regarding communication emanating from organizations. To understand sports organizations truly from a communicative perspective, one must look at the messages these organizations send to their various publics. This requires looking at and embracing the literature in the areas of advertising, marketing, media, and public relations. Second, scholars in other disciplines such as small group, sport psychology, and the sociology of sport have been studying aspects of communication in sports organizations for quite some time. It is time the communication discipline brings its theoretical sensitivities to these conversations. Third, communication scholars interested in sports and organizational communication have not entered these sports organizations to study their questions. It is time to move beyond the analysis of archival data and begin to study the communicative activities of the members of sports organizations.

Earlier, this section offered two areas needing additional consideration in research on the community of sport. First, there is a need for more work that considers when and how individual members (e.g., coaches, players, general managers) of sporting organizations engage external audiences. Second, more communication scholars should be critically examining the external discourses of organizations in light of the economic structures and hierarchical power relationships in which they exist. In addition, in order to rectify the criticisms discussed in the previous paragraph, scholars must first embrace the work of those examining the messages emanating from sports organizations and work with them to understand all aspects of the intersection of communication and organizing sport. For example, one could explore both the sense-making processes of organizational stakeholders as they create messages for their various publics and the publics' understandings of those messages. One could look at how a marketing campaign for a local professional franchise or collegiate team is created and whether or not that campaign rings true for the intended audiences. That study would reveal much about the process of how communication and sport are organized.

Second, scholars should read the literature about communication phenomena being studied in other disciplines and begin to bring communication theories and approaches to these topics. For example, in the area of goal setting, communication scholars could begin to look more closely at the language of goal setting and how variations in the language of goals might affect an individual's commitment to or identification with that goal. One could bring communication expertise in the area of storytelling and narrative to the discussion of motivation and performance and record how various managers and coaches couch negative and positive feedback. More specifically, scholars should examine whether the delivery of negative feedback in a story has a greater likelihood of being internalized by the recipient than negative feedback delivered nonnarratively. A sports team might offer a perfect setting for such a study because most teams have an oral culture and verbal feedback has a constant presence.

Finally, communication scholars must begin to enter sports organizations and study all of the phenomena examined in other organizations. This, however, might be the biggest challenge. The boundaries of most professional and amateur organizations seem almost impermeable. Management—be they coaches, owners, or administrators—rarely tolerate distractions in regard to their athletes and support personnel. Research needs to crack these boundaries. Perhaps not enough attempts have been made—yet the payoffs could be tremendous. For example, it would seem that managers and coaches of most team sports deal not only with the continual prospect of change, but also with the challenges of a diverse roster as part of their jobs. As a result, a study of successful coaches and managers and sports organizations, in the same vein that Hawkins and Tolzin (2002) studied leadership on a minor-league baseball team, could inform nonsports organizations about how to communicatively handle change and diversity. As with the other areas reviewed in this chapter, there is much work to be done with regard to understanding how the community of sport conducts and is affected by communication and organizing sport.

CONCLUSION

This chapter reviewed selective and illustrative literature that examines the communicative activities of the community of sport. Bringing this literature together in a cohesive statement reveals the significant and intimate connection that exists between communication and sport and highlights the potential for continued scholarship that explores the intersection of the two. Several lines of research were inspected, drawing from disparate sources and across disciplines, to integrate existing knowledge about communication and sport. To make sense of this body of work, four interrelated communicative activities were discussed: enacting, (re)producing, consuming, and organizing sport. These four activities function to signal membership or exclusion from, participation in, exposure to, experience with, and co-construction of the community of sport.

There is much to learn about this community, much that we as communication scholars can observe and discover with regard to the role and function of communication in constituting, shaping, and sustaining what it means to play, watch, discuss, and experience sport. These processes occur within a community that interfaces with sport in multiple and complex ways, across time, and in varied social settings. This is a dynamic, purposeful, and influential community that merits the attention of communication scholars. Research holds the potential for building upon and complementing existing knowledge about sport by recognizing the subtleties and nuances by which message exchange, everyday talk, narrative, rhetorical texts, and the like give meaning to the experience of sport. As a new and expanding domain for communication studies, there is much territory here available for exploration. This territory provides considerable prospects for the application of our constructs and theories as well as meaningful opportunities to address socially significant issues embedded within the community of sport, such as violence and aggression at youth sporting events, the gender and racial stereotypes created and perpetuated in sportscasts and consumed by sports fans, and the influence and impact of sports media conglomerates. This chapter introduces and illuminates these possibilities and invites the discipline to get in the game and play ball.

REFERENCES

Aden, R. C. (1994). Back to the garden: Therapeutic place metaphor in *Field of Dreams*. *Southern Communication Journal, 59,* 307–317.

Aden, R. C. (1995). Nostalgic communication as temporal escape: *When It Was a Game*'s re-construction of a baseball/work community. *Western Journal of Communication, 59,* 20–38.

Anderson, P. M. (1997). Playing the stadium game. *Journal of Sport and Social Issues, 21,* 103–111.

Anderssen, N., & Wold, B. (1992). Parental and peer influences on leisure-time physical activity in young adolescents. *Research Quarterly for Exercise and Sport, 63*(4), 341–349.

Andrews, D. L. (1999). Whiter the NBA, whiter America? *Peace Review, 11,* 505–510.

Arms, R. L., Russell, G. W., & Sandilands, M. L. (1979). Effects on the hostility of spectators of viewing aggressive sports. *Social Psychology Quarterly, 42,* 275–279.

Armstrong, K. L. (2002). Race and sport consumption motivations: A preliminary investigation of a Black consumers' sport motivation scale. *Journal of Sport Behavior, 25,* 309–330.

Armstrong, S. (2001). Are you a "transformational" coach? *Journal of Physical Education, Recreation, & Dance, 72*(3), 44–48.

Baade, R. A. (1996). Professional sports as catalysts for metropolitan economic development. *Journal of Urban Affairs, 18*(1), 1–17.

Bandura, A. (1986). *Social foundations of thought and action: A social cognitive theory.* Englewood Cliffs, NJ: Prentice Hall.

Bandura, A., Underwood, B., & Fromson, M. E. (1975). Disinhibition of aggression through diffusion of responsibility and dehumanization of victims. *Journal of Research in Personality, 9,* 253–269.

Bernhardt, P. C., Dabbs, J. M., Fielden, J. A., & Lutter, C. D. (1998). Testosterone changes during vicarious experiences of winning and losing among fans at sporting events. *Physiology and Behavior, 65,* 59–62.

Billings, A. C., & Eastman, S. T. (2002). Gender, ethnicity, and nationality: Formation of identity in NBC's 2000 Olympic coverage. *International Review for the Sociology of Sport, 37,* 349–368.

Billings, A. C., Eastman, S. T., & Newton, G. D. (1998). Atlanta revisited: Prime-time promotion in the 1996 Olympic games. *Journal of Sports and Social Issues, 22,* 65–78.

Billings, A. C., Halone, K. K., & Denham, B. E. (2002). "Man" that was a "pretty" shot: An analysis of gendered broadcast commentary of the 2000 Men's and Women's NCAA Final Four basketball tournaments. *Mass Communication & Society, 5,* 295–315.

Bineham, J. L. (1991). Some ethical implications of team sports in politics. *Communication Reports, 4,* 35–42.

Birrell, S. (1989). Racial relations theories and sport: Suggestions for a more critical analysis. *Sociology of Sport Journal, 6,* 212–227.

Birrell, S. & Rintala, J. (1984). Fair treatment for the active female: A content analysis of *Young Athlete* magazine. *Sociology of Sport Journal, 1,* 231–250.

Black, S. J., & Weiss, M. R. (1992). The relationship among perceived coaching behaviors, perception of ability, and motivation in competitive age-group swimmers. *Journal of Sport and Exercise Psychology, 14,* 309–325.

Boyd, J. (2000). Selling home: Corporate stadium names and the destruction of commemoration. *Journal of Applied Communication Research, 28,* 330–346.

Bremmer, D. S., & Kesselring, R. G. (1993). The advertising effect of university athletic success: A reappraisal of the evidence. *Quarterly Review of Economic and Finance, 33,* 409–421.

Brown, A. (1998). (Ed.). *Fanatics: Power, identity and fandom in football.* London: Routledge.

Brown, B. R., Baranowski, M. D., Kulig, J. W., Stephenson, J. N., & Perry, B. (1996). Searching for the Magic Johnson effect: AIDS, adolescents, and celebrity disclosure. *Adolescence, 31,* 253–260.

Brown, C., & Paul, D. M. (2002). The political scoreboard of professional sports facility referendums in the United States, 1984–2000. *Journal of Sport and Social Issues, 26,* 248–267.

Bryant, J., & Raney, A. A. (2000). Sports on the screen. In D. Zillmann & P. Vorderer (Eds.), *Media entertainment: The psychology of its appeal* (pp. 153–174). London: Erlbaum.

Burnett, J., Menon, A., & Smart, D. T. (1993). Sports marketing: A new ball game with new rules. *Journal of Advertising Research, 33,* 21–35.

Butterfield, F. (2000, July 11). A fatality, parental violence and youth sports. *New York Times,* p. A14.

Campbell, E., & Jones, G. (2002). Sources of stress experienced by elite male wheelchair basketball players. *Adapted Physical Activity Quarterly, 19,* 82–99.

Case, R. (1999). Leader member exchange theory and sport: Possible applications. *Journal of Sport Behavior, 21,* 387–396.

Caution, G. (1984). The effects of TV advertisements on Black children. *Psychiatric Forum, 12,* 72–81.

Celozzi, M. J., Kazelskis, R., & Gutsch, K. U. (1981). The relationship between viewing televised violence in ice hockey and subsequent levels of personal aggression. *Journal of Sport Behavior, 4,* 157–162.

Charbonneau, D., Barling, J., & Kelloway, E. K. (2001). Transformational leadership and sports performance: The mediating role of intrinsic motivation. *Journal of Applied Social Psychology, 31,* 1521–1535.

Chase, M. A., & Drummer, G. M. (1992). The role of sport as a social status determinant for children. *Research Quarterly for Exercise and Sport, 63,* 418–424.

Christopherson, N., Janning, M., & McConnell, E. D. (2002). Two kicks forward, one kick back: A content analysis of media discourses on the 1999 women's World Cup soccer championship. *Sociology of Sport Journal, 19,* 170–188.

Cialdini, R. B., Borden, R. J., Thorne, A., Walker, M. R., Freeman, S., & Sloan, L. R. (1976). Basking in reflected glory: Three (football) field studies. *Journal of Personality and Social Psychology, 34,* 366–375.

Coates, D., & Humphreys, B. R. (1999). The growth effects of sport franchises, stadia, and arenas. *Journal of Policy Analysis and Management, 18,* 601–624.

Cole, C., & Hribar, A. (1995). Celebrity feminism: Nike style, post-Fordism, transcendence, and consumer power. *Sociology of Sport Journal, 12,* 347–369.

Creedon, P. J. (1998). Women, sport, and media institutions: Issues in sports journalism and marketing. In L. A. Wenner (Ed.), *Mediasport* (pp. 88–99). London: Routledge.

Crompton, J. L. (1995). Economic impact analysis of sports facilities and events: Eleven sources of misapplication. *Journal of Sport Management, 9,* 14–35.

Daddario, G. (1992). Swimming against the tide: *Sports Illustrated*'s imagery of female athletes. *Women's Studies in Communication, 15,* 49–64.

Davis, L. R., & Harris, O. (1998). Race and ethnicity in U.S. sports media. In L.A. Wenner (1st Ed.), *MediaSport* (pp. 154–169). New York: Routledge.

Delgado, F. (1997). Major league soccer: The return of the foreign sport. *Journal of Sport and Social Issues, 21,* 285–297.

Denham, B. E., Billings, A. C., & Halone, K. K., (2002). Differential accounts of race in broadcast commentary of the 2000 NCAA men's and women's Final Four basketball tournaments. *Sociology of Sport Journal, 19,* 315–332.

Dewar, A. (1993). Sexual oppression in sport: Past, present and future alternatives. In A. G. Ingram & J. W. Loy (Eds.), *Sport in social development* (pp. 147–165). Champaign, IL: Human Kinetics Books.

Di Berardinis, J. D., Barwind, J., Flaningam, R. R., & Jenkins, V. (1983). Enhanced interpersonal relation as predictor of athlete performance. *International Journal of Sport Psychology, 14*(4), 243–251.

Dietz-Uhler, B., Harrick, E. A., End, C., & Jacquemotte, L. (2000). Sex differences in sport fan behavior and reasons for being a sport fan. *Journal of Sport Behavior, 23,* 219–231.

Duncan, J. (1997). Focus group interviews with elite young athletes, coaches and parents. In J. Kremer, K. Trew, & S. Ogle (Eds.), *Young people's involvement in sport* (pp. 152–177). London: Routledge.

Duncan, M. C., & Brummett, B. (1989). Types and sources of spectating pleasure in televised sports. *Sociology of Sport Journal, 6,* 195–211.

Duncan, M. C., & Hasbrook, C. A. (1988). Denial of power in televised women's sports. *Sociology of Sport Journal, 5,* 1–21.

Duncan, M. C., & Messner, M. A. (1998). The media image of sport and gender. In L. A. Wenner (Ed.), *Mediasport* (pp. 170–185). London: Routledge.

Dunning, E. (1999). *Sport matters: Sociological studies of sport, violence and civilization.* London: Routledge.

Duquin, M. (1982). The importance of sport in building women's potential. *Journal of Physical Education, Recreation and Dance, 53*(3), 18–20.

Dwyer, J. J., & Fischer, D. G. (1990). Wrestlers' perceptions of coaches' leadership as predictors of satisfaction with leadership. *Perceptual and Motor Skills, 71,* 511–517.

Eastman, S. T., & Billings, A. C. (1999). Gender parity in the Olympics: Hyping women athletes, favoring men athletes. *Journal of Sport and Social Issues, 23,* 140–170.

Eastman, S. T., & Billings, A. C. (2000). Sportscasting and sports reporting: The power of gender bias. *Journal of Sport and Social Issues, 24,* 192–213.

Eastman, S. T., & Billings, A. C. (2001). Biased voices of sports: Racial and gender stereotyping in college basketball announcing. *Howard Journal of Communications, 12*(4), 183–204.

Eastman, S. T., Brown, R. S., & Kovatch, K. L. (1996). The Olympics that got real? Television's story of Sarajevo. *Journal of Sport and Social Issues, 20,* 366–391.

Eastman, S. T., & Otteson, J. L. (1994). Promotion increases ratings, doesn't it? The impact of program promotion in the 1992 Olympics. *Journal of Broadcasting & Electronic Media, 38,* 307–322.

Edwards, H. (1969). *Revolt of the Black athlete.* New York: Free Press.

Engen, D. E. (1995). The making of a people's champion: An analysis of media representations of George Foreman. *Southern Communication Journal, 60,* 141–151.

Entine, J. (2000). *Taboo: Why Black athletes dominate sports and why we're afraid to talk about it.* New York: Public Affairs.

Farrell, T. B. (1989). Media rhetoric as social drama: The Winter Olympics of 1984. *Critical Studies in Mass Communication, 6,* 158–182.

Fiddick, T. (1989). Beyond the domino theory: The Vietnam war and metaphors of sport. *Journal of American Culture, 12,* 79–87.

Fink, J. S., & Kensicki, L. J. (2002). An imperceptible difference: Visual and textual constructions of femininity in *Sports Illustrated* and *Sports Illustrated for Women*. *Mass Communication & Society, 5,* 317–340.

Fishwick, L., & Greendorfer, S. (1987). Socialization revisited: A critique of the sport-related research. *Quest, 39,* 1–8.

Fortunato, J. A. (2000). Public relations strategies for creating mass media content: A case study of the National Basketball Association. *Public Relations Review, 26,* 481–497.

Frank, M. G., & Gilovich, T. (1988). The dark side of self- and social perception: Black uniforms and aggression in professional sports. *Journal of Personality and Social Psychology, 54,* 74–85.

Gantz, W., & Wenner, L. A. (1991). Men, women, and sports: Audience experiences and effects. *Journal of Broadcasting and Electronic Media, 35,* 233–243.

Gantz, W., & Wenner, L. A. (1995). Fanship and the television sports viewing experience. *Sociology of Sport Journal, 12,* 56–74.

Garcia, J. A. (1995). The future of sports merchandising licensing. *Communication/Entertainment: Hastings Communication and Entertainment Law Journal, 18*(1), 219–244.

Gerbner, G., Gross, L., Morgan, M. & Signorielli, N. (1986). Living with television: The dynamics of the cultivation process. In J. Bryant & D. Zillman (Eds.), *Perspectives on media effects* (pp. 17–40). Hillsdale, NJ: Erlbaum.

Gould, D., Hodge, K., Peterson, K., & Giannini, J. (1989). An exploratory examination of strategies used by elite coaches to enhance self-efficacy in athletes. *Journal of Sport and Exercise Psychology, 11,* 128–140.

Gwinner, K. P., & Eaton, J. (1999). Building brand image through event sponsorship: The role of image transfer. *Journal of Advertising, 28*(4), 47–58.

Hallmark, J. R., & Armstrong, R. N. (1999). Gender equity in televised sports: A comparative analysis of men's and women's NCAA Division I basketball broadcasts, 1991–1995. *Journal of Broadcasting & Electronic Media, 43,* 222–235.

Halone, K. K. (2003, April). *The structuration of sports broadcast commentary: Implicating the system and structure of mediated athletic performance.* Paper presented at the annual conference of the Southern States Communication Association, Birmingham, AL.

Hanrahan, S., & Gallois, C. (1993). Social interactions. In R. N. Singer, M. Murphey, & L. K. Tennant (Eds.), *Handbook of research on sport psychology* (pp. 623–646). New York: Maxwell Macmillan International.

Hansen, A. D. (1999). Narrating the game: Achieving and coordinating partisanship in real time. *Research on Language and Social Interaction, 32,* 269–302.

Harris, O. (1993). African-American predominance in collegiate sport. In D. D. Brooks & R. C. Althouse (Eds.), *Racism in college athletics: The African American athlete's experience* (pp. 51–74). Morgantown, WV: Fitness Information Technology.

Harrison, K., & Fredrickson, B. L. (2003). Women's sports media, self objectification, and mental health in Black and White adolescent females. *Journal of Communication, 53,* 216–232.

Hawkins, K., & Tolzin, A. (2002). Examining the team/leader interface: Baseball teams as exemplars of postmodern organizations. *Group and Organization Management, 27,* 97–112.

Heath, S. B. (1991). "It's about winning!": The language of knowledge in baseball. In L. B. Resnick, & J. M. Levine (Eds.) *Perspectives on socially shared cognition* (pp. 101–124). Washington, DC: American Psychological Association.

Heath, S. B., & McLaughlin, M. W. (1994). The best of both worlds: Connecting schools and community youth organizations for all-day, all-year learning. *Educational Administration Quarterly, 30,* 278–300.

Higgs, D. T., & Weiler, K. H. (1994). Gender bias and the 1992 Summer Olympic Games: An analysis of television coverage. *Journal of Sport and Social Issues, 18,* 234–246.

Hightower, R., Brady, M. K., & Baker, T. L. (2002). Investigating the role of the physical environment in hedonic service consumption: An exploratory study of sporting events. *Journal of Business Research, 55,* 697–707.

Hirt, E. R., Zillmann, D., Erickson, G. A., & Kennedy, C. (1992). Costs and benefits of allegiance: Changes in fans' self-ascribed competencies after team victory versus defeat. *Journal of Personality and Social Psychology, 63,* 724–738.

Hopkins, N., Reicher, S., & Levine, M. (1997). On the parallels between social cognition and the "new racism." *British Journal of Social Psychology, 36,* 305–329.

Horine, L. (1990). The Johari-Window—Solving sport management communication problems. *Journal of Physical Education, Recreation, and Dance, 61,* 49–51.

Horne, J., Tomlinson, A., & Whannel, G. (1999). *Understanding sport: An introduction to the sociological and cultural analysis of sport.* New York: Routledge.

Irwin, R. L., Zwick, D., & Sutton, W. A. (1999). Assessing organizational attributes contributing to marketing excellence in American professional sport franchises. *Journal of Consumer Marketing, 6,* 603–615.

Jacobs, D., & Singell, L. (1993). Leadership and organizational performance: Isolating links between managers and collective success. *Social Science Research, 22,* 165–189.

Jansen, S. C., & Sabo, D. (1994). The sport/war metaphor: Hegemonic masculinity, the Persian Gulf War, and the new world order. *Sociology of Sport Journal, 11,* 1–17.

Jimerson, J. B. (2001). A conversation (re)analysis of fraternal bonding in the locker room. *Sociology of Sport Journal, 18,* 317–339.

Kane, M. J. (1995). Resistance/transformation of the oppositional binary. *Journal of Sport and Social Issues, 19,* 191–218.

Kassing, J. W., & Barber, A. M. (2000, February). *"It's not whether you win or lose": An initial investigation of sportsmanship messages provided to youth athletes.* Paper presented at the annual conference of the Western States Communication Association, Sacramento, CA.

Kassing, J. W. & Infante, D. A. (1999). Aggressive communication in coach-athlete dyads. *Communication Research Reports, 16,* 110–120.

Kassing, J. W., & Meân, L. J. (2001, November). *Charting the communication geography of youth sporting events: A message analysis.* Paper presented at the annual conference of the National Communication Association, Atlanta, GA.

Katz, E., & Lazarsfeld, P. F. (1955). *Personal influence: The part played by people in the flow of mass communication.* New York: Free Press.

Kenow, L., & Williams, J. M. (1999). Coach-athlete compatibility and athlete's perception of coaching behaviors. *Journal of Sport Behavior, 22,* 251–260.

Kinkema, K. M. & Harris, J. C. (1998). Mediasport studies: Key research and emerging issues. In L. A. Wenner (Ed.), *Mediasport* (pp. 27–54). London: Routledge.

Knoppers, A. (1989). Coaching: An equal opportunity occupation? *Journal of Physical Education, Recreation and Dance, 60,* 38–43.

Knoppers, A. (1992) Explaining male dominance and sex segregation in coaching: Three approaches. *Quest, 44,* 210–227.

Knoppers, A., & Anthonissen, A. (2001). Meanings given to performance in Dutch sport organizations: Gender and racial/ethnic subtexts. *Sociology of Sport Journal, 18,* 302–316.

Koivula, N. (1999). Gender stereotyping in televised media sport coverage. *Sex Roles, 40,* 589.

Lakoff, G. (1987). *Women, fire and dangerous things: What categories reveal about the mind.* Chicago: University of Chicago Press.

Larson, J. F., & Rivenburgh, N. K. (1991). A comparative analysis of Australian, U.S., and British telecasts of the Seoul Olympic ceremony. *Journal of Broadcasting and Electronic Media, 35,* 75–94.

Lefebvre, L. M., & Cunningham, J. D. (1977). The successful football team: Effects of coaching and team cohesiveness. *International Journal of Sport Psychology, 8,* 29–41.

Lenskyj, H. (1986) *Out of bounds: Women, sport and sexuality.* Toronto, Canada: Women's Press.

Liukkonen, J., Laakso, L., & Telama, R. (1996). Educational perspectives of youth sport coaches: Analysis of observed coaching behaviors. *International Journal of Sport Psychology, 27,* 439–453.

Lord, M. (2000, May 15).When cheers turn into jeers. *U.S. News & World Report,128,* 52.

Lorenz, K. (1963). *The so-called evil: On the natural history of aggression.* Vienna: Borotha-Schoeler.

Lough, N. L. (2001). Mentoring connections between coaches and females athletes. *Journal of Physical Education, Recreation, & Dance, 72*(4), 30–34.

Maingueneau, D. (1999). Analysing self-constituting discourses. *Discourse Studies, 1,*175–199.

Maltz, D. N., & Borker, R. (1982). A cultural approach to male-female miscommunication. In J. J. Gumpertz (Ed.), *Language and social identity* (pp. 196–216). Cambridge, UK: Cambridge University Press.

McCarthy, D., & Jones, R. L. (1997). Speed, aggression, strength, and tactical naiveté. *Journal of Sport and Social Issues, 21,* 348–362.

McChesney, R. W. (1999). *Rich media, poor democracy: Communication politics in dubious times.* Urbana: University of Illinois Press.

McDaniel, S. R. (1999). An investigation of match-up effects in sport sponsorship advertising: The implications of consumer advertising schemas. *Psychology & Marketing, 16,* 163–184.

McDermott, S. T., Hocking, J. E., Johnson, L., & Atkin, C. K. (1989). Adolescents' responses to sports figure product endorsement. *Southern Communication Journal, 54,* 350–363.

McGinley, M., Kremer, J., Trew, K., & Ogle, S. (1998). Socio-cultural identity and attitudes to sport in Northern Ireland. *Irish Journal of Psychology, 19,* 464–471.

McGuire, R. T., & Cook, D. L.(1985). The influence of others and the decision to participate in youth sports. *Journal of Sport Behavior, 6,* 9–16.

Meân, L. (2001). Identity and discursive practice: Doing gender on the football pitch. *Discourse and Society, 12,* 789–815.

Meân, L. J., Kassing, J. W., Gebhard, K. L, & Burkhart, K. A. (2002, November). *Making mamma and daddy proud: Youth athletes' constructions of parent and fan behavior.* Paper presented at the annual conference of the National Communication Association, New Orleans, LA.

Meân Patterson, L. J. (2003). Everyday discursive practices and the construction of gender: A study at the "grass roots." In A. Schoor, W. Campbell, & M. Schenk (Eds.), *Communication research and media science in Europe* (pp. 497–515). Berlin, Germany: Mouton De Gruyter.

Meehan, E. R. (1993). Heads of household and ladies of the house: Gender, genre, and broadcast ratings, 1929–1990. In W. S. Solomon & R. W. McChesney (Eds.), *Ruthless criticism: New perspectives in U.S. communication history* (pp. 204–221). Minneapolis: University of Minnesota Press.

Messner, M. A. (1988). Sports and male domination: The female athlete as contested ideological terrain. *Sociology of Sport Journal, 5,* 197–211.

Messner, M. A., Duncan, M. C., & Jensen, K. (1993). Separating the men from the girls: The gendered language of televised sports. In D. S. Eitzen(Ed.), *Sport in Contemporary Society* (219–233). New York: St. Martin's Press.

Messner, M. A., Duncan, M. C., & Wachs, F. L. (1996). The gender of audience building: Televised coverage of women's and men's NCAA basketball. *Sociological Inquiry, 66,* 422–440.

Midrigal, R. (2001). Social identity effects in a belief-attitude-intentions hierarchy: Implications for corporate sponsorship. *Psychology & Marketing, 18*(2), 145–161.

Miles, J. A., & Greenberg, J. (1993). Using punishment threats to attenuate social loafing effects among swimmers. *Organizational Behavior and Human Decision Processes, 56,* 246–265.

Mullin, B. J., Hardy, S., & Sutton, W. A. (2000). *Sport marketing* (2nd ed.). Champaign, IL: Human Kinetics.

Nelson, J. (1984). The defense of Billie Jean King. *Western Journal of Speech Communication, 48,* 92–102.

Nelson, T. F., & Wechsler, H. (2003). School spirits: Alcohol and collegiate sports fans. *Addictive Behaviors, 28,* 1–11.

Nielsen Media Research. (1998). *1998 report on television.* New York: Author.

Nunn, S., & Rosentraub, M. S. (1997). Sports wars: Suburbs and center cities in a zero-sum game. *Journal of Sport and Social Issues, 21,* 65–82.

O'Donnell, H. (1994). Mapping the mythical: A geopolitics of national sporting stereotypes. *Discourse and Society, 5,* 345–380.

Orlick, T., & Botterill, C. (1975). *Every kid can win.* Chicago: Nelson-Hall.

Parrott, R., & Duggan, A. (1999). Using coaches as role models of sun protection for youth: Georgia's "Got Youth Covered" project. *Journal of Applied Communication Research, 27,* 107–119.

Perse, E. M. (1992). Predicting attention to local television news: Need for cognition and motives for viewing. *Communication Reports, 5,* 40–49.

Pratt, S. R., & Eitzen, D. S. (1989). Contrasting leadership styles and organizational effectiveness: The case of athletic teams. *Social Science Quarterly, 70,* 311–320.

Prisuta, R. H. (1979). Televised sports and political values. *Journal of Communication, 29*(1), 94–102.

Rada, J. (1996). Color blind-sided: Racial bias in network television's coverage of professional football games. *Howard Journal of Communications, 7,* 231–240.

Real, M. R. (1975). Super Bowl: Mythic spectacle. *Journal of Communication, 75*(1), 31–43.

Real, M. R., & Mechikoff, R. A. (1992). Deep fan: Mythic identification, technology, and advertising in spectator sports. *Sociology of Sport, 9,* 323–339.

Riggs, K. E., Eastman, S. T., & Golobic, T. S. (1993). Manufactured conflict in the 1992 Olympics. *Critical Studies in Mass Communication, 10,* 253–272.

Roberts, G. C., Treasure, D. C., & Hall, H. K. (1994). Parental goal orientation and beliefs about the competitive-sport experience of their child. *Journal of Applied Social Psychology, 24,* 631–646.

Rothenbuhler, E. W. (1988). The living room celebration of the Olympic Games. *Journal of Communication, 38*(1), 61–81.

Rothenbuhler, E. W. (1989). Values and symbols in orientations to the Olympics. *Critical Studies in Mass Communication, 6,* 138–157.

Rowe, D., Lawrence, G., Miller, T., & McKay, J. (1994). Global sport? Core concern and peripheral vision. *Media, Culture, and Society, 16,* 662–667.

Rybacki, K. C., & Rybacki, D. J. (1995). Competition in the comic frame: A Burkean analysis of vintage sports car racing. *Southern Communication Journal, 61,* 76–90.

Sabo, D., Jansen, S. C., Tate, D., Duncan, M. C., & Leggett, S. (1996). Televising international sport: Race, ethnicity, and nationalistic bias. *Journal of Sport and Social Issues, 20,* 7–21.

Sargent, S. L., Zillmann, D., & Weaver, J. B. (1998). The gender gap in the enjoyment of televised sports. *Journal of Sport and Social Issues, 22,* 46–64.

Scodari, C. (1993). Operation desert storm as "wargames": Sport, war, and media intertextuality. *Journal of American Culture, 16,* 1–4.

Seefeldt, V. D. (1999, April). *Challenges for the educators of athletic coaches in the 21st century.* Paper presented at the annual conference of the Association of American Health and Physical Educators, Boston, MA.

Seefeldt, V. D., & Ewing, M. E. (2000). Youth sports in America: An overview. *President's Council on Physical and Sports Research Digest, 2*(11), 1–10.

Shapiro, M. J. (1989). Representing world politics: The sport/war intertext. In J. Derian & M. J. Shapiro (Eds.), *International/intertextual relations* (pp. 69–96). Lexington, MA: Lexington Books.

Shields, D. L. L., Gardner, D. E., Bredemeier, B. J. L., & Bistro, A. (1997). The relationship between leadership behaviors and group cohesion in team sports. *Journal of Psychology, 131,* 196–210.

Shugart, H. A. (2003). She shoots, she scores: Mediated constructions of contemporary female athletes in coverage of the 1999 U.S. women's soccer team. *Western Journal of Communication, 67,* 1–31.

Sinclair, D. A., & Vealey, R. S. (1989). Effects of coaches' expectations and feedback on the self-perceptions of athletes. *Journal of Sport Behavior, 12,* 77–91.

Singer, R. N., Hausenblas, H. A., & Janelle, C. M. (Eds.). (2001). *Handbook of sport psychology* (2nd ed.). New York: Wiley.

Sklair, L. (1991). *Sociology of the global system.* London: Harvester Wheatsheaf.

Smith, R. E., & Smoll, F. L. (1990). Self-esteem and children's reactions to youth sport coaching behaviors: A field study of self-enhancement processes. *Developmental Psychology, 26,* 987–993.

Smith, R. E., Smoll, F. L., & Barnett, N. P. (1995). Reduction of children's sport performance anxiety through social support and stress-reduction training for coaches. *Journal of Applied Developmental Psychology, 16*, 125–142.

Snyder, E. E., & Spreitzer, E. (1989). *Social aspects of sport.* Englewood Cliffs, NJ: Prentice Hall.

Stabile, C. A. (2000). Nike, social responsibility, and the hidden abode of production. *Critical Studies in Media Communication, 17*, 186–204.

Staffo, D. F. (1989). Enhancing coach-media relations. *Journal of Physical Education, Recreation, and Dance, 60*(7), 25–28.

Staples, R., & Jones, T. (1985). Culture, ideology and Black television images. *Black Scholar, 16*(3), 10–20.

Stephenson, D. (2002). Women, sport, and globalization. *Journal of Sport and Social Issues, 26*, 209–225.

Sugden, J., & Tomlinson, A. (1994). Soccer culture, national identity and the World Cup. In J. Sugden & A. Tomlinson (Eds.), *Hosts and champions: Soccer cultures, national identities and the USA World Cup.* Aldershot, UK: Arena.

Sullivan, P. J., & Feltz, D. L. (2001). The relationship between intrateam conflict and cohesion within hockey teams. *Small Group Research, 32*, 342–355.

Sutton, W. A. (1987). Developing an initial marketing plan for intercollegiate athletic programs. *Journal of Sport Management 1*, 146–158.

Sutton, W. A., Irwin, R. L., & Gladden, J. M. (1998). Tools of the trade: Practical research methods for events, teams and venues. *Sport Marketing Quarterly 7*(2), 45–49.

Tankard, J. W. (2001). The empirical approach to the study of media framing. In S. D. Reese, O. H. Gandy, & A. E. Grant (Eds.), *Framing public life* (pp. 95–106). Mahwah, NJ: Erlbaum.

Theberge, N. (2000). Gender and sport. In J. Coakley & E. Dunning (Eds.), *Handbook of sports studies* (pp. 322–322). Thousand Oaks, CA: Sage.

Thorngren, C. M. (1990). A time to reach out: Keeping the female coach in coaching. *Journal of Physical Education, Recreation and Dance, 61*, 57–60.

Thornton, J. S. (1991). Springing youth athletes from the parental pressure cooker. *Physician and Sportsmedicine, 19*, 92–95.

Trujillo, N. (1991). Hegemonic masculinity on the mound: Media representations of Nolan Ryan and American sports culture. *Critical Studies in Mass Communication, 8*, 290–308.

Trujillo, N. (1992). Interpreting (the work and talk of) baseball: Perspectives on ballpark culture. *Western Journal of Communication, 56*, 350–371.

Trujillo, N. (2000). Baseball, business, politics, and privilege: An interview with George W. Bush. *Management Communication Quarterly, 14*, 307–316.

Trujillo, N., & Krizek, B. (1994). Emotionality in the stands and in the field: Expressing self through baseball. *Journal of Sport and Social Issues, 18*, 303–325.

Tuggle, C. A., & Owen, A. (1999). A descriptive analysis of NBC's coverage of the centennial Olympics. *Journal of Sport and Social Issues, 23*, 171–182.

Turman, P. D. (2001). Situational coaching styles: The impact of success and athlete maturity level on coaches' leadership styles over time. *Small Group Research, 32*, 576–594.

Turman, P. (2003a). Athletic coaching from an instructional communication perspective: The influence of coach experience on high school wrestlers' preferences and perceptions of coaching behaviors across a season. *Communication Education, 23*, 73–86.

Turman, P. (2003b). Coaches and cohesion: The impact of coaching techniques on team cohesion in the small group sport setting. *Journal of Sport Behavior, 26*, 86–104.

Van Dijk, T. A. (1993). Principles of critical discourse analysis. *Discourse and Society, 4*, 249–283.

Wann, D. L., Lane, T. M., Duncan, L. E., & Goodson, S. L. (1998). Family status, preference for sport aggressiveness, and sport fan motivation. *Perceptual and Motor Skills, 86*, 1419–1422.

Wann, D. L., Shelton, S., Smith, T., & Walker, R. (2002). Relationship between team identification and trait aggression: A replication. *Perceptual and Motor Skills, 94*, 595–598.

Wanta, W., & Elliott, W. R. (1995). Did the "Magic" work? Knowledge of HIV/AIDS and the knowledge gap hypothesis. *Journalism & Mass Communication Quarterly, 72,* 312–312.

Way, N., & Gillman, D. A. (2000). Early adolescent girls' perceptions of their relationships with their fathers: A qualitative investigation. *Journal of Early Adolescence, 20,* 309–331.

Weiss, M. R., & Friedrichs, W. D. (1986). The influence of leader behaviors, coach attributes, and institutional variables on performance and satisfaction of collegiate basketball teams. *Journal of Sport Psychology, 8,* 332–346.

Westre, K., & Weiss, M. (1991). The relationship between perceived coaching behaviors and group cohesion in high school football teams. *Sport Psychologist, 5,* 41–54.

Whannel, G. (1992). *Fields in vision: Television sport and cultural transformation.* London: Routledge.

Whitson, D. (1984). Sport and hegemony: On the construction of the dominant culture. *Sociology of Sport Journal, 1,* 64–78.

Wong, E. (2001, May 6). New rules for soccer parents. *New York Times,* pp. 1, 42.

Wonsek, P. L. (1992). College basketball on television: A study of racism in the media. *Media, Culture, and Society, 14,* 449–461.

Wood, J. T. (1996). She says/he says: Communication, caring, and conflict in heterosexual relationships. In J. T. Wood (Ed.), *Gendered relationships* (pp. 149–162). Mountain View, CA: Mayfield.

Woodard, W. M. (1990, November 17). It's more than just the shoes. *Black Enterprise.*

Woolger, C., & Power, T. G. (1993). Parent and sport socialization: Views from the achievement literature. *Journal of Sport Behavior, 16,* 171–190.

Yiannakis, A. (1991). Training the sport marketer: A social science perspective. *Journal of Sport Behavior, 14,* 61–69.

Zacharatos, A., Barling, J., & Kelloway, E. K. (2000). Development and effects of transformational leadership in adolescents. *Leadership Quarterly, 11,* 211–226.

Zillmann, D., & Bryant, J. (1994). Entertainment as media effect. In D. Zillmann & J. Bryant (Eds.), *Media effects: Advances in theory and research* (pp. 437–461). Hillsdale, NJ: Erlbaum.

Zillmann, D., Bryant, J., & Sapolsky, B. S. (1989). Enjoyment from sports spectatorship. In J. H. Goldstein (Ed.), *Sports, games, and play: Social and psychological viewpoints* (2nd ed., pp. 241–278). Hillsdale, NJ: Erlbaum.

Zillmann, D., Johnson, R. C., & Day, K. D. (2000). Attribution of apparent arousal and proficiency of recovery from sympathetic activation affecting excitation transfer to aggressive behavior. In E. T. Higgins & A. W. Kruglanski (Eds.), *Motivational science: Social and personality perspectives* (pp. 416–424). Philadelphia: Psychology Press.

CHAPTER CONTENTS

11 Speech Community: Reflections Upon Communication

TRUDY MILBURN

Baruch College/The City University of New York

From Hymes (1962) onward, communication scholars, anthropologists, linguists, sociolinguists, and scholars in ethnic studies have not only used the term *speech communities*, but have extended its significance. The purpose of this review is to examine the ways various authors have defined and used the term, in order to understand its evolution. Speech community boundaries have been defined by demographic features, such as place or space, shared language use, and shared meanings. Each condition is explored and analyzed in turn. The review raises four issues: Labels used to describe speech community refer usually to specific demographic features of the community itself, rather than features of communication; the composition of a speech community is usually defined a priori; the idea of a speech community as a homogeneous entity does not exist; and researchers often focus on member codes as the key component of a speech community. Given these issues, consideration should be given to refining speech community as a unit of analysis so that it remains a meaningful construct to study.

No one would claim that there is a one-to-one relationship between languages and social systems, yet we continue to think of speech communities as discrete, culturally homogeneous groups whose members speak closely related varieties of a single language (Gumperz, 1969/1971, p. 230).

Communication scholars examine what people say to one another and the consequences. When they seek to examine the patterned ways people communicate, then they focus either on universal communication use or on particular ways that specific groups of people use communication. The latter focus is often referred to as cultural, intercultural, or cross-cultural communication. The ways specific groups communicate is also the specific purview of researchers in the ethnography of communication tradition. Those who conduct research in this

Correspondence: Trudy Milburn, Department of Communication Studies, Baruch College/The City University of New York, One Bernard Baruch Way, Box B8-240, New York, NY 10010; email: Trudy_Milburn@baruch.cuny.edu tradition vary in how much they emphasize the group composition itself over the practices examined. Even though many make the claim that how people communicate indicates who they are (e.g., group identities), there are variations among ethnography of communication (ethnocomm) reports regarding how the identity of the group under investigation is defined. That is, how one delineates who is being studied is still a pressing research question.

Fitch (1994) has argued persuasively to consider ethnography of communication as a productive way to examine traditional areas within the discipline, such as interpersonal communication. In the past 10 years, several researchers have examined interpersonal communication through an ethnography of communication perspective. The boundaries implied by the term *speech community*, often considered to be the basic unit of analysis, have surprisingly not been used in many studies. To take Fitch's (1994) call to include an ethnocomm perspective seriously, and even extend it to other traditional areas within the discipline (e.g., organizational communication, rhetoric and public debate, the area formerly known as mass media, or other mediated forms of communication) is to pause to consider the starting place of this research.

This review comes in the midst of several ongoing debates and tensions: between scholars regarding the questions of who counts as a member of a community and who remains outside of those boundaries, and between those who argue for the cohesiveness of any particular community and those who argue for recognizing the multiplicity of memberships that any particular member of a community can claim. Within these two camps, scholars also find different ways of conceptualizing communication. In the first, they examine communication rules and norms and foreground the codes through which participants come to make sense of their habitual actions. In the second camp, multiple identities constructed by multiple labels for who one is and what one does are foregrounded. Here communication itself is often understood to be a vehicle for expressing these differences.

Given these tensions, it behooves scholars to examine a unit of analysis that is often associated with the stable sense of a group. This unit of analysis is speech community and has a history of use by communication and other language scholars. By examining the ways that researchers have employed the term, one begins to explore the very tension between commonality and differences that is a central concern within the communication discipline. Delineating a particular moment in time about which to make a meaningful claim about a group of people is challenging because communication itself is understood as a living process that never quite seems to sit still.

Needless to say, the literature about speech communities has broad-reaching implications for the field of communication. From Hymes (1962) onward, many of the journals in the field have not only used the term, but extended its significance. The idea of speech communities has been shaped further by writings in other fields, particularly linguistics, sociolinguistics (Bowie, 2001; Lo, 1999; Milroy, 2002), anthropology (Hill, 1992; Kroskrity, 1993), and ethnic studies (Chaston, 1996; Dyers, 1999; Saohatse, 1998; Smitherman, 1997), to name a few.

This review examines the ways communication scholars have defined the speech community under investigation. This examination will yield two outcomes: a compilation of studies that demonstrate the attention given to community boundaries, as well as a refinement of the term itself as it has been used by a community of scholars.

The utility of speech community as a unit of analysis is indicated by the way researchers presently report about its function in their analyses. Some of the questions that will be addressed have both theoretical and methodological implications for examining communication practices within communities: (a) Are researchers employing the term speech community as solely a data collection technique? (b) Are researchers using the term theoretically and not methodologically? and (c) Are researchers using the notion of speech community as a predefined research tool primarily rather than discovering how members of communities label and enact community?

This review will not catalog all studies that claim to be ethnographies or ethnographies of communication in order to try to determine who is being studied. Only authors who claim to be speaking about a speech community explicitly in their title or article's key words have been chosen. Some studies that do not fit these search criteria have been included because they are programmatic pieces, or the topic under investigation is primarily a speech community.

It is important to characterize the way the term community is employed by communication researchers in general; therefore, a brief review of additional articles from communication journals that refer to community in their title or key words will be included. Within this group of articles, the current study inquires about the particular features that make this group a community. For example, when an author refers to the *Chicano community* or the *homosexual community,* what communication patterns are present that help the author make the claim that these groups of people are in fact communities? Further, what unifies or binds a group to suggest a sense of community? Finally, whereas an author may make research claims about a group that suggests that it constitutes a community, is it also the case that members of such groups self-identify as a particular type of community?

The search criteria described above yielded approximately 70 studies that have used the term speech community. In order for an item to be included, it met the following criteria: (a) The author characterized the group or target of study as a speech community; and (b) the author focused on one or more aspects of the language use of the speech community. Before undertaking a review of current literature, a chronological history of the term from some programmatic statements will be explicated.

CHRONOLOGICAL HISTORY OF SPEECH COMMUNITY

Hymes (1962, 1964a, 1964b, 1972, 1974) is often cited as the founder of the project initially called ethnography of speaking and subsequently refined to ethnography of communication. The cornerstone of ethnographic studies was, and remains, the group of speakers described as a speech community. Hymes (1964a) gave credit to Bloomfield for his comparative method and early descriptions of the term speech community. Bloomfield (1933) defined a speech community broadly as "a group of people who interact by means of speech" (as cited in Murray, pp. 123–142). Murray (1998) described Bloomfield's definition as including all members who speak a language, such as Russian, while noting the difficulty that bilingualism brings to the boundaries of any such speech community.

The group of speakers itself primarily composed the speech community. While drawing on the way that the notion of speech community, and similar terms, were then employed, Hymes (1964a, 1964b) sought to create a more specific definition for the purposes of a "new project" that combined linguistics with anthropology. The idea that ethnography of communication should take the community as its starting point, rather than "linguistic form, a given code, or speech itself" (p. 3), was an argument that Hymes (1964b) needed to make in order to draw attention away from research in linguistics primarily that makes language as central and focuses instead on the anthropological notions of a group of people that *situates* and makes *meaningful* any language practice. It was in this way that Hymes (1964b) argued that communication, rather than simply language, was the most important focus.

Hymes (1964a) cited Gumperz (1962) as being among users of the familiar term linguistic community. Gumperz (1962/1971) defined a linguistic community as

> a social group which may be either monolingual or multilingual, held together by frequency of social interaction patterns and set off from surrounding areas by weaknesses in the lines of communication. Linguistic communities may consist of small groups bound together by face-to-face contact or may cover large regions, depending on the level of abstraction we wish to achieve. (p. 101)

Gumperz (1962/1971) is recognized as having employed a specific definition of linguistic community; however, in his own article, Gumperz (1964/1971) frequently used the two terms speech community and linguistic community interchangeably.

Hymes (and Gumperz) wanted to draw attention to the way that sociality and language were related. This refocusing became not so much about making universal claims about a language's speakers but rather became a way for investigators to examine how different groups who use a similar language are able to use language distinctly. These distinctions were both a way to mark the group itself (e.g., who counts as a member is someone who can use language in such a way) as well as to mark the particular ways of language in use. A speech community, according to Gumperz (1968/1971), is comprised of human aggregates who regularly and frequently use shared signs and are set apart from other human aggregates by their particular use of language. Previously Gumperz (1964/1971) had included "over a significant span of time" (p. 151) in this basic definition. The focus is on language use, rather than language rules per se. Hymes (1972) described the speech community as comprised of people who share "rules for the conduct and interpretation of speech, and rules for the interpretation of at least one linguistic variety" (p. 54).

Another significant component of the definition pertained to the group of speakers themselves. Hymes (1964b) noted that speech communities are "dynamic" and "complex" rather than "monolithically uniform" (p. 5). Hymes (1964b) stated: "[W]hat seems like variation and deviation from the standpoint of a single linguistic code, emerge as structure and pattern from the standpoint of the communicative economy of the group in whose habits the code exists" (p. 3).

Following Hymes' (1962) programmatic essay, speech community has continued to retain its central position of the ethnography of communication. Hymes (1964b) argued for a change of emphasis from what had been traditionally examined within linguistics and anthropology to a recognition that "the place, boundaries, and organization, of language, and other communicative means in a community . . . be taken as problematic" (p. 11). Further, Hymes (1964b) wanted his new research program to focus on the "cultural consequences of a community" (p. 12). He stated that

the starting point is the ethnographic analysis of the communicative habits of a community in their totality, determining what counts as communicative events, and as their components, and conceiving no communicative behavior as independent of the set framed by some setting or implicit question. (p. 13)

This "totality of communicative behavior" was echoed in Gumperz (1964/1971) to distinguish his approach from homogeneous language research. To highlight the variety of speech within a given system, Gumperz (1966/1971) defined a "linguistic or verbal repertoire" as "the totality of linguistic forms regularly employed within the community in the course of socially significant interaction. Repertoires in turn can be regarded as consisting of speech varieties, each associated with particular kinds of social relationships" (p. 182).

In seeking out patterned ways of speaking, Hymes (1974) sought to create a systematic methodology for comparing different speech communities. He believed that unless researchers made note of similar characteristics across groups by using comparable means to study them, it would be difficult if not impossible to make comparisons between these groups and specific cultures.

The framework Hymes (1972, 1974) developed was based upon the theoretical premise that, to understand general features of language, researchers should systematically compare how its different components are used in specific contexts. The examination of situated language use allowed for the unearthing of patterns that otherwise would not be readily identified within some of the more traditional frameworks. Within his framework, Hymes (1974) stated that "the starting point is the ethnographic analysis of the communication conduct of a community" (p. 9). He proposed basic units that can be applied to the communication styles of a variety of different cultures (Hymes, 1974). The framework included several social units (e.g., speech community, speech situation, speech event, communicative act, communicative style, and ways of speaking); however, speech community was the first and primary unit of analysis.

Arguing for a more robust use of the term speech community, Hymes (1964a) maintained that often a speech community is assumed by the researcher. Further, he stated that when the features of a particular community's composition appear very obvious, or homogenous, perhaps that community may not seem to warrant the rigor of defining its community boundaries because they are taken for granted. The problem with these unlabeled, assumed groups may occur later, as people question the distinctions within the group, or the political reasons for making such an assumed grouping (e.g., such arguments have been waged against using the term *Americans* as a label for everyone living in the United States because of the diversity of groups within this population). These arguments led Labov, Cohen, Robins, and Lewis (1968) to undertake research that explicitly examined different forms of spoken English in the largest, most diverse city in the United States, New York. By labeling some of the speech they encountered nonstandard English (NSE), Labov et al. demonstrated that language use, even when considering the same language, is not as homogeneous or standard as was often assumed.

Within this early research program, the definition of speech community included a group of speakers—who shared situated communication practices that are made meaningful by examining language in use and its socializing function—and, although variation may exist within any given speech community, the language practices themselves, which have cultural consequences that can only be compared by using an analytically rigorous framework.

Thereafter, three distinct strands of research emerged from these early theorists. Roughly speaking, Hymes's work led to ethnocomm (and education research not covered here), Gumperz led to sociolinguistic research, and Labov (1964) led to more linguistic research. After Hymes (1962) began the program of ethnography of speaking, with the primary unit of analysis as speech community, there emerged a number of researchers who heeded his call and developed research studies that focused on this unit.

Speech Community in Communication Studies

Within the field of communication, Philipsen's (1975) landmark essay about Teamsterville in the *Quarterly Journal of Speech* ushered in the speech community unit of analysis and the program of ethnography of communication. In this essay, Philipsen (1975) described a speech community in "Hymesian terms" as those who are "privy to understandings shared by members" and who "have access to the culture" (p. 14). This description focused on the way members of a community share common resources. By beginning the report with a description of the speech community, Philipsen (1975) echoed Hymes's and Gumperz's call to focus on communication practices within a situated community. By drawing together particular ways of speaking within this "Teamsterville" speech community, Philipsen (1975) explicitly related communication to community.

The most prominent features of the speech community as described by Philipsen (1975) included gendered ways of speaking (e.g., speaking like a man) and the location or places where such speech was more likely to occur versus the places where it was deemed socially inappropriate for men's speech. Philipsen (1992) has since described the way by which he came to understand a speech community as not only a place, but a place alive with significance and meaning for its participants.

> When I first entered Teamsterville, the community appeared to me as merely a series of *uncon-nected streets, buildings, people and activities*. By the time I left it over three years later, it was, for me, not just a setting, but a scene, a place suffused with activity, with meaning, with signifi-cance, not only for me, but more importantly for those who had grown up there and those who lived there permanently. As a student of community, what eventually struck me most about Teamsterville and my experiences in it was that one way to think about this community was as a *speech community, a universe of discourse with a finely organized, distinctive pattern of meaning and action*" (p. 4). [italics added]

Philipsen's (1992) research emphasized how a speech community is a unit of analysis that is important both to the researcher and to its members or participants as a keenly felt and lived-in place. What began for the researcher as a geographic location, or a site of investigation, became meaningful through people's descrip-tions of it, their manifest relation with it. Group identity was based upon the places members frequented—their homes, their streets—and it was these different as-pects of location that were embodied in everyday conversations. The meaningful-ness of the term speech community relates to both the way that researchers define the patterned use of language as a speech community as well as the bounded sense of what counts as important to the people in that community. A speech community, then, is clearly not defined solely or even primarily in terms of its geographic boundaries. As Philipsen (1992) stated, it is when places are spoken of as mean-ingful in a consistent and patterned way by a group that the interaction between geography and speech community becomes intertwined.

Philipsen (1992) stated that he was drawing upon Hymes (1974) when he de-scribed his project as one that considered speech communities to be comprised of diverse patterns that form a recognizable system. These patterns, Philipsen (1992) believed, are easiest to recognize when one steps into a different society and hears sounds that are not readily accessible from one's own speech community.

For Philipsen, then, the very term speech community was descriptive of the particular patterned ways that communities use communication. Further, Philipsen (1992) included in his definition of speech community structured language prac-tices. Even though he incorporated diverse speaking instances, he argued that, combined, they formed a system for organizing the structure of speech production. In this definition an important distinction is made between a social community and a speech community. Seemingly similar in many ways, they also contain impor-tant differences.

Philipsen (1992) pointed out that "[i]n every speech community there is a social pattern of language use—that is, some ordering in what is actually done in the speech activity of a community. And there is a cultural ideology—that is, a system of beliefs and prejudices about communication" (p. 13). Philipsen also addressed the way that people make sense of speech as further refinement of the idea of a speech community. This sense making also seems to be related to shared beliefs within any such speech community.

According to Philipsen (1992), it is also important to distinguish between a culture and social community. He defined culture as "a system of meanings, an organized complex of symbols, definitions, premises, and rules" (p. 14). Philipsen stressed that what makes a culture is not a geographic location but a shared code. For Philipsen, then, a community "consists of a group of people who are bound together in some relation of shared sentiment and mutual responsibility" (p. 14). The code itself is made meaningful by the community that enacts it. The code itself both constrains and enables communicative action.

For Philipsen, then, speech communities radiated meanings following Hymes. They were comprised of members who shared access to culture, common resources, and ways of speaking. Speech communities could begin to be defined by place, but that sense of place became deeper as an investigator began to understand the patterned practices that comprised the social system of members' beliefs, also known as their cultural code.

Following in Philipsen's Footsteps

Following the line of research begun by their mentor, Carbaugh and Fitch have applied the ideas of the speech community concept to a broader range of groups as well as extended its use. Both in theory and methodology, these researchers have commented on the relationship between communication and speech communities.

Based on Philipsen's ideas of community members sharing a common culture, Carbaugh (1993, 1996) juxtaposed community with notions of the individual. In his book review in *QJS*, Carbaugh (1993) described the work of four ethnographies of communication, Basso (1990), Goodwin (1990), Katriel (1991), and Johnstone (1990). He discussed the way in which the authors decided whether or not to position the group under investigation as a speech community. He suggested that each author under review investigated "situated communication practice in its local place, explicating the general way in which communication is patterned by a social group, within its own context" (p.101). According to Carbaugh (1993), the social group under investigation by Basso was the "Western Apache;" for Katriel it was "contemporary Israel" and Israeli children; for Goodwin, the research focused on a "particular speech community of peers" (p. 106) that was designated as the "Maple Street children's group and their neighborhood of inner-city Philadelphia, Pennsylvania" (p. 106). Finally, Carbaugh described Johnstone's speech community as "Fort Wayne people." In each of these communities, communication practices are examined.

Carbaugh's attention to the communication patterns presented by each author, such as Johnstone's description of the connection between stories and places for constructing personal and communal identities, marked the importance of relating the speech community to its members' practices. By reiterating Goodwin's recommendation to ground communication inquiry in "social groups, speech communities, or peer groups" (p.108), Carbaugh (1993) reified its importance.

In other work, Carbaugh (1996) described social relationships as part of the context for communication, but did not specify the boundaries of a speech community. Instead, his research attended to shared patterns of speech on a cultural level. Following Philipsen (1992), Carbaugh (1996) found within the project of ethnography of communication a way to talk about various tensions felt by individuals acting within particular cultural scenes. Carbaugh (1993, 1996) does not specifically use the term speech community in his own ethnographic investigations. He created instead another term, cultural discourses, and described these as, at least partially, related to the practices of a community (see Carbaugh, Gibson, & Milburn, 1997).

By contrast, Fitch (1994) argued for the use of ethnography of speaking in interpersonal communication research and highlighted the value recognizing features that distinguish speech communities bring to interpersonal studies. To combat long-held assumptions of universality, Fitch (1994) detailed the specific features of what constitutes a speech community. She drew specifically on the idea that "each cultural system should be studied on its own terms to discover the ways of speaking that are meaningful within the speech community" (p. 115). Within each community, members use shared symbols to communicate. Fitch's (1994) claim that "meaning is negotiated through language use within a speech community" (p. 118) is significant in that meaning is not already assumed, but constructed through the process of speaking. This idea was a departure from Philipsen's description, whereby shared meaning is an assumed part of the speech community's resources for interpreting specific symbols. The unifying features in Fitch's (1994) definition of speech community include "shared valued ways of speaking" (p. 118) and the ability to negotiate meaning.

On the other hand, she drew on Philipsen (1992) when she claimed that "the relationship of persons to a speech community is a matter that may be empirically established by familiarity with, as well as use of, the ways of speaking that define the group" (Fitch, 1994, p. 119). In reality, not all research that purports to examine a speech community does this. Finally, Fitch (1994) highlighted two key features when discussing speech community: the material practices (i.e., discourse) and the "specific definition of members and boundaries of the social group(s) whose messages influence the perceptions and experiences of persons" (p. 130). These features are applied to and used as evidence of a speech community within communication studies.

More recently, Fitch (1999) has offered a compelling comparison among three groups of researchers, among them Hymes, Carbaugh, and Philipsen, who she claimed employ the term speech community in slightly different ways. Fitch (1999) argued that Hymes (1974) left the boundaries and membership of speech communities intentionally vague. She further asserted that as "the term *ethnography* has been applied to an ever wider range of qualitative research" the types of groups or interactions that might be considered a speech community have little consistency. She outlined three definitions of what counts as a speech community:

> 1. A group of people whose members have contact with one another and through their interaction develop shared practices and symbols (the Hymesian view).
> 2. A network of people who have something significant in common (such as geographical location or age) and thus share a language space, but may have cleavages between them (such as race, class or gender) such that some members have no contact with some others (a sociological oriented view).
> 3. A string of people who share a symbolic code of speaking practices and meanings for those practices, although they may be separated by distance as well as race, class, gender, age, and so forth (a Philipsen/Katriel/Carbaugh view). (Fitch, 1999, p. 46).

Fitch (1999) established these distinctions in order to argue that an Internet listserv may count as a speech community, even if participants interact infrequently or never, because members brought "certain shared resources for interaction" to the list from which a "shared code might be constructed" (p. 47). The distinctions she made are useful for categorizing research about speech communities.

It is important to underscore that the boundaries of a speech community are frequently designated by researchers rather than delineated by the participants/ members of such a community. This is one element Fitch's (1994, 1999) categorization of speech communities does not address. How people come to see themselves as members of any particular community and differentiate between their (or researchers') community as opposed to any other community is an area that has received scant attention in recent research on speech community. Increasingly important is research tracing the ways that participants label themselves as members of a particular community, describing the boundary conditions of such a community (often using geographic or container metaphors), and accounting for actions as occurring both within and for such a community, as well as those actions being held accountable from other delineated members of the community.

In order to address the literature that stems from this lineage, the following articles provide additional instances of the way to which speech communities are referred and how the concept is employed. This is similar to the method of finding a native term (Carbaugh, 1989b) within the ethnography of communication tradition. As such, how the authors represented the speech community they made claims about is the central concern of this next section. This method of investigation follows a model proposed by Katriel and Philipsen (1990), in which they determine what participants mean when they use the term communication. Along these lines, this review examines talk (or writing) about speech communities to determine what the authors mean when they use the term.

Instances of talk about speech community are cataloged following in the ethnography of communication research tradition. Once the instances of such communication are identified, their context, or in what realm they co-occur, helps to determine the meaning(s) of such a term and its importance to the participants who use such language. If such a community identifies itself by such terms, then this community will be so labeled. When no such references were present, the label applied to this speech community follows norms proposed by the methodology itself. This may seem to indicate a tautological position; however, there are three reasons to employ such a methodology here. First, it seems the clearest way to validate or to legitimize a research method is in its use. Secondly, when one attends carefully to the method in an article, one refines its features for subsequent use. Thirdly, examining a body of literature for signs of a speech community, as Fitch (1994) called our attention to in her review, can help us to examine specific features to compare and evaluate future research.

CURRENT USES OF SPEECH COMMUNITY: PLACE, LABEL, CODE

Out of the current literature, roughly three categories seem to capture the use of the term. In the first of the three categories, the authors place primary emphasis on the place in which their study was undertaken. Most often, place is described as a geographic location, such as a country, region, or municipality, or place is described as a physical location such as a front stoop (such as Philipsen, 1975) or particular building. The second category includes articles that refer mainly to the in-group labels given to the group. For these authors, the use of members' terms that connote their community is most important. The third group treats a speech community as comprised of a cultural code. In this set, the authors foreground the beliefs and values demonstrated in particular speaking practices. Each of these categories are defined and described below.

Place and Space

One of the unquestionable contributions to the definition of speech community made by Philipsen (1976) was the attention paid to participants' use of, and meaning attributed to, the spaces and places they frequent. Others have subsequently attended carefully to this feature in their examination of particular cultural groups (also see Carbaugh & Berry, 2001). How members use their spaces and places in meaningful ways is clearly tied to their sense of identity as a community. The next set of articles (Aleman, 2001; Braithwaite, 1997a; Saohatse, 1998; Shue & Beck, 2001; Tagliamonte & Hudson, 1999) call attention to the defining features of place for particular speech communities. The specifics of place are detailed to convey a sense of how place itself is made in, and makes meaningful, the communicative practices of each speech community.

In the first article, Shue and Beck (2001) focus on the importance of the physical space of the dance studio in creating the speech community. They described the environment or learning site of the classroom and dance studio. This context indicates the importance of the physical space, which remains an implicit component of the speech community. For example, the dance instructors encouraged members to express freely their creativity and emotions by making suggestions about how to interpret each dance, and by addressing one another through family metaphors, such as little sister. The confidence of body image and self-expression, however, is often in conflict with messages present in the physical space of the studio, where wall-to-wall mirrors are often used as a means for evaluating how one looks and performs in relation to others.

Aleman (2001) also took seriously the concept of place in the definition of speech community in an analysis of a retirement community. She used ethnography of communication as her framework for conducting participant-observation research. In defining speech communities, she suggested that public spaces were a defining feature of the particular speech community under investigation. Given this definition, the author employed the speech community concept to describe the relationship between residents and the physical space of a hotel in which they lived, focusing on their use of public and private space areas. The author clearly related a way of speaking, in this case described as complaining, as it occurred in relation to the space (e.g., dining halls) and the meaning that the practice of complaining enacted, such as loss of control over surroundings and the strain of social living.

Saohatse (1998) uses the term speech community as it referred to the talk that occurred within the physical setting of a hospital. As this talk emerged in multiple languages, the implication was that a speech community is comprised of those who participate in interaction regardless of whether they share a way of speaking. That participants shared institutional tasks included in giving and receiving care became the key component of a speech community for this author. These shared practices in the hospital, then, indicated the presence of a speech community. The author also discussed the diverse composition of languages present in the larger, geographic community, which would seem to conflict with the hospital community because the patients were drawn from this region. The common experience of being in a hospital, however, facilitated communication because the relationship among members is so task oriented.

Several authors have described much larger physical boundaries of a speech community. For instance, a country was the situated place that bound members for Matsumura (2001). He suggested that investigators examine linguistic competence in one's home country before being immersed in a second language, or target, speech community. On the other hand, Tagliamonte and Hudson (1999) discussed the limitations of countries as significant boundaries of speech communities. They suggested that it is the demographic category of age that binds members more firmly to a speech community, where a particular style of speaking extends geographic limits. Similarly, Dubois and Melancon (1997) argued that physical region cannot be used solely to define a speech community. Additionally, Braithwaite (1997a) described how the speaking patterns of one Native American tribe transcended the boundaries of a particular community college and extended to the broader, tribal cultural practices.

Even though it is often the case that features of a particular space or place are significant and meaningful to participants, there are also several instances that demonstrate how speech community membership transcends place. Several researchers begin with a geographical or physical location as their primary means for identifying a speech community. Some reflect more on the relationship between the physical location and the speaking practices of the group in question more than others.

An emerging line of investigation has focused on the economic conditions of the participants. For instance, when pinpointing the features of the speech community under investigation, Linnes (1998) began with a geographic location of the city of Houston, but then further refined it to a particular neighborhood in the city. Next, the idea of participants' socioeconomic status is foregrounded as participants are described as part of the middle-class community. Additional evidence is found in the work of Huspeck and Kendall (1991), who described the lumber industrial workers, and Huspeck (1994), who described the working class community of the Pacific Northwest.

Another aspect of the space/place paradigm is the way ethnicity and race are described and situated in geographic locales. For instance, Chaston, (1996) described the Chicano speech community comprised of Mexican Americans in the Southwest. Linnes (1998) included race in his description of a speech community who demonstrated the importance of talking Black or talking White depending upon the topic of conversation. Linnes then compared this to another speech community residing in the same city, the German community comprised of bilingual German-English speakers.

Within this set of articles, the prominent reference to speech community has been that of place or space. The physical or geographic region of speakers not only describes a prominent feature of a speech community, it is also the primary way some speech communities create their sense of identity and community. Additional features of these speech communities include economic opportunities (or lack thereof) as well as ethnic features of members that are frequently described as bound to a place.

Researcher Labeling of Speech Communities

Even though the main feature of a speech community discussed thus far has been the place or geographic location of participants, these boundaries have been most frequently delineated by researchers rather than members themselves (see Dubois & Melancon, 1997, for an exception). There are a variety of researchers (e.g., Baumann, 1996; Fought, 1999; Jacobs, 1998; Milburn, 2002; and Smitherman, 1997) who are taking very seriously the labels that members give to their own communities. These researchers use member labels as the prominent feature of their descriptions of the speech community.

Smitherman (1997), for example, referred to the hip hop nation, which she claimed specifies urban youth culture that is mostly Black but also includes Latinos. She also uses the labels African American speech community and Black speech community to refer to the same speech community. The distinctions, however, became somewhat blurred as she referred to hip hop nation as part of the larger Black speech community when focusing on the linguistic practices employed by members. These practices also have various labels, including African American language (AAL), Black English, African American vernacular English (see Labov et al., 1968, and Linnes, 1998, above), and Ebonics. With these various labels, the speech practices of this speech community functioned both as a resistant language and as a linguistic bond of the culture (Smitherman, 1997). She stated: "As we move to the 21st century, it is clear that African America continues to constitute itself as a distinct speech community, with its own linguistic rules and sociolinguistic norms of interaction" (Smitherman, 1997, p. 9). Even though Smitherman described various labeling practices, she did not discuss how the various researcher-generated labels were used by participants or informed their communicative practices.

In their article about the Cajun community, Dubois and Melancon (1997) described the difficulty of defining the Cajun community based on the old categories of geography, race, religion, ancestry, region, or surname. In this article, the authors cited Labov primarily for his definition of speech community. They explained that Labov (1966, 1969, 1972a, 1972b) "showed that a speech community is defined through any homogenous usage of forms and elements" (p. 64). They also refer to the way that Hymes (1972, 1974) "added" the notion that members share "strong feelings of belonging to a local territory" (p. 64). Further, these authors recognized the various ways speech community has been employed in other sociolinguistic research: from groups that share common ways of speaking to groups that interact within a geographic area.

The definition of a true Cajun or one who can claim membership in the Cajun speech community was based upon the requirements that one either be fluent or semifluent in the Cajun language or have Cajun ancestry. By asking members directly about the labels they prefer and the requirements for membership, the authors were able to find some unique responses. For instance, Dubois and Melancon (1997) reported that "a few, largely younger respondents felt that the notion of a Cajun community consisted only of such abstractions as *la joie de vivre*" (italics in original, p. 87). Whereas the authors consider this phrase an abstraction, it also seems to indicate that there is a native term for being captured by the language. The idea that members of a particular community can self-identify how boundary conditions are made, rather than be defined by a team of researchers, is one of the most appealing conclusions of this work.

In her article about Chicano English, Fought (1999) explicitly discussed the idea that the community itself should define what features are relevant to consider it a speech community. Fought (1999) described the way that Eckert (1989) used the member terms *jocks* and *burnouts* as labels for their speech communities. She noted that researchers would not know about these labels unless they were discovered through ethnographic investigation. Fought (1999) then discussed the importance of gang membership for many groups (as far back as Labov), and particularly salient in the Los Angeles area under investigation. Initially paying particular attention to member labels, the author nonetheless continued by describing her research as an examination of a minority community. Even though there are some inconsistencies with her use of member labels, Fought (1999) employed several native terms in her research. For instance, speech community members used the phrase "low income' to describe those members who live in apartments, as opposed to those who lived in houses. This member label referred back to the importance of place as well as economics as prominent features of the linguistic practices that define speech community.

Similarly, Jacobs (1998) discussed the use of "queer" among the lesbian and gay community of Toronto, Canada. The use of a particular label and the variety of reasons for the acceptance of the queer label is explored. When Jacobs referred to the lesbian and gay community as part of the larger speech community, it becomes unclear whether the terms are member labels or author labels. For instance, it seems clear that the author switched from an emphasis on member labels by introducing the concept of the dominant culture's speech community, clearly a researcher label. This inconsistency highlights the tenuous hold of member labels as a primary unit of analysis in the hierarchy of research terms.

Research by Carbaugh, Gibson, and Milburn (1997) and Milburn (2002) described the way participants employ the term community when referencing in- and out-group members. Specifically, Puerto Rican Center members use the self-label (i.e., our community). This label plays a significant role in determining who is able to claim "legitimate membership as a participant in 'our community'" (Carbaugh, Gibson, & Milburn, 1997, p.11). The community is the label used by members to refer to those who are outside the boundaries of the particular speech community. By focusing on participants' language use and speaking practices, Milburn, like Dubois and Melacon (1997), privileged member labels of their own community.

Another researcher who made this point is Baumann (1996), who attended quite carefully to member's descriptions of their speech communities. For example, in Baumann's ethnographic investigation, he spoke with, and listened to, residents of one geographically marked location in London called Southall. It was from this geographically defined place that he came to study and describe community. He argued that he did not take as given the existence of a unified culture nor a unified community. He did admit to making the initial assumption that there might be a culture or community found in a physical locale. As he listened to their talk, these residents labeled multiple communities and delineated the boundaries of each according to a variety of features, many of which included ethnic distinctions. Consequently, Baumann used residents' own language to describe and refer to the Afro-Caribbean community, the Muslim community, the Hindu and Sikh communities, and the White community, which was distinguished by its lack of clear designating labels or unifying features. In addition to ethnicity, he found that religious, migratory, and labor labels were used by residents to differentiate communities and sub-communities. By demonstrating the multiple ways that residents referred to one another and distinguish one group from another, Baumann helped preserve the way that a term will serve a variety of different purposes according to how it is employed by participants. Further, Baumann contested the adequacy of the term *culture* as meaningful, given the extremely varied composition and discourses of Southallians.

Considering the diverse groups living within a geographic area, the boundaries of community can be found by attending to members' labels and other boundary practices. What constitutes culture and the relationship between its boundaries and those of a particular community are often not clearly designated. Perhaps researchers are hastily suggesting that cultural features of discourse are present when, in fact, they are merely describing community practices specifically.

Given the various ways that members seem to self-identify, it is also informative to examine more specifically the labels researchers use to describe the specific speech community under investigation. For instance, as mentioned previously, Fitch (1994) argued that culture and conversation are key aspects of speech community. The particular speech communities she cited were referred to by either (a) geographic location, such as continent (Africa or North American), country, or region/city, (b) ethnicity or race, or (c) both—rather than labeled by researchers based on features of speaking or communication practices themselves. Fitch (1994) seemed to raise this issue of labeling by advocating a closer examination of the "communication style of African Americans at the level of speech communities," for instance, in order to show "the variability of meaning attached to particular ways of speaking as those relate to the shared experiences and resulting premises of different groups of people" (p. 129).

Some researchers have paid particular attention to members' labels when defining the speech community under investigation. These same researchers also seem to utilize location and other demographic characteristics to refer to the speech community itself. A focus on situated communication practices within speech communities, rather than demographic markers such as age, class, or geographic origin, should prompt future researchers to use either member labels for their group or their communication practices.

Cultural Codes

The final way that speech communities have been defined is according to its members' use of particular codes. By focusing on the way communication is coded, researchers with this focus are able to acknowledge the multiple communities in which people may have membership while paying particular attention to instances in which the use of language, through a particular code, is made to represent membership in a specific community. In this section, the articles under review (Braithwaite, 1997b; Coutu, 2000; Fitch, 1994; Hastings, 2001; Lo 1999; Sequeira, 1993) reveal how cultural codes create speech communities.

Sequeira (1993) provided a model by which researchers can use the concept of code as part of their definition of the speech community under investigation. In this article, Sequeira discussed terms of address use in an American speech community. When she described the "social meaning" of address term use, Sequeira noted that there was a "commitment to *community*" (p. 279, italics in original). She further claimed that "understanding 'community' is knowing which address forms carry public, interpersonal force" (p. 279). Further, she noted how the use of familiar address terms set this community apart from outsiders who might even have found the practice offensive. The communication practices formed part of the boundaries for this group of speakers and provided certain options that may seem to constrain or predispose members to select among certain forms of address over others. Sequeira, however, insisted that the speech community did not determine members' particular choices.

By reflecting upon how the moral code, values, and norms create a sense of member identity, Sequeira (1994) recognized how these features function to bind members to the speech community. Sequeira initially lauded the importance of defining a speech community through reference to their codes; however, she referred to the group itself as a Christian community or community of believers rather than using a label related to their speaking practices.

Fitch (1998) investigated the way code is conducted in conversations by detailing interaction between some members of a middle-class, urban Colombian speech community and another speech community labeled the southern United States. In order to describe the prominent codes members used and oriented to in their conversation, Fitch referred to one conversational participant, J, by noting that his practices were sensible from within his speech community. While claiming to analyze the selected conversations to determine the cultural codes of communication to which participants oriented, Fitch (1998) reverted to the familiar sense of place as a designator of what constitutes speech community membership. As Fitch (1998) noted, she was once a member of the same speech community as J, but does not live there now.

Braithwaite (1997b) offered another example of the way speech community is created through the use of a common code. Code may be displayed in the process of enacting particular communication rituals. Braithwaite established three criteria for evidence of a speech community. Members either share (a) aspects of linguistic variation, (b) communication rules for speaking, or (c) shared meanings for interpreting speech. When members overtly state their goals as creating and enacting a sense of community, they employ specific forms of communication. Specifically, this study described and analyzed one particular ritual form (called a *ritual of legitimacy*) where the topic of conversation among participants often referred to members' need to create a sense of togetherness or community among all Vietnam veterans. Analysis of this particular form of interaction, Braithwaite claimed, revealed much about the communicative world of Vietnam veterans, and about how speech was used explicitly to form a sense of communal identity.

Lo (1999) argued that because no community is linguistically homogenous, researchers should focus on the way conversational participants *codeswitch* to determine speech community membership. As there are degrees of membership in any speech community, members also have degrees of shared orientations towards norms. She further argued that different speakers' beliefs about what kinds of speaking practices are permissible relate to their acceptance of comembers. Within any conversation, participants need to assume that they share certain norms for speaking in order to understand when and why conversational participant codeswitch. As a result, the practice of codeswitching itself can be said to be indicative of comembership. Any given act of codeswitching can help position participants as socially validated group members who share a common identity.

Lo (1999) explained that there may be some speech communities for whom members do not reciprocate codeswitching, but that the practice itself potentially creates and affirms shared speech community membership. Lo did claim that when one encounters an instance where codeswitching is not reciprocated, that provides an opportunity to examine how speech community membership is negotiated in the process of conversation. For example, Lo described the way three people codeswitched during a conversation and the role this codeswitching played in helping participants understand to which speech community any given speaker might belong: "For Chazz, his participation in this Korean American community is his way of being maximally authentically Chinese, in fact, more Chinese than if he were to be an active participant in what he considers to be degenerate contemporary Chinese American culture" (p. 475). She noted that Chazz's choice of code helped determine whether his conversational participants understood and allowed him to use such a code in mixed code-preferring company. The article clearly demonstrated how speech community membership is an interactional achievement based upon how participants use and interpret codes.

Like Lo, Coutu (2000) called attention to the existence of competing codes in any community. She began with a published nonfiction text to argue that its discourse is part of a particular speech community. By not conforming to the usual boundaries of place, Coutu gave little credence to that as a necessary or sufficient condition for speech community membership. Coutu used speech community specifically as part of her methodology to situate the codes of its members. Her examination of the competing, coded practices within the American speech community under investigation helped Coutu to argue that several top government officials, McNamara in particular, did not share a code with the larger group. Implicit within this article, is the claim that it is to speech communities that any one member must account about his or her actions. Communicative actions, then, take place within an evaluative system, whereby any particular member's actions may be held accountable by other members. When members recognize the communication codes of shared beliefs and values that comprise the speech community, then they also recognize the obligation to account for untoward actions properly to continue to be counted as a member.

Coutu concluded by reiterating the presence of competing codes within speech communities and urging for recognition that the conflict between codes is an area that can be fruitfully examined to learn how members make sense of any particular code. Coutu suggested that future research follow Hymes's (1962) call for comparative work in the ethnography of communication based on how similarities and differences of code use by individual members is accomplished and evaluated by each speech community.

Hastings (2001) also discussed the importance of examining cultural codes when defining speech community membership. She, however, referred to the specific, local place surrounding the speech community under investigation. Hastings described the emergence of a speech community that she labeled Indian strangers comprised of graduate students in a college town in the United States. She focused her definition of this speech community on those persons who share both origin (i.e., Asian Indian) and certain normative and code rules for speaking. She summarized these rules as (a) be who you are and (b) be interdependent. These rules created the distinctions among this new speech community and other communities. Even though Hastings did not focus explicitly on the tension between a unified speech community and a speech community comprised of various members who communicate based upon various rules, she did display individual members' tensions as they engaged in social dramas, whereby those who were members ridiculed those persons who could be considered members based on the loose affiliation requirement of being Asian Indian, but did not act in socially sanctioned ways. That particular actions should be understood as able to count as valid and preferable (rather than permissible) tended to favor the unified perspective of speech community. How members used rules for communication to enact and evaluate speech community membership was skillfully displayed.

The way codes create speech communities is perhaps most evident in different forms of mediated communication. Several authors (e.g., Al-Khatib, 2001; Sawyer, 2002; and Spitulnik, 1997) described the way code is enacted based on the communication channel used and how the channel helped to create a particular sense of speech community.

In her discussion of mediated communities, and in particular radio use in Zambia, Spitulnik (1997) described the limitations of defining a speech community as comprised of people who share linguistic knowledge and frequently interact. She focused on the way people in large, urban societies rely upon mass-mediated forms of communication to learn the common codes. Spitulnik suggested that speech communities should be examined for *frequency* (i.e., in the rate of consumption of the same media as others) and *density* (i.e., in terms of large-scale exposure to such common forms of communication). These key features, she argued, provide "common linguistic reference points" (p. 163) and should be considered the key features of speech communities.

Similarly, Sawyer (2002) addressed the use of television texts to argue that a speech community is comprised of people who share similar practices. Sawyer described the practice of making references to television in speech as one that functions to "create a sense of community or shared identification between people who share a 'common pop-cultural landscape'" (p. 5). She further pointed out that the practice is not so much of a particular speech community, but that, through its use, participants actually create a sense of community. Sawyer also described the practice of telereferencing as operating through a restricted code (citing Bernstein, 1972), which works to create a sense of community because the knowledge of particular meanings are restricted to the few who have access to a set of common texts.

Even though participants' codes figure prominently in the relationship between speech communities and forms of mediated communication for the previous authors, Al-Khatib (2001) discussed the language-switching process itself in three television programs designed for different Arabic audiences. The author described how participants in a Jordanian speech community modified their speech not based upon what their audience could understand, but upon what their audience expected to hear. Similarly, Neethling (2000) described the code switching that occurs within speech communities based on new codes being promoted by sports teams and advertisements.

COMMUNITY REFERENCE IN COMMUNICATION JOURNALS

After reviewing of articles that employ the concept of speech communities, a comparison will be made with articles that refer to groups as communities rather than speech communities. This comparison helps determine how authors describe the relationship between communication and community when they do not use the unit of analysis speech community. Several articles from communication journals between 1991 and 2001 were selected because they use the key words *speech* and *community* or *language* and *community*. The articles selected were not written from an ethnography of communication perspective (nor within the tradition of speech communities); however, they each covered the same areas as those previously mentioned, such as the place, label, or communication practices of a given community. Within any given article, community itself was described by a combination of these features interchangeably. Each category proposed above (i.e., geographic, member labels, and cultural codes), therefore, will be used to make comparisons within this set of articles.

First, several articles refer to the geographic region of the community under investigation. Pousada (1991) examined east Harlem, New York; Cortes-Conde (1994) investigated a community located in the Buenos Aires, Argentina; Robinson and Varley (1998) discussed a language community in Africa; and Dyer (2002) referred to Scotland as the site of her research. Of these, only east Harlem is a narrow geographic location. Of the others, three made claims about entire countries, and the final one is a largely populated city in a large country. There are, however, other articles that use the notion of place more specifically. Of these, Aden (1995) and Marshall (2001) are exemplary.

Aden (1995) discussed the idea of community as a place and the way that such a community relates to its members' identity. The author explored the relationship between work communities and residential communities through a discussion of how economic changes affected baseball players or workers and those who

attended baseball games. The economic changes, including the increased importance placed on players' salaries and the effects of unionization, altered the identities explored. The author described the way people make sense of their communities as interpretive communities that are located in particular places, particularly
homes. The importance of place and a sense of home put this definition of community in concert with Philipsen's (1975) early definition of speech community as
enacted in a particular place.

Similarly, Marshall (2001) argued that communities are defined by a sense of
place affected by economic conditions in her article about the changing conditions
within fishing communities. The members of the particular community she examined all practiced fishing as a form of livelihood. Given changing economic conditions, however, the community itself was in the process of being redefined. Marshall
suggested that communities are engaged in a continual process of reworking, or
reimagining themselves. Her findings seem to indicate that communities are bound
by a sense of connectivity and connections; however, she also noted the tensions
that exist among members between the desire for mobility (to seek more favorable
economic conditions) and the value of rootedness and familial lineage. Finally,
this author described the spatial-bound parameters and place-bound relationships
as no longer forming such tight boundary conditions.

In these articles, then, communities selected for research are often done by
geographic location. At the same time, those who make claims about the strength
of these communities also note that the changing economic conditions of a certain
place alter its composition and communication patterns.

In relation to the notion of member labels, several articles ascribe a label to the
group under investigation. Pousada (1991) used the label the Puerto Rican community of east Harlem, as well as a poor, working class community, as a more
specific descriptor; Cortes-Conde (1994) used the label Anglo Argentine community and the Spanish-speaking community more specifically; Lee (1995) labeled a
particular community a small town; Brookey (1996) discussed the homosexual
community; and LaWare (1998) referred to the Chicano community in Chicago.
These authors all refer to the group under question by a variety of features, including geography (as mentioned above), ethnicity, nationality, and sexuality.

This group of authors also used different researcher labels for the type of community under investigation. These labels included *interpretive community* (Aden,
1995), *language community* (Robinson & Varley, 1998), and *dialogic community*
(Zoller, 2000). Given that the group of articles did not make use of the research
term speech community, it is interesting to note that the terms in use share similar
features. The interpretive community referred to the way members create shared
meaning of events and places. The language community (although recognizably
sharing roots with speech community in the early work of linguists) referred to the
decisions about which language to use that are made by determining what language members have in common in a geographic region comprised of multiple
languages. The dialogic community, likewise, indicated that participants in a new
community had to create for themselves not only their community label, but also

the definition and boundaries of such a community. This process was aided by trainers (one label for one participant group) and initiators or charterers who helped begin the new community.

Finally, some features of a cultural code, athough never used explicitly by any of these authors, seem to be present in these authors' findings. Particularly salient are notions of values and beliefs of particular communities. For instance, Pousada (1991) indicated that the strong belief in education motivates the community to approach the school (noted as a different community by label and speech practices). Cortes-Conde (1994) discussed the practice of codeswitching and preference for the use of English or Spanish as being related to larger cultural practices. Lee (1995) argued that the small town community, although demonstrated in speech patterns such as sluggishness, also contains very clear values and beliefs such as a desire to appear respectable. Brookey (1996) discounted the existence of a real homosexual community but did suggest that members of such a community nonetheless retain distinctness even though they share some common substance. LaWare (1998) argued for the importance of including a community's preference for the medium of communication (in this case, visual mural artwork) as a way of expressing identity. Finally, Marshall (2001) discussed the ways communities are constantly in the process of reimagining themselves while valuing rootedness and familial lineage. These articles all focus on communication practices; how these practices are patterned and how they relate to and are valued by the community itself are the key features of the methodological term, speech code.

What these articles describe are various ways to conceptualize community. They each raise an issue that is prominently dealt with in the previously described definitions of the basic unit of analysis, speech community. These issues include (a) the geographic and economic features of the community; (b) the ethnic or racial features members orient to when interacting with members their community; and (c) the specific language use and ways various media affect its use in particular communities. What this set of articles does not do as well is to describe language use with reference to the common code used by participants of the communities under investigation. The relationship between community and communication is closely examined by these authors; however, it remains unclear why they do not use the unit speech community in their analyses.

Even if the term speech community is not employed, there are strands of the concept present here strikingly similar to those investigated under the rubric of speech community. Perhaps one suggestion is that these authors are not claiming to belong to the Hymes' program of investigation, ethnography of communication. This may be true for several of these authors, but there are two inconsistencies. The first is that several of these authors do cite Labov, who was among those early investigators of the basic unit. Secondly, even among those who claim they are committed to the program of research of ethnography of communication, not all consistently employ the term speech communities. As mentioned above Carbaugh (1989a, 1994, 1996), for instance, did not use the term speech community in his descriptions' communication codes, but rather referred to the communal function of language that bound members together. In fact, because of his shared commitments to the program of ethnography of communication, his research is often cited for its contribution to the definition of the basic term speech communities (see Fitch, 1999). One is therefore left asking: What utility value does the unit of analysis speech community hold for future communication researchers?

DISCUSSION

This review has raised roughly four issues. First, authors since Hymes and Gumperz have often used descriptive labels for the speech community under investigation that refer to specific demographic information (e.g., most frequently race or ethnicity, geography, income or socio-economic status, gender, age, or sexuality). The labels researchers use to designate particular community groups seem to indicate the relative importance of these demographic features over the speech practices that such group members employ. (The only exception is Smitherman, 1997, who refers to the speaking practice in the speech community labeled hip hop nation.). The emphasis on demographic features in our labeling has important research implications: By emphasizing demographics we run the risk of stating demographics as facts rather than constructs that are made meaningful through the communication practices that we are examining.

The second related finding relates to how researchers define the composition of a speech community. In most of the studies examined in this review, the composition of a particular speech community had been defined a priori. One cannot label a speech community in advance without such a label being directly tied to the different ways in which it is enacted through conversations. That is, one can only designate a speech community as such when the features that define it have been revealed by one's research.

The third finding is that the idea of a speech community as a homogeneous entity does not exist. A widely held assumption is that a speech community is defined by a particularly salient and consistent pattern of communication. What emerges, however, is great variation in how the pattern is enacted by the members of the speech community. Scholars often describe competing or conflicting ways of speaking within and among communities. What makes any one group cohesive enough to earn the label of speech community may upon closer examination prove to be areas of tension and contradiction within that group. In fact, members of the speech community may themselves be in an ongoing process of determining if and how they remain part of the same speech community. This reflects the dynamic (i.e., nonstatic) nature of communication (see Lo, 1999, for an excellent discussion of this point.) This area also needs additional research.

The fourth issue is the prevalence of a focus on member codes as the key component of a speech community. These codes have been variously defined (see Bernstein, 1972; Carbaugh, 1994, 1996; Fitch, 1994, 1998, 1999; Huspeck, 1994; and Philipsen, 1987, 1992, for further elaboration). Some researchers define codes by the rules governing language use. Others define code as the beliefs and values that help determine meaningful practices among members of a speech community. The latter is preferable because it emphasizes the meaning that members create through interactions as opposed to their being an assumed set of meanings that are mechanically ascribed to one language or another.

An implication of these four issues is the question of how we might refine speech community as a unit of analysis so that it remains a meaningful construct to study. There are similarities between how researchers have used the terms community and speech community. Are the two terms in essence referring to the same thing, or is there something to be gained by using the term speech community? The difference lies in how the term speech community makes evident the inseparable relationship between speech and community. Furthermore, the concept of speech community tends to stress the importance of what members themselves find meaningful about their communities and their communication practices.

In sum, after closely examining several different uses of speech communities and considering several organizational schemes (particularly Fitch, 1994, 1999), three categories seem to encompass its recurrent uses in the literature:

1. Speech communities are bound by the significance of their geography or place. Locations are described as containing communicative action or fostering particular modes of being a member (Basso, 1990; Lakoff & Johnson, 1980; Philipsen, 1975, 1989; Schegloff, 1971).

2. Participants consider themselves members of a "community" that they label as such (Carbaugh, Gibson, & Milburn, 1997; Fitch, 1999; Gumperz, 1968; Hymes, 1972, 1974). Participants may also use labels for their distinct communicative practices and for persons whom they deem outsiders.

3. Coded practices are what forms a community, regardless of geographic region, shared space, or label (Fitch, 1994). Conversational participants may use a code from any number of communities in which they are a part. However, the use of any such code helps interactants to recognize particular speech community membership(s) (Braithwaite, 1997b; Coutu, 2000; Lo, 1999; Hastings, 2001; Sequeira, 1993). Implied within the concept of code are the beliefs and values of particular actions. Communicative actions are undertaken by speech community members, so the speech community is the entity that holds individual actors accountable (Buttny, 1993; Coutu, 2000; Hastings, 2001; Scott & Lyman, 1968). Speech communities form part of a system of meanings that can be used to evaluate any particular action.

CONCLUSIONS

This review has been undertaken to determine the way current researchers have employed the term speech community. Historically, this unit of analysis was used in the formation of one specific program of research, ethnography of speaking, and it is clear that it remains a cornerstone upon which many researchers base their claims.

It is important to reiterate that Hymes's and Gumperz's starting places for their unit of analysis, speech community, stemmed from concerns similar to those today. One primary concern remains that careful and consistent use of analytic terms, particularly a term like speech community, can help make more precise the descriptions of communication practices of particular groups, both in terms of their boundaries and their own labels. Speech communities began as a complex unit. Not only did the term refer to the particular group of speakers under investigation, it also referred to the variety of ways they used language and the continuity in their language use according to rules and norms enacted situationally. Furthermore, the term described the cultural resources that community members drew upon to make sense of their communication practices. It may seem that this complexity has been forsaken, as many of the authors reviewed here seemed to refer mainly to the features of place, label, or cultural code. Still, another perspective on the articles reviewed is that, by choosing such a particular focus, they actually help refine some of the most significant features of the term. Speech communities are fruitfully explored by attending to the sense of space or place, member labels, and the cultural codes by which they make their practices meaningful to one another.

Another issue today is how to build community or communities. In this regard, the speech community research is almost solely concerned with communities already in existence. It is important, however, to appreciate the way communities have come to exist and the function(s) of communication within them. Furthermore, how particular individuals partake in a community, or come to have a sense of community is most apparent in the ways members come together (in a shared space or place), in the way they choose to label their group, and in the cultural code shared by participants.

Many people seem to belong to several heterogeneous groups with overlapping boundaries and group memberships. In this regard, it is of vital importance to recall early research that sought to examine the ways communities are set apart by their language use. When one person's community constitutes the fringe of another person's membership, we begin to recognize the ever-widening (or narrowing) set of community relationships that are increasingly complex and difficult to define. One community may encompass another or many others, determined by individual need or circumstance. Researchers need to recognize these seemingly fluid boundaries and take seriously the way communication operates in their formation or dissolution: People speak intercommunally, rather than just interculturally.

The future of speech community as a research unit lies in how scholars foreground membership. That is, it is not enough to locate persons who seem to form a cohesive unit, but how particular persons create membership or community identities in any talk is extremely important (see Hester & Elgin, 1997). By carefully examining interaction, one can begin to understand how conversational participants identify members and determine who counts as a member (see also Weider &

Pratt, 1990). This echoes Rudd (1995) as he advocated for reformulating the concept of speech community as having multiple identities within any given community, rather than "as if it produced one collective identity" (p. 220).

Today, there is a greater recognition of the multiple impacts upon speech communities, from uncertain and changing economic conditions to issues of sexuality to different forms of mediating communication. Given each of these impacts, the position of place, not just as a geographic or physical proximity concept, but the way members construct a sense of place as a communal location (as an actual space or metaphor for the boundaries of community) remains a primary concern. As groups are less and less defined by proximity and more and more defined through mediated forms of communication, the speech community continues to be a necessary and useful term because it helps identify the ways members use local knowledge (Morgan, 2001) to make sense of what is happening around them. The primary way this is done is through communication. With all of these changing impacts, it is increasingly important to continue examining speech communities to learn more about how members incorporate these conditions into their definitions and meanings of their community membership.

REFERENCES

Aden, R. C. (1995). Nostalgic communication as temporal escape: *When it was a game*'s re-construction of a baseball/work community. *Western Journal of Communication, 46*(1), 20–38.

Aden, R. C., Rahoi, R. L., & Beck, C. S. (1995, Fall). "Dreams are born on places like this": The process of community formation at the *Field of Dreams* site. *Communication Quarterly, 43* (4), 368–380.

Aleman, M. W. (2001). Complaining among the elderly: Examining multiple dialectical oppositions to independence in a retirement community. *Western Journal of Communication, 65*(1), 89–112.

Al-Khatib, M. A. (2001). Audience design revisited in a diglossic speech community: A case study of three TV programs addressed to three different audiences. *Multilingua, 20,* 393–414.

Anderson, B. (1983). *Imagined communities: Reflections on the origin and spread of nationalism.* London: Verso.

Basso, K. H. (1990). *Western Apache language and culture: Essays in linguistic anthropology.* Tucson: University of Arizona Press.

Baumann, G. (1996). *Contesting culture: Discourses of identity in multi-ethnic London.* Cambridge, UK: Cambridge University Press.

Beck, C. S. (1995). You make the call: The co-creation of media text through interaction in an interpretive community of Giants' fans. *Electronic Journal of Communication, 5*(1).

Bernstein, B. (1972). A sociolinguistic approach to socialization; with some reference to educability. In J. J. Gumperz & D. Hymes (Eds.), *Directions in sociolinguistics: The ethnography of communication* (pp. 465–497). New York: Holt, Rinehart, & Winston.

Bowie, D. (2001, December). The Diphthongization of /ay/: Abandoning a southern norm in southern Maryland. *Journal of English Linguistics, 29,* 329–346.

Braithwaite, C. A. (1997a). Sa'ah Naaghai Bik'eh Hozhoon: An ethnography of Navajo educational communication practices. *Communication Education, 46,* 219–233.

Braithwaite, C. A. (1997b, Fall). "Were YOU there?": A ritual of legitimacy among Vietnam veterans. *Western Journal of Communication, 61,* 423–447.

Braithwaite, C. A. (1990). Communicative silence: A cross cultural study of Basso's hypothesis. In D. Carbaugh (Ed.), *Cultural communication in intercultural context* (pp. 321–328). Hillsdale, NJ: Erlbaum.

Britain, D. (2001). Where did it all start? Dialect contact, the "Founder Principle" and the so-called (-own) split in New Zealand English. *Transactions of the Philological Society, 99*(1), 1–27.

Britain, D., & Trudgill, P. (1999). Migration, new-dialect formation and sociolinguistic refunctionalisation: Reallocation as an outcome of dialect contact. *Transactions of the Philological Society, 97*, 245–257.

Brookey, R. A. (1996). A community like "Philadelphia." *Western Journal of Communication, 60*(1), 40–56.

Burke, K. (1950). *A rhetoric of motives.* New York: Prentice Hall.

Buttny, R. (1993). *Social accountability in communication.* London: Sage.

Carbaugh, D. (1988). Cultural terms and tensions in the speech at a television station. *Western Journal of Speech Communication, 52*, 216–237.

Carbaugh, D. (1989a). *Talking American: Cultural discourses on Donahue.* Norwood, NJ: Ablex.

Carbaugh, D. (1989b) Fifty terms for talk: A cross cultural study. *International and Intercultural Communication Annual, 13*, 93–120.

Carbaugh, D. (Feb. 1993). Communal voices: An ethnographic view of social interaction and conversation. *Quarterly Journal of Speech, 79*, 99–130.

Carbaugh, D. (1994). Personhood, positioning, and cultural pragmatics: American dignity in cross-cultural perspective. In S. A. Deetz (Ed.), *Communication yearbook 17* (pp. 159–186). Thousand Oaks, CA: Sage.

Carbaugh, D. (1996). *Situating selves: The communication of social identities in American scenes.* Albany: State University of New York Press.

Carbaugh, D., & Berry, M. (2001). Communicating history, Finnish and American discourses: An ethnographic contribution to intercultural communication inquiry. *Communication Theory, 11*, 352–366.

Carbaugh, D., Gibson, T. A., & Milburn, T. (1997). A view of communication and culture: Scenes in an ethnic cultural center and a private college. In B. Kovacic (Ed.), *Emerging theories of human communication* (pp. 1–24). Albany: State University of New York Press.

Chaston, J. M. (1996, Sept.–Dec.). Sociolinguistic analysis of gender agreement in article/noun combinations in Mexican American Spanish in Texas. *Bilingual Review, 21*(3), 195–203.

Cortes-Conde, F. (1994). English as an instrumental language: Language displacement in the Anglo-Argentine community. *Bilingual Review, 19*(1), 25–39.

Coutu, L. M. (2000). Communication codes of rationality and spirituality in the discourse of and about Robert S. McNamara's *In Retrospect. Research on Language and Social Interaction, 33*(2), 179–211.

Dubois, S., & Melancon, M. (1997). Cajun is dead—Long live Cajun: Shifting from a linguistic to a cultural community. *Journal of Sociolinguistics, 1*(1), 63–93.

Dyer, J. (2002). We all speak about the same round here: Dialect leveling in a Scottish-English community. *Journal of Sociolinguistics, 6*(1) 99–116.

Dyers, C. (1999). Xhosa students' attitudes towards Black South African languages at the University of the Western Cape. *South African Journal of African Languages,19*(2),73–83.

Eckert, P. (1989). *Jocks & burnouts: Social categories and identity in high school.* New York: Teachers College, Columbia University.

Eckert, P. (1991). *New ways of analyzing sound change.* San Diego, CA: Academic Press.

Fitch, K. (1994). Culture, ideology, and interpersonal communication research. In S. A. Deetz (Ed.), *Communication Yearbook 17* (pp. 104–135). Thousand Oaks, CA: Sage.

Fitch, K. L. (1998). Text and context: A problematic distinction for ethnography. *Research on Language and Social Interaction, 31*(1), 91–107.

Fitch, K. (1999). Pillow talk? *Research on Language and Social Interaction, 32*(1–2), 41–50.

Fitch, K. L. (2003). Cultural persuadables. *Communication Theory, 13*(1), 100–123.

Fought, C. (1999). A majority sound change in a minority community: /u/-fronting in Chicano English. *Journal of Sociolinguistics, 3*(1), 5–23.

Goodwin, M. H. (1990). *He-said-she-said: Talk as social organization among Black children.* Bloomington: Indiana University Press.

Gumperz, J. J. (1971). Types of linguistic communities. In A. S. Dil (Ed.), *Language in social groups* (pp. 97–113). Stanford, CA: Stanford University Press. (Original work published 1962)

Gumperz, J. J. (1971). Linguistic and social interaction in two communities. In A. S. Dil (Ed.), *Language in social groups* (pp.151–176). Stanford, CA: Stanford University Press. (Original work published 1964)

Gumperz, J. J. (1971). Linguistic repertoires, grammars, and second language instruction. In A. S. Dil (Ed.), *Language in social groups* (pp 177–189). Stanford, CA: Stanford University Press. (Original work published 1966)

Gumperz, J. J. (1971). The speech community. In A. S. Dil (Ed.), *Language in social groups* (pp. 114–128). Stanford, CA: Stanford University Press. (Original work published1968)

Gumperz, J. J. (1971). Communication in multilingual societies. In A. S. Dil (Ed.), *Language in social groups* (pp. 230–250). Stanford, CA: Stanford University Press. (Original work published 1969)

Gumperz, J. J. (1971). *Language in social groups.* Stanford, CA: Stanford University Press.

Gumperz, J. J. (1982). *Language and social identity.* Cambridge, UK: Cambridge University Press.

Hastings, S. O. (2001). Social drama as a site for the communal construction and management of Asian Indian "stranger" identity. *Research on Language and Social Interaction, 34,* 309–335.

Hester, S., & Elgin, P. (Eds.). (1997). *Culture in action: Studies in membership categorization analysis.* Washington, DC: University Press of America.

Hill, J. H. (1992). The flower world of old Uto-Aztecan. *Journal of Anthropological Research, 48*(2), 117–145.

Huspeck, M. (1994) Oppositional codes and social class relations. *British Journal of Sociology, 45*(1), 79–102.

Huspeck, M., & Kendall, K. E. (1991). On withholding political voice: An analysis of the political vocabulary of a "nonpolitical" speech community. *Quarterly Journal of Speech, 77,* 1–19.

Hymes, D. (1962). The ethnography of speaking. In T. Gladwin & W. Sturtevant (Eds.), *Anthropology and Human Behavior* (pp. 15–53). Washington, DC: Anthropological Society of Washington.

Hymes, D. (1964a). *Language in culture and society: A reader in linguistics and anthropology.* New York: Harper & Row.

Hymes, D. (1964b). Introduction: Toward ethnographies of communication. *American Anthropologist, 66*(2), 1–34.

Hymes, D. (1972). Models of the interaction of language and social life. In J. Gumperz & D. Hymes (Eds.), *Directions in sociolinguistics: The ethnography of communication* (pp. 35–71). New York: Holt, Rinehart, & Winston.

Hymes, D. (1974). *Foundations in sociolinguistics: An ethnographic approach.* Philadelphia: University of Pennsylvania Press.

Hymes, D. (1980). *Language in education: Ethnolinguistic essays.* Washington, DC: Center for Applied Linguistics.

Jacobs, G. (1998). The struggle over naming: A case study of "queer" in Toronto, 1990–1994. *World Englishes, 17*(2), 193–202.

Johnstone, B. (1990). *Stories, community and place: Narratives from middle America.* Bloomington: Indiana University Press.

Johnstone, B. (1999). Uses of southern-sounding speech by contemporary Texas women. *Journal of Sociolinguistics, 3*(4), 505–522.

Katriel, T. (1991). *Communal webs: Communication and culture in contemporary Israel.* Albany: State University of New York Press.

Katriel, T., & Philipsen, G. (1990). "What we need is communication": "Communication" as a cultural category in some American speech. In D. Carbaugh (Ed.), *Cultural communication and intercultural contact* (pp. 77–94). Hillsdale, NJ: Erlbaum.

Kroskrity, P. V. (1993). Aspects of syntactic and semantic variation within the Arizona Tewa speech community. *Anthropological Linguistics, 35*(1–4), 250–274.

Labov, W. (1964). Phonological correlates of social stratification. *American Anthropologist, 66*(6), 164–176.

Labov, W. (1966). *The social stratification of English in New York City.* Washington, DC: Center for Applied Linguistics.

Labov, W. (1969). Contraction, deletion and inherent variabilitiy of the English corpula. *Language, 45*, 715–762.

Labov, W. (1972a). *Language in the inner city: Studies in black English vernacular*. Philadelphia: University of Pennsylvania Press.

Labov, W. (1972b). *Sociolinguistic patterns*. Philadelphia: University of Pennsylvania Press.

Labov, W. (1994). *Principles of linguistic change*. Oxford, UK: Blackwell.

Labov, W., Cohen, P., Robins, C., & Lewis, J. (1968). *A study of the non-standard English of Negro and Puerto Rican speakers in New York City*. Washington, DC: U.S. Department of Health, Education & Welfare Bureau of Research.

Lakoff, G., & Johnson, M. (1980). *Metaphors we live by*. Chicago: University of Chicago Press.

LaWare, M. R. (1998). Encountering visions of Aztlan: Arguments for ethnic pride, community activism and cultural revitalization in Chicano murals. *Argumentation & Advocacy, 34*(3), 140–154.

Lee, R. (1995). Electoral politics and visions of community: Jimmy Carter, virtue, and the small town myth. *Western Journal of Communication, 60*(1), 39–60.

Linnes, K. (1998). Middle-class AAVE versus middle-class bilingualism: Contrasting speech communities. *American Speech, 73*, 339–367.

Lo, A. (Nov. 1999). Codeswitching, speech community membership, and the construction of ethnic identity. *Journal of Sociolinguistics, 3*, 461–480.

Marshall, J. (2001). Connectivity and restructuring: Identity and gender relations in a fishing community. *Gender, Place and Culture, 8*, 391–401.

Matsumura, S. (2001). Learning the rules for offering advice: A quantitative approach to second language socialization. *Language Learning, 51*, 635–679.

Milburn, T. (2000). Enacting "Puerto Rican time" in the United States. In M. J. Collier (Ed.), *Constituting cultural difference through discourse: the international and intercultural communication annual, 23*, (pp. 47–76). Thousand Oaks: Sage.

Milburn, T. (2002). Collaboration and the construction of Puerto Rican community. In M. P. Orbe, T. McDonald, & T. Ford-Ahmed (Eds.), *Building diverse communities* (pp. 287–303). Cresskill, NJ: Hampton Press.

Milroy, L. (2002). Introduction: Mobility, contact and language change: Working with contemporary speech communities. *Journal of Sociolinguistics, 6*(1), 3–16.

Morgan, M. M. (2001). Community. In A. Duranti (Ed.), *Key terms in language and culture*. Malden, MA: Blackwell.

Murray, S. O. (1998). *American sociolinguistics: Theorists and theory groups*. Amsterdam: John Benjamins.

Neethling, S. J. (2000). An onomastic renaissance: African names to the fore. *South African Journal of African Languages, 20*(3), 207–217.

Philipsen, G. (1975). Speaking "like a man" in Teamsterville: Culture patterns of role enactment in an urban neighborhood. *Quarterly Journal of Speech, 61*, 13–22.

Philipsen, G. (1976). Places for speaking in Teamsterville. *Quarterly Journal of Speech, 62*, 15–25.

Philipsen, G. (1987). The prospect for cultural communication. In L. Kincaid (Ed.), *Communication theories: Eastern and western perspectives* (pp. 245–254). New York: Academic Press.

Philipsen, G. (1989). Speech and the communal function in four cultures. *International and Intercultural Communication Annual, 13*, 79–92. Thousand Oaks, CA: Sage.

Philipsen, G. (1992). *Speaking culturally: Explorations in social communication*. Albany: State University of New York Press.

Pousada, A. (1991). Community participation in bilingual education as part of language policy. *Bilingual Review, 16*(2–3), 159–171.

Robinson, C. D. W., & Varley, F. (1998, June). Language diversity and accountability in the South: Perspectives and dilemmas. *Journal of Sociolinguistics, 2*, 189–204.

Rudd, G. (1995). The symbolic construction of organizational identities and community in a regional symphony. *Communication Studies, 46*(3–4), 201–221.

Saohatse, M. C. (1998). Communication problems in multilingual speech communities. *South African Journal of African Languages, 18*(4), 111–118.

Sawyer, M. S. (2002, April). Telereference: The use of television texts to create community. Paper presented at the Eastern Communication Association annual conference, New York, NY.

Schegloff, E. A. (1971). Notes on a conversational practice: Formulating place. In D. Sudnow (Ed.), *Studies in social interaction*. New York: Free Press.

Scott, M. B., & Lyman, S. M. (1968). Accounts. *American Sociological Review, 33*, 46–62.

Sequeira, D. L. (1993). Personal address as negotiated meaning in an American church community. *Research on Language and Social Interaction, 26*, 259–285.

Sequeira, D. L. (1994). Gifts of tongues and healing: The performance of charismatic renewal. *Text and Performance Quarterly, 14*, 126–143.

Shue, L. L., & Beck, C. S. (2001). Stepping out of bounds: Performing feminist pedagogy within a dance education community. *Communication Education, 50*(2), 125–143.

Smitherman, G. (1997). The chain remains the same. *Journal of Black Studies, 28*(1), 3–25.

Spitulnik, D. (1997). The social circulation of media discourse and the mediation of communities. *Journal of Linguistic Anthropology, 6*(2), 161–187.

Tagliamonte, S., & Hudson, R. (1999). Be like et al. beyond America: The quotative system in British and Canadian youth. *Journal of Sociolinguistics, 3*(2), 1–26.

Trudgill, P. (1986). *Dialects in contact*. Oxford, UK: Blackwell.

Weider, D. L., & Pratt, S. (1990). On being a recognizable Indian among Indians. In D. Carbaugh (Ed.), *Cultural communication and intercultural contact* (pp. 45–64). Hillsdale, NJ: Erlbaum.

Zoller, H. M. (2000). "A place you haven't visited before": Creating the conditions for community dialogue. *Southern Communication Journal, 65*(2–3), 191–207.

AUTHOR INDEX

SUBJECT INDEX

ABOUT THE EDITOR

PAMELA J. KALBFLEISCH (Ph.D., Michigan State University, 1985) is professor and director of the School of Communication at the University of North Dakota. Her research reflects an active interest in interpersonal communication and communication in close relationships, covering such topics as social support, mentoring relationships, deceptive communication, and gender issues. Her published research is found in International Communication Association publications *Communication Theory, Human Communication Research* and the *Journal of Communication*, as well as in publications such as *Health Communication, Communication Education, Journal of Applied Communication Research, Howard Journal of Communication*, and the *Journal of Language and Social Psychology*. She edited *Interpersonal Communication: Evolving Interpersonal Relationships*, and with Michael J. Cody, coedited *Gender, Power, and Communication in Human Relationships*, both books published by Lawrence Erlbaum Associates. She authored the *Persuasion Handbook* published by Kendall Hunt, and she has authored and coauthored numerous book chapters and monographs. Kalbfleisch also guest edited a special issue of *Communication Theory* on "Building Theories in Interpersonal Communication," and she serves as associate editor and review board member for nine scholarly publications. She rides quarter horses and competitively paddles outrigger canoes whenever horses or oceans are available.

ABOUT THE CONTRIBUTORS

SOPHIA ACORD graduated with honors from Swarthmore College and is pursuing advanced studies in artistic expression and public culture at the University of Essex.

ANDREW C. BILLINGS (Ph.D., Indiana University, 1999) is an assistant professor in the Department of Communication & Culture at Clemson University. His research considers gender and ethnicity as it relates to televised sport. His research has been published in the *Journal of Communication, Mass Communication & Society, Television & New Media,* and the *Howard Journal of Communication.*

ROBERT S. BROWN (Ph.D., Rhetoric/Public Address, Indiana University, 1996) is an associate professor of communication arts at Ashland University in Ohio, where he also directs the sport communication major. Recent publications include a chapter examining the role of baseball as propaganda during World War II entitled "Baseball Carries On" in the 2002 Hampton Press book *Take Me Out to the Ballgame: Communicating Baseball,* and an essay, cowritten with Lisa Strange, entitled "The Bicycle, Women's Rights, and Elizabeth Cady Stanton" in the September–October 2002 issue of *Women's Studies.* Brown's most recent efforts have been in the preparation of his book, *Case Studies in Sport Communication,* released in December 2003.

WALTER J. CARL (Ph.D., University of Iowa, 2001) is currently an assistant professor in the Department of Communication Studies at Northeastern University in Boston, MA. His research focuses on social interaction and relationships in various institutional and organizational contexts in order to better understand how organizational actors manage their identities and organizational change. Recent publications include his dissertation and a manuscript on managing legitimacy and constructing entrepreneurial identities in multilevel marketing discourse.

KIKU DASGUPTA is a graduate student in communication at Rutgers University.

KALPANA DAVID is a graduate student in communication at Rutgers University.

AARON DIMOCK (M.A., University of Colorado) is a Ph.D. candidate in the Communication Department at the University of Colorado at Boulder. He is interested is bringing the fields of rhetoric and language and social interaction together. In his dissertation he is studying a series of cases in which city councils in the U.S. deliberated about resolutions concerning the war in Iraq. His past research has examined the ways juvenile offenders construct their identity and the implications those identities have for defining appropriate and inappropriate action.

STEVE DUCK (Ph.D., 1971, University of Sheffield, England) is currently the Daniel and Amy Starch Distinguished Research Chair at the University of Iowa. He is interested in daily life conduct as it influences and bleeds into relationships, and his recent work is about the ways in which everyday conversation and activity lay the basis for relational experience. He has written 40 books on relationships, including the *Human Relationship Reader* (with Bill Dragon) and *The Relationship Book*, currently in press with Sage.

PAIGE EDLEY (Ph.D., Rutgers University, 1997) is an assistant professor at Loyola Marymount University in Los Angeles, CA. Her research interests include the intersections of power, gender, and identity in organizations, alternative forms of organizing, work-life balance, and women-owned businesses. She has published multiple book chapters on home-based businesses, women-owned businesses, corporate colonization of the body in international ballet companies, and the use of technology in work-family balance, as well as articles in journals such as *Management Communication Quarterly, Women and Language*, and *Argumentation and Advocacy*.

LAWRENCE FREY (Ph.D., University of Kansas, 1979) is professor and associate chair of the Department of Communication at the University of Colorado at Boulder. His interests include group communication, applied communication (with a focus on social justice), health communication, and communication research methods (both quantitative and qualitative). His research seeks to understand how participation in communicative practices makes a difference in people's individual and collective lives, especially for those who are most underresourced and marginalized. He has investigated that theme in a residential facility for people living with AIDS and is currently studying a cancer center. He is the author/editor of 10 books, 3 special journal issues, and more than 50 published book chapters and journal articles, and is the recipient of 9 distinguished scholarship awards. He is a past president of the Central States Communication Association and a recipient of the Outstanding Young Teacher Award from that organization.

KIRK HALLAHAN (Ph.D., University of Wisconsin-Madison, 1995) is associate professor of journalism and technical communication at Colorado State University, Fort Collins. He joined the faculty in 1996, after serving 3 years on the faculty of the University of North Dakota. For 19 years, he was a public relations practitioner in California. He is the recipient of several professional and academic awards, including the Jackson, Jackson & Wagner Behavioral Science Prize presented by the Public Relations Society of America Foundation. His recent research has focused on theories of communities and publics in public relations and online public relations.

KELBY K. HALONE (Ph.D., University of Oklahoma, 1998) is an assistant professor at the School of Communication Studies, College of Communication &

Information, University of Tennessee, Knoxville. His research agenda theoretically examines the pragmatic intersection of relational processes and organizing processes, how such processes become communicatively manifest at micro- and macrolevels, and how such processes interactively contribute to cultural dynamics underlying relational, group, and organizational health. Previous publications have appeared in such journals as *Mass Communication & Society, International Journal of Listening, Communication Reports,* and *Sociology of Sport Journal.*

KRISTEN HARRISON (Ph.D., University of Wisconsin-Madison, 1997) is an assistant professor in the Department of Speech Communication at the University of Illinois in Urbana-Champaign. Her research focuses on the effects of mass media exposure on young people's development of a sense of body image and eating disorders. As a William T. Grant Scholar, she is currently conducting longitudinal research to determine if early childhood media exposure contributes to the development of self-esteem and body image problems in girls and boys. She is also conducting an analysis of the nutritional content of foods advertised during the television programs children watch most frequently. She plans to add obesity to the list of outcomes she will be investigating in future research. Her work has been published in the *Journal of Sport and Social Issues, Journal of Communication,* and *Communication Research.*

RENEE GUARRIELLO HEATH (M.A., Washington State University, 1997) is a Ph.D. student in the Department of Communication at the University of Colorado at Boulder. She spent 5 years associated with a community collaboration in Northwest Washington before returning to academia to conduct research in that area. Her research interests are specific to community collaboration, bridging studies of communication in groups, organizations, and civic leadership. Research conducted for her M.A. thesis was published in the *Journal of Applied Communication Research.* She has presented papers on communication and collaboration at both the International Communication Association and the National Communication Association conferences. She recently received a Residence Life Academic Teaching Award from the University of Colorado at Boulder.

ANNIKA HYLMÖ (Ph.D., Purdue University, 2001) is an assistant professor at Loyola Marymount University in Los Angeles, CA. Her award-winning research examines organizational cultures, telecommuting, life balance within and outside of formal organizational contexts in different national contexts, expatriate employees and their families, and expressions of diversity. She has published multiple book chapters on the experiences of telecommuting and in-house employees, and on the experiences of internationally mobile children (third-culture kids), in addition to monographs in *Communication Monographs.*

JEFFREY W. KASSING (Ph.D., Kent State University, 1997) is an associate professor and director of graduate studies in the Department of Communication

Studies at Arizona State University West. His research interests focusing on communication and sport include aggressive communication within coach-athlete relationships, parents' communication at youth sporting events, and the construction of identity as it relates to women's participation in sport. Additionally, he has conducted research that examines employee dissent, superior/subordinate communication, as well as the communicative nature of corporal punishment. His research has been published in *Management Communication Quarterly, Communication Studies,* and *Communication Research Reports.*

JAMES E. KATZ is a professor of communication at Rutgers University. He is coauthor of *Social Consequences of Internet Use: Access, Involvement and Expression* (MIT Press 2002) and coeditor of *Internet and Health Communication: Experience and Expectations* (Sage, 2000). He also has published joint articles on social aspects of mobile phone use with Ronald E. Rice.

ROBERT L. KRIZEK (Ph.D., Arizona State University, 1995), is an associate professor and director of graduate studies in the Department of Communication at Saint Louis University. He teaches and conducts research in the areas of organizational culture, sport communication, communication in third places, and ethnographic methodologies. In addition to research into socialization and storytelling in organizational contexts, he examines the personal and cultural significance of nonroutine public events (including sport stadium closings) through the examination of the personal narratives of those in attendance. His work has appeared in five recent anthologies as well as in the *Quarterly Journal of Speech, Management Communication Quarterly, Journal of Applied Communication Research, Journal of Sport and Social Issues, Adolescence,* and other journals. His most recent publication is a chapter entitled "Ethnography as the Excavation of Personal Narrative" in Robin Clair's 2003 edited volume, *Expressions of Ethnography*, published by SUNY Press.

LINDSEY L. MEÂN (Ph.D., 1995, University of Sheffield, England) was on faculty as a senior lecturer at Manchester Metropolitan University in the United Kingdom until recently, when she accepted a visiting post at Arizona State University West. Her research interests include language, gender, diversity, sport, social discourses and representations. She has recently published work in *Discourse & Society* and in the edited book *Communication Research and Media Science in Europe,* which considers the construction of gender through discursive practices occurring during athletic activities. In addition she is the coauthor, with Angela Goddard, of the Routledge text *Language and Gender.*

TRUDY MILBURN (Ph.D., University of Massachusetts, Amherst, 1998) is currently an assistant professor in the Communication Studies Department at Baruch College/The City University of New York. Her current research interests include (a) theoretical/methodological considerations of the intersection between ethnography of communication and conversation analysis; (b) questions regarding "community" as both a unit of analysis as well as its composition; and (c) questions exploring membering and identity constitution, particularly gendered and ethnic identities, in interactions. Her work has been published in such journals as *Communication Studies, Iowa Journal of Communication,* and *International and Intercultural Communication Annual,* as well as in chapters of several books.

LAWRENCE J. MULLEN (Ph.D., 1992, University of Iowa) is an associate professor of communication studies in the Hank Greenspun School of Communication at the University of Nevada, Las Vegas. His research interests are eclectic, but tend to emphasize aspects of visual communication and visual literacy. Sports broadcasting, prescription drug advertising, post-September 11 corporate advertising, political imagery, and pictorial learning are among those interests. Articles on these topics can be found in *Iowa Journal of Communication, Communication Studies, Journal of Broadcasting and Electronic Media,* and *Critical Studies in Mass Communication.* Mullen is currently working on a book that examines the relationship between communication and community in his adopted hometown of Las Vegas, Nevada. The author would like to thank David R. Henry, Eric W. Rothenbuhler, and Barbara A. Spanjers for their critiques and suggestions on earlier versions of this article.

VICTORIA ANN NEWSOM (M.A., Bowling Green State University, 2000) is a doctoral candidate in the School of Communication Studies at Bowling Green State University. Her dissertation research is a study focused on her theory of "contained empowerment" as it exists in third wave feminisms. Her research centers on the negotiation of power, gender, and identity in communication and communication technologies. She examines performances of identity, power, and gender in a variety of marginalized groups, including feminists, webloggers, women in the Middle East North Africa Region, and historic reenactors and anachronists. She has published book chapters and articles in journals such as *FemSpec* and *Feminist Media Studies.*

RONALD E. RICE is a professor of communication at Rutgers University. He is coauthor of *Social Consequences of Internet Use: Access, Involvement and Expression* (MIT Press 2002) and co-editor of *Internet and Health Communication: Experience and Expectations* (Sage, 2000). He has also published joint articles on social aspects of mobile phone use with James E. Katz.

GREGORY SHEPHERD (Ph.D., University of Illinois) is professor and director of the School of Communication Studies at Ohio University. His primary teaching and scholarly interests are in communication theory, interpersonal communication, and American pragmatism. He is a winner of the Central States Communication Association Outstanding Young Teacher Award and a W. T. Kemper Fellowship for Teaching Excellence. He is coeditor (with Eric Rothenbuhler) of *Communication and Community* (2001, Erlbaum) and is the author of many book chapters and essays, including articles appearing in *Communication Monographs, Human Communication Research, Journal of Communication, Communication Studies, Southern Journal of Communication, Communication Research, Journal of Social Psychology, Management Communication Quarterly,* and *Journal of Research and Development in Education.*

JEFFREY ST. JOHN (Ph.D., University of Washington) is assistant professor in the School of Communication Studies at Ohio University, Athens, OH. His research interests include communication theory, legal argument, and public sphere studies. He teaches a graduate course in communication theory and undergraduate courses in argumentation, legal theory, political communication, and freedom of speech. His recent work has been published in the *Proceedings of the Fifth Conference of the International Society for the Study of Argumentation* (2002) and in *Rhetoric & Public Affairs* (2003).

LAURA STAFFORD (Ph.D., University of Texas at Austin, 1985) is an associate professor in the School of Communication and Journalism at Ohio State University. Research interests include relational maintenance and family communication. Current publications include "The Role of Family Communication in Middle Childhood" in *The Handbook of Family Communication* and "A Longitudinal Study of Relational and Individual Well-being" in the *Journal of Social and Personal Relationships,* coauthored with Susan L. Kline and Caroline Rankin.

KAREN TRACY (Ph.D., University of Wisconsin, 1981) is professor of communication at the University of Colorado at Boulder. She is a discourse analyst interested in communicative dilemmas, multiple-goal situations, and issues of identity-work. Her research focuses on problems in education- and justice-linked institutions. She is the author of *Colloquium: Dilemmas of Academic Discourse,* and *Everyday Talk: Building and Reflecting Identities* and is currently working on a book about the challenges of school board meetings in American society.

PAUL D. TURMAN (Ph.D., University of Nebraska, Lincoln, 2000) is an assistant professor of communication studies at the University of Northern Iowa. His major research interests center on the examination of coaching from an instructional communication perspective. Specifically his research has examined how various communication variables (e.g., power, immediacy, leadership style) influence a variety of outcomes associated with sport participation (i.e., cohesion, affective learning). Currently, he is examining how high school coaches use regret messages to increase athlete performance during pregame and halftime speeches. His research has been published in the *Journal of Sport Behavior, Communication Education,* and the *Journal of Small Group Behavior.*